MW01070757

THE PAPERS OF JOSEPH SMITH

VOLUME 1

AUTOBIOGRAPHICAL AND HISTORICAL WRITINGS

Joseph Smith, by Alvin Gittens. Oil. 1959. LDS Church.

THE PAPERS OF JOSEPH SMITH

VOLUME 1
AUTOBIOGRAPHICAL AND HISTORICAL WRITINGS

EDITED BY
DEAN C. JESSEE

Deseret Book Company
Salt Lake City, Utah

Library of Congress Cataloging-in-Publication Data

Smith, Joseph, 1805–1844.
The papers of Joseph Smith / edited by Dean C. Jessee.
p. cm.
Bibliography: p.
Includes index.

Contents: v. 1. Autobiographical and historical writings.
1. Smith, Joseph, 1805–1844. 2. Mormon Church–Presidents–Biography. 3. Church of Jesus Christ of Latter-day Saints–Presidents–Biography. 4. Mormon Church–History–Sources. 5. Church of Jesus Christ of Latter-day Saints–History–Sources. I. Jessee, Dean C. II. Title.
BX8695.S6A3 1989a
289.3'092–dc20
[B] 89–11720
ISBN 0-87579-199-9 CIP

Printed in the United States of America

10 9 8 7 6 5 4 3 2 1

CONTENTS

Acknowledgments ix
General Introduction xi
Guide to Editorial Procedures xxxvii
Joseph Smith Chronology xxxix
Joseph Smith Family xlv
Introduction to Volume 1 xlvii

History [1832] 1
Letter to Oliver Cowdery, 1834 11
History, 1834–1836 15
"Journal Extract," 1839 210
History [1839 Draft] 230
History, 1839 265
Orson Pratt, *A Interesting Account,* 1840 387
Orson Hyde, *Ein Ruf aus der Wüste,* 1842 402
"Church History," 1842 427
Pittsburgh Gazette Interview, 1843 438
I. Daniel Rupp, *An Original History,* 1844 445
Alexander Neibaur Report, 1844 459

Maps 463
Biographical Register 471
Works Cited 526
Index 543

ILLUSTRATIONS

Joseph Smith Frontispiece
History [1832], Joseph Smith Letterbook, p. 1 2
Birthplace of Joseph Smith, Sharon,
Windsor County, Vermont 4
History, 1834-1836, A-1, p. 9 16
Oliver Cowdery 34
History 1834-1836, A-1, p. 121 126
Kirtland Temple 194
Kirtland Temple drawing 195
Liberty Jail 222
Exchange Row, site of Egbert B. Grandin
Printing Office 240
Reconstruction of Peter Whitmer, Sr., home 245
History, 1839, A-1, p. 1 266
Sidney Rigdon 326
Orson Pratt 388
Orson Hyde 426
John Wentworth 428
David Nye White 439
Nauvoo Temple 441
Israel Daniel Rupp 446
Nauvoo 455
Alexander Niebaur 460
Alexander Niebaur Diary, 24 May 1844 462

ACKNOWLEDGMENTS

This edition of the Papers of Joseph Smith is made possible by the help and cooperation of many people. I give special acknowledgment to officials of The Church of Jesus Christ of Latter-day Saints who made available sources from the Church archives where the bulk of the Joseph Smith papers are housed. I am indebted to administrators at Brigham Young University for resources provided by that institution, including research grants that have helped facilitate this work. I appreciate Ronald K. Esplin, director of the Joseph Fielding Smith Institute for Church History at the University, who was instrumental in getting the project started, and has given freely of his talents and knowledge as this work progressed.

In addition, many others have provided invaluable assistance, generously sharing their expertise and specialized skills in a variety of areas. These include: Leonard J. Arrington, Maureen Ursenbach Beecher, Jill Mulvay Derr, William G. Hartley, Richard L. Jensen, Carol Cornwall Madsen, Marilyn Rish Parks, and Ronald W. Walker, my colleagues in the Smith Institute at Brigham Young University; Donald L. Enders, James L. Kimball, Jr., Glenn N. Rowe, William W. Slaughter, Steven Ray Sorenson, Richard E. Turley, Jr., and Ronald G. Watt at the LDS Church Historical Department in Salt Lake City; Noel Barton, Sandra J. Pitts, and Raymond S. Wright at the LDS Family History Library, Salt Lake City; Richard L. Anderson, Mark E. Davies, Chad J. Flake, Marvin H. Folsom, Keith W. Perkins, and David J. Whittaker at Brigham Young

University; Richard P. Howard, RLDS Church Historian; Eleanor Knowles, Jack M. Lyon, Ronald A. Millett, Patricia J. Parkinson, Kent Ware, and Emily Watts at Deseret Book Company, Salt Lake City; and Steven R. Thomas, University of Utah.

In addition to the LDS Church archives, other repositories have provided valuable material and assistance, including: Brigham Young University Library; Carnegie Library of Pittsburgh, Pennsylvania Department; Chicago Historical Society; Historical Society of Pennsylvania; the LDS Church Family History Library; Library of Congress; Reorganized Church of Jesus Christ of Latter Day Saints Library-Archives; and the Utah State Historical Society.

This edition of the Joseph Smith Papers has also benefited from the guidelines and experience developed during the renaissance in editing historical and literary works in America over the past forty years that has produced more than 250 book and microform editions of the papers of individuals and institutions.

In acknowledging my indebtedness to many people for their help, I nevertheless remain solely responsible for the content and for any errors that may appear in the pages that follow.

GENERAL INTRODUCTION

Joseph Smith is best known as the prophet-founder of Mormonism. The story of his life begins in a log cabin in the valley of the White River in eastern Vermont in the fifth year of Thomas Jefferson's presidency; moves into western New York amidst the religious turmoil of what Whitney Cross labeled the "burned-over district," where the boy Joseph became concerned "for the welfare of my mortal soul"; enlarges with his visions of the 1820s; and emerges into the world of public controversy with the printing of the Book of Mormon and the founding of the church in 1830. Then, after fourteen years of contending for his message in a hostile world and trying to establish a permanent gathering place for his followers, first in New York, then in Ohio, Missouri, and Illinois, he was shot to death by a mob with blackened faces who stormed the jail at Carthage, Illinois, where he was being detained.[1]

A listing of the Mormon leader's accomplishments would include his publication of the Book of Mormon and more than a hundred other revelations, including restored writings of Moses and Enoch, and an autobiographical record of Abraham. He also produced a revision of the Bible, began publication of his own *History of the Church*, and created personal records

1. Whitney R. Cross, *The Burned-over District: The Social and Intellectual History of Enthusiastic Religion in Western New York, 1800-1850* (New York: Cornell University Press, 1950); Joseph Smith 1832 History, see p. 1.

that form the basis for investigating his life and times. He initiated a vigorous missionary outreach in the British Isles and America; directed the establishment of communities in Ohio, Missouri, and Illinois; and oversaw the building of two temples. Besides his ecclesiastical responsibilities, he served as mayor of Nauvoo, Illinois, and as commander of its militia, and he was campaigning for the presidency of the United States at the time of his death.[1]

Few who knew Joseph Smith regarded him with indifference. Though his message attracted intense devotion and support, it also aroused strong opposition. Shortly before his death, he wrote, "The envy and wrath of man have been my common lot all the days of my life; . . . deep water is what I am wont to swim in." The cause of the antagonism that dogged his efforts seemed mysterious to him, unless, as he wrote, "I was ordained from before the foundation of the world for some good end, or bad, as you may choose to call it." But despite the turmoil that followed him, his sense of mission buoyed him up: "If I had not actually got into this work and been called of God, I would back out. But I cannot back out: I have

---

1. Works dealing with Joseph Smith and the beginnings of Mormonism include the following: The Book of Mormon: Another Testament of Jesus Christ, trans. Joseph Smith, Jr., rev. ed. (Salt Lake City: The Church of Jesus Christ of Latter-day Saints, 1986); The Doctrine and Covenants of the Church of Jesus Christ of Latter-day Saints, rev. ed., (Salt Lake City: The Church of Jesus Christ of Latter-day Saints, 1986); Joseph Smith, *History of the Church of Jesus Christ of Latter-day Saints*, ed. Brigham H. Roberts (Salt Lake City: Deseret Press, 1964); Brigham H. Roberts, *A Comprehensive History of the Church of Jesus Christ of Latter-day Saints* (Salt Lake City: The Church of Jesus Christ of Latter-day Saints, 1930), vols. 1, 2. Richard L. Bushman, *Joseph Smith and the Beginnings of Mormonism* (Urbana and Chicago: University of Illinois Press, 1984); Lucy Smith, *Biographical Sketches of Joseph Smith the Prophet and his Progenitors for many Generations* (Liverpool: Published for Orson Pratt by S. W. Richards, 1853); Donna Hill, *Joseph Smith: The First Mormon* (Garden City, New York: Doubleday and Company, 1977); Richard L. Anderson, *Joseph Smith's New England Heritage* (Salt Lake City: Deseret Book Company, 1971); Larry C. Porter, "A Study of the Origins of the Church of Jesus Christ of Latter-day Saints in the States of New York and Pennsylvania, 1816-1831," (Ph.D. diss., Brigham Young University, 1971).

no doubt of the truth." "I know of a certainty of eternal things." He was convinced of his eventual triumph, "for the Lord hath spoken it."[1]

Despite the adversity and tribulation of his life, and his living in a society seen by outsiders as generally possessing an excessive gravity, "a dull and gloomy character" that made "a toil of pleasure," Joseph Smith was not a somber, forbidding person. In an introspective part of his history, he admitted weaknesses and "foolish errors" but asserted that he was not guilty of any "great or malignant sins," for a disposition to commit such was not part of his nature. However, he confessed, "I was guilty of levity and sometimes associated with jovial company," adding that those who knew him were acquainted with his "native cheery temperament."[2]

People who met the Prophet for the first time were often surprised by his affable nature. "He didn't appear exactly as I expected to see a Prophet of God. However, I was not stumbled at all. I found him to be a friendly, cheerful, pleasent, agreable man. I could not help likeing him," wrote a New England convert upon meeting the Mormon leader for the first time in 1835. And Thomas Ford, governor of Illinois, whose contact with Joseph Smith spanned the years of turmoil that immediately preceded the Prophet's death, said, "It must not be supposed . . . that he was a dark and gloomy person, with a long beard, a grave and severe aspect, and a reserved and saintly carriage of his person; on the contrary, he was full of levity, even to boyish romping."[3]

---

1. Joseph Smith to the Saints, 1 September 1842, Joseph Smith Papers, LDS Church Archives, Salt Lake City, Utah; see D&C 127:2; Diary of Joseph Smith, 6 April 1843, Ms., Joseph Smith Papers, LDS Church Archives, published in Smith, *History of the Church*, 5:336.

2. Edward Pessen, *Jacksonian America: Society, Personality, and Politics* (Homewood, Illinois: The Dorsey Press, 1978), 10-11; Joseph Smith History, see p. 273 note 1 below.

3. "A Biographical Sketch of the Life of Jonathan Crosby written by himself," 13, Ms., Utah Historical Society; Thomas Ford, *History of Illinois from its Commencement as a State in 1818 to 1847* (Chicago: S.G. Griggs and Company, 1854), 2:213-14.

In 1843, a Boston newspaper correspondent—whose conception of prophets was one of gray-haired old men with long beards, wearing animal skins, living in caves, and being too sanctified to appear in human society except just long enough to deliver their message from heaven, and then crying out with such sanctity that everybody would know they were holy—noted that Joseph Smith was far different from what he had expected: "I could not help noticing that he dressed, talked and acted like other men, and in every respect appeared exactly the opposite of what I had conjured up in my imagination a prophet [to be]."[1]

As a religious leader, Joseph Smith has profoundly influenced many who knew him, and others who have studied him since his death. After visiting Nauvoo in 1842, James G. Bennett, editor of the *New York Herald*, wrote that the Mormon Prophet was "undoubtedly one of the greatest characters of the age," and he compared him in talent, originality, and moral courage to the "great spirits that have hitherto produced the revolutions of past ages." He noted that in this age of irreligion and materialism, "some such singular prophet . . . is required to preserve the principle of faith, and to plant some new germs of civilization," and while a naturalistic philosophy spreads through the country, "Joe Smith is creating a spiritual system, combined also with morals and industry, that may change the destiny of the race." The mayor of Boston, Josiah Quincy, who met Joseph Smith two years later, observed that future generations might well identify him as the American of the nineteenth century who "has exerted the most powerful influence upon the destinies of his countrymen." Quincy noted that Joseph was accepted by thousands as "a direct emissary from the Most High" and could not be disposed of by "pelting his memory with unsavory epithets." His influence "throws

1. Unidentified correspondent to the *Boston Bee*, 24 May 1843, published in Smith, *History of the Church*, 5:406-8.

him into relief before us . . . as a phenomenon to be explained. . . . The possibilities of the Mormon system are unfathomable." And the twentieth-century Roman Catholic scholar Gustave Weigel said, "It is easy for scoffers to ridicule the man for some of the things he did but his productivity marks him as a man of genius. He had very little schooling . . . yet he was a combination of practical wisdom, great daring and rich imagination. He was clearly a leader of men, with a great confidence in himself which repeated failures could not destroy."[1]

A non-Mormon who saw Joseph Smith only once said, "I never met his equal in all my life. . . . His manners, movements and whole deportment made a deep and lasting impression upon me, and convinced me that he was not the impostor and wicked man he had been represented by his enemies to be; to me he appeared to be a good, honest and noble-hearted man, and from all I have ever learned about him since, I have not had occasion to change my opinion about him."[2]

A convert to Mormonism who lived in the Smith home for a time saw him not only in public but as a private citizen in the role of husband, father, and neighbor: "I witnessed his earnest and humble devotions both morning and evening in his family. I heard the words of eternal life flowing from his mouth, nourishing, soothing, and comforting his family, neighbours, and friends. . . . I could form some kind of an opinion about Joseph Smith as a natural man. . . . I could believe him to be a man of God from his conversation, from

1. James G. Bennett, "The Mormons – A Leaf From Joe Smith," *New York Herald*, 3 April 1842; Josiah Quincy, *Figures of the Past From the Leaves of Old Journals*, (Boston: Roberts Brothers, 1883), 376-77; Gustave Weigel, S.J., *Churches in North America: An Introduction* (Baltimore: Helicon Press, 1961), 90.

2. Andrew Jenson and Edward Stevenson, *Infancy of the Church* (Salt Lake City, 1889), 51, quoting L. C. Bidamon. For other contemporary accounts of Joseph Smith see Marvin Hill, "Joseph Smith the Man: Some Reflections on a Subject of Controversy," *BYU Studies* 21 (Spring 1981): 175-86.

his acts, from his dealings." To the Saints who accepted his mission and followed his leadership, he was regarded as having "done more, save Jesus only, for the salvation of men in this world than any other man that ever lived in it."[1]

For thousands who joined the movements he led, Joseph Smith brought a dimension to life and a meaning to the human experience that had long been missing from religion. Efforts to define his personality and understand his thought continue more than a century after his death.

The Importance of the Papers of Joseph Smith

Speaking to a large assembly in Nauvoo, Illinois, less than three months before he died, Joseph Smith no doubt surprised some who heard him when he remarked, "You don't know me; you never knew my heart. No man knows my history. I cannot tell it: I shall never undertake it. I don't blame anyone for not believing my history. If I had not experienced what I have, I would not have believed it myself."[2] The Prophet's writings indicate that this statement was not intended to imply lack of interest, neglect, or duplicity in the records he produced. Rather, it conveys the reality that even under the best circumstances the picture of his life, as with all history, is incomplete—and he saw his life as so unusual that even a complete factual record might appear fictional. Try as he did to preserve a careful record, important elements of his past lay beyond the range of normal experience; and neither the methods of record keeping in his day nor his forced removal from state to state lent themselves to a systematic and comprehensive archive.

1. Discourse of Orson Pratt at Salt Lake City, Utah, 10 July 1859, published in *The Journal of Discourses*, 26 vols. (Liverpool, England, 1853-1886), 7:176-77; D&C 135:3, authored by John Taylor.

2. Diary of Joseph Smith, 7 April 1844, Ms.; Thomas Bullock report of Joseph Smith discourse, 7 April 1844, Ms., Joseph Smith Papers, LDS Church Archives. The quotation is a blend of the reports of the address by Willard Richards, who kept the Prophet's diary at that time, and by Thomas Bullock.

While some of Joseph Smith's contemporaries left more substantial records than he did, none were more committed to history. Indeed, his influence was the central motivation behind the records of early Mormonism. However, his papers were produced in a setting where procedures for recording events were practically nonexistent by present standards, and circumstances arose that hampered his own efforts. Although his life has been the subject of great interest, his papers, the raw materials for dependable biography, have never been brought together or published in their entirety.

And yet, the papers of Joseph Smith provide the basic resource for understanding the man and for measuring the credibility of his claim that he had seen God and had been directed to translate a new record of American religious history containing the testimony of New-World prophets, that he had been commissioned with authority to found a church, and that a dispensation of divine truth had been introduced in which he played a fundamental role. In describing the "rise and progress" of the work in which he had "the honor under God of being the founder," the Prophet informed a Chicago newspaper editor that a heavenly messenger declared to him in 1823 that "the preparatory work for the second coming of the Messiah was speedily to commence, that the time was at hand when the gospel in all its fulness was to be preached in power unto all nations that a people might be prepared for the millennial reign."[1]

The Prophet saw his mission as laying the foundation for a new order—the establishment of Zion, the gathering of the pure and honest from among all nations, the beginnings of a society that would herald a thousand years of peace upon the earth under divine leadership. "The building of Zion is a cause that has interested the people of God in every age," he wrote

1. "Church History," *Times and Seasons* 3 (1 March 1842): 707; see p. 427.

in 1842. "It is a theme upon which prophets, priests and kings, have dwelt with peculiar delight; they have looked forward with joyful anticipation unto the day in which we live . . . but they died without the sight. We are the favored people that God has made choice of to bring about the Latter-day glory . . . when the Saints of God will be gathered in one, from every nation and kindred and tongue. . . . a work that is destined to bring about the destruction of the powers of darkness, the renovation of the earth, the glory of God, and the salvation of the human family." The Prophet later told a congregation of his followers, "I intend to lay a foundation that will revolutionize the whole world. . . . It will not be by sword or gun that this kingdom will roll on—the power of truth is such that all nations will be under the necessity of obeying the Gospel."[1]

Joseph Smith's testimony that significant events occurred in western New York in the 1820s and that divine messengers communicated with him, as they did with prophets in biblical times, to inaugurate a new era has been followed by the rise of one of the world's most rapidly growing religions, and it has created more than casual interest in his life and thought. Historian of religion Sidney Ahlstrom has observed that Mormonism has persistently escaped definition, that "the transformation brought about by numerical growth, economic adaptation, internal divisions, external hostility, and heroic exploits renders almost useless the usual categories of explanation." He added that one cannot be sure if the movement initiated by Joseph Smith "is a sect, a mystery cult, a new religion, a church, a people, a nation, or an American subculture; indeed, at different times and places it is all of these."

---

1. Joseph Smith discourse reported by Thomas Bullock, Nauvoo, Illinois, 12 May 1844, Ms. LDS Church Archives; "The Temple," *Times and Seasons* 3 (2 May 1842): 775-76; see also, Ronald K. Esplin, "Joseph Smith's Mission and Timetable: 'God Will Protect Me Until My Work Is Done,' " in *The Prophet Joseph: Essays on the Life and Mission of Joseph Smith*, eds. Larry C. Porter and Susan Easton Black (Salt Lake City: Deseret Book Company, 1988), 280-319.

Nevertheless, Joseph Smith's work "can be likened to a fast-growing hardwood towering above the sectarian underbrush of the burnt-over district." And Jan Shipps, the Methodist scholar of comparative religions, has defined Mormonism as "a new religious tradition" containing important elements not part of traditional Christianity although adhering to its scriptural past—just as early Christians parted from the way of the Jews.[1]

Following Joseph Smith's announcement that he had been called as prophets were in biblical times, and the persistent and steady rise to prominence of the movement he introduced, every scrap of information dealing with him is read with care, and the papers he produced have become the object of more than passing interest.

Joseph Smith and Record Keeping

The inspiration that initiated Joseph Smith's prophetic mission took place in the 1820s. But it was not until 1832—in his twenty-seventh year—that he took pen in hand to write the story of his life. During that year he commenced two records: the first, discontinued shortly after he started it, was intended to contain "an account of his marvilous experience and of all the mighty acts which he doeth in the name of Jesus Christ . . . and also an account of the rise of the church of Christ in the eve of time according as the Lord brought forth and established by his hand." The second marked the beginning of his diary keeping, when, on November 27, he began writing in a small blank book "to keep a minute acount of all things that come under my observation." In conjunction with his diary, he also began copying letters, revelations, and other

1. Sidney E. Ahlstrom, *A Religious History of the American People* (New Haven and London: Yale University Press, 1972), 508-9; Jan Shipps, *Mormonism: The Story of a New Religious Tradition* (Urbana and Chicago: University of Illinois Press, 1985).

documents into what became the Church's earliest record books.[1]

Before 1832, Joseph Smith's literary output had consisted of the Book of Mormon, a few letters and other documents, and a large number of revelations written in what Richard Bushman has termed "his prophetic voice," where the speaker "stands above and outside Joseph, sharply separated emotionally and intellectually" from him.[2] By the time of the Prophet's death in June 1844, a substantial number of records consisting of correspondence, diaries, revelations, and historical writings pertaining to his life and thought had been created and collected.

Since an understanding of Joseph Smith depends upon the records he kept, the reader must be aware of limitations that restrict the perception of him and that have tended to distort the image of him reflected in the documents that bear his name. To begin with, one finds extensive gaps in the records of his life. Joseph Smith's background and orientation help explain the lack of his writings before 1830 and the nature of those produced thereafter. The consciousness of history that motivated generations of the John Adams family to create and preserve extensive records[3] did not exist in the Smith family. The reason for this is primarily due to the different backgrounds of the two families.

Born and reared under conditions of poverty and hard manual labor that limited the time available for education and literary pursuits, Joseph Smith produced all of his writings in

---

1. Dean C. Jessee, "Joseph Smith and the Beginning of Mormon Record Keeping," in *The Prophet Joseph Smith*, eds., Porter and Black, 138-60.

2. Bushman, *Joseph Smith and the Beginnings of Mormonism*, 93.

3. Edward Everett Hale remarked that probably nowhere else in the world could "the history of a great nation . . . be so studied in the [records] of one family." As quoted by Lyman H. Butterfield, "The Adams Papers," in "Publishing the Papers of Great Men: A Session at the Sixty-Ninth Annual Meeting of the American Historical Association 30 December 1954," *Daedalus* 86 (May 1955): 64-65.

the last fifteen years of his life after he had been motivated by a revelation to do so and after he had become a subject of public controversy. He noted that "indigent circumstances" required hard labor for the support of a large family, and all who were able were required to work. "Therefore we were deprived of the bennifit of an education," he wrote, except for basics of reading, writing, and arithmetic, "which constituted my whole literary acquirements." His brother William later said that although Joseph was "illiterate to some extent," it was a mistake to say he was entirely unlettered. "In syntax, orthography, mathematics, grammar, geography with other studies in the common schools of his day he was no novice, and for writing he wrote a plain inteligible hand."[1]

When Joseph was six years old, his family moved from Royalton, Vermont, to Lebanon, New Hampshire. Before that, according to his mother, the children had "in a great measure, been debarred from the privilege of schools." The prospects at Lebanon seemed good for correcting that situation, and the parents worked hard to assist their children. Hyrum, the second son, was sent to the academy at Hanover, and the other school-age children enrolled in a common school. But prosperity and opportunity to learn were cut short by a typhoid epidemic that prostrated the family, including Joseph, who suffered through a year of sickness made worse by a debilitating leg operation. When health returned, the family economy was so low that the Smiths were "compelled to strain every energy to provide for . . . present necessities."[2] Following this illness, the family moved to Norwich, Vermont, where they and their neighbors experienced three successive years of crop failure that produced a near famine, forcing upon the Smiths another move, this time to western New York.

---

1. Charles Knecht, "Notes Written on 'Chamber's Life of Joseph Smith,' by William Smith," (1925), 17, Typescript, LDS Church Archives.

2. Lucy Smith, *Biographical Sketches*, 60, 66.

Settling in Palmyra in 1816, the Smiths united their strength to pay for a hundred acres of land and establish themselves in a new community. William Smith later recalled that while living on their New York farm, they "cleared sixty acres of the heaviest timber I ever saw, . . . trees you could not conveniently cut down."[1] In addition, the family maintained fifteen hundred maple trees from which they gathered sap and made sugar and molasses, and the boys hired out as laborers in the town. Through all this, record keeping was not part of the Joseph Smith, Sr., family tradition. Not until later in their lives did members of the family write about their experience.

Another factor that has limited the perception of Joseph Smith, especially during the formative years of Mormonism, was the problem of defining and developing a system of record keeping, once an 1830 revelation had commanded that responsibility. Only gradually were procedures developed for producing and preserving records. But even after a basic historical structure was in place, many important occurrences were missed entirely. Substantial amounts of the Prophet's writings and speeches, especially before 1842, were not recorded or were lost.

Of more than two hundred and fifty known occasions when Joseph Smith addressed an assembly or spoke in the hearing of others, reasonably adequate reports of only about one-fifth of his discourses were recorded. In many instances, nothing more was preserved than the subject and the fact of his having spoken. The lack of reference to his early religious experiences in early Mormon sources may be attributed, at least in part, to irregularities in record keeping.

For example, William W. Phelps reported hearing the Prophet give in 1835 an address entitled "This is My Beloved Son: Hear Ye Him." Phelps noted that it was one of the greatest

---

1. J. W. Peterson, "William B. Smith's Last Statement," *Zion's Ensign* 5 (1894), 6.

sermons he had ever heard, lasting about three hours. But no record of it was made. Later that year, during a period covered by one of Joseph's most detailed diaries, a visitor to Kirtland, Ohio, made inquiry of the Mormon leader about the origin of the church. Joseph gave "a brief relation of my experience while in my juvenile years, say from 6 years old up to the time I received the first visitation of Angels which was when I was about 14 years old and also the visitation that I received afterward concerning the book of Mormon." Again, neither the Prophet nor the scribe employed to record the event added further detail.[1]

Writing to the Saints in Canada in 1836, Parley Pratt told of an important meeting he had attended in the Kirtland Temple. One week prior to the gathering, an announcement went out that the Prophet would speak about the coming forth of the Book of Mormon, the establishment of the Church, and his own experience. According to Pratt, "a vast concourse assembled at an early hour. Every seat was crowded and 4 or 5 hundred people stood up in the aisles. Br. S[mith] gave the history of these things relating many particulars of the manner of his first visions &c. The spirit and power of God was upon him in bearing testimony insomuch that many if not most of the congregation were in tears. As for myself I can say that all the reasonings in uncertainty and all the conclusions drawn from the writings of others . . . however great in themselves dwindle into insignificance when compared with the living testimony when your eyes see and your ears hear from the living oracles of God." Beyond the Pratt letter no other report of the discourse has been found.[2]

In 1837, Wilford Woodruff heard Joseph Smith speak in

1. Diary of William W. Phelps, 2 June 1835, Ms., LDS Church Archives; Diary of Joseph Smith, 14 November 1835.

2. Parley Pratt to the Elders of the Church of Latter day Saints and Brethren in Canada, 27 November 1836, Ms., Parley P. Pratt Papers, LDS Church Archives.

the Kirtland Temple at a time when many who opposed him were in the audience. He spoke "several hours . . . in the power of God . . . as Moses did anciently," and the opposers were "put to silence" for they saw that "he stood in the power of a Prophet."[1] Yet this prolific diarist added nothing further to his report. Nor have other accounts of the event surfaced.

Another element that has in some instances warped or colored the perception of Joseph Smith reflected in his papers was his dependence upon others to help keep his records. Like busy men of other times, the Mormon leader depended upon clerks to do most of his writing. Thus, a substantial part of his diaries are not his own thoughts. Most of his writings were the product of a policy he articulated to Willard Richards in 1843, that "a man to be a great man . . . must not dwell upon small things, though he may enjoy them." This he explained to mean, "A prophet cannot be a scribe."[2]

Throughout much of the papers of Joseph Smith, his philosophy of record keeping has effectually shielded the present reader from the mind and heart of the Prophet. After 1836, very little of the material in his diaries was dictated, and in his papers as a whole only an occasional letter or series of diary entries are in his own hand. The variety in the Smith papers, fluctuating between holograph, dictated, and ghostwritten prose, creates a challenge for those who seek his personality or face issues of actual authorship.

The completeness and accuracy with which Joseph Smith's life and thought are known depend upon the skill of his clerks and the reader's ability to understand what they wrote. For instance, an 1838 Smith journal, kept by George W. Robinson, contains these lines written on September 4: "Prest. Rigdon & myself commenced this day the study of Law under General

1. Diary of Wilford Woodruff, 19 February 1837, Ms., Wilford Woodruff Papers, LDS Church Archives.

2. Diary of Joseph Smith, 4 March 1843.

Atchison & Doniphan. They think by dilligent application we can be admitted to the bar in twelve months." Considering that Robinson was keeping the journal for Joseph, early editors of his *History* assumed from this entry that Rigdon and Smith began studying law on that day. But a careful look at Robinson's use of first and second person construction in this part of the diary suggests that it was Rigdon and Robinson who commenced the study of law on September 4, and not Joseph Smith.

Similarly, the editors assumed that the first-person usage in the Smith diary kept by James Mulholland in 1839 reported the Prophet's own activity. Hence, the published *History*, based upon Joseph Smith's diaries, indicates that Joseph traveled from Commerce, Illinois, to Quincy and back between May 14 and 19: "I returned to Quincy [from Commerce] so kept no minute [record] of course, I got back here Sunday evening the 19th May." However, Wilford Woodruff, who arrived in Commerce on May 18, wrote that his first stop was with the Smith family. Woodruff's account supports a rereading of the first-person statement in the diary, which suggests that the diary is actually Mulholland's own explanation of why he did not record the events of that week.

Much of both the quality and the quantity of the Joseph Smith diaries depended upon the ability and diligence of his clerks. A comparison of overlapping journal entries, and reports of discourses where more than one scribe kept a record, indicate a wide range of competence and diligence. James Mulholland kept a small diary for the Prophet in 1838 covering the period from September 3 to October 6. The Mulholland record overlaps the journal kept for Joseph by Robinson in 1838 through eight days. A comparison of the two records shows Mulholland to have been observing Joseph from a distance. And the record he kept leaves the impression that he may not have been well enough oriented in his responsibility to report essentials. He saw the Mormon leader's goings and comings each day but apparently did not have the personal contact to learn any detail. Yet, even on September 4, when Mulholland records having had a meal with the Prophet, their time together did not produce a more substantial report for the day.

The Smith diary kept by Mulholland is essentially a list of arrivals and departures. On September 7, he "saw him leave home about sun rising and heard, and saw him at home between 10 and 11 oclock same night," with no further explanation as to where Joseph had gone or what had transpired. Robinson, on the other hand, reported at some length that the Prophet had traveled to Raglin's, near the Caldwell County line, where a hearing was held in the Adam Black case that resulted in Joseph, and Lyman Wight, being bound over for trial on a $500 bond.

Where Robinson's report is available during that critical summer of 1838, the reader gets a more complete picture of Joseph Smith's activities. But after the Robinson journal ends, the Mulholland record provides little detail. A reconstruction of the Prophet's activities based on his diary kept by Mulholland in September and October 1838, at the height of the Missouri crisis, gives the impression of Joseph riding leisurely about the countryside while Rome burned: "At home at breakfast and before, saw him ride out a horseback about 1/2 past 8 oclock morning. Returned home about 5 oclock evening." (September 24.) "At home morning early also at breakfast between 7 & 8 oclock. Saw him ride out between 10 & eleven oclock and saw him at home again 9 oclock evening." (September 26.) A comparison of the two records shows that while Mulholland was the better penman and copyist, Robinson produced a more detailed report. But more important, they reflect the unevenness of Joseph Smith's diary not only in portraying his personality but in many instances even a basic summary of his daily activity.

Another barrier that limits the view of Joseph Smith stems

from the difficulty of accurately reporting what he said. There is little evidence that he spoke from a prepared text. The surviving manuscript record supports an 1830 revelation stating that God would give him "in the very moment what [he should] speak and write." (D&C 24:6.) In 1843 he told an audience, "I am not like other men; my mind is continually occupied with the business of the day, and I have to depend entirely upon the living God for everything I say on such occasions as these."[1] Occasionally, he changed the topic of an address as he arose to face his audience.[2] In the absence of prepared drafts for speeches, or technical means to record them, incomplete surviving reports by those who heard him are the only sources for what he said.

Pitman shorthand, a method developed in England in 1837, provided a major nineteenth-century breakthrough in writing speed and accuracy. But no one in the Mormon community mastered the skill in time to produce a verbatim account of a Joseph Smith discourse. The reports of his speeches were the product of the longhand, speed writing, and memory skills of those who heard him. These varied from brief to lengthy summaries, many of them reported in the diaries of those who heard him.

A comparison of the same discourse by different reporters (see for example the Woodruff and Richards reports of 21 February 1843, or Brigham Young and Wilford Woodruff reports on 14 May 1843) shows the difference in capacity and ability between scribes. And in cases where gaps were left in reports for later expansion, the time lapse made it difficult to reconstruct specific details. George A. Smith, in editing many of the reports of discourses for the Prophet's history more than

1. Diary of Joseph Smith, 13 August 1843.
2. Ibid., 11 June 1843.

a decade later, noted that his work "was an immense labor, requiring the deepest thought and the closest application."[1]

Another force that came to bear upon the structure of the Smith papers was the unsettled conditions in which he lived. Chaotic times were not productive of an extensive collection of his papers, and this helps explain the gaps in his diaries and history. The Joseph Smith History speaks of long imprisonments, vexatious and long-continued lawsuits, the treachery of some of his clerks, the untimely death of others, and his own poverty as circumstances that impeded his record keeping. Add to this the heavy burden of administration. In June 1840, he memorialized the Nauvoo high council to relieve him from "the anxiety and trouble necessarily attendant on business transactions" and to provide appropriate means to hire clerks to help him in the important work of record keeping. In 1843 when noise from a school class hindered the work on his history, he advised the caretaker of the school to seek out another location as the "history must go ahead before anything."[2]

If everything known about Joseph Smith is conditioned by the documentary foundation upon which that knowledge rests, a careful ordering and evaluation of his papers is important. A study of his autograph writings reveals dimensions of his personality that have been diluted or are missing completely in the works attributed to him but produced by other minds.[3] One finds in his personal writings, for example, a cosmic view of life and events that evoked a spontaneous outpouring of his

1. George A. Smith to Wilford Woodruff, 21 April 1856, Ms., Historian's Office Papers, LDS Church Archives.

2. Diary of Joseph Smith, 19 May 1843; Memorial to the High Council of the Church, 18 June 1840, in Joseph Smith Letterbook, 2:148-50, Ms., Joseph Smith Papers, LDS Church Archives.

3. A significant study of Joseph Smith's literary style is Elinore H. Partridge, "Characteristics of Joseph Smith's Style," Task Papers in LDS History, No. 14, 1976. Typescript. See also, her "Nineteenth-century Spelling: The Rules and Writers," *Ensign* 5 (August 1975): 75-80.

feelings. After being awakened one November night to see "the signs in the heavens," he wrote in his diary, "I arrose and beheld to my great Joy the stars fall from heaven yea they fell like hail stones a litteral fullfillment of the word of God as recorded in the holy scriptures and a sure sign that the coming of Christ is clost at hand Oh how marvellous are thy works Oh Lord and I thank thee for thy mercy unto me thy servent Oh Lord save me in thy kingdom for Christ sake Amen." Frequently, his autograph writings contain expressions of gratitude and imploring for divine favor: "Oh may God grant that I may be directed in all my thoughts. Oh bless thy servent, Amen."[1]

Another element of the Prophet's personality reflected in his holograph writings is one that derived from personal spiritual experience, contemplation, and a more than casual study of holy writ. He taught that "the things of God are of deep import and time and experience and careful and ponderous and solemn thought can only find them out." His prose reveals an extraordinary religious sense. Delayed at Greenville, Indiana, while traveling from Missouri to Ohio in 1832, Joseph wrote of visiting a grove "just back of the town almost every day where I can be secluded from the eyes of any mortal and there give vent to all the feelings of my heart in meditation and prayer"—a place where he sought "consolation of him who is alone able to console me," where he "communed with him who is altogether lovely."[2]

The scriptural syntax, images, and examples he used reveal a mind well-schooled in the Bible: "the cloud is gethering around us with great fury and all pharohs host or in other words all hell and the combined powrs of Earth are Marsheling their forces to overthrow us. . . . We must wait on God to be

1. Diary of Joseph Smith, 13 November 1833; 27 November 1832.

2. Joseph Smith to the Church, 20 March 1839; Joseph Smith to Emma Smith, 6 June 1832; Joseph Smith to William W. Phelps, 31 July 1832.

gratious and call on him with out ceaseing to make bare his arm for our defence."[1] Biblical quotations and illustrations abound in his writings and discourses.

One also finds in the Joseph Smith writings an attitude of wonder, admiration, and awe for the physical universe, for nature, for events occurring about him on the earth. Reflecting upon his early life on one occasion, he wrote, "I looked upon the sun the glorious luminary of the earth and also the moon rolling in their majesty through the heavens and also the stars shining in their courses and the earth also upon which I stood and the beast[s] of the field and the fowls of heaven and the fish of the waters and also man walking forth upon the face of the earth in majesty and in the strength of beauty whose power and intelligence in governing the things which are so exceeding great and marvelous even in the likeness of him who created them and when I considered upon these things my heart exclaimed, well hath the wise man said, it is a fool that saith in his heart there is no God."[2]

Another personal attribute reflected in Joseph Smith's writings was his deep concern for family, friends, and, indeed, all humanity. He taught that "love is one of the leading characteristics of Deity, and ought to be manifested by those who aspire to be the Sons of God. A man filled with the love of God is not content with blessing his family alone but ranges through the world, anxious to bless the whole of the human family."

After a careful study of the Prophet's autograph writings, Elinore Partridge concluded that despite the fact that he had a limited education and little time to study literary skills, his writings reflect characteristics of the finest masters of the English language: he was well-schooled in the King James Bible; he had a keen sense of detail as seen in the descriptive nature

1. Joseph Smith to William W. Phelps and others, 18 August 1833.
1. Joseph Smith, History, 1832. See p. 1.

of his prose; he had a good narrative sense and was able to communicate in a way that held the interest of his audience; and he wrote in a conversational style. Partridge noted the enormous sense of joy and vitality that permeated his writings. "In contrast to the dark visions of Calvinism and the dry, rational theology of Unitarianism, Joseph Smith's pronouncements emphasize the wonder of existence and the love of humanity." And in contrast to "threats of wrath, judgment, and damnation" in some of the writings of early Mormonism, there is in the Prophet's prose "an undercurrent of understanding and compassion." And although moments of discouragement and anger do occur, they are tempered with "trust in God, love for his family, and hope for the future."[1]

Efforts to Publish Joseph Smith's Papers

The Joseph Smith papers are primarily housed in the archives of the LDS Church in Salt Lake City, Utah, but significant segments and individual items are located in other repositories, and in private hands. The collection consists of a dozen volumes containing diary and autobiographical material beginning with the year 1832 and continuing, with substantial gaps, until his death in 1844; three copybooks containing correspondence, revelations, and other documents; several hundred items of loose correspondence, revelations, financial records, discourses, and other writings; manuscripts pertaining to the Book of Mormon, the Books of Abraham and Moses, a Bible revision; and the manuscript of his History of the Church.

Joseph Smith's documentary History of the Church, begun in 1838 and completed in 1856, was the first attempt to publish a work based on a large portion of his papers. His diaries formed the basis for the History narrative, interspersed with correspondence and other papers in their chronological se-

1. Partridge, "Characteristics of Joseph Smith's Style," 19-20.

quence according to a pattern he established. The History appeared serially in Church periodicals between 1842 and 1856 and was eventually edited and published by Church historian B. H. Roberts in six volumes at the beginning of the twentieth century. Although the Joseph Smith History incorporated a significant number of his papers, it was not a comprehensive publication of the available source material. Nor did the editorial standards of the time always preserve the integrity of the sources.

Following publication of the Smith History, more than half a century elapsed before portions of his papers were published using more accurate methods of editorial skill. Most notable of these is the edition of his Nauvoo discourses published by Andrew F. Ehat and Lyndon W. Cook in 1980, and Scott H. Faulring's edition of most of the Joseph Smith diaries in 1987.[1]

The Present Edition

When Julian Boyd's first volume of the Thomas Jefferson papers appeared in 1950, it was the fifth time an edition of the writings of America's second president had been published since his death in 1826. Work on the Jefferson papers prompted President Harry S. Truman to direct the National Historical Publications Commission to prepare a plan for making available "the public and private writings of men whose contributions to our history are now inadequately represented by published works." This action by the president initiated what has been described as the "most monumental editorial task ever undertaken in this country."[2] In 1951, the commission

---

1. Andrew F. Ehat and Lyndon W. Cook, *The Words of Joseph Smith: The Contemporary Accounts of the Nauvoo Discourses of the Prophet Joseph* (Provo, Utah: Religious Study Center, Brigham Young University, 1980); Scott H. Faulring, *An American Prophet's Record: The Diaries and Journals of Joseph Smith* (Salt Lake City: Signature Books, 1987).

2. Haskell M. Monroe, "Some Thoughts for an Aspiring Historical Editor," *American Archivist* 32 (April 1969): 148, 150.

initially recommended the comprehensive publication of the papers of five of the Founding Fathers (Franklin, John Adams, John Quincy Adams, Madison, and Hamilton) in addition to the Jefferson papers then under way. They believed that publication of the papers of America's great men and women would give "added strength and inspiration to the people." The commission added that in times like these "when the democratic world is seriously threatened by enemies within and without its borders . . . an understanding of the American heritage and of the ideas and ideals upon which it rests is vitally important."[1] Since these words were written, the publication of the papers of nearly a hundred prominent Americans has been undertaken.[2]

Dumas Malone has noted that these enterprises are "without parallel in our history and unequalled in the Western World." Their net result will be to make available "more knowledge of the greatest men of the early Republic than was available to their own contemporaries. . . . No country in the world will have so complete a record of its beginnings. No country could hope to have one that is more honest." As these works emerge, with their wealth of information, Esmond Wright observed, "It is quite likely that the whole of American history may need rewriting."[3]

Some of the papers of America's Founding Fathers are being published for the fourth or fifth time, each edition building upon the previous one to take advantage of new materials and methods. Thomas Jefferson's papers, for example, were first published in 1829 (three years after his death) in four

1. Jesse Lemisch, "The Papers of Great White Men," *Maryland Historian* 11 (Spring 1975): 44.

2. National Historical Publications and Records Commission, *Historical Documentary Editions* (Washington, D.C.: National Archives, 1986).

3. Dumas Malone, "Tapping the Wisdom of the Founding Fathers," *New York Times Magazine*, 27 May 1954, 25-26; Esmond Wright, "Making History," *The Listener* 63 (15 November 1962): 803.

volumes by Thomas Jefferson Randolph. This was followed by the nine-volume Henry Washington edition in 1853-54; the ten-volume Paul Leicester Ford edition in 1892-99; the twenty-volume Lipscomb and Bergh edition in 1903-4; and, finally, the current edition begun by Julian Boyd in 1950, contemplated for sixty-five volumes. Since there is no history without documents, these published works have proven invaluable for understanding the life and times of those who produced them. These publications are the fulfillment of Jefferson's sense of the importance of preserving the national heritage, when he encouraged the preservation of important manuscripts and records "by such a multiplication of copies, as shall place them beyond the reach of accident."[1]

By contrast, the papers of Joseph Smith have never been published, or even listed, in their entirety, and yet his image continues to increase in the ranks of the world's great leaders. No study of Joseph Smith or Mormonism can hope to succeed without recourse to his papers, so centrally was he involved in the history of his people. If, as he and his followers have maintained, he was the recipient of a new dispensation of divine authority, his life and thought are of fundamental importance. Heretofore, his *History of the Church* has served as the best source for a study of his life and times. However, limitations in format, completeness, and accuracy underscore the need for a comprehensive edition of his papers. This printing of the historical and autobiographical writings and diaries of Joseph Smith in three volumes comprises the first series in what we hope can become a comprehensive publication of his papers.

The present work had its inception in 1972 under the administration of the Church Historian, Leonard Arrington, when groundwork was laid for publishing the personal writings of Joseph Smith, comprising that portion of the Prophet's pa-

1. Quoted by Haskell Monroe in "Some Thoughts," p. 147.

pers written by his own hand, and other material known to have been dictated by him. This work was published by Deseret Book Company in 1984 under the title *The Personal Writings of Joseph Smith*. As a collection of that part of his papers that most accurately portrays his own personality, the *Personal Writings* will continue to serve a need. The present phase of editing the Joseph Smith papers began in 1985 in the Joseph Fielding Smith Institute for Church History at Brigham Young University, under the direction of Ronald K. Esplin, and will, so far as possible, include everything that has appeared over Joseph Smith's name, whether he did the actual writing himself or directed others to write for him.

GUIDE TO EDITORIAL PROCEDURES

The editorial procedure governing this edition of the Papers of Joseph Smith is derived from the position that an individual's personality is a reflection of the totality of his being, including his handwritten prose. Hence, in formulating rules for the present edition, I have emphasized preserving the integrity of the original sources. To accomplish this, I have adopted rules that will reproduce the original text as near as typography will allow.

Very little of the visual element of writing (the formation of letters and words and their placement on the page) can be transcribed in print short of a photographic facsimile. But the literary content (the message conveyed by the writing, including the spelling, punctuation, crossed-out words, insertions, and so on), can be fairly accurately transcribed.

Recognizing the impossibility of reproducing in type the visual characteristics of handwriting, I have employed a uniform format for paragraph indentation and placement of date, salutation, and signature of correspondence. Occasional photographs will show the visual dimension of the writing. An exception to the strict preservation of literary content is a uniform expansion and italicizing of diary dates.

The following additional guidelines govern the presentation of the text:

All Joseph Smith holograph writing (material written in his own hand) is in this typeface.

Handwriting other than Joseph Smith's follows a slash mark and note identifying the writer: /[15] .

All spelling, punctuation, and capitalization have been retained as they appear in the original manuscripts. Where the manuscript is unclear, current usage is given.

Insertions that are part of the original text are enclosed in angle brackets at the place of insertion: ⟨heavy⟩. If placement of non-careted insertions affect meaning, such instances are noted.

Canceled material is retained as in the original: ~~stone~~ .

Missing or unintelligible letters or words are indicated by dots and dashes within brackets—dots [..] representing the approximate number of missing letters, and dashes [– –] the approximate number of missing words.

Editorial insertions that enlarge the original text or supply missing or unintelligible words are enclosed in brackets: H[eber].

Editorial comments not part of the text are enclosed in brackets and italicized: [*page torn*].

Underlined words appear in italics: *several.*

Shorthand has been deciphered where possible and enclosed in braces: {married}.

Bracketed page numbers designate the end of each page of the copy text: [p. 1]. Unnumbered pages are numbered editorially: [p.[1]].

Superscript letters are lowered: J^r to Jr.

Each volume of the Joseph Smith Papers will contain a biographical register of persons mentioned in the text of the volume, a list of sources cited, and its own index. The final volume of the work will contain a combined register of names, bibliography, index, and a calendar of the Joseph Smith Papers.

JOSEPH SMITH CHRONOLOGY

1805	Dec 23	Born at Sharon, Windsor County, Vermont.
1811		Family moved to Lebanon, New Hampshire.
1813		Contracted typhus fever; leg operation.
1816		Family moved to Palmyra, New York.
1820	Spring	First Vision.
1823	Sep 21	First visitation from Moroni.
	Nov 19	Death of brother Alvin.
1827	Jan 18	Married Emma Hale at Bainbridge, New York.
	Sep 22	Obtained Book of Mormon plates.
	Dec	Moved to Harmony, Pennsylvania.
1828		116 pages of Book of Mormon manuscript lost.
	Jun 15	Son born; died same day.
1829	May-Jun	Priesthood received.
	Jun	Finished Book of Mormon translation.
1830	Mar	Book of Mormon published.
	Apr 6	Church organized.
	Jun	Visions of Moses revealed.
	Dec	Writings of Moses revealed.
1831	Jan	Moved to Kirtland, Ohio.
	Spring	Commenced revision of the Bible.
	Apr 30	Twins born; lived only three hours.
	May 9	Adopted Murdock twins (Joseph and Julia).
	Jun 19	Started for Jackson County, Missouri.
	Jul	Revelation designating site for city of Zion (D&C 57).
	Sep 12	Moved to Hiram, Ohio.
	Dec	Preached in area of Kirtland-Ravenna, Ohio, to counteract effects of anti-Mormon *Ohio Star* articles.

1832	Jan 25	Sustained president of High Priesthood at Amherst, Ohio, conference.
	Feb 16	Revelation of postmortal state of mankind (D&C 76).
	Mar 24	Tarred and feathered by mob at Hiram, Ohio.
	Mar 29	Adopted son, Joseph M., died.
	Apr 1	Started for Missouri.
	Jun	Arrived back at Kirtland after delay at Greenville, Indiana.
	Oct	Traveled to Albany, New York City, and Boston, with Newel K.Whitney.
	Nov 6	Returned to Kirtland. Son, Joseph III, born.
	Dec 25	Revelation on war (D&C 87).
1833	Feb 27	Revelation known as the Word of Wisdom (D&C 89).
	Mar 18	First Presidency finally organized.
	Jul 23	Cornerstone for Kirtland Temple laid.
	Oct 5	Left Kirtland on proselyting mission to Canada.
	Nov 4	Returned to Kirtland.
	Nov 25	News of expulsion of Saints from Jackson County, Missouri.
1834	Feb 17	High council organized at Kirtland.
	Feb 26	Left Kirtland to proselyte volunteers for Zion's Camp.
	Mar 28	Returned to Kirtland.
	Apr 1-3	Attended court at Chardon in Hurlbut case.
	Apr 12	Fishing on Lake Erie.
	Apr 22	Conference at Norton, Ohio.
	May 5	Left Kirtland for Missouri at head of Zion's Camp.
	Jun 19	Arrived in Clay County, Missouri.
	Aug 1	Returned to Kirtland, Ohio.
	Oct	Visited Saints in Michigan.
	Nov	Participated in school of elders at Kirtland.
1835	Feb 14	Organization of Quorum of Twelve.
	Feb 28	Organization of Quorum of Seventy.
	Mar 28	Revelation on priesthood (D&C 107).
	Jul	Egyptian mummies and papyrus purchased.
	Oct 8-11	Attended father during his illness.
	Nov	Studying Hebrew and Greek.
1836	Mar 27	Dedicated Kirtland Temple.
	Apr 3	Vision of Savior in Kirtland Temple.

	May 17	Met grandmother, Mary Duty, at Fairport and accompanied her to Kirtland.
	Jun 20	Son Frederick born.
	Jul 25	Left Kirtland for the East.
	Jul 30	Visited part of New York City burned in 1835 fire.
	Sep	Returned to Kirtland.
	Nov 2	Kirtland Safety Society Bank established.
1837	Apr 6	Solemn assembly in Kirtland Temple.
	May	Denounced by dissenters at Kirtland.
	May 30	Acquitted in Grandison Newel case.
	Jun	Seriously ill.
	Jul 23	Revelation to the Twelve (D&C 112).
	Aug	Visited Saints in Canada.
	Sep 3	Conference in Kirtland; three of Twelve rejected.
	Sep 27	Left Kirtland for Missouri.
	Nov 7	Conference at Far West, Missouri.
	Dec	Returned to Kirtland, dissension in Church.
1838	Jan 12	Left Kirtland to escape mob violence.
	Mar 14	Arrived with family at Far West, Caldwell County, Missouri.
	Apr 30	Writing history.
	May 14	Plowed garden.
	May 19	Selected site for new settlement, Adam-ondi-Ahman.
	Jun 2	Son Alexander born.
	Aug 6	Election-day fight at Gallatin, Missouri.
	Oct 11	Led harassed Saints from DeWitt, Carroll County, Missouri to Far West, Caldwell County.
	Oct 27	Extermination order issued by Governor Boggs.
	Oct 30	Haun's Mill massacre.
	Oct 31	Surrendered to Missouri militia at Far West; imprisoned.
	Nov 1	Sentenced to death; opposition by General Doniphan prevented execution.
	Nov 4	Arrived under guard at Independence, Jackson County,Missouri.
	Nov 12	Court of inquiry at Richmond, Ray County.
	Dec 1	Imprisoned at Liberty, Clay County.
1839	Apr 6	Taken from Liberty jail to Gallatin, Daviess County, for trial.

	Apr 11	Indicted; granted change of venue to Boone County.
	Apr 15	En route to Boone County, allowed to escape by guards.
	Apr 22	Reunited with family at Quincy, Illinois.
	May 10	Moved to Commerce (later renamed Nauvoo), Hancock County, Illinois.
	Jun	Involved in resettlement of Saints at Nauvoo.
	Jul 21-22	Administered to sick.
	Oct 29	Left Nauvoo to present Mormon grievances to federal government.
	Nov 28	Arrived at Washington, D.C.
	Nov 29	Visited President Martin Van Buren.
	Dec	Visited Saints in Philadelphia and New Jersey.
1840	Feb	Left Washington, D.C., for home.
	Mar 4	Arrived at Nauvoo.
	Sep 14	Death of father, Joseph Smith, Sr.
1841	Jan 30	Elected Trustee-in-trust.
	Feb 1	Elected to Nauvoo city council.
	Feb 4	Elected lieutenant general of Nauvoo Legion.
	Apr 5	Sealed to Louisa Beaman.
	Apr 6	Laid cornerstone for Nauvoo Temple.
	May 2	Entertained Stephen A. Douglas.
	Jun 4	Arrested on old Missouri charges.
	Jun 9-10	Trial before Judge Douglas at Monmouth, Illinois; acquitted.
	Jul 3	Patriotic address to Nauvoo Legion.
	Aug 7	Brother, Don Carlos, died at age of twenty-six.
	Aug 12	Spoke to visiting Sac and Fox Indians at Nauvoo.
	Sep 14	Attended military parade at Montrose, Iowa.
	Nov 8	Dedicated baptismal font in Nauvoo Temple.
1842	Jan 5	Commenced selling goods at his new store in Nauvoo.
	Jan 15	Correcting proof for new edition of Book of Mormon.
	Mar 1	Commenced publication of Book of Abraham.
	Mar 15	Officiated at installation of Nauvoo masonic lodge; received first degree of masonry.

	Mar 15	Became editor of *Times and Seasons*.
	Mar 17	Organized Female Relief Society.
	Mar 27	Engaged in baptisms for dead in Mississippi River.
	Apr	Forced to apply for bankruptcy.
	May 4	Introduced temple endowment.
	May 7	Life endangered during review of Nauvoo Legion.
	May 14	Working in garden after city council meeting.
	May 19	Elected mayor of Nauvoo.
	Aug 8	Arrested for complicity in Boggs assassination attempt; forced into hiding.
	Sep 16	Sitting for portrait.
	Dec 13	Chopped and hauled wood.
	Dec 26	Second arrest in Boggs case.
1843	Jan 5	Acquitted in Boggs case by Judge Nathaniel Pope.
	Jan 18	Fifteenth wedding anniversary; enjoyed day with invited guests at dinner.
	Feb 3	Studied German; read proof on Doctrine and Covenants.
	Feb 8	Went sliding on ice with son Frederick.
	Feb-Mar	Attended mother during her illness.
	Mar 4	Sealed to Emily Partridge.
	Mar 13	Wrestled William Wall; blessed twenty-seven children in evening.
	Apr 23	Took his children on pleasure ride in carriage.
	May 1	Sealed to Lucy Walker.
	May 16	Traveled to Ramus, Hancock County, Illinois.
	May 28	Sealed to Emma for time and eternity.
	Jun 3	Pleasure trip to Quincy, Illinois with family and friends on Mississippi River.
	Jun 13	Left Nauvoo to visit relatives at Dixon, Illinois.
	Jun 23	Arrested at Dixon by officers disguised as missionaries.
	Jun 30	Arrived at Nauvoo.
	Jul 1	Discharged by Nauvoo court.
	Jul 12	Revelation on marriage recorded (D&C 132).
	Aug 31	Moving into new residence, Nauvoo Mansion.

	Sep 4	Attended circus with family.
	Sep l6	Reviewed Nauvoo Legion.
	Sep 28	Introduced fulness of priesthood ordinances.
	Dec 25	Entertained fifty couples on Christmas Day.
1844	Jan 29	Elected candidate for U.S. presidency.
	Feb 20	Instructed Twelve to investigate location for Saints in California or Oregon.
	Mar 11	Organized Council of Fifty.
	Mar 18	Studying German.
	Apr 3	Presided at municipal court hearing.
	Apr 5	Attended dedication of Nauvoo masonic temple.
	Apr 7	Delivered King Follett funeral discourse.
	Apr 26	Life threatened by Nauvoo dissenters.
	May 10	Prospectus of Nauvoo *Expositor* distributed by dissenters.
	May 17	Nominated for U.S. presidential candidate at Nauvoo convention.
	Jun 7	Nauvoo *Expositor* published.
	Jun 10	Ordered destruction of Nauvoo *Expositor* press.
	Jun 12	Arrested on charge of riot for destroying press.
	Jun 18	Placed Nauvoo under martial law.
	Jun 25	Surrendered at Carthage, Hancock County, to face riot charge.
	Jun 27	Shot to death by mob at Carthage jail.

JOSEPH SMITH'S FAMILY

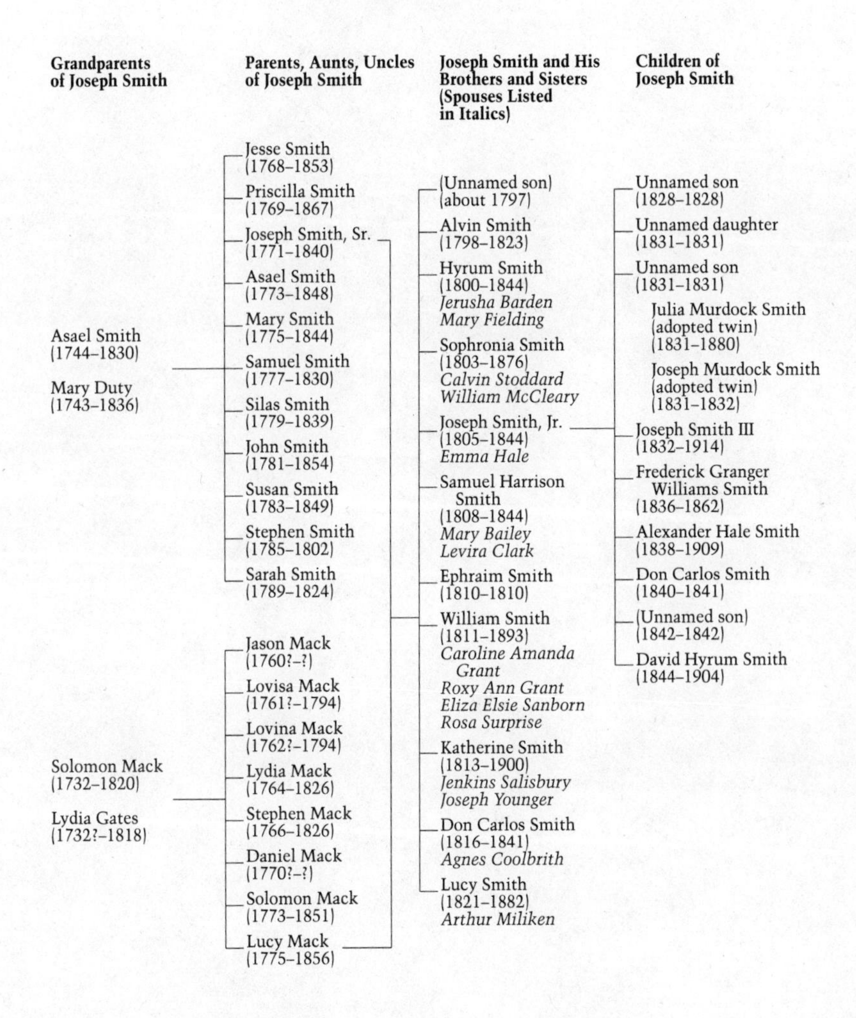

INTRODUCTION TO VOLUME 1

Joseph Smith's interest in record keeping may have been initially aroused as he read statements of personal history and advice by members of his family, and as he worked on the Book of Mormon. But his actual involvement in record keeping followed a revelation he delivered to the newly organized Church of Christ at Fayette, New York, on 6 April 1830, which began with the words, "Behold, there shall be a record kept among you." From instructions that followed, the Prophet outlined the general direction and form the record-keeping process should take—that it was the responsibility of the Church to produce "a history and a general church record of all things that transpire in Zion," including a record of its inhabitants, "their manner of life, their faith, and works."[1]

The early records of the Church reflect the efforts made by the Prophet to establish an effective record-keeping enterprise

---

1. Both of Joseph Smith's grandfathers wrote personal statements for their posterity. See Asael Smith's statement, 10 April 1799, MS. LDS Church Archives; and Solomon Mack, *A Narraitve [sic] of the Life of Solomon Mack* (Windsor, Vermont: Printed at the expence of the author, [1811?]); both of which are published in Richard L. Anderson, *Joseph Smith's New England Heritage* (Salt Lake City: Deseret Book Company, 1971), 31-61; 124-40. For record keeping as a Book of Mormon theme see Richard L. Bushman, "The Book of Mormon in Early Mormon History," in *New Views of Mormon History: A Collection of Essays in Honor of Leonard J. Arrington,* edited by Davis Bitton and Maureen U. Beecher, (Salt Lake City: University of Utah Press, 1987), 3-18. The quotations here are from D&C 21:1; 47; 85:1-4; 128:2-4.

and produce a history of his own life and labors. Among these are a number of false starts in the writing of a history, produced during the 1830s, as Joseph Smith and those involved with him in writing the Church history attempted to create a suitable model.[1] The writings in this volume represent the early efforts of Joseph Smith and others close to him to produce a record of his life and the beginnings of the work he established. Written between 1832 and 1844, the twelve items published here do not fall into a neat series easily distinguished from other writings Joseph produced, nor can they all be seen as having clearly emanated from his mind. The decision to group these writings together to the exclusion of everything else rested upon their substance, Joseph's personal involvement, the extent to which they tell the story of his life and earliest religious experience, and whether or not they fit naturally into other segments of his papers, such as his diaries or correspondence. Categorized here as autobiographical and historical writings, these documents were produced under a wide range of circumstances and reflect varying degrees of proximity to the Prophet's mind. The 1832 history is the only one of the twelve items that contains holograph material. The remaining works contain information only he knew, and they were either dictated or written from information he had supplied.

The general antagonism that followed a public awareness of Joseph Smith's early visions and involvement with the Book of Mormon continued throughout his life. Seldom has a historical figure met with such sustained misinformation and distortion in the public press. The writings produced here were written primarily to inform sincere inquirers about his life and mission, to tell his side of the story, including those religious

1. Jessee, "Joseph Smith and the Beginning of Mormon Record Keeping"; and "The Writing of Joseph Smith's History," *BYU Studies* 11 (Spring 1971): 439-73; Howard C. Searle, "Early Mormon Historiography: Writing the History of the Mormons 1830-1858" (Ph.D. diss., UCLA, 1979).

experiences that were central in his life and were the focus of his critics.

The materials presented in this volume appear in the order of their creation. This order documents Joseph Smith's efforts to prepare, as commanded in 1830, an adequate record of his life's work and provides the reader a sense of the development of his history-keeping efforts.

Those wishing a more chronological approach to Joseph Smith's life may consider reading in the following order:

1. History [1832] (p. 1): Joseph Smith's birth to translation of the Book of Mormon.
2. Letter to Oliver Cowdery, 1834 (p. 11): birth and character.
3. History, 1839 (p. 265): birth to late 1832.
4. History, 1834–1836 (p. 15): late 1834 to early 1836.
5. "Journal Extract," 1839 (p. 210): 1838–1839.

Add to this, two brief summaries of his life and mission:

6. "Church History," 1842 (p. 427).
7. *An Original History*, 1844 (p. 445).

HISTORY [1832]

MS. Joseph Smith Letterbook 1, pp. 1-6, Joseph Smith Papers, LDS Church Archives, Salt Lake City, Utah. The non-holograph portions of the manuscript are in the handwriting of Frederick G. Williams.

Editorial Note

The earliest historical record mentioned in the annals of Mormon history is attributed to Oliver Cowdery, Joseph Smith's clerk during the writing of much of the Book of Mormon. In 1831, when John Whitmer was selected historian, because Cowdery had been "appointed to another office," he noted that Cowdery had written "the commencement of the church history" beginning with the finding of the Book of Mormon plates to 12 June 1831, and that his (Whitmer's) work would continue the narrative from that time. But like his predecessor, Whitmer's tenure as historian was short-lived. (The Cowdery history is either lost or may refer to Cowdery documents copied into early records. See Jessee, "Joseph Smith and the Beginning of Mormon Record Keeping"; D&C 47:3; F. Mark McKiernan and Roger D. Launius, eds., *An Early Latter Day Saint History: The Book of John Whitmer* [Independence, Mo., 1980], 25, 56.)

Apparent laxity, or disagreement as to the nature of the work, brought an admonition from Joseph Smith to the historian, Whitmer, in 1832 to "remember the commandment to keep a history of the church and the gathering" and to "show himself approved" in the responsibilities of his calling. (Joseph Smith to Hyrum Smith, 31 July 1832.) Possibly disappointed with previous efforts to write a history, or recognizing the need for his personal involvement, Joseph produced a manuscript in 1832 that he intended as a history of his own life and the rise of the Church. This document is the earliest extant attempt by the Prophet to write a history of his life, and his only autobiographical work containing his own handwriting.

The manuscript consists of six pages written in brown ink on the first three leaves of what later became Joseph Smith's first letterbook.

Page 1

A History of the life of Joseph Smith Jr. an account
of his marvilous experience and of all the mighty acts
which he doeth in the name of Jesus Christ the son
of the living God of whom he beareth record
and also an account of the rise of the church of
Christ in the eve of time according as the Lord brought
forth and established by his hand firstly he receiving
the testamony from on high seccondly the ministering of Angels thirdly the reception of
the holy Priesthood by the ministring of
Aangels to adminster the letter of the Gospel
—the Law and commandments as they were given unto him—
and the ordinencs, forthly a confirmation
and reception of the high Priesthood after
the holy order of the son of the living God pow-
-er and ordinence from on high to preach
the Gospel in the administration and demonstra-
-tion of the spirit the Kees of the Kingdom of God
confered upon him and the continuation of the
blessings of God to him &c ——
I was born in the town of Charon in the State of Vermont
North America on the twenty third day of December
AD 1805 of goodly Parents who spared no pains
to instructing me in the christian religion at the age of
about ten years my Father Joseph Smith Seignior
moved to Palmyra Ontario County in the State of
New York and being in indigent circumstances were
obliged to labour hard for the support of a large
Family having nine chilldren and as it requir-
-ed the exertions of all that were able to render
any assistance for the support of the Family
therefore we were deprived of the bennifit of an
education suffice it to say I was mearly instruc-
-ted in reading and writing and the ground rules of
Arithmatic which constuted my whole lite-
-rary acquirements. At about the age of twelve
years my mind become seriously imprest

History, 1832, Joseph Smith Letterbook 1, p. 1. Handwriting of Frederick G. Williams and Joseph Smith. LDS Church Archives.

The pages, which measure 32 1/2 x 20 cm., were afterward cut from the volume. Although the manuscript is undated, a writing date of 1832 can be determined from the fact that Williams, according to his own statement, began writing for Joseph on 20 July that year. Furthermore, the dates of the beginning entries in the letter book, and the start of Joseph's first diary on 27 November, suggest that by that date the writing of this history had been discontinued. (Statement of Frederick G. Williams, n.d., MS. FGW Papers, LDS Church Archives; further detail on the dating of this manuscript is in Jessee, "Early Accounts of the First Vision," *BYU Studies*, 9 [Spring 1969]: 277-78.)

The 1832 History is an autobiographical narrative covering the period from Joseph Smith's birth to the translation of the Book of Mormon.

A History of the life of Joseph Smith Jr. an account of his marvilous experience and of all the mighty acts which he doeth in the name of Jesus Ch[r]ist the son of the living God of whom he beareth record and also an account of the rise of the church of Christ in the eve of time according as the Lord brough⟨t⟩ forth and established by his hand ⟨firstly⟩ he receiving the testamony from on high seccondly the ministering of Angels thirdly the reception of the holy Priesthood by the ministring of Aangels to adminster the letter of the Gospel—⟨—the Law and commandments as they were given unto him—⟩ and the ordinencs, forthly a confirmation and reception of the high Priesthood after the holy order of the son of the living God power and ordinence from on high to preach the Gospel in the administration and demonstration of the spirit **the Kees of the Kingdom of God confered upon him and the continuation of the blessings of God to him &c— I was born in the town of Charon [Sharon] in the ⟨State⟩ of Vermont North America on the twenty third day of December AD 1805 of goodly Parents[1] who spared no pains to instructing me in ⟨the⟩ christian religion at the age of about ten years**

1. On the Joseph Smith family background see Anderson, *Joseph Smith's New England Heritage.*

Birthplace of Joseph Smith, Sharon, Windsor County, Vermont, 29 December 1907. George E. Anderson Collection. LDS Church Archives.

my Father Joseph Smith Siegnior moved to Palmyra[1] Ontario County in the State of New York and being in indigent circumstances were obliged to labour hard for the support of a large Family having nine chilldren[2] and as it required the exertions of all that were able to render any assistance for the support of the Family therefore we were deprived of the bennifit of an education suffice it to say I was mearly instructid in reading ~~and~~ writing and the ground ⟨rules⟩ of Arithmatic which constuted my whole literary acquirements. At about the age of twelve years my mind become seriously imprest [p. 1] with regard to the all importent concerns for the wellfare of my immortal Soul which led me to searching the scriptures believeing as I was taught, that they contained the word of God thus applying myself to them and my intimate acquaintance with those of different denominations led me to marvel excedingly for I discovered that ⟨they did not ~~adorn~~⟩ ~~instead~~ of adorn~~ing~~ their profession by a holy walk and Godly conversation agreeable to what I found contained in that sacred depository this was a grief to my Soul thus from the age of twelve years to fifteen I pondered many things in my heart concerning the sittuation of the world of mankind the contentions and divi[si]ons the wicke[d]ness and abominations and the darkness which pervaded the ~~of the~~ minds of mankind my mind become excedingly distressed for I become convicted of my sins and by searching the scriptures I found that ~~mand~~ ⟨mankind⟩ did not come unto the Lord but that they had apostatised from the true and liveing faith and there was no society or denomination that built upon the gospel of Jesus Christ as recorded in the new testament and I felt to mourn for my own sins

---

1. A description of Palmyra in the time of Joseph Smith is in Milton V. Backman, Jr., *Joseph Smith's First Vision: The First Vision in its Historical Context* (Salt Lake City: Bookcraft, Inc., 1971), 34-40.

2. See chart on page xlv.

and for the sins of the world for I learned in the scriptures that God was the same yesterday to day and forever that he was no respecter to persons[1] for he was God for I looked upon the sun the glorious luminary of the earth and also the moon rolling in their magesty through the heavens and also the stars shining in their courses and the earth also upon which I stood and the beast of the field and the fowls of heaven and the fish of the waters and also man walking forth upon the face of the earth in magesty and in the strength of beauty whose power and intiligence in governing the things which are so exceding great and [p. 2] marvilous even in the likeness of him who created ~~him~~ ⟨them⟩ and when I considered upon these things my heart exclaimed well hath the wise man said ~~the~~ ⟨it is a⟩ fool ⟨that⟩ saith in his heart there is no God my heart exclaimed all all these bear testimony and bespeak an omnipotant and omnipreasant power a being who makith Laws and decreeeth and bindeth all things in their bounds who filleth Eternity who was and is and will be from all Eternity to Eternity and when I considered all these things and that ⟨that⟩ being seeketh such to worship him as worship him in spirit and in truth therefore I cried unto the Lord for mercy for there was none else to whom I could go and ~~to~~ obtain mercy and the Lord heard my cry in the wilderness and while in ⟨the⟩ attitude of calling upon the Lord ⟨in the 16th year of my age⟩ a piller of ~~fire~~ light above the brightness of the sun at noon day come down from above and rested upon me and I was filled with the spirit of god and the ⟨Lord⟩ opened the heavens upon me and I saw the Lord and he spake unto me saying Joseph ⟨my son⟩ thy sins are forgiven thee. go thy ⟨way⟩ walk in my statutes and keep my commandments behold I am the Lord of glory I was crucifyed for the world that all those who believe on my name may have Eternal life ⟨behold⟩ the world lieth in sin

1. Hebrews 13:8; Acts 10:34-35.

~~and~~ at this time and none doeth good no not one they have turned asside from the gospel and keep not ⟨my⟩ commandments they draw near to me with their lips while their hearts are far from me and mine anger is kindling against the inhabitants of the earth to visit them acording to th[e]ir ungodliness and to bring to pass that which ⟨hath⟩ been spoken by the mouth of the prophets and Ap[o]stles behold and lo I come quickly as it [is] written of me in the cloud ⟨clothed⟩ in the glory of my Father and my soul was filled with love and for many days I could rejoice with great Joy and the Lord was with me but [I] could find none that would believe the hevnly vision nevertheless I pondered these things in my heart ~~about that time my mother and~~ but after many days [p. 3] I fell into transgressions and sinned in many things which brought a wound upon my soul[1] and there were many things which transpired that cannot be writen and my Fathers family have suffered many persicutions and afflictions[2] and it came to pass when I was seventeen years of age I called again

---

1. Joseph Smith publicly addressed the subject of his transgressions in 1834. See pp. 13-14.

2. Among the "persecutions and afflictions" suffered by the family was an effort by unprincipled people to harrow up their feelings after the death of Alvin Smith as reflected in an item published in the local newspaper:

"To the Public.

"Whereas reports have been industriously put in circulation, that my son Alvin had been removed from the place of his interment and dissected, which reports, every person possessed of human sensibility must know, are peculiarly calculated to harrow up the mind of a parent and deeply wound the feelings of relations—therefore, for the purpose of ascertaining the truth of such reports, I, with some of my neighbors, this morning repaired to the grave, and removing the earth, found the body which had not been disturbed.

"This method is taken for the purpose of satisfying the minds of those who may have heard the report, and of informing those who have put it in circulation, that it is earnestly requested they would desist therefrom; and that it is believed by some, that they have been stimulated more by a desire to injure the reputation of certain persons than a philanthropy for the peace and welfare of myself and friends.

"JOSEPH SMITH"

The notice was published in the *Wayne Sentinel* (Palmyra, New York), 30 September; 6, 13, 20, 27 October; and 3 November 1824.

upon the Lord and he shewed unto me a heavenly vision for behold an angel of the Lord came and stood before me and it was by night and he called me by name and he said the Lord had forgiven me my sins and he revealed unto me that in the Town of Manchester Ontario County N.Y. there was plates of gold upon which there was engravings which was engraven by Maroni & his fathers the servants of the living God in ancient days and deposited by the commandments of God and kept by the power thereof and that I should go and get them and he revealed unto me many things concerning the inhabitants of[1] the earth which since have been revealed in commandments & revelations and it was on the 22d day of Sept. AD 1822 and thus he appeared unto me three times in one night and once on the next day and then I immediately went to the place and found where the plates was deposited as the angel of the Lord had commanded me and straightway made three attempts to get them and then being excedingly frightened[2] I supposed it had been a dreem of Vision but when I considred I knew that it was not therefore I cried unto the Lord in the agony of my soul why can I not obtain them behold the angel appeared unto me again and said unto me you have not kept the commandments of the Lord which I gave unto you therefore you cannot now obtain them for the time is not yet fulfilled therefore thou wast left unto temptation that thou mightest be made acquainted with the power of the advisary therefore repent and call on the Lord thou shalt be forgiven and in his own due time thou shalt obtain them [p. 4] for now I had been tempted of the advisary and saught the Plates to obtain riches and kept not the commandment that I should have an eye single to the glory of God therefore I was chastened

1. MS. repeats "of."

2. Further detail on his effort to obtain the plates is in accounts of Lucy Smith, *Biographical Sketches*, 85-86; and Joseph Knight, Dean C. Jessee, "Joseph Knight's Recollection of Early Mormon History," *BYU Studies* 17 (Autumn 1976): 31.

and saught diligently to obtain the plates and obtained them not untill I was twenty one years of age and in this year I was married to Emma Hale Daughter of Isaach Hale who lived in Harmony Susquehana County Pensylvania on the 18th [of] January AD 1827, on the 22d day of Sept of this same year I obtained the plates and ~~the~~ in December following we mooved to Susquehana[1] by the assistence of a man by the name of Martin Haris who became convinced of the visions and gave me fifty Dollars to bare my expences and because of his faith and this rightheous deed the Lord appeared unto him in a vision and shewed unto him his marvilous work which he was about to do **and ⟨he⟩ imediately came to Su[s]quehanna and said the Lord had shown him that he must go to new York City with some of the c[h]aracters so we proceeded to coppy some of them and he took his Journy to the Eastern Cittys[2] and to the Learned ⟨saying⟩ read this I pray thee and the learned said I cannot but if he would bring the plates[3] they would read it but the Lord had fo⟨r⟩bid it and he returned to me and gave them to ⟨me to⟩ translate and I said ~~I said~~ [I] cannot for I am not learned but the Lord had prepared ~~spect-ticke~~ spectacles for to read the Book therefore** I commenced translating the characters and thus the Prop[h]icy of Is⟨ia⟩ah was fulfilled which is writen in the 29 chapter concerning the book and it came to pass that after we had translated 116 pages that he desired to carry them to read to his friends that peradventure he might convince them of the truth therefore I inquired of the Lord and the Lord said unto me that he must not take them and I spoke unto him (Martin) the word of the Lord [p. 5] and he said inquire again and I inquired again and

1. Joseph Smith's stay in Susquehanna County, Pennsylvania, is discussed in Porter, "Origins of the Church," chapter 4.

2. On Harris's trip to the east see Stanley B. Kimball, "The Anthon Transcript: People, Primary Sources and Problems," *BYU Studies* 10 (Spring 1970): 325-64.

3. MS. reads "blates."

also the third time and the Lord said unto me let him go with them only he shall covenant with me that he will not shew them to only but four persons and he covenented withe Lord that he would do according to the word of the Lord therefore he took them and took his journey unto his friends to Palmira Wayne County & State of N York and he brake the covenent which he made before the Lord and the Lord suffered the writings to fall into the hands of wicked men and Martin was chastened for his transgession and I also was chastened ~~also~~ for my transgression for asking the Lord the third time wherefore the Plates was taken from me by the power of God and I was not able to obtain them for a season[1] and it came to pass after much humility and affliction of soul I obtained them again when [the] Lord appeared unto a young man by the name of Oliver Cowdry and shewed unto him the plates in a vision and also the truth of the work and what the Lord was about to do through me his unworthy servant therefore he was desirous to come and write for me[2] to[3] translate now my wife had writen some for me to translate and also my Brother Samuel H Smith but we had be come reduced in property and my wives father was about to turn me out of doors & I had not where to go and I cried unto the Lord that he would provide for me to accomplish the work whereunto he had commanded me [p. 6]

---

1. The chastisement of Martin Harris and Joseph Smith is found in Doctrine and Covenants sections 3 and 10.

2. Oliver Cowdery's clerical work on the Book of Mormon began on 7 April 1829. Most of the surviving pages of the original Book of Mormon manuscript are in his handwriting. See Dean C. Jessee, "The Original Book of Mormon Manuscript," *BYU Studies* 10 (Spring 1970): 259-78.

3. "to" written over "and" in MS.

LETTER TO OLIVER COWDERY, 1834

Joseph Smith to Oliver Cowdery, Latter Day Saints' Messenger and Advocate *1 (December 1834): 40.*

Editorial Note

Dissent against the orthodox creeds of Christendom has always produced opposition against those who dissented. In addition, the skepticism with which many of Joseph Smith's contemporaries reacted to his claims of divine favor shows the extent to which the scientific revolution had made inroads upon American society by the 1820s. If an earlier generation may have accepted the Mormon Prophet's claims with less rancor, by the early nineteenth century religious leaders denounced as superstition anything like revelation, spiritual gifts, dreams, healings, and so on, and particularly claims of direct communication with God on rational as well as religious grounds. (Richard Bushman, *Joseph Smith and the Beginnings of Mormonism*, 6, 7. See also, Keith Thomas, *Religion and the Decline of Magic* [New York, 1971], chapter 22.)

It is not surprising, then, that Joseph's declaration of divine communication met with hostility. A prevalent theme in publications that discredited the Mormon leader almost from the beginning of his public career was the charge of laziness and deceit. Among those whose writings established the framework of nineteenth-century anti-Mormon rhetoric were Abner Cole, a Palmyra, New York, newspaper editor, and the tandem of Eber D. Howe and Doctor Philastus Hurlbut (a publisher and disgruntled ex-Mormon), who joined efforts in the area of Painesville, Ohio.

In 1829 Abner Cole had commenced a small weekly paper in Palmyra titled *The Reflector*, using the same *Wayne Sentinel* press upon which the Book of Mormon was then being printed. Three months before the Book of Mormon came off the press, Cole published pirated extracts from it in his paper. Forced to desist when faced with the threat of legal action, Cole vented his wrath against Joseph Smith in a series of articles published in his paper in 1830-31 in which he portrayed Joseph as an unprincipled, shiftless, ignorant character. (Russell R. Rich, "The Dogberry Papers and the Book of Mormon," *BYU Studies* 10 [Spring 1970]: 315-19; "The Book of Pukei," *The Reflector* (Palmyra, New York), 12 June; 7 July 1830; Joseph W. Barnes, "Obediah Dogberry: Rochester Freethinker," *Rochester History* 36 [July 1974]: 1-24.)

Two years later, Philastus Hurlbut, a native of Vermont, had met the Prophet in Kirtland, Ohio, where the two men discussed the Book of Mormon and Hurlbut was baptized. But soon after his conversion and ordination to the office of an elder, Hurlbut was excommunicated for immoral conduct. This experience led him to join with anti-Mormons in Kirtland in vigorous opposition to Joseph Smith.

After threatening the Prophet's life, which netted him a $200 court fine and a restraining order to keep the peace, Hurlbut was sent by the local anti-Mormon committee to obtain information that would show "the bad character of the Mormon Smith Family," divest Joseph of "all claims to the character of an honest man," and place him at an "immeasurable distance from the high station he pretends to occupy." To accomplish his task, Hurlbut traveled in Ohio, New York, and Pennsylvania collecting statements disparaging to the Smith name. It was Hurlbut who introduced the Spalding theory of Book of Mormon origins, claiming that the book's story line was borrowed from a romance written by one Solomon Spalding of Conneaut, Ohio, and reworked with its religious content by Sidney Rigdon into the present Book of Mormon. In 1834 the fruits of Hurlbut's work appeared in Eber D. Howe's *Mormonism Unvailed*. (Max H. Parkin, "Conflict at Kirtland: A Study of the Nature and Causes of External and Internal Conflict of the Mormons in Ohio Between 1830 and 1838" [Salt Lake City, 1966], 120-28; Richard Bushman, *Joseph Smith and the Beginnings of Mormonism*, 126-27; Lester E. Bush, Jr., "The Spalding Theory Then and Now," *Dialogue* 10 [Autumn 1977]: 40-69.)

Concurrent with the appearance of the Howe book, the Mormon paper in Kirtland, Ohio, the *Latter Day Saints' Messenger and Advocate*, began what was intended to be "a full history of the rise of the church" in an effort to counter the distorted reports that had circulated. The editor of the paper, Oliver Cowdery, wrote in his introduction that "no sooner had the messengers of the fulness of the gospel, began to proclaim its heavenly precepts, and call upon men to embrace the same, than they were vilified and slandered by thousands who never saw their faces, and much less knew aught derogatory of their characters, moral or religious—Upon this unfair and unsaint like manner of procedure they have been giving in large *sheets* their own opinions of the incorrectness of our system, and *attested* volumes of our lives and characters." (*Latter Day Saints' Messenger and Advocate* [Kirtland, Ohio] 1 [October 1834]: 13, 41-42.)

Aware of the prospective history, Joseph Smith sent Oliver Cowdery a brief sketch of his birth and a statement about his character that was published in the December issue of the paper.

Brother O. Cowdery: Having learned from the first No. of the Messenger and Advocate, that you were, not only about to "give a history of the rise and progress of the church of the Latter Day Saints;" but, that said "history would necessarily embrace my life and character," I have been induced to give you the time and place of my birth; as I have learned that many of the opposers of those principles which I have held forth to the world, profess a personal acquaintance with me, though when in my presence, represent me to be another person in age, education, and stature, from what I am.

I was born, (according to the record of the same, kept by my parents,) in the town of Sharon, Windsor Co. Vt. on the 23rd of December, 1805.

At the age of ten my father's family removed to Palmyra, N.Y. where, and in the vicinity of which, I lived, or, made it my place of residence, until I was twenty one—the latter part, in the town of Manchester.

During this time, as is common to most, or all youths, I fell into many vices and follies; but as my accusers are, and have been forward to accuse me of being guilty of gross and outragious violations of the peace and good order of the community, I take the occasion to remark, that, though, as I have said above, "as is common to most, or all youths, I fell into many vices and follies," I have not, neither can it be sustained, in truth, been guilty of wronging or injuring any man or society of men; and those imperfections to which I alude, and for which I have often had occasion to lament, were a light, and too often, vain mind, exhibiting a foolish and trifling conversation.

This being all, and the worst, that my accusers can substantiate against my moral character, I wish to add, that it is not without a deep feeling of regret that I am thus called upon in answer to my own conscience, to fulfill a duty I owe to myself, as well as to the cause of truth, in making this public confession of my former uncircumspect walk, and unchaste conversation: and more particularly, as I often acted in violation of those holy precepts which I knew came from God. But as the "Articles and Covenants" of this church[1] are plain upon this particular point, I do not deem it important to proceed further. I only add, that I do not, nor never have, pretended to be any other than a man "subject to passion," and liable, without the assisting grace of the Savior, to deviate from that perfect path in which *all* men are commanded to walk!

By giving the above a place in your valuable paper, you will confer a lasting favor upon myself, as an individual, and, as I humbly hope, subserve the cause of righteousness.

I am, with feelings of esteem, your fellow laborer in the gospel of our Lord.

JOSEPH SMITH JR.

---

1. The "Articles and Covenants," a statement of fundamental principles, beliefs, and practices for the Church, served as a constitution, a standard of conduct and procedure. It was routinely read at early Church conferences, used by lay members as a standard for behavior, and carried by missionaries to teach procedure and policy. The revelation was eventually published as section 20 in the Doctrine and Covenants. See Robert J. Woodford, "The Historical Development of the Doctrine and Covenants," Ph.D. diss., Brigham Young University, 1974, 1:286-351. On its larger impact see David J. Whittaker, "The 'Articles of Faith' in Early Mormon Literature and Thought," in *New Views of Mormon History,* edited by Bitton and Beecher, 63-92.

HISTORY, 1834–1836

MS. History of the Church, A-1, 1-187, Joseph Smith Papers, LDS Church Archives.

Editorial Note

In 1834 Oliver Cowdery, who had performed extensive clerical work for Joseph Smith after meeting him in 1829, began writing in a big, leather-bound book, a record the Prophet later referred to as his "large journal." (Diary of Joseph Smith, 29 October 1835.) Following the uncompleted 1832 History, Oliver Cowdery's work was the next in a continuing effort to produce a history of Joseph Smith's life and the beginnings of the Church.

The 1834 History begins with a genealogy of the Church presidency, Joseph Smith, Oliver Cowdery, Sidney Rigdon, and Frederick G. Williams. However, information is given only under the names of the first two presidents, while succeeding pages remain blank except for the names of Rigdon and Williams at the top of the pages.

The genealogy then gives way to a diary-type narrative, continued in Oliver Cowdery's handwriting, under the heading "Chapter 1," and the date, 5 December 1834, which in turn was terminated after four pages following the entry of 6 December on page 20 of the manuscript. Then follow twenty-four blank pages numbered consecutively from 21 to 45.

Another change of format occurs in the manuscript starting on page 46 under the date of September 1834. In the handwriting of Frederick G. Williams, another Joseph Smith scribe, the narrative continues as a copy of a series of eight letters by Oliver Cowdery to William W. Phelps. These had commenced publication in the October 1834 *Messenger and Advocate.*

Oliver Cowdery's letters were written in the romantic style of nineteenth-century history. According to their published introduction, they

Genealogy of President Joseph Smith junior

Joseph Smith junior was born in the town of Sharon, Windsor County Vermont, December 23, AD. 1805.

Emma Hale was born in the town of Harmony, Susquehanna County, Pennsylvania, July 10, AD. 1804.

Joseph Smith junior, and Emma Hale, were married in the town of Bainbridge, County of Chenango, New-York, January 18, AD. 1827.

June 15 1828, a Son was born unto Joseph Smith junior. Harmony, Pennsylvania. — Died the same hour

April 30, 1831, A Son and daughter were born unto Joseph Smith jr in Kirtland, Geauga County, Ohio. — Lived three hours.

Joseph Smith 3rd was born in Kirtland, Ohio, November 6, 1832.

Joseph S. and Julia Murdock were born in Orange, Cuyahoga Co. Ohio, April 30, 1831, and adopted into Joseph Smith jr's family at the age of nine days. — Joseph S. Murdock died in Hiram Portage Co. Ohio, March 29, 1832. Age 11 months

History, 1834-1836, A-1, p. 9. LDS Church Archives.

were intended to be "a full history of the rise of the church of the Latter Day Saints, and the most interesting parts of its progress, to the present time."

To assure accuracy, Oliver Cowdery noted that "our brother, J. Smith Jr. has offered to assist us. Indeed, there are many items connected with the fore part of this subject that render his labor indispensible. With his labor and with authentic documents now in our possession, we hope to render this a pleasing and agreeable narrative, well worth the examination and perusal of the Saints." (*Messenger and Advocate*, 1 [October 1834]: 13.)

Shortly after the work of copying the Oliver Cowdery letters began, Joseph Smith hired a new scribe, Warren Parrish. On the day Parrish was employed, the Prophet retrieved his "large journal" from Frederick Williams, and, after returning home, he noted that Parrish "commenced writing in my Journal a history of my life, concluding President Cowdery's 2d letter to W.W. Phelps, which president Williams had begun." (Diary of Joseph Smith, 29 October 1835.)

After the eighth Oliver Cowdery letter had been copied into the "large journal," the "history" underwent still another format change. Under the date of September 1835, Warren Parrish prefaced the new material with an explanation that since the subject of the history, Joseph Smith, was "becoming daily more and more noted, the writer deemed it proper to give a plain, simple, yet faithful narration of every important item in his every-day occurrences."

The History then included entries from Joseph Smith's diary beginning 22 September 1835 and continuing through 17 January 1836, written in the third person. Following the entry of 17 January 1836, this History, like that which preceded it, was discontinued.

The third-person copy of the Joseph Smith diary is included here in its entirety, in addition to the first-person original later on. One reason for this is because the copy of the diary contains scribal additions that do not appear in the first-person account.

More significant, however, is the need to present the diary, as it was copied into the 1834-36 History, in its context as part of the continuing effort of Joseph Smith and those who helped him produce a history of his life and the work in which he was engaged.

A comparison of the *Messenger and Advocate* Oliver Cowdery material copied into this history, with the published original, indicates a lack of precision in preserving spelling, punctuation, paragraphing, and some wording. The word changes are given in the notes.

/[1]Genealogy of President Joseph Smith Junior.[2]

Joseph Smith Junior was born in the town of Sharon, Windsor County Vermont, December 23, A.D. 1805.

Emma Hale was born in the town of Harmony, Susquehanna County, Pennsylvania, July 10, A.D. 1804.

Joseph Smith Junior, and Emma Hale, were married in the town of Bainbridge, County of Chenango, New-York, January 18, A.D. 1827.

June 15, 1828, a son[3] was born unto Joseph Smith Junior. Harmony, Pennsylvania. (Died the same hour.

April 30, 1831, A son and daughter[4] were born unto Joseph Smith Jr. in Kirtland, Geauga County, Ohio. (Lived three hours.

Joseph Smith 3rd was born in Kirtland, Ohio, November 6, 1832.

Joseph S. and Julia Murdock were born in Orange, Cuyahoga Co. Ohio, April 30, 1831, and adopted into Joseph Smith Jr's family at the age of nine days. (Joseph S. Murdock died in Hiram, Portage Co. Ohio, March 29, 1832. Age 11 months.[5] [p. 9]

Joseph Smith sen. was born in the town of Topsfield, County of Essex, Massachusetts, July 12, A.D. 1772.[6]

Lucy Mack was born in the town of Gilsom, County of Cheshire, New Hampshire, July 8, 1776.[7]

Joseph Smith Sen. and Lucy Mack were married in Tunbridge, Orange Co. Vt. January 24, 1796.

---

1. Beginning of Oliver Cowdery's handwriting.

2. The headings designating genealogy of the presidency on each page are written in red ink. The genealogy data that follows is written in double columns in the manuscript. All of the text is written in the left column, except the portion of those paragraphs that follow the (.

3. The gravestone did not show a name for this child.

4. According to Emma Smith, the twins were unnamed.

5. See below, p. 378.

6. Birthdate should be 1771.

7. Gilsum, New Hampshire town records give birthdate of 8 July 1775. (Richard L. Anderson, *Joseph Smith's New England Heritage*, 162.)

Alvin Smith, born in Tunbridge, Vt. February 11, 1798. (Died in Manchester Ontario Co. N.Y. Nov. 19, 1825[1]–Aged–27, years–9 months–8 days.

Hyrum Smith, born in Tunbridge Vt. February 9, 1800.

Sophron[i]a Smith, born in Tunbridge Vt. May 16, 1803.

Joseph Smith Jr, born in Sharon, Windsor Co. Vt. Dec. 23, 1805.

Samuel H. Smith, born Tunbridge Vt. March 13, 1808.

Ephraim Smith, born in Royalton, Windsor Co. Vt. March 13, 1810. (Died Royalton, Vt. March 24, 1810. Aged–12 days.

William Smith, born in Royalton Vt. March 13, 1811.

Katharine Smith, born in Lebanon, Grafton Co. N.H. July 28, 1813.

Don Carlos Smith, born in Norwich, Windsor Co. Vt. March 25, 1816.

Lucy Smith, born in Palmyra, Ontario Co. N.Y. July 18, 1821. [p. 10]

Genealogy of President Oliver Cowdery.

Oliver Cowdery was born in the town of Wells, Rutland Co. Vermont, Friday, October 3, 1806.

Elizabeth Ann Whitmer was born in the town of Fayette, Seneca County, New York, Sunday, January 22, 1815.

Oliver Cowdery and Elizabeth Ann Whitmer were married in Kaw Township, Jackson Co. Missouri, [Zion][2] Dec. 18, 1832.

Maria Cowdery was born in Kirtland, Geauga County, Ohio, fifteen (15) minutes past 9 o'clock A.M. Friday, August 21, 1835.[3] [p. 11]

---

1. Alvin Smith died 19 November 1823.
2. Brackets in MS.
3. This paragraph is in a different Oliver Cowdery handwriting than the surrounding text.

Genealogy of President Oliver Cowdery.

[*Remainder of p. 12 blank*]

Genealogy of President Sidney Rigdon.

[*Remainder of p. 13 blank*]

Genealogy of President Sidney Rigdon.

[*Remainder of p. 14 blank*]

Genealogy of President Frederick G. Williams.

[*Remainder of p. 15 blank*]

Genealogy of President Frederick G. Williams.

[*Remainder of p. 16 blank*]

December 1834

Chapter 1.

5 December 1834 · Friday

According to the direction of the Holy Spirit, President Smith, assistant Presidents, Rigdon and Williams, assembled for the purpose of ordaining ⟨first⟩ High Counsellor Cowdery to the office of assistant President of the High and Holy Priesthood in the Church of the Latter-Day Saints.[1]

---

1. Brigham H. Roberts indicates that the purpose of this meeting was to recognize Oliver Cowdery as second Elder in the Church, a position to which he had been designated by revelation and by ordination. (See Smith, *History of the Church*, 2:176; D&C 20:3-4.)

In addition to those named here, Joseph Smith, Sr., and Hyrum Smith were ordained assistant presidents (counselors) on December 6 (see p. 25). After Oliver Cowdery left the Church, the office of assistant president was held by Hyrum Smith beginning 24 January 1841. Following Hyrum's death, the office was not continued. (Robert Glen Mouritsen, "The Office of Associate President of the Church of Jesus Christ of Latter-day Saints," M.A. thesis, Brigham Young University, 1972; Dennis Michael Quinn, "Organizational Development and Social Origins of the Mormon Hierarchy, 1832-1932: A Prosopographical Study" [M.A. thesis, University of Utah, 1973], 275, 277.)

It is necessary, for the special benefit of the reader, that he be instructed ⟨into, or⟩ concerning the power and authority of the above named Priesthood.

First. The office of the President is to preside over the whole Church; to be considered as at the head; to receive revelations for the Church; to be a Seer, ~~and~~ Revelator ⟨and Prophet– ⟩ having all the gifts of God:– taking ⟨Moses⟩ for an ensample. Which is ~~Second~~ the office and station of the above President Smith, according to the calling of God, and the ordination which he has recieved.

Second. The office of Assistant President is to assist in presiding over the whole Church, and to officiate in the abscence of the President, according to ~~their~~ ⟨his⟩ rank and appointment, viz: President Cowdery, first; President Rigdon Second, and President Williams Third, as they ~~are~~ ⟨were⟩ severally called. The office of this Priesthood is also to act as Spokesman—taking Aaron for an ensample.

The virtue of the[1] ⟨above⟩ Priesthood is to hold the keys of the kingdom of heaven, or the Church militant.

The reader may further understand, that ~~Presidents~~ ⟨the⟩ reason why ~~President~~ ⟨High Counsellor⟩ Cowdery was not previously ordained ⟨to the Presidency,⟩ was, in consequence of his necessary attendance in Zion,[2] to assist Wm. W. Phelps in conducting the printing business; but that this promise was made by the angel while in company with President Smith, at the time they received the office of the lesser priesthood.[3] And further: The circumstances and situation of the Church re-

---

1. "the" written over "this."

2. Zion refers to the gathering place of the Latter-day Saints in Missouri. A July 1831 revelation designated Missouri as "the place for the city of Zion," for the gathering of the saints, and Independence as the center place and site for

3. Reference is made to the restoration of the Aaronic Priesthood. See pp. 290-291.

quiring, Presidents Rigdon and Williams were previously ordained, to assist President Smith.

After this short explination, we now proceed to give an account of the acts, promises, and blessings of this memorable Evening:

First. After assembling, we received a rebuke for our former low, uncultivated, and disrespectful manner of communication, and salutation, with, and unto each other, by the voice of the Spirit, saying unto us: Verily, condemnation resteth upon you, who are appointed to lead my Church, and to be saviors of men: and also upon the church: And there must needs be a repentance and a refor[m]ation among you, in all things, in your ensamples before the Church, and before the world, in all your manners, habits and customs, and salutations one toward another—rendering unto every man the respect due the office, ~~and~~ calling, and priesthood, whereunto I the Lord have appointed, and ordained you. Amen. [p. 17]

It is only necessary to say, relative to the foregoing reproof and instruction, that, though it was given in sharpness, it occasioned gladness and joy, and we were willing to repent and reform, in every particular, according to the instruction given. It is also proper to remark, that after the reproof was given, we all confessed, voluntarily, that such had been the manifestations of the Spirit a long time since, in consequence of which the rebuke came with greater sharpness.

Not thinking to evade the truth, or excuse, in order to escape censure, but to give proper information, a few remarks relative to the situation of the Church previous to this date, is necessary. Many, on hearing the fulness of the gospel, embraced it with eagerness; ⟨yet,⟩ at the same time were unwilling to forego their former opinions and notions relative to church government, and the rules and habits proper for the good order, harmony, peace, and beauty of a people destined, with the protecting care of the Lord, to be an ensample and light of the world. They did not dispise government; but there was a disposition to organize that government according to their own notions, or feelings. For example: Every man must be subjected to wear a particular fashioned coat, hat, or other garment, or else an accusation was brought that we were fashioning after the world. Every one must be called by their given name, without respecting the office or ordinance to which they had been called: Thus, President Smith was called Joseph, or brother Joseph; President Rigdon, brother Sidney, or Sidney, &c. This manner of address gave occasion to the enemies of the truth, and was a means of bringing reproach upon the Cause of God. But in consequence of former prejudices, the Church, many of them, would not submit to proper and wholesome order. This proceeded from a spirit of enthusiasm, and vain ambition—a desire to compel others to come to certain rules, not dictated by the will of the Lord; or a jealous fear, that, were men called by thier respective titles, and the ordinance of heaven honored in a proper manner, some were in a way to be exalted above others, and their form of government disregarded. In fact, the true principle of honor in the Church of the Saints, that the more a man is exalted, the more humble he will be, if actuated by the Spirit of the Lord, seemed to have been overlooked; and the fact, that the greatest is least and servant of all, as said our Savior, never to have been thought of, by numbers. These facts, for such they were, when viewed in their proper light, were sufficient, of themselves to cause men to humble themselves before the Lord; but when communicated by the Spirit, made an impression upon our hearts not to be forgotten. [p. 18]

Perhaps, an arrangement of this kind in a former day would have occasioned some unpleasant reflections, in the minds of many, and at an ~~early~~ ⟨earlier⟩ period, in this church, others to have forsaken the cause, in consequence of weakness, and unfaithfulness; but that the leaders of the church should wait so long before stepping forward according ⟨to⟩ the manifestation of the Spirit, deserved a reproof. And that the church should be chastened, for their uncultivated manner of salutation, is also just. But to proceed with the account of the interview.

After addressing the throne of mercy, President Smith laid hands upon High Counsellor Cowdery, and ordained him to the Presidency of the High priesthood in the Church, saying:

Brother, In the name of Jesus Christ of Nazareth, who was crucified for the sins of the world, that we through the virtue of his blood might come to the Father, I lay my hands upon thy head, and ordain thee a President of the high and holy priesthood, to assist in presiding over the Church, and bearing the keys of this kingdom—which priesthood is after the order of Melchizedek—which is after the order of the Son of God—And now, O Father, wilt thou bless this thy servant with wisdom, knowledge, and understanding—give him, by the Holy Spirit, a correct understanding of thy doctrine, laws, and will—Commune with him from on high—let him hear thy voice, and receive the ministring of the holy angels—deliver him from temptation, and the power of darkness—deliver him from evil, and from those who may seek his destruction,— be his shield, his buckler, and his great reward—endow him with power from on high, that he may write, preach, and proclaim the gospel to his fellowmen in demonstration of the Spirit and of power—may his feet never slide—may his heart never feint—may his faith never fail. Bestow upon him the blessings of his fathers Abraham, Isaac, Jacob, and of Joseph—Prolong his life to a good old age, and bring him in peace to his end, and to rejoice with thy saints, even the sanctified, in the celestial kingdom; for thine is the kingdom, the power, and the glory, forever. Amen.

Presidents Rigdon and Williams, confirmed the ordinance and blessings by the laying on of hands and prayer, after which each were blessed with the same blessings and prayer.

Much light was communicated to our minds, and we were instructed into the order of the Church of the saints, and how they ought to conduct in respecting and reverencing each other.

The praise of men, or the honor of this world, is of no benefit; but if a man is respected in his calling, and considered to be a man of righteousness, the truth may have an influence, many times, by which means they may teach the gospel with success, and lead men unto the kingdom of heaven. [p. 19]

6 December 1834 · Saturday

Presidents Smith, Cowdery, and Rigdon assembled with High Counsellors Joseph Smith Sen. Hyrum Smith,[1] and Samuel H. Smith, in company with Reynolds Cahoon, Counsellor to the Bishop, High Priest William Smith, and ⟨Elder⟩ Don C. Smith.

The meeting was opened by prayer, and a lengthy conversation held upon the subject of introducing a more refined order into the Church. On further reflection, the propriety of ordaining others to the office of Presidency of the high priesthood was also discussed, after which High Counsellor Hyrum Smith was ordained ⟨to⟩ the Presidency under the hands of President Smith, and High Counsellor Joseph Smith, Sen. under the hands of President Rigdon. The others present were blessed under the hands of Presidents J. Smith Jr. Cowdery, and Rigdon, and the meeting closed, after a happy season, and a social intercourse upon the great subject of the gospel and the work of the Lord in this day.

[*remainder of p. 20 blank*]

---

1. The first high council of the Church was created at Kirtland, Ohio, on 17 February 1834 for the purpose of "settling important difficulties which might arise in the church." Among the original twelve appointees were Joseph Smith's father, Joseph Smith, Sr., and the Prophet's brother Samuel Harrison. On 24 September 1834 Hyrum Smith was added to the council to take the place of Sylvester Smith, who was released on that day. (D&C 102; Smith, *History of the Church*, 2:165.)

[*pages 21 to 45 blank*]

/[1]September 1834

The following communication was designed to have been published in the last No. of the star[2]; but owing to a press of other matter it was laid over for this No. of the Messenger and ad[v]ocate. Since it was writen, upon further reflection, we have thought that a full history of the rise of the church of the Latter Day Saints, and the most interesting parts of its progress, to the present time, would be worthy the perusal of the Saints.– If circumstances admit, an article on this subject will appear in each subsequent No. of the Messenger and advocate, until

1. End of Oliver Cowdery's handwriting and beginning of Frederick G. Williams's hand.

2. *The Evening and the Morning Star* was the first paper published by the Church. It was printed by William W. Phelps at Independence, Missouri, beginning in June 1832, and it continued through fourteen issues until July 1833, when a mob destroyed the press. A council held in Kirtland, Ohio, 11 September 1833, consisting of Frederick Williams, Sidney Rigdon, Newel Whitney, Joseph Smith, and Oliver Cowdery, resolved that a printing office be established in Kirtland under the name of F.G. Williams & Co. to commence a new publication, the *Latter Day Saints' Messenger and Advocate.* The council also resolved to continue publication of the *Star,* which would be printed in Kirtland until it could be transferred to its former location in Missouri. The press at Kirtland produced ten issues of the *Star* between December 1833 and September 1834, at which time the *Messenger and Advocate* was begun. In addition, beginning in January 1835, the Kirtland press reprinted the Independence issues of the *Star,* but with a revised text of the revelations. (Smith, *History of the Church,* 1:409; Richard Howard, *Restoration Scriptures: A Study of Their Textual Development* [Independence: Herald Publishing House, 1969], 201-2; Andrew Jenson, *Encyclopedic History of the Church of Jesus Christ of Latter-day Saints* [Salt Lake City: Deseret News, 1941], 239-40; 492-93.)

The narrative here, written in the form of eight letters by Oliver Cowdery to William W. Phelps, was published in eight issues of the *Messenger and Advocate* between October 1834 and October 1835. The letters were republished in the *Times and Seasons* between November 1840 and May 1841 (all except No. VII); the *Gospel Reflector* (15 March 1841): 137-75; and *Letters by Oliver Cowdery to W.W. Phelps on the Origin of the Book of Mormon and the Rise of the Church of Jesus Christ of Latter-day Saints* (Liverpool: Thomas Ward and John Cairns, 1844).

the time when the church was driven from Jackson Co. Mo. by a lawless banditti; & such other remarks as may be thought appropriate and interesting.

That our narrative may be correct, and particularly the introduction, it is proper to inform our patrons, that our brother J. Smith Jr. has offered to assist us. Indeed, there are many items connected with the fore part of this subject that render his labor indispensible. With his labor and with authentic documents now in our possession, we hope to render this a pleasing and agreeable narrative, well worth the examination and perusal of the Saints.–

To do ⟨Justice to⟩ this subject will require time and space: we therefore ask the forbearance of our readers,[1] assuring them that it shall be founded upon facts.

Norton, Medina Co. Ohio,[2] Sabbath evening, September 7, 1834.

Dear Brother [Phelps].– Before leaving home, I promised, if I tarried long, to write; and while a few moments are now allowed me for reflection aside from the cares and common conversation of my friends in this place, I have thought that were I to communicate them to you, might, perhaps, if they should not prove especially beneficial to yourself, by[3] confirming you in the faith of the gospel, at least be interesting, since it has pleased our heavenly Father to call us both to rejoice in the same hope of eternal life. And by giving them publicity, some thousands who have embraced the same covenant, may learn something more particular upon the rise of this church, in this last time. And while the gray evening is fast changing into a settled darkness, my heart responds with the happy

1. "readears" in MS.

2. On 5 September 1834, Oliver Cowdery had left his home in Kirtland, Ohio, with Joseph Smith to attend a conference at New Portage, Medina County, Ohio, on 8 September.

3. "by" repeated in MS.

millions who are in the presence of the Lamb, and are past the power of temptation, in rendering thanks, though feebly, to the same parent.

Another day has passed, into that, to us boundless ocean. Eternity! where nearly six thousand years have gone before; and what flits across the mind like an electric shock is, that it will never return! [p. 46] whether it has been well improved or not; whether the principles emenating from HIM who "hallowed" it, have been observed; or whether, like the common mass of time, it has been heedlessly spent, is not for me to say—one thing I can say—it can never be recalled!– it has rolled in to assist in filling up the grand space decreed in the mind of its Author, till nature shall have ceased her work, and time its accustomed revolutions—when its lord shall have completed the gathering of his elect, and with them enjoy that sabbath which shall never end!

On Fryday, the 5th in company with our brother Joseph Smith Jr. I left Kirtland for this place (New Portage,) to attend the conference previously appointed. To be permited, once more, to travel with this brother, occasions reflections of no ordinary kind. Many have been the fatiagues and privations which have fallen to my lot to endure, for the gospel's sake, since 1828 with this brother. Our road has frequently been spread with the "fowlers snare," and our persons saught with the eagerness, of the savage's ferocity, for innocent blood, by men, either heated to desperation by the insenuation[s] of those who professed to be "guides and way marks," to the kingdom of glory, or the individuals themselves!– This, I confess, is a dark picture to spread before our patrons, but they will pardon my plainness when I assure them of the truth, In fact, God has so ordered, that the reflections which I am permited to cast upon my past life, relative to a knowledge of the way of salvation, are rendered "doubly endearing." Not only have I been graciously preserved from wicked and unreasonable men, with this our brother, but I have seen the fruit of perseverance in proclaiming the everlasting gospel, immediately after it was declared to the world in these last days, in a manner not to be forgotten while heaven gives my common intellect. And what serves to render the reflection past expression on this point is, that from his hand I received baptism, by the direction of the angel of God[1] – the first received into this church, in this day.

Near the time of the setting of the sun, sabbath evening, April 5th. 1829, my natural eyes for the first time beheld this brother. He then resided in Harmony, susquehanna county Penn. On monday the 6th. I assisted him in aranging some business of a temporal nature, and on tuesday the 7th. commenced to write the book of Mormon.[2] These were days never to be forgotten – to ⟨sit⟩ ~~assist~~ under the sound of a voice dictated by the inspiration of heaven, awakened the utmost gratitude of this bosom! Day after day I continued, uninterrupted, to [p. 47] write from his mouth, as he translated with the Urim and Thummim, or, as the Nephites should have said, ["]Interpreters," the history, or reccord, called "the book of Mormon.["]

To notice, in few words, the interesting account given by Mormon, and his faithful son Moroni, of a people once beloved and favored of heaven, would supercede my present design: I shall therefore defer this to a future period, and as I said in the introduction, pass more directly to some few incidents immediately connected with the rise of this church, which may be entertaining to some thousands who have stepped

1. See p. 290; also Richard L. Anderson, "The Second Witness of Priesthood Restoration," *Improvement Era* 71 (September 1968): 15-24.

2. The surviving fragment of the original Book of Mormon manuscript is in the LDS Church Archives in Salt Lake City, and a complete copy of the second manuscript, known as the printer's manuscript, is in the RLDS Church Archives at Independence, Missouri. These show that Oliver Cowdery did most of the writing on both manuscripts.

forward, amid the frowns of biggots and the callumny of hypocrites, and embraced the gospel of Christ.

No men in their sober senses, could translate and write the directions given to the Nephites, from the mouth of the saviour of the precise manner in which men should build up his church, and especially, when corruption had spread an uncertainty over all forms and systems practiced among men without desiring a privilege of showing the willingness of the heart by being burried in the liquid grave, to answer a "good concience by the resurection of Jesus Christ.["]

After writing the account given of the savior's ministry to the remnant of the seed of Jacob, upon this continent,[1] it was easily to be seen, as the prophet said would be, that darkness covered the earth and gross darkness the minds of the people.

On reflecting further, it was as easily to be seen, that amid the great strife and noise concerning religeon, none had authority from God to administer the ordinances of the gospel For, the question might be asked, have men authority to administer in the name of Christ, who deny revelation? when his testamony is no less then the spirit of prophecy? and his religeon bared, built, and sustained by immediate revelations in all ages of the world, when he has had a people on earth? If these facts were burried, and carefully concealed by men whose craft would have been in danger, if once permited to shine in the faces of men, they were no longer to us; and we only waited for the commandment to be given, "arise and be baptized."

This was not long desired before it was realized. The Lord, who is rich in[2] mercy, and ever willing to answer the consistent prayer of the humble, after we had called upon him in a fervent manner, aside from the abodes of men, condescended to [p. 48] manifest to us his will. On a sudden, as from the midst

1. 3 Nephi.
2. "is" in MS.

of eternity, the voice of the redeemer spake peace to us, while the vail was parted and the angel of God came down clothed with glory, and delivered the anxiously looked for message, and the keys of the gospel of repentance!–[1] What Joy! what wonder! what amazement! while the world were wracked and distracted—while millions were grouping [groping] as the blind for the wall, and while all men were resting upon uncertainty, as a general mass, our eyes beheld—our ears heard. As in the "blaze of day"; yes more—above the glitter of the may sun beam, which then shed its brilliancy over the face of nature! Then his voice, though mild, pierced to the center, and his words, ["]I am thy fellow servant," dispelled every fear. We listened—we gazed—we admired! Twas the voice of the angel from glory—twas a message from the Most High! and as we heard we rejoiced, while his love enkindled upon our souls, and we were wrapt in the vision of the Almighty! Where was room for doubt? No where: uncertainty had fled, doubt had sunk, no more to rise, while fiction and deception had fled forever!

But, dear brother think further think for a moment, what Joy filled our hearts, and with what surprise we must have bowed, (for who would not have bowed the knee for such a blessing?) when we received under his hand the holy priesthood, as he said, ["]upon ⟨you⟩ my fellow servants, in the name of Messiah I confer this priesthood, and this authority, which shall remain upon earth, that the sons of Levi may yet offer an offering unto[2] the Lord in righteousness!"

I shall not attempt to paint to you the feelings of this heart, nor the majestic beauty and glory which surrounded us on this occasion; but you will believe me when I say, that earth, nor men, with the eloquence of time cannot begin to clothe language in as interesting and sublime a manner as this holy

1. Joseph Smith's account of these events is on pp. 290-291.
2. "into" in MS.

personage. No, nor has this earth power to give the Joy, to bestow the peace, or comprehend the wisdom which was contained in each sentence as they were delivered by the power of the holy spirit! Man may deceave his fellow man; deception may follow deception, and the children of the wicked one may have power to seduce the foolish and untaught, till naught but fiction feeds the many, and the fruit of falshood carries in its current the giddy to the grave; but one touch [p. 49] with the finger of his love, yes, one ray of glory from the upper world, or one word from the mouth of the savior, from the bosom of eternity strikes it all into insignifficance, and blasts[1] it forever from the mind! The assurence that we were in the presence of an angel; the certainty that we heard the voice of Jesus, and the truth unsullied as it flowed from a pure personage, dictated by the will of God, is to me, past description, and I shall ever look upon this expression of the Saviors goodness with wonder and thanksgiving while I am permited to tarry, and in those mansions where perfection dwells and sin never comes, I hope to adore in that day which shall never cease!

To day the church in this place assembled, and were addressed on the great and important subject of salvation by brother Jared Carter, followed by brother Sidney Rigdon. The cheering truths ably and[2] eloquently advanced by these brethren were like "apples of gold. in baskets of silver."–

⟨The saints listened with attention, after which bread was broken, and we offered another memorial to our Lord that we remembered him.⟩[3] I must close for the present: my candle is quite extinguished. And all nature seems locked in silence, shrouded in darkness, and enjoying that repose so necessary to this life. But the period is rolling on when night will close,

1. "blots" in *Messenger and Advocate.*
2. MS. reads "any."
3. This insertion is written on a small slip of paper attached to the page with sealing wax and marked for insertion here.

and those who are found worthy will inherit that city where neither the light of the sun nor moon will ⟨be⟩ necessary! "for the glory of God will ~~be~~ bright in[1] it, and the Lamb will be the light thereof."

O COWDERY.

TO W.W. PHELPS, ESQR.

P.S. I shall write you again on the subject of the Conference. O.C. I will hereafter give you a full history of the rise of this church, up to the time stated in my introduction; which will necessarily embrace the life and character of this brother. I shall therefore leave the[2] history of baptism, &c. till its proper place.

Letter II.

TO W.W. PHELPS, ESQR.
DEAR BROTHER:–

In the Last Messenger and Advocate I promised to commence a more particular or minute history of the rise and progress of the church of the Latter Day Saints; and publish for the benefit of enquirers and all who are disposed to learn. There are certain facts relative to the works of God [p. 50] worthy the consideration and observance of every individual, and every society:– They are that he never works in the dark – his works are always performed in a clear, intelligible manner: and another point is, that he never works in vain. This is not the case with men; but might it not be? When the Lord works, he accomplishes his purposes, and the effects of his power are to be seen afterward. In view of this, suffer me to make a few remarks by way of introduction. The works of man may shine for a season with a degree of brilliancy, but time changes their comp[l]exion; and whether it did or not, all would be the same

1. *Messenger and Advocate* reads "lighten" in place of "bright in."
2. "thy" in MS.

Oliver Cowdery. Charles W. Carter Collection. LDS Church Archives.

in a little space, as nothing except that which was erected by the hand which never grows weak, can remain when corruption is consumed.

I shall not be required to adorn and beautify my narrative with a relation of the faith of Enoch, and those who assisted him to build up Zion, which fled to God—on the mountains of which was commanded the blessing, life forever more—to be held in reserve to add another ray of glory to the grand retinue, when worlds shall rock from their base to their center; the nations of the righteous rise from the dust, and the blessed millions of the church of the first born shout his triumphant coming, to receive his kingdom, over which he is to reign till all enemies are subdued. Nor shall I write the history of the Lords church raised up according to his own instruction to Moses and Aaron; of the perplexities and discouragements which came upon Israel for their transgressions, their organization upon the land of Canaan, and their overthrow and dispersion among all nations, to reap the reward of their eniquities, to the appearing of the Great Shepherd, in the flesh.

But there is, of necessity a uniformity so exact; a manner so precise, and ordinances so minute, in all ages and generations whenever God has established his church among men, that should I have occasion to recur to either age, and particularly to that characterized by the advent of the Messiah, and the ministry of the apostles of that church; with a cursory view of the same till it lost its visibility on earth; was driven into darkness, or till God took the holy priesthood unto himself wher[e] it has been held in reserve to the present century, as a matter of right [p. 51] in this free country, I may take the privilege. This may be doubted by some—indeed by many—as an admission of this point would overthrow the popular systems of the day. I cannot reasonably expect, then, that the large majority of professors will be willing to listen to my argument for a moment, as a careful, impartial and faithful investigation of the doctrines which I believe to be correct, and the principles cherished in my bosom—and believed by this church—by every honest man must be admited as truth.

Of this I may say as Tertullian said to the emperor when writing in defence of the saints in his day: "Whoever looked well into our religeon that did not embrace it?"[1]

Common ~~understanding~~ undertakings and plans of men may be overthrown or destroyed by opposition. The systems of this world may be exploded or annihilated by oppression or falshood; but it is the reverse with pure religeon. There is a power attendant on truth that all the arts and designs of men cannot fathom; there is an increasing influence which rises up in one place the moment it is covered in another, and the more it is traduced, and the harsher the means employed to effect its extinction, the more numerous are its votaries.– It is not the vain cry of "delusion" from the giddy multitude; it is not the snears of biggots; it is not the frowns of zealots, neither the rage [of] princes, kings, nor emperors, that can prevent its influence.

The fact is as Tertullian said, no man ever looked carefully into its co[n]sistency and propriety without embracing it. It is impossable: That light which enlightens man, is at once enraptured: that intelligence which existed before the world was, will unite, and that wisdom in the Divine economy will be so conspicuous, that it will be embraced, it will be observed, and it must be obeyed!

Look at pure religion whenever it has had a place on earth, and you will always mark the same characteristics in all its features. Look at truth (without which the former could not exist,) and the same pecul[i]arities are apparent. Those who have been guided by them have always shown the same principles; and those who were not, have as uniformly sought to destroy their influence.

---

1. Tertullian (ca. 155-220) was a Christian writer-theologian-polemicist, born at Carthage in north Africa.

Religion has had its friends and its enemies; its advocates and its opponents. But the thousands of years which have [p. 52] come and gone, have left it unaltered; millions[1] who have embraced it, and are now enjoying that bliss held forth in its promises, have left its principles unchanged, and its influence upon the honest heart, unweakened. The many oppositions which have encountered it; the millions of calumnies, the numberless repro[a]ches, and the myriads of falshoods, have left its fair form unimpaired, its beauty untarnished, and its excellence as excellent; while its certainty is the same, and its foundation upheld by the hand of God!

One peculiarity of men I wish to notice in the early part of my narrative—so far as my acquaintance and knowledge of men and their history extends, it has been the custom of every generation, to boast of, or extol the acts of the former. In this respect I wish it to be distinctly understood that I mean the righteous,—those to whom God communicated his will. There has ever been an apparent blindness common to men, which has hind[e]red their discovering the real worth and excellence of individuals while residing with them; but when once deprived of their society, worth and councel, they are[2] ready to exclaim, "how great and inestimable were their qualities, and how precious is their memory."

The vilest and most corrupt are not exempted from this charge: even the Jews, whose former principles had become degenerated, and whose religion was a mere show, were found among that class who were ready to build and garnish the sepulchurs of the prophets, and condemn their fathers for putting them to death; making important boasts of their own righteousness, and of their assurance of salvation, in the midst of which they rose up with one consent, and treacherously and shamefully betrayed, and crucified the savior of the world! No

1. "the" precedes "millions" in *Messenger and Advocate*.
2. "were" in *Messenger and Advocate*.

wonder that the enquirer has turned aside with disgust, nor marvel that God has appointed a day when he will call the nations before him, and reward every man according to his works!

Enoch walked with God and was taken home with out tasting death.—[1] Why were not all converted in his day and taken with him to glory? Noah, it is said, was perfect in his generation:[2] and it is plain that he had communion with his maker, and by his direction accomplished a work the parallel of which is not to be found in the annals of the world! Why were not the world converted, that the flood might have been ~~destroyed~~ stayed? Men, from the days of our father Abraham, have talked, boasted, and extolled his faith: and he is even represented in the scriptures:– ["]The father of [p. 53] the faithful."[3] Moses talked with the Lord face to face; received the great moral law, upon the bases of which those of all civillized governments are founded; led Israel forty years, and was taken home to receive the reward of his toils[4]—then Jacob could realize his worth. Well was the question asked by our lord, "How can the children of the bride chamber mourn while the bridegroom is with them?["][5] It is said, that he travelled and taught the righteous principles of his kingdom three years, during which he chose twelve men, and ordained them apostles, &c.[6] The people saw and heard—they were particularly benefited, many of them, by being healed of infirmities, and diseases; of plagues, and devils:[7] they saw him walk upon the water,[8] they saw the winds and waves calmed at his command;[9]

1. Genesis 5:24.
2. Moses 8:27.
3. Galatians 3:8-9.
4. Moses 1:31; Exodus 20; Deuteronomy 34:5-7.
5. Matthew 9:15.
6. Matthew 10:1-5.
7. See Matthew 8.
8. Mark 6:46-50.
9. Matthew 8:23-27.

they saw thousands fed to the full with a pittance,[1] and the very powers of darkness tremble in his presence and like others before them considered it as a dream, or a common occurrence, till the time was fulfilled, and he was offered up. Yet while he was with them he said you shall desire to see one of the days of the Son of Man, and shall not see it.[2] He knew calamity would fall upon that people, and the wrath of heaven overtake them to their overthrow, and when that devoted city was surrounded with armies, well may we conclude that they desired a protector possessing sufficient power to lead them to some safe place aside from the tumult of a seige.

Since the apostles fell asleep all men who profess a belief in the truth of their mission, extol their virtues and celebrate their fame. It seems to have been forgotten that they were men of infermities and subject to all the feelings, passions, and imperfections common to other men. But it appears, that they as others were before them, are looked upon as men of perfection, holiness, ~~and~~ purity, and goodness, far in advance of any since. So were the characters of the prophets held in the days of the[3] apostles. What can be the difference in the reward, whether a man died for righteousness sake in the days of Abel, Zecharias, John the twelve apostles chosen at Jerusalem, or since? Is not the life of one equally as precious as the other? and is not the truth, Just as true?

But in reviewing the lives and acts of men in past generations, whenever we find a righteous man among them, there always were excuses for not giving heed or credence to his testamony. The people could see his imperfections; or, if no imperfections, supposed ones, and were always ready to frame an excuse upon that for not believeing.– No matter how pure

1. Mark 6:32-44.
2. Luke 17:22.
3. "these" in *Messenger and Advocate.*

the principles, nor how precious the teachings—an excuse was wanted—and an excuse was had. [p. 54]

The next generation, perhaps, was favored with equally as righteous men, who were condemned upon the same principles of the former while the acts and precepts of the former were the boasts of the multitude; when in reality, their doctrines were no more pure, their exertions to turn men to righteousness no greater, neither their walk any more ~~perfect~~ circumspect—the grave of the former is considered to be holy, and his sepulcher is garnished while the latter is deprived a dwelling among men, or even an existence upon earth! Such is a specimen of the depravity and inconsistency of men, and such has been their conduct toward the righteous in centuries past.

When John the son of Zecharias came among the Jews, it is said that he came neither eating bread nor drinking wine. In another place it is said that his meat was locusts and wild honey.[1] The Jews saw him, heard him preach, and were witnesses of the purity of the doctrines advocated—they wanted an excuse, and they soon found one—"He ~~soon found~~ hath a devil!"—[2] And who among all generations, that valued his salvation, would be taught, by or follow one possessed of a devil?

The savior came in form and fashion of a man; he ate, drank, and walked about as a man, and they said "Behold, a man gluttonous, and a wine bibber, a friend of publicans and sinners!"[3] You see an excuse was wanting, but not long wanting till it was found—who would follow a disscipated leader? or who, among the righteous Pharisees would acknowledge a man who would condscend to eat with publicans and sinners? This was too much—they could not endure it. An individual teaching the doctrines of the kingdom of heaven, and declaring

1. Matthew 3:4.
2. Matthew 11:18.
3. Luke 7:34.

that that kingdom was nigh, or that it had already come, must appear different from others, or he could not be received. If he were athirst he must not drink, if faint he must not eat, and if weary he must not rest, because he had assumed the authority to teach the world righteousness, and he must be different in manners, and in consitution, if not in form, that all might be attracted by his singular appearance: that his singular demeanor might gain the reverence of the people, or he was an imposter—a false teacher—a wicked man—a sinner—and an accomplice of Beelzebub, the prince of devils!

If singularity of appearance, or difference of manners would command respect, certainly John would have been reverenced, and heard. To see one coming from the wilderness, clad with camel's hair, drinking neither wine nor strong drink, nor yet eating common food, must have awakened the curiosity of the curious, to the fullest extent. But there was one peculiarity in this man common to every righteous man before him, for which the people hated him, and for which he lost his life—he taught holiness, proclaimed [p. 55] repentance and baptism for the remission of sins, warned the people of the consequences of eniquity, and declared that the kingdom of heaven was at hand—All this was too much! To see one dressed so rediculously eating no common food, neither drinking wine like other men; stepping in advance of the learned and reverend Pharisees, wise doctors, and righteous scribes, and declaring at the same time, that the Lords Kingdom would soon appear, could not be borne—he must not teach—he must assume—he must not attempt to lead the people after him—"He hath a devil."

The Jews were willing, (professedly so) to believe the ancient prophets, and follow the directions of heaven as delivered to the world by them; but when one came teaching the same doctrine, and proclaiming the same things, only that they were nearer, they would not hear. Men say if they could see they would believe, but I have thought the reverse, in this respect—If they cannot see they will believe.

One of two reasons may be assigned as the cause why the messengers of truth have been rejected—perhaps both. The multitude saw their imperfections, or supposed ones, and from that framed an excuse for rejecting them, or else in consequence of the corruption of their own hearts, when reproved, were not willing to repent, but saught to make a man an offender for a word: or for wearing camels hair, eating locusts, drinking wine, or showing friendship to publicans and sinners!

When looking over the sacred scriptures we seem to forget that they were given through men of imperfections, and subject to passions. It is a general belief that the ancient prophets were perfect—that no stain, or blemish ever appeared upon their characters while on earth, to be brought forward by the opposer as an excuse for not believing. The same is said of the apostles; but James said that Elias [Elijah][1] was a man subject to like passions as themselves, and yet he had that power with God that in answer to his prayer it rained not on the earth by the space of three years and a half.[2]

There can be no doubt but those to whom he wrote looked upon the ancient prophets as a race of beings superior to any in those days; and in order to be constituted a prophet of God, a man must be perfect in every respect.—

The idea is, that he must be perfect according to their signification of the word. If a people were blessed with prophets, they must be the individuals who were to prescribe the Laws by which they must be governed, even in their private walks. The generation following were ready to suppose, that those men who believed the word of God were as perfect as those to whom it was delivered supposed they must be, and were as forward to prescribe the rules by which they were governed,

1. Brackets in MS.
2. James 5:17.

or rehearse laws and declare them to be the governing principles of the prophets, as though they themselves held the keys of the mysteries of heaven, and had searched the archives of the generations of the world.

You will see that I have made mention of the Messiah, of his mission into [p. 56] the world, and of his walk and outward appearance, but do not understand me as attempting to place him on a level with men, or his mission or a parallel with those of the prophets and apostles—far from this. I view his mission such as none other could fill; that he was offered without spot to God a propitiation for our sins; that he rose triumphant and victorious over the grave, and him that has ⟨the⟩ power of death.–

This man could not do—It required a perfect sacrafice—man is imperfect—It required a spotless offering—man is not spotless—It required an infinite atonement—man is mortal!

I have, then as you will see, made mention of our Lord, to show that individuals teaching truth, /[1]whether perfect or imperfect have been looked upon as the worst of men. and that even our Saviour the great Shepherd of Israel was mocked and derided and placed on a parallel with the prince of devils; and the prophets and apostles though at this day, looked upon as perfect as perfection, were concidered the basest of the human family by those among whom they lived. It is not rumor, though it is wafted by every gale, and retriated[2] by every zephyr upon which we are to found our Judgments of ones merits or demerits: If it is we erect an altar upon which we sacrafice the most perfect of men, and establish a criterion by which the "vilest of the vile" may escape censure.

But lest I weary you with too many remarks upon the history of the past, after a few upon the propriety of a narative of the description I have proposed, I shall proceed.—Editor.

---

1. Frederick G. Williams's handwriting ends and Warren Parrish's begins.
2. "reiterated" in *Messenger and Advocate*.

Letter III.

To W.W. Phelps Esqr.
Dear Brother:–

after a silence of another month, agreeabley to my[1] promise I proceed upon the subject I proposed in the first No. of the Advocate. Perhaps an apology for brevity may not be improper, here, as many important incidents consequently transpiring in the organization and establishing of a society like the one whose history I am about to give to the world, are overlooked or lost, and soon buried with those who were the actors, will prevent my giving those minute and particular reflections which I have so often wished migh[t] have characterized the "Acts of the apostles," and the ancient Saints.

But such facts as are within my knowledge will be given without any reference to inconsistencies, in the minds of others [p. 57] or impossibilities, in the feelings of such as do not give credence to the system of salvation and redemption so clearly set forth and so plainly written over the face of the sacred scriptures:

Upon the propriety, then, of a narative of this kind, I have briefly to remark: It is known to you, that this church has suffered reproach and persecution, from a majority of mankind who have heard but a rumor, since its first organization. and further, you are also conversant with the fact, that no sooner had the messengers of the fulness of the gospel began to proclaim its heavenly precepts, and call upon men to embrace the same, than they were vilified and slandered by thousands who never saw their faces and much less knew aught derogatory of their characters, moral or religious – upon this unfair and unsaint like manner of p[r]ocedure they have been giving in large sheets their own opinions of the incorrectness of our system, and attested volum[e]s of our lives and characters.

1. "my" repeated in MS.

Since, then, our opposers have been thus kind to introduce our cause before the public, it is no more than just that a correct account should be given; and since they have invariably sought to cast a shade over the truth, and hinder its influence from gaining ascendency, it is also proper that it should be vindicated, by laying before the world a correct statement of[1] events as they have transpired from time to time.

Whether I shall succeed so far in my purpose as to convince the publick of the incorrectness of those scurulous reports which have inundated our land, or even but a small portion of them, will be better ascertained when I close than when I commence; and I am content to submit it before the candid for perusal, & before the Judge of all for inspection, as I most assuredly believe that before Him I must stand and answer for the deeds transacted in this life.

Should I, however, be instrumental in causing a few to hear before they judge, and understand both sides of this matter before they condemn, I shall have the satisfaction of seeing them embrace it as I am certain that one is the inevitable fruit of the other.

But to proceede:

You will recollect that I informed you, in my letter published in the first No. of the Messenger and Advocate, that this history would necessarily embrace the life and character of our esteemed friend and brother, J. Smith Jr. one of the presidents of this church and for information on that part of the [p. 58] subject, I refer you to his communication of the same published in this paper.[2] I shall, therefore, pass over that till I come to the 15th year of his life.

It is necessary to p[r]emise this account by relating the situation of the public mind relative to religion at this time: one Mr. [George] Lane a presiding Elder of the Methodist

1. MS. repeats "of."
2. See pp. 13-14.

church, visited Palmyra, and vicinity. Elder Lane was a talented man possessing a good share of literary endowments, and apparent humility. there was a great awakening, or excitement raised on the subject of religion and much enquiry for the word of life.[1] Large additions were made to the Methodist, Presbyterian, and Baptist churches. Mr. Lane's manner of communication was peculiarly calculated to awaken the intellect of the hearer, and arouse the sinner to look about him for safety—much good instruction was always drawn from his discourses on the scriptures, and in common with others, our brother's mind became awakened.[2]

For a length of time the reformation seemed to move in a harmonious manner, but, as the excitement ceased, or those who had expressed anxieties, had professed a belief in the pardoning influence and condescension of the Saviour a general strug[g]le was made by the leading characters of the different sects, for prosolytes. Then strife seemed to take the place of that apparent union and harmony which had previously characterized the moves and exhortations of the old professors, and a cry—I am right—you are wrong—was introduced in their stead.

In this general strife for followers, his mother, one sister, and two of his natural brothers, were persuaded to unite with the Presbyterians.[3] This gave opportunity for further reflection;

1. On the religious climate in Joseph Smith's locality see Backman, *Joseph Smith's First Vision*, chapter 3; also his *American Religions and the Rise of Mormonism* (Salt Lake City: Deseret Book Company, 1965); Ahlstrom, *A Religious History of the American People*, part IV.

2. Questions of a revival in the vicinity of Palmyra, New York, in 1819-20; George Lane's involvement; and the dating of Joseph Smith's First Vision are discussed in Larry Porter, "Reverend George Lane—Good 'Gifts,' much 'Grace,' and Marked 'Usefulness,'" *BYU Studies* 9 (Spring 1969): 321-40; and Marvin Hill, "The First Vision Controversy: A Critique and Reconciliation," *Dialogue: A Journal of Mormon Thought* 15 (Summer 1982): 31-46.

3. See Milton V. Backman, Jr., and James B. Allen, "Membership of Certain of Joseph Smith's Family in the Western Presbyterian Church of Palmyra," *BYU Studies* 10 (Summer 1970): 482-84.

and as will be seen in the sequel, laid a foundation, or was one means of laying a foundation for the attestation of the truths, or professions of truth, contained in that record called the word of God.

After strong solicitations to unite with one of those different societies, and seeing the apparent proselyting disposition manifested with equal warmth from each, his mind was led to more seriously contemplate the importance of a move of this kind. To profess godliness without its benign influence upon the heart, was a thing so foreign from his feelings, that his spirit was not at rest day nor night. To unite with a society professing to be built upon the only sure foundation, [p. 59] and that profession be a vain one, was calculated, in its verry nature, the more it was contemplated, the more to arouse the mind to the serious consequences of moving hastily, in a course fraught with eternal realities. To say he was right, and still be wrong, could not profit; and amid so many, some must be built upon the sand.

In this situation where could he go? if he went to one he was told they were right, and all others were wrong—if to another, the same was heard from those: all professed to be the true church; and if not they were certainly hypocritical, because, if I am presented with a system of religion, and enquire of my teacher whether it is correct, and he informs me that he is not certain, he acknowledges at once that he is teaching without authority, and acting without a commission!

If one profess a degree of authority or preference in consequence of age or right, and that superiority was without evidence, it was insufficient to convince a mind once aroused to that degree of determination which at that time operated upon him. And upon fa[r]ther reflecting, that the Saviour had said that the gate was strait and the way narrow that lead to life eternal, and that few entered there; and the[1] way was broad,

1. "that" precedes "the" in *Messenger and Advocate*.

and the gate wide which lead to destruction, and that many crowded its current,[1] a proof from some source was wanting to settle the mind and give peace to the agitated bosom. It is not frequent that the minds of men are exercised with proper determinations relative to obtaining a certainty of the things of God.– They are too apt to rest short of that assurance which the Lord Jesus has so freely offered in his word to man, and which so beautifully characterizes his whole plan of salvation, as revealed to us.

Letter IV.

TO W.W. PHELPS, ESQR.
DEAR BROTHER:–

In my last, published in the 3d No. of the Advocate I apologized for the brief manner in which I should be obliged to give, in many instances, the history of this church. Since then yours[2] [p. 60] of Christmas has been received. It was not my wish to be understood that I could not give the leading items of every important occurrence. at least so far as would effect my duty to my fellowmen, in such as contained important information upon the subject of doctrine, and as would render it intelligbly plain; but as there are, in a great house, many vessels, so in the history of a work of this magnitude, many items which would be interesting to those who follow, are forgot[t]en. In fact, I deem every manifestation of the Holy Spirit, dictating the hearts of the saints in the way of righteousness, to be of importance, and this is one reason why I plead an apology.

You will recolect that I mentioned the time of a religious ex⟨c⟩itement, in Palmyra and vicinity to have been in the 15th year of our brother J. Smith Jr's age—that was an error in the type—it should have been in the 17th.–[3]

1. Matthew 7:13-14.
2. MS. repeats "yours."
3. Cowdery's confusion in dating the Palmyra revivals may reflect the difficulty of a secondary retelling of another's experience.

You will please remember this correction, as it will be necessary for the full understanding of what will follow in time. This would bring the date down to the year 1823.

I do not deem it to be necessary to write further on the subject of this excitement. It is doubted by many whether any real or essential good ever resulted from such excitements, while others advocate their propriety with warmth.

The mind is easily called up to reflection upon a matter of such deep importance, and it is just that it should be; but there is a regret occupying the heart when we consider the deep anxiety of thousands, who are lead away with a vain imagination, or a groundless hope, no better than the idle wind or the spider's web.

But if others wer[e] not benefited, our brother was urged forward and strengthened in the determination to know for himself of the certainty and reality of pure and holy religion.– And it is only necessary for me to say, that while this excitement continued, he continued,[1] to call upon the Lord in secret for a full manifestation of divine approbation, and for, to him the all important information if a Supreme being did exist, to have an assurance that he was accepted of him. This, most assuredly, was correct–it was right. The Lord has said, long since, and his word remains steadfast, that to him who knocks it shall be opened,[2] & whosoever will, may come and partake of the waters of life freely.

To deny a humble penitent sinner a refreshing draught from [p. 61] this most pure of all fountains, and most desirable of all refreshments, to a thirsty soul, is a matter for the full performance of which the sacred record stands pledged. The Lord never said–"Come unto me all ye that labor, and are heavy laden, and I will give you rest,"[3] to turn a deaf ear to

1. MS. repeats "he continued."
2. Matthew 7:7.
3. Matthew 11:28.

those who were weary, when they call upon him. He never said, by the mouth of the prophet "Ho, everyone that thirsts, come ye to the waters," without passing it as a firm decree, at the same time, that he that should after come, should be filled with joy unspeakable. Neither did he manifest by the Spirit to John upon the isle—"Let him that is athirst, come," and command him to send the same abroad, under any other consideration, than that "whosoever would, might take of the water of life freely,"[1] to the remotest ages of time, or while there was a sinner upon his footstool.

These sacred and important promises are looked upon in our day as being given, either to another people, or in a figurative form, and consequently require spiritualizing, notwithstanding they are as conspicuously plain, and are meant to be understood according to their literal reading, as those passages which teaches us of the creation of the world, and of the decree of its Maker to bring its inhabitants to judgment. But to proceed with my nar⟨r⟩ative.—

On the evening of the 21st of September, 1823, previous to retiring to rest, our brother's mind was unusually wrought up on the subject which had so long agitated his mind—his heart was drawn out in fervent prayer, and his whole soul was so lost to every thing of a temporal nature, that earth, to him, had lost its charms,[2] and all he desired was to be prepared in heart to commune with some kind messenger who could communicate to him the desired information of his acceptance with God.

At length the family retired, and he, as usual, bent his way, though in silence, where others might have rested their weary frames "locked fast in sleep's embrace;" but repose had fled, and accustomed slumber had spread her refreshing hand over others beside him—he continued still to pray—his heart,

1. Revelation 21:6.
2. "claims" in *Messenger and Advocate.*

though once hard and obdurate, was softened, and that mind which had often flitted,[1] like the "wild bird of passage," had settled upon a determined basis not to be decoyed or driven from its purpose.

In this situation hours passed unnumbered—how many or how few I know not, neither is he able to inform me; but supposes it must have been eleven or twelve, and perhaps later, as the noise and bustle of the family, in retiring, had long since [p. 62] ceased.– While continueing in prayer for a manifestation in some way that his sins were forgiven; endeavouring to exercise faith in the scriptures, on a sudden a light like that of day, only of a purer and far more glorious appearance and brightness, burst into the room.– Indeed to use his own description, the first sight was as though the house was filled with consuming and unqu[e]nchable fire. This sudden appearance of a light so bright, as must naturally be expected, occasioned a shock or sensation, visible to the extremities of the body. It was, however, followed with a calmness and serenity of mind, and an overwhelming rapture of Joy that surpassed understanding, and in a moment a personage stood before him.

Notwithstanding the room was previously filled with light above the brightness of the sun, as I before described, yet there seemed to be an additional glory surrounding or accompanying this personage, which shone with an increased degree of brilliancy, of which he was in the midst; and though his countenance was as lightning, yet it was of a pleasing, in[n]ocent and glorious appearance, so much so, that every fear was banished from the heart, and nothing but calmness pervaded the soul.

It is no easy task to describe the appearance of a messenger from the skies—indeed, I doubt their being an individual clothed with perishable clay, who is capable to do this work.

---

1. A correction of "fitted" in *Messenger and Advocate*.

To be sure, the Lord appeared to his apostles after his resurrection, and we do not learn as they were in the least difficultied to look upon him; but from John's description upon Patmos, we learn that he is there represented as most glorious in appearance; and from other items in the sacred scriptures we have the fact recorded where angels appeared and conversed with men, and there was no difficulty on the part of the individuals, to endure their presence; and others where their glory was so conspicuous that they could not endure. The last description or appearance is the one to which I refer, when I say that it is no easy task to describe their glory.

But it may be well to relate the particulars as far as given The stature of this personage was a little above the common size of men in this age; his garment was perfectly white, and had the appearance of being without seam. [p. 63]

Though fear was banished from his heart, yet his surprise was no less when he heard him declare himself to be a messenger sent by commandment of the Lord, to deliver a special message and to witness to him that his sins were forgiven, and that his prayers were heard; and that the scriptures might be fulfilled, which say—"God has chosen the foolish things of the world to confound the things which are mighty: and base things of the world, and things which are despised, has God chosen; yea, and things which are not, to bring to nought things which are that no flesh should glory in his presence.["][1] Therefore, says the Lord, I will proceed to do a marvelous work among this people, even a marvelous work and a wonder; the wisdom of their wise shall perish, and the understanding of their prudent shall be hid;[2] for according to his covenant which he made with his ancient saints, his people, the house of Israel must come to a knowledge of the gospel, and own that Messiah whom their fathers rejected, and with them the fulness of the

1. 1 Corinthians 1:27-29.
2. Isaiah 29:14.

Gentiles be gathered in to rejoice in one fold under one Shepherd."

"This cannot be brought about untill first certain preparatory things are accomplished, for so has the Lord purposed in his own mind. He has therefore chosen you as an instrument in his hand to bring to light that which shall perform his act, his strange act, and bring to pass a marvelous work and a wonder. Wherever the sound shall go it shall cause the ears of men to tingle, and wherever it shall be proclaimed, the pure in heart shall rejoice, while those who draw near to God with their mouths, and honor him with their lips, while their hearts are far from him, will seek its overthrow, and the destruction of those by whose hands it is carried. Therefore, marvle not if your name is made a derission, and had as a by-word among such, if you are the instrument in bringing it, by the gift of God, to the knowledge of the people."

He then proceeded and gave a general account of the promises made to the fathers, and also gave a history of the aborigenes of this country, and said they were literal descendants of Abraham. He represented them as once being an enlightned and intelligent people, possessing a correct knowledge of the gospel, and the plan of restoration and redemption. He said this history [p. 64] was written and deposited not far from that place, and that it was our brother's privilege, if obedient to the commandments of the Lord, to obtain and translate the same by the means of the Urim and Thummim, which were deposited for that purpose with the record.

"Yet," said he, "the scripture must be fulfilled before it is translated, which says that the words of a book, which were sealed, were presented to the learned;[1] for thus has God determined to leave men without excuse, and show to the meek that his arm is ⟨not⟩ short[e]ned that it cannot save."

A part of the book was sealed, and was not to be opened

1. Isaiah 29:11.

yet. The sealed part, said he, contains the same revelation which was given to John upon the isle of Patmos, and when the people of the Lord are prepared, and found worthy, then it will be unfolded unto them.

On the subject of bringing to light the unsealed part of this record, it may be proper to say, that our brother was expressly informed, that it must be done with an eye single to the glory of God; if this consideration did not wholly characterize all his procedings in relation to it, the adversary of truth would overcome him, or at least prevent his making that proficiency in this glorious work which he otherwise would.

While describing the place where the record was deposited, he gave a minute relation of it, and the vision of his mind being opened at the same time, he was permitted to view it critically; and previously being acquainted with the place, he was able to follow the direction of the vision, afterward, according to the voice of the angel, and obtain the book.

I close for the present by subscribing myself as ever, your brother in Christ

OLIVER COWDERY

Letter V.

TO W.W. PHELPS, ESQR.
DEAR BROTHER:–

Yours of the 6th ult. is received and published in this No. It contains so many questions, that I have thought I would let every man answer [p. 65] for himself; as it would occupy a larger space to answer all of them than would be proper to devote at this time. When I look at the world as it is, and view men as they are, I am not much surprised that they oppose the truth as many, perhaps, and indeed, the more I see the less I marvle on this subject. To talk of heavenly communications, angels visits, and the inspiration of the Holy Spirit, now, since the apostles have fallen asleep, and men interp[r]et the word of God without the aid of either the Spirit or angels, is a novel thing among the wise, and a piece of blasphemy among the craft-men. But so it is, and it is wisdom that it should be so, because the Holy Spirit does not dwell in unholy temples, nor angels reveal the great work of God to hypocrites. You will notice in my last, on rehearsing the words of the angel, where he communicated to our brother—that his sins were forgiven, and that he was called of the Lord to bring to light, by the gift of inspiration, this important inteligence, an item like the following—"God has chosen the foolish things of the world, and things which are despised, God has chosen;" &c. This, I conceive to be an important item—Not many mighty and noble were called in ancient times, because they always knew so much that God could not teach them, and a man that would listen to the voice of the Lord and follow the teachings of heaven, always was despised, and concidered to be of the foolish class—Paul prooves this fact, when he says, ["]we are made as the filth of the world—the off-scouring of all things unto this day."[1]

I am aware, that a rehearsal of visions of angels at this day, is as inconsistent with a portion of mankind as it formerly was, after all the boast of this wise generation in the knowledge of the truth: but there is a uniformity so complete, that on the reflection, one is led to rejoice that it is so.

In my last I gave an imper[f]ect description of the angel, and was obliged to do so, for the reason, that my pen would fail to desribe an angel in his glory, or the glory of God. I also gave a few sentences which he uttered on the subject of the gathering of Israel. &c.

Since writing the former, I have thought it would, perhaps, be interesting to give something more full on this important subject, as well as a revelation of the gospel. That these holy personages should feel a deep interest in the accomplishment

1. 1 Corinthians 4:13.

[p. 66] of the glorious purposes of the Lord, in his work in the last days, is consistent, when we view critically, what is recorded of their sayings in the holy Scriptures.

You will remember to have read in daniel—"And at that time, [the last days][1] shall Michael stand up, the great prince, who stands for the children of thy people;"[2] and also in Revelations—"I am thy fellow servant, and of thy brethren the prophets."[3] Please compare these sayings with that singular expression in Heb. "Are they [angels][4] not all mininstering Spirits, sent forth to minister for them who shall be heirs of salvation?"[5] And then let me ask nine questions: first

Are the angels now in glory, the former prophets and servants of God? secondly: Are they brethren of those who keep his commandments on earth? and thirdly have brethren & fleshly kindred in the Kingdom of God, feelings of respect and condescension enough to speak to each other, though one may be in heaven and the other on the earth?

Fourthly: If angels are ministering spirits, sent forth to minister for those who shall be heirs of salvation, will they not minister for those heirs? and fifthly, if they do, will any one know it?

Sixthly: will Michael, the archangel, the great prince, stand up in the last days for Israel? Seventhly: will he defend them from their enemies? Eightly, will he lead them, as they were once lead; and ninthly, if so, will he be seen? These questions I leave without answering, because the reasoning is so plain, and so many might be brought, that, they must be at hand in the heart and mind of every saint. But to the gospel, and then to the gathering?

The great plan of redemption being prepared before the fall

1. Brackets in MS.
2. Daniel 12:1.
3. Revelation 22:9.
4. Brackets in MS.
5. Hebrews 1:14.

of man, and the salvation of the human family being as precious in the sight of the Lord at one time as at another, before the Messiah came in the flesh and was crucifyed, as after the gospel was preached, and many were found obedient to the same. This gospel being the same from the beginning, its ordinances were also unchangable. Men were commanded to repent and be baptised by water in the name of the Lord: and were then blessed with the Holy Spirit. The Holy Spirit being thus given, men were enabled to look forward to the time of the coming of the Son of Man, and to rejoice in that day, because through that sacrifice they looked for a remission of their sins, and for their redemption. [p. 67]

Had it not been for this plan of salvation, which God devised before the fall, man must have remained miserable forever, after transgressing the first commandment, because, in consequence of that transgression he had rendered himself unworthy the presence of his maker. He being therefore cast out, the gospel was preached, and this hope of eternal life was set before him, by the ministering of angels who delivered it as they were commanded.

Not only did the ancients look forward to the time of the coming of the Messiah in the flesh, with delight, but there was another day for which they sought, and for which they prayed. Knowing, as they did, that the fall had brought upon them death, and that man was sensual and evil, they longed for a day when the earth might again rest, and appear as in the beginning—when evil might be unknown upon its face, and all creation enjoy one undisturbed peace for a thousand years.

This being sought for in faith, it pleased the Lord to covenant with them to roll on his purposes untill he should bring it to pass—and though many generations were to be gathered to their fathers, yet the righteous, those who should, in their lives, embrace the gospel, and live obedient to its requirements, rise and inherit it during this reign of peace.

From time to time the faithful servants of the Lord have

endeavored to raise up a people who should be found worthy to inherit this rest; (for it was called the rest of the righteous or the day of the Lord's rest, prepared for the righteous;) but were not able to sanctify them, that they could endure the presence of the Lord, excepting Enoch, who, with his people, for their righteousness, were taken into heaven, with a promise that they should yet see that day when the whole earth should be covered with glory.

Moses labored diligently to effect this object, but in consequence of the transgressions and rebellions of the children of Israel, God swore in his wrath that they should not enter into his rest; and in consequence of this decree, and their transgressions since, they have been scattered to the four winds, and are thus to remain till the Lord gathers them in by his own power.

To a remnant of them the gospel was preached by the [p. 68] Messiah in person, but they rejected his voice, though it was raised daily among them. The apostles continued to hold forth the same; after the crucifixion & resurection of the Lord Jesus, untill they would hear it no longer; and then they were commanded to turn to the Gentiles.

They however labored faithfully to turn that people from error; that they might be the happy partakers of mercy, and save themselves from the impending storm that hung over them. They were commanded to preach Jesus Christ night and day—to preach through him the resurection from the dead—to ~~preach~~ declare that all who would embrace the gospel, repent and be baptized for the remission of their sins, should be saved—to declare that this was the only sure foundation on which they could build and be safe—that God had again visited his people in consequence of his covenant with their fathers, and that if they would, they might be the first who should receive these glad tidings, and have the unspeakable joy of carrying the same to all people; for before the day of rest comes, it must go to all nations, kindred and toungs.

But in consequence of their rejecting the gospel, the Lord suffered them to be again scattered; their land to be wasted and their beautiful city to be troden down of the Gentiles, untill their time should be fulfilled.

In the last days, to fulfill the promises to the ancient prophets, when the Lord is to pour out his Spirit upon all flesh, he has determined to bring to light his gospel, to the Gentiles, that it may go to the house of Israel. This gospel has been perverted and men have wandered in darkness. That commission given to the apostles at Jerusalem, so easy to be understood, has been hid from the world, because of evil, and the honest have been lead by the designing, till there are none to be found who are practising the ordinances of the gospel, as they were anciently delivered.

But the time has now arived, in which, according to his covenants, the Lord will manifest to the faithful that he is the same to-day, and forever, and that the cup of suffering of his people, the house of Israel, is nearly fulfilled; and that the way may be prepared before their face he will bring to the knowledge of the people the gospel, as it was preached [p. 69] by his servants on this land, and manifest to the obedient the truth of the same, by the power of the Holy Spirit; for the time is near when his sons and daughters will prophesy, old men dream dreams, and young men see vissions, and those who are thus favored will be such as embrace the gospel as it was delivered in old times, and they shall be blessed with signs following.

Farther on the subject of the gathering of Israel.– This was perfectly understood by all the ancient prophets. Moses prophesied of the affliction which should come upon that people even after the coming of the Messiah, where he said: ["]and evil will befall you in the latter days; ⟨because ye will do evil in the sight of the Lord⟩ to provoke him to anger through the work of your hands.["][1] connecting this with a prophecy in the song which follows; which was given to Moses in the tabernacle—remembering the expression—"in the latter days"– where the Lord foretels all their evil, and their being received to mercy, to such as seek the peace of Israel much instruction may be gained. It is as follows:–

["]I will heap mischiefs upon them; I will spend my arrows upon them. They shall be burnt with hunger, and devoured with burning heat: I will also send the teeth of beasts upon them, with the poison of serpents of the dust. The sword without, and terror within, shall destroy both the young man and the virgin, the suckling with the man of gray hairs."[2]

But after all this, he will judge their enemies and avenge them of theirs; for he says:

"if I whet my glittering sword, and my hand take hold on judgment, I will render vengance to my enemies, and will reward them that hate me. I will make my arrows drunk with blood, and my sword shall devour flesh."[3]

After all this—after Israel has been restored, and afflicted and his enemies have also be[e]n chastised, the Lord says: ["]Rejoice O ye nations, with his people: for he will avenge the blood of his servants, and will render vengance to his adversaries, and will be merciful unto his land and to his people."[4]

I will give a fu[r]ther detail of the promises to Israel, hereafter, as rehearsed by the angel. Accept assurance of my esteem as ever. [p. 70]

---

1. Deuteronomy 31:29.
2. Deuteronomy 32:23-25.
3. Deuteronomy 32:41-42.
4. Deuteronomy 32:43.

Letter VI.

To W.W. Phelps, Esqr.
Dear Sir:–

Yours of the 24th February is received and inserted in this No. of the Advocate. When reviewing my letter No. 3, I am lead to conclude, that some expressions contained in it are calculated to call up past scenes, and perhaps, paint them to the mind, in a manner differently than otherwise were it not that you can speak from experience of their correctness.

I have not space you know, to go into every particular item noticed in yours, as ⟨that⟩[1] would call my attention too far or too much, from the great object lying before me, — the history of this church;– but one expression, or quotation contained in your last strikes the mind (and I may add — the heart,) with so much force, that I cannot pass without noticing it: It is a line or two from that little book contained in the Old Testament, called "Ruth." It says:

["]Entreat me not to leave thee, or to return from following after thee: for whither thou goest, I will go; and where thou lodgest, I will lodge, thy people shall be my people, and thy God my God."[2]

There is a something breathed in this, not known to the world. The great, as many are called, may profess friendship, and covenant to share in each other's toils, for honors and riches of this life, but it is not like the sacrifice offered by Ruth. She forsook her friends, she left her nation, she longed not for the altars of her former gods, and why? because Israels God was God indeed? and by joining herself to Him a reward was offered, and an inheritance promised with him when the earth was sanctified, and peoples, nations and toungs serve him acceptably? And the same covenant of Ruth's, whispers the

1. Insertion in another hand.
2. Ruth 1:16.

same assurance in the same promises, and the same knowled[g]e of the same God.

~~There is a something breathed in this, not known to the world. The great, as many are called, may~~

I gave, in my last, a few words, on the subject of a few items, as spoken by the angel at the time the knowledge of the record of the Nephites was communicated to our [p. 71] brother, and in consequence of the subject of the gospel and that of the gathering of Israel's being so connected, I found it difficult to speak of the one without mentioning the other; and this may not be improper, as it is evident, that the Lord has decreed to bring forth the fulness of the gospel in the last days, previous to gathering Jacob, but a preparatory work, and the other is to follow in quick succession.

This being of so much importance, and of so deep interest to the saints, I have thought best to give a farther detail of the heavenly message, and if I do not give it in the precise words, shall strictly confine myself to the facts in substance.

David said (Ps. C.) ["]make a joyful noise unto the Lord, all ye lands, that is, all the earth. Serve the Lord with gladness: come before his presence with singing.["][1] This he said in view of the glorious period for which he often prayed, and was anxious to behold, which he knew could not take place untill the knowledge of the glory of God covered all lands, or all the earth. Again he says, (Ps. 107) ["]O give thanks unto the Lord, for he is good! For his mercy endureth forever. Let the redeemed of the Lord say so, whom he has redeemed from the hand of the enemy; and gathered out of the lands from the east, and from the west from the north and from the south.– They wandered in the wilderness in a solitary way; they found no city to dwell in. Hungry and thirsty, their souls fainted in them. Then they cried unto the Lord in their trouble, and he

1. Psalm 100:1-2.

delivered them out of their distresses; and led them in the right way that they might go to the city of habitations.["][1]

Most clearly was it shown to the prophets,[2] that the righteous should be gathered from all the earth: He knew that the children of Israel were led from Egypt, by the right hand of the Lord, and permitted to possess the land of Canaan, though they were rebellious in the desert but he farther knew, that they were not gathered from the east, the west, the north and the south, at that time; for it was clearly manifested that the [p. 72] Lord himself would prepare a habitation, even as he said, when he would lead them to a city of refuge. In that, David saw a promise for the righteous, [see 144, Ps][3] when they should be delivered from those who oppressed them, and from the hand of strange children, or the enemies of the Lord; that their sons should be like plants grown up in their youth, and their daughters like corner-stones, polished after the similitude of a beautiful palace. It is then that the sons and daughters shall prophesy, old men dream dreams, and young men see visions. At that time the garners of the righteous will be full, affording all manner of store. It was while contemplating this time, and viewing this happy state of the righteous, that he further says: ["]The Lord shall reign forever, even thy God, O Zion, unto all generations—Praise ye the Lord![")[4]

Isaiah who was on the earth at the time the ten tribes of Israel were led away captive from the land of Canaan, was shown, not only their calamity and affliction, but the time w[h]en they were to be delivered. After reproving them for their corruption and blindness, he prophesies of their dispersion. He says, ["]Your country is desolate, your cities are burnt with fire: Your land strangers devour[5] in your presence and it is

1. Psalm 107:1-7. "habitation" in *Messenger and Advocate.*
2. "prophet" in *Messenger and Advocate.*
3. Brackets in MS.
4. Psalm 146:10.
5. "it" follows "devour" in *Messenger and Advocate.*

thus made desolate, being overthrown by strangers.["] He further says while speaking of the iniquity of that people. ["]Thy princes are rebellious and companions of thieves: every one loves gifts, and follows after rewards: They judge not the fatherless, neither does the cause of the widow come unto them. Therefore, says the Lord, the Lord of hosts, the mighty One of Israel, Ah, I will ease me of my adversaries, and avenge me of my enemies.["][1] But after this calamity has befallen Israel, and the Lord has poured upon them his afflicting judgments, as he said by the mouth of Moses—["]I will heap mischiefs upon them I will spend my arrows upon them.– They shall be afflicted with hunger, and devoured with burning heat, and with bitter destruction: I will also send the teeth of beasts upon them, with the poison of serpents of the earth["][2]—he will also fulfill this [p. 73] further prediction uttered by the mouth of Isaiah. ["]I will turn my hand upon thee, and purely purge away thy dross, and take way all thy tin: and I will restore thy Judges as at the first, and thy counsellors as at the beginning: afterward you shall be called, the city of righteousness, the faithful city.["][3] Then will be fulfilled, also, the sayings of David: ["]And he led them forth by the right way, that they might go to a city of habitation.["][4]

Isaiah continues his prophecy concerning Israel, and tells them what would be done for them in the last days; for thus it is written: ["]The word that Isaiah the son of Amos saw concerning Juda and Jerusalem. And it shall come to pass in the last days, that the mountain of the Lord's house shall be established in the top of the mountains, and shall be exalted above the hills;– and all nations shall flow unto it. And many people shall go and say, come ye, and let us go up to the

1. Isaiah 1:7; 23-24.
2. Deuteronomy 32:23-24.
3. Isaiah 1:25-26.
4. Psalm 107:7.

mountain of the Lord, to the house of the God of Jacob; and he will teach us of his ways and we will walk in his paths; for out of Zion shall go forth the law, and the word of the Lord from Jerusalem.– And he shall judge among the nations, and shall rebuke many people: and they shall beat their swords into ploughshares, and their spears into pruning hooks: nation shall not lift up the sword against nation, neither shall they learn war any more. And the Lord will creat[e] upon every dwelling place of his people in Zion, and upon their assemblies, a cloud and smoke by day, and the shining of a flaming fire by night: for upon all the glory shall be a defence, or above, shall be a covering and a defence. And there shall be a tabernacle for a shadow in the day-time from the heat, and for a place of refuge, and for a covert from storm and from rain.["][1] And his people shall dwell safely, they shall possess the land forever, even the land which was promised to their fathers for an everlasting inheritance: for behold says the Lord by the mouth of the prophet: ["]The day will come that I will sow the house of Israel with the seed of man, and with the seed of beast. And it shall come to pass, that like as I have watched over them, to pluck up, and to break down, and ⟨and to throw down and to destroy and⟩ to afflict; so will I watch over them, to [p. 74] build and to plant, says the Lord.["][2]

For this happy situation and blessed state of Israel, did the prophets look, and obtained a promise, that though the house of Israel and Juda, should violate the covenant, the Lord in the last days would make with them a new one: not according to the one which he made with their fathers in the day that he took them by the hand to lead them out of the land of Egypt; which said the Lord, ["]my covenant they broke, although I was a husband and a father unto them: but this shall be the covenant that I will make with the house of Israel: After

1. Isaiah 2:1-4; 4:5-6.
2. Jeremiah 31:27-28.

those days, says the Lord, I will put my law in their inward parts, and will write it in their hearts; and I will be their God, and they shall be my people.["][1]

For ["]thus says the Lord, I will bring again the captivity of Jacob's tents, and have mercy on his dwelling places; and the city shall be builded upon her own heap, and the palace shall remain after the manner thereof. And out of them shall procede thanksgiving, and the voice of them that make merry:– and I will multiply them and they shall not be few; I will also glorify them and they shall not be small. Their ~~and they shall~~ children also shall be as afore time, and their congregation shall be established before me, and I will punish all that opress them. Their nobles shall be of themselves, and their governor shall procede from the midst of them.["][2]

["]At the same time, says the Lord, will I be the God of all the families of Israel, and they shall be my people;[. . .] I will bring them from the north country, and gather them from the coasts of the earth;["][3] ["]I will say to the north Give up, and to the south, keep not back:– bring my sons from far, and my daughters from the ends of the earth.["][4]

And in those days, and at that time, says the Lord though Israel and Juda have been driven and scattered, they shall come together,[5] they shall even come weeping: for with supplications will I lead them:[6] they shall go and seek the Lord their God. They shall ask the way to Zion, with their faces thitherward, [p. 75] and say, Come, and let us join ourselves to the Lord, in a perpetual covenant that shall not be forgoten; and watchmen upon Mount Ephraim shall say, arise, and let us go up

1. Jeremiah 31:32-33.
2. Jeremiah 30:18-21.
3. Jeremiah 31:1,8.
4. Isaiah 43:6.
5. Jeremiah 50:4-5.
6. Jeremiah 31:9.

to Zion, unto the holy mount of the Lord our God;[1] for he will teach us of his ways, and instruct us to walk in his paths. That the way for this to be fully accomplished, may be prepared, the Lord will utterly destroy the toung of the Egyptian sea, and with his mighty wind shake his hand over the river[2] smite it in its seven streams, and make men go over dry-shod. And there shall be a high way for the remnant of his people, which shall be left from Assyria; like as it was to Israel when they came up out of the land of Egypt.[3]

And thus shall Israel come: not a dark corner of the earth shall remain unexplored, nor an Island of the seas be left without being visited; for as the Lord has ~~said~~ removed them into all corners of the earth, he will cause his mercy to be as abundantly manifested in their gathering as his wrath in their dispersion, untill they are gathered according to the covenant.

He will, as he said by the prophet, send for many fishers and they shall fish them; and after will I send for many hunters, who shal[l] hunt them;[4] not as their enemies have to afflict, but with glad tidings of great joy, with a message of peace, and a call for their return.

And it will come to pass, that though the house of Israel has forsaken the Lord, and bowed down and worshiping other gods, which were no gods, and been cast out before the face of the world, they will know the voice of the Shepherd when he calls upon them this time; for soon his day of power comes, and in it his people will be willing to harken to his counsel; and even now are they already beginning to be stired up in their hearts to search for these things, and are daily reading the anci[e]nt prophets, and are marking the times, and seasons

1. Jeremiah 31:6.
2. "and" follows "river" in *Messenger and Advocate*.
3. Isaiah 11:15-16.
4. Jeremiah 16:16.

of their fulfilment. Thus God is preparing the way for their return.

But it is necessary that you should understand, that what is to be fulfilled in the last days, Is not [p. 76] only for the benefit of Israel, but the Gentiles, if they will repent and embrace the gospel, for they are to be remembered also in the same covenant, and are to be fellow heirs with the seed of Abraham, inasmuch as they are so by faith—for God is no respecter to[1] persons. This was shown to Moses, when he wrote—["]Rejoice, O ye nations, with his people!["][2]

In consequence of the transgression of the Jews at the coming of the Lord, the Gentiles were called into the Kingdom, and for this obediance, are to be favored with the gospel in its fulness first, in the last days: for it is written The first shall be last, and the last first.[3] Therefore, when the fulness of the gospel, as was preached by the rig[h]teous, upon this land, shall come forth, it shall be declared to the Gentiles first, and whoso will repent shall be delivered, for they shall understand the plan of salvation and restoration for Israel, as the Lord manifested to the ancients.– They shall be baptized with water and with the Spirit—they shall lift up their hearts with joy and gladness, for the time of their redemption shall also roll on, and for their obediance to the faith they shall see the house of Jacob come with great glory, even with songs of everlasting joy, and with him partake of salvation.

Therefore, as the time draws near when the sun is to be darkened, the moon turned[4] to blood, and the stars fall from heaven,[5] the Lord will bring to the knowledge of his people his commandments and statutes, that they may be prepared to stand when the earth shall reel to and fro as a drunken man,

1. "of" in *Messenger and Advocate*.
2. Deuteronomy 32:43.
3. Matthew 19:30.
4. *Messenger and Advocate*: "turn."
5. Revelation 6:12-13.

earthquakes cause the nations to tremble, and the destroying angel goes forth to waste the inhabitance at noon-day: for so great are to be the calamities which are to come upon the inhabitants of the earth, before the coming of the Son of Man the second time, that w[h]oso is not prepared cannot abide; but such as are found faithful, and remain, shall be gathered with his people and caught up to meet the Lord in the clouds,[1] and so shall they inherit eternal life.

I have now given you a rehe⟨a⟩rsal of what was communicated to our brother, when he was directed to go and obtain [p. 77] the record of the Nephites.[2] I may have missed in arrangement in some instances, but the principle is preserved, and you will be able to bring forward abundance of corroborating scripture upon the subject of the gospel and of the gathering.

You are aware of the fact, that to give a minute rehearsal of a lengthy interview with a heavenly messenger, is verry difficult unless one is assisted immediately with the gift of inspiration. There is another item I wish to notice on the subject of visions. The spirit you know, searches all things, even the deep things of God. When God manifests to his servants those things that are to come, or those which have been, he does it by unfolding them by the power of that Spirit which comprehends all things, always; and so much may be shown and made perfectly plain to the understanding in a short time, that to the world, who are ocupied all their life to learn a little, look at the relation of it, and are disposed to call it false.

You will understand then, by this, that while those glorious things were being rehearsed, the vision was also opened, so

---

1. *Messenger and Advocate*: "cloud."

2. On the sources dealing with this vision see Richard L. Anderson, "Confirming Records of Moroni's Coming," *Improvement Era* 73 (September 1970): 4-9.

that our brother was permitted to see and understand much more fully and perfectly[1] than I am able to communicate in writing. I know much may ⟨be⟩ conveyed to the understanding in writing, and many marvellous truths set forth with the pen, but after all it is but a shadow, compared to an open vision of seeing, hearing and realizing eternal things. And if the fact was known, it would be found, that of all the heavenly communications to the ancients, we have no more in comparison than the alphabet to a quarto vocabulary. It is said, and I believe the account, that the Lord show[e]d the brother of Jared (Moriancumer) all things which were to transpire from that day to the end of the earth, as well as those which had taken place. I believe that Moses was permitted to see the same, as the Lord caused them to pass, in vission before him as he stood upon the mount;[2] I believe that the Lord Jesus told many things to his apostles which are not written, and after his ascension unfolded all things unto them; I believe that Nephi, the son of Lehi, whom the Lord brought out of Jerusalem, saw the same; I believe that the twelve upon this continent, whom the Lord chose to preach his gospel, when he came down to manifest to this branch of the house of Israel, [p. 78] that he had other sheep, who should hear his voice, were also permitted to behold the same mighty things transpire in vision before their eyes; and I believe that the angel Moroni, whose words I have been rehearsing, w[h]o communicated the knowledge of the record of the Nephites, in this age, saw also, before he hid up the same unto the Lord, great and marvelous things, which were to transpire when the same should come forth; and I also believe, that God will ⟨give⟩ line upon line precept upon precept to his saints, until all these things will be unfolded to them, and they finally sanctified and brought into

1. *Messenger and Advocate:* "much more full and perfect."
2. See Ether 3:25-26; Moses 1:8, 27-29.

the Celestial glory, where tears will be wiped from all faces, and sighing and sorrowing flee away!

May the Lord preserve you from evil and reward you richly for all your afflictions, and crown you in his kingdom. Amen.

Accept, as ever, assurances of the fellowship and esteem of your unworthy brother in the gospel.

Letter VII.

To W.W. Phelps, Esqr.
Dear Brother:–

Circumstances having heretofore intervened to prevent my addressing you previously upon the history of this church you will not attribute the neglect to any want on my part, of a disposition to prosecute a subject so dear to me and so important to every saint, living as we do in the day when the Lord has begun to fulfill his covenants to his long-dispersed and afflicted people.

Since my last yours of May and June have been received. It will not be expected that I shall digress so far from my object, as to go into particular explanations on different items contained in yours; but as all men are deeply interested on the great matter of revelation, I indulge a hope that you will present such facts as are plain and uncontrovertible, both from our former scriptures and the book of Mormon, [p. 79] to show that such is not only consistent with the character of the Lord, but absolutely necessary to the fulfilment of that sacred volume, so tenaciously admired by professors of religion – I mean that called the bible.

You have, no doubt, as[1] well as myself, frequently heard those who do not pretend to an "experimental" belief in the Lord Jesus, says, with those who do, that, (to use a familiar phrase,) "any tune can be played upon the bible:"– What is

1. MS. reads "ase."

here meant to be conveyed, I suppose, is, that proof can be adduced from that volum[e], to support as many different systems as men please to choose: one saying this is the way, and the other, this is the way, while the third says, that it is all false, and that he can "play this tune upon it." If this is so, alas for our condition: admit this to be the case, and either wicked and designing men have taken from it those plain and easy items, or it never came from Deity, if that Being is perfect and consistent in his ways.

But although I am ready to admit that men, in previous generations, have with polluted hands and corrupt hearts, taken from the sacred oracles many precious items which were plain of comprehension, for the main purpose of building themselves up in the trifling things of this world, yet, when it is carefully e[x]amined a straight forward consistency will be found, sufficient to check the vicious heart of man and teach him to revere a word so precious, handed down to us from our fathers, teaching us that by faith we can approach the same benevolent Being, and receive for ourselves a sure word of prophecy, which will serve as a light in a dark place, to lead to those things within the vail, where peace, righteousness and harmony, in one uninterrupted round, feast the inhabitants of those blissful regions in endless day.

Scarce can the reflecting mind be brought to contemplate these scenes, without asking, for whom are they held in reserve, and by whom are they to be [p. 80] enjoyed? Have we an interest there? Do our fathers, who have waded through affliction and adversity, who have been cast out from the society of this world, whose tears have, times without number, watered their furrowed faces, while mourning over the corruption of their fellow-men, an inheritance in those mansions? If so, can they without us be made perfect? Will their joy be full till we rest with them? And is their efficacy and virtue sufficient, in the blood of a Saviour, who groaned upon Calvary's summit, to expiate our sins and cleans[e] us from all unrighteousness?

I trust, that as individuals acquainted with the gospel, through repentance, baptism and keeping the commandments of that same Lord, we shall eventually, be brought to partake in the fulness of that which we now only participate—the full enjoyment of the presence of our Lord.

Happy indeed, will be that hour to all[1] saints, and above all to be desired, (for it never ends,) when men will again mingle praise with those who do always behold the face of our Father who is in heaven.

You will remember that in my last I brought my subject down to the evening, or night of the 21st of September, 1823, and gave an outline of the conversation of the angel upon the important fact of the blessings, promises and covenants to Israel, and the great manyifestations of favor to the world, in the ushering in of the fulness of the gospel, to prepare the way for the second advent of the Messiah, when he comes in the glory of the Father with the holy angels.

A remarkable fact is to be noticed with ⟨regard⟩ to this vision. In ancient times the Lord warned some of his servants in dreams: for instance, Joseph, the husband of Mary, was warned in a dream to take the young child and his mother, and flee into Egypt; also, the wise men were warned of the Lord in a dream not to return to Herod; and when "out of ⟨Egypt⟩ the Son was called" the angel of the Lord appeard in a dream to Joseph again: [p. 81] also he was warned in a dream to turn aside into the parts of Galilee.[2] Such were the manifestations to Joseph, the favoured descendant of the father of the faithful in dreams, and in them the Lord fulfilled his purposes: But the one of which I have been speaking is what would have been called an open vision. And though it was in the night, yet it was not a dream. There is no room for conjecture in this matter, and to talk of deception would be to sport with

1. "the" follows "all" in *Messenger and Advocate*.
2. Matthew 2:12-13, 22.

the common sense of every man who knows when he is awake, when he sees and when he does not see.

He could not have been deceived in the fact that a being of some kind appeared to him; and that it was an heavenly one, the fulfillment of his words, so minutely, up to this time, in addition to the truth and word of salvation which has been developed to this generation, in the book of Mormon, ought to be conclusive evidence to the mind of every man who is privileged to hear of the same. He was awake, and in solem[n] prayer, as you will bear in mind, when the angel made his appearance; from that glory which surrounded him the room was lit up to a perfect brilliancy, so that darkness wholly disappeared: he heard his words with his ears, and received a joy and happiness indiscribable by hearing that his own sins were forgiven, and his former transgressions to be remembered against him no more, if he then continued to walk before the Lord according to his holy commandments. He also saw him depart, the light and glory withdraw, leaving a calmness and peace of soul past the langauge of man to paint—was he deceived?

Far from this; for the vision was renewed twice before morning, unfolding farther and still farther the mysteries of godliness and those things to come. In the morning he went to his labour as us[u]al, but soon the vision of the heavenly messenger was renewed, [p. 82] instructing him to go immediately and view those things of which he had been informed, with a promise that he should obtain them if he followed the directions and went with an eye single to the glory of God.

Accordingly he repaired to the place which had thus been described. But it is necessary to give you more fully the express instructions of the angel, with regard to the object of this work in which our brother had now engaged—He was to remember that it was the work of the Lord, to fulfil certain promises previously made to a branch of the house of Israel, of the tribe of Joseph, and when it should be brought forth must be done expressly with an eye, as I said before, single to the glory of God, and the welfare and restoration of the house of Israel.

You will understand, then, that no motive of a pecuniary or earthly nature, was to be suffered to take the lead of the heart of the man thus favoured. The allurements of vice, the contaminating influence of wealth, without the direct guidance of the Holy Spirit, must have no place in the heart nor be suffered to take from it that warm desire for the glory and kingdom of the Lord, or instead of obtaining, disapointment and reproof would most assuredly follow. Such was the instruction and this the caution.

Alternately, as we could naturally expect, the thought of the previous vision was ruminating in his mind, with a reflection of the brightness and glory of the heavenly messenger; but again a thought would start across the mind on the prospects of obtaining so desirable a treasure—one in all human probability sufficient to raise him above a level with the common earthly fortunes of his fellow men, and relieve his family from want, in which, by misfortune and sickness they were placed.

It is verry natural to suppose that the mind would revolve upon those scenes which had passed, when those who had acquired a little of this world's goods, by industry and economy, with the blessings of health or friends, or by art and intrigue [p. 83] from the pockets of the day-labourer, or the widow and the fatherless, had passed by with a stif neck and a cold heart, scorning the virtuous because they were poor, and Lording over those who were subjected to suffer the miseries of this life.

Alternately did these, with a swift reflection of the words of the holy messenger, "Remember, that he who does this work, who is thus favored of the Lord, must do it with his eye single to the glory of the same, and the welfare and restoration of the scattered remnants of the house of Israel"—rush upon his mind with the quickness of electricity. Here was a strugle indeed; for when he calmly reflected upon his errand, he knew that if God did not give, he could not obtain; and again, with the thought or hope of obtaining, his mind would be carried back to its former reflections[1] of poverty, abuce,—wealth, grandure and ease, until before arriving at the place described, this wholly occupied his desires;[2] and when he thought upon the fact of what was previously shown him, it was only with an assurance that he should obtain, and accomplish his desires in relieving himself and friends from want.

A history of the inhabitants who peopled this continent, previous to its being discovered to Europeans by Columbus, must be interesting to every man; and as it would develop the important fact, that the present race were descendants of Abraham, and were to be remembered in the immutable covenant of the Most High to that man, and be restored to a knowledge of the gospel, that they, with all nations might rejoice, seemed to inspire further thoughts of gain and income from such a valuable history. Surely, thought he every man will sieze with eagerness, this knowledge, and this incalculable incom[e] will be mine. Enough to raise the expectations of any one of like inexperience, placed in similar circumstances. But the important point in this matter is, that man does not see as the Lord, neither are his purposes like his. The small things of this life are but dust in comparison with salvation [p. 84] and eternal life.

~~Alternately did these,~~ It is sufficient to say that such were his reflections during his walk of from two to three miles: the distance from his father's house to the place pointed out. And to use his own words it seemed as though two invisible powers were influencing or striving to influence his mind—one with the reflection that if he obtained the object of his pursuit, it would be through the mercy and condescention of the Lord, and that

1. *Messenger and Advocate*: "reflection."
2. *Messenger and Advocate*: "desire" here and two lines below.

every act or performance in relation to it, must be in strict accordance with the instruction of that personage, who communicated the inteligence to him first; and the other with the tho'ts and reflections like those previously mentioned—contrasting his former and present circumstances in life with those to come. That precious instruction recorded on the sacred page—pray always—which was expresly impressed upon him, was at length entirely forgotten, and as I previously remarked, a fixed determination to obtain and agrandize himself, ocupied his mind when he arrived at the place where the record was found.

I must now give you some description of the place where, and the manner in which these records were deposited.

You are acquainted with the mail road from Palmyra, Wayne Co. to Canandaigua, Ontario Co. N.Y. and also, as you pass from the former to the latter place, before arriving at the little village of Manchester, say from three to four, or about four miles from Palmyra, you pass a large hill on the east side of the road.[1] Why I say large, is because it is as large perhaps, as any in that country. To a person acquainted with this road, a description would be unnecessary, as it is the largest and rises the highest of any on that rout. The north end rises quite sudden until it assumes a level with the more southerly extremity, and I think I may say an elevation higher than at the south a short distance, say half or three fourths of a mile. As you pass toward canandaigua it lessens gradually until the surface assum⟨es⟩ [p. 85] ~~a level with the more southerly extremity, and I think I may,~~ its common level, or is broken by other smaller hills or ridges, water courses and ravines. I think I am justified in saying that this is the highest hill for some distance round, and I am certain that its appearance, as it rises so suddenly from a plain on the north, must attract the notice of the traveller as he passes by.

1. See map on p. 470.

At about one mile west rises another ridge of less height, running parallel with the former, leaving a beautiful vale between. The soil is of the first quality for the country, and under a state of cultivation, which gives a prospect at once imposing, when one reflects on the fact, that here, between these hills, the entire power and national strength of both the Jaredites and Nephites were destroyed.

By turning to the 529th and 530th pages of the book of Mormon you will read Mormon's account of the last great struggle of his people, as they were encamped round this hill Cumorah. (it is printed Camorah, which is an error.)[1] In this vally fell the remaining strength and pride of a once powerful people, the Nephites—once so highly favored of the Lord, but at that time in darkness, doomed to suffer extermination by the hand of their barbarous and uncivilized brethren. From the top of this hill, Mormon, with a few others, after the battle, gazed with horror upon the mangled remains of those who, the day before, were filled with anxiety, hope or doubt. A few had fled to the South, who were hunted down by the victorious party, and all who would not deny the Saviour and his religion, were put to death. Mormon himself, according to the record of his son Moroni, was also slain.

But a long time previous to this[2] disaster it appears from his own account, he foresaw approaching destruction. In fact, if he perused the records of his fathers, [p. 86] which were in his possession, he could have learned that such would be the case. Alma who lived before the coming of the Messiah, prophesies this. He, however, by divine appointment, abridged from those records, in his own style and language, a short account of the more important and prominent items, from the days of Lehi to his own time, after which he deposited, as he says, on

1. References are to the first edition. See Mormon 6 in the current edition.
2. "national" follows "this" in *Messenger and Advocate*.

the 529th page,[1] all the records in this same hill, Cumorah and after gave his small record to his son Moroni, who, as appears from the same, finished, after witnessing the extinction of his people as a nation.

It was not the wicked who overcame the righteous; far from this: it was the wicked against the wicked, and by the wicked the wicked were punished.– The Nephites who were once enlightened, had fallen from a more elevated standing as to favour and privilege before the Lord in consequence of the righteousness of their fathers, and now falling below, for such was actually the case, were suffered to be overcome, and the land was left to the possession of the red men, who were without inteligence, only in the affairs of their wars; and having no records, only preserving their history by tradition from father to son, lost the account of their true origin, and wandered from river to river, from hill to hill, from mountain to mountain, and from sea to sea, till the land was again peopled, in a measure, by a rude, wild, revengful, warlike and barbarous race. Such are our indians.

This hill, by the Jaredites, was called Ramah:[2] by it, or around it pitched the famous army of Coriantumr their tents. Coriantumr was the last king of the Jaredites. The opposing army were to the west, and in this same vally, and near by, from day to day, did that mighty race spill their blood, in wrath, contending, as it were, brother against brother, and father, against son. In this same spot, in full view from the top of this same hill, one may gaze with astonishment upon the ground which was twice covered with the dead and dying of our fellow men. Here may be seen where once sunk to nought the pride and strength of two mighty nations; and here [p. 87] may be contemplated, in solitude, while nothing but the faithful record of Mormon and Moroni is now extant to inform us

1. First edition. Mormon 6:6 in later editions.
2. Ether 15:11.

of the fact, scenes of misery and distress—the aged, whose silver locks in other places and at other times would command reverence; the mother, who in other circumstances would be spared from violence; the infant, whose tender cries would be regarded and listened to with a feeling of compassion and tenderness; and the virgin, whose grace, beauty and modesty, would be esteemed and held inviolate by all good men and enlightened and civilized nations, alike disregarded and treated with scorn!– in vain did the hoary head and man of gray hairs ask for mercy; in vain did the mother plead for compassion; in vain did the helpless and harmless infant weep for verry anguish, and in vain did the virgin seek to escape the ruthless hand of revengeful foes and demons in human form—all alike were trampled down by the feet of the strong, and crushed beneath the rage of battle and war! Alas, who can reflect upon the last struggles of great and populous nations, sinking to dust beneath the ⟨hand of Justice and retribution without⟩ weeping over the corruptions of the human heart, and sighing for the hour when the clangor of arms shall no more be heard, nor the calamities of contending armies no more experienced for a thousand years? Alas, the calamity of war, the extinction of nations, the ruin of kingdoms, the fall of empires and the disolution of governments! O the misery, distress and evil attendant on these! Who can contemplate like scenes without sorrowing, and who so destitute of commiseration as not to be pained that man has fallen so low, so far beneath the station in which he was created?

In this vale lie commingled, in one mass of ruin the ashes of thousands, and in this vale was destined to consume the fair forms and vigerous systems of tens of thousands of the human race—blood mixed with blood, flesh with flesh, bones with bones and dust with dust! When the vital spark which [p. 88] animated their clay had fled, each lifeless lump lay on one common level—cold and inanimate. Those bosoms which had burned with rage against each other for real or suposed injury, had now ceased to heave with malice; those arms which were, a few moments before nerved with strength, had alike become paralized and those hearts which had been fired with revenge, had now ceased to beat, and the head to think—in silence, in solitude, and in disgrace alike, they have long since turned to earth, to their mother dust, to await the august, and to millions, awful hour, when the trump of the Son of God shall echo and reecho from the skies, and they come forth, quickened and immortalized, to not only stand in each other's presence, but before the bar of him who is Eternal!

With sentiments of pure respect, I conclude by subscribing myself your brother in the gospel,

OLIVER COWDERY.

Letter VIII.

DEAR BROTHER,—

In my last I said I should give, partially, a "description of the place where, and the manner in which these records were deposited:" the first promise I have fulfilled, and must proceed to the latter:

The hill of which I have been speaking, at the time mentioned, presented a varied appearance: the north end rose suddenly from the plain, forming a promontory without timber, but covered with grass. As you passed to the south you soon came to scattering timber, the surface having been cleared by art or by wind; and a short distance further left, you are surrounded with the common forest of the country. It is necessary to observe, that even the part cleared was only occupied for pasturage, its steep ascent and narrow summit not admitting the plow of the husbandman, with any degree of [p. 89] ease or profit. It was at the second mentioned place where the record was found to be deposited, on the west side of the hill, not far from the top down its side; and when myself visited the place in the year 1830, there were several trees standing: enough to cause a shade in summer, but not so much as to prevent the surface being covered with grass—which was also the case when the record was first found.

Whatever may be the feeling of men on the reflection of past acts which have been performed on certain portions or spots of this earth, I know not, neither does it add or diminish to nor from the reality of my subject. When Moses heard the voice of God, at the foot of Horeb, out of the burning bush, he was commanded to take his shoes off his feet, for the ground on which he stood was holy.[1] The same may be observed when Joshua beheld the "Captain of the Lord's host" by Jericho[2]—And I confess that my mind was filled with many reflections; and though I did not then loose my shoe, yet with gratitude to God did I offer up the sacrifice of my heart.

How far below the surface these records were placed by Moroni, I am unable to say; but from the fact they had been some fourteen hundred years buried, and that too on the side of a hill so steep, one is ready to conclude that they were some feet below, as the earth would naturally wear more or less in that length of time. But they being placed toward the top of the hill, the ground would not remove as much as at two-thirds, perhaps. Another circumstance would prevent a wearing ~~away~~ of the earth: in all probability, as soon as timber had time to grow, the hill was covered, after the Nephites were destroyed, and the roots of the same would hold the surface. However, on this point I shall leave every man to draw his own conclusion, and form his own speculation, as I only promised to give a description of the place at the time the records were found [p. 90] in 1823.– It is sufficient for my present purpose to know, that such is the fact: that in 1823, yes, 1823, a man with whom I have had the most intimate and personal acquaintance, for almost seven years, actually discovered by the vision of God, the plates from which the book of Mormon,

1. Exodus 3:2-6.
2. Joshua 5:14-15.

as much ~~as much~~ as it is disbelieved, was translated! Such is the case, though men rack their verry brains to invent falshood, and then waft them upon every breeze, to the contrary notwithstanding.

I have now given sufficent on the subject of the hill Cumorah—it has a singular and imposing appearance for that country, and must exite the curious enquiry of every lover of the book of Mormon: though I hope never like Jerusalem and the sepulcher of our Lord, the pilgrims. In my estimation, certain places are dearer to me for what they now contain than for what they have contained. For the satisfaction of such as believe I have been thus particular, and to avoid the question being a thousand times asked, more than any other cause, shall procede and be as particular as heretofore. The manner in which the plates were deposited:

First, a hole of sufficient depth, (how deep I know not) was dug. At the bottom of this was laid a stone of suitable size, the upper surface being smooth. At each edge was placed a large quantity of cement, and into this cement, at the four edges of this stone, were placed, erect, four others, their bottom edges resting in the cement at the outer edges of the first stone. The four last named, when placed erect, formed a box, the corners, or where the edges of the four came in contact, were also cemented so firmly that the moisture from without was prevented from entering. It is to be observed, also, that the inner surface of the four erect, or side stones was smoothe. This box was sufficiently large to admit a breast-plate, such as was used by the ancients to defend the chest, &c. from the arrows and weapons of their enemy. From the bottom of the box, or from the breast-plate, arose three small pillars composed of the same description of cement used on the edges; and upon these three pillars was [p. 91] placed the record of the children of Joseph, and of a people who left the tower far, far before the days of Joseph, or a sketch of each, which had it not been for this, and the never failing goodness of God, we might have perished in our sins, having been left to bow down before the altars of the Gentiles and to have paid homage to the priests of Baal! I must not forget to say that this box, containing the record was covered with another stone, the bottom surface being flat and the upper, crowning. But those three pillars were not so lengthy as to cause the plates and the crowning stone to come in contact. I have now given you, according to my promise, the manner in which this record was deposited; though when it was first visited by our brother, in 1823, a part of the crowning stone was visible above the surface while the edges were concealed by the soil and grass, from which circumstances you will see, that however deep this box might have been placed by Moroni at first, the time had been sufficient to wear the earth so that it was easily discovered when once directed, and yet not enough to make a perceivable difference to the passer-by. So wonderful are the works of the Almighty, and so far from our finding out are his ways, that one who trembles to take his holy name into his lips, is left to wonder at his exact providences, and the fulfilment of his purposes in the event of times and seasons.

A few years sooner might have found even the top stone concealed, and discouraged our brother from attempting to make a further trial to obtain this rich treasure, for fear of discovery; and a few latter might have lef[t] the small box uncovered, and exposed its valuable contents to the rude calculations and vain speculations of those who neither understand common language nor fear God.

But such would have been contra[r]y to the words of the ancients and the promises made to them: and this is why I am left to admire the works and see the wisdom in the designs of the Lord [p. 92] in all things manifested to the eyes of the world: they show that all human inventions are like the vapors, while his word endures forever and his promises to the last generation.

Having thus digressed from my main subject to give a few

items for the special benefit of all, it will be necessary to return, and proceed as formerly.–

And if any suppose I have indulged too freely in reflections, I will only say that it is my opinion, were one to have a view of the glory of God which is to cover Israel in the last days, and know that these, though they may be thought small things, were the beginning to effect the same, they would be at a loss where to close, should they give a moment's vent to the imaginations of the heart

You will have woundered, perhaps, that the mind of our brother should be occupied with the thoughts of the goods of this world, at the time of arriving at Cumorah, on the morning of the 22nd of September, 1823, after having been rapt in the visions of heaven during the night, and also seeing and hearing in open day; but the mind of man is easily turned, if it is not held by the power of God through the prayer of faith, and you will remember that I have said that two invisible powers were operating upon his mind during his walk from his residence to Chumorah, and that the one urging the certainty of wealth and ease in this life, had so powerfully wrought upon him, that the great object so carefully and impressively ⟨named by the angel had entirely⟩ gone from his recollection that only a fixed determination to obtain now urged him forward. In this, which occasioned a failure to obtain, at that time, the record, do not understand me to attach blame to our brother: he was young, and his mind easily turned from correct principles, unless he could be favoured with a certain round of experience. And yet, while young, untraditionated and ⟨un⟩taught in the systems of the world, he was in a situation to be lead into the great work of God, and be qualified to [p. 93] perform it in due time.

After arriving at the repository, a little exertion in removing the soil from the edges of the top of the box, and a light pry, brought to his natural vision its contents. No sooner did he behold this sacred treasure than his hopes were renewed, and he supposed his success certain; and without first attempting to take it from its long place of deposit, he thought, perhaps, there might be something more, equally as valuable, and to take only the plates, might give others an opertunity of obtaining the remainder, which could he secure, would still add to his store of wealth. These, in short, were his reflections, without once thinking of the solemn instruction of the heavenly messenger, that all must be done with an express view of glorifying God.

On attempting to take possession of the records a shock was produced upon his system, by an invisible power, which deprived him in a measure, of his natural strength. He desisted for an instant, and then made another attempt, but was more sensibly shocked than before. What was the occasion of this he knew not—there was the pure unsulied record, as had been described—he had heard of the power, of enchantment, and a thousand like stories, which held the hidden treasures of the earth,[1] and suposed that physical exertion and personal strength was only necessary to enable him to yet obtain the object of his wish. He therefore made the third attempt with an increased exertion, when his strength failed him more than at either of the former times, and without premeditation he exclaimed, "why can I not obtain this book?" ["]because you have not kept the commandments of the Lord", answered a voice, within a seeming short distance. He looked, and to his astonishment, there stood the angel who had previously given him the directions concerning this matter.[2] [p. 94] In an instant, all the former instructions, the great inteligence con-

1. On treasure seeking in early America see Ronald W. Walker, "The Persistent Idea of American Treasure Hunting," *BYU Studies* 24 (Fall 1984): 429-59; Jon Butler, "Magic, Astrology and the Early American Religious Heritage, 1600-1760," *The American Historical Review* 84 (April 1979): 317-46.

2. On Joseph Smith's attempt to obtain the plates, see also Lucy Smith, *Biographical Sketches*, 85-86, and Jessee, "Joseph Knight's Recollection of Early Mormon History."

cerning Israel and the last days, were brought to his mind: he thought of the time when his heart was fervently engaged in prayer to the Lord, when his spirit was contrite, and when his holy messenger, from the skies unfold the wonderful things connected with this record. He had come, to be sure, and found the word of the angel fullfilled concerning the reality of the record but he had failed to remember the great end for which they had been kept, and in consequence could not have power to take them into his possession and bear them away.

At that instant he looked to the Lord in prayer, and as he prayed darkness began to disperse from his mind and his soul was lit up as it was the evening before, and he was filled with the Holy Spirit; and again did the Lord manifest his condescension and mercy: the heavens were opened and the glory of the Lord shone round about and rested upon him. While he thus stood gazing and admiring, the angel said, "Look!" and as he thus spake he beheld the prince of darkness, surrounded by his innumerable train of associates.

All this passed before him, and the heavenly messenger said, "All this is shown, the good and the evill, the holy and impure, the glory of God and the power of darkness, that you may know hereafter the two powers and never be influenced or overcome by that wicked one Behold, whatever entices and leads to good and to do good, is of God, and whatever does not is of that wicked one: It is he that fills the hearts of men with evil, to walk in darkness and blaspheme God; and you may learn from henceforth, that his ways are to destruction, but the way of holiness is peace and rest. You now see why you could not obtain this record; that the commandment was strict, and that if ever these sacred things are obtained they must be by prayer and faithfulness in obeying the Lord. They are not deposited here for [p. 95] the sake of accumulating gain and wealth for the glory of this world: they were seald by the prayer of faith, and because of the knowledge which they contain they are of no worth among the children of men, only for their knowledge. On them is contained the fulness of the gospel of Jesus Christ, as it was given to his peopel on this land, and when it shall be brought forth by the power of God it shall be carried to the Gentiles, of whom many will receive it, and after will the seed of Israel be brought into the fold of their Redeemer by obeying it also. Those who kept the commandments of the Lord on this land, desired this at his hand, and through the p[r]ayer of faith obtained the promise, that if their descendants should transgress and fall away, that a record might be kept and in the last days come to their children. These things are sacred, and must be kept so, for the promise of the Lord concerning them must be fulfilled. No man can obtain them if his heart is impure, because they contain that which is sacred; and besides, should they be entrusted in unholy hands the knowledge could not come to the world, because they cannot be interpreted by the learning of this generation; consequently, they would be considered of no worth, only as precious metal. Therefore, remember, that they are to be translated by the gift and power of God. By them will the Lord work a great and a marvelous work: the wisdom of the wise shall become as nought, and the understanding of the prudent shall be hid, and because the power of God shall be displayed those who profess to know the truth but walk in deceit, shall tremble with anger; but with signs and with wonders, with gifts and with healings, with the manifestations of the power of God, and with the Holy Ghost, shall the hearts of the faithful be comforted. You have now beheld the power of God manifested and the power of Satan: you see that there is nothing that is desirable in the works of darkness; that they cannot [p. 96] bring happiness; that those who are overcome therewith are miserable, while on the other hand the righteous are blessed with a place in the Kingdom of God where joy unspeakable surrounds them. There they rest beyond the power of the enemy of truth, where no evil can disturb them. The glory of God crowns them, and they continually feast upon his goodness and enjoy his smiles. Behold, notwithstanding you have seen this great display of power, by which you may ever be able to detect the evil one, yet I give unto you another sign, and when it comes to pass then know that the Lord is God and that he will fulfil his purposes, and that the knowledge which this record contains will go to every nation, and kindred and toung and people under the whole heaven.– This is the sign: When these things begin to be known, that is, when it is known that the Lord has shown you these things, the workers of iniquity will seek your overthrow: they will circulate fals-hoods to destroy your reputation, and also will seek to take your life; but remember this, if you are faithful, and shall hereafter continue to keep the commandments of the Lord, you shall be preserved to bring these things forth; for in due time he will again give you a commandment to come and take them. When they are interpreted the Lord will give the holy priesthood to some, and they shall begin to proclaim this gospel and baptize by water, and after that they shall have power to give the Holy Ghost by the laying on of their hands. Then will persecution rage more and more; for the iniquities of men shall be rev[e]aled, and those who are not built upon the Rock will seek to overthrow this church; but it will increase the more opposed, and spread farther and farther, increasing in knowl-edge till they shall be sanctified and receive an inheritance where the glory of God will rest upon them; and when this takes place, and all things are prepared, the ten tribes of Israel will be revealed in the north country, whither they have been for a long season; and when this is fulfilled will be brought to pass that saying of the prophet– 'And the Redeemer shall come to Zion, and unto them that turn from transgression in [p. 97] Jacob, saith the Lord'[1] —But, notwithstanding the workers of iniquity shall seek your destruction the arm of the Lord will be extended, and you will be borne off conqueror if you keep

1. Isaiah 59:20.

all his commandments. Your name shall be known among the nations, for the work which the Lord will perform by your hands shall cause the rightious to rejoice and the wicked to rage: with the one it shall be had in honor, and with the other in reproach; yet, with these it shall be a terror because of the great and marvelous work which shall follow the coming forth of this fulness of the gospel. Now, go thy way, rem[em]bering what the Lord has done for thee, and be diligent in keeping his commandments, and he will deliver thee from temptations and all the arts and devises of the wicked one.– Forget not to pray, that thy mind may become strong, that when he shall manifest unto thee, thou mayest have power to escape the evil, and obtain these precious things." Though I am unable to paint before the mind, a perfect description of the scenery which passed before our brother, I think I have said enough to give you a field for reflection which may not be unprofitable. You see the great wisdom in God in leading him thus far, that his mind might begin to be more matured, and thereby be able to judge correctly, the spirits. I do not say that he would not have obtained the record had he went according to the direction of the angel—I say that he would; but God knowing all things from the beginning, began thus to instruct his servant. And in this it is plainly to be seen that the adversary of truth is not sufficient to overthrow the work of God. You will remember that I said, two invisible powers were operating upon the mind of our brother while going to Cumorah. In this, then, I discover wisdom in the dealings of the Lord: it was impossible for any man to translate the book of Mormon by the gift of God, and endure the afflictions, and [p. 98] temptations, and devices of satan, without being overthrown unless he had been previously benefited with a certain round of experience: and had our brother obtained the record the first time, not knowing how to detect the works of darkness, he might have been deprived of the blessings of sending forth the word of truth to this generation. Therefore, God knowing that satan would thus lead his mind astray, began at that early hour, that when the full time should arive, he might have a servant prepared to fulfill his purpose. So, however afflicting to his feelings this repuls[e] might have been, he had reason to rejoice before the Lord and be thankful for the favors and mercies shown; that whatever other instruction was necessary to the accomplishing this great work, he had learned, by experience, how to discern betwe[e]n the spirit of Christ and the spirit of the devil.

From this time to September, 1827, few occurrences worthy of note transpired. As a fact to be expected, nothing of importance could be recorded concerning a generation in darkness.– In the mean time our brother of whom I have been speaking, passed the time as others, in laboring for his suport. But in consequence of certain fals and slanderous reports which have been circulated, justice would require me to say something upon the private life of one whose character has been so shamefully traduced. By some he is said to have been a lazy, idle, vicious, profligate fellow. These I am prepared to contradict, and that too by the testimony of many persons with whom I have been intimately acquainted, and know to be individuals of the strictest veracity, and unquestionable integrity. All these strictly and virtually agree in saying, that he was an honest, upright, virtuous, and faithfully industrious young man. And those who say to the contrary can be influenced by no other motive than to destroy the reputation of one who never injured any man in either property or person

While young, I have been informed he was afflicted with sickness;[1] but I have been told by those [p. 99] for whom he has labored, that he was a young man of truth and industrious habits. And I will add further that it is my conviction, if he never had been called to the exalted station in which he now occupies, he might have passed down the stream of time with ease and in respectability, without the foul and hellish toung

1. See p. 268, note 1.

of slander ever being employed against him. It is no more than to be expected, I admit, that men of corrupt hearts will try to traduce his character and put a spot upon his name: indeed, this is according to the word of the angel; but this does not prohibit me from speaking freely of his merits, and contradicting those falshoods—I feel myself bound so to do, and I know that my testimony, on this matter, will be received and believed while those who testify to the contrary are crumbled to dust, and their words swept away in the general mass of lies when God shall purify the earth!

Connected with this, is the character of the family: and on this I say as I said concerning the character of our brother—I feel myself bound to defend the innocent always when oportunity offers. Had not those who are notorious for lies and dishonesty, also assailed the character of the family I should pass over them here in silence; but now I shall not forbear. It has been industriously circulated that they were dishonest, deceitful and vile.[1] On this I have the testimony of responsible persons, who have said and will say, that this [is] basely false; and besides, a personal acquaintance for seven years, has demonstrated that all the difficulty is, they were once poor, (yet industrious,) and have now, by the help of God, arisen to note, and their names are like to, (indeed they will,) be handed down to posterity, and had among the righteous.– They are industrious, honest, virtuous and liberal to all. This is their character; and though many take advantage of their liberality, God will reward them; but this is the [p. 100] fact, and this testimony shall shine upon the records of the saints, and be ⟨recorded on the archives of heaven to be⟩ read in the day of eternity, when the wicked and perverse, who have vilely slandered them without cause or provocation, reap their reward

1. See, for example, Eber D. Howe, *Mormonism Unvailed* (Painesville, Ohio: Printed and published by the author, 1834), 11-12, 248-49, 261, 267-68.

with the unjust, where there is weeping, wailing and gnashing of teeth!– if they do not repent.

Soon after this visit to Cumorah, a gentleman from the south part of the State, (Chenango County,) employed our brother as a common laborer, and accordingly he visited that section of ⟨the⟩ country; and had he not been accused of digging down all, or nearly so the mountains of Susquehannah, or causing others to do it by some art of necromancy, I should leave this, for the present, unnoticed. You will remember, in the mean time, that those who seek to vilify his character, say that he has always been notorious for his idleness. This gentleman, whose name is [Josiah] Stowel, resided in the town of Bainbridge, on or near the head waters of the Susquehannah river. Some forty miles south, or down the river, in the town of Harmony, Susquehannah county, Pa. is said to be a cave or subteraneous recess, whether entirely formed by art or not I am uninformed, neither does this matter; but such is said to be the case,– where a company of Spaniards, a long time since, when the country was uninhabited by white setlers, excavated from the bowels of the earth ore, and coined a large quantity of money; after which they secured the cavity and evacuated, leaving a part still in the cave, purposing to return at some distant period. A long time elapsed and this account came from one of the individuals who was first engaged in this ⟨mining⟩ buisness. The country was pointed out and the spot minutely described. This I believe, is the substance, so far as my memory serves, though I shall not pledge my verasity for the correctness of the account as I have given.– Enough however, was credited of the Spaniard story, to exite the belief of many that there was a fine sum of the precious metal lying coined in this subteraneous vault, among whom was [p. 101] our employer; and accordingly our brother was required to spend a few months with some others in excavating the earth, in pursuit of this treasure.[1]

1. On Joseph Smith's involvement in treasure-digging see Bushman, *Joseph*

While employed here he became acquainted with the family of Isaac Hale, of whom you read in several of the productions of those who have sought to destroy the validity of the book of Mormon.[1] It may be necessary hereafter, to refer you more particularly to the conduct of this family, as their influence has been considerably exerted to destroy the reputation of our brother, probably because he married a daughter of the same, contrary to some of their wishes, and in connection with this, to certain statements of some others of the inhabitants of that section of count[r]y. But in saying this I do not wish to be understood as uttering aught against Mrs. Smith, (formerly Emma Hale.) She has most certainly evinced a decidedly correct mind and uncommon ability of talent and judgment, in a manifest willingness to fulfill, on her part, that passage in sacred writ.– "and they twain shall be one flesh",[2] – by accompanying her husband, against the wishes and advise of her relatives, to a land of strangers: and however I may deprecate their actions, can say in justice, her character stands as fair for morality, piety and virtue, as any in the world. Though you may say, this is a digression from the subject proposed, I trust I shall be indulged, for the purpose of satisfying many, who have heard so many slanderous reports that they are ⟨led to believe them true because they are⟩ not contradicted; and besides, this generation are determined to oppose every item in the form or under the pretence of revelation, unless it comes throug[h] a man who has always been more pure than Michael the great prince; and as this is the fact, and my opposers have put me to the necessity, I shall be more prolix, and have no doubt, before I give up the point, shall prove to your satisfac-

---

Smith and the Beginnings of Mormonism, 64-80; Richard L. Anderson, "The Mature Joseph Smith and Treasure Searching," *BYU Studies* 24 (Fall 1984): 489-560.

1. An Isaac Hale affidavit, dated 20 March 1834, was published in Howe, *Mormonism Unvailed*, 262-66.

2. Genesis 2:24.

tion, and to that of every man, that the translator of the book of Mormon is worthy the appelation of a seer and [p. 102] a prophet of the Lord. In this I do not pretend that he is not a man subject to passions like other men, beset with infirmities and encompassed with weaknesses; but if he is, all men were so before him, and a pretence to the contrary would argue a more than mortal, which would at once destroy the whole system of the religion of the Lord Jesus; for he anciently chose the weak ~~things~~ to overcome the strong, the foolish to confound the wise, (I mean considered so by this world,) and by the foolishness of preaching to save those who believe.

On the private character of our brother I need add nothing further, at present, previous to his obtaining the records of the Nephites, only that while in that country, some verry officious persons complained of him as a disorderly person, and brought him before the authorities of the county; but there being no cause of action he was honorably acquited.[1]

From this time forward he continued to receive instructions concerning the coming forth of the fulness of the gospel, from the mouth of the heavenly messenger, until he was directed to visit again the place where the records was deposited.

For the present I close, with a thankful heart that I am permitted to see thousands rejoicing in the assurance of the promises of the Lord, confirmed unto them through the obediance of the everlasting covenant.

As ever your brother in the Lord Jesus

---

1. Reference is made to an 1826 hearing in South Bainbridge, New York, in which Joseph Smith had been charged with being a "glass looker." See Bushman, *Joseph Smith and the Beginnings of Mormonism*, 74-76; Marvin Hill, "Joseph Smith and the 1826 Trial: New Evidence and New Difficulties," *BYU Studies* 12 (Winter 1972): 223-33; and Gordon Madsen, "Joseph Smith at Bainbridge: The Trial and the Law" (paper read at the 23rd Annual Conference of the Mormon History Association, Logan, Utah, 7 May 1988, forthcoming in *BYU Studies*).

Oliver Cowdery

To W.W. Phelps.

~~To the Elders of the Church of the Latter Day Saints~~

~~At the close of my letter in the September No. of the "Messenger and Advocate," I promise[d] to continue the subject there commenced: I do so with a hope that it may be a benefit and a means of assistance to the elders in their labours, while [p. 103] they are combatting the prejudices of a crooked and perverse generation, by having in their possession, the facts of my religious principles, which are misrepresented by almost all those whose crafts are in danger by the same, and also to aid those who are anxiously inquiring, and have been excited to do so from rumor, in accertaining correctly, what my principles are.~~

~~I have been drawn into this course of proceeding, by persecution, that is brought upon us from false rumor, and misrepresentations concerning my sentiments.~~

~~But to proceed, in the letter alluded to. The principles of repentance and baptism for the remission of sins, are not only set forth, but many passages of scriptures, were quoted, clearly illucidating the subject, let me add, that I do positively rely upon the truth and veracity of those principles inculcated in the new testament, and then pass from the above named items, on to the item or subject of the gathering, and show my views upon this point: which is an item which I esteem to be of the greates[t] importance to those who are looking for salvation in this generation, or in these what may be called "the latter times,"~~[1]

---

1. The preceding three paragraphs and heading were canceled in the MS. by writing "Error" through the text. The canceled lines are from *Messenger and Advocate*, 2 (November 1835): 1.

[*remainder of p. 104 blank*]

September 1835

/[1]Here the reader will observe that the narrative assumes a different form. The subject of it becoming daily more and more noted, the writer deemed it proper to give a plain, simple, yet faithful narration of every important item in his every-day occurrences. Therefore, he trusts, that to the man of God, no apology will be necessary for such a course especially when he takes into consideration, that he writes, not so much for the benefit of his co[n]temporaries as for that of posterity. The candid, reflecting mind will also realize, how highly we all estimate every species of intelligence or correct information we can obtain relative to the ancient Prophets & Apostles, through whom the Most-High condescended to reveal himself to the children of men. Such revelations, therefore, as may at any time be given through him will be inserted, and the characters of other men, from their necessary connexion with him, will in some instances be plainly pourtrayed; but the digression from the main thread of the narrative, when short, will, the writer trusts, constitute that pleasing variety, those lights and shades, that picture of human life on which the eye rests with most pleasure. The ear, and the mind of both reader and hearer, will be relieved from that formal sameness, or tiresome monotony, that characterize a dull tale of no merit, and enable future generations, to duly appreciate the claims the subject of this narrative may ⟨have⟩ had, on his co[n]temporaries for their implicit reliance on what he taught them.

---

1. This marks the termination of Warren Parrish's handwriting and the beginning of Warren A. Cowdery's hand.

22 September 1835 · Tuesday

This day he labored, with his friend and brother in the Lord, Oliver Cowdery, in obtaining and writing blessings. They were thronged a part of the time with company, so that their labor was rather retarded; but they obtained many precious things and their souls were blessed, to that degree, that they were constrained to cry out in ecstacy, O. Lord, may thy Holy Spirit, be with thy servants forever. Amen.

23 September 1835 · Wednesday

This day he was at home, writing blessings for his beloved brethren. He was hindered by multitudes of visitors, but remarked, that the Lord had blessed their souls this day, and may God grant to continue his mercies unto my house this night for Christ's sake. This day his soul had desired the salvation of brother Ezra Thayer. His soul was also drawn out in love for brother [p. 105] Noah Packard, who came to his house and loaned the Chapel Committee, one thousand dollars, for the building of the House of the Lord[1] in this place. O may God bless him an hundred fold, even of this worlds goods, for this act of virtuous liberality. He then as if soliloquizing, writes in his journal. My heart is full of desire this day, to be blessed of the God of Abraham, with prosperity, until I shall be able to pay all my debts, for it is the delight of my soul to be honest, O Lord, that thou knowest right well! help me, and I will give to the poor.

This day three of his brethren (viz.) Wm. John & Joseph Tibbits [Tippets] called on him to bid him farewell, having set out on a journey to Missouri,[2] the place designated by the Lord,

---

1. MS. repeats "house of the."

2. On 28 November 1834, the Kirtland high council met to consider a letter presented to them by John, Joseph, and William Tippets, Church members from Lewis, Essex County, New York, listing money and property totaling $848.40 sent by the Church in Essex to purchase land in Missouri. Desiring the counsel

for the gathering of the Saints in these last days.[1] A number of brethren came in to pray with them. Brother David Whitmer took the lead and truly prayed in the spirit, and to use the expression of the subject of our narrative, a glorious time succeeded his prayer, joy filled our hearts and we blessed them & bid them God speed. We promised them a safe journey and bid them adieu for a season. O may God grant them long life and good days. These blessings I ask for them, in the name of Christ, Amen.[2]

24 September 1835 · Thursday

This day the High Council of the Church met at his house to take into consideration the afflictions of Zion, and to devize means for her redemption.[3] It was the voice of the spirit of the Lord, that a petition be sent to the governor of the state of Missouri,[4] praying for his assistance in his official capacity, in restoring those to their possessions in Jackson County, who had previously been driven from them by a lawless mob.

---

of the Church leaders, the men were advised to remain in Kirtland during the winter and make part of their money available for Church use to be repaid the following year. At the high council meeting of 24 August 1835, the Tippetses were directed to go to Missouri the coming fall "to purchase land for the church in Essex." This entry marks their departure. (Kirtland, Ohio High Council Minutes, 28 November 1834; 24 August 1835, MS., LDS Church Archives, Salt Lake City, Utah.)

1. D&C 57:1-3.

2. In the MS. this paragraph is also headed with the same date (September 23) as the previous one.

3. After a July 1831 revelation had designated the area of Jackson County, Missouri, as Zion, the gathering place of the Latter-day Saints, Church members began migrating to that place in anticipation of establishing a holy city and a temple. However, economic, social, and religious differences between the Mormon community and old settlers gave rise to antagonism and finally violence. In 1833 the Mormon population of Jackson County was driven from the county. (See Warren Jennings, "The Expulsion of the Mormons from Jackson County, Missouri," *Missouri Historical Review* 64 [October 1969]: 41-63; and Jennings, "Zion is Fled: The Expulsion of the Mormons from Jackson County, Missouri" [Ph.D. diss., University of Florida, 1962].)

4. Governor Daniel Dunklin.

The brethren had a good time, and covenanted to struggle for this, their favorite object, until death dissolve this union; and if one falls, the rest are not to abandon the pursuit, but struggle on, until the ultimate object is attained, which, they prayed that God would grant unto them, in the name of Jesus Christ.

He drew an article for his brethren to sign who were willing to go next Spring and assist in the redemption of Zion.[1] He felt to ask God in the name of Jesus, that eight hundred or one thousand men, well armed would volunteer to accomplish that great work.[2]

25 September 1835 · Friday

This day he remained at home, and nothing of note transpired during the day. [p. 106]

26 September 1835 · Saturday

This evening, the "Twelve,["] having returned from the East in the morning,[3] he met them, and conversed upon some

1. John Whitmer wrote of the meeting in which this transaction took place: "We met in counsel at the house of J. Smith, Jr., the seer, where we according to a previous commandment given, appointed David Whitmer captain of the Lord's Host, and Presidents F.G. Williams and Sidney Rigdon his assistants and President W.W. Phelps, myself and John Corrill, as an assistant quorum, and Joseph Smith, Jr., the seer, to stand at the head and be assisted by Hyrum Smith and Oliver Cowdery. This much for the war department, by revelation." (John Whitmer, "The Book of John Whitmer: Kept by Commandment," ch. 17., MS., RLDS Church Archives, Independence, Missouri.)

2. In the MS. this paragraph is also headed with the same date (September 24) as the previous one.

3. On 12 March 1835, less than a month after the Quorum of Twelve had been selected, they were called on a mission to the eastern states to "hold conferences in the vicinity of the several branches of the Church for the purpose of regulating all things necessary for their welfare." The Twelve left Kirtland on 4 May and returned 26 September 1835. ("A Record of the Transactions of the Twelve Apostles of the Church of Christ of Latter day Saints from the Time of their Call to the Apostleship Which was on the 14th Day of February AD. 1835," 4, MS., LDS Church Archives.)

matters of difficulty which were resting between some of them and President S. Rigdon, and all things were settled satisfactorily.[1]

27 September 1835 · Sunday

He attended meeting: Brethren, Thomas B. Marsh, David W. Patten, Brigham Young & Heber C. Kimball preached, and broke bread. The Lord condescended to pour out his spirit, and the souls of his servants were edified.

28 September 1835 · Monday

High Council met and tried F.G. Bishop:[2] he was reproved, repented and was reordained. Lorenzo Lewis was tried for fornication and cut off from the church.

29 September 1835 · Tuesday

High Council met to day and tried brother Allen Avery,[3] who on an investigation was acquitted from any charge. P.H. Young was also tried and acquitted.[4] Lorenzo Young was also

1. On this date the presidency, consisting of Joseph Smith, Sidney Rigdon, David Whitmer, William Phelps, John Whitmer, Hyrum Smith, and Oliver Cowdery, met to consider two charges against the Twelve: one from a Warren A. Cowdery letter containing reports "derogatory to the character and teaching" of the Twelve while on their mission to the East, and another from William McLellin and Orson Hyde expressing dissatisfaction with Sidney Rigdon. The charges growing out of the Cowdery letter were found to be false, and the McLellin and Hyde matter was satisfactorily resolved. (Kirtland Council Minutes, 26 September 1835. See also Diary of Joseph Smith, 16 January 1836.)

2. On this date Bishop was charged with "advancing heretical doctrines . . . derogatory to the character of the Church." (Kirtland Council Minutes, 28 September 1835.)

3. The charge against Avery was for rebelling against the decision of the elder's court that took away his license. However, Avery came forward, readily complied with the requisitions of the council, and was restored to his office. (Kirtland Council Minutes, 29 September 1835.)

4. Phineas was accused of "unchristian like conduct" in transactions involving the transfer of copies of the Book of Mormon during an 1835 proselyting journey, but the council found no cause for action, and he was acquitted. (Kirtland Council Minutes, 29 September 1835.)

tried, confessed his error and was forgiven.[1] In all these cases, the subject of this narrative acted in the part of the defense for the accused, to plead for mercy. The Lord appeared to bless his soul, and the council was also greatly blessed. He congratulated himself that much good would result from the two days he had been laboring in church business.

30 September 1835 · Wednesday

He stayed at home and visited many who came to enquire after the work of the Lord.

1 October 1835 · Thursday

He stayed at home and labored on the Egyptian Alphabet[2] in company with his brethren O. Cowdery & W.W. Phelps. The system of Astronomy was unfolded.

2 October 1835 · Friday

He wrote a letter to be published in the Messenger & Advocate.[3]

---

1. A charge had been brought against Lorenzo by W.W. Phelps in 1835 for teaching that "poor men ought not to raise up seed or children" but that marriage relations were nevertheless acceptable. The charge was dismissed. (Kirtland Council Minutes, 29 September 1835.)

2. In July 1835 the Kirtland Saints purchased Egyptian mummies from one Michael Chandler, who had come to Kirtland from the East after hearing of Joseph Smith's notoriety as a linguist. A "Grammar & Alphabet of the Egyptian Language" in the handwriting of William W. Phelps and Warren Parrish appears to have been the product of early study of these ancient materials. (Smith, *History of the Church*, 2:235-36; "Grammar and Alphabet of the Egyptian Language," 1 vol., MS., LDS Church Archives. See also, Hugh Hibley, "The Meaning of the Kirtland Egyptian Papers," *BYU Studies* 11 [Summer 1971]: 350-99; Nibley, *The Message of the Joseph Smith Papyri: An Egyptian Endowment* [Salt Lake City: Deseret Book Company, 1975]; Edward H. Ashment, "The Facsimiles of the Book of Abraham: A Reappraisal," *Sunstone* 4 [December 1979]: 33-48; Nibley, "The Facsimiles of the Book of Abraham: A Response by H.W. Nibley to E.H. Ashment," *Sunstone* 4 [December 1979]: 49-51.)

3. Commencing in the September issue of the *Messenger and Advocate*, being published in Kirtland under the editorship of John Whitmer, Joseph Smith pro-

3 October 1835 · Saturday

He attended, and held a High Council in the case of Elder John Gould for giving credence to false and slanderous reports, instigated and propagated to injure brother Sidney Rigdon, also to investigate the case of Dean Gould, son of John Gould, for threatning S. Rigdon and other Elders. After due reflection on the part of the accused, they both confessed, and were acquitted.[1] In the afternoon of the same day, he waited on the Twelve, most of them at his own house, exhibited to them the ancient records in his possession, and gave explanations of the same. This day he observed, passed off with the blessings of the Lord.

4 October 1835 · Sunday

He started early in the morning with one of his brethren, by the name of John Carrill [Corrill], to hold a meeting in Perry. When about a mile from home, they saw two deer which gave a turn to their thoughts upon the subject of the Creation of God. [p. 107] They conversed freely upon many topicks, the day passed off in a very agreeable manner, and the Lord blessed their souls. When they arrived at Perry they were disappointed of a meeting, through some mismanagement, but they conversed freely with Corrill's relatives, which apparently allayed much prejudice in their minds. He truly felt to ask the Lord to have mercy on their souls.

---

duced three letters in successive issues with the intent "that perhaps the elders traveling through the world . . . may be aided in a measure, in doctrine, and in the way of their duty." ("To the Elders of the Church of Latter Day Saints," *Messenger and Advocate* 1 [September 1835]: 179-82; 2 [November 1835]: 209-12; 2 [December 1835]: 225-30; Smith, *History of the Church*, 2:253-72.)

1. The council considered charges against the two Goulds by Reynolds Cahoon—John for "making expressions . . . calculated to do injury to the . . . cause . . . and manifesting a very strong dissatisfaction against the teachings of the Presidency of the Church"; and Dean for "using wrong expressions and threatening the Elders of the Church," specifically Sidney Rigdon. At this meeting "the wound was healed." (Kirtland Council Minutes, 3 October 1835.)

5 October 1835 · Monday

He returned home, and being much fatigued, from riding in the rain, he spent the remainder of the day in reading & meditation. In the evening he attended a High Council of the twelve Apostles. He had, as he stated, a glorious time, and gave them many instructions concerning their duties for time to come. He told them it was the will of God that they should take their families to Missouri next season, also that they should attend the solemn assembly[1] of the first Elders, for the organization of the school of the Prophets,[2] attend to the ordinance of washing of feet, and prepare their hearts in all humility for an endowment with power from on high. To this they all assented with one accord, and appeared to be grea[t]ly rejoiced. He felt to pray God to spare the lives of these twelve to a good old age, for Christ, the Redeemer's sake, Amen.

---

1. In December 1832, a "solemn assembly" was announced (D&C 88:70), where an "endowment" of spiritual power, a day of Pentecost, was anticipated for the faithful "first laborers" in the kingdom in order that they might be "prepared and able to overcome all things." The gathering was to be preceded by a period of preparation consisting of study classes and participation in ordinances of washing and anointing. (See Lyndon Cook, *The Revelations of the Prophet Joseph Smith: A Historical and Biographical Commentary of the Doctrine and Covenants* [Provo, Utah: Seventies Mission Bookstore, 1981], 182-83; Milton V. Backman, Jr., *The Heavens Resound: A History of the Latter-day Saints in Ohio 1830-1838* [Salt Lake City: Deseret Book Company, 1983], chapter 16.)

2. To better qualify the elders of the Church for building the kingdom and to prepare for the anticipated "solemn assembly," a school, known as the "school of the prophets" or "school of the elders," was organized at Kirtland, Ohio. Beginning in 1833, the school continued during four winter seasons. The 1835-36 session of the school met between November 2 and March 29. An important part of the school, which generally met in the printing office, was the study of Hebrew. (Cook, *Revelations*, 185-91.)

Heber C. Kimball noted that four hundred attended the school in the winter of 1835: "Some studied grammar and other branches. We also employed the celebrated Hebrew teacher Mr. Seixas, who gave us much insight in a short time, into that language. . . . The Elders and church had been previously commanded to seek learning and study the best books, and get a knowledge of countries, kingdoms, languages &c., which inspired us with an untiring thirst after knowledge." (Heber C. Kimball, "Journal and Record of Heber Chase Kimball an Apostle of Jesus Christ of Latter Day Saints," 34-35, MS. Heber C. Kimball Papers, LDS Church Archives.)

6 October 1835 · Tuesday

He staid home, and Elder– Stevens[1] came to his house and loaned F.G. Williams and Co.[2] six hundred dollars, which greatly relieved the Company from its pecuniary embarrassments. May God bless and preserve his soul forever. In the afternoon he called to visit his father, who was very sick with a fever: he was some better toward evening and the subject of this memoir spent the rest of the day in reading and meditation

7 October 1835 · Wednesday

He went to visit his father and found him very low: he administred some mild herbs to him, agreeably to the commandment of the Lord to his servants in these last days, and earnestly prayed that God would have mercy upon him & restore him immediately to health, for Christ the Redeemer's sake. This day his own natural brother, Hyrum Smith and Newel K. Whitney set out in the stage for the City of Buffalo, in the State of New York, to purchase goods to replenish the store called the committee store.[3] May the Lord be propitious,

---

1. Possibly Jonathan Stevens, who, along with his two sons Uzziel and Lyman and his son-in-law John E. Page, was told by the Kirtland high council in August 1835 to settle his family in Kirtland and then go forth to preach the gospel. (Kirtland Council Minutes, 24 August 1835.)

2. In 1831 a "literary firm" had been organized to oversee Church publications. Two years later, after the destruction of the Church press in Missouri, Oliver Cowdery established another press in Kirtland, Ohio, under the firm name "Frederick G. Williams and Company." The year 1835 was a busy one for the printing company. The press published the first edition of the Doctrine and Covenants and was publishing a hymn book and three newspapers, the *Latter Day Saints' Messenger and Advocate*, the *Northern Times* (a political paper supporting Andrew Jackson), and reprints of the *The Evening and the Morning Star*, published earlier in Missouri. By October 1835, heavy expenses and minimal returns had brought the company to the brink of collapse. (Lyndon Cook, *Joseph Smith and the Law of Consecration* [Provo, Utah: Grandin Book Company, 1985], 47-51; Backman, *The Heavens Resound*, 70-71.)

3. In December 1832, less than two years after Joseph Smith arrived in Kirtland, a revelation commanded the building of a temple. Begun in 1833 and finished in 1836, the edifice was built at great sacrifice to the Latter-day Saints.

grant them health strength, a prosperous journey and a safe, expeditious return to the bosom of their families and society of their friends. He here pronounced a blessing and a prophecy upon N.K. Whitney He said blessed of the Lord is brother Whitney, even the Bishop of the Church of Latter-day Saints, for the Bishoprick shall never be [p. 108] taken away from him while he liveth. and the time cometh when he shall overcome all the narrow-mindedness of his heart, and all his covetous desires that so easily beset him. He shall deal with a liberal hand to the poor, the needy, the sick and afflicted the widow and the fatherless. Marvelously and miraculously shall the Lord his God provide for him, even, that he shall be blessed with a fulness of the good things of this earth, and his seed after him from generation to generation. And it shall come to pass, that according to the measure that he metes out with a liberal hand unto the poor, so shall it be measured to him again by the hand of his God, even an hundred fold. Angels shall guard his habitation and protect the lives of his posterity; and they shall become very numerous on the earth. Whomsoever he blesseth, shall be blessed and whosoever he curseth shall be cursed. When his enemies seek to hurt or destroy him, let him rise up and curse them and the hand of God shall be upon his enemies in judgement: They shall be utterly confounded and brought to desolation. Therefore, he shall be preserved unto the utmost, for his life shall be precious in the sight of the Lord. He shall rise up and shake himself as a Lion. As a Lion riseth out of his nest and roareth until he shaketh the hills, as a Lion goeth forth among the lesser beasts, so shall the goings forth of him be whom the Lord hath anointed

---

In June 1833, Hyrum Smith, Reynolds Cahoon, and Jared Carter were appointed a committee to direct the construction of the temple. Workers on the temple received compensation through Bishop Newel K. Whitney, who supervised the committee's storehouse. (Backman, *The Heavens Resound*, chapter 9; Smith, *History of the Church*, 2:333.)

to exalt the poor and humble the rich. Therefore, his name shall be on high and his rest among the sanctified.

8 October 1835 · Thursday

He staid at home and attended his sick father with anxiety; nothing worthy of notice transpired

9 October 1835 · Friday

This day passed much as the preceding, he waited on his father, and nothing occurred worthy of notice.

10 October 1835 · Saturday

Visited the house of his father and found him failing very fast.

11 October 1835 · Sunday

Visited his father again, who was very sick. While the subject of this narrative was in secret prayer in the morning, the Lord said, my servant, thy father shall live. He waited on him all this day, with his desires raised to God in the name of Jesus Christ, that he would restore to health again, that he might be blessed with his company and advice, esteeming it one of the greatest earthly blessings to be favored with the society of parents, whose mature years and experience, render them capable of giving [p. 109] the most salutary advice. At evening David Whitmer came and united with J. Smith Junr in calling on the Lord in mighty prayer, in the name of Jesus Christ, and laid their hands on him and rebuked the disease, and God heard and answered their prayer to the great joy and satisfaction of their souls His aged sire arose, dressed himself, shouted and praised the Lord. He called his Brother Wm. who had retired to rest, that he might join with them in songs of praise to the Most High.

12 October 1835 · Monday

He rode to Willoughby (a small village about two miles and a half from Kirtland) in company with his wife, to purchase goods at W. Lyon's Store. On his return he found a Mr. Bradley, who had been thrown from his waggon, lying across the road, and apparently much injured by his fall.

13 October 1835 · Tuesday

He visited his father, who was very much recoverd from his sickness; indeed, so much so as to cause his friends to marvel at the might, power, and condescension of God in answering prayer in his behalf.

14 October 1835 · Wednesday

He was at home through the day.

15 October 1835 · Thursday

He labored in his father's orchard, gathering fruit.

16 October 1835 · Friday

He was called into the printing office to settle some difficulties which had occurred in it. At evening of the same day he baptized Ebenezer Robinson,[1] and his own words in his

1. Of his baptism by Joseph Smith, Robinson wrote, "At dinner that day, (Oct. 16, 1835) Joseph Smith, Jr. finished his meal a little before the others at the table, and went and stood in the doorway (the door being open, it being a warm pleasant day,) with his back to the door jamb, when we arose and went and stood before him, and looking him in the face said, 'do you know what I want?' when he replied, 'No, without it is to go into the waters of Jordan.' We told him that was what we wanted, when he said he would attend to it that afternoon. We then went to the printing office together, he to his council room which adjoined the room where we worked, and we to our work in the printing office. We worked until well on to the evening, feeling very anxious all the time, for it seemed that we could not live over night without being baptized; after enduring it as long as we could, went to the door of their room, and gently

journal, are the Lord poured out his spirit upon us and we had a good time.

17 October 1835 · Saturday

He called his family together, arranged some of his domestic concerns, and dismissed his boarders.

18 October 1835 · Sunday

He attended meeting in the Chapel, confirmed several who had been baptized,[1] and blessed several children, with the blessings of the new and everlasting covenant. Elder P.P. Pratt preached in the forenoon and John F. Boynton in the afternoon. It was truly an interesting time.[2]

19 October 1835 · Monday

He was at home and exhibited the Egyptian Records of antiquity to a number of persons who called to see them.

20 October 1835 · Tuesday

He was at home during the day, but preached in the school house in the evening.

---

opened it, (a thing we had never presumed to do before.) As soon as Mr. Smith saw us he said, 'yes, yes, brethren, Brother Robinson wishes to be baptized, we will adjourn and attend to that.' We repaired to the water, (the Chagrin river which flows through Kirtland,), and, after a season of prayer, Brother Joseph Smith, jr., baptized us by immersion." (Ebenezer Robinson, "Items of Personal History of the Editor," *The Return* [Davis City, Iowa] 1:74.)

1. One of those confirmed on October 18 was Ebenezer Robinson.

2. John Whitmer adds this detail on October 18: "This day assembled in the House of the Lord as usual, and the Spirit of the Lord descended upon J. Smith, Jr., the seer, and he prophesied saying, the Lord has showed me this day by the Spirit of revelation that the distress and sickness that has heretofore prevailed among the children of Zion will be mitigated from this time forth. And it came to pass that some of the first elders or presidents of the church received a prophetic blessing by revelation through the means prepared in the last days to receive the word of the LORD, J. Smith, Jr. Therefore Joseph dictated blessings for himself, Hyrum Smith, Sidney Rigdon, F.G. Williams, Oliver Cowdery, David Whitmer, W.W. Phelps, and myself, as you will find recorded in the Patriarchal blessing book in Kirtland, Ohio, Book A." (Whitmer, "Book of John Whitmer," ch. 17.)

21 October 1835 · Wednesday

He was at home during the day and nothing of much moment transpired.

22 October 1835 · Thursday

He was at home attending to his domestic concerns.

23 October 1835 · Friday

He was at home. Nothing worthy of note occurred.[1] [p. 110]

24 October 1835 · Saturday

Mr. Goodrich and his lady called on him to see the ancient Egyptian Records, and also went to Doct. F.G. Williams, to see the Mummies. Brethren Hawks[2] & Carpenter from Michigan called and tarried with him over the sabbath and attended meeting

25 October 1835 · Sunday

He attended meeting. President S. Rigdon preached in the forenoon and Elder Lyman Johnson in the afternoon; after which, Elder S. Brownson [Seymour Brunson] joined brother Wm. Perry and Sister Eliza Brown in matrimony, and the subject of this narrative blessed them with long life and prosperity in the name of Jesus Christ. At evening he attended a prayer meeting, opened it and exhorted his brethren and sisters about an hour. The Lord poured out his spirit and some glorious things were spoken in the gift of tongues, and interpreted concerning the redemption of Zion.

---

1. A prayer offered this day was recorded following the 27 November 1835 entry on p. 147.

2. Possibly Joseph B. Hawkes (1799-1862), born at Buxton, New York, and living in Pontiac, Oakland County, Michigan, in 1834, and in Far West, Caldwell County, Missouri, in 1836. (Family Group Records Collection.)

26 October 1835 · Monday

Went to Chardon to attend the County Court, in company with three of his Brothers (viz.) Hyrum, Samuel & Carloss. His Brother Samuel was summoned before this court for not doing Military duty[1] and was fined because they had not their conference minutes with them, for testimony to prove that F.G. Williams was clerk of the conference. This testimony, they would have carried with them, had it not been for the neglect of their Council, or Lawyer, who did not notify them that it was necessary to his success in the suit. This act of the Attorney, he felt as did his brethren, was a want of fidelity to his client, apparent indeed, and a bare insult practiced upon him on account of his religious faith, that the ungodly might

1. The Militia Act of 1792 had required the enrollment of every free, white male citizen between the ages of eighteen and forty-five to serve in his state militia. This service required the attendance of each member of the militia equipped at his own expense at a muster lasting from one to six days, depending upon the state, for purposes of training. Failure to comply resulted in a fine, which was the means of enforcing compulsory military service. However, the law exempted "all post-officers, and stage drivers . . . employed in the care and conveyance of the mail . . . all ferrymen employed at any ferry on the post road; all inspectors of exports; all pilots; all mariners actually employed in the sea service . . . and all persons who now are or may hereafter be exempted by the laws of the respective states." In addition, most states exempted state and local officials, clergymen, teachers, and students in college. (United States, *Statutes at Large*, vol. 1, 264-65, 271-72; William H. Riker, *Soldiers of the States: The Role of the National Guard in American Democracy* [Washington, D.C.: Public Affairs Press, 1957], 27-29; Lena London, "The Militia Fine, 1830-1860," *Military Affairs* 15 [1951]: 133-44; Robert Reinders, "Militia and Public Order in Nineteenth Century America," *Journal of American Studies* 11 [April 1977]: 81-101.)

In October 1835, the case of George Metcalf, Paymaster of the 1st Brigade, 2nd Regiment, 9th Division, Ohio Militia, vs. Samuel H. Smith came before the court at Chardon, Geauga County, Ohio. At a court of inquiry held 25 September 1833, Smith had been fined $1.75 for failing to attend company and regimental musters in 1833. Represented by his attorney, Benjamin Bissel, Samuel Smith sought dismissal of the charges against him on various technical grounds and that he was a minister of the gospel, and hence not subject to the military requirement. However, the court sustained the charges against Smith and ordered him to pay the fine and court costs. (Geauga County, Ohio, Court of Common Pleas, Final Record, Book S, 95-101.)

have an unlawful power over him, and trample him and our feelings under their unhallowed feet. In consequence of this omission of duty a fine of twenty dollars including costs, was imposed upon his brother, and to cancel it and the expenses attending the suit he was obliged to sell his cow. The subject of this narrative, felt to say in the name of Jesus Christ, that the money thus unjustly taken, shall be a testimony against them, and canker their flesh as fire.

27 October 1835 · Tuesday

In the morning he was called to his Brother Samuel Smith's to visit his wife,[1] who was confined and in a dangerous situation. His brother Carloss went to Chardon after Doctor F.G. Williams. He went himself out into the field and bowed in mighty prayer before the Lord, beseeching him in the name of Jesus Christ in her behalf. The word of the Lord came unto him, saying, my servant Frederick shall come and deal prudently, and mine handmaiden shall be delivered of a living child and be spared. [p. 111] The Doctor came in about an hour; and in the course of two hours after she was safely delivered.[2] Thus what God had manifested to him, was fulfilled every whit. On the evening of the same day he preached in the school-house to a crowded congregation.

28 October 1835 · Wednesday

He was at home during the day employed in domestic concerns.

29 October 1835 · Thursday

Warren Parrish began to write for him at $15.00 per month, and received $16.00 in advance out of the Store, known by

1. Mary Bailey (1808-1841).
2. Susanna Bailey Smith (1835-1905), the first child of Samuel and Mary Bailey Smith.

the name of the Committee Store. His father & mother Smith visited at his house this day. Bishop E. Partridge returned this day from a long journey to the East. It is proper here to note that his clerk, W. Parrish, agreed, subsequently to board himself, for which he was to have four dollars more per month, making $19. The subject of this memoir was then summoned to appear before the High Council of the Church, which was then sitting to give his testimony in the case of David Elliott who was arraigned before that tribunal for whipping his own daughter unreasonably. His testimony was in Elliott's favor. He then returned to his writing room, thence to Dr. William's after his large journal[1] and on returning, he made some observations to his scribe relative to the plan of a city which is to be built up hereafter on[2] this ground consecrated for a stake of Zion.[3] It is proper here to notice that during his absence at the Doctor's Bishop E. Partridge came in, accompanied with President W.W. Phelps. He was much rejoiced to see them. He returned home and his scribe commenced writing in his journal a history of his life; concluding President O. Cowdery's 2d letter to W.W. Phelps, which, President Williams had be-

---

1. The "large journal" referred to here is the volume containing this text; it was labeled "A-1" and was later used for the manuscript of Joseph Smith's 1839 History. Frederick G. Williams's involvement is seen from his handwriting on pages 26-43.

2. "on" repeated in MS.

3. A discussion of Joseph Smith's master plan for Kirtland is found in Parkin, "Conflict at Kirtland," 210-12; and in Ronald K. Esplin, "The Emergence of Brigham Young and the Twelve to Mormon Leadership, 1830-1841" (Ph.D. diss., Brigham Young University, 1981), chapter 5.

According to Wilford Woodruff, "Joseph presented us in some degree the plot of the city of Kirtland . . . as it was given him by vision. It was great, marvelous and glorious. The city extended to the east, west, north, and south. Steam boats will come puffing into the city. Our goods will be conveyed upon railroads from Kirtland to many places and probably to Zion. Houses of worship would be reared unto the most high. Beautiful streets was to be made for the saints to walk in, Kings of the earth would come to behold the glory thereof, and many glorious things not now to be named would be bestowed upon the saints." (Diary of Wilford Woodruff, 6 April 1837.)

gun.[1] Bishop Whitney and his wife with his father & mother[2] called to see him. The Bishop's parents had but recently come from the East, and had called to make some enquiry concerning the coming forth of the Book of Mormon. Bishop Partridge and some others came in; and he then set down and related to them the history of the coming forth of the Book, the administration of the Angel to him and the rudiments of the Gospel of Christ. They appeared to be well satisfied, and he expected to baptize them in[3] a few days, at least, such were his feelings although they made no request of that kind at the time of the interview. He then went to the council in the case of Elliott where he had previously been called as testimony.[4] The Presidency adjourned, and on his return Elder J. Boynton, observed that long debates were indulged. He replied [p. 112] that it was generally the case that too much altercation was indulged on both sides, and their debates protracted to an unprofitable length. He was now called to his supper. After being seated around the table, Bishop Whitney observed to Bishop Partridge, that the thought had just occurred to his mind, that perhaps, in about one year from that time they might be seated together, around a table in the land of Zion. His wife observed, on hearing this remark, she hoped it might be the case, that not only they, but the rest of the company present might be seated

1. The "history" referred to is this manuscript. See page 43 for the point at which Joseph Smith's scribe, Warren Parrish, began writing.

2. Samuel Whitney and Susanna Kimball Whitney.

3. "in" repeated in MS.

4. The high council met at Edmund Bosley's to consider a charge made by William Smith against David Elliott and his wife for "beating and whipping" their fifteen-year-old daughter. During the hearing, Joseph Smith testified he "was satisfied that the girl was at fault, and that the neighbors were trying to create a difficulty." The council ruled, however, that "the complaint was not without foundation," that Elliott had "acted injudiciously and brought a disgrace upon himself, upon his daughter & upon the Church, because he ought to have trained his child in a way that should not have required the rod at the age of 15 years." After confessing their wrongdoing and promising to improve, the accused were "restored to fellowship." (Kirtland Council Minutes, 29 October 1835.)

around a table in that land of promise. The same sentiment was reciprocated by the company round the table, to which his full soul seemed to respond his hearty amen, praying God to grant it in the name of Jesus Christ. After supper he went again to the High Council, accompanied at this time, with his wife, and some others that belonged to his household. He was solicited to take a seat with the Presidency, and preside in the case of Sister [Mary Cahoon] Elliott.[1] He did so, his mother was[2] called as testimony and began to relate circumstances that had previously been brought before the church and settled. He objected against such testimony. The Complainant, Wm. Smith arose and accused him of invalidating or doubting his mother's testimony, which he had not done, nor had he any desire to do so. He told his Brother Wm. he was out of place and asked him to set down: but he refused; the request was repeated and Wm. became enraged. He was finally ordered to set down, but said he would not, unless he was knocked down. By this time he (President J.S. Junr.) became wounded and agitated in his feelings on account of the wilful and wicked stubbornness of his brother Wm. and was about to leave the house; But his aged father who was present, requested him not to do so. He hearkened to his advice, the house was brought to order, after much debate upon the subject and the council resumed business. Brother Elliot & his wife were both acquitted of the charges against them.

30 October 1835 · Friday

He was at home. This day Mr. Francis Porter, a member of the Methodist Episcopal Church from Jefferson County N.Y. called to make some inquiry about lands in this place, whether there are any farms for sale that are valuable, and whether a

1. Mary Cahoon Elliott faced the same charge previously brought against her husband, and with the same result.
2. "mother was" repeated in MS.

member of our church could move into this vicinity and enjoy his own possessions and property without making it common stock.

He had been requested to do so by some brethren, who live in LeRay, Jefferson County N.Y. He replied that he had a valuable farm joining the Temple lot that he would sell, and that there are other lands for sale in this place, that there is no common stock business, among us, and that [p. 113] every man enjoys his own property; or he can if he be disposed consecrate liberally or illiberally to support the poor & needy or to the building up of Zion. He also inquired how many members there were in this church. He was told there were about five or six hundred who communed at our chapel and that perhaps, there were one thousand in this vicinity.

At evening the subject of this narrative was presented with a letter from his brother Wm. Smith, the purport of which was that he was censured by the brethren, in consequence of what took place in the council the preceding evening; he also wished to have the cause of censure removed to the satisfaction and understanding of all, that he might not unjustly be censured or made to suffer in his feelings. He then considered that he had been materially injured. He (J.S. Jnr) replied that he thought they parted with the best of feelings, and that he was not accountable for the dissatisfaction of others. Wm. was invited by Joseph, to call and talk with him, assuring him that he would converse in the spirit of meekness on the subject, and give him all the satisfaction he could. This reply was by letter and a copy retained.

31 October 1835 · Saturday

In the morning his Brother Hyrum Smith called in and said he had been much trou[b]led all night, and had not slept any. He said something was wrong, and while they were conversing his brother Wm. came in according to his (Joseph's) request last night. His brother Hyrum observed that he must go to the store. He was invited by Joseph to stay; he replied that he could go and do his business and return: He did so, and during his absence Wm. introduced the subject of their difficulties at the council. Joseph told him he did not want to converse upon that subject until Hyrum returned. He soon came in, and it was proposed to relate the o[c]urrences of the council before named, and wherein he (Joseph) had done wrong he would confess it and ask his forgiveness; and then he (Wm.) should relate his story and make confession wherein he had done wrong, and then leave it to brother Hyrum Smith & brother Parrish to decide the matter between them, and he would agree to the decision and be satisfied therewith. Wm. observed that he had not done wrong and that Joseph was always determined to carry every point whether right or wrong, and, therefore, he could not stand [p. 114] an equal chance with him. This was truly an insult. It was indirectly accusing him of wilful stubbornness and wicked obstinacy: however he did not reply to him in a harsh manner, knowing his brother's irascible disposition, but tried to reason with him and show him the propriety of a compliance with his request. He finally succeeded with the assistance of his brother Hyrum, in obtaining his assent to the proposition he had made. He (Joseph) then related the circumstances as they occurred, and wherein he had done wrong he confessed it and asked him to forgive him. Wm. then made his statements justifying himself, wholly not only in transgressing the rules of the council, but in treating the Presidency with utter contempt. After he had closed, brother Hyrum began to make some remarks in the spirit of meekness. Wm. became enraged, Joseph now joined his br. Hyrum in trying to calm the stormy feelings of Wm. But, neither reason nor argument were of any avail. He insisted that they intended to add abuse to injury. His passion increased; he arose abruptly and said he wanted no more to to do with them or the church and they might take his license for he would have nothing to do with them. He rushed out of the door in a fit of rage, his brothers trying to prevail on him to stop, but all their entreaties had no effect to soften his heart or subdue his passion. He went away in a rage and soon sent his license to his brother Joseph. He appeared to be under the influence of the Adversary of righteousness, and consequently, to spread the leaven of iniquity among the brethren of the Church. He succeeded in prejudicing the mind of his brother Samuel. He was also soon heard in the highway exclaiming against his br. Joseph; which would make his enemies to greatly rejoice. Where the matter would end he knew not, but he prayed God to forgive them, and give them humility and unfeigned repentance. The feelings of his heart he could not express on that occasion. He could prevail nothing with them; he could only pray his Heavenly Father to open their eyes that they may discover where they stand, and extricate themselves from the snare into which they had fallen.

After dinner he in company with his wife, children and brother Carloss and some others rode out on a visit to brother [Shadrach] Roundy's who lived near the village of Willoughby in Cayahoga County. He expressed himself as having had an agreeable visit, and as soon as he returned, he was called upon to baptize Mr. Samuel Whitney, wife and daughter.[1] After baptism, he with others returned to their [p. 115] house and offered our thanks to the Most High. While in prayer he obtained an evidence that his brother Wm. would return to the church and confess the wrong he had done.

1 November 1835 · Sunday

Verily, thus saith the Lord unto his servant Joseph Smith Junr. mine anger is kindled against my servant Reynolds Cahoon, because of his iniquities, his covetous and dishonest

1. The parents and sister of Newel K. Whitney, who had arrived in Kirtland on 29 October.

principles, in himself and family; and ⟨if⟩ he doth not purge them away and set his house in order, ⟨~~chastizement awaiteth him~~⟩ therefore, if he repent not chastizement awaiteth him, even as it seemeth good in my sight. Therefore go and declare unto him this word. He (the subject of this narrative) went immediately and delivered this message according as the Lord had commanded him. He even called him in and read what the Lord had said concerning him. He acknowledged that it was verily so, and expressed much humility. He then went to meeting. Elder Carrill [Corrill] preached a fine discourse In the P.M. President Wm. W. Phelps continued the services of the day by reading the 5th Chapter of Matthew, also the law regulating the High Council and made some remarks upon them. The eucharist was administred. he (Joseph) then confirmed a number who had been baptized, and blessed a number of children in the name of Jesus Christ, with the new and everlasting Covenant Notice was then given that the Elder's school would commence the next day. He then dismissed the meeting.

2 November 1835 · Monday

He was engaged in regulating the affairs of the school. He then had his team harnessed, and he, S. Rigdon O. Cowdery, F.G. Williams, his scribe, and a number of others, went to Willoughby to hear Doct. Piexotto [Peixotto] deliver a lecture on the theory and practice of Physic. They called at Mr. Cushman's had their horses put in the stable, took dinner, attended the lecture and was treated with marked respect, throughout. They then returned home. Lyman Wight[1] came in to the place to day from Zion & George Smith & Lyman Smith from the East.[2] The question was then agitated, which should go to

1. Wight had left Missouri in September 1835 and arrived in Kirtland, Ohio, on 2 November to attend the School of the Prophets.

2. On 5 June 1835, George A. and his second cousin, Lyman Smith, had been sent on a proselyting mission: "We traveled about two thousand miles on

New-York to make arrangements respecting a book-bindery. The question was at length referred to him for a decision. The word of the Lord came thus unto him, saying, It is not my will that my servant, Frederick should go to New York, but inasmuch as he wishes to go and visit his relatives, that he may warn them to flee the wrath to come let him go and see them, for that purpose, and let that be his only business. And behold in this thing he shall be blessed [p. 116] with power to overcome their prejudices. Verily thus saith the Lord, Amen.

3 November 1835 · Tuesday

Thus came the word of the Lord unto him concerning the Twelve, behold they are under condemnation because they are not sufficiently humble, in my sight, and in consequence of their covetous desires, in that they have not dealt equally with each other, in the division of the monies which came into their hands, nevertheless some of them dealt equally, therefore, they shall be rewarded. But verily I say unto you they must all humble themselves before me, before they will be accounted worthy to receive an endowment, to go forth in my name unto all nations. As for my servant William, let the Eleven humble themselves in prayer and in faith and wait on me in patience and my servant William shall return and I will make him a polished shaft in my quiver, in bringing down the wickedness and abominations of men and there shall be none mightier than he in his day and generation, nevertheless, if he repent not speedily, he shall be brought low and shall be chastened, and sorely for all his iniquity which he has committed against me. Nevertheless the sin which he hath sinned against me, is not even now more grievous than the sin with which my

---

foot, without purse or scrip, through the eastern part of Ohio, the western part of Pennsylvania and New York; held about eighty meetings, baptized eight, and preached from house to house continually." The two missionaries arrived back in Kirtland on November 2. ("Sketch of the Autobiography of George Albert Smith," *Deseret News*, 18 August 1858.)

servant David W. Patten, my servant Orson Hyde, and my servant Wm. E. McLelin, have sinned against me, and the residue are not sufficiently humble before me. Behold the parable which I spake concerning a man having twelve sons. For what man among you having twelve sons and is no respecter to them and they serve him obediently and he saith unto the one be thou clothed in robes and sit thou here, and to the other be thou clothed in rags and sit thou there. And looketh upon his sons and saith I am just.[1] Ye will answer and say no man, and ye answer truly. Therefore ⟨verily⟩ thus saith the Lord your God. I appointed these Twelve, that they should be equal in their ministry and in their portion, and in their evangelical rights. Wherefore they have sinned a very grievous sin, inasmuch as they have made themselves unequal, and have not hearkned unto my voice. Therefore, let them repent speedily and prepare their hearts for the solemn assembly, and for the great day which is to come. Verily thus saith the Lord. Amen.[2] [p. 117]

He then went to assist in organizing the Elders school: called to order and made some appropriate remarks on the object of the school, and the great necessity there was of rightly improving time and reigning up our minds to a sense of the great object that lies before us, (viz.) That glorious endowment that God has in store for the faithful. He then dedicated the school in the name of the Lord Jesus Christ. After the school was dismissed, he attended a patriarchal meeting at his brother Samuel Smith's. his wife's parents[3] were blessed, also his own child and named Susanna. At evening he preached in the school house to a crowded congregation.

1. D&C 38:26.
2. A discussion of the context of this revelation is in Esplin, "The Emergence of Brigham Young and the Twelve," chapter 4.
3. Joshua Bailey and Hannah Boutwell Bailey.

4 November 1835 · Wednesday

He was at home in the morning, but attended school, during the school hours; made good progress in studies. In the evening he lectured on Grammar at home. On this day King Follet arrived in this place from Zion.

5 November 1835 · Thursday

He attended school. This day Isaac Morley[1] came in from the East. He was called in the morning to visit Thomas Burdick, who was sick. He took his scribe with him and they prayed for, and laid their hands upon him in the name of the Lord Jesus The disease was rebuked. Wm. E. McLelin and Orson Hyde came in and desired to hear the revelation concerning the "Twelve"[2] His Scribe read it to them. They expressed some little dissatisfaction but after examining their own hearts, they acknowledged it to be the word of the Lord, and said they were satisfied. After school Elder Brigham Young came in and being one of the Twelve, he desired also to hear it read. After hearing it he appeared perfectly satisfied. In the evening he lectured on Grammar.

6 November 1835 · Friday

He was at home in the morning, but attended school during the school hours of the day. spent the evening at home. It may not be improper here to remark that in the morning he was introduced to a man from the East. After hearing the name, Joseph Smith, he remarked that he was nothing but a man, i[n]timating by this expression that he had imbibed the idea, that a person through whom the Lord revealed himself, must be something more than a man. He appeared to have forgotten that all the ancient Prophets were but men, particularly what

1. See note 2, p. 123.
2. See entry of 3 November 1835.

St. James said of the Prophet, Elias, that he was a man of like passions as we are, yet he had that power with God, that he prayed that it might not rain on the earth, and it rained not for three years and six months. And again in answer to his prayer, the Lord gave rain and the earth brought forth her fruits.[1] Indeed, such is the [p. 118] darkness and ignorance of this generation, that it is a thing incredible that a man should have any intercourse with his Maker.

7 November 1835 · Saturday

He spent the day at home attending to his domestic concerns. The word of the Lord came unto him, saying, behold I am well pleased with my servant, Isaac Morley and my Servant Edward Partridge because of the integrity of their hearts in laboring in my vineyard for the salvation of the souls of men.[2] Verily I say unto you their sins are forgiven them; Therefore, say unto them in my name, that it is my will that they should tarry for a little season and attend the school, and also the solemn assembly for a wise purpose in me, even so Amen.

8 November 1835 · Sunday

He went to meeting in the morning at the usual hour. In the fore noon Z[erubbabel]. Snow preached a very interesting discourse. In the after noon J[oseph]. Young preached; and after preaching Isaac Hill came forward to make some remarks, by way of confession. He had previously been excommunicated from the Church, for lying, and for an attempt to seduce a female. His confession was not satisfactory to the mind of the subject of these memoirs. John Smith then rose and made some remarks, touching the proceedings of the High Council

1. James 5:17-18.

2. Partridge and Morley had been sent on a proselyting mission in the East in May 1835. They had left Kirtland on June 2 and returned in late October having baptized three and preached eighteen times.

in the case of said Hill. He observed that the council decided, that he should make a public confession of his crime and have it published in the Messenger & Advocate. He proposed that Mr. Hill should now make his confession before the congregation, and then immediately observed that he had forgiven Mr. Hill, which seemed rather to militate against the statement he first made, which doubtless was rather to be attributed to an error of the head than the heart. President S. Rigdon then arose and made some remarks in opposition to those made by the preceding speaker, and were directly calculated to destroy his influence and bring him into disrepute in the eyes of the Church. This was not right; he also misrepresented Mr. Hill's case and spread darkness rather than light upon the subject. A vote of the Church was then called on his case and he was restored without any further confession; that he should be received into the Church by baptism, which was administered accordingly. After he (J.S.) came home from meeting, he took up a labor with his Uncle John Smith, and convinced him that he was wrong in some of his remarks respecting I. Hill, and he confessed it. He then went and labored with President Rigdon, and succeeded also in convincing him of his error, which [p. 119] he confessed. The word of the Lord then came unto him that President Wm. W. Phelps and President J. Whitmer were under condemnation before the Lord for their errors. He also commenced a labor with J. Carrill for not partaking of the sacrament, and he made his confession. He also reproved his wife for leaving the meeting before sacrament. she made no reply but manifested contrition by weeping.

9 November 1835 · Monday

After breakfast Mary Whitcher came in and wished to see him: her request was granted. She gave a relation of her grievances which, for the time being, were unfathomable, and if true they were sorrowful indeed. He prayed his Heavenly Father to bring the truth of her case to light, that the reward due to evil doers may be given them, and that the afflicted and oppressed, may be delivered. While sitting in his house this morning between the hours of ten and eleven, a man came in and introduced himself to him calling himself Joshua, the Jewish Minister,[1] His appearance was something singular, having, a beard about three inches in length which is quite gray. his hair was also long and considerably silvered with age. He had the appearance of a man about 50 or 55 years old. He was tall and straight, slender frame, blue eyes, thin visage, and fair complexion. He wore a green frock coat and pantaloons of the same color. He had on a black fur hat with a narrow brim. When speaking he frequently shuts his eyes and exhibits a kind of scowl upon his countenance. He (Joseph) made some inquiry after his name, but, received no definite answer. The conversation soon turned upon the subject of Religion, and after the subject of this narrative had made some remarks concerning the bible, he commenced giving him a relation of the circumstances, connected with the coming forth of the Book of Mormon, which were nearly as follows. Being wrought up in my mind respecting the subject of Religion, and looking at the different systems taught the children of men, I knew not who was right or who was wrong, but considered it of the first importance to me that I should be right, in matters of so much moment, matter[s] involving eternal consequences. Being thus perplexed in mind I retired to the silent grove and there bowed down before the Lord, under a realizing sense, (if the bible be true) ask and you shall receive, knock and it shall be opened, seek and you shall find, and again, if any man lack wisdom, let [him ask] of God who giveth to all men liberally & upbraideth not. Information was what I most desired [p. 120] at this time, and with a fixed determination to obtain it, I called on the Lord for the first time in the place above stated,

1. Robert Matthews, alias Robert Matthias, alias Joshua the Jewish minister.

at this time, and with a fixed determination to obtain it, I called on the Lord for the first time in the place above stated, or in other words, I made a fruitless attempt to pray my tongue seemed to be swolen in my mouth, so that I could not utter, I heard a noise behind me like some one walking towards me, I strove again to pray, but could not; the noise of walking seemed to draw nearer, I sprang upon my feet and looked round, but saw no person or thing that was calculated to produce the noise of walking. I kneeled again, my mouth was opened and my tongue loosed; I called on the Lord in mighty prayer. A pillar of fire appeared above my head; which presently rested down upon me, and filled me with unspeakable joy. A personage appeared in the midst of this pillar of flame, which was spread all around and yet nothing consumed. Another personage soon appeared like unto the first: he said unto me thy sins are forgiven thee. He testified also unto me that Jesus Christ is the son of God. I saw many angels in this vision. I was about 14 years old when I received this first communication. When I was about 17 years I had another vision of angels; in the night season after I had retired to bed; I had not been asleep, but was meditating upon my past life and experience. I was well aware I had not kept the commandments, and I repented heartily for all my sins and transgressions, and humbled myself before him whose eye surveys all things at a glance. All at once the room was illuminated above the brightness of the sun; an angel appeared before me, his hands and feet were naked pure and white, he stood between the floors of the room, clothed with purity inexpressible. He said unto me I am a messenger sent from God, be faithful and keep his commandments in all things. He told me also of a sacred record which was written on plates of gold. I saw in the vision the place where they were deposited. He said to me the Indians were the literal descendants of Abraham. He explained many of the prophecies to me; one of which I will mention which is in Malachi 4th chapter. Behold the day of the Lord cometh &c. He also informed me that the Urim & Thummim was hid up with the record, and that God would give me power to translate it with the assistance of this instrument; he then gradually vanished out of my sight or the vision closed. while meditating on what I had seen. The Angel appeared to me again, and related the

History, 1834-1836, A-1, p. 121. Entry of 9 November 1835.
Handwriting of Warren A. Cowdery.

or in other words, I made a fruitless attempt to pray My tongue seemed to be swoolen in my mouth, so that I could not utter. I heard a noise behind me like some one walking towards me: I strove again to pray, but could not; the noise of walking seemed to draw nearer; I sprang upon my feet and looked round, but saw no person, or thing that was calculated to produce the noise of walking. I kneeled again, my mouth was opened and my tongue loosed; I called on the Lord in mighty prayer. A pillar of fire appeared above my head; which presently rested down upon me, and filled me with unspeakable joy. A personage appeared in the midst of this pillar of flame, which was spread all around and yet nothing consumed. Another personage soon appeared like unto the first: he said unto me thy sins are forgiven thee. He testified also unto me that Jesus Christ is the son of God. I saw many angels in this vision. I was about 14 years old when I received this first communication. When I was about 17 years I had another vision of angels; in the night season, after I had retired to bed; I had not been asleep, but was meditating upon my past life and experience. I was well aware I had not kept the commandments, and I repented heartily for all my sins and transgressions, and humbled myself before him, whose eye surveys all things at a glance. All at once the room was illuminated above the brightness of the sun; an Angel appeared before me; his hands and feet were, naked, pure and white; he stood between the floors of the room, clothed with purity inexpressible. He said unto me I am a Messenger sent from God, be faithful and keep his commandments in all things. He told me also of a sacred record which was written on plates of gold. I saw in the vision the place where they were deposited. He said to me the Indians were the literal de[s]cendants of Abraham. He explained many of the prophecies to me; one of which I will mention, which is in Malachi 4th chapter. Behold, the day of the Lord cometh ⟨(&c⟩ He also informed me that the Urim & Thummim was hid up with the record, and that God would give me power to translate it with the assistance of this instrument; he then gradually vanished out of my sight or the vision closed. while meditating on what I had seen, The Angel appeared to me again, and related the [p. 121] same things and much more, also the third time bearing the same tidings and departed. During the time I was in this vision I did not realize any thing around me, except what was shown to me in this communication. After the vision had all passed, I found that it was nearly day light; The family soon arose, and got up also. On that day while in the field at work with my father, he asked me if I was sick, I replied, I had but little strength. He told me to go to the house. I started and went part of the way, and was finally deprived of my strength and fell; but how long I remained I do not know. The Angel came to me again and commanded me to go and tell my father what I had seen & heard. I did so. The old man wept and told me that it was a vision from God, and to attend to it. I went and found the place where the plates were, according to the direction of the Angel, I also saw them and the Angel as before. The powers of darkness strove hard against me. I called on God. The Angel told me, that the reason why I could not obtain the plates at this time, was because I was under transgression, but to come again in one year from that time. I did so but did not obtain them, also the third and the fourth year the last of which time I obtained them, and translated them into ⟨the⟩ english language by the gift and power of God and have been preaching it ever since.

While President Smith was relating this brief history of the establis[h]ment of the Church of Christ in these last days, Joshua seemed to be highly entertained. After he had gone through he observed to him (Joshua) that the hour of worship and time to dine had now arrived, and asked him to tarry, to which he consented. After dinner the conversation was resumed, & Joshua proceeded to make some remarks on the Prophecies as follows. He observed that he was aware that, he

(Joseph) could bear stronger meat than many others, therefore he should open his mind the more freely. Daniel has told us that he is to stand in his proper lot in the latter days. According to his vision he had a right to shut it up and also to open it again after many days, or in the latter times. Daniel's image whose head was gold, and body, arms legs and feet were composed of the different materials described in his vision, represents the different governments [p. 122] The golden head was to represent Nebuchadnezzar, King of Babylon; the other parts other kings and forms of government,[1] which I shall not now mention in detail, but confine my remarks more particularly to the feet of the image. The policy of the wicked spirit is to seperate what God has joined together, and unite what he has seperated, which he has succeeded in doing to admiration, in the present state of society, which is like unto iron & clay. There is confusion in all things both political and religious and notwithstanding all the efforts that are made to bring about a union, society remains disunited, and all attempts to unite it are as fruitless as to attempt to unite[2] iron and clay.

The feet of the image is the government of these United States. Other nations ⟨& kingdoms⟩ are looking up to her for an example of union, freedom and equal rights, and, therefore, worship her like as Daniel saw in the vision, although they are beginning to lose confidence in her, on seeing the broils and discord that distract her political and religious horizons. This image is characteristic of all governments and institutions, or most of them; as they begin with a head of gold and terminate in the contemptible feet of iron and clay. They make a splendid appearance at first, promising much more than they can perform, and finally end in degradation and sink in infamy. We should not only start to come out of Babylon, but we should

1. Daniel 2.
2. MS. repeats "it are as fruitless as to attempt to unite."

leave her entirely, lest we be overthrown in her ruins. We should, therefore, keep on improving and reforming. Twenty four hours for improvement now, is worth as much as a year was, a hundred years ago. The spirit of the Fathers was cut down, or those that were under the altar, are now rising, this is the first resurrection. the Elder that falls first will rise last. We should not form any opinion only for the present, and leave the result of futurity with God. I have risen up out of obscurity, but was looked up to, when but a youth in temporal things. It is not necessary that God should give us all things at first, or in his first commission to us, but in his second John saw the Angel deliver the gospel in the last days,[1] which would not be necessary if it were already in the world: This expression would be inconsistent. The small lights that God has given are sufficient to lead us out of Babylon [p. 123] and when we get out we shall have the greater light. He told Joshua that he did not perfectly understand him concerning the resurrection, and wished him to be more explanatory on that subject: he replied that he did not feel impressed by the spirit to unfold it further at that time, but perhaps, he might at some other time.—President Smith then withdrew to transact some business with a gentleman that had called to see him. Joshua informed W. Parrish Smith's scribe that he was born in the town of Cambridge Washington County in the State of New York. He said that all the Rail-Roads, Canals and other improvements, are performed by spirits of the resurrection. The silence, spoken of by John the Revelator, he said, which is to be in Heaven for the space of half an hour,[2] is between 1830 & 1851, during which time the judgements of God will be poured out: After that time there will be peace. Curiosity to see a man that was said to be a Jew, induced many to call during the day, and more particularly at evening. Suspicions

1. Revelation 14:6.
2. Revelation 8:1.

were entertained that said Joshua was none other than the noted Matthias of New York City, about whom so much had been said in the public prints on account of the trials he underwent in that place before courts of justice. The crimes alle⟨d⟩ged against him were murder, manslaughter, contempt of Court, and whipping his daughter, for the two last of which he was found guilty was imprisioned and came out about four months since After some equivocating he confessed that he was really Matthias. After supper it was proposed that Matthias should deliver a lecture to those present. He did so sitting in his chair He commenced, by saying, God said let there be light and there was light, which he dwelt upon through his discourse. He made some very excellent remarks but his mind was evidently filled with darkness. After he dismissed his meeting & the congregation dispersed, he conversed freely upon the circumstances that tra[n]spired in New York. His name is Robert Matthias. He says that Joshua is his priestly name. During all this time no one contradicted his sentiments. The object of President Smith, was to draw out all he could concerning his faith. The next morning–

10 November 1835 · Tuesday

He resumed the conversation and desired him to enlighten his mind with his views respecting the [p. 124] resurrection. He says he possesses the spirit of his fathers, that he is the literal decendant of Matthias the Apostle, who was chosen in the place of Judas that fell,[1] and that his spirit is recussitated in him, and that this is the way or scheme of Eternal life; this transmigration of soul or spirit from Father to Son. He told Matthias that his doctrine was of the Devil. That he in reality was possessed of a wicked and deformed spirit. Notwithstanding, he professed to be the spirit of truth itself, and said also

1. Acts 1:15-26.

that he possessed the soul of Christ. He tarried until the next day.

11 November 1835 · Wednesday

After breakfast Joshua was told that his God was the Devil and could stay no longer, but he must depart, and so for once says the subject of these memoirs I cast out the Devil in bodily shape.

Here it may not be improper to mention that on the 9th A[lvah]. Beaman came to ask advise relative to purchasing land, in this place or in Missouri. As he could not arrange his business to go to Missouri next spring he was advized to buy and settle here until he arrange his mind and then go to Zion if he chose to do so. President Smith was at home this day except during school hours. He spent the evening around his own fireside teaching his family the science of grammar. The weather was now cold, the wind high and it commenced snowing.

12 November 1835 · Thursday

He attended school again during the school hours. Rain and snow continued to fall. The snow by that time was about one inch in depth. the wind high and the weather extremely unpleasant. The laborers who had commenced finishing the out side of the Lord's House were obliged to break off from their business on the 11th at the commencement of this storm. The job of finishing the out side of the House was let to A[rtemus]. Millet & L[orenzo]. Young for $1000. They progressed rapidly, in it. Jacob Bump has the Job of plastering the inside throughout for $1500. He commenced on the 9th and still continues, the inclemency of the weather ⟨to the contrary⟩ notwithstanding. This evening (12) President Smith met with a council of the "Twelve" by their request. Nine of them were present. Council opened by singing and prayer and he then remarked to them nearly as follows: I am happy in the enjoyment of this opportunity in meeting this council on this occasion. I am satisfied that [p. 125] the spirit of the Lord is here, and I am satisfied with all the [brethren present][1] and I need not say to you that you have my utmost confidence, and that I intend to uphold you to the uttermost, for I am well aware that you have to sustain my character against the vile calumnies and reproaches of this ungodly generation, and that you delight in so doing. Darkness prevails; it is in a great degree now as it was when Christ was about to be crucified. The powers of darkness strove to obscure the glorious sun of righteousness, that then began to dawn upon the world, and was soon to burst in great blessings upon the heads of the faithful; and let me tell you, brethren, That great blessings await us at this time, and will soon be poured out upon us if we are faithful in all things: for we are even entitled to greater blessings than they were, because they had the person of Christ with them to instruct them in the great plan of salvation. His personal presence we have not, therefore we need the greater faith on account of our peculiar circumstances. I am determined to do all I can to uphold you, although I may do many things inadvertantly that are not right in the sight of God. You want to know many things that are before you, that you may know how to prepare yourselves for the great things that God is about to bring to pass. But there is one great deficiency or obstruction in the way, that deprives us of the greater blessings, and in order to make the foundation of this church complete, and permanent, we must remove this obstruction, which is to attend to certain duties to which we have not attended. I supposed I had established this church on a permanent foundation when I went to Missouri, and indeed I did so, for if I had been taken away it would have been enough. But as I yet live, therefore, God requires more at my hands. The item to which

1. Omission in MS. supplied from Joseph Smith Diary.

I wish the more particula[r]ly to cite your minds this night is the ordinance of washing of feet. This we have not done as yet, but it is as necessary now as it was in the days of the Saviour, and we must have a place prepared that we may attend to this ordinance aside from the world. We have not desired much from the hand of the Lord, with that faith and obedience that we ought. Yet we have enjoyed great blessings, but we are not so sensible of them as we should be [p. 126] When or where has God suffered one of the witnesses or first Elders of this church to fall? Amidst all the calamities and judgements that have befallen the inhabitants of the earth, his Almighty arm has sustained us. Men & Devils have raged but they have raged in vain. We must have all things prepared and call our solemn assembly as the Lord has commanded us, that we may be able to accomplish his great work. It must be done in God's own way. The House of the Lord must be prepared and the solemn assembly be called and organized in it, according to the order of the House of God: & in it we must attend to the ordinance of washing of feet. This ordinance was never intended for any but official members: it is calculated to unite our hearts, that we may be one in feeling & sentiment, and that our faith may be strong so that Satan can not overthrow us, nor have any power over us. The endowment about which you are so anxious, you cannot comprehend now, nor could the Angel Gabriel explain it to the understanding of your dark minds, but strive to be prepared in your hearts, be faithful in all things, that when we meet in the solemn assembly that is, such as God shall name out of all the official members, will meet, and we must be clean every whit. Let us be faithful and silent, brethren, and if God gives you a manifestion keep it to yourselves, be watchful and prayerful and you shall have a prelude of those joys that God will pour out on that day. Do not watch for iniquity in each other, if you do, you will not get an endowment, for God will not bestow it on such: but if we are faithful, and live by every word that proceeds forth from the mouth of God I will venture to prophecy that we shall get a blessing that will be worth our grateful acknowledgements and everlasting remembrance. If we should live as long as John the Revelator our blessings will be such as we have not realized before, nor in this generation.

The order of the House of God has been, and ever will be the same, even after Christ comes, and after the termination of the Thousand years it will be the same, and we shall finally enter the Celestial kingdom of God and enjoy it forever. You need an endowment, brethren, in order that you may be prepared and able to overcome all things, and then those who reject your testimony will be damned. The sick will be healed, the lame made to walk the deaf to hear and the blind to see through your instrumentality. But let me tell you, that you will not have power after the endowment, to heal those who have not faith, nor to benefit them [p. 127] for you might as well expect to benefit a Devil in Hell as such an one. Such ones are possessed of his spirit and are willing to keep it, for they are habitations of Devils and are only fit for his society. But when you are endowed and prepared to preach the Gospel to all nations, kindreds & tongues in their own languages, you must faithfully warn all, bind up the law and seal up the testimony, and the destroying angel will follow close at your heels and execute his tremendous mission upon the children of disobedience, and destroy the workers of iniquity: while the Saints will be gathered out from among them, and stand in holy places ready to meet the Bride-Groom when he comes.

I feel disposed to speak a few words more to you, my brethren, concerning the endowment, all who are prepared and are sufficiently pure to abide the presence of the Lord, will see him in the solemn assembly.

The brethren expressed their gratification for the instructions he had given them. He closed by prayer, returned home and retired to rest.

13 November 1835 · Friday

He attended school During school hours. After school a Mr. Messenger of Bainbridge Chenango County N.Y. came in to make some inquiry about H[ezekiah]. Peck's family. Messenger was a Universalian Minister, and the conversation was soon turned upon Religion. He [went] with him to President Rigdon's and spent the evening in conversation. Preached the gospel to him, bore testimony to him of what they had seen & heard. He attempted to raise some objections, but the force of truth bore him down, and he was silent although unbelieving

14 November 1835 · Saturday

Thus came the word of the Lord unto me saying. Verily thus saith the Lord unto my servant Joseph concerning my servant Warren [Parrish], behold, his sins are forgiven him because of his desires to do the works of righteousness, therefore, inasmuch as he will hearken unto my voice, he shall be blessed with wisdom and with a sound mind, even above his fellows. Behold, it shall come to pass in his day, that he shall see great things shew forth themselves ~~in him~~ unto my people; he shall see much of my ancient records and shall know of hidden things, and shall be endowed with a knowledge of hidden languages, and if he desires, and shall [p. 128] seek it at my hand, he shall be privileged with writing much of my word as a scribe unto me for the benefit of my people.

Therefore, this shall be his calling until I shall order it otherwise in my wisdom: and it shall be said of him in a time to come, behold Warren, the Lord's Scribe, for the Lord's Seer whom he hath appointed in Israel. therefore, if he will keep my commandments he shall be lifted up at the last day, even so. Amen.

A gentleman called this afternoon, by the name of Erastus Holmes of Newbury Clemon [Newberry, Clermont] Co. Ohio, to make inquiry about the establishment of the Church of the

Latter Day Saints, and to be instructed more perfectly in the doctrine & principles of it. He (Smith) commenced and gave him a brief relation of his experience while in his youthful days, say from the age of six years up to the time he received the first visitation of Angels which was when he was about 14 years old. He also gave him an account of the revelations he ~~had~~ afterward received concerning the coming forth of the Book of Mormon, and a succinct account of the rise and progress of the church up to this date. He listened very attentively and seemed highly gratified. and expressed a determination to unite with the Church. He truly appeared to be a sincere inquirer after truth, which rendered his society endearing.

15 November 1835 · Sunday

He, (President Smith) and his friend, Holmes, of whom mention has been made above, went to meeting, which was held in the school-house. President Rigdon preached on the subject of men's being called to preach the gospel and their qualifications &c. He was happy in the delivery, and in his peculiar, entertaining manner gave an interesting, instructing discourse. Holmes appeared to be well satisfied. He has been a member of the Methodist Church and was excommunicated for receiving the Elders of the Church of the Latter-Day-Saints into his house. In the afternoon before partaking of the Sacrament, the case of Isaac Hills, an offending brother, was called up & agitated. This case was settled after much controversy and Hills retained in the Church by his making a humble acknowledgement before the Church, and consenting to have his Confession published in the Messenger & Advocate. Sacrament was then admininstered and congregation [p. 129] dismissed at a late hour.

16 November 1835 · Monday

President Smith was at home this day and dictated a letter for the Messenger & Advocate.[1] Also one to Harvey Whitlock.

1. See note 3, p. 102.

Elders Beaman, [Elial?] Strong & others called to see him in the course of the day.

Here follows the Copy of a long letter from H. Whitlock.

Dear Sir,

Having a few leisure moments, I have at last concluded to do what my judgement has long dictated would be right, but the allurements of many vices, have long retarded the hand, that would wield the pen, that would make intelligent the communication that I wish to send you. And even now, that ambition which is a prevailing and predominant principle among the great mass of natural men, forbids that plainness of sentiment with which I wish to write. For know assuredly, Sir, to you I wish to unbosom the secrets of my heart, as before the Omnicient Judge of all the earth.

Be not surprized when I declare unto you, as the Spirit will bear record, that my faith is firm and unshaken in the things of the Everlasting Gospel as it is proclaimed by the servants of the Latter-Day-Saints. Dear brother Joseph (if I may be allowed the expression) when I consider the happy times, the peaceful moments, and pleasant seasons, I have enjoyed with you and this people; contrasted with my now degraded state, together with the high and exalted station, I have held before God: and the abyss into which I have fallen is a subject that swells my heart too big for utterance, and language is overwhelmed with feelings, and looses its power of description. And as I desire to know the will of God concerning me I believe it is my duty to make known unto you my real situation. I shall, therefore, dispassionately, proceed to give a true and untarnished relation; I need not tell you that in former times I have preached the word, and endeavored to be instant in Season and out of season, to reprove rebuke exhort, and faithfully discharge that trust reposed in me. But, Oh! with what grief, and lamentable sorrow & anguish do I have to relate that

I have fallen from that princely station whereunto our God has called me. Reasons why are unnecessary. May the fact suffice, and believe me when I tell you I have sunk myself (since my last separation from this Body) [p. 130] in crime of the deepest dye, and that I may the better you to understand what my real sins are, I will mention, (although pride forbids it) some that I am not guilty of. My hands have not been stained with innocent blood, neither have I lain couched around the cottages of my fellow men to seize and carry off the booty; nor have I slandered my neighbor, nor born false testimony, nor taken unlawful hire, nor oppressed the widow nor fatherless, neither have I persecuted the saints. But my hands are swift to do iniquity and my feet are fast running in the paths of vice and folly, and my heart, quick to devise wicked imaginations. Nevertheless I am impressed with the sure thought that I am fast hastening to a whole world of disembodied beings, without God and with but one hope in the world; which is to know that to err is human, but, to forgive is Divine. Much I might say in relation to myself and the original difficulties with the Church, which I will forbear and inasmuch as I have been charged with things that I was not guilty of, I am now more than doubly guilty, and am now willing to forgive and forget, only let me know that I am within the reach of mercy. If I am not I have no reflections to cast, but say that I have sealed my own doom and pronounced my own sentence. If the day is passed by with me may I here beg leave to entreat of those who are toiling up the rugged asscent, to make their way to endless felicity, and delight to stop not for anchor here below, follow not my example, but steer your course onward in spite of all the combined powers of earth and Hell, for know that one mistep here is only retrievable by a thousand groans & tears before God. Dear brother Joseph, let me entreat you on the reception of this letter, as you regard the salvation of my soul, to inquire at the hand of the Lord in my behalf for I this day in presence of God, do covenant to abide the word that may be given, for I am willing to receive any chastisement that the Lord sees I deserve. Now hear my prayer & suffer me to break forth in the agony of my soul. O ye angels, that surround the throne of God, Princes of Heaven, that excell in strength, ye who are clothed with transcendent brightness, plead O plead for one of the most wretched of the sons of men. O ye Heavens whose azure arches rise immensely high, and stretch immeasurably wide grand amphitheatre of nature, throne of the Eternal God, bow to hear the prayer of a poor wretched bewildered way wanderer to eternity. O, Thou Great Omnicient & omnipresent [p. 131] Jehovah, Thou who sitteth upon the throne before whom all things are present. Thou Maker, Moulder and Fashioner of all things, visible and invisible, breathe O breathe into the ears of thy servant, the Prophet, words suitably adapted to my case and situation. Speak once more make known thy will concerning me, which favors I ask in the name of the Son of God, Amen.

N.B. I hope you will not let any business hinder you from answering this letter in haste.

Yours Respectfully
Harvey Whitlock

To Joseph Smith

Kirtland Nov. 16th 1835

Brother Harvey Whitlock,

I have received your letter ⟨of⟩ the 28th of Sept. 1835 and I have read it twice, and it gave sensations that are better imagined than described, let it suffice that I say the very flood-gates of my heart were broken up: I could not refrain from weeping. I thank God that it has entered into your heart to return to the Lord and to his people, if it so be that he will have mercy upon you.

I have inquired of the Lord concerning your case. These

words came to me. Verily thus saith the Lord unto you: Let him who was my servant Harvey, return unto me, and unto the bosom of my church, and forsake all the sins, wherewith he has offended against me, and pursue from henceforth a virtuous and upright life, and remain under the directions of those I have appointed to be pillars, and heads of my Church, and behold saith the Lord your God, his sins shall be blotted out from under Heaven, and shall be forgiven from among men, and shall not come up in mine ears nor be recorded as a memorial against him. but I will lift him up as out of deep mire, and he shall be exalt[ed] upon the high places, and shall be counted[1] worthy to stand among princes, and shall yet be made a polished shaft in my quiver, of bringing down the strong hold of wickedness among those who set themselves up on high, that they may take council against me and against my anointed ones, in the [p. 132] last days. Therefore let him prepare himself speedily and come unto you, even to Kirtland, and inasmuch as he shall hearken to all your counsel, from henceforth he shall be restored, unto his former state and shall be saved unto the uttermost, even as the Lord your God liveth, Amen.

Thus you see, my dear brother, the willingness of our Heavenly Father to forgive sins and restore to favor, all those who are willing to humble themselves before him and confess their sins and forsake them, and return to him with full purpose of heart acting no hypocrisy to serve him to the end.

Marvel not that the Lord has condescended to speak from the Heavens and give you instructions, whereby you may learn your duty, he has heard your prayers and witnessed your humility, and holds forth the hand of paternal affection for your return, The angels rejoice over you while the saints are willing to receive you again into fellowship.

I hope on the receipt of this you will lose no time in coming

1. MS. reads "county."

to Kirtland, for if you get here in season you will have the privilege of attending the school of the Prophets, which has already commenced, and also receive instruction in doctrine and principle from those whom God has appointed, whereby you may be qualified to go forth and declare the true doctrines of the Kingdom according to the mind and will of God. And when you come to Kirtland, it will be explained to you why God has condescended to give you a revelation according to your request.

Please give my respects to your family and be assured I am yours in the new and everlasting covenant.

JOSEPH SMITH JUNR.

On the same evening (viz. the 16th[)] a council was called at his house, to advise with Alvah Beaman on the subject of his moving to Missouri. The subject of these memoirs had previously told him that the Lord had said that he had better go next Spring, however, to gra[t]ify him a council was called. It met agreeably to his request. President D. Whitmer arose after the council was ready to proceed to business, and observed that the spirit manifested to him that it was his duty to go, and others also bore the same testimony. The same night (16) he (J.S. Junr.) received the word of the Lord on the case of Erastus Holmes who called on the 14 [p. 133] He had desired him to inquire at the hand of the Lord whether it was his duty to be baptized here or wait till he returned home. The Word of the Lord came to him (J.S. Junr.) that Mr. Holmes had better not be baptized here, and that he had better not return by water also that there were three men seeking his destruction, and to beware of his enemies.

17 November 1835 · Tuesday

He exhibited the Alphabet of the ancient Egyptian Records to Mr. Holmes & some others, went with him to F.G. William's to see the Mummies, after which he (Holmes) to[ok] leave, by giving the parting hand and started for home, being strong in the faith of the Gospel of Christ, and apparently determined to obey its requirements.

He, of whom we write more particularly, returned home after his friend Holmes had taken leave, and spent the day in comparing and dictating letters. In the evening he preached at the school House, from thence he went home and retired to rest.

18 November 1835 · Wednesday

He was at home in the A.M. until about 11 o clock, at which time, he set out with his wife, mother and his scribe to go to Preserved Harris'. He had been requested to attend at said Harris' by a request of the family and preach the funeral sermon of Harris' father.[1] The congregation were very attentive. We returned after meeting, to his own house, having had a pleasant ride ⟨al⟩though the weather was cool, and the occasion of his ride a melancholy one.

In the evening Bishop Whitney, his wife, father, mother and Sister in law came ~~to visit him~~ in and gave him & his wife a pressing invitation to go with them on visit to his father Smith's /[2]When they arived they found that some of the young Eldrs were about engaging in a debate upon the subject of miracles. After an interesting debate of three hours or more, during which time much talent was displayed, it was decided by the presidents of the school in the negative: Which was a righteous decision.

He discovered in this investigation to[o] much warmth manifested, to[o] much zeal for mastery, to[o] much of that enthusiasm that characterizes a lawyer at the bar, who is determined on victory right or wrong.

1. Nathan Harris (1758-1835).

2. End of Warren A. Cowdery's handwriting and beginning of Warren Parrish's.

He therefore ⟨availed⟩ himself of this favourable opportunity to drop a few words upon this subject by way of advise, that they might improve their minds, and cultivate their powers of intilect in a proper manner, that they might not incur the displeasure of heaven, that they should [p. 134] handle sacred things very sacredly; and with due deference to the opinions of others, and with an eye single to the glory of God.

19 November 1835 · Thursday

In company with Dr. F G. Williams he went to see how the workmen prospered in finishing the house of the Lord.

On his return he met with br's Lloyd & Lorenzo Lewis[1] who he had been informed were much dissatisfied; but found that this was not the fact, as touching the faith of the church but with the conduct of some of the members. He returned home and spent the day in translating the Egyptian records. The weather is warm & pleasant.

20 November 1835 · Friday

He continued translating & made rapid progress At evening Pres. Cowdery returned from New York bringing ~~with him~~ a quantity of Hebrew books, for the benefit of the school, he presented him with a Hebrew bible, lexicon & Grammar, also a Greek & English lexicon.– Pres. Cowdery had a prosperous journey, according to the prayers of the saints

21 November 1835 · Saturday

He spent the day at home, in examining & studying his Hebrew books.– At evening he met with the class to make some arangments about a teacher, it was decided by the voice of the school that we would send to New York for a Jew, to teach us the Hebrew language having asertained that Dr. Piex-

1. See entry of 28 September 1835.

otto was not qualified to give us the knowledge we wished to acquire.

22 November 1835 · Sunday

He attended meeting at the usual hour: Eldr. Simeon Carter preach[ed] from Math. 7th ch.– At our evening meeting Eldr. Jackson Squires who had withdrawn from the church made application to return to the fold of Christ. We organized into a regular council, and after much altercation upon the subject, & keen rebuke Eldr. Squires was restored by the voice of the council & church, and the clerk ordered to give him his licence.–[1] On this night we had a snow storm

23 November 1835 · Monday

Several brethren called to converse with him & see the records. To day he received a letter from Jared Carter. His leasure moments he devoted to study, meditation, & prayer.

24 November 1835 · Tuesday

He spent the A.M. in instructing those that called to inquire respecting the things of God in the last days. In the P.M. he translated some of the ancient manuscripts.– This evening he had an invitation to attend a wedding at his brother Hyrum Smith's to solemnize the rights of matrimony between Newel Knights & Lydia Goldthwait. His wife & some others accompanied [p. 135] him when they arived, they found a respectable company assembled, the interview was opened by singing &

1. Andrew Jackson Squires, having joined the Mormon church in the early 1830s, been ordained an elder, and "preached the gospel successfully," had joined the Methodists for a time but desired to return to fellowship in the Church. At this council convened to hear his case, Joseph Smith spoke on the "impropriety of turning away from the truth," and Sidney Rigdon spoke on the "folly of fellowshipping any doctrine or spirit aside from that of Christ." After a repentant expression, Squires was again restored to fellowship and his office as elder. (Kirtland Council Minutes, 22 November 1835.)

prayer, Pres. Smith then requested the bridegroom, & bride, to arise & join hands, and then proceeded to make some remarks, upon the subject of mariage as follows; that it was an institution of heaven first solemnized in the garden of Eden by God himself, by the authority of everlasting priesthood. The following is in substance the ceremony delivered on that occasion—calling them by name you covenant to be each others companions during your lives, and discharge the duties of husband & wife in all respects, to which they gave their assent. He then pronounced them husband & wife in the name of God with many blessings, after which he dismissed the audiance & returned home –The weather is freezing cold and snow on the ground

25 November 1835 · Wednesday

He spent the day in translating.– To day Eldrs [David] Harvey Redfield & Jesse Hitchcock arived here from Missouri; the latter says that he has no doubt, but that a dose of poison was administered to him in a boll of milk by the hand of an enemy, with the intention to kill him. It sickened him & he vomited it up, & thus the Lord verified his word ~~to him~~ and delivered him. "If they drink any deadly thing it shall not hurt them."[1]

26 November 1835 · Thursday

We spent the day in transcribing Egyptian characters from the papyrus. Our br. at this time is labouring under a severe affliction in concequence of a violent cold. May the Lord deliver him from his indisposition, that he may the more successfully persue the avocation, where unto God has called him.

1. Mark 16:18.

27 November 1835 · Friday

He was severely afflicted with his cold, yet able to attend to his domestic concerns, & determined to overcome in the name of the Lord Jesus. He spent the day in reading Hebrew at home. Eldr. Parrish his scribe being indisposed in concequence of having taken cold called on Pres. J. Smith Jun. to pray for & lay hands on him in the name of the Lord; He did so and in return Eldr. Parrish prayed for & laid hands on him, this reciprocal kindness was heard and graciously answered upon both their heads by our Heavenly Father in relieving them from their affliction.

The following prayer was offered to the God of heaven on the 23d day of October 1835, by the individuals whose names are [p. 136] inserted below viz Joseph Smith Jun., Oliver Cowdery, David Whitmer, Hyrum Smith, John Whitmer, Sidney Rigdon, Samuel H. Smith Frederick G. Williams & Wm W. Phelps, who assembled on the above mentioned day at 4 oclock P.M. and united in prayer with one voice before the Lord for the following blessing.

That the Lord will give us means sufficient to deliver us from all our afflictions and difficulties, wherein we are placed by means of our debts; that He will open the way & deliver Zion in the appointed time and that without the shedding of blood; that He will hold our lives precious, and grant that we may live to the common age of man, and never fall into the hands ~~of our enemies~~ nor power of the mob in missouri, nor any other place; that he will also preserve our posterity, that none of them fall even to the end of time; that he will give us the blessings of the earth sufficient to carry us to Zion and that we may purchase inheritances in that land, even enough to carry on and accomplish the work unto which he has appointed us; and also that he will assist all others who desire according to his commandments to go up and purchase inheritances and all this easily & without perpexity and trouble;

and finaly that in the end he will save us in his c[e]lestial kingdom. Amen.

OLIVER COWDERY (CLERK

28 November 1835 · Saturday

He spent the morning in company & correcting his journal.– Eldr. Josiah Clark called this morning to ⟨see⟩ him, he lives in Cam[pb]el County, Kentucky, about 3 miles above Cincinnati, he had been biten by a mad dog some three or four years since, & had spent much upon physicians and received some benefit by so doing; but is much afflicted notwithstanding; he came here that he might receive the benefit of the united prayers of the church; accordingly, we prayed for and laid our hands on him in the name of the Lord Jesus Christ, & anointed him with oil, & rebuked his affliction praying our Heavenly Father to hear and answer our prayers according to our faith in him, even so, Amen. [p. 137]

29 November 1835 · Sunday

This morning he went to meeting at the usual hour Eldr. Isaac Morley occupied the desk in the A.M. & Bp. Edward Partrige in the P.M. Their discourses were well adapted to the times in which we live, and the circumstances, under which we are placed; their words were truly words of wisdom "like apples of gold in pictures of silver," spoken in the unaffected simple accents of a child; yet sublime as the voice of an angel. The saints appeared to be much pleased with the beautiful discourses of these two fathers in Israel. After these servises closed, three of the Zion brethren came forward and received their blessing. Solon Foster was ordained to the office of an Eldr. The Lord's supper was then administered, and the meeting closed. Our brother returned home and spent the evening in his family circl[e], around the social fire side.– The weather continues cold and stormy.

30 November 1835 · Monday

The snow continues falling and is already sufficiently deep to make good sleighing This is uncommon for this country, at this season of the year. He spent the day in writing, or in other words dictating a letter for the Messenger & Advocate on the subject of the gathering in the last days from Matthew 13th ch.[1] This afternoon Henry Capron called to see him Mr. Cap[r]on is an old acquaintance of his from Manchester New York. He showed him the ancient records and explained them to him.

1 December 1835 · Tuesday

This is a delightful morning indeed; Pres. Joseph made preparations to ride to Painsville, his wife & children with some others of his household, accompanied him. When we were passing through Mentor street, we overtook two men with a team, & politely asked them to let us pass; they granted our request, and as we passed them, they abruptly bawled out to Pres. Smith do you get any revelations lately, with an addition of blackguard & vulgarity, to us uninteligable. This is a fair specimine of the character of the inhabitants of Mentor; who have rendered themselves notorious, for mobing & persecuting the saints; [p. 138] and are ready to scandalize, & traduce, the characters of men, who never laid a straw in their way, and, in fact men whose faces they never saw, and against whom they cannot bring an accusation either of a temporal or spiritual nature; except our firm belief in the fulness of the gospel. And we were led to marvle at the longsuffering, and great condesention of our Heavenly Father, in permitting these ungodly wretches to possess this goodly land, which is indeed as beautifully situated, & and its soil as fertile, as any in this

1. See *Messenger and Advocate* 2 (December 1835): 225-30. This was the last of a three-part installment. See p. 102, note 3.

region of country, and its inhabitants wealthy, even blessed above measure in temporal things; and feign would God bless them with spiritual blessings, even eternal life, were it not for their evil hearts of unbelief, and we are inclined to mingle our cries with ~~the souls of~~ those saints, who have suffered the like treatment before us; whose souls are under the altar, praying for vengance upon those who dwell upon the earth.

And we rejoice in our hearts, that the time is at hand when those who persist in wickedness, will be swept from the earth with the besom of distruction, and the earth become an inheritance for the poor & the meek.–

When we arived at Painsville we called at sister Harriet How[e']s, and lef[t] Mrs. Smith & family to visit while we rode into town ~~to do some buisiness,~~ we called on br. H[orace]. Kingsbury, and also at the bank, and at various other places, and after accomplishing our buisiness we returned & dined with sister How[e]; & took the parting hand & returned home. We had a fine ride, and agreeable visit; the sleighing is good and weather pleasant.

2 December 1835 · Wednesday

Nothing of much importance transpired, suffice it to say that he of whom we write, spent the day in the society of his family, manageing his domestic concerns, visiting, & receiving visitors, and instructing such, as desired a knowledge of the things of God.

3 December 1835 · Thursday

He was at home, and indited a letter to David Dort Rochester Michigan, also another [p. 139] to Almira [Mack] Scoby Liberty Clay County Missouri. At evening he & his wife were invited to attend a wedding at Thomas Carrico's to solemnize the rights of matrimony between Eldr. W. Parrish, & Martha H. Raymond; when we arived we found a very pleasant &

respectable company waiting: we opened our interview by singing & prayer; Pres. Smith then delivered an appropriate address upon the subject of matrimony; he then invited the parties who were to be joined in wedlock to arise, and solemnized the institution in a brief, & explicit manner, and pronounced them husband & wife in the name of God according to the articles & covenants of the Church of Latter day Saints; closed by singing & prayer, took some refreshment and retired, having spent the evening agreeably.

4 December 1835 · Friday

To day he got a note of three hundred & fifty dollars discounted at Painsville bank by giving the following names with his own.– viz. F G. Williams & co. N K. Whitney J[ohn]. Johnson & Vinson Knights. He settled with Eldr. Knights & paid him two hundred & fifty dollars: He also settled with his brother Hiram Smith; & has the means to pay a debt due Job Lewis, which he has been much perplexed about; and he feels hartily to thank God, that He has thus graciously smiled upon him, & blessed him with such a multiplicity of blessings, & thus far crowned our feeble efforts with success: And we ask our Heavenly Father in the name of Jesus Christ, to enable us to extricate ourselves, from all embarasments whatever, that we may not be brought into disrepute in any respect; that our enemies may not have any power over us.– He spent the day at home, devoted some time in studying the Hebrew language.– This has been a warm & rainy day; the snow is melting fast.–This evening a Mr. John Holister of Portage County Ohio called to see Pres. Smith upon the all important subject of religion; said Holister is a member of the close communion baptist church, he said that his object in calling on us, was to enquire concerning our faith, [p. 140] having heard many reports of an unfavourable character, he desired now to know the truth of the matter.

He appeared to be an honest inquirer. Pres. Smith spent the evening with him, in conversation, & found him to be a candid man; but without any peculiarities about him except his simplicity, he tarried over night [with] us, and acknowledged in the morning, that although he had thought that he knew something about religion, he was now convinced, that he knew but little, which was the greatest trait of wisdom which he displayed.

5 December 1835 · Saturday

This morning the weather is cold & the snow is gently dropping from the heavens, & there is a prospect of sleighing again.– Presdts. Cowdery & Williams called and spent the fore noon in studying Hebrew with us.— Our author Pres. Smith is labouring under a slight indisposition of health; but after taking a little repose, he resumed his wonted cheerfulness and throug[h] the blessings of God was abled to attend to his business. on this day he received a letter from Reuben McBride dated at Villanovia New York, and another from Parley Pratt's mother in law,[1] dated at Herkimer Co. N.Y. of no consequence as to what it contained but cost us 25 cents for postage; he mentioned this because it [is] a common occurrence, and he is subjected to a great expense in this way,[2] by those who he

1. Thankful Cooper Halsey.

2. On this date, Joseph Smith inserted a notice in the *Messenger and Advocate* to inform his friends and all others "that whenever they wish to address me thro' the Post Office, they will be kind enough to pay the postage on the same. My friends will excuse me in this matter, as I am willing to pay postage on letters to hear from *them*; but am unwilling to pay for insults and menaces,— consequently, must refuse all, unpaid."

Between 1816 and 1845 the cost for sending a single sheet letter less than thirty miles was six cents; not over 80 miles, ten cents; not over 150 miles, 12 1/2 cents; and not over 400 miles, 18 3/4 cents. Greater distances cost 25 cents. Letters of two or more sheets required additional postage in proportion. If a letter weighed more than an ounce, the postage quadrupled. For many, postal communication was a luxury. Prior to 1847, when postage stamps were authorized, the collection of postage from the addressee had led to many abuses, including

knows nothing about, only that they are destitute of good manners, for if people wish to be benefited by his counsel & instruction, common respect, and good breeding would dictate them to pay the postage on their letters.

6 December 1835 · Sunday

He as usual attended meeting, being ever constant at the shrine of public & private devotion, setting an example of unremitting, & untiring zeal and piety teaching, & enforcing, both by precept, and example, the principles, & doctrines, of the holy religion he professes.[1]

Eldr. Gideon Carter occupied the desk in the morning and delivered an interesting discourse. In the P.M. an exhortation was delivered, and the Lords supper administered. br. Draper came forward to make a [p. 141] confession for having left the meeting abruptly as we were about to partake of the Lord's supper and disturbed the peace & quiet of the congregation. But his confession was not satisfactory, it seemed to be affected and superficial: He was therefore delivered over to the bufitings of satan until he should [humble][2] himself before the Lord, & repent of his sins and confess them before the church.

7 December 1835 · Monday

Received a letter from Milton Holmes and was much rejoiced to hear of his prosperity in proclaiming the gospel in the west; he wrote him a letter in which he requested br. Holmes to return to this place:– spent the day in reading Hebrew—Mr. John Hollister called to take the parting hand

---

the payment by the addressee for letters containing offensive and insulting messages. (Arthur E. Summerfield, *U.S. Mail: The Story of the United States Postal Service* [New York: Holt, Rinehart and Winston, 1960], 45-46; Clyde Kelly, *United States Postal Policy* [New York and London: D. Appleton and Co., 1932], 57-58.)

1. This paragraph is a clerical comment not found in the Joseph Smith Diary.
2. Bracketed word supplied from Joseph Smith Diary.

with Pres. Smith and remarked that he had been in darkness all his days, but had now found the true light and intended to obey it; a number of brethren also call[ed] this evening to see the ancient records, which he exibited & explained to their satisfaction.

8 December 1835 · Tuesday

He spent the day in his family circle, receiving & waiting upon those who called to visit him; his few leisure moments he devoted to study. This evening as usual, he preach[ed] at the school house had great liberty in speaking. the power of God in a wonderful manner rested upon the audiance. After the servises closed Eldr. [Leonard] Rich proposed to the brethren, to assist Pres. Smith in getting his supply of wood for the winter, to which they cheerfully assented, and fixed on tomorrow for the day.

9 December 1835 · Wednesday

At home. This morning the south wind blows strong and chilly, ~~and~~ the sky is overcast and the clouds portend a storm at hand.

Eldr. Packard called and made our author, a present of a twelve dollar note, which he held against him;[1] Eldr. James Aldrich also sent him a note of twelve dollars by the hand of Eldr. J. Hitchcock.—Also the brethren whose names are written below opened their hearts in great liberality & paid him at the

1. The settlement of debt in a largely barter economy required that anyone who performed services or supplied goods to others had to keep a record of each transaction. When two people settled their accounts, each brought his own record and both signed the resulting settlement. Often when a debt was acquired, a handwritten record was made on a scrap of paper. These notes became a sort of scrip and circulated until retired by cash, labor, or barter. As in the case here of Joseph Smith and Noah Packard, the debt could be settled by the creditor presenting his copy of the note as a gift to the debtor. (See James M. McCabe, "Early Ledgers and Account Books: A Source for Local Vermont History," *Vermont History* [Winter 1969]: 5-12.)

Committee's store [p. 142] the sums set oposite their respective names, as follows.

John Carrill	$5.00
Levi Jackman	3.25
Elijah Fordham	5.25
James Emmett	5.00
Newel Knights	2.00
Truman Angell	3.00
Wm. Felshaw	3.00
Emer Harris	1.00
Truman Jackson	1.00
Samuel Rolph	1.25
Elias Higby	1.00
Albert Brown	3.00
Wm. F. Cahoon	1.00
Harlow Crozier	.50
Salmon Gee	.75
Harvey Stanley	1.00
Zemira Draper	1.00
George Morey	1.00
John Rudd	.50
Alexander Badlam	1.00
Warren Parrish	5.00

My heart swells with gratitude inexpressible when I realize the great condescension of my Heavenly Father in opening the hearts of these my beloved brethren to administer so liberally, to the wants of the servant, of the Most High; and we hear him breaking forth in the the following accents of prayer and praise to God.– I ask the[e] my Heavenly Father in the name of Jesus to smile propiciously upon these my brethren and multiply blessings without number upon their heads—and bless me O Lord [with] great grace and wisdom from heaven, and dispose of me to the best advantage for the benefit of my brethren and the building up of thy kingdom on the earth; and whether in life, or in death, in prosperity, or in adversity, in time, or in eternity, I say in my heart, O Lord, let me enjoy the society of such brethren.– To day Eldr Tanner[1] brought him half of a fatned hog for the benefit of his family; and a few days since Eldr. Roundy presented him with a quarter of beef; thus we se[e] the word of the Lord verified, that He will not se[e] the righteous forsaken, nor his seed begging bread.

10 December 1835 · Thursday

A delightful morning indeed, and fine sleighing. This morning the brethren met according to previous arangement, to chop & draw wood for him, and have been very active, and industrious and have probably supplied him with wood for the winter; for which kindness his heart swells [p. 143] with gratitude, which flow[s] forth in blessings upon the heads of his brethren, in substance as follows.

I am sincerely thankful to each and every one of you my brethren, for this testimony of your respect and goodness manifested toward me; and in the name of Jesus Christ I invoke the rich benediction of heaven to rest upon them, & their families, and I ask my Heavenly Father to preserve their healths, that they may [have] strength of body, to persue successfully, their several avocations in life, & the use and activity of their limbs; also power of intelect & sound minds, that they may treasure up wisdom understanding & inteligence above measure, that they may readily desern between the righteous & the wicked between him that serveth God & him that serveth him not, and be preserved from plagues pestilence and famine, from the power of the destroyer that that wicked one touch them not, and give unto them wisdom & strength, to elude the grasp of all their enemies, that they may be able to counteract the designs & purposes of wicked ~~designing~~ men and

1. Probably John Tanner (1778-1850).

prepare the way before them, O God that they may journey to the land of Zion and be established on their inheritances, to enjoy undisturbed peace and happiness for ever, and ultimately be crowned with everlasting life in the celestial Kingdom of God, which favours, & blessings I ask in the name of Jesus of Nazereth Amen. This after noon he was called in company with Pres. D. Whitmer to visit Sister Angeline Works, they found her ver[y] sick and much deranged; they prayed for and laid hands on her in the name of the Lord that she might be restored to her senses and healed; the former, was immediately done, but the latter was progressive, she was much better when we left.– On their return[1] they found the brethren engaged in extinguishing a fire that had broken out, in a board kiln near the chapel; after contending with this distructive [p. 144] element, for about one hour they succeeded in conquering it. there was a large quantity of lumber in the kiln, three forths of which, was consumed, the committee have sustained a very conciderable loss by this fire.

There was about 200 brethren engaged on this occasion who deserve much credit for the activity & interest they manifested.– The finishing of the house of the Lord, will necessarily be protracted, on account of this accident, as the lumber that was lost, was designed for that purpose.[2] This evening a number of brethren called at Pres. Smith's to see the ancient manuscripts and were much pleased with their interview.

11 December 1835 · Friday

A fire broke out in a shoemaker's shop owned by Orison [Orson] Johnson, but was soon extinguished by the active exertions of the brethren; on it's appearance the family were much alarmed, the shop being connected with their dwelling house; they carried their furniture into the streets, but not

1. MS. reads "returned."
2. This sentence not in Joseph Smith Diary.

much damage was sustained. This is a pleasant morning,[1] the atmosphere is serene & healthy; our author spent the day at home in reading, meditation, and prayer, and instructing those who called for advise. To day Eldr. Daily[2] & wife lef[t] for home.

12 December 1835 · Saturday

He devoted the morning to reading; at about 12 oclock a number of young persons called to see the Egy[p]tian records, he resquested his scribe (W. Parrish) to exibit them; he did so, one of the young ladies who had been examining them, was asked by the subject of this narative, if the manuscripts had the appearance of antiquity, to which she replied with an air of contempt in the negative: on hearing this he was surprised at the ignorance she manifested, and very justly remarked to her that she was an anomaly in creation, for all the wise and learned that had ever examined them, without hesitation pronounced them ancient: He further observed that it was downright ignorance, bigotry, superstition, & wickedness, that caused her to make the remark and that it was worthy of record, for after generations to gaze upon, because it is a fair specimine of the [p. 145] prevailing spirit of the times, showing that priestcraf[t] has it's victims, also in this age, like those in ages past, that would not believe, though one should rise from the dead. This evening he attended a debate at his brother Wm. Smith's; The question propounded was as follows.– was it, or was it not, necessary for God to reveal himself to man to render them happy. He (Joseph) was on the affirmative, and the last one to speak on that side of the question: But while list[e]ning [to] the ingenious arguments of the contending parties, he & Eldr. Carrill (who was his opponent in this debate) was called

1. Remainder of this sentence not in Joseph Smith Diary.
2. Possibly Moses Daley (1794-1865).

away to visit the sick, and neither of them had the opportunity of speaking on that occasion.[1]

13 December 1835 · Sunday

At the usual hour, viz. 10 oclock he attended meeting at the school-house on the flats. Eldr. Jesse Hitchcock preached a very feeling discourse indeed; in the after noon Eldr. Peter Whitmer related his experiance, after which Pres. F G. Williams, related his also; they both spoke of many things connected with the rise and progress of this church of Christ, which were highly interesting and the saints listened with attention. After these servises closed the sacrament of the Lord's supper was administered, under the superintendance of Pres. David Whitmer, who presided over the meeting during the day. Pres. Joseph (our author) then made some remarks respecting prayer meetings, and our meeting was brought to a close by invoking heavens blessings upon the audiance.

He returned home and ordered his horses saddled and himself, & scribe rode to Mr. Jennings[2] where he had been envited to solemnize the marriage contract, between Mr. Ebenezer Robinson, & Miss Angeline Works. After these cere-

1. Important in the development of adult education in America were the lyceums, mechanics' institutes, and agricultural societies that flourished in Jacksonian America. During this period, hundreds of informal associations were established for the purpose of improving the social, intellectual, and moral fabric of society. The lyceum movement, with its lectures, dramatic performances, class instruction, and debates, contributed significantly to the education of adult Americans in the nineteenth century and provided the cultural framework for the Kirtland, Ohio, debates and schools. (See Edward W. Stevens, Jr., "Science, Culture, and Morality: Educating Adults in the Early Nineteenth Century," in *"Schools and The Means of Education Shall Forever Be Encouraged": A History of Education in the Old Northwest, 1787-1880,* edited by Paul H. Mattingly and Edward W. Stevens, Jr. [Athens, Ohio: Ohio University Libraries, 1987]: 69-83; Carl Bode, *The American Lyceum: Town Meeting of the Mind* [New York: Oxford University Press, 1956].)

2. Possibly Ebenezer Jennings, living in Chester, Geauga County, Ohio, in 1830 and a property owner at Kirtland in 1832. (U.S. Census: Geauga County, Ohio, 1830; 1832 Geauga County, Ohio, tax list.)

monies were concluded we rode to Mr. [Isaac] Mc Withy's the distance of about 3 miles from town, where he had been solicited to attend and join in marrage Mr. E[dwin]. Webb & Miss E[liza] A. Mc Withy: The parents and many of the connexions of both parties were present, with a large and respectable company of friends, who were invited as [p. 146] guests: The necessary arangements were made, and the company came to order, and the Groom & Bride with their attendants politely came forward and and took their seats; our interview was then opened by singing & prayer, & having been invited to make some preliminary remarks upon the subject of matrimony, he delivered an interesting lecture of about 40 minutes in length, during which time all present appeared highly gratified with the exception of two individuals who manifested a spirit of grovling contempt, which he was constrained to reprove and sharply rebuke. He then sealed the matrimonial ceremony in the name of God and pronounced the blessings of heaven upon the heads of the young pair, praying that they may be blessed with long life & prosperity, and ultimately with everlasting life in the Kingdom of God.

a sumptuous feast was then spread and the company were invited to seat themselves at the table two by two, male, and female, commencing with the eldest, and the interview throughout was conducted with propriety & decorum; and our hearts were made to rejoice while together and cheerfulness smiled on every countinance we spent the evening agreeably, until the tolling 9 oclock, announced to us that the time to retire, had arived: we pronounced a blessing upon the company and returned home.–

To day the board-kiln took fire again, in consequence of bad management.

14 December 1835 · Monday

This morning a number of brethren from New York called to visit him, and see the records. Eldr. [Martin] Harris also returned this morning from visiting his family who live in Palmyra N.Y. also a brother Eaton[1] of the same place a very worthy brother made him a visit. Sister Harriet How[e] of Painsville also visit[ed] us to day.– after dinner Pres. Smith & his family attended a funeral at Sylvester Smith's who had lost his youngest child.–[2] This evening [met] agreeably to [p. 147] previous notice, to make arangements to guard against fire, and organized a company for that purpose, they also counseled on others affairs of a temporal nature.– To day Samuel Branum,[3] called at his house much afflicted with a swelling on his arm; he had been prayed for, but lacked faith to be healed, and at this time his pain was intolerable; Sister Emma Smith (wife of our author) who is ever ready to alleviate the distresses of the afflicted, administered to his swolen limb such applications as occured to her mind, and succeeded, in checking the inflamation, and his arm was saved, and restored to health, through the blessings of God. He (Joseph) spent the ⟨day⟩ at home in reading, and waiting upon friends who called to see him.

15 December 1835 · Tuesday

Spent the day at home, and as usual was blessed with much company, some of which called to see the records.– This afternoon Eldr. Orson Hyde handed a letter to him, the purport of which is that, he is dissatisfied with the committee[4] as it respects their dealing with him in merchandise; that they do not deal as liberally with him as they do with ⟨Eldr.⟩ Wm. Smith,

1. Frazier Eaton, according to the Joseph Smith Diary.
2. Sylvester M. Smith died at the age of eleven weeks and four days.
3. There is no reference to a Samuel Branum in early Mormon sources. The name may be a corruption of Samuel Brannan, who later figured prominently in the settlement of San Francisco, California. If so, he would have been fifteen when he visited Joseph Smith on December 14.
4. The committee consisting of Hyrum Smith, Reynolds Cahoon, and Jared Carter.

he also requested him (Joseph) to reconcile the revelation given to the 12, since their return from their eastern mission.– That unless these things with others named in the letter alluded to, could be reconciled to his mind, his honour would not stand united with them. This I believe is the amount of Eldr. Hydes letter, although much was written, in justification of the course he had taken. On reading this letter his feelings were inexpressible, knowing that he had dealt in righteousness with him in all things; and endeavoured to promote his happiness and well being, and do him good, as much as lay in his power.

He was therefore concious that the reflections cast upon him by Eldr. Hyde were ungrateful, & unjust, and founded in jealousy; that the [p. 148] adversary of righteousness, is striving, with his subtle devises and evil influence, to destroy him by causing a division among the 12 Apostles that God has chosen in these last days, to open the gospel Kingdom among all nations, kindred, toungs, and people. But with his usual descission of mind and firm reliance on Him, who possesses all wisdom, & knows the thoughts & intents of every heart, we hear him making the following appeal to the throne of grace, that God may deliver him (Eldr. Hyde) from the power of that wicked one, that his faith fail not in this hour of temptation, & darkness, and prepare him, with the rest of his fellow labourers in the vinyard of the Lord, to receive an induement [endowment], in the habitation of the most High, as God shall see fit, to call them into the solemn assembly of the saints, from time to time, until his kingdom becomes universal, and time is no more

16 December 1835 · Wednesday

The weather is extremely cold.– This morning he went to the council room, to lay before the presidency the letter that he received from Eldr. O. Hyde, but when he arived he found that he had lost said letter, he made search for it in vain, however he related the substance of it to that body; but they had not time to attend to it on account of other business; and accordingly laid it over ⟨until⟩ monday evening following.– He returned home. Eldrs McLellen Young & Carter call[ed] to visit him he was much pleased with the interview; he exhibited, & explained the Egy[p]tian records to them, and many things concerning the dealings of God, with the ancients especially the system of astronomy as taught by Abraham, which is contained upon these manuscripts; they were much gratified with this inteligence.– This evening he went to his brother Wm. Smith's to take part in the debate, that was commenced on last Saturday evening, upon the question before named, viz. was it necessary for God to reveal himself to the world &c. [p. 149]

After the debate was concluded, and a descision given in favour of the affirmative, some altercation was had upon the impropriety of continuing the school. He and his brother Hyrum Smith were descidedly of the opinion that it would not result in good. Their brother Wm. strenuously opposed them and insisted on having another question propounded, asserting that he was in his own house and should insist on continuing the school regardless of consequences, and at length he became much inraged especially at his brother Joseph, and committed violence upon his person, and others who interfered to stay him, in his wicked course. After his passion had abated a little, and his stormy feelings were partialy tranquilized Joseph, returned home, grieved beyond expression, at ⟨the⟩ wickedness of his brother, who Cain like had sought to kill him, and had conciderably wounded him, notwithstanding the exertions of his brethren to prevent it; nevertheless he prayed God to forgive him inasmuch as he would heartily repent and humble himself before the Lord.

17 December 1835 · Thursday

This morning he was very unwell on account of the unhappy occurrence that took place on the preceeding evening at his brother Williams;– Eldr. Hyde called and presented him with a copy of the letter that he handed him on last tuesday, which he had lost; the following is a true copy.

DEC. 15TH 1835

PRES. SMITH

Sir you may esteem it a novel circumstance to receive a written communication from me at this time.

My reasons for writing are the following. I have some things which I wish to communicate to you, and feeling a greater Liberty to do it by writing alone by myself I take this method; and it is generally the case that you are thronged with [p. 150] business, and not convenient to spend much time in conversing upon subjects of the following nature.

Therefore let these excuses paliate the novelty of the circumstance and patiently hear my recital. After the committee had received their store of fall & winter goods, I went to Eldr. Cahoon and told him that I was destitute of a cloak and wanted him to trust me until spring for materials to make one.

He told me that he would trust me until Jany. but must then have his pay, as the payments for the goods become due at that time. I told him that I knew not from whence the money would come and I could not promise it so soon. But in a few ~~days~~ weeks after I unexpectedly obtained the money to buy a cloak, and applyed immediately to Eldr. C. for one and told him that I had the cash to pay for it, but he said that the materials for cloaks were all soald, and that he could not accommodate me; and I will here venture a guess, that he has not realized the cash for one cloak pattern. A few weeks after this I called on Eldr. Cahoon again and told him that I wanted ~~some~~ cloth for some shirts, to the amount of four or five dollars. I told him that I would pay him in the spring and sooner if I could; he let me have it. Not long after, my school was established, and some of the hands who laboured on the house attended, and wished to pay me at the committees store for their tuition. I called at the store to see if any negotiation could be made and they take me off where I owed them; but no such negotiation could be made. These with some other circumstances of like character called for the following reflections. In the first place I gave the committee two hundred & seventy five dollars in cash, besides some more, and during the last season have traveled through the middle and eastern States, to support and uphold the Store, and in so doing, have reduced myself to nothing in a pecuniary point. Under these circumstances [p. 151] this establishment refused to render me that ~~assistance~~ accommodation which a worldlings establishment would have gladly done, and one too which never received a donation from me, nor in whose favour I never raised my voice, or exerted my influence. But after all this, thought I, it may be right, and I will be still,– until not long since I asertained that Eldr. Wm. Smith could go to the Store and get what ever he pleased, and no one to say why do ye so; until his account has amounted to seven hundred dollars or there abouts, and that he was a silent partner in the concern, yet not acknowledged as such, fearing that his creditors would make a haul upon the Store. While we were abroad this last season we strained every nerve to obtain a little something for our families, and regularly divided the monies equally for ought that I know, not knowing that William had such a fountain at home, from whence to draw his support. I then called to mind the revelation[1] in which myself, McLellen, & Patten, were chastned, and also the ~~revelation~~ quotation in that revelation of the parable of the twelve sons; as if the original meaning refered directly to the twelve Apostles of the church of Latter day Saints. I would now ask if each one of the twelve, has not an equal right to the same accomodations from that Store, provided they are alike faithful? If not with such a com-

1. See pp. 120-121.

bination mine honour be not thou united. If each one has the same right, take the basket off from our noses or put one to Williams nose; or if this cannot be done, reconcile the parable of the twelve sons, with the superior priviliges that William has. Pardon me if I speak in parables or in parody.

A certain shepherd had twelve sons and he sent them out one day to go and gather his flock which were scattered upon the mountains and in the valleys afar off. They were all obediant to their fathers mandate; and at evening they returned with the flock. And one son received wool [p. 152] enough to make him warm and comfortable; and also received of the flesh and milk of the flock. The other eleven received not so much as one kid to make merry with their friends.

These facts with some others, have disqualifed my mind for studying the Hebrew language at present, and believing as I do, that I must sink or swim, or in other words take care of myself; I have thought that I should take the most efficient means in my power to get out of debt; and to this end I proposed taking the school. But if I am not thought competent to take the charge of it, or worthy to be placed in that station, I must devise some other means to help myself, althoug[h] having been ordained to that office under your own hands, with a promise that it should not be taken from me.–

Conclusion of the whole matter is such, I am willing to continue, and do all I can, provided we can share equal benefits one with the other, and upon no other principles whatever. If one has support from the "public crib" let them all have it. But if ~~I am willing~~ one is pinched, I am willing to be, provided we are all alike.

If the principles of impartiality and equality can be observed by all, I think that I will not peep again

If I am damned it will be for doing what I think is right. There has been two applications made to me, to go into business, since I talked of taking the school. But it is in the world, and I had rather remain in Kirtland if I can consistently.

All I ask is *Right*
I am Sir with Respect Your obt. Servt.

ORSON HYDE

TO PRESIDENT J. SMITH JR.
KIRTLAND GEAUGA CO. OHIO. [p. 153]

Eldr. O. Hyde called and read the foregoing letter himself and Pres. Smith explained upon the objections named in it, and satisfied his mind upon every objectionable point, and Eldr. Hyde remarked after they had got through, that he was more than satisfied, with his explannations, and would attend the Hebrew school, and on parting gave him his hand, with every expression of friendship that a gentleman and a christian could manifest, which our author reciprocated with cheerfulness, declareing at the same time, that he entertained the best of feelings for him, and most cordially forgave him the ingratitude, which was manifested in his letter, knowing that it was for want of correct information, that his mind was disturbed as far as his reflections related to ~~me~~ Joseph. But the committee had not dealt, in righteousness with him in all things; but all is now amicably adjusted and setled, and no hardness exists between them.

This evening his father & mother called to see him upon the subject of the difficulty that transpired at their house on wednesday evening, between him and his brother William. They were sorely afflicted in mind, and almost heart broken on the account of that occurrence. The subject of our narative conversed with his parents and convinced them that he was not to ⟨be⟩ blame[d] for taking the course he did with his brother William on that occassion. But that he had acted in righteousness with him in all things.

He invited his parents to come and live with him, which they concented to do, as soon as it is practicable.

18 December 1835 · Friday

He was at home; his brother Hyrum called to see him, and read a letter that he received from William, in which he asked his (Hyrum's) forgiveness for the abuse he offered him at the debate. He tarried most of the fore noon and conversed freely with Joseph upon the subject of the difficulty existing between him [p. 154] and their brother William. He said he was perfectly satisfied with the course Joseph had taken, with his brother William, in rebukeing him in his wickedness. But he is deeply wounded in his feeling on account of the conduct of William and although he ⟨feels⟩ all the tender sympathy and fine feelings, of a brother toward him, yet he can but look upon his conduct, as an abomination in the sight of God: And said Joseph (as his brother Hyrum took the parting hand with him,) I could pray in my heart that all my brethren were like unto my beloved brother Hyrum, for truly he possesses the mildness of a Lamb, and the integrity of a Job; and in short the meek and quiet spirit, of Jesus Christ; and I love him with that love, that is stronger than death, for I never had occasion to rebuke him, nor he me, which he declared when he left me to day.

The following is a copy of a letter from Eldr. William Smith

December 18th 1836

Br. Joseph—

Though I do not know but I have forfeited all right and title to the word brother in consequence of what I have done, for I concider myself, that I am unworthy to be called one, after coming to myself, and reflecting upon what I have been doing, I feel as though it was my duty, to make an humble confession to you, on account of what took place at my house the other evening but I shall [leave] this part of the subject for the present. I was called to an account yesterday by the quorum of the 12, for my conduct; or in other words they desired to know my mind and determinations and what I intended to do. I told them that on reflection upon the many difficulties that I had had, with the church & the much disgrace I had brought upon myself in consequence of my bad conduct; and also that my health would not admit of my going to school, to make any preperation for the induement [endowment], and that I was not able to travel; therefore it would be better for them to appoint one in my stead, that would be better able to fill that important station than myself: And by doing [p. 155] this they throw me into the hands of the church, and leave me where I was before I was chosen among the twelve.

Then I would not be in a situation to bring so much disgrace upon the cause,[1] when I fell into temptations. And perhaps by this means I might obtain salvation. You know dear brother my passions and the danger of falling from so high a station: and therefore I chose to withdraw from the office of the Apostleship, while there is salvation for me, and remain a member in the church. I feel afraid if I do not, it will be worse for me some other day.

And again my health is poor and it is necessary that the office should not be idle. And again I say, you know my passions and I am fearful that it will be worse for me by, and by; do so, if the Lord will have mercy on me, and let me remain a member in the church, and travel & preach, when I am able. do not think that I am your enemy, for what I have done. perhaps the inquiry may arise in your mind, why I do not rem[em]ber the many good deeds you have done for me; or if I do remember them, why it is that I should treat you so basely.—when I reflect upon the injuries I have done you, I must confess that I cannot account for my conduct. I feel truly sorry for what I have done and humbly ask your forgiveness. I have not confidence as yet, to come and see you, for I feel ashamed of what I have been doing; and as I feel now I feel as though all the confession that I could make verbally, or by writing, would not be sufficient to atone for my transgression. Be this as it may, I am willing to make all the restitution you shall

1. MS. reads "casuse."

require, if I can stay in the church as a member, I will try to make all the satisfaction I possibly can.

YOURS WITH RESPECT
WILLIAM SMITH

P.S. do not cast me off, but strive to save me in the church as a member: I do heartily repent of what I have done to you, and ask your forgiveness.– I consider my transgression the other evening, of no small magnitude. But it is done and I cannot help it now—I know brother Joseph you are always willing to forgive; but I sometimes think when I reflect upon the many injuries I have done you [p. 156] as though a confession was not sufficient; but have mercy on me this once, and I will try to do so no more.

The quorum of the 12, called a council yesterday and sent for me, and I went over. This council was called together without my knowledge, or concent.–

YOURS WM. S.

KIRTLAND FRIDAY DECEMBER 18TH 1836

Answer to the foregoing letter. A Copy
BR. WILLIAM

Having received your letter I now proceed to answer it. I shall first proceed to give a brief narration of my feelings and emotions, since the night I first came to the knowledge of your having a debating-school at your house; which was at the time I called with Bishop Whitney & family—This was the first that I knew any thing about it, and from that time I took an interest in them; and was delighted with it, and formed a determination to attend the school for the purpose of obtaining, and with the idea of imparting the same, through the assistance of the spirit of the Lord; if by any means I should have faith to do so, and with this intent I went to the School on Wednesday night. Not with the idea of breaking up the school; neither did it enter into my heart, that there was any wrangling or jealousys in your heart, against me.

However previous to my leaving home there were feelings of solemnity rolling across my heart, which were unaccountable to me. These feelings continued by times to depress my spirits, and seemed to manifest that all was not right, even after the school commenced, and during the debate. Yet I strove to believe that all would work together for good. I was pleased with the arguments, & ingenuity manifested and did not feel to cast any reflections, upon any one that had spoken. But I felt that it was the duty of old men that set as presidents, to be as grave at least as young men. And that it was our duty to smile at solid arguments, and sound reasoning; and be impressed with solemnity, which should be expressed in our countinance [p. 157] when folly, and that which militates against truth and righteousness, rears it[s] deformed head

Therefore in the spirit of my calling, and in view of the authority of the priesthood which has been confered upon me, it was my duty to reprove whatever I considered to be wrong; fondly hoping in my heart, that all parties, would think it right; and therefore humble themselves, that satan might not take the advantage of us, and hinder the progress of our school. Now brother William I want you should bear with me, notwithstanding my plainness.

I would say to you then, that my feeling[s] were grieved when you interupted Eldr. Mc Lellen in his speech. I thought that you should have considered your relation to him in your Apostleship: and not have manifested any divission of sentiment, between you & him, for the surrounding multitude to take the advantage of.

Therefore by way of entreaty on account of the anxiety I had for you, & your influence ⟨& welfare⟩ in society, I said unto you do not have any feeling, or something to that amount.—Why I am thus particular, is that if you have misunderstood my feelings or motives toward you; you may be corrected. But to proceed.– After the school was ~~commenced~~ closed brother Hyrum requested the privilege of speaking; you objected. However you said if he would not abuse the school, he might speak, observing at the same time that you would not allow any man to abuse the school in your house. You had no reason dear brother to suspect that Hyrum would abuse the School.

Therefore my feelings were mortified, at those unnecessary observations. I undertook to reason with you; but you manifested an inconsiderate and stubborn spirit: I then dispared of benefiting you on the account of the spirit you manifested; which drew from me the expression that you was as ugly as the devil.

Father then commanded silence and I formed the de[te]rmination to obey his mandate, and was about to leave the house, with the impression that you was under the influence of a wick[ed] spirit [p. 158] you replyed that you, would say what you pleased, in your own house. Father replyed say what you please; but let the rest hold their toungs. Then a reflection rushed through my mind of the anxiety and care I had for you, and your family, in doing what I did in finishing your house and providing flower for your family &c. And also father had possession in the house as well as yourself. And when at any time have I transgressed the commandments of my father or sold my birthright? that I should not have ⟨the⟩ privilege of speaking in my father's house, or in other words in my fathers family, or in your house, (for so we will call it; and so it shall be,) that I should not have the privilege of reproving a younger brother?

Therefore I said I will speak for I built the house, and it is as much mine as yours, or something to that effect, (I should have said that I helped to finish the house.) I said it merely to show that it was not the right spirit, that would rise up for trifling matters, and undertake to put me to silence.

I saw that your indignation was kindled against me, and you made towards me; I was not then to be moved, and I thought to pull off my loose coat, least it should tangle me, and you be left to hurt me. But not with the intention of hurting you. But you was to[o] soon for me; and having once fallen into the hands of a mob and wounded in my side,[1] and now into the hands of a brother, my side gave way: and after having been rescued from your grasp, I left your house, with feelings that were indiscribable. The scenery had now changed and all those fond expectations, that I had cherished (when going to your house,) of brotherly kindness, charity forbearance, and natural affection, that binds us in duty, not to make each other an offender for a word.

But alas! abuse, anger, malice, hatred, and rage, are heaped upon me, by a brother; and with marks of violence upon my body, with a lame side, I left your habitation bruised and wounded; and not only oppressed with these, but more severely so in mind being born down under the reflection of my disappointment. I returned home, not able to sit down or rise up without help. But through the blessing of God I am [p. 159] now better.– I have received your letter and perused it with care; I have not entertained a feeling of malice against you; I am older than yourself, and have endured more suffering, having been mar⟨r⟩ed by mobs, with the labours of my calling, with a series of persecution and injuries, continually heaped upon me, all serve to debiletate my system. And it may be that I cannot boast of being stronger than you: If I could, or could not, would this be an honour, or dishonour to me? If I like David could boast of slaying a Goliath, who defied the armies of the living God;[2] or like Paul, of contending with a Peter face to face,[3] with sound and iresistable arguments, it might be an honour. But to mangle the flesh or seek revenge upon one who

1. Probably a reference to the mobbing at Hiram, Ohio, on 24 March 1832. See pp. 374-377.

2. 1 Samuel 17:10.

3. Galatians 2:11.

never done you any wrong, cannot be a source of sweet reflection to you, nor me, neither to our honerable father & mother, brothers & sisters.

And when we reflect upon the care and unremitting diligence our parents have wa[t]ched over us by night, & by day, and how many hours of sorrow, and painful anxiety they have spent over our cradles and by our bedsides, in sickness and in health. How careful ought we to be of their feelings in their old age? It surely cannot be a source of sweet reflection to us, to say or do any thing that would bring down their grey hairs with sorrow to the grave. In your letter you asked my forgiveness, which I readily grant; but it seems to me that you still retain an idea that I have ~~done~~ given you reason to be angry, or dissatisfied with me.

Grant me the privilege then of saying, that however hasty, or harsh, I might have spoken at any time to you, it has been for the express purpose of endeavouring to warn exhort, admonish & rescue you from falling into difficulties & sorrows which I fore saw that you were plunging yourself, by giving way to that wicked spirit, which you call your passions, which you should curb and break down, and put under your feet, which if you do not, you never can be saved, (in my view) in the Kingdom of God.

The Lord requires the will of his creatures to be swallowed up in his will. [p. 160] You desire to remain in the church, but to forsake your Apostleship This permit me to tell you is a stratigem of the evil one. When he has gained one advantage, he lays a plan for ~~an~~ another; but by rising up and maintaining your Apostleship and by making one tremendious effort, you may overcome your passions and please God. And by forsakeing your apostleship, you say that you are not willing to make that sacrafice that God requires at your hand. And by so doing you ⟨will⟩ incur his displeasure, and without pleasing God, do not think that it will be any better for you. When a man falls one step he must regain that step, or fall another he then has still more to regain or eventually all is lost.

I desire brother William that you would humble yourself. I feel for you, and freely forgive you all; and you know my unshaken and unchangable disposition. I know in whom I trust. I stand upon the rock, the floods cannot, no they shall not overthrow me. You know the doctrine I teach is true, and you know that God has blessed me. I brought salvation to my fathers house, as an instrument in the hand of God, when they were in a miserable situation. You also know that it is my duty to admonish you when you do wrong. This liberty I shall always take, and you shall have the same privilege.– I take the privilege to admonish you because of my birthright, and I grant you the privilege because it is my duty to be humble and receive rebuke, and instruction from a brother or a friend.

As it regards what course you shall persue hereafter I do not pretend to say; I leave you in the hands of God and his church. Make your own decision, I will do you good although you marr me, or slay me; by so doing my garments shall be clear of your sins. And if at any time you should consider me to be an impostor, for heavens sake leave me in the hands of God, and not think to take vengance upon me yourself.– Tyrany, userpation, and to take men's rights, ever has been, and ever shall be, banished from my heart.– And now may God have mercy upon my fathers house; may God [p. 161] take away enmity, from between me, and them and may all blessings be restored, and the past errors be forgotten forever, may humble repentance bring us both to thee O God, and under thy power and protection, and to a crown to enjoy the society of father, mother, Alvin, Hyrum, Sophronia, Samuel, Catharine, Carloss, Lucy, the Saints and all the sanctified in peace forever, is the prayer of Your brother

JOSEPH SMITH JUN.

TO WM. SMITH–

19 December 1835 · Saturday

He was at home and wrote the above letter, or rather indited it, to his brother William concerning whom he had many solemn feelings and he prayed hartily, that the Lord ~~will~~ cast him not off, but that he may return to the God of Jacob & magnify his apostleship and calling, may this be his happy lot for the Lord of Glory sake, Amen.

20 December 1835 · Sunday

He spent the day at home, in the society of his family, with whom he enjoyed great comfort & satisfaction. He also had many serious reflections, which were profitable.– br's Palmer, & Taylor, called to day to see him, to whom he exhibited the sacred records, to their joy, and satisfaction, and for whom he prayed as follows.– O may God have mercy upon thes[e] men, and keep them in the way of everlasting life in the name of Jesus Christ, Amen.

21 December 1835 · Monday

He spent this day in endeavouring to treasure up wisdom, & knowledge for the benefit of my calling; The day passed off very pleasantly, for which, his soul flowed out in thankfulness to the Lord for his mercy and blessings to himself, & family, in sparing their lives, and administering to all their wants; O continue thy parental care over him, & his family, for Jesus sake.

22 December 1835 · Tuesday

He continued his studies at home, [p. 162] with his heart raised in prayer to the Lord to give him learning, especially a knowledge of languages, and endue him with qualifications, to magnify, and adore his great and exalted name. This evening he delivered an address, to the church, the Lord blessed him with utterance & power; and the saints were edifyed.– His scribe[1] being indisposed at this time, in consequence of a cold, he prayed thus for him.– O may God heal him, for his kindness to me, O my soul be thou greatful to him, & bless him, and he shall be blessed of God forever; I believe him to be a faithful friend of mine, therefore my soul delighteth in him, Amen.

JOSEPH SMITH JUNR.

23 December 1835 · Wednesday

He spent the fore noon at home, in studying the Greek language, and in waiting upon brethren who called to visit him;– in the afternoon, in company with ~~Pres O Cow~~ Eldr. Leonard Rich, he called at Pres. O. Cowdery's to visit his relatives; but had not a very agreeable visit, for he found them filled with prejudice against the work of the Lord, and their minds blinded with superstition and ignorance.

24 December 1835 · Thursday

Spent the A.M. at home, in reading, meditation, & prayer, in the P.M. he assisted in laying out a road across his farm. The commissioner who had been appointed by the County court superintended the same.

25 December 1835 · Friday

This Christmas day, he spent at home in his family circle, and injoyed great satisfaction and comfort, for which he blessed the name of the Lord of Hosts; For the privilege of spending this day of the year, in the bosom of his family, he had not enjoyed for a long time before.

1. Warren Parrish.

26 December 1835 · Saturday

To day in company with Pres. F G. Williams & Eldr. W. Parrish, who were convened at his own house he commenced regularly, & systematically, to study the venerable Hebrew language; we had paid some little attention to it before.– Eldr. Lyman Sherman called and requested the word of the Lord, throug[h] his servant Joseph, our author; he (Sherman) said that he had been wrought upon for a long time to make known [p. 163] his feelings to him, (Joseph) with an assurance from the Lord that he would give him a revelation which should make known his duty.

The following is a revelation given to Lyman Sherman Through Joseph Smith Jun. this 26th day of Dec. 1835[1]

Verily thus saith the Lord unto you my servant Lyman, your sins are forgiven you because you have obeyed my voice in coming up hither this morning to receive counsel of him whom I have appointed.

Therefore let your soul be at rest concerning your spiritual standing and resist no more my voice, and arise up and be more careful henceforth in observing your vows, which you have made, and do make, and you shall be blessed with exceeding great blessings. Wait patiently until the time when the solemn assembly shall be called, of my seventy, then you shall be rem[em]bered with the first of mine elders and receive right by ordination with the rest of mine elders whom I have chosen.

Behold this is the promise of the father unto you, if you continue faithful; and it shall be fulfilled upon you in that day that you shall have right to preach my gospel, wheresoever I shall send you from henceforth from that time. Therefore strengthen your brethren in all your exhortations, in all your prayers, and in all your doings, and behold, and lo, I am with you forever, Amen.

1. See D&C 108.

27 December 1835 · Sunday

At⟨the⟩usual hour he attended meeting at the school-house. Pres. Cowdery delivered a very able discourse, which was edifying to the saints, and calculated to administer grace to all enquiring minds. In the after part of the day Pres. Hyrum Smith, & Bish. Partrige delivired each, a short an[d] interesting lecture; after which the sacrament of the Lord's supper was administered and our meeting dismissed.

28 December 1835 · Monday

Having prefered a charge against Eldr. Almon Babbit,[1] for traduceing his character, he was called before the high council with his witnesses, & substantiated his charges [p. 164] against him; and Eldr. Babbit in part acknowledged his fault, but not satisfactory to the council, and after parleying with him a long time, and granting him every indulgence that could be required in righteousness, the council adjourned without obtaining a full confession from him.

On this day the quorum of the seventy met, to render an account of their travels and ministry, since they were ordained to the apostleship. The meeting was interesting indeed, and his heart was made glad while he listened to the relations of those, who had been labouring in the vinyard of the Lord with such marvelous success, and he prayed God to bless them with an increas[e] of faith, and power, and keep them all with the indurance of faith, in the name of Jesus Christ to the end

29 December 1835 · Tuesday

At about 10 oclock A.M. in company with his wife, father & mother, (who had come to live with him,) ~~also his scribe~~

---

1. Babbitt was brought before the high council for "misrepresenting" the Prophet "to certain of the brethren." His case was not resolved until 2 January 1836, when he reconciled his difficulty and was "restored to fellowship." (Kirtland Council Minutes, 28 December 1835; 2 January 1836.)

~~accompanied them. A large~~ he went to br. Oliver Olneys, to attend a blessing meeting; his scribe also accompanied them. After the company had assembled and were seated, his father Joseph Smith sen. (who is ordained to the office of a patriarch in the church of Latter-day Saints, to confer blessings by the spirit of prophesy.) arose and made some preliminary remarks which were very applicable to the occasion; a hymn was then sung, after which he opened the meeting by an able address, to the throne of grace. Fifteen persons came forward and received each, a patriarchal blessing under his hands, as the spirit gave utterance[1]

The servises then were closed, as they commenced viz. by singing & prayer. A table was then spread and crowned with the bounties of the earth; and after invoking the benediction of heaven upon the rich repast, we fed sumptuously upon the same, and suffice it to say, that we had a glorious meeting, throughout, and he was highly pleased with the harmony and decorum that existed among the brethren and sisters. We returned home at evening. He then repaired to thc school-house where [p. 165] he preached to a crowded audiance, who listened with attention while he delivered a lecture of about 3 hours in length; he had great liberty in speaking.

We were afterwards informed that there were some persons present, who are of the calvinistic faith; if so we have no doubt but some of our authors sayings set to them like a garment that, was well fited, as he exposed their craft, and abominations, to a nicety, and that too, in the language of the scriptures. And his prayer to God is that it may be like a nail in a sure place, driven by the Master of assemblies.

To day Col. Chamberlain's Son called to see him, a respectable gentleman.

---

1. Among those receiving blessings at this time were Lyman Wight, Ezra Hayes, and George Morey.

30 December 1835 · Wednesday

He spent the day in reading hebrew at the council room, with his scribe, in whose company he delighted, & who had sufficiently recovered his health, to attend to his usual avocation.

31 December 1835 · Thursday

After attending to his domestic concerns, he retired to the council room, in the ~~post office~~ printing office, in order to persue his studies.

The council of the twelve convened in an upper room under the same roof, and sent for him and some of the rest of the ⟨first⟩ presidency to meet with them, to take into consideration the subject of the council, that is to be holden on Saturday next, and to make some arangments respecting it.– In the afternoon he attended at the Lord's House to give some directions concerning, the finishing of the upper rooms, and more especially the west room which he intends occupying for a translating room which will be prepared this week.[1]

1 January 1836 · Friday

On the introduction of the new year, his heart is filled with greatful praise to God, for his kind care that has been over him and his family in preserving their lives while an~~n~~other year has rolled away. They have been sustained and upheld in the midst of a wicked, and pervers generation and exposed to all the afflictions temptations and miseries that are incident to human life; for which [p. 166] he felt to humble himself, as it were in dust and ashes before the Lord.– But notwithstanding the gratitude that filled his heart, on retrospecting the past year, with the multiplied blessings that have crowned

1. See Kirtland Temple floor plan on p. 195; also Diary of Joseph Smith, 4 January 1836.

his head; his heart is pained, and his peace distrubed when he reflects upon the difficulties that exists in his fathers family

The Devil has made a violent attack upon his brother William Smith & his brother in law Calvin Stoddard, and the powers of darkness seem to hover over their minds and obscure the light of truth: and not only theirs but a gloomy shade appears to be cast over the minds of some more of his brothers & sisters, which prevents them from seeing thing[s] as they really are. And the powers of earth & hell seem combined to overthrow us, and the church by causing a division in his fathers family. Indeed the adversary is bringing into requisition all his subtlety to prevent the saints from being endued [endowed]; by causing divisions among the twelve, also among the seventy, and bickerings & jealousies among the Elders, & official members, and thus the leaven of iniquity foments & spreads among the lay members of the church.– But Joseph determined in his heart, that no exertion on his part should be wanting to adjust, and amicably dispose of, and settle, all family difficulties on this day; that the ensuing year, & years, be they many, or few, may be spent in righteousness before the Lord. And he declared that he feels confident, that the cloud will burst, and satan's kingdom be laid in ruins, with all his black designs; and the saints come forth like gold seven times tried in the fire, being made perfect throug[h] temptations & sufferings: and the blessings of heaven, & earth, will be multiplied upon our heads, which may God grant for his Sons sake, Amen.

This morning his brother Wm. Smith called to see him upon the subject of their difficulties; they retired to a private room with their father, ~~and~~ their uncle John Smith, their brother Hyrum Smith, & Eldr. Martin Harris; their aged father then opened the interview by prayer [p. 167] after which he expressed his feelings on the occasion in a very feeling and pathetic manner; even with all the sympathy of a father whose feelings were deeply wounded on account of the difficulty that was existing in his family: and while he was speaking the spirit of God rested down upon them in mighty power and their hearts melted down in contrition and humility before the Lord. William made an humble confession and asked his brother Joseph's forgivness for having abused him; and wherein Joseph had been out of the way he asked his forgiveness, and indeed the spirit of confession and forgiving, was mutual among us all, and we entered into a covenant with each other, before the Lord, & the Holy Angels, and the brethren present, to strive from hence forward, to build each other up in righteousness in all things, and not listen to evil reports concerning each other; but like brethren of the same household, go to each other with our grievances in the spirit of meekness and be reconciled, and strive to promote our own happiness, and the happiness of our fathers family, & the happiness of our own families, and in short the happiness, and well being of all. His wife, mother and scribe, was then called in to partake of our joys to whom we related the covenant we had entered into, and while gratitude swelled our bosoms, tears flowed from our eyes.– Joseph was then requested to close our interview, which he did by prayer, and truly it was a time of rejoicing, and ⟨a⟩ jubillee to his fathers family.

2 January 1836 · Saturday

A council had been called to set in judgment, on a complaint prefered against Eldr. Wm. Smith, by Eldr. Orson Johnson.[1] At 9 oclock this morning agreeably to previous arangments, Pres. Smith attended this council. The council organized and proceeded to business: but before entering on the trial, his brother William arose and humbly confessed the

---

1. On 29 December 1835, Johnson had brought charges against William Smith of "unchristian like conduct in speaking disrespectfully of President Joseph Smith . . . and the revelations & commandments given through him" and for "attempting to inflict personal violence." (Kirtland Council Minutes, 29 December 1835.)

charges prefered against him, and the forgiveness of the council, and the whole congregation. A vote was then called to know whether his confession was sattisfactory, and whether the [p. 168] brethren would extend the hand of fellowship to him again. With cheefulness the whole congregation raised their hands to receive him.– Eldr. Almon Babbit also confessed the charge which our author had prefered, ~~against~~ and sustained against him, before a previous council,[1] and was received into fellowship; and some other business was transacted in harmony and union and a mutual good feeling seemed to prevail among the brethren, and our hearts were made glad on the occasion, and there was joy in heaven and our souls magnifyed the Lord for his goodness and mercy manifested to us. The council adjourned by prayer.

3 January 1836 · Sunday

He attended meeting at the usual hour. President Rigdon delivered an interesting lecture upon the subject of revelation – in the P.M. he (Joseph) confirmed about 10 or 12 individuals who had been baptized, among whom was M[arvel].C. Davis who had previously belonged to the church. His brother William made his confession to day, the church cheerfully forgave, and cordially received him into fellowship again:– The Lord['s] supper was administered and William gave out an appointment to preach in the evening at early candle light, and preached accordingly. This has been a day of rejoicing to him, of whom we write; the cloud that has been hanging ove[r] his mind has burst with great blessings upon his head and satan has been foiled in his attempts to destroy him and the church by causing divisions & jealousys to arise in the hearts of some of the brethren, and we unitedly thank our Heavenly Father for the union and harmony that now exists in the church.

1. See entry of 28 December 1835.

4 January 1836 · Monday

He met in the west school-room in the chape[l], to assist in organizeing the Hebrew class. Dr. Piexotto who had engaged to teach our Hebrew school agreed to wait on us to day, and deliver his introductory lecture.– yesterday he sent word to us that he could not come until Wednesday next; a vote was called to know wether the class would submit to such treatment or not, and carried in the negative [p. 169] Eldr. Sylvester Smith was appointed to inform the said Dr. Piexotto that his servises were not wanted; and Eldrs Wm Mc Lellen & Orson Hyde were appointed by the voice of the school to go to Hudson Seminary,[1] to hire a teacher and notwithstanding our disapointment we concluded to go on with our school and do the best we can until we can obtain a teacher. By the voice of the class Pres. Joseph Smith Jnr. was solicited to take charge of school for the time being, to which he concented.– This being the first day that this room was occupied, we thought meet to dedicate it to God, which was solemnized by the venerable patriarch Joseph Smith Sen.– This evening we met at the chapel to make arangements for a singing school; after some altercation, a judicious arangement was entered into, and a committe of 6 was chosen to take charge of the singing department.

This is a rainy unpleasant time, and the roads are extremely mud[d]y.

5 January 1836 · Tuesday

He attended the Hebrew school, & made several divissions in the class, had some debate with Eldr. Orson Pratt respecting

1. The Western Reserve College at Hudson, Summit County, Ohio, about twenty-eight miles south of Kirtland, was founded in 1826. The curriculum of the college in the 1830s was theology, languages, philosophy, and mathematics. (William H. Perrin, ed., *History of Summit County, Ohio* (Chicago, 1881), 446-66.)

the Hebrew pronunciations which was unpleasant, he manifested a stubbourn spirit, which grieved Joseph much.

6 January 1836 · Wednesday

At 9 oclock A.M. he repaired to the school room, and spent most of the fore noon in setling the difficulty that took place the preceeding day between him and Eldr. Pratt, and after much controversy he confessed his fault and asked the forgiveness of the whole school, which was cheerfully, & readily granted by all.– Eldr. Mc Lellen returned from Hudson and reported to the school that he had engaged a man to teach 40 schollars for the term of 7 weeks at 320 Dollars, to commence about fifteen days from this time. His name is Joshua Seixas a Jew by birth & education and highly celebrated as a Hebrew teacher, and proposes to give us sufficient knowledge of the language to read and translate it, in the above mentioned time; or at least to those who attend to his instruction and diligently apply themselves to study [p. 170]

At a conference held at the schoolhouse on Saturday the 2nd Inst. the following individuals were appointed by the voice of the conference to be ordained to the office of Eldrs, in the church of Latter day Saints.– They were ordained under the hands of Pres. J. Smith Jn.—viz.

Vincent [Vinson] Knight
Thomas Grover
Elisha [Elijah] Fordham
Hyram Dayton
Samuel James
John Herrott [Herritt]

7 January 1836 · Thursday

He attended a sumptuous feast at Bp. N K. Whitneys; this feast was after the order of the Son of God, the lame, the halt, & blind were invited according to the instructions of the Saviour. Our meeting was opend by singing and prayer, the Bishops father & mother were bless[ed], and several others with a patriarchal blessing.

We then received a bountiful refreshment furnished by the liberality of the Bishop; the company was large and respectable. Before we parted the Lord poured out his spirit upon us in mighty power, and some of the songs of Zion were sung, and our hearts were made glad while partaking of an antipast of those joys that will be poured upon the heads of the saints when they are gathered together upon mount Zion, to enjoy each others society forever; even all the blessings of heaven and earth, where there will be none to molest or make us afraid.—He returned home and spent the evening in the bosom of his family.

8 January 1836 · Friday

He spent the day in the Hebrew School, and made rapid progress in his studies, and advanced the students in theirs.

9 January 1836 · Saturday

While at school in the A.M. he received the following note.—

Thus saith the voice of the spirit to me if thy brother Joseph Smith Jn. will attend the feast at thy house this day at 12 oclock, the poor & lame will rejoice at his presence, & also think themselves honoured

Yours in friendship & love

N K. WHITNEY

9TH JANY 1836 [P. 171]

He dismissed his class in order to comply with the Bp's. request, his wife, father, & mother accompanied him. A large company assembled, and a number were blessed under the hands of the patriarch, & indeed the Lord blessed us all, we had a good time. He spent the evening at home.

10 January 1836 · Sunday

He attended meeting; Eldr. [Solomon] Wilber Denton & Eldr. [Wilkins] J. Salisbury preached in the fore noon:— In the

P.M. his brother's Samuel & Carloss Smith delivered each a discourse; all these young Eldrs did well concidering their advantages & experiance and bid fair to make useful men in the vinyard of the Lord.[1] The Lords supper was administered and the meeting dismissed. At the intermission to day three were received into the church by baptism.

11 January 1836 · Monday

There being no school to day he injoyed the sweets of the social fireside with his family; however many brethren visited him among whom was Alva Beeman of Gen⟨n⟩essee Co. New York, who had come to attend the solemn assembly.– I delight (says Joseph) in the society of my friends & brethren & pray that the blessings of heaven and earth may be multiplied upon their heads.

12 January 1836 · Tuesday

To day he called on the presidency of the church and made arangements to meet tomorrow at 10 oclock A.M. to take into concideration the subject of the solemn Assembly. This afternoon a young man called to see the Egyptian records and on viewing them, he expressed great satisfaction and appeared very anxious to know how to translate them.– also a man was introduced to him by the name of Russel We[a]ver from Cambray Niagary Co. New York; This man is a preacher in the Christian or Unitarian Church. Mr. Wever remarked that he had but few minutes to spend with me, we imediately entered into conversation, and had some little debate upon the subject of prejudice, but soon came [p. 172] to an understanding, he spoke of the gospel and said he believed it, adding at the same time that it was ~~the power~~ good tidings of great joy.– Pres. Smith replyed that it was one thing to proclaim good tidings,

1. Salisbury was 26; Samuel Smith, 27; and Don Carlos Smith, 19.

and another to tell what those tidings consisted in; he waived the conversation and retired.– He was introduced by Joseph Rose

13 January 1836 · Wednesday

At 10 oclock A.M. he met in council with all the presidency of Kirtland, & Zion, together with their counsellors,[1] (or their

1. The presidency at Kirtland had consisted of Joseph Smith, Sen., Sidney Rigdon, and Hyrum Smith, and at Zion (Missouri), of David Whitmer, John Whitmer, and William W. Phelps. (Smith, *History of the Church*, 2:364.)

One of the purposes of the meeting was to fill vacancies in the leadership of the Church. The Kirtland High Council left this report: "The grand council met this day in the attic story of the printing office, consisting of the following Authorities, (viz.) Presidents Joseph Smith Senior, Sidney Rigdon, Hyrum Smith, David Whitmer, John Whitmer, Joseph Smith Junr. and W.W. Phelps. Also the Twelve Apostles, The High Council of Zion and a part of the high council of Kirtland.

"The Bishop of Zion and his counsellors, also the Bishop of Kirtland and one Counsellor and one to be appointed instead of Hyrum Smith now belonging to the Presidency.

"Council opened by prayer of J. Smith Senior. J. Smith Junr. presiding. Elder Vinson Knight was nominated by the Bishop of Kirtland as a counsellor to fill the vacancy in his court occasioned by the elevation of Hyrum Smith to the presidency. The move was seconded and carried by a unanimous vote of all.

"Bishop Whitney then proceeded to ordain Elder Knight to the high Priesthood and also to be a counsellor. After which all the congregation said Amen with a loud voice. After singing a Hymn they adjourned for one hour.

"At the expiration of the time met again pursuant to adjournment and proceeded to fill the vacancies in the high council. The standing high counsellors were John Smith, John Johnson, Orson Johnson, Martin Harris, Samuel H. Smith, Jared Carter and Joseph Coe.

"The names of those who had been called to fill other offices were Joseph Smith Senr. Hyrum Smith Orson Hyde Luke Johnson and Oliver Cowdery. It was then moved, seconded and voted unanimously that Elder J.P. Green be appointed a high counsellor in the place of Oliver Cowdery. Elder Thomas Grover was nominated in the room of Elder Luke Johnson. This motion was carried unanimously by all the quorums present. It was then moved, seconded, and voted unanimously that Noah Packard be a counsellor in the room of Hyrum Smith. Moved, Seconded and voted that Elder Joseph Kingsbury be appointed a high counsellor in the room of Orson Hyde. Moved, seconded and carried that Samuel James, be appointed a high counsellor in the room of Joseph Smith Senior. Motioned seconded and voted that Joseph Smith Senr. S. Rigdon and Hyrum Smith proceed to ordain the foregoing persons to the respective offices

legal representatives), the presidents of the seventy and many of the Eldrs. of the church of Latter day Saints, came to order

---

to which they had been appointed.

"1st Proceeded to ordain Elder John P. Green.

"We lay our hands on thy head and ordain thee to this high and conspicuous office and pray that our heavenly Father will give thee great wisdom in counsel and make thee of deep penetration, and fill thy heart with compassion and love that all thy decisions may be just and true

"Brother Grover, we ordain thee to be an high priest in the Church of Christ and pray that thou mayest have all the power of thy ministry, we also ordain thee a high counsellor in the High Council at Kirtland, and we pray that thou mayest have great wisdom and be very useful in the church and through faithfulness thou shalt have all the blessings of heaven and of earth and no man shall take them from thee.

"Noah Packard we also ordain thee to be a high priest and pray that thou mayest be a minister in Righteousness and go forth and proclaim the gospel with great power. We also ordain thee to be a high counsellor in the high council of Kirtland and we say if thou art faithful great blessings shall be given to you.

"Joseph Kingsbury, We ordain thee to be an high priest and pray that thy crown be made to shine as the stars that thou mayest always bear off the gospel triumphaly in the face of all opposition. We also ordain thee to be a high counsellor at that stake at Kirtland, praying that you may have the spirit of these offices to which you are now ordained, and this shall be the case through your faithfulness.

"Samuel James, We ordain thee to be an high priest in the Church of the Latter day Saints, and pray that all the powers of thy mind may be enlisted in building up the kingdom of God, that thou mayest be consecrated to God from this very hour: We also ordain thee to be a high counsellor at the stake of Kirtland and we say to thee, if thou wilt be faithful, thou shalt have all the blessings pertaining to the offices to which you have been ordained and no power shall take them from thee. Amen.

"Alvah Beeman and Isaac McWithy were appointed counsellors pro tem in the place of Elders John Murdock and Solomon Hancock who were absent in the council of Zion.

"Thomas Carrico was appointed Door Keeper in the house of the Lord by unanimous vote of the assembly.

"Motioned, seconded and voted unanimously that J. Smith Junr. S. Rigdon, Hyrum Smith, W.W. Phelps and David Whitmer be a committee to draft a code of rules or laws for the regulation of the house of the Lord in times of worship.

"Nominated, Seconded and carried unanimously that no whispering shall be allowed in the council nor any loud talking by any one except when called upon, or when he asks the privilege of so doing.

"President Rigdon rose up and made some general remarks in relation to the building up of the Kingdom of God, which were very appropriate and timely. He then closed by prayer.

"Adjourned till Friday the 15th inst at 9 o clock A.M. to meet in the stone house. Orson Hyde, Clerk" (Kirtland Council Minutes, 13 January 1836.)

and sung Adam-ondi-Ahman and opened by prayer offered up by Joseph Smith sn. Pres. Joseph Smith Jun. presided on the occasion.– The council being thus organized and opened, he arose and made some preliminary remarks in general terms to[u]ching the authoritys of the church; also laying before them the business of the day, which was to supply some deficiencies in the several quorums, which were occasioned by the calling of the twelve & seventy &c. After some altercation upon the subject as to the most proper manner to proceed Eldr. Vinson Knight was nominated and seconded to fill the bishops quorum in Kirtland.

The vote of the presidency was called and carried ~~in the~~ unanimously,– vote of the high council of Zion was then called & carried also,– vote of the twelve was called and carried,– vote of the council of the seventy was called and carried,– vote of the bishop of Zion & his council was called & carried, and Eldr. Knight was received by the unanimous voice & consent of all the authoritys of the church as a counsellor in the bishops council in Kirtland to fill the place of Hyrum Smith who is ordained to the presidency.– Eldr. Knight was then ordained under the hands of Bp. N K. Whitney to the office of a councillor also to the high priesthood.– Council adjourned for one hour, by sing[ing] come let us rejoice in the day of salvation &c.– Council assembled at 1, oclock P.M. and proceeded to business—John P. Greene was nominated & seconded, as councilor in the high council of Kirtland to fill the place of O. Cowdery who is ordained to the presidency—a vote was called of the several quorums in their respective order and carried unanimously [p. 173] Eldr. Thomas Grover was nominated & seconded to supply the place of Eldr. Luke Johnson in the high council of Kirtland, vote called and carried unanimously. Eldr. Noah Packard was nominated & seconded to supply the place of Eldr. Sylvester Smith in the high council of Kirtland, vote call[ed] of the respective authorities and carried unanimously.

Eldr. Joseph Kingsbury was nominated & seconded to fill the place of Eldr. Orson Hyde in the high council of Kirtland, vote called and carried unanimously Eldr. Samuel James was nominated & seconded to supply the place of Joseph Smith Sen. —vote called and carried unanimously.

The newly elected counsellors were then called forward and ordained in order as they were elected under the hands of Presidents J. Smith Jn S. Rigdon & H. Smith to the office of high priests and counsellors in the high council of Kirtland the Stake of Zion.

Many great and glorious blessings were pronounced upon the heads of these councillors by Pres. Rigdon who was mouth on the occasion.– Next proceeded to supply the deficiencies in the Zion high council Eldr.s Alva Beeman & Isaac Mc Withy were nominated & seconded to fill the places of Eldrs. John Murdock and Solomon Hancock for the time being. —vote was called and carried unanimously.

Eldr. Nathaniel Milliken, & Thomas Carrico, were nominated & seconded to serve as door keepers in the house of the Lord, vote called and carried unanimously by the whole assembly. Presdt's J. Smith Jn., S. Rigdon, W.W. Phelps, D. Whitmer, & H. Smith, were nominated & seconded to draft rules & regulations to govern the house of the Lord; vote was called and carried by the unanimous voice of the whole assembly. The question was then agitated whether whispering should be allowed in our councils & assemblies; a vote was called and carried unanimously in the negative, that not only whispering, but loud talking shall be prohibited in our assemblies except by those who are called upon, or ask permission to speak [p. 174] upon any consideration whatever; and that no man shall be interupted while speaking unless he is speakin[g] out of place, and every man shall be allowed to speak in his turn.– Eldr. N. Milliken refused to serve as door keeper in the house of the Lord on account of his ill health and was released by the voice of the assembly.

Pres. S. Rigdon made a request to have some of the presidency pray for & lay hands upon him and rebuke a severe affliction with which he was afflicted in his face, chiefly nights;– Presdts H. Smith & D. Whitmer, prayed for & laid hands on him and rebuked his affliction in the name of the Lord Jesus, the whole assembly responded Amen. Eldr. D W. Patten also made a request in behalf of his wife, our author, offered up a prayer in her behalf, & the whole assembly responded Amen. The minuets of the council were read and council adjourned until Friday 15th Inst. at 9. oclock A.M. at the school room in the upper part of the Chapel.– Pres. Rigdon arose and made some very appropriate remarks touching the enduement [endowment] and dismissed ~~by~~ the assembly by prayer–

W. PARRISH (SCRIBE

This (says Joseph) has been one of the best days I ever spent, there has been an entire unison of feeling expressed in all our proceedings during this day and it has been good for us to be here, in this heavenly place in Christ Jesus, and although much fatiegued with the labours of the day; yet my spiritual reward has been very great.– He returned home and spent the evening.

14 January 1836 · Thursday

At 9 oclock A.M. he met the Hebrew class at the schoolroom in the Chapel and made some arangments about our anticipated teacher Mr. J. Seixas.– He then repaired to the council room in the printing office, to meet with his colleagues who were appointed with himself to draft ~~resolutions~~ rules & regulations to be observed in the house of the Lord in Kirtland, built by the church of latter day saints in the year of our Lord 1834, as follows.– [p. 175]

1st– It is according to the rules & regulations of all regular and legal organized bodies to have a president to keep order.

Kirtland Temple, Kirtland, Lake County, Ohio, c.1907.
George E. Anderson Collection. LDS Church Archives.

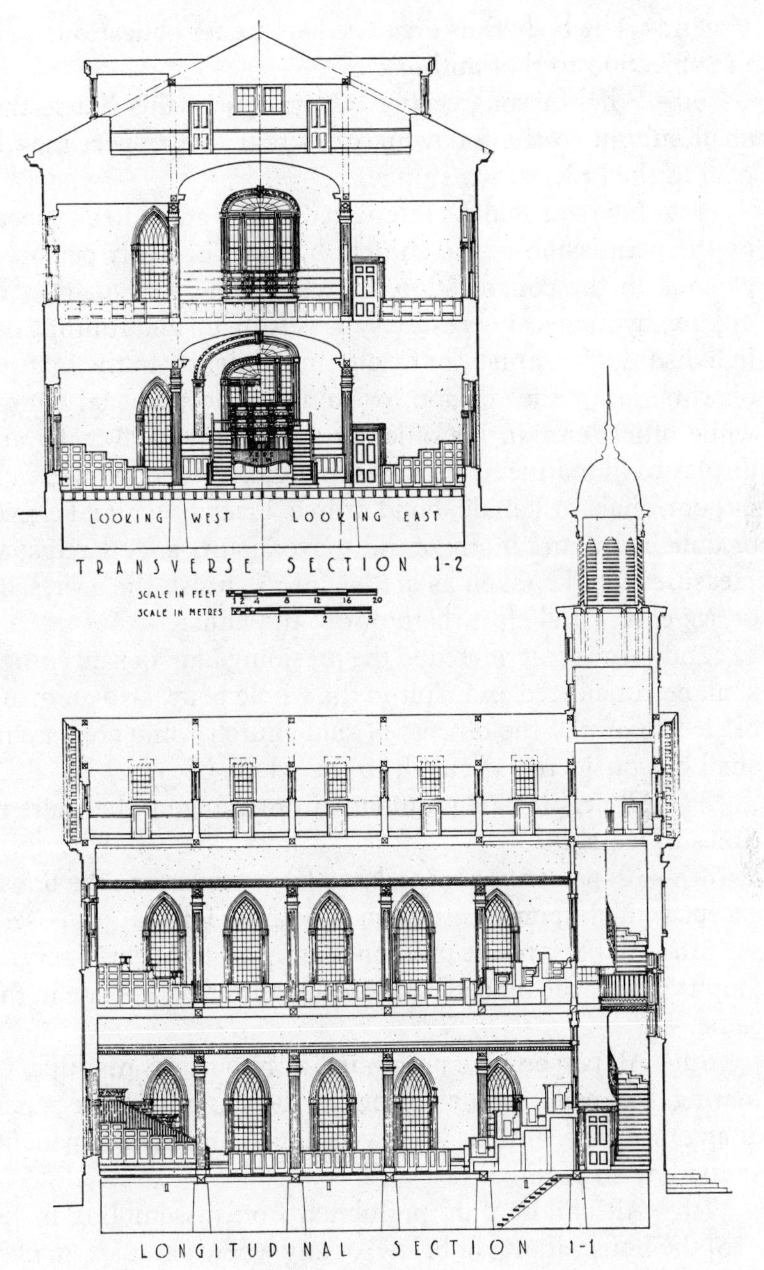

Kirtland Temple drawing. Library of Congress, Washington, D.C.

2nd– The body thus organized are under obligations to be in subjection to that authority.

3d– When a congregation assembles in this house they shall submit to the following rules that due respect may be paid to the order of worship. viz.

1st– No man shall be interupted who is appointed to speak by the permission of the church, by any disorderly person or persons in the congregation, by whispering, by laughing, by talking, by manaceing gestures, by getting up and running out in a disorderly manner, or by offering indignity to the manner of worship, or the religion, or to any officer of said church while officiateing in his office in any wise whatever, by any display of ill manners, or ill breeding, from old, or young, rich, or poor, male or female, bond or free, black or white, believer or unbeliever, and if any of the above insults are offered such measures will be taken as are lawful to punish the aggressor, or aggressors and eject them out of the house.

2nd– An insult offered to the presiding Eldr. of said church shall be concidered an insult to the whole body, also an insult offered to any of the officers of said church while officiateing shall be considered an insult to the whole body.

3d– All persons are prohibited from going up the stairs in times of worship.

4th– All persons are prohibited from exploreing the house except waited upon by a person appointed for that purpose.

5th– All persons are prohibited from going into the several pulpits except the officers who are appointed to officiate in the same.

6th– All persons are prohibited from cutting, marking, or maring, the inside, or outside of the house, with a knife pencil or any other instrument whatever, under pain of such penalty as the law shall inflict.

7th– All children are prohibited from assembling in [p. 176] the house above, or below, or any ~~where~~ part of it, to play or for recreation at any time, and all parents guardians or mastures, shall be emeniable for all damage that shall accrue in consequence of their children.

8th– All persons whether believers or unbelievers shall be treated with due respect by the authorities of the church.

9th– No imposition shall be practiced upon any member of the church by depriving them of their rights in the house.

Council adjourned sine die. – Our author returned home this afternoon Pres. O. Cowdery returned from the City of Columbus the metropolis of this State (Ohio).[1]

At evening himself & wife were invited to attend on a matrimonial occasion at Mrs. Wilcox where he was solicited to solemnize the marriage contract between Mr. John Webb & Mrs. Catharine Wilcox; also Mr. Thomas Carrico & Miss Eliza[be]th Baker, at the same place. The crowded assembly were seated, and the interview opened by singing & prayer suited to the occasion; after which he made some remarks in relation to the duties that are incumbent on husbands & wives; in particular the great importance there is in cultivating the pure principles of the institution in all its bearings and relations to each other and society in general.– He then invited them to arise and join hands, and pronounced the ceremony according to the rules & regulations of the Church of Latter-day Saints; and pronounced such blessings upon their heads as the Lord put into ~~their~~ his heart, even the blessings of Abraham Isaac & Jacob, and dismissed by singing and prayer.– We then took some refreshment and our hearts were made glad with the fruit of the vine. This is according to the pattern set us by ~~the~~ our Saviour himself when he graced the marriage in Cana of Gallilee and turned the water into wine that they might

1. On 10 October 1835, Oliver Cowdery had been elected by the Geauga County Democratic Convention as a delegate to the state convention held at Columbus on 8 January 1836. He left Kirtland on 3 January. (Diary of Oliver Cowdery for dates indicated. The diary is published in Leonard J. Arrington, "Oliver Cowdery's Kirtland, Ohio, 'Sketch Book,'" *BYU Studies* 12 [Summer 1972]: 410-26.)

make themselves joyful, and we feel disposed to patronize all the institutions of heaven.[1] Pres. Smith took leave of the audiance and retired.

15 January 1836 · Friday

At 9. oclock A.M. he met in council agreeably to adjournment, at the council room in the Chapel, & organized the authorities of the church agreeable to their respective offices in the same. He then made [p. 177] some observations respecting the order of the day and the great ~~importance~~ responsibility we are under, to transact all our business in righteousness before the Lord, inasmuch as our descisions will have a bearing upon all mankind and upon all generations to come. The song Adam ondi Ahman was sung & council opened by prayer; & proceeded to business by reading the rules & regulations to govern the house of the Lord, as drafted by the committee chosen for that purpose.[2] The vote of the pres-

---

1. John 2:1-11.

The revelation referred to as the Word of Wisdom (D&C 89), given to the Latter-day Saints in February 1833, was not consistently observed until the twentieth century; hence, references to occasional use of wine and other substances forbidden by the revelation are found in nineteenth-century Mormon sources. (See Paul H. Peterson, "An Historical Analysis of the Word of Wisdom" [M.S. thesis, Brigham Young University, 1972]; Thomas G. Alexander, *Mormonism in Transition: A History of the Latter-day Saints, 1890-1930* [Urbana and Chicago: University of Illinois Press, 1986], chapter 13.)

2. The purpose of this meeting and of the one two days previous, which constituted a gathering of the entire Church leadership, was to fill gaps in the organization of the Church leadership and, since the first temple was nearing completion and would soon be dedicated, make regulations to govern the conduct of those who entered that holy edifice.

According to the minutes of the Kirtland High Council, after the meeting convened, Joseph Smith "proceeded to give many good instructions in relation to the order & manner of conducting the council and also delivered a solemn charge to the counsel after which he opened by prayer and presided as before.

"President J. Smith Junr one of the committee to draft rules for the regulation of the House of the Lord, made the report of said committee by reading the rules they had drafted three times. They were approved and unanimously adopted, and the counsil adjourned one hour.

"Met at the expiration of the time aforesaid and proceeded to business without

idency was called upon these rules; some exceptions were taken by Pres. O. Cowdery which he withdrew on an explanation, and the vote passed unanimously.– The subject was then laid before the high council of Kirtland and after some altercation their vote was called and unanimously passed in favour of the rules.– The investigation was then thrown before the high council of Zion; some inquiry was made upon some particular items, which were soon settled, and their vote called and passed unanimously in favour of them.– The quorum of the twelve investigated the subject next, and their vote called & unanimously passed in favour of them.– Council adjourned for one hour.

1. oclock. P.M. council called to order & proceeded to business. The subject of the rules & regulations to govern the house of the Lord, came next in order before the quorum of the seventy, their vote called and carried unanimously.

The question was then thrown before the bishop in Kirtland & his councillors, their vote called & carried in the affirmative.– The above named bill having now passed unanimously through all the quorums, in their order, it is received & established as a law to govern the house of the Lord in Kirtland.– In the investigation which has been had today upon the above mentioned subject; he (Joseph) saw that many who had deliberated upon it, were darkened in their minds respecting it; which drew forth the following remarks from him, concerning the privileges of the authorities of the church; that they should each speak in his turn, and in his place, and in

---

ceremony. Motioned and seconded that the Laws regulating the house of the Lord go into effect from this time, and that Elder John Corril take it upon him to see that they are enforced, giving him the privelege of calling as many as he choose to assist him." (Kirtland Council Minutes, 15 January 1836.)

Oliver Cowdery summarized the events of January 15 in his diary: "The several Quorums of the authorities of the Church met today, and transacted important business preparatory to the endowment. The Spirit of the Lord was in our midst." (Diary of Oliver Cowdery, 15 January 1836; published in Leonard J. Arrington, "Oliver Cowdery's Kirtland, Ohio, 'Sketch Book.' ")

his time & season, that their may be perfect order in all things, and that every man before he makes an objection to any item that is thrown before them for their consideration, should be certain that he [p. 178] can throw light upon the subject, rather than spread darkness, and that his objection be founded in righteousness: which may be done, by applying ourselves diligently to study & know the mind & will of the Lord; whose spirit always makes manifest, and demonstrates to the understanding of all who are in possession of its benign influence.

Eldr. Carloss Smith was nominated & seconded to be ordained president of the high priesthood to preside over that quorum in Kirtland, a vote was called of all the respective quorums and unanimously passed.

Eldr. Alva Beeman was nominated and seconded to officiate as president of the Eldrs. in Kirtland; The vote of the several authorities was call[ed], and unanimously passed.

William Cowdery was nominated & seconded to officiate as president over the priests of the Aaronic priesthood in Kirtland the vote of the assembly was called beginning at the bishops council and passing through the several authorities until it come to the first presidency and received their sanction having been carried unanimously in all the other quorums.

Oliver Olney was nominated & seconded to preside over the teachers in Kirtland; the vote was call[ed] and unanimously passed through all the assembly.

Ira Bond was nominated and seconded to preside over the deacons in Kirtland;– vote called & passed unanimously.

Eldr. Carloss Smith was called forward to the seat of the presidency and ordained to the office whereunto he had been elected; and many blessings pronounced upon his head, by Joseph Smith Jun. S. Rigdon & H. Smith who were appointed to ordain him.

Eldr. Beeman also received his ordination & blessing under the hands of the presidency.

Bishop N K. Whitney & his councillors then proceeded to ordain those that had been elected to fill the several quorums of the Aaronic priesthood; & pronounced such blessings upon their heads, as the Lord put into their hearts.

Next proceeded to appoint door keepers to serve in the house of the Lord. The officers of the several quorums were nominated & seconded, and vote carried, that each should [p. 179] serve in his turn as doorkeeper in the Lords house.– also Nathaniel Milliken, Thomas Carrico, Samuel Rolph, & Amos R. Orton were elected to the office of doorkeepers.

Nominated & seconded that the presidency of the high council hold the keys of the inner & outer courts of the Lords house in Kirtland, except the key to one of the vestrys, which is to be held by the bishopric of the Aaronic priesthood.– The vote of the assembly called & carried unanimously.

Nominated & seconded that John Carrill [Corrill] be appointed to take immediate charge of the house of the Lord in Kirtland The vote of the assembly called & passed unanimously.

Pres. Rigdon then arose and delivered his charge to the assembly; his remarks were few and appropriate.

Council adjourned by prayer.–

W. PARRISH (SCRIBE

16 January 1836 · Saturday

By request he met with the council of the twelve, in company with his colleagues F G. Williams & S. Rigdon.– Council organized and opened by singing & prayer offered up by Thomas B. Marsh president of the twelve. He arose and requested the privilege in behalf of his colleagues of speaking, each in his turn until they all had spoken without being interupted; which was cheerfully granted by the presidency.– Eldr. Marsh proceeded to unbosom his feelings touching the mission of the twelve; but more particularly respecting a certain letter which they received from the presidency of the high council in Kirtland, while they were attending a conference in the State of Maine. He also cast some reflections on the account of the twelve having been placed in our council on friday last, below the high councils of Kirtland & Zion having been previously placed in our assemblies next [to] the presidency.– He also remarked that their feelings were hurt on account of some remarks made by Pres. H. Smith on the trial of Glad[d]en Bishop who had been previously tried before the council of the twelve while on their mission in the east;[1] who had by their request thrown his case before the high council in Kirtland for investigation; and from some remarks made by the presidency the twelve drew the conclusion that their proceedings [p. 180] with him were in some degree discountinanced.[2]

Eldr. Marsh then gave way to his brethren and they arose and spoke in turn until they had all spoken acquiessing in the observations of Eldr. Marsh and made some additions to his remarks as follows,– That the letter in question which they received from the presidency, in which two of their number were suspended, and the rest severely chastened, ~~and~~ was upon testimony that was unwarantable also that particular stress, was laid upon a certain letter which the presidency had received from Dr. Warren A. Cowdery of Freedom New York, in which

1. Reference is made to the May 4–September 26, 1835, mission of the Twelve in which they traveled through the eastern states and New England holding conferences and regulating the affairs of the Church.

2. The March 1835 revelation that defined and established the interrelationship between the presiding quorums of the Church designated the First Presidency, the Quorum of Twelve, and the stake high councils as equal in authority. (D&C 107:22-24, 36-37.) For a time after their appointment as a quorum, as the nature and scope of their apostolic calling was being defined, the Twelve, individually and collectively, confronted Joseph Smith with issues that concerned their relationship to him, the First Presidency, and the high council. The meeting on 16 January was an attempt to resolve some of these issues. (For a discussion of this context see Esplin, "The Emergence of Brigham Young and the Twelve," chapter 4.)

he prefered charges against the twelve which were false; and upon which the presidency had acted, in chastning them.[1]

And therefore the twelve had come to the conclusion that the presidency had lost confidence in them; and that whereas the church in Kirtland had caressed them at the time of their appointment to the apostleship; they now treated them coolly and appeared to have lost confidence in them also.– They spoke of their having engaged in the work, or at least some of them almost from it's commencement and had borne the burden in the heat of the day, and passed through many trials, & hardship, and that the presidency ought not to suspect their fidelity nor loose confidence in them, neither to have chastened them upon such testimony as was lying before them.

They also urged the necessity of an explanation upon the letter which they received from the presidency, and the propriety of their having information as it respects their duties authority &c. That they might come to understanding in all things, that they might act in perfect unison and harmony before the Lord and be prepared for the enduement.– Also that the twelve had prefered a charge against Dr. Cowdery for his unchristian conduct, which the presidency had disregarded.– also that Pres. O. Cowdery on a certain occasion, made use of language to one of the twelve that was unchristian, and unbecoming any man; and that they would not submit to such treatment.

The remarks of all the twelve, were made in a very forcible, determined, & explicit manner, yet cool, & deliberate. [p. 181] Pres. Smith arose and observed ~~that~~ to the twelve, that the

1. While the Twelve were on their mission to the east in 1835, they were censured by the Presidency for neglecting "to teach the Church in Freedom, New York the necessity of contributing of their earthly substance for the building of the House of the Lord" in Kirtland. The censure was based upon a letter sent them by Warren Cowdery. In a note of reconciliation, published in the February 1836 *Messenger and Advocate*, Cowdery apologized, stating he had afterward learned that his observations were ill-founded.

presidency had sat and heard them patiently, and in their turn should expect to be heard patiently by them also.– And first he remarked that it was necessary that the twelve should state whether they were determined to persevere in the work of the Lord, whether the presidency are able to satisfy them or not.– The president of the twelve call[ed] a vote of his quorum, upon this question, which was unanimously carried in the affirmative. Our author then assured them that he had not lost confidence in them, and that they had no reason to suspect his confidence; and that he would be willing to be weighed in the scale of truth to day, with them in this matter, and risk the event in the day of judgment.

And as it respects the chastning contained in the letter in question, which he acknowledged might have been expressed in language to[o] harsh; which was not intentional, and therefore he asked their forgivness in as much as he had injured their feelings in concequence of it.– But nevertheless said he the letter that Eldr. Mc Lellen sent back to Kirtland, while the twelve were at the east, was harsh also and he was willing to set the one against the other. He next proceeded to explain the subject of the duty of the twelve, ~~which is next the~~ and their authority; which is next to that of the first presidency; and that the organization of the council on the 15th Inst, on which occasion the high council of Kirtland was seated next [to] the presidency; was because the business to be transacted on that day, was business that particularly related to that body.– Not because they were first in office; therefore the arrangement was [the] most judicious that could be made on that occasion.

And furthermore he observed that the twelve are not subject to any other authority in the church, except the first presidency. He also remarked to the twelve that he did not countinance the harsh language of Pres. Cowdery to them; neither did he countinance it in himself, nor any other man; although he had sometimes indulged in it, & spoken to[o] harsh from the impuls[e] of the moment, and wherein he had [p. 182] wounded their feelings by so doing, he asked their forgiveness.– For said he I truly love you brethren, with a perfect love, and will hold you up with all my heart, in all righteousness before the Lord, & before all men.– be assured brethren I am willing to stem the torrent of all opposition in your behalf, in storms, in tempests, in thunder, in lightning, by sea & by land, in the wilderness, among fals[e] brethren, or mobs, or wherever God in his providence may call me for your support or defence, and I am determined that neither h[e]ights, nor depths, principalities, nor powers, things present, or to come, nor any other creature shall seperate me from you. And I will now covenant with you before God this day that I will not listen to nor credit any derogatory report against any of you, to condemn you upon any testimony beneath the heavens, save that which is infalable, until I can see you face to face and know of a surety of the things whereof you are accused.

I believe you to be men of God, therefore I place unlimited confidence in you. And I ask the same confidence on your part brethren, when I tell you any thing, for I will not declare any thing to you, that I do not know to be truth. But I have allready consumed more time in my remarks than I intended when I arose, and I will now give way to my colleagues.– Pres. Rigdon arose and acquiessed in what Pres. Smith had said & acknowledged to the twelve that he had not done as he ought in not attending to the charges that were put into his hands by them against Doct. W A. Cowdery, he frankly acknowledged ~~his duty~~ that he had neglected his duty in that thing for which he asked their forgiveness, and pledged himself to attend to it immediately if they desired him to do so. Pres. Rigdon also observed to the twelve that if he had at any time spoken or reproved to[o] harsh, and had injured their feelings in cons[e]quence thereof, he asked their forgivness. Pres. F G. Williams arose and acquiessed in the sentiments expressed by Presdt's, Smith & Rigdon [p. 183] and said many good things.

The Pres. of the twelve then called a vote of that body to know whether they were perfectly satisfied with the explanation which ~~we had given~~ had been given them, and whether they would enter into the covenant which the presidency proposed to make with them; which was most readily manifested in the affirmative, by raising their hands to heaven, in testimony of their willingness and desire to enter into this covenant and their entire satisfaction with the explanation of the presidency upon all the difficulties that were on their minds.– The presidency, scribe, & twelve, all took each other by the hand in confirmation of the covenant they had mutually entered into, and there was a perfect unison of feeling expressed, and their hearts overflowed with blessings which they pronounced upon each others heads as the spirit gave them utterance; may God enable them all to perform their vows & covenants with each other in all fidelity & righteousness before Him, that their influence may be felt among the nations of the earth in mighty power, even to rend the kingdoms of darkness in sunder, and triumph over priestcraft and spiritual wickedness in high places, & break in pieces all kingdoms that are opposed to the kingdom of Christ, and spread the light & truth of the everlasting gospel from the rivers to the ends of the earth.

Eldr. Beeman called upon Pres. Smith for counsel upon the subject of his returning; he desired to know whether it would be wisdom for him to go before the Solemn Assembly or not. The subject was laid before the council, who advised Eldr. Beeman to tarry until after the assembly

Council adjourned by singing & prayer.

W. PARRISH (SCRIBE

17 January 1836 · Sunday

Pres. Smith attended meeting at the usual hour, a large congregation assembled; he [p. 184] proceeded to organize the several quorums present; first the presidency, then the twelve,

& all of the seventy who were present, also the counsellors of Kirtland, & Zion. Pres. S. Rigdon then arose and remarked to the audiance that instead of preaching as usual the time would be occupied by the quorums in speaking each in his turn, until they had all spoken commencing with the presidency. The Lord poured out his spirit upon the congregation, as the brethren began to confess their faults one to another, & tears flowed from our eyes, & some of our hearts were to[o] big for utterance; (to use the language of our author,) the gift of toungs came upon us like the rushing mighty wind, and my soul was filled with the glory of God.– In the P.M. Pres. Smith joined three couple in the bonds of matrimony, in the publick congregation; the Lord's supper was administered and the congregation dismissed.– Pres. Smith was then invited to attend a feast at Eldr. Cahoon's which was prepared on the occasion, and had a good time while partaking of the rich repast that was spread before us; and verily said he, it is good for brethren to dwell together in unity, it is like the dew upon the mountains of Israel where the Lord commanded blessings even life for ever more.– He returned home and spent the evening.

18 January 1836 · Monday

He attended the Hebrew school:– on this day the Eldrs was removed into an upper room in the Lord's house prepared for that purpose

Copy of a letter from Doct. Piexotto to his scribe

WILLOUGHBY JANY 5TH 1836.

TO ELDR. W. PARRISH

Sir I have received an open note from Mr. Sylvester Smith informing me that your school concidered itself dissolved from all engagements with me, for this I was [p. 185] not unprepared. But he adds that I must excuse him for saying that I appear to be willing to trifle with you in regard to appointments, time, &c– This insinuation is unworthy of me beneath my sence of honour, and I could hope unwarranted by any mean suspicion of your whole body.– I wrote for books to New York by Mr. Cowdery,– not but ~~what~~ I could have taught the rudiments without them,– but because I wished to make my instructions philosophically availing as well as mere elementary. In this object I thought myself confirmed by *you*; my books have not come as yet & are probably lost – of the pecuniary value I seek not.– I borrowed a book of Eldr. Boynton & told him believing him to be responsible that wednesday would be best for me to deliver a publick lecture owing to my engagements here. I here was *officially* informed when the school was to be *opened* by me.– The addition of insult to abuse may be gratifying to small minds, mine is above it, scorns and repud[i]ates it – I am very respectfully

YOUR VERY OBT. SERVT.
DANIEL L M. PIEXOTTO

The answer

KIRTLAND JANY 11TH 1836

DR. PIEXOTTO

Sir I received yours of the 5th Inst. in which you manifested much indignation and considered your *honour* highly insulted by us as a body, if not by me as an individual, and deprecated our conduct because we informed you that you appeared willing to trifle with us, as it respects our engagements with you to teach our Hebrew class. I have acted in this matter as agent for the school; the time agreed upon for you to commence, was not to be protracted, at farthest later than [p. 186] Dec. 15th & the class have ever till now, considered themselves bound by the engagement I made with you.– When Cowdery & myself called, you set a time that you would come to Kirtland & have our agreement committed to writing, but did not come, some were displeased. I excused you; some days elapsed & we heard nothing from you: at length Dr. Williams called & you specified another time that you would come, which is some 2, or 3, weeks since; the class were again disappointed, again I plead an excuse for you; on last saturday week (the 2nd Inst.) our class met and agreed to organize on Monday morning the 4th Inst. at 9 oclock A.M. and by the voice of the school I was appointed to wait on you, and advertize your *honour* that we were ready, and should expect you to attend at that hour; presuming that you would be ready at that late period to fulfill your engagements if you ever intended to; and accordingly I called, and informed you of the arangements we had made, but on account of your arangements at the medical university I was willing to exceed my instructions, and let you name the hour that you would wait on us on that day, which was at 4. oclock P.M.[1] [p. 187]

---

1. The MS. ends abruptly at this point. The text continues in the 1835-36 Diary of Joseph Smith.

"JOURNAL EXTRACT," 1839

"Extract From the Private Journal of Joseph Smith Jr.," Times and Seasons *1 (November 1839): 2-9.*

Editorial Note

After an 1831 revelation to Joseph Smith designated Jackson County, Missouri, as the place "consecrated for the gathering of the saints" and the building of "the city of Zion," and specified Independence as "the center place" where a temple would be built, Latter-day Saints began migrating in large numbers to western Missouri. Their social, religious, and economic values and practices differed from those of other Missouri residents, creating a conflict that eventually led to the expulsion of the Mormons from the state. The situation grew to a climax at Far West, Caldwell County, on 31 October 1838 when Joseph Smith and other Mormon leaders entered the camp of Missouri militia commander Samuel Lucas, under a flag of truce, to discuss ways to defuse the volatile situation. However, instead of being given a conference, the Mormons were arrested and confined. Thus began nearly six months of imprisonment for the Prophet, most of which was spent in a cold, dark jail at Liberty in Clay County. The next spring, after making his way to Illinois following his confinement, Joseph wrote a summary of his Missouri experience. (D&C 57:1-3; The Mormon sojourn in Missouri and the causes of the conflict are treated in Jennings, "The Expulsion of the Mormons from Jackson County"; Max H. Parkin, "A History of the Latter-day Saints in Clay County, Missouri, from 1833 to 1837" [Ph.D. diss., Brigham Young University, 1976]; Leland H. Gentry, "A History of the Latter-day Saints in Northern Missouri from 1836-39" [Ph.D. diss., Brigham Young University, 1965]; and Dean Jessee, " 'Walls, Grates, and Screeking Iron Doors': The Prison Experience of Mormon Leaders in Missouri, 1838-1839," in *New Views of Mormon History:*

A Collection of Essays in Honor of Leonard J. Arrington, ed. Davis Bitton and Maureen Ursenbach Beecher [Salt Lake City: University of Utah Press, 1987]; Richard L. Anderson, "Atchison's Letters and the Causes of Mormon Expulsion from Missouri," *BYU Studies* 26 [Summer 1986]: 3-47; Jessee and David J. Whittaker, "The Last Months of Mormonism in Missouri: The Albert Perry Rockwood Journal," *BYU Studies* 28 [Winter 1988]: 5-41.)

One of the first undertakings of the Latter-day Saints after establishing a new gathering place in Hancock County, Illinois, in 1839 was the publication of a monthly paper, the *Times and Seasons*. Edited by Ebenezer Robinson and Don Carlos Smith, the first issue appeared in November 1839 with the promise, "We shall . . . endeavor to give a detailed history of the persecution and suffering, which the members of the church of Jesus Christ of Latter Day Saints, has had to endure in Missouri, and elsewhere, for their religion."

The first article to appear in the paper after the editor's prospectus was an "Extract, From the Private Journal of Joseph Smith Jr.," containing a personal account of his 1838-39 Missouri experience and the sufferings of his people, beginning with his arrival at Far West on 14 March 1838 and ending with his arrival in Illinois in April 1839. Although the title refers to a private journal of the Prophet, no manuscript source for the "extract" is known. His statement in the text, "I have now resided in this neighborhood for several weeks" (referring to Quincy, Illinois), indicates that the account was written shortly after Joseph's arrival at Quincy, Illinois, in 1839.

On the fourteenth day of March, in the year of our Lord one thousand eight hundred and thirty eight, I with my family, arrived in Far West, Caldwell county Missouri, after a journey of more than one thousand miles, in the winter season, and being about eight weeks on our Journey; during which we suffered great affliction, and met with considerable persecution on the road.[1] However, the prospect of meeting my friends in the west, and anticipating the pleasure of dwelling in peace, and enjoying the blessings thereof, buoyed me up under the

1. Some of the difficulties encountered during this midwinter trip to Missouri are reviewed in the Diary of Joseph Smith, 29 December 1842; see also Smith, *History of the Church*, 3:1-3; 5:211.

difficulties and trials which I had then to endure. However, I had not been there long before I was given to understand that plots were laid, by wicked and designing men for my destruction, who sought every opportunity to take my life; and that a company on the Grindstone forks of Grand river, in the county of Daviess, had offered the sum of one thousand dollars for my scalp: persons of whom I had no knowledge whatever, and who, I suppose, were entire strangers to me; and in order to accomplish their wicked design, I was frequently waylaid &c.; consequently, my life was continually in jeopardy.

I could hardly have given credit to such statements, had they not been corroborated by testimony, the most strong and convincing; as shortly after my arrival at Far West, while watering my horse in Shoal Creek, I distinctly heard three or four guns snap, which were undoubtedly intended for my destruction; however, I was mercifully preserved from those who sought to destroy me, by their lurking in the woods and hiding places, for this purpose.

My enemies were not confined alone, to the ignorant and obscure, but men in office, and holding situations under the Governor of the State,[1] proclaimed themselves my enemies, and gave encouragement to others to destroy me; amongst whom, was Judge [Austin A.] King, of the fifth Judicial circuit, who has frequently been heard to say that I ought to be beheaded on account of my religion. Expressions such as these, from individuals holding such important offices as Judge King's, could not fail to produce, and encourage persecution against me, and the people with whom I was connected. And in consequence of the prejudice which existed in the mind of this Judge, which he did not endeavor to keep secret, but made it as public as he could, the people took every advantage they possibly could, in abusing me, and threatening my life; re-

1. Lilburn W. Boggs (1798-1861).

gardless of the laws, which [p. 2] promise protection to every religious society, without distinction.

During this state of things I do not recollect that either myself, or the people with whom I was associated, had done any thing to deserve such treatment, but felt a desire to live at peace, and on friendly terms, with the citizens of that, and the adjoining counties, as well as with all men; and I can truly say, "for my love they were my enemies," and "sought to slay me without any cause," or the least shadow of a pretext.

My family was kept in a continual state of alarm, not knowing, when I went from home, that I should ever return again; or what would befall me from day to day. But notwithstanding these manifestations of enmity, I hoped that the citizens would eventually cease from their abusive and murderous purposes, and would reflect with sorrow upon their conduct in endeavoring to destroy me, whose only crime was in worshipping the God of heaven, and keeping his commandments; and that they would soon desist from harrassing a people who were as good citizens as the majority of this vast republic—who labored almost night and day, to cultivate the ground; and whose industry, during the time they were in that neighborhood, was proverbial.

In the latter part of September, A.D. 1838, I took a journey, in company with some others, to the lower part of the county of Caldwell, for the purpose of selecting a location for a Town. While on my journey, I was met by one of our brethren from Dewitt, in Carroll county, who stated that our people, who had settled in that place, were, and had been for some time, surrounded by a mob, who had threatened their lives, and had shot at them several times; and that he was on his way to Far West, to inform the brethren there, of the facts. I was surprised on receiving this intelligence, although there had, previous to this time, been some manifestations of mobs, but I had hoped that the good sense of the majority of the people, and their respect for the constitution, would have put down any spirit of persecution, which might have been manifested in that neighborhood.[1]

Immediately on receiving this intelligence, I made preparations to go to that place, and endeavor if possible, to allay the feelings of the citizens, and save the lives of my brethren who were thus exposed to their wrath. I arrived at Dewitt, about the first of October, and found that the accounts of the situation of that place were correct, for it was with much difficulty, and by travelling unfrequented roads, that I was able to get there; all the principal roads being strongly guarded by the mob, who refused all ingress as well as egress. I found my brethren, (who were only a handfull, in comparison to the mob, by which they were surrounded,) in this situation, and their provisions nearly exhausted, and no prospect of obtaining any more.

We thought it necessary to send immediately to the Governor, to inform him of the circumstances; hoping, from the Executive, to receive the protection which we needed, and which was guaranteed to us, in common with other citizens. Several Gentlemen of standing and respectability, who lived in the immediate vicinity, (who were not in any wise connected with the church of Latter Day Saints,) who had witnessed the proceedings of our enemies; came forward and made affidavits to the treatment we had received, and concerning our perilous situation; and offered their services to go and present the case to the Governor themselves. A messenger[2] was accordingly despatched to his Excellency, who made known to him our situation. But instead of receiving any aid whatever, or even sympathy from his Excellency, we were told that "the quarrel was between the Mormons and the mob," and that "we might

---

1. The strife in Carroll County, Missouri, is discussed in Gentry, "History of the Latter-day Saints in Northern Missouri," 194-212.

2. The messenger, A.C. Caldwell, of DeWitt, returned with his report on 9 October. (Smith, *History of the Church*, 3:157.)

fight it out." In the mean time, we had petitioned the Judges to protect us. They sent out about one hundred of the militia, under the command of Brigadier General [Hiram G.] Parks; but almost immediately on their arrival, General Parks informed us that the greater part of his men under Capt. [Samuel] Bogart had mutinied, and that he should be obliged to draw them off from the place, for fear they would join the mob; consequently he could afford us no assistance. [p. 3]

We had now, no hopes whatever, of successfully resisting the mob, who kept constantly increasing: our provisions were entirely exhausted and we being wearied out, by continually standing on guard, and watching the movements of our enemies; who, during the time I was there, fired at us a great many times. Some of the brethren died, for want of the common necessaries of life, and perished from starvation; and for once in my life, I had the pain of beholding some of my fellow creatures fall victims to the spirit of persecution, which did then, and has since prevailed to such an extent in Upper Missouri—men too, who were virtuous, and against whom, no legal process could for one moment, be sustained; but who, in consequence of their love to God— attachment to his cause—and their determination to keep the *faith,* were thus brought to an untimely grave.

Many houses belonging to my brethren, were burned; their cattle driven away, and a great quantity of their property destroyed by the mob. Seeing no prospect of relief, the Governor having turned a deaf ear to our entreaties, the militia having mutinied, and the greater part of them ready to join the mob; the brethren came to the conclusion to leave that place, and seek a shelter elsewhere; they consequently took their departure, with about seventy waggons, with the remnant of the property they had been able to save from their matchless foes, and proceeded to Caldwell. During our journey, we were continually harrassed and threatened by the mob, who shot at us several times; whilst several of our brethren died from the fatigue and privations which they had to endure, and we had to inter them by the wayside, without a coffin, and under circumstances the most distressing.

On my arrival in Caldwell I was informed by General [Alexander W.] Doniphan of Clay county, that a company of mobbers eight hundred strong, were marching towards a settlement of our people's in Daviess county. He ordered out one of the officers to raise a force and march immediately to what he called Wight's town and defend our people from the attacks of the mob, until he should raise the militia in his, and the adjoining counties to put them down. A small company of militia who were on their route to Daviess county, and who had passed through Far West, he ordered back again, stating that they were not to be depended upon, as many of them were disposed to join the mob; and to use his own expression, were "damned rotten hearted." According to orders Lieut. Colonel [George M.] Hinkle marched with a number of our people to Daviess county to afford what assistance they could to their brethren. Having some property in that county and having a house building there, I went up at the same time. While I was there a number of houses belonging to our people were burned by the mob, who committed many other depredations, such as driving off horses, sheep, cattle hogs &c. A number, whose houses were burned down as well as those who lived in scattered and lonely situations, fled into the town for safety, and for shelter from the inclemency of the weather, as a considerable snow storm had taken place just about that time; women and children, some in the most delicate situations, were thus obliged to leave their homes, and travel several miles in order to effect their escape. My feelings were such as I cannot describe when I saw them flock into the village, almost entirely destitute of clothes, and only escaping with their lives. During this state of affairs General Parks arrived at Daviess county, and was at the house of Colonel Lyman Wight, when the intelligence was brought, that the mob were burning houses; and also when women and children were fleeing for safety. Colonel Wight who held a commission in the 59th regiment under his (General Parks) command, asked what was to be done. He told him that he must immediately, call out his men and go and put them down. Accordingly, a force was immediately raised for the purpose of quelling the mob, and in a short time were on their march with a determination to drive the mob, or die in the attempt; as they could bear such treatment no longer. The mob having learned the orders of General Parks, and likewise being aware of the determination of the oppressed, they broke up their encampments and fled. The mob seeing that they could not succeed by force, now [p. 4] resorted to stratagem; and after removing their property out of their houses, which were nothing but log cabins, they actually set fire to their own houses, and then reported to the authorities of the state that the Mormons were burning and destroying all before them.

On the retreat of the mob from Daviess, I returned to Caldwell, hoping to have some respite from our enemies, at least for a short time; but upon my arrival there, I was informed that a mob had commenced hostilities on the borders of that county, adjoining to Ray co. and that they had taken some of our brethren prisoners, burned some houses and had committed depredations on the peaceable inhabitants. A company under the command of Capt. Patten, was ordered out by Lieutenant Col. Hinckle to go against them, and stop their depredations, and drive them out of the county. Upon the approach of our people, the mob fired upon them, and after discharging their pieces, fled with great precipitation, with the loss of one killed and several wounded. In the engagement Capt Patten, (a man beloved by all who had the pleasure of his acquaintance,) was wounded and died shortly after. Two others were likewise killed and several wounded. Great excitement now prevailed, and mobs were heard of in every direction who seemed determined on our destruction. They burned the houses in the country and took off all the cattle they could find. They destroyed cornfields, took many prisoners, and threatened death to all the Mormons. On the 28 of Oct. a large company of armed soldiery were seen approaching Far West. They came up near to the town and then drew back about a mile and encamped for the night. We were informed that they were Militia, ordered out by the Governor for the purpose of stopping our proceedings; it having been represented to his excellency, by wicked and designing men from Daviess, that we were the aggressors, and had committed outrages in Daviess &c They had not yet got the Governors orders of *extermination*, which I believe did not arrive until the next day. On the following morning, a flag was sent, which was met by several of our people, and it was hoped that matters would be satisfactorily arranged after the officers had heard a true statement of all the circumstances. Towards evening, I was waited upon by Colonel Hinckle who stated that the officers of the Militia desired to have an interview with me, and some others, hoping that the difficulties might be settled without having occasion to carry into effect the exterminating orders, which they had received from the Governor. I immediately complied with the request, and in company with Elders Rigdon and Pratt, Colonel Wight, and Geo. W. Robinson, went into the camp of the militia. But judge of my surprise, when instead of being treated with that respect which is due from one citizen to another, we were taken as prisoners of war, and were treated with the utmost contempt.[1] The officers would not converse with us, and the soldiers, almost to a man, insulted us as much as they felt disposed, breathing out threats against me and my companions. I cannot begin to tell the scene which I there witnessed. The loud cries and yells of more than one thousand

1. Hinkle later denied he had betrayed the Mormon leaders. (See letter of G.M. Hinkle to W.W. Phelps, 14 August 1844, published in S.J. Hinkle, "A Biographical Sketch of G.M. Hinkle," *Journal of History* 13 [October 1920]: 448-53.)

voices, which rent the air and could be heard for miles; and the horrid and blasphemous threats and curses which were poured upon us in torrents, were enough to appal the stoutest heart.[1] in the evening we had to lie down on thc cold ground surrounded by a strong guard, who were only kept back by the power of God from depriving us of life. We petitioned thc officers to know why we were thus treated, but they utterly refused to give us any answer, or to converse with us. The next day they held a court martial, and sentenced us to be shot, on Friday morning, on the public square, as an ensample to the Mormons. However notwithstanding their sentence, and determination, they were not permitted to carry their murderous sentence into execution.

Having an opportunity of speaking to General [Robert] Wilson, I inquired of him the cause why I was thus treated, I told him I was not sensible of having done any thing worthy of such treatment; that I had always been a supporter of the constitution and of Democracy. His answer was "I know it, and that is the reason why I want to kill you or have you killed." The militia then went into the town and without any restraint whatever, plundered the [p. 5] houses, and abused the innocent and unoffending inhabitants. They went to my house and drove my family out of doors. They carried away most of my property and left many destitute.— We were taken to the town, into the public square; and before our departure

1. Parley Pratt later described the arrest: "The haughty general rode up, and, without speaking to us, instantly ordered his guard to surround us. They did so very abruptly, and we were marched into camp surrounded by thousands of savage looking beings, many of whom were dressed and painted like Indian warriors. These all set up a constant yell, like so many bloodhounds let loose upon their prey, as if they had achieved one of the most miraculous victories that ever graced the annals of the world. If the vision of the infernal regions could suddenly open to the mind, with thousands of malicious fiends, all clamoring, exulting, deriding, blaspheming, mocking, railing, raging and foaming like a troubled sea, then could some idea be formed of the hell which we had entered." (Parley Pratt, Jr., ed., *Autobiography of Parley P. Pratt*, 186-87.)

from Far West, we, after much entreaties, were suffered to see our families, being attended all the while with a strong guard; I found my wife and children in tears, who expected we were shot by those who had sworn to take our lives, and that they should see me no more. When I entered my house, they clung to my garments, their eyes streaming with tears, while mingled emotions of joy and sorrow were manifest in their countenances. I requested to have a private interview with them a few minutes, but this privilege was denied me. I was then obliged to take my departure, but who can realize my feelings which I experienced at that time; to be torn from my companion, and leaving her surrounded with monsters in the shape of men, and my children too, not knowing how their wants would be supplied; to be taken far from them in order that my enemies might destroy me when they thought proper to do so. My partner wept, my children clung to me and were only thrust from me by the swords of the guard who guarded me. I felt overwhelmed while I witnessed the scene, and could only recommend them to the care of that God, whose kindness had followed me to the present time; and who alone could protect them and deliver me from the hands of my enemies and restore me to my family.

I was then taken back to the camp and then I with the rest of my brethren, viz: Sidney Rigdon, Hyram Smith, Parley P. Pratt, Lyman Wight, Amasa Lyman, and George W. Robinson, were removed to Independence, Jackson county. They did not make known what their intention or designs were in taking us there; but knowing that some of our most bitter enemies resided in that county, we came to the conclusion that their design was to shoot us, which from the testimony of others, I do think was a correct conclusion. While there, we were under the care of Generals [Samuel] Lucas and Wilson, we had to find our own board, and had to sleep on the floor with nothing but a mantle for our covering, and a stick of wood for our pillow. After remaining there a few days we were ordered by General [John B.] Clark to return; we were accordingly taken back as far as Richmond, and there we were thrust into prison and our feet bound with fetters. While in Richmond, we were under the charge of Colonel [Sterling] Price from Chariton county, who suffered all manner of abuse to be heaped upon us. During this time my afflictions were great, and our situation was truly painful.[1] After remaining there a few days we were taken before the court of inquiry, but were not prepared with witnesses, in consequence of the cruelty of the mob, who threatened destruction to all who had any thing to say in our favor: but notwithstanding their threats there were a few who did not think their lives dear so that they might testify to the truth, and in our behalf, knowing we were unlawfully confined; but the court who was predjudiced against us, would not suffer them to be examined according to law, but suffered the State's Attorney to abuse them as he thought proper. We were then removed to Liberty jail in Clay county, and there kept in close confinement in that place for more than four months.[2] While there, we petitioned Judge [Joel] Turnham for a writ of habeas corpus, but on account of the predjudice of the jailor all communication was cut off; at length however, we succeeded in getting a petition conveyed to him, but for fourteen days we received no answer. We likewise petitioned the other Judges but with no success. After the expiration of fourteen days Judge Turnham ordered us to appear before him, we went and took a number of witnesses, which caused us considerable expense and trouble; but he altogether refused to hear any of our witnesses. The lawyers

---

1. Parley Pratt's description of the imprisonment and court of inquiry at Richmond, Missouri, including a rebuke of the guards by Joseph Smith, is in Parley Pratt, Jr., ed., *Autobiography of Parley P. Pratt*, chapter 26. See also Joseph Smith to Emma Smith, 12 November 1838.

2. On Joseph Smith's Missouri imprisonment see Jessee, " 'Walls, Grates and Screeking Iron Doors'."

Liberty Jail, Liberty, Clay County, Missouri, c.1878. Photograph by J.T. Hicks. Photograph was given to Joseph F. Smith by Josie Schweich, granddaughter of David Whitmer. LDS Church Archives.

which we had employed refused to act; being afraid of the people. This being the case, we of course could not succeed, and were consequently remanded back to our prison house.— We were sometimes visited by our friends whose kindness and attention, I shall ever remember with feelings of lively gratitude, but frequently we were not suffered to have that privilege. Our victuals were of the coarsest [p. 6] kind, and served up in a manner which was disgusting. We continued in this situation, bearing up under the injuries and cruelties we suffered as well as we could, until we were removed to Daviess county, where we were taken in order to be tried for the crimes with which we had been charged. The grand jury (who were mostly intoxicated,) indicted us for treason, &c. &c.

While there, we got a change of venue to Boon county, and were conducted on our way to that place by a strong guard. The second evening after our departure the guard got intoxicated, we thought it a favorable opportunity to make our escape; knowing that the only object of our enemies was our destruction; and likewise knowing that a number of our brethren had been massacred by them on Shoal creek,[1] amongst whom were two children; and that they sought every opportunity to abuse others who were left in that state; and that they were never brought to an account for their barbarous proceedings, but were winked at, and encouraged, by those in authority. We thought that it was necessary for us, inasmuch as we loved our lives, and did not wish to die by the hand of murderers and assassins; and inasmuch, as we loved our families and friends, to deliver ourselves from our enemies, and from that land of tyrany and oppression, and again take our

1. Haun's Mill, a small Mormon community on Shoal Creek in Caldwell County, was attacked on 30 October 1838 by a large number of Missouri state militia under the command of Colonel Thomas Jennings. The attack, which left some seventeen Mormons dead, was marked by acts of vicious cruelty. (See LeSueur, *The 1838 Mormon War*, 162-68; Alma R. Blair, "The Haun's Mill Massacre," *BYU Studies* 13 [Autumn 1972]: 62-67.)

stand among a people in whose bosoms dwell those feelings of republicanism and liberty which gave rise to our nation: — Feelings which the inhabitants of the state of Missouri were strangers to. — Accordingly we took the advantage of the situation of our guard and took our departure, and that night we traveled a considerable distance. We continued on our journey both by night and by day, and after suffering much fatigue and hunger, I arrived in Quincy Illinois, amidst the congratulations of my friends and the embraces of my family.[1]

I have now resided in this neighborhood for several weeks as it is known to thousands of citizens of Illinois, as well as of the State of Missouri, but the authorities of Mo., knowing that they had no justice in their crusade against me, and the people with whom I was associated, have not yet to my knowledge, taken the first step towards having me arrested.

Amongst those who have been the chief instruments, and leading characters, in the unparallelled persecutions against the church of Latter Day Saints; the following stand conspicuous, viz: Generals Clark, Wilson, and Lucas, Colonel Price, and Cornelius Guilliam [Gilliam]. Captain Bogart also, whose zeal in the cause of oppression and injustice, was unequalled, and whose delight has been to rob, murder, and spread devastation amongst the Saints. He stole a valuable horse, saddle and bridle from me; which cost two hundred dollars, and then sold the same to General Wilson. On understanding this I applied to General Wilson for the horse, who assured me, upon the honor of a gentleman, and an officer, that I should have the horse returned to me; but this promise has not been fulfilled.

All the threats, murders, and robberies which these, officers

1. The escape of Joseph Smith and his fellow prisoners occurred on 15 April 1839 as they were traveling near Yellow Creek in Chariton County, Missouri. Joseph arrived at Quincy, Illinois, on 22 April. (Jessee, " 'Walls, Grates, and Skreeking Iron Doors'.")

have been guilty of, are entirely looked over by the Executive of the state; who, to hide his own iniquity, must of course shield and protect those whom he employed, to cary into effect his murderous purposes.

I was in their hands as a prisoner about six months, but notwithstanding their determination to destroy me, with the rest of my brethren who were with me; and although at three different times (as I was informed) we were sentenced to be shot, without the least shadow of law, (as we were not military men,) and had the time, and place appointed for that purpose; yet, through the mercy of God, in answer to the prayers of the saints, I have been preserved, and delivered out of their hands, and can again enjoy the society of my friends and brethren, whom I love: and to whom I feel united in bonds that are stronger than death: and in a state where I believe the laws are respected, and whose citizens, are humane and charitable.

During the time I was in the hands of my enemies; I must say, that although I felt great anxiety, respecting my family and friends; who were so inhumanly treated and abused; and who had to mourn the loss of the husbands and children, who had been slain; and after having been robbed of [p. 7] nearly all that they possessed be driven from their homes, and forced to wander as strangers in a strange country, in order, that they might save themselves and their little ones, from the destructions they were threatened with in Missouri; yet, as far as I was concerned, I felt perfectly calm, and resigned to the will of my heavenly Father. I knew my innocency, as well as that of the saints; and that we had done nothing to deserve such treatment from the hands of our oppressors: consequently, I could look to that God, who has the hearts of all men in his hands. and who had saved me frequently from the gates of death for deliverance: and notwithstanding that every avenue of escape seemed to be entirely closed, and death stared me in the face, and that my destruction was determined upon, as far as man was concerned; yet, from my first entrance into the camp, I felt an assurance, that I with my brethren and our families should be delivered. Yes, that still small voice, which has so often whispered consolation to my soul, in the depth of sorrow and distress, bade me be of good cheer, and promised deliverance, which gave me great comfort: and although the heathen raged, and the people imagined vain things, yet the Lord of hosts, the God of Jacob, was my refuge; and when I cried unto him in the day of trouble, he delivered me; for which I call upon my soul, and all that is within me, to bless and praise his holy name: For although I was "troubled on every side, yet not distressed; perplexed, but not in dispair; persecuted, but not forsaken; cast down, but not destroyed."[1]

The conduct of the saints under their accumulated wrongs and sufferings, has been praise-worthy; their courage, in defending their brethren from the ravages of mobs; their attachment to the cause of truth, under circumstances the most trying and distressing, which humanity can possibly endure; their love to each other; their readiness to afford assistance to me, and my brethren who were confined in a dungeon; their sacrifices in leaving the state of Missouri, and assisting the poor widows and orphans, and securing them houses in a more hospitable land; all conspire to raise them in the estimation of all good and virtuous men; and has secured them the favor and approbation of Jehovah; and a name, as imperishable as eternity. And their virtuous deeds, and heroic actions, while in defence of truth and their brethren: will be fresh and blooming; when the names of their oppressors shall either be entirely forgotten, or only remembered, for their barbarity and cruelty. Their attention and affection to me, while in prison, will ever be remembered by me; and when I have seen them thrust away, and abused by the jailor and guard, when they came to do any kind offices, and to cheer our minds while we were in the gloomy prison house, gave me feelings, which I cannot

1. 2 Corinthians 4:8-9.

describe, while those who wished to insult and abuse us, by their threats and blasphemous language, were applauded and had every encouragement given them.

However, thank God, we have been delivered; and although, some of our beloved brethren, have had to seal their testimony with their blood; and have died martyrs to the cause of truth; yet,

Short, though bitter was their pain,
Everlasting is their joy.

Let us not sorrow as "those without hope," the time is fast approaching, when we shall see them again, and rejoice together, without being affraid of wicked men: Yes, those who have slept in Christ, shall he bring with him, when he shall come to be glorified in his saints, and admired by all those who believe: but to take vengeance upon his enemies, and all those who obey not the gospel. At that time, the hearts of the widow and fatherless shall be comforted, and every tear shall be wiped from off their faces.

The trials they have had to pass through, shall work together for their good, and prepare them for the society of those, who have come up out of great tribulation; and have washed their robes, and made them white in the blood of the Lamb. Marvel not then, if you are persecuted, but remember the words of the Savior, "The servant is not above his Lord, if they have persecuted, me, they will persecute you also;"[1] and that all the afflictions through which the saints have to pass, are in fulfillment of the words of [p. 8] the prophets, which have spoken since the world began. We shall therfore do well to discern the signs of the times, as we pass along, that the day of the Lord may not "overtake us as a thief in the night."[2] Afflictions, persecutions, imprisonments and deaths, we must expect according to the scriptures, which tell us, that the blood

1. Matthew 10:24; John 15:20.
2. D&C 106:4.

of those whose souls were under the alter, could not be avenged on them that dwell on the earth, untill their brethren should be slain, as they were.[1]

If these transactions had taken place among barbarrians, under the authority of a despot; or in a nation, where a certain religion is established according to law, and all others proscribed; then there might have been some shadow of defence offered. But can we realize that in a land which is the cradle of Liberty and equal rights, and where the voice of the conquerors, who had vanquished our foes, had scarcely died away upon our ears, where we frequently mingled with those who had stood amidst the "battle and the breeze," and whose arms have been nerved in the defence of their country and liberty: whose institutions are the theme of philosophers and poets, and held up to the admiration of the whole civilized world. In the midst of all these scenes, with which we were surrounded, a persecution, the most unwarrantable, was commenced; and a tragedy, the most dreadful, was enacted, by a large portion of the inhabitants, of one of those free and independent States, which comprise this vast republic; and a deadly blow was struck at the institutions, for which our Fathers had fought many a hard battle, and for which, many a Patriot had shed his blood; and suddenly, was heard, amidst the voice of joy and gratitude for our national liberty, the voice of mourning, lamentation and woe. Yes, in this land, a mob, regardless of those laws, for which so much blood had been spilled, dead to every feeling of virtue and patriotism, which animated the bosom of freemen; fell upon a people whose religious faith was different from their own; and not only destroyed their homes, drove them away, and carried off their property, but murdered many a free born son of America. A tragedy, which has no parallel in modern, and hardly in ancient times; even the face

1. Revelation 6:9-11.

of the Red man would be ready to turn pale at the recital of it.

It would have been some consolation, if the authorities of the State had been innocent in this affair, but they are involved in the guilt thereof; and the blood of innocence, even of *children*, cry for vengeance upon them. I ask the citizens of this vast republic, whether such a state of things is to be suffered to pass unnoticed, and the hearts of widows, orphans and patriots, to be broken, and their wrongs left without redress? No! I invoke the genius of our constitution, I appeal to the patriotism of Americans, to stop this unlawful and unholy procedure; and pray that God may defend this nation from the dreadful effects of such outrages. Is there not virtue in the body politic? Will not the people rise up in their majesty, and with that promptitude and zeal, which is so characteristic of them, discountenance such proceedings, by bringing the offenders to that punishment which they so richly deserve; and save the nation from that disgrace and ultimate ruin, which otherwise must inevitably fall upon it?

JOSEPH SMITH JR.

HISTORY [1839 DRAFT]

MS. LDS Church Archives. This MS. is written on nine leaves of unlined paper measuring 16" × 12 1/2" folded to make an 8" × 12 1/2" document of thirty-six pages. A filing notation on the front, apparently in the hand of Willard Richards, reads "Early part of the history commencing with Joseph and Oliver's Baptism."

Editorial Note

Following the discontinuance of the 1834-36 History, two years elapsed before Joseph Smith again turned to the writing of his history. Beginning on 27 April 1838, less than two months after he had arrived at Far West, Caldwell County, Missouri, from Kirtland, Ohio, the Prophet, his counselors in the Presidency, and clerk George W. Robinson worked several days on a narrative that became the opening pages of the multivolume Joseph Smith *History of the Church*. (Diary of Joseph Smith, 27 April–4 May 1838.) Having resolved the question of format that had complicated previous attempts to write a history, the Prophet and his associates began the 1838 chronicle as an autobiographical narrative that eventually took the form of a daily journal – the whole work interspersed with copies of letters, revelations, and other documents inserted in their chronological sequence. (See Joseph Smith, *History of the Church*.)

The incomplete draft presented here was evidently written in Illinois in 1839 as a continuation of the work begun the previous year in Missouri. I have dated it 1839 instead of 1838 because it is in the handwriting of James Mulholland, and not George W. Robinson, who was the clerk assisting Joseph Smith during the work in April and May 1838 referred to above. According to Mulholland's diary, his tenure as scribe for the Prophet in Missouri did not begin until 3 September 1838, and it continued until 5 October that year. (Diary of James Mulholland, MS. LDS Church Archives.) The only known product of his work in Missouri is the sketchy diary he kept for Joseph during that time period. Joseph Smith's arrest and imprisonment beginning 31 October 1838 indicates a further improbability of involvement with Mulholland on the History until after the Prophet's arrival in Illinois in April 1839. When Mulholland resumed writing for Joseph Smith in Illinois the following year, he was specific in distinguishing between general clerical work and work on the History. His first reference to writing on the history was 10 June 1839. (See editorial note, pp. 266-267.)

This manuscript covers events in Joseph Smith's life and the early Church from the time of his baptism in May 1829 to the incident involving Hiram Page's seer stone in September 1830.

Immediately upon our coming up out of the water after we had been baptized,[1] we experienced great and glorious blessings from our Heavenly Father. No sooner had I baptized Oliver Cowdery than the Holy Ghost fell upon him and he stood up and prophecied many things which should ⟨shortly⟩ come to pass. And again so soon as I had been baptized by him, I also had the Spirit of prophecy when standing up I prophecied concerning the rise of this Church and many other things connected with the Church ~~of Christ~~ and ~~with~~ this generation of the children of men.[2] We were filled with the Holy Ghost, and rejoiced in the God of our Salvation. Our minds being now enlightened, we began to have the Scriptures laid open to our understandings, and the true meaning and intention of their more mysterious passages revealed unto us, in a manner which we never could attain to previously, nor ever before had thought of. In the mean time ~~however~~ we were forced to keep ⟨secret⟩ ~~these things entirely secret in our bosoms, viz:~~ the cir-

1. Because beginning pages of this manuscript have not survived, the account fails to give the setting in which the events being described took place. In his finished draft of this history, Joseph Smith notes that while translating the Book of Mormon at Harmony, Pennsylvania, in 1829, the question of baptism came up, whereupon he and Oliver Cowdery went a short distance into the woods to pray and inquire of the Lord. In response to their petition, a heavenly messenger appeared "in a cloud of light," declaring himself to be John the Baptist. The messenger conferred upon them the priesthood of Aaron and instructed them to baptize each other. See pp. 290-291.

2. Oliver Cowdery's description of this experience is on pp. 30-32.

cumstances of our having been baptized and having received this ~~Aaronic~~ priesthood ~~And this on account of~~ ⟨owing to⟩ a spirit of persecution which had ~~been~~ ⟨already⟩ manifested in the neighborhood, ~~for some time previous,~~ We had been threatened with being mobbed, from time to time and this too by professors of religion, and their intentions of mobbing us, were only counteracted by the influence of my wife's father's family,⟨(under Divine Providence)⟩ who had became very friendly to me and were opposed to mobs, and were willing that I should be allowed to continue the work of translation[1] without interruption: and therefore offered and promised us protection from all unlawful proceedings, as far as in them lay. After a few days however feeling it to be our duty we commenced to reason, out of the Scriptures, with our acquaintances and friends, as we happened to meet with them. About this time my brother Samuel H. Smith came to visit us. We ~~soon~~ informed him of what the Lord was [p.[1]] about to do for the Children of men, and to reason with him out of the Bible, we also showed him that part of the work which we had translated, and laboured to persuade him concerning the Gospel of Jesus Christ which was now about to be revealed in its fullness. He however was not very easily persuaded of these things, but after much enquiry and explanation he retired to the woods, in order that by secret and fervent prayer he might obtain of a merciful God, wisdom to enable him to judge for himself: The result was that he obtained revelation for himself sufficient to convince him of the truth of our assertions to him, and on the [*blank space*] day of that same month[2] in which we had been baptized and ordained, Oliver Cowdery baptized him, and he returned to his father's house greatly glorifying and praising God, being filled with the Holy Spirit. Not many days afterwards, my brother Hyrum Smith came to us to en-

1. Written over "translating."
2. Samuel H. Smith was baptized on 25 May 1829.

quire concerning these things when ~~upon~~ ⟨at⟩ his earnest request, I enquired of the Lord through the Urim and Thummin,[1] and received for him the folowing.

Revelation given to Hyrum Smith, at Harmony, Susquehana County, Pensylvania May, 1829.

Book of Covcnants pagc 167[2]

About the same time, ~~with my brother Hyrum~~ came an old gentleman to visit us. of whose name I wish to make honorable mention; Mr Joseph Knight Senr. of Colesville, Broom County, Pen, who having heard of the manner in which we were occupying our time, very kindly and considerately brought us, a quantity of provisions, in order that we might not be interrupted in the work ⟨of translation⟩ by the want of such necessaries of life. And I would just mention [p.[2]] here (as in duty bound) that he several times after wards brought us supplies, (a distance of ⟨at⟩ least thirty miles) which enabled us to continue the work, when otherwise we must have relinquished it for a season. Being very anxious to know his duty, as to this work, I enquired of the Lord for him, and obtained as follows.

Revelation given to Joseph Knight Senr. at Harmony, Susquehana County Pensylvania May 1829.

Book of Covenants Page 169[3]

Shortly after ~~my having~~ commencing[4] to translate, I became

---

1. Joseph Smith stated that "through the medium of the Urim and Thummim" he translated the Book of Mormon "by the gift and power of God." (See p. 431.) The term *Urim and Thummim* has occasionally been used to refer to a stone or stones used to translate or impart the word of God. (See Richard Van Wagoner and Steve Walker, "Joseph Smith: 'The Gift of Seeing,' " *Dialogue* 15 [Summer 1982]: 49-68.)

2. This and following references in this manuscript are to the first edition of the Doctrine and Covenants, published in 1835 at Kirtland, Ohio. See current edition of the Doctrine and Covenants section 11.

3. See D&C 12.

4. Written over "commenced."

acquainted with ~~the f~~ Mr Peter Whitmer ~~Senr~~ of ⟨Fayette⟩ Seneca County, New York and also with ⟨some of⟩ his family. In the beginning of the month of June, his Son David Whitmer came to the place where we were residing, ⟨and brought⟩ with ⟨him⟩ a two horse waggon, for the purpose, of ~~prevailing upon~~ ⟨having⟩ us — ~~to~~ accompany him to his father's place, ⟨and there remain untill we finished the work⟩ He proposed that we should have[1] our board free of charge, and the assistance of one of his brothers to write for me, as also his own assistance when it might answer. Having much need of such timely aid in ~~such~~ an undertaking so arduous, and being informed that the people in the neighborhood were anxiously waiting ~~to g~~ the opportunity to enquire into these things. We ~~consented~~ accepted the invitation, and accompanied Mr Whitmer to his father's house,[2] and there ~~remained~~ ⟨resided⟩ untill the translation was finished, and the copy right secured. Upon our arrival, we found Mr Whitmer's family very anxious concerning the work, and very friendly towards ourselves. They continued so, boarded and lodged us according to ~~the~~ proposal, and John Whitmer, in particular, assisted [p.[3]] us very much in writing ~~&c~~ during the remainder of the work, ~~The family in [-]~~ in the mean time ~~however~~ David, John and Peter Whitmer became ~~very zealous in the cause~~ ⟨our zealous friends and assistants in the work,⟩ and ⟨being⟩ anxious to know their respective duties, and ⟨having⟩ desired with much earnestness that I should enquire of the Lord concerning them I did so through the means of the Urim and Thummin and obtained for them the following revelations in succession.

---

1. Written over "go."

2. Joseph Smith arrived at the Whitmer home near Fayette, New York, from Harmony, Pennsylvania, in June 1829.

The Whitmers had moved to the Fayette area from Pennsylvania between 1807 and 1809. For detail on the Whitmer family in Seneca County see Porter, "Origins of the Church," chapter 6.

3 revelations, Book of Covenants Page 169[1]

We found the people ~~in~~ ~~general~~ ~~of Fayette~~ of Seneca Co. in general, friendly, and disposed to enquire in to the truth of these strange matters, which now began to be noised abroad. Many opened their houses ⟨to us,⟩ in order that we might have an opportunity of meeting with their friends for the purpose of instruction, and explanation. We met with many willing to hear us, and wishful to find out the truth as it is in Christ Jesus, and apparently willing to obey the ~~truth~~ ⟨Gospel⟩ when once, fairly convinced and satisfied in their own minds; and in this same month ~~(June)~~ of June, My Brother Hyrum Smith, ~~and~~ David Whitmer and Peter Whitmer Jr were baptized, the two former by myself, and the latter by Oliver Cowdery. From this time forth, many became believers, and were baptized whilst we continued to instruct and persuade as many as ~~expressed desires~~ applied for information, ~~[. . . .]~~, In the course of the work of translation, ⟨~~we~~⟩ ~~became~~ we ascertained that three[2] ~~work~~ especial witness[es] were to be provided by the Lord, to whom he would grant, that they should ~~have a~~ see the plates from which this work, (The Book of Mormon) should be translated, and that these witness[es] should bear ~~testimony of the same publickly to~~ record of the same [p.[4]] as will be found recorded Book of Mormon Page [*blank space*] second Edition and Page [*blank space*] first edition—[3] ~~almost~~ So soon as we had made this discovery, it ⟨almost immediately⟩ occurred to, Oliver Cowdery David Whitmer and the aforementioned Martin Harris who had come to see us, and make inquiry how we got along with our work of translation; that they would have me enquire of the Lord, to know if they might not obtain

1. D&C 14, 15, 16.
2. Written over "this."
3. References to witnesses in the first edition of the Book of Mormon are in the Second Book of Nephi, Chapter 8, p. 86; and Ether, Chapter 2, p. 548. In the current edition see 2 Nephi 11:3 and Ether 5:2-4.

of him to be allowed to be these three witnesses and ~~at length~~ ⟨finally⟩ they became so very solicitous, and teazed me so much almost without intermission for some time, that I at length complied, and through the Urim and Thummin I obtained ⟨of the Lord⟩ for them the folowing

Revelation to Oliver Cowder[y] &c,
Book of Covenants Page 171[1]

Not many days after the above revelation was given, we four, viz. Martin Harris, ⟨David Whitmer⟩ Oliver Cowdery and myself, agreed to retire into the woods, and try to obtain by ~~faithful, and~~ fervent and humble prayer, the fulfillment of the promises given in this revelation (that they should have a view of the plates &c,) We accordingly made choice of a ~~retired~~ piece of woods convenient to ~~Fat~~ Mr Whitmer's house to which we retired and, having knelt down, we began to pray in much faith, to Almighty God, to bestow upon us a realization of those promises. ~~It was deci had been arranged by us pre~~ According to previous arrangement, I commenced by vocal prayer to our Heavenly Father, ~~and in suce~~ and was followed by each of the—~~other three~~ ⟨rest⟩ in succession, we however did not yet receive any answer or manifestation of the divine favour in our behalf. We again observed the same order of prayer each calling on and praying fervently to God in regular rotation. but with the same ⟨unbeneficial⟩ result as before. Upon our again failing, Martin Harris proposed that he should withdraw himself from us believing, as he expressed himself, that his presence was the cause of our not obtaining the object [p.[5]] of our desires at that time. He accordingly withdrew from us, and we k[n]elt down again, and had not been many minutes engaged in prayer when presently we beheld a light above us in the air of exceeding brightness and behold an angel stood before us; in his hands he held the plates which we had been

1. D&C 17.

praying ~~to God to~~ ⟨for those to⟩ have a view of. he turned over the plates one by one so that we could see them, and discern the engravings thereon distinctly, He addressed himself to David Whitmer, and said ~~unto him~~ "David, blessed is ~~God~~ ⟨The Lord⟩ and ~~all those who~~ ⟨he that⟩ keeps his commandments." When immediately afterwards we heard a voice from out ⟨of⟩ the bright light above us, saying "these plates have been revealed by the power of God, and they have been translated by the power of God, the translation of them which you have seen is correct, and I command you to bear record of ~~the truth thereof.~~ ⟨what you now see and hear⟩ ~~Immediately afterwards~~ I ⟨now⟩ ~~left these two,~~ [left] David, and Oliver, and went in pursuit of Martin Harris, whom I found at a considerable distance fervently engaged in prayer, he soon told me however that he had not yet prevailed with the Lord, and earnestly requested of me, to join him in prayer, ~~to the intention~~ that he also might realize the same blessings, which we had just received. We now joined in prayer, and obtained our desires, for before we had yet finished, the same vision was opened to our view~~(~~ at least it was, again to me, and I once more beheld ⟨and heard⟩ the same things. whilst at the same moment, Martin Harris cried out apparently in an extasy of Joy, " 'tis enough. 'tis enough mine eyes have beheld, mine eyes have beheld", and jumping up he shouted Hosanna, ~~and~~ blessed God, and otherwise rejoiced excceedingly. Having thus, through the mercy of God, obtained ~~to~~ these glorious manifestations,[1] it now remained [p.[6]] for those three individuals to fulfill the commandment which they had received to bear record of these things, in order to accomplish which they drew up and subscribed their names to the folowing document.

---

1. Personal descriptions of their experience by Oliver Cowdery, David Whitmer, and Martin Harris are given in Richard L. Anderson, *Investigating the Book of Mormon Witnesses* (Salt Lake City: Deseret Book Company, 1981), chapters 4, 6, and 8.

The Testimony of three witnesses.

Soon after these things had transpired the following testimony was obtained from those whose names are subscribed thereto.

"And also the Testimony of Eight Witnesses"[1]

~~During all this time however~~ ⟨Meantime⟩ we continued to translate, ⟨at intervals⟩ when ~~we were~~ not necessitated to attend to the ⟨numerous⟩ enquirers[2] ~~of the numbers~~ that now began to visit us, some for the sake of finding the truth, others for the purpose of putting hard questions, and trying to confound us, ~~we had several~~ among the~~se~~ latter class ⟨were⟩ several learned Priests, ~~to visit us,~~ generally for the purpose of disputation. However the Lord continued to pour out upon us his Holy Spirit and as often as we had need, he gave us in that moment what to say, so that although, unlearned, and inexperienced in religious controversies, yet were we able to confound these learned Rabbi's of the day, whilst at the same time we were enabled, to convince the honest in heart, that we had obtained to the true & everlasting gospel of Jesus Christ, so that almost daily we administered the ordinance of baptism for the remission of sins to such as believed. We now became anxious to have that promise ~~which conferred upon~~ ⟨realized to⟩ us, which the angel ~~had~~ that conferred upon us the Aaronick Priesthood ~~upon us,~~ had given us, viz, that provided we continued faithful, ~~the~~ we should also have the Melchesidec Priesthood, which holds the authority of the laying on of hands for the gift of the Holy Ghost. [p.[7]] We had for some time made this a subject of humble prayer, and at length we got together in the Chamber of Mr Whitmer's house in order more particularly to seek of the Lord information, and if possible obtain

1. The testimony of the witnesses was published at the end of the first edition of the Book of Mormon. Their testimony introduces the text in modern editions.

2. Written over "enquiries."

what we now so earnestly desired. ~~We had not been long~~ After some time spent in solemn and fervent prayer, the word of the Lord came unto us, in the Chamber, commanding us, that I should ordain Oliver Cowdery to be an Elder in the Church of Jesus Christ, and that he also should ordain me to the same office,[1] and that after having been thus ordained, we should ~~th~~ proceed to ordain others to the same office, according as it should be made known unto us, from time to time, ~~We~~ also commanding us, that as soon as practicable we should call together all those who had already been baptized by us, to bless bread, and break it with them, also to take wine, bless it, and drink it with them doing all these things in the name of the Lord, but to defer our own ordination untill we had called ~~the Chur~~ together our brethren and had their sanction, and[2] been accepted by them as their teachers, after which we were commanded to proceed to ordain each other and ~~then~~ call out such men as the spirit should dictate unto us, and ordain them, and then attend to the laying on of hands for the Gift of the Holy Ghost,[3]

The following commandment will further illustrate the nature of our calling to this Priesthood as well as others who were yet to be sought after.

Revelation Page 172[4]

We continued to receive instruction concerning our duties from time to time, and among ~~the~~ many things the folowing directions, fixing the time of our anticipated meeting together ⟨for the purpose of being organised⟩ were given by the Spirit of prophecy and revelation

---

1. On the dating and circumstances surrounding the Melchizedek Priesthood restoration see Larry C. Porter, "Dating the Melchizedek Priesthood," *Ensign* 9 (June 1979): 5-10; William G. Hartley, "Upon You My Fellow Servants," in *The Prophet Joseph*, edited by Porter and Black, 55-57.

2. Written over "th."

3. Additional detail pertaining to the meeting at Whitmers' is in the Joseph Smith letter of 4 September 1842. See D&C 128:21.

4. D&C 18.

Exchange Row, site of Egbert B. Grandin Printing Office, Book Bindery, Bookstore and Circulating Library, Palmyra, Wayne County, New York, c.1907. The printing office where the Book of Mormon was published was located on the third floor. George E. Anderson Collection. LDS Church Archives.

Section 2nd[1] [p.[8]]

Mean time our translation drawing to a close, we went to Palmyra, and agreed there ⟨with Mr⟩ Egbert Granden to print ~~and publish~~ five thousand ⟨copies⟩ for three thousand Dollars, and about this time secured the copy right.[2] I would mention here also in order to correct a misunderstanding, which has gone abroad concerning the title page of the Book of Mormon, that it is not a composition of mine or of any other man's who has lived or does live in this generation, but that it is a literal translation taken from the last leaf of the plates, on the left hand side of the collection of plates, the language running same as ~~the~~ ⟨all⟩ Hebrew writing ~~language~~ in general. And that no error can henceforth possibly exist I give here the Title so far as it is a translation.

Title Page—
Revelation page 174[3]

Whilst the Book of Mormon was in the hands of the printer, we still continued to bear testimony ~~and preach~~ to such as would hear as far as we had opportunity. ~~And~~ ⟨We⟩ made known also to those ~~-~~ who had already been baptized, that we had received commandment to organize the Church ⟨Revelation Page 177—[4]: and accordingly ⟨we⟩ met to gether, ⟨(being ~~about 30~~ ⟨six⟩ in number) besides a number who were beleiving —[5]

1. D&C 20. The problem of the sequence and dating of section 20 is treated in David J. Whittaker, "The 'Articles of Faith' in Early Mormon Literature and Thought," in *New Views of Mormon History*, edited by Bitton and Beecher, 64-65.

2. The copyright was obtained 11 June 1829.

3. D&C 19.

4. D&C 21.

5. There are several different lists of those comprising the six. See Richard L. Anderson, "Who Were the Six Who Organized the Church on 6 April 1830?" *Ensign* 10 (June 1980): 44-45. Anderson identifies seven lists produced by Joseph Smith, Brigham Young, Joseph Knight, Jr., and David Whitmer. Another list is given by William McLellin in *The Ensign of Liberty of the Church of Christ*, 1 (March 1847): 2. Brigham Young, Joseph Knight, and David Whitmer all name Joseph Smith, Oliver Cowdery, Hyrum Smith, and Samuel H. Smith; Brigham Young and William McLellin both name Joseph Smith, Sr.; McLellin is the only one to include Joseph's mother, Lucy Smith.

met with us⟩ on Tuesday the Sixth day of Aprile ~~in the year of our~~ A.D. ~~A thousand E~~ One thousand, Eight hundred and[1] thirty, and proceeded, as follows, at the house of the above mentioned Mr. Whitmer—[2] Having opened the meeting by solemn prayer to our Heavenly Father ⟨and the ~~meeting Ch~~ brethren & Sisters having by unanimous vote, accepted us as &c⟩ I proceeded to lay my hands upon Oliver Cowdery—and ordained him an Elder of the Church of Jesus Christ of Latter Day Saints, after which he ordained me also to the office of an Elder of said Church. We then took bread, blessed it, & brake it with them, also wine, blessed it, and drank it with them. We then laid our hands on each individual member of the Church present, to confirm them members of the Church of Jesus Christ, and that they might receive the Holy Ghost, when immediately the Holy Ghost was poured out upon ~~the~~

1. Written over "&."

2. Early Church sources are contradictory on the site of the 6 April 1830 Church organization. Some, including the Book of Commandments, chapters 17-22 (D&C 23, 21), give the location as Manchester, Wayne County, New York; others, such as the *Evening and Morning Star*, May 1834, 160, follow the traditional text here, designating the Whitmer home in Fayette, Seneca County, New York. The problem may stem from clerical errors in early sources and imprecise methods of copy editing, the time lapse between the event and the recording of it, and the definition of what constituted church organization in the minds of those who first wrote about it. David Whitmer's 1887 statement may help clarify the discrepancy: "Now, when April 6, 1830 came, we had then established three branches of the 'Church of Christ,' in which three branches were about seventy members: One branch was at Fayette, N.Y.; one at Manchester N.Y., and one at Colesville, Pa. It is all a mistake about the church being *organized* on April 6, 1830, as I will show. We were as fully *organized*—spiritually—before April 6th as we were on that day. The reason why we met on that day was this; the world had been telling us that we were not a regularly organized church, and we had no right to officiate in the ordinances of marriage, hold church property, etc., and that we should organize according to the laws of the land. On this account we met at my father's house in Fayette, N.Y. on April 6, 1830, to attend to this matter of organizing according to the laws of the land." (David Whitmer, *An Address to All Believers in Christ* (Richmond, Missouri, 1887), 33; see also Richard L. Anderson, "The House Where the Church Was Organized," *Improvement Era* 73 [April 1970]: 16-25; John K. Carmack, "Fayette: The Place the Church Was Organized," *Ensign* 19 [February 1989]: 14-19; Hartley, "Upon You My Fellow Servants," 57-60.)

~~whole community~~ us all ~~in a miraculous manner~~ ⟨to a greater or less degree.⟩ Some [p.[9]][1] prophecied, ~~many spoke with new tongues, and some ⟨several⟩ of our number were ⟨so⟩ completely overpowered for a time, that we were obliged to lay them upon beds &c &c, and when bodily sensibility was restored to them they shouted Hosannas to God and the Lamb—& declared that the Heavens had been opened unto them, ⟨especialy N Knights⟩ that they had seen Jesus Christ sitting at the right hand of the Majesty on high, and many other great and glorious things. Either at this time or very shortly after was the following were ⟨with others⟩ called to the priesthood & ordained to the respective offices, according as the Spirit made it manifest, viz Joseph Smith Senior, Hyrum Smith, John Whitmer, Peter Whitmer, Christian Whitmer Samuel Smith, Martin Harris.~~

We afterwards called out and ordained ~~Several~~ ⟨some others⟩ of the brethren to the respective offices of the Priesthood, according as the Spirit made manifest unto us. ⟨ ~~Revelation~~ ⟩ As may reasonably ⟨be⟩ expected, such scenes as these were calculated, to inspire our hearts with Joy unspeakable, at the same time that we felt ourselves almost over whelmed, with awe and reverence for that Almighty Being, by whose grace we had been called to be instrumental in bringing about for the Children of men, the enjoyment of such glorious blessings, as were now at this time poured out upon us. To find ourselves engaged in the very same order of things which were observed by the Holy Apostles of old, To realize the importance and solemnity of the above mentioned proceedings, and to witness ⟨& feel⟩ with our own natural senses, the like glorious manifestions of the powers of the Priesthood; the gifts and blessings of the Holy Ghost, ~~which we had often read of as a things~~ and the goodness and grace of a merciful God, unto such as obey the

1. At the bottom of page 9 and continuing along the bottom of page 10 is this note: "Father Smith Martin Harris baptized this evening 6th April. [p.[9]] Mother Smith & Sister Rockwell 2 or 3 days afterward." [p.[10]]

everlasting gospel of our Lord Jesus Christ, combined to create within us sensations of rapturous gratitude, which may be felt, but ~~whi~~ cannot be described.

After a considerable time spent in such ⟨a⟩ happy manner, we dismissed; with the pleasing knowledge, that we now individually were members of—and had been acknowledged of God, The ~~organized~~ Church of Jesus Christ, organized in [p.[10]] accordance with commandments and revelations given by him to ourselves, in these last days; as well as according to the order of the Church of Christ, as found recorded in the New Testament.

Several persons who attended this meeting, but who had ⟨not⟩ as yet been baptized, came forward shortly after, and were received into the Church having on that occasion got entirely convinced of the truth of the work. Among the rest Father Smith, Martin Harris Mother Smith.

Revelation page 176[1]—& Revelation 178[2]

On Sunday April 11th 1830, ~~Oliver Cowdery preached~~ ⟨we held a public meeting by appointment at⟩ ~~Mr~~ Whitmer's Fayette Seneca Co. N.Y., when Oliver Cowdery preached the first ⟨real⟩ public sermon, which was delivered by any ⟨member⟩ ~~Elder~~ of our Church, we had a crowded audience, and the same day he baptized the following persons viz: Hiram Page Katharine Page, Christian Whitmer, Anne Whitmer, Jacob Whitmer, & Elizabeth Whitmer and Mary Page, and on the 18th of said month Peter Whitmer Senr. Mary Whitmer, William Jolly Elizabeth Jolly—Vincent Jolly—Richd B. [Ziba] Peterson, and Elizabeth Ann Whitmer. ~~Jun 1rst Conference June 10th 1830 David Whitmer baptized John Poorman, John Jolly Julia Anne~~

1. D&C 23.
2. D&C 22.

Photograph of a reconstructed early nineteenth-century cabin at the site of the original Peter Whitmer, Sr., home in Fayette, Seneca County, New York. Place where the Church was organized.

~~Jolly and Harriett Jolly—Jerushee Smith, Kathrine Smith—Wm Smith, Don C. Smith, Porter Rockwell, Caroline Rockwell and Electa Rockwell, The last eleven were all baptized in Seneca lake—~~

During this month of ~~June~~ ⟨April⟩, I went ~~in company with Oliver Cowdery~~ ⟨on a visit⟩ to the residence of Mr Joseph Knight's—of Colesville—Broom Co. N.Y with whom I had been forme[r]ly well acquainted, as well as with his family and in the Neighborhood generally—Mr Knight & his family were Universalists—but were as usual glad to see ~~us~~ ⟨me⟩ and very friendly and willing to reason on the subject of religion, We held several meetings in the neighborhood, we had many friends and some enemies—our meetings were well ⟨attended⟩ however, and many began to pray fervently to Almighty God to give them wisdom to understand the truth; Among those who attended our meetings regularly, was Newel Knights, son to Joseph Knights, He and I had frequent conversations on this important subject of the plan of man's eternal salvation, we had got into the habit of praying much at our meetings [p.[11]] and Newel had ~~said~~ promised me on a certain day, that he would that evening take up his cross and pray vocally in the meeting the same evening — The evening came and the meeting was held, but when ~~it came to~~ Newel~~s~~ was asked to pray, he begged to be excused. I tried to prevail upon him and encourage him to pray ~~when he brought up as figure the following, "Suppose that a man travelling along the road, sho~~ he replied that when he got out in the woods by himself he should there take up his cross. I endeavored to persuade him that where so many were ~~there,~~ ready & willing to assist him there was the place for him to pray — and that for my part I would & could help him by my faith, provided he would only, make an attempt to pray. He now brought up the follow[ing] figure, suppose I should be traveling along the road & through carelessness get into a mudhole and a number of men came along, it is natural to expect, that I should be so much ashamed that I would rather wait untill they would go past & then try to get out myself.– To this I replied that provided he should get into a situation of the kind~~, [..]nd~~ that it was most likely he would require help, but that no person would help him out of a mud hole, unless he would show a willingness to assist himself also. All arguments were however useless, he deferred praying untill next morning—when he then retired into the woods, where according to his own account afterwards he made several attempts to pray, but could scarcely do so, feeling as he said, that he had not done his duty, but that he should have taken up his cross in the presence of others, he began to feel uneasy and felt worse both in mind and body, untill upon reaching his own house, his appearance was such as to alarm his wife very much—he requested her to go and bring me to him, I went and found him suffering very much in his mind, and his body acted upon in a most strange manner, His visage and limbs distorted & twisted into every possible shape and appearances, and finally he was caught up off the floor of the apartment and tossed about most fearfully. his situation was soon made known to his neighbors and relatives and in a short time as many as eight or nine grown persons had got together to witness the scene. After he had thus suffered for some time, I succeeded in getting hold of him by the hand, when almost immediately he was able to speak, and requested with great earnestness that I should cast the Devil out of him, that [p.[12]] he knew that he was in him, and that he also knew that I could cast him out, I replied "If you know that I can, it shall be done". And almost unconsciously I ~~commanded~~ rebuked the Devil, and commanded him ~~to leave him~~ in the name of Jesus Christ to depart from him. When immediately Newel spoke out and said that he saw the Devil leave him and vanish from his sight—⟨This was the first miracle wrought in this Church⟩ The scene was now entirly changed, for ~~very~~ ⟨as⟩ soon as the Devil, had departed, from this our friend his countenance became natural, his distortions of body ceased, and almost immediately the Spirit of God descended upon him, to such a degree that the visions of eternity were opened to his view and he beheld great and glorious things—he afterward related his experience of this as follow[s], "I now began to feel a most pleasing sensation resting upon me, and immediately the visions of Heaven were opened to my view. I felt ⟨myself⟩ attracted ⟨up⟩wards ~~it,~~ and remained for some time enwrapt ~~in the~~ ⟨in⟩ contemplation in so much that I knew not what was going on in the room, but by and by I felt some weight pressing upon my shoulder and the side of my head, which served to recall me to a sense of my situation—and I found that the Spirit of the Lord had actually lifted me off the floor, ~~and that I had removed the floor of the Chamber above,~~ and that my shoulder & head were pressing against the beams"

All this was witnessed by many to their great astonishment, and satisfaction when the[y] Saw the Devil thus Cast out of a human being and the power of God and His Holy Spirit thus made manifest. So soon as consciousness returned, his bodily weakness was such that we were obliged to put him to bed, and wait upon him some time. As may be expected such a scene as this contributed much to make believers of those who witnessed it, and the greater part finally became members of the Church.

I soon after returned to Fayette Seneca Co-- and as the Book of Mormon had now been for some time published,[1] we found quite enough to occupy our time. No small stir was created by its appearance great opposition, much persecution, to those who believed in its authenticity was generally the case—but on the other hand, many were friendly and anxious to hear so that we continued to preach and give information

1. The first notice of publication of the Book of Mormon appeared in the *Wayne County Sentinel* (Palmyra, New York), 26 March 1830. After publishing the title page, under the heading "The Book of Mormon," the paper reported, "The above work, containing about 600 pages, large Duodecimo, is now for sale, wholesale and retail, at the Palmyra Bookstore, by Howard & Grandin."

as far as in our power, ~~On the day in which the Church~~ [p.[13]] ~~was organized, we had agreed to hold a conference of the Church the first day of June following~~

~~About~~ ⟨During⟩ the last week of May the above mentioned Newel Knights came to visit us at Fayette and was baptized by ~~Oliver Cowdery~~ David Whitmer.

On the First day of June the Church met in conference according to appointment made on the day of our organization.[1] Our numbers being about thirty, many however attended who were either believing or wishful to hear. Having opened by singing and prayer, we partook together of the emblems of the body and blood of our Lord Jesus Christ. We then ⟨called out &⟩ ordained Several to ~~the~~ various offices in the Church, and proceeded to confirm a number who had been lately baptized,– The Holy Ghost was poured out upon us in a miraculous manner, many of our number prophecied, others had the heavens opened to their view, and whilst several were so overcome that we had to lay them on beds, &c. Amongst the rest, was ~~the aforementioned~~ Brother Newel Knights, who was overcome, and laid on a bed because he was unable to help himself–according to his own relation of his experience,[2] He could not understand why we laid him on the bed, he felt ⟨no sensibility of weakness⟩ ~~strong~~, his heart ⟨was⟩ filled with Love, Glory & pleasure unspeakable, and could (as he thought) discern all that was going on in the room, when all of a sudden, a vision of the futurity burst upon him, He saw there ⟨represented⟩ the great work which through my instrumentality was

1. The date of this conference was 9 June 1830. The meeting was held in the Whitmer log home in Fayette, New York, where the Church had been organized on 6 April. Minutes of this first conference are recorded in the Far West Record. (Donald Q. Cannon and Lyndon W. Cook, eds., *Far West Record: Minutes of The Church of Jesus Christ of Latter-day Saints, 1830-1844* [Salt Lake City: Deseret Book Company, 1983], 1-2.)

2. The Diary of Joseph Smith, 4-5 July 1839, dates Newel Knight's contribution and indicates he was probably the source for the text in this part of the manuscript.

yet to be accomplished, He saw Heaven opened and beheld the Lord Jesus Christ, sitting [at] the right hand of the majesty on high, and had it made plain to his understanding that the time would come when he should be admitted into his presence to enjoy his society for ever and ever, When their bodily strength returned to them, they shouted Hosannas to God, and the Lamb, & rehearsed the glorious things which they had seen and felt, whilst yet in the spirit. (Comments upon the whole we had a [*remainder of [p. [14]] blank*]

[*Top of page blank*]

About this time David Whitmer baptized the following viz: John Poorman, John Jolly, Julia Anne Jolly—and Harriette Jolly Jerushee Smith Kathrine Smith Wm Smith, Don C. Smith—Porter Rockwell—Caroline Rockwell and Electa Rockwell in Seneca Lake.

Immediately after the conference, I ⟨thence returned to my own house & farm⟩ (in company with my wife) Oliver Cowdery—John Whitmer—& David Whitmer) ~~returned~~ journeyed ⟨again⟩ on a visit to Mr Knights, Broom Co. We found a number in the neighborhood still believing and now anxious, to be baptized, accordingly we appointed a meeting on the ⟨next⟩ Sabbath day,[1] intending to attend to the ordinance. On the afternoon previous, we had erected a dam across a stream in order to form a place for baptism, but during the night a mob collected (at the instigation of sectarian Priests of the neighborhood) and tore away our dam, which hindered our intentions of baptizing those who wished at this time. We however held our meeting, Oliver Cowdery preached, & many of us bore record & testimony to the truth of the book of Mormon, the doctrine of repentance, &c. Amongst our Audience were those who had torn down our dam the night previous, & seemed wishful to give us trouble, but did not untill after our meeting

1. 27 June 1830.

had been dismissed, when they immediately commenced talking to those who they considered our friends—to try to turn them against us and our doctrines. [p.[15]]

⟨And⟩ a young woman ⟨named Emily Coburn [Colburn]⟩ a sister in law to Newel Knight was ~~forcibly~~ taken upon a power of attorney, and ⟨forcibly⟩ carried out of the neighborhood because her relations understood her to be in the way of believing our doctrine. Early however on Monday morning[1] we wer[e] on the alert, and got together ~~quite early in th~~ before our enemies were aware we soon repaired the dam, and proceeded to baptize—when the following thirteen persons were baptized for the remission of their sins under the hands of Oliver Cowdery. viz: Emma Smith, Hezekiah Peck & wife,[2] Joseph Knight~~s~~ & wife[3] William Stringham & wife[4] Joseph Knight~~s~~ Jr Aron Culver & wife[5] Levi Hale [Hall],[6] Polly Knight, ⟨&⟩ Julia Stringham.

Before we had yet finished the baptism of these, the same mob began again to collect together, and shortly after we had done and retired to the house of Joseph Knight, the mob ~~had~~ amounted to about fifty men. They now surrounded the House, raging with anger, and apparently wishful to commit violence upon us, some of them asked questions, others threatened us, and annoyed us so much that we thought it wisdom to leave and go to the house of Newel Knight. They followed us there also, and it was with great perseverance and prudence that we were enabled to keep them in bounds ~~untill we succeeded in confirming those who had been baptized, some~~ ⟨Numbers⟩ of the brethren had to constantly keep the door and keep

1. 28 June 1830.
2. Martha Long Peck.
3. Polly Peck Knight.
4. Esther Knight Stringham.
5. Esther Peck Culver.
6. That is, Levi Hall. Newel Knight in his diary refers to Levi Hall, which is substantiated by the Windsor, Broome County, New York census.

them in talk, ⟨&⟩ answer their various and unprofitable questions, so long as they were inclined to stay. I talked to them considerable, but in general to no purpose. We had appointed a meeting on the evening of the same day, for the purpose of confirmation, the time appointed had arrived and our friends had nearly all collected together, when to my surprise I was visited by a constable, and arrested by him, on ⟨a⟩ warrant on a charge of being a disorderly person,[1] of setting the country in an uproar by preaching the Book of Mormon, and various other such like charges. The constable informed me soon after he had arrested me that the plan of those who had got out this warrant, was to get me into the hands of the mob who were now lying in ambush[2] for me [p.[16]] but that he was determined to save me from them, as he had found me to be a different kind of person, from what had been represented to him. We ~~got into~~ had a waggon to travel in and ~~he~~ soon found that he had told me the truth in this matter, for not far from Mr Knight's house the waggon was surrounded by the mob, who seemed only to await some signal from the constable, but to their great disappointment—he gave the horse the whip, ~~and left them far behind~~ and drove me out of their reach, however whilest we were driving pretty quickly along one of our wheels came off, which left us very nearly once more in their power, as they were in close pursuit, however we managed to get the wheel on again, and once more left them behind, he drove on to ⟨a town⟩ which was then called south Bainbridge, ⟨in Chenango Co⟩ where he lodged me for the time being in an upper room in a Tavern there, and in order that all might be right with me, and himself also, he slept ~~all~~ during the night,

1. A bill by Constable Ebenezer Hatch, dated 4 July 1830, totaling $2.37 1/2 for serving a warrant on Joseph Smith, keeping him twenty-four hours, and subpoenaing five witnesses, is in the courthouse at Norwich, Chenango County, New York. The bill identifies the constable and helps date the hearing. (Bushman, *Joseph Smith and the Beginnings of Mormonism*, 160-61.)

2. MS.: "anbust."

with his feet against the door, and a loaded musket by his side whilst I occupied a bed, which was [in] the room. have[ing] declared that if we were interrupted, he would fight for me and defend me as far as in his power.

A court was here convened on the [*blank*] day of [*blank*] for the purpose of investigating those charges which had been preferred against me.[1] A great excitement prevailed, on account of the scandalous falsehoods which had been circulated, the nature of which will come out in the sequel. In the mean time as soon as Mr. Joseph Knights had heard of my arrest, he immediately repaired to two of his neighbours respectable farmers ⟨viz: Esq. James Davidson and John Reed men⟩ renowned for their integrity and well versed in the laws of their country, and retained them on my behalf in the coming trial. At length the trial commenced amidst a multitude of spectators who in general evinced a belief that I was guilty of all that had been ~~hatched~~ reported concerning me. and of course were very zealous that I should be punished, according to my crimes—Mr Josiah Stoal, ⟨among many witnesses⟩ (of whom I have heretofore spoken) was called up and ~~examined,~~ ⟨questioned nearly⟩ as follows, Did not the prisoner Joseph Smith have a horse of you? Ansr. Yes, Did ⟨not⟩ he go to you and tell you, that an angel had appeared unto him, and authorized him to get the horse from you. Answer No, he told me no such story [p.[17]] Well! How[2] had he the horse of you? ⟨Ans⟩ He bought him of me, as another man would do. Q. Have you had your pay? Ansr. That is not your business. The question being again put, the witness replied, I hold his note for the price of the horse, which I consider as good as the pay—for I am ⟨well⟩ acquainted with him and know him to be an honest man, and

1. The day following his arrest, Joseph Smith was brought before Justice Joseph Chamberlain on complaint of being a "disorderly person." According to Chamberlain's bill, the hearing took place on 1 July 1830, and twelve witnesses were called. (Bushman, *Joseph Smith and the Beginnings of Mormonism*, 161.)

2. "how" repeated in MS.

if he wishes—I am ready to let him have another horse on the same terms. Mr. Jonathan Thompson was next called up, and examined. Question, Has not Joseph Smith, the prisoner had a yoke of oxen of you, Ansr. Yes, Did he not ⟨obtain them by⟩ telling you that he had a revelation to the effect that he was to have them? Ansr. No, he did ⟨not⟩ mention a word of the kind concerning the oxen, he purchased them, same as another man would. After a few more such attempts, the court was ~~adjourned untill~~ ⟨detained for a time⟩ in order that two young[1] women ⟨(daughters to Mr Stoal)⟩[2] might be sent for, with whom I had often kept ⟨~~often~~⟩ company; in order if possible to elicit something from them that might be made a pretext against me. The court again sat, and the ⟨young⟩ Ladies were ⟨separately⟩ examined touching my Character, Conduct, ~~and~~ in general, but particularly as to my behaviour towards them, both in public and in private. When they both bore such testimony in my favor as left my enemies without a pretext on their account. Several attempts were now made to prove something against me, and even circumstances which ⟨were alleged to have⟩ had taken place in Broom Co were brought forward, but which my lawyers would not admit of being here brought against me. In order therefore that I should if possible be made [to] appear guilty of something. The Court was detained over untill a warrant was obtained from Broom County. and served upon me just immediately after I had been acquitted and set at liberty by this court. The Constable who served this warrant, had no sooner done so than he began to abuse and insult me, and so unfeeling was he with me, that although, I had been kept all the day in court with out anything to eat since the morning yet he hurried me off to Broom County, a distance of about

1. "you" written before "young" in MS.
2. Probably Rhoda and Miriam Stowell.

15 miles before he allowed me time ⟨to⟩ eat anything. [p.[18]][1] About this time we were over against my own house, I wished to be allowed to go home for the night ⟨offering security for safety⟩ but would not [–]. He then took me to a Tavern, and gathered in a number of men who used every means to abuse, ridicule, and insult me. They spit upon me, pointed their fingers at me, saying to me, prophesy–prophesy, and in many ⟨other~~s~~⟩ ways did the[y] insult me. I applied for something to eat, The constable ordered me some crusts of bread and some water which was the only fare I that night received~~; and I at length got some respite from my persecutors, being furnished with a bed in the second story of the house.~~ At length the constable and I retired to bed, he made me lie next the wall, and he lay down beside me, ~~and lest I might escape, he~~ ⟨and⟩ put his arms around me, and upon my moving in the least, would clench me fast, fearing I intended to escape from him:[2]

Next day I was brought before the Magistrate's Court of Broom Co, and put upon my trial. My former faithful friends and lawyers were again at my side, my former persecutors were again arrayed against me. ~~Among the latter was one Mr Seymour a zealous professor and advocate of the presbyterian creed, who had made himself conspicuous against me, and had been all along ⟨both⟩ during the former and present trial~~

---

1. Unrelated to the text here, the following lines appear at the top of p. 19 of the MS. in the handwriting of Frederick G. Williams:

"Scriptures on Covenants
Genesis

IX Section 20th and 21 Par 28th Par.
X Section 12 Paragraph, –
XI Section 5th Paragraph, – 8 Par. 9th Par 10th Par – 11th Par."

Since p. 19 is part of the center fold of the leaves upon which this History is written, it appears that prior to using these pages for the present document, they were briefly intended for another purpose. Folded in the opposite direction, the right side of the center page would have been the first page of another work. Lined in pencil, p. 19 is the only page so marked in the otherwise unlined manuscript.

2. At this point in the manuscript, the notation "Burch, a lawyer for the prosecution" is set off from the rest of the text with an encircling line.

Many witnesses were again called forward and examined. Some of whom swore to the most palpable falsehoods, and like to the false witnesses which had appeared against me on the former trial, they contradicted themselves, so plainly that the court would not admit their testimony, ~~and after using~~ Others were called who ~~proved~~ shewed by their zeal that they were willing enough to prove something against me, but all they could do, was to ~~prove~~ tell somethings which some body else had told them, in this frivolous and vexatious manner did they proceed for a considerable [p.[19]] time, when finally, Newel Knight was called up ~~for~~ ⟨and⟩ examined by Lawyer [William] Seymour,[1] (who was a Presbyterian, ⟨and (who had been especially sent for on this occasion —⟩ and had shown great zeal, lest the people should be deluded by me, and false doctrines propagated in the neighborhood.) to the following effect. What is your name? Ansr. Newel Knight. Did the prisoner Joseph Smith, Cast the Devil out of you? ⟨Ansr⟩ No sir — Why have not you had the Devil cast out of you? Ansr. Yes Sir. And had not Joe Smith some hand in its being done? Ansr. Yes Sir. And did not he cast him out of you? Ansr. No Sir, it was done by the power of God, and ~~he was~~ Joseph Smith was the instrument made use of on the occasion, He commanded him out of me in the name of Jesus Christ. And are you sure that it was the Devil? Ansr. Yes Sir. Did you see him after he was cast out of you? Ansr. Yes sir, I saw him — Pray, what ⟨did⟩ he look like? (Here one of my lawyers, informed the witness that he need not answer the question) The witness replied, I believe I need not answer your last question, but I will do it provided I be allowed to ask you one question first, and you answer me. Viz: Do you Mr Seymour ~~profess~~ understand the things of the

1. Referring to the Joseph Smith Colesville hearing, John S. Reed said the prosecution employed the "ablest lawyer" in the county. ("Some of the Remarks of John S. Reed, Esq., as Delivered Before the State Convention," *Times and Seasons* 5 [1 June 1844]: 551.)

Spirit? Ans. No I do not pretend to such big things. Well then said Knight, 'Twould be of no use to tell you, what the Devil looked like. for it was a Spiritual sight, and of course you would ⟨not⟩ understand it, were I to tell you of it. The lawyer dropped his head, whilst the loud laugh of the assembled ~~audience~~ ⟨multitude⟩ proclaimed his discomfiture. Mr Seymour now addressed the Court, and in a long & violent harangue endeavored to blacken my character, and bring me out guilty of the charges which had been brought against me, among other things, he brought up the story of my having been a money digger and in this manner proceeded in hopes to influence the Court and the people against me. ~~My Lawyers followed in my behalf~~ Mr Davidson and Mr Reed followed in my behalf. ~~They showed~~ [p.[20]] they held forth in its true colors, the nature of the prosecution, the malignancy of intention, and apparent disposition to persecute their client, rather than to afford him justice. They took up the different arguments which had been brought by the Lawyers for the prosecution and having shewed their utter futility & misapplication. then ~~tok~~ proceeded to scrutinize the evidence which had been adduced, and ⟨each⟩ in his turn, thanked God that he had been engaged in so good a cause as that of defending t~~he Character (cause) of~~ a man, whose character stood so[1] well the test of such a~~n~~ scrutinizing enquiry. In fact these men (although not regular lawyers) were upon this occasion ~~en~~able~~d~~ to put to silence their opponents—and convince the court that I was innocent. They spoke like men inspired of God, whilst the~~ir~~ lawyers who were arrayed against me, trembled under the~~ir~~ sound of their voice, and quailed before them like criminals before a bar of Justice. The majority of all[2] who had attended, had now began to find that nothing could be sustained against me. Even the Constable who had arrested me and who had treated me so badly—now came and

1. Written over "the."
2. Written over "the."

apologized to me, and asked my forgiveness of his behaviour towards me. and so far was he changed that he informed me, that the mob were determined; that if the court acquitted me, that they would have me, and rail ride me and tar & feather me, and further told me that he was willing to favor me so, that he would lead me out in safety by a private way.

The court finding the charges against me not sustained—~~acqu~~ I was acquitted to the great satisfaction of my friends and vexation of my enemies; who were now once more set for me, but through the instrumentality of my new friend the Constable I was enabled to escape them, and make my way in safety to my wife's sister's house. where I found my wife—with whom I next day returned home to my own house.

~~Af~~ After some few days however, Oliver Cowdery and myself again returned to Colesville for the purpose of confirming those whom we had [p.[21]] thus been forced to abandon for a time. We had scarcely however arrived at Mr Knights when the mob was seen collecting together to oppose us, and we considered it wisdom to leave for home, which we did without having waited even to refresh ourselves, by something to eat. our enemies pursued us, and it was often times as much as we could do to elude them, however we managed to get home, after having traveled all night, except a short time which we were forced to rest ourselves under a large tree by the wayside, sleeping and watching alternately. And thus were we persecuted on account of ⟨our⟩ religious faith—in a country the Constitution of which guarantees to every man the indefeasable right to worship God according to the dictates of his own conscience. and by men too who were professors of religion, and who were not backward to maintain this right for themselves, though they thus wantonly could deny ⟨it to⟩ us. ~~the same privilege~~ for instance one ⟨Cyrus⟩ McMaster, a presbyterian of high standing in his Church, was one of the chief instigators of these persecutions, and told me personally ⟨~~[—]~~⟩ that he believed me culpable without Judge or Jury. The celebrated Doctr. [Nathan] Boynton,[1] ⟨also presbyterian⟩ was another instigator of the business. And a young man ⟨named [Abram Willard] Benton &⟩ of the same ⟨religious⟩ Faith swore out the first warrant ~~John Whitmer now came to live with me and write for me.~~ against me,

~~Revelation Page 111 & Page 178 & Page 179~~

Notwithstanding however all the rage of our enemies, still we had much consolation, and many things occurred to strengthen our faith, and cheer our hearts amidst our trials and persecutions. after we had returned home after our trial, the Church at Colesville, were, as might be expected, very anxious concerning our again visiting them, during which time, Sister Knight, (wife to Newel Knight)[2] had a dream which enabled her to say that we would ~~soon~~ visit them that day, which really came to pass, for a few hours after she had told her dream we arrived and thus was our faith much strengthened, concerning the things of the last days mentioned by the Prophet Joel—of dreams & visions—[3]

After our return to my ⟨own⟩ house as above mentioned, we received the following Revelations,

Rev page 111—page 179 page 178—[4]

Shortly afterwards, Oliver Cowdery returned to Mr Whitmer's, and[5] John Whitmer (who was now living with me) and myself began to arrange & copy the revelations and commandments which we had received from time [p.[22]] ~~Septer 1rst we met in general conference of the Church—at Mr Whitmers Fayette~~ to time from our Heavenly Father, which engaged our attention for some time. Whilst thus (and otherwise at

1. MS. reads "Boyington."
2. Sally Colburn Knight (1804-1834).
3. Joel 2:28-29.
4. D&C 24, 26, 25.
5. "and" written over "house."

intervals) employed in the work appointed me by my great Creator, I received a letter from Oliver Cowdery, the contents of which gave me both sorrow and uneasiness. Not having that letter now in my possession I cannot of course give it here in full but merely an extract, of the most prominent part, which I can yet; and expect long to remember. It was ~~as follows.~~ to the effect that, he had discovered an error, in one of the commandments, see book of Covenants Section 2nd paragraph 7th[1] "and truly manifest by their works that they have received of the Spirit of Christ unto the remission of their Sins." the above quotation he said was erroneous, and ⟨added I⟩ commanded~~ed~~ you in the name of God, To erase those words from that commandment, "that no priestcraft be amongst us."

I immediately wrote to him in reply, in which I asked him, by what authority he took upon him to command me to alter or erase, to add or diminish to or from a revelation or commandment from the Almighty God.

I shortly after paid him a visit when I found that he had persuaded Father Whitmer and most of the family that the above was an error—And it was with great difficulty, and much labour that I prevailed with any of them to reason calmly on the subject, however Christian Whitmer at length got convinced that it was reasonable and according to scripture and finally with his assistance I succeeded ⟨in⟩ bringing not only all the Whitmer family but also Oliver himself to acknowledge that they had been in error & that the above quotation was in accordance with the rest of the commandment. Early in the

1. D&C 20:37. Cowdery's reaction to an alteration in this revelation is best understood in light of his own involvement in its composition. An 1829 revelation to Cowdery, written in his own hand, commands him to write "the articles of the Church of Christ" and contains segments now published in section 20. Hence, an alteration to the document might have violated his sense of propriety in this instance. (See Whittaker, "The 'Articles of Faith' in Early Mormon Literature and Thought," 64-65; and Woodford, "The Historical Development of the Doctrine and Covenants," 286-351. The 1829 Cowdery revelation is transcribed in Woodford.)

month of August Newel Knights and his wife paid us a visit at our place in Harmony. Neither his wife nor mine had been as yet confirmed, and it was proposed that we should ⟨have sacrament together &⟩ confirm them; before he & his wife should leave us. ~~and that we~~

In order to prepare for these things I set out—to go to procure some wine for the occasion. I had however gone but a short distance when I was met by a heavenly messenger, and had the following revelation. the first paragraph of which was written at this time, & the remainder in Septer following

Page 179[1] [p.[23]]

Agreeable to this revelation we prepared some wine of our own make, ~~and~~ ⟨and⟩ held our meeting which consisted only of five; viz: Newel Knight & wife myself & wife and John Whitmer. We partook together of the sacrament after which we confirmed the two sisters into the Church, and spent the evening in a glorious manner. The Spirit of the Lord was poured out upon us and we praised God & rejoiced exceedingly.

About this time[2] a ~~bitter~~ spirit of persecution began to ⟨be⟩ manifested towards us in the neighborhood where I resided—and was commenced & originated by a man of[3] the Methodist persuasion, who professed to be a minister of God.[4] He came to understand that my Father in law was friendly and enquiring earnestly into the work, and knowing that if he could ⟨get⟩ him and his family turned against me, my friends in that place would be few, accordingly he went to him and told him false-hoods, of the most shameful nature which turned them en-

1. D&C 27.
2. August 1830.
3. "of" written over "who"
4. A leader of the opposition against Joseph Smith in Harmony, Pennsylvania, was Nathaniel C. Lewis, brother-in-law of Isaac Hale, and "the pioneer Methodist" in that area. (Porter, "Origins of the Church," 169-70.)

tirely against me insomuch that he would not so much as visit us or give us any more protection &c &c—

Towards the latter end of August, I (in Company with John & David Whitmer, and my brother Hyrum Smith) visited the Church at Colesville, N.Y. Well knowing the determined hostility of our enemies in that quarter and also knowing that it was our duty to visit the Church ⟨we⟩ had called upon our Heavenly Father in mighty prayer, that he would grant us an opportunity of meeting with ~~the Church~~ them, that he would blind the eyes of our enemies so that they would not know us,~~ on this occasion,~~ & that we might ⟨on⟩ this ~~time~~ ⟨occasion⟩ ~~escape~~ ⟨return⟩ unmolested.

Our prayers were not in vain, for when ~~Saturday afternoon~~ ⟨within a little⟩ distance of Mr Knight's place, we encountered a large company working at the public road, among whom were many of our most bitter enemies they looked earnestly at us, but not knowing us, ~~then left us our course clear and we arrived~~ ⟨we passed on without interruption.⟩ We that evening assembled the Church, and confirmed them, partook of the sacrament, and held a happy meeting, having much reason to rejoice in the God of our Salvation and sing Hosannas to his holy name. Next morning we set out on our return home, and although our enemies had offered a reward of five dollars, to any one who would let them know of the arrival of Joe Smith, yet did we get clear out of the Neighborhood, without the least annoyance. and without our enemies having heard of our— ~~arrival~~ ⟨visit⟩ at all, and arrived at home in safety. Some few days afterwards however Newel Knight came to my place when we learnt from him, that very shortly after our departure the mob had heard of our having been there, when the[y] immediately collected together and had threatened the brethren and very much annoyed ⟨them⟩ during all that day, Meantime Brother Knight had came prepared ⟨with his waggon⟩ to move me and my wife ~~out of this neighborhood~~ to Fayette N.Y. [p.[24]] Mr Whitmer having invited us to go and live with him, on account of the great persecution which had ⟨been⟩ got up against us, at Harmony Pa. We arrived at Fayette, during the last week of August, amidst the congratulations of our brethren and friends.

To our great grief however we found that Satan had been, lying in wait to deceive, and seeking whom he might devour. Brother Hyram Page had got in his possession a certain stone ⟨by⟩ which he obtained to certain revelations concerning the upbuilding of Zion the order of the Church and so forth, but which were entirely at variance with the order of Gods House, as it is laid down ~~both in ancient and our modern~~ in the scriptures. and our own late revelations.

As a conference meeting had been appointed for the 1rst September I ~~did~~ ⟨thought it wisdom⟩ not to do much more than converse with the brethren on the subject untill the conference ~~was~~ ⟨should be⟩ held. Finding however that many of the brethren (especially the Whitmer family and Oliver Cowdery) were believing much in the things which were set forth by this stone, a few of us got together and succeeded in obtaining the following revelations, which gave us much information on that & other subjects connected with our respective duties.

Rev page 181 – and page 112[1]

Conference at length assembled,[2] the subject of the Stone &c was brought up, and after considerable discussion, reasoning and investigation Hyrum agreed to renounce the stone and its author, and the brethren unanimously agreed to renounce them also – We now partook of sacrament – confirmed and ordained many, and attended to a great variety of Church business ~~during~~ ⟨on⟩ that and the following day. During which

1. D&C 28, 29.
2. Minutes of this conference, dated 26 September 1830, are published in Cannon and Cook, *Far West Record*, 3.

time we had much of the power of God manifested, The Holy Ghost poured out upon us and obtained the following revelations –

page 182 & page 183[1] [p.[25]]

1. D&C 30, 31.

HISTORY, 1839

MS. History of the Church, A-1, pp. 1-240, Joseph Smith Papers, LDS Church Archives, Salt Lake City.

A scrap of paper different from the pages of the MS. has been attached with sealing wax inside the front cover, with the words: "In Memory of Alvin Smith Died the 19th Day of November In the 25 year of his age year 1824 Joseph Smith Joseph In Memory of Alvin S" The writing appears to be that of Hyrum Smith. A "3" has been written over the "4" in different ink correcting the year of Alvin's death.

Editorial Note

The manuscript of Joseph Smith's History presented here is the finished version of the preceding draft. In addition, it includes the text of the beginning missing pages of that manuscript and also material that continued beyond it.

The manuscript of the History in six volumes, some 2,300 pages, of which the text here is the first 240 pages, was published serially between 1842 and 1858, beginning in the *Times and Seasons* in Nauvoo, Illinois, and continuing in England and Utah in the *Millennial Star* and *Deseret News*. In 1880, extracts from the first eighteen pages were included in the corpus of LDS scripture as part of the *Pearl of Great Price*, when that work was canonized at the October general conference of the Church. The installments of the History that had appeared in the Church newspapers over sixteen years were finally brought together, edited, and published as the Joseph Smith *History of the Church* in six volumes between 1902 and 1912 by the Church historian, Brigham H. Roberts. (See Searle, "Early Mormon Historiography.")

Work began on this manuscript in 1839 after Joseph Smith had arrived in Illinois from Missouri. He and his clerk, James Mulholland, took the large volume containing the aborted 1834-36 History material, turned the book over so the back became the front cover of the new

Owing to the many reports which have been put in circulation by evil disposed and designing persons in relation to the rise and progress of the Church of Jesus Christ of Latter day Saints, all of which have been designed by the authors thereof to militate against its Character as a Church, and its progress in the world I have been induced to write this history so as to disabuse the publick mind, and put all enquirers after truth into possession of the facts as they have transpired in relation both to myself and the Church as far as I have such facts in possession.

In this history I will present the various events in relation to this Church in truth and righteousness as they have transpired, or as they at present exist, being now the eighth year since the organization of said Church. I was born in the year of our Lord One thousand Eight hundred and five, on the twenty third day of December, in the town of Sharon, Windsor County, State of Vermont. My father Joseph Smith Senior left the State of Vermont and moved to Palmyra, Ontario, (now Wayne) County, in the State of New York when I was in my tenth year.

In about four years after my father's arrival at Palmyra, he moved with his family into Manchester in the same County of Ontario. His family consisting of eleven souls, namely, My Father Joseph Smith, My Mother Lucy Smith whose name previous to her marriage was Mack, daughter of Solomon Mack, My brothers Alvin (who died Nov 19th 1823 in the 25 year of his age) Hyrum, Myself, Samuel Harrison, William, Don Carloss, and my Sisters Sophonia, Cathrine and Lucy. Sometime in the second year after our removal to Manchester, there was in the place where we lived an unusual excitement on the subject of religion. It commenced with the Methodists, but soon became general among all the sects in that region of country, indeed the whole district of Country seemed affected by it and great

History, 1839, A-1, p. 1 (numbering from back of book).
Handwriting of James Mulholland.

history, and began writing. Labeled "A-1," the volume became the first of six, continued consecutively to "F-1," that would contain the complete manuscript of the documentary History of the Church.

The History begins as an autobiographical narrative and eventually merges into a journal format based primarily on the text of Joseph Smith's diaries. Included in the narrative are copies of correspondence, revelations, and other documents in their chronological order. Mulholland wrote that he "commenced again to write for the Church" on 22 April 1839. On 10 June he noted that Joseph Smith "began to study and prepare to dictate history," and the following day "commenced to dictate and I [Mulholland] to write history." (Diary of James Mulholland.) As indicated in the editorial note to the previous manuscript, the 10 June dictation may refer to a continuation of that manuscript which was then recopied into the present form.

Only the beginning autobiographical portion of volume A-1 is given here. This material covers Joseph Smith's experience from his birth to the point where his first diary becomes the basis for the text of the History on 27 November 1832. Since the revelations were not included by Mulholland in the preceding draft and are part of an intended later publication of the Joseph Smith papers, the text of the revelations in volume A-1 is not included here. As in the preceding draft, the reader is referred instead to the published revelations in the current edition of the Doctrine and Covenants.

/[1]Owing to the many reports which have been put in circulation by evil disposed and designing persons in relation to the rise and progress of the Church of ⟨Jesus Christ of⟩[2] Latter day Saints, all of which have been designed by the authors thereof to militate against its character as a church, and its progress in the world; I have been induced to write this history so as to disabuse the publick mind, and put all enquirers after truth into possession of the facts as they have transpired in relation both to myself and the Church as far as I have such facts in possession.

In this history I will present the various events in relation

1. James Mulholland handwriting.

2. Insertion in different ink and handwriting than surrounding text; probably Willard Richards.

to this Church in truth and righteousness as they have transpired, or as they at present exist, being now the eighth year since the organization of said Church. I was born in the year of our Lord One thousand Eight hundred and five, on the twenty third day of December, in the town of Sharon, Windsor County, State of Vermont. ⟨see page Note A 131⟩[1] My father

---

1. This insertion and the note it refers to are in the handwriting of Willard Richards. They were added in December 1842 after Richards began assisting Joseph Smith as a secretary. The material that constitutes note "A" is found on pp. 131-32 of the History manuscript:

"When I was 5 years old or thereabouts I was attacked with the Typhus Fever, and at one time, during my sickness, my father dispaired of my life. The Doctors broke the fever, after which it settled under my shoulder & ~~the Dr.~~ ⟨Dr. Parker⟩ caled it a sprained shoulder & anointed it with bone ointment, & freely applied the hot shovel, when it proved to be a swelling under the arm which was opened, & discharged freely, after which the disease removed & desended into my left Leg & ancle & terminated in a fever sore of the worst kind, and I endured the most acute suffering for a long time under the care of Drs Smith, Stone & Perkins, of Hanover.

At one time eleven Doctors came from ~~the~~⟨Dartmouth⟩ medical college, at Hanover New Hampshire, for the purpose of amputation, but, young as I was, I utterly refused to give my assent to the operation, but I consented to their Trying an experiment by removing a ⟨large portion⟩ ~~great~~ of the bone from my left leg, which they did, & fourteen additional peices of bone afterwards worked out before my leg healed, during which time I was reduced so very low that my mother could carry me with ease, & after I began to get about I went on crutches till I started for the State of New York ⟨where⟩ ~~In the mean time~~ my father had gone ~~to the State of New York~~ for the purpose of preparing a place for the removal of his family, which he affected by sending a man after us by the name of Caleb Howard, who, after he had ~~got~~ started on the Journey with my mother & family spent the money he had rec[e]ived of my father in drinking & gambling &c.— We fell in with a family by the name of Gates who were travelling west, & Howard drove me from the waggon & made me travel in my weak state through the snow 40 miles per day for several days, during which time I suffered the most excrutiating weariness & pain, & all this that Mr Howard might enjoy the society of two of Mr Gates' Daughters which he took on the waggon where I should have Rode, & thus he [p. 131] continued to ⟨do⟩ day day after day through the Journey, & when my brothers remonstrated with Mr Howard for his treatment to me, he would knock them down with the butt of his whip.— When we arrived at Utica, N. York Howard threw the Goods out of the waggon into the street & attempted to run away with the Horses & waggon, but my mother seized the horses by the reign[s], &, calling witnesses forbid his taking them away as they were her property. On our way from Utica I was left to ride on the last ~~waggon~~ ⟨sleigh⟩ in the company, ⟨(the Gates family were in sleighs)⟩ but when that came

Joseph Smith Senior ⟨see Note E page 2. adenda. My Father⟩[1] left the State of Vermont and moved to Palmyra, Ontario, (now Wayne) County, in the State of New York when I was in my tenth year. ⟨or thereabouts.⟩[2]

In about four years after my father's arrival at Palmyra, he moved with his family into Manchester in the same County of Ontario. His family consisting of eleven souls, namely, My Father Joseph Smith, My Mother Lucy Smith whose name previous to her marriage was Mack, daughter of Solomon Mack, My brothers Alvin (who ⟨died Nov. 19th: 1823 in the 25 year of his age.⟩[3] ~~is now dead~~) Hyrum, Myself, Samuel-Harrison, William, Don Carloss, and my Sisters Soph[r]onia, Cathrine and Lucy. Sometime in the second year after our removal to Manchester, there was in the place where we lived an unusual excitement on the subject of religion. It com-

---

up I was knocked down by the driver, one of Gate's sons, & left to wallow in my blood until a stranger came along, picked me up, & carried me to the Town of Palmyra.– Howard having spent all our funds My Mother was compelled to pay our landlords bills from Utica to Palmyra, in bits of cloth, clothing &c the last payment being made with the drops [earrings] taken from sister Sophron[i]a's ears, for that purpose. Although the snow was generally deep through the country during this Journey we performed the whole ⟨on⟩ ~~except~~ wheels, except the first two days, when we were accompanied by My Mothers mother, Grandmother, ⟨Lydia Mack⟩ who was injured by the upsetting of the sleigh, & not wishing to accompany her friends west, tarried by the way with her friends in Vermont, & we soon after heard of her death supposing that she never recovered from the injury received by the overturn of the sleigh." (In the above insertion, "Lydia Mack" is in another hand and ink. A parallel account of Joseph Smith's leg operation is his mother's report in Lucy Smith, *Biographical Sketches*, 62-66; see also, LeRoy S. Wirthlin, "Joseph Smith's Boyhood Operation: An 1813 Surgical Success," *BYU Studies* 21 (Spring 1981): 131-54.)

1. Insertion in the hand of Willard Richards.

2. This insertion is in the handwriting of Willard Richards.

Addendum, note E, page 2, in an unidentified hand, following page 553 of the text of this manuscript, contains this note on Joseph Smith's ancestry: "Joseph Smith ⟨Sen.⟩ was born July 12th 1771, in Topsfield, ⟨Essex county⟩ Massachusetts his father Asael Smith was born March 7th, 1744 Topsfield Massachusetts his father Samuel Smith was born Jan'y 26th, 1714 Topsfield Massachusetts his father Samuel Smith was born Jan'y 26th, 1666, Topsfield his father Robert Smith came from England."

3. Insertion in the handwriting of Willard Richards.

menced with the Methodists, but soon became general among all the sects in that region of country, indeed the whole district of Country seemed affected by it and great [p. 1] multitudes united themselves to the different religious parties, which created no small stir and division among the people, Some crying, "Lo here" and some Lo there. Some were contending for the Methodist faith, Some for the Presbyterian, and some for the Baptist; for notwithstanding the great love which the converts to these different faiths expressed at the time of their conversion, and the great Zeal manifested by the respective Clergy who were active in getting up and promoting this extraordinary scene of religious feeling in order to have everybody converted as they were pleased to call it, let them join what sect they pleased yet when the Converts began to file off some to one party and some to another, it was seen that the seemingly good feelings of both the Priests and the Converts were ~~mere pretence~~ more pretended than real, for a scene of great confusion and bad feeling ensued; Priest contending against priest, and convert against convert so that all their good feelings one for another (if they ever had any) were entirely lost in a strife of words and a contest about opinions.

I was at this time in my fifteenth year. My Fathers family w~~as~~⟨ere⟩[1] proselyted to the Presbyterian faith and four of them joined that Church, Namely, My Mother Lucy, My Brothers Hyrum, Samuel Harrison, and my Sister Soph[r]onia.

During this time of great excitement my mind was called up to serious reflection and great uneasiness, but though my feelings were deep and often pungent, still I kept myself aloof from all these parties though I attended their several meetings ⟨as often⟩[2] as occasion would permit. But in process of time my mind became somewhat partial to the Methodist sect, and I felt some desire to be united with them, but so great was the

1. Alteration in different hand and ink; probably Willard Richards.
2. Insertion in different hand and ink; probably Willard Richards.

confusion and strife amongst the different denominations that it was impossible for a person young as I was and so unacquainted with men and things to come to any certain conclusion who was right and who was wrong. My mind at different times was greatly excited ~~for~~ the cry and tumult were so great and incessant. The Presbyterians were most decided against the Baptists and Methodists, and used all their powers of either reason or sophistry to prove their errors, or at least to make the people think they were in error. On the other hand the Baptists and Methodists in their turn were equally Zealous in endeavoring to establish their own tenets and disprove all others.

In the midst of this war of words, and tumult of opinions, I often said to myself, what is to be done? Who of all these parties are right? Or are they all wrong together? And if any one of them be right which is it? And how shall I know it?

While I was laboring under the extreme difficulties caused by the contests of these parties of religionists, I was one day reading the Epistle of James, First Chapter and fifth verse which reads, "If any of you lack wisdom, let him ask of God, that giveth to all men liberally and upbraideth not, and it shall be given him. Never did any passage of scripture come with more power to the heart of man than[1] this did at this time to mine. It seemed to enter with great force into every feeling of my heart. I reflected on it again and again, knowing that if any person needed wisdom from God, I did, for how to act I did not know and unless I could get more wisdom than I then had would never know, for the teachers of religion of the different sects understood the same [p. 2] passage of Scripture so differently as ⟨to⟩ destroy all confidence in settling the question by an appeal to the Bible. At length I came to the conclusion that I must either remain in darkness and confusion or else I must do as James directs, that is, Ask of God. I at last came

1. MS. reads "that."

to the determination to ask of God, concluding that if he gave wisdom to them that lacked wisdom, and would give liberally and not upbraid, I might venture. So, in accordance with this, my determination to ask of God, I retired to the woods to make the attempt. It was on the morning of a beautiful clear day early in the spring of Eighteen hundred and twenty. It was the first time in my life that I had ⟨made⟩ such an attempt, for amidst all ⟨my⟩ anxieties I had never as yet made the attempt to pray vocally.

After I had retired into the place where I had previously designed to go, having looked around me and finding myself alone, I kneeled down and began to offer up the desires of my heart to God. I had scarcely done so, when immediately I was ⟨siezed⟩ upon by some power which entirely overcame me and ⟨had⟩ such astonishing influence over me as to bind my tongue so that I could not speak. Thick darkness gathered around me and it seemed to me for a time as if I were doomed to sudden destruction. But exerting all my powers to call upon God to deliver me out of the power of this enemy which had siezed upon me, and at the very moment when I was ready to sink into despair and abandon myself to destruction, not to an imaginary ruin but to the power of some actual being from the unseen world who had such a marvelous power as I had never before felt in any being. Just at this moment of great alarm I saw a pillar ⟨of⟩ light exactly over my head above the brightness of the sun, which descended ~~gracefully~~ gradually untill it fell upon me. It no sooner appeared than I found myself delivered from the enemy which held me bound. When the light rested upon me I saw two personages (whose brightness and glory defy all description) standing above me in the air. One of ⟨them⟩ spake unto me calling me by name and said (pointing to the other) "This is my beloved Son, Hear him." My object in going to enquire of the Lord was to know which of all the sects was right, that I might know which to join. No sooner therefore did I get possession of myself so as to be able to speak, than I asked the personages who stood above me in the light, which of all the sects was right, (for at this time it had never entered into my heart that all were wrong) and which I should join. I was answered that I must join none of them, for they were all wrong, and the Personage who addressed me said that all their Creeds were an abomination in his sight, that those professors were all corrupt, that "they draw near to me with their lips but their hearts are far from me, They teach for doctrines the commandments of men, having a form of Godliness but they deny the power thereof." He again forbade me to join with any of them and many other things did he say unto me which I cannot write at this time. When I came to myself again I found myself lying on ⟨my⟩ back looking up into Heaven. ⟨B See Note P 132⟩[1] Some few days after I had this vision I happened to be in company with one of the Methodist Preachers who was very active in the before mentioned religious excitement and conversing with him on the subject of religion I took occasion to give him an account of the vision which I had had. I was greatly surprised at his behaviour, he treated my communication not only lightly but with great contempt, saying it was all of the Devil, that there was no such thing as visions or revelations in these days, that all such things had ceased with the [p. 3] apostles and that there never

1. This insertion is in the hand of Willard Richards as is the note to which it refers on pages 132-33 of this manuscript: "When the light had departed I had no strength, but soon recovering in some degree. I went home. & as I leaned up to the fire piece. Mother Enquired what the matter was. I replied never mind all is well.– I am well enough off. I then told my mother I have learned for myself that Presbyterianism is not true.– It seems as though the adversary was aware at a very early period of my life that I was destined to prove a disturber & [p. 132] annoyer of his kingdom, or else why should the powers of Darkness combine against me, why the oppression & persecution that arose against me, almost in my infancy?"

According to Richards's diary, this note was written on 2 December 1842, which explains why it does not appear in the History in the *Times and Seasons* which began publication in March that year. (Willard Richards Diary, 2 December 1842. MS., LDS Church Archives.)

would be any more of them. I soon found however that my telling the story had excited a great deal of prejudice against me among professors of religion and was the cause of great persecution which continued to increase and though I was an obscure boy only between fourteen and fifteen years of age ⟨or thereabouts,⟩[1] and my circumstances in life such as to make a boy of no consequence in the world, yet men of high standing would take notice sufficient~~ly~~ to excite the public mind against me and create a hot persecution, and this was common ⟨among⟩ all the sects: all united to persecute me. It has often caused me ~~m~~ serious reflection both then and since, how very strange it was that an obscure boy of a little over fourteen years of age and one too who was doomed to the necessity of obtaining a scanty maintainance by his daily labor should be thought a character of sufficient importance to attract the attention of the great ones of the most popular sects of the day so as to create in them a spirit of the bitterest persecution and reviling. But strange or not, so it was, and was often cause of great sorrow to myself. However it was nevertheless a fact, that I had had a vision. I have thought since that I felt much like ~~as~~ [2]Paul ~~did~~ when he made his defence before King Aggrippa[3] and related the account of the vision he had when he saw a light and heard a voice, but still there were but few who beleived him, some said he was dishonest, others said he was mad, and he was ridiculed and reviled, But all this did not destroy the reality of his vision. He had seen a vision he knew he had, and ⟨all⟩ the persecution under Heaven could not make it otherwise, and though they should persecute him unto death yet he knew and would know to his latest breath that he had both seen a light and heard a voice speaking unto him and all the world could not make him think or believe otherwise. So it

1. Insertion in the hand of Willard Richards.
2. Cancellation in ink; following one in pencil.
3. Acts 26.

was with me, I had actualy seen a light and in the midst of that light I saw two personages, and they did in reality speak ⟨un⟩to me, or one of them did, And though I was hated and persecuted for saying that I had seen a vision, yet it was truc and while they were persecuting me reviling me and speaking all manner of evil against me falsely for so saying, I was led to say in my heart, why persecute ⟨me⟩[1] for telling the truth? I have actually seen a vision, "and who am I that I can withstand God" or why does the world think to make me deny what I have actually seen, for I had seen a vision, I knew it, and I knew that God knew it, and I could not deny it, neither dare I do it, at least I knew that by so doing ⟨I⟩ would offend God and come under condemnation. I had now got my mind satisfied so far as the sectarian world was concerned, that it was not my duty to join with any of them, but continue as I was untill further directed, ~~for~~ I had found the testimony of James to be true, that a man who lacked wisdom might ask of God, and obtain and not be upbraided. I continued to pursue my common avocations in life untill the twenty first of September, One thousand Eight hundred and twenty three, all the time suffering severe persecution at the hand of all classes of men, both religious and irreligious because I continued to affirm that I ⟨had⟩ seen a vision. During the space of time which intervened between the time I had the vision and the year Eighteen hundred and twenty three, (having been forbidden to join any of the religious sects of the day, and being of very tender years and persecuted by those who ought to have been my friends, and to have treated me kindly [p. 4] and if they supposed me to be deluded to have endeavoured in a proper and affectionate manner to have reclaimed me) I was left to ~~all kinds of~~ temptations, and mingling ⟨with⟩ ~~all kinds of~~ society I frequently ⟨fell⟩ into many foolish errors and displayed the

1. Insertion penciled in another hand.

weakness of youth and the ~~corruption~~ ⟨foibles⟩[1] of human nature which I am sorry to say led me into divers temptations ~~to the gratification of many appetites~~ offensive in the sight of God. ⟨see Note C. p. 133⟩[2] In consequence of these things I often felt condemned for my weakness and imperfections; when on the evening of the above mentioned twenty first of september, after I had retired to my bed for the night I betook myself to prayer and supplication to Almighty God for forgiveness of all my sins and follies, and also for a manifestation to me that I might know of my state and standing before him. For I had full confidence in obtaining a divine manifestation as I had previously had one. While I was thus in the act of calling upon God, I discovered a light appearing in the room which continued to increase untill the room was lighter than at noonday ~~and~~ ⟨when⟩ immediately a personage ⟨appeared⟩ at my bedside standing in the air for his feet did not touch the floor. He had on a loose robe of most exquisite whiteness. It was a whiteness beyond any⟨thing⟩ earthly I had ever seen, nor do I believe that any earthly thing could be made to appear so exceedin[g]ly white and brilliant, His hands were naked and his arms also a little above the wrists. So also were his feet naked as were his legs a little above the ankles. His head and neck were also bare. I could discover that he had no other clothing on but this robe, as it was open so that I could see into his bosom.

---

1. Insertion in another hand and ink; probably Willard Richards.
2. This insertion in the text, as also the note to which it refers, on page 133 of the manuscript, is in the hand of Willard Richards: "In making this confession, no one need suppose me guilty of any great or malignant sins: a disposition to commit such was never in my nature; but I was guilty of Levity, & sometimes associated with Jovial company &c, not consistent with that character which ought to be maintained by one who was called of God as I had been; but this will not seem very strange to any one who recollects my youth & is acqu⟨aint⟩ed with my native cheery Temperament."

Richards wrote these lines on 2 December 1842; hence, like notes A and B, this insertion does not appear in the *Times and Seasons* publication of the *History* that commenced in March of that year. (Diary of Willard Richards, 2 December 1842.)

Not only was his robe exceedingly white but his whole person was glorious beyond description, and his countenance truly like lightning. The room was exceedingly light, but not so very bright as immediately around his person. When I first looked upon him I was afraid, but the fear soon left me. He called me by name and said unto me that he was a messenger sent from the presence of God to me and that his name was Nephi ⟨Moroni⟩.[1] That God had a work for me to do, and that my ⟨name⟩ should be had for good and evil among all nations kindreds and tongues. or that it should be both good and evil

---

1. The name "Moroni" has been inserted, possibly by Brigham H. Roberts, who prepared this History for publication at the turn of the century, and who keyed the insertion to these words at the bottom of the page: "Evidently a clerical error; see Book Doc & Cov., Sec 50, par 2 [1835 Kirtland edition]; Sec 106, par 20 [1842 Nauvoo edition]; also Elders' Journal Vol. 1, page 43. Should read Moroni." These are references in which Joseph Smith, during his lifetime, designated Moroni as the messenger who appeared. The *Doctrine and Covenants* citations are found in sections 27:5 and 128:20 of the current edition.

With regard to the apparent discrepancy between the names of Nephi and Moroni in early references to the messenger who appeared to Joseph Smith in September 1823, the 1832 History refers to Moroni but can be read to support either position. (See above, p. 8.)

Brigham Young wrote, "There is really no discrepancy in the history about these names. It was Moroni who delivered the sacred records and Urim and Thummim to Joseph; but Nephi also visited him." (Brigham Young to Brigham Young, Jr., 24 April 1866, Brigham Young Letterbook 8:327-30, MS., Brigham Young Papers, LDS Church Archives.)

Orson Pratt noted that "the discrepancy in the history . . . may have occurred through the ignorance or carelessness of the historian or transcriber. It is true, that the history reads as though the Prophet himself was writing: but . . . many events recorded were written by his scribes who undoubtedly trusted too much to their memories, and the items probably were not sufficiently scanned by Bro. Joseph before they got into print." (Orson Pratt to John Christensen, 11 March 1876, MS., LDS Church Archives.)

In recommending alterations in early Church publications, Church historians Orson Pratt and Joseph F. Smith emphasized, "The contradictions in regard to the name of the angelic messenger who appeared to Joseph Smith occurred probably through the mistakes of clerks in making or copying documents, and, we think should be corrected. . . . From careful research we are fully convinced that Moroni is the correct name. This also was the decision of the former historian, George A. Smith." (Orson Pratt and Joseph F. Smith to John Taylor, 18 December 1877, MS., LDS Church Archives.)

spoken of among all people. He said there was a book deposited written upon gold plates, giving an account of the former inhabitants of this continent and the source from whence they sprang. He also said that the fullness of the everlasting Gospel was contained in it as delivered by the Saviour to the ancient inhabitants. Also that there were two stones in silver bows and these (~~put~~ ⟨stones fastened⟩ ~~in~~to a breast plate) ~~which~~ constituted what is called the Urim & Thummin deposited with the plates, and ⟨the possession and use of these stones⟩[1] ~~that~~ was what constituted seers in ancient or former times and that God ⟨had⟩ prepared them for the purpose of translating the book. After telling me these things he commenced quoting the prophecies of the old testament, he first quoted part of the third chapter of Malachi and he quoted also the fourth or last chapter of the same prophecy though with a little variation from the way it reads in our Bibles. Instead of quoting the first verse as reads in our books he quoted it thus, "For behold the day cometh that shall burn as an oven, and all the proud ⟨yea⟩ and all that do wickedly shall burn as stubble, for ⟨the~~y~~ day⟩[2] that cometh shall burn them saith the Lord of hosts, that it shall leave them neither root nor branch." And again he quoted the fifth verse thus, "Behold I will reveal unto you the Priesthood by the hand of Elijah the prophet before the coming of the great and dreadful day of the Lord." He also quoted the next verse differently. [p. 5] "And he shall plant in the hearts of the children the promises made to the fathers, and the hearts of the children shall turn to their fathers, if it were not so the whole earth would be utterly wasted at his coming." In addition to these ~~quotations~~ he quoted the Eleventh Chapter of Isaiah saying that it was about to be fulfilled. He quoted also

1. This and previous insertions in this sentence are in the handwriting of Willard Richards.

2. The alteration of "they" and addition of "day" are in a different hand and ink.

the third chapter of Acts, twenty second and twenty third verses precisely as they stand in our new testament. He said that that prophet was Christ, but the day had not yet come when "they who would not hear his voice should be cut off from among the people," but soon would come.

He also quoted the second chapter of Joel from the twenty eighth to the last verse. He also said that this was not yet fulfilled but was soon to be. And he further stated the fullness of the gentiles was soon to come in. He quoted many other passages of scripture and offered many explanations which cannot be mentioned here. Again he told me that when I got those plates of which he had spoken (for the time that they should be obtained was not yet fulfilled) I should not show ⟨them⟩ to any person, neither the breastplate with the Urim and Thummin only to those to whom I should be commanded to show them. If I did I should be destroyed. While he was conversing with me about the plates the vision was opened to my mind that I could see the place where the plates were deposited and that so clearly and distinctly that I knew the place again when I visited it.

After this ~~conversation~~ communication I saw the light in the room begin to gather immediately around the person of him who had been speaking to me, and it continued to do so untill the room was again left dark except just round him, when instantly I saw as it were a conduit open right up into heaven, and he ascended up till he entirely disappeared and the room was left as it had been before this heavenly light had made its appearance.

I lay musing on the singularity of the scene and marvelling greatly at what had been told me by this extraordinary messenger, when in the midst of my meditation I suddenly discovered that my room was again beginning to get lighted, and in an instant as it were, the same heavenly messenger was again by my bedside. He commenced and again related the very same things which he had done at his first visit without the least variation which having done, he informed me of great judgements which were coming upon the earth, with great desolations by famine, sword, and pestilence, and that these grievous judgments would come on the earth in this generation: Having related these things he again ascended as he had done before.

By this time so deep were the impressions made on my mind that sleep had fled from my eyes and I lay overwhelmed in astonishment at what I had both seen and heard:

But what was my surprise when again I beheld the same messenger at my bed side, and heard him rehearse or repeat over again to me the same things as before and added a caution to me, telling me that Satan would try to tempt me (in consequence of the indigent circumstances of my father's family) to get the plates for the purpose of getting rich, This he forbid me, saying that I must have ~~mo~~ no other object in view in getting the plates but to glorify God, and must not be influenced by any other motive but that of building his kingdom, otherwise I could not get them. After this third visit he again ascended up into heaven as before and I was again left to ponder on the [p. 6] strangeness of what I had just experienced, when almost immediately after the heavenly messenger had ascended from me the third time, the cock crew, and I found that day was approaching so that our interviews must have occupied the whole of that night. I shortly after arose from my bed, and as usual went to the necessary labors of the day, but in attempting to labor as at other times, I found my strength so exhausted as rendered me entirely unable. My father who was laboring along ⟨with⟩ me discovered something to be wrong with me and told me to go home. I started with the intention of going to the house, but in attempting to cross the fence out of the field where we were, my strength entirely failed me and I fell helpless on the ground and for a time was quite unconscious of any thing. The first thing that I can recollect was a voice speaking unto me calling me by name. I looked up and beheld the same messenger standing over my head surrounded by light as before. He then again related unto me all that he had related to me the previous night, and commanded me to go to my father and tell him of thc vision and commandments which I had received.

I obeyed. I returned back to my father in the field and rehearsed the whole matter to him. He replyed to me, that it was of God, and to go and do as commanded by the messenger. I left the field and went to the place where the messenger had told me the plates were deposited, and owing to the distinctness of the vision which I had had concerning it, I knew the place the instant that I arrived there.*[1] Under a ~~stound~~ stone of considerable size, lay the plates deposited in a stone box, This stone was thick and rounding in the middle on the upper side, and thinner towards the edges, so that the middle part of it was visible above the ground, but the edge all round was covered with earth. Having removed the earth ~~off the edge of the stone,~~ and obtained a lever which I got fixed under the edge of the stone, and with a little exertion raised it up, I looked in and there indeed did I behold the plates, the Urim and Thummin and the Breastplate as stated by the messenger The box in which they lay was formed by laying stones together in some kind of cement, in the bottom of the box were laid two stones crossways of the box, and on these stones lay the plates and the other things with them. I made an attempt to take them out but was forbidden by the messenger and was again informed that the time ⟨for⟩ bringing them forth had not yet arrived, neither would untill four years from that time, but

1. The asterisk, added by James Mulholland, is keyed to an attached note in the manuscript containing these words on one side: "I mentioned to President Smith that I considered it necessary that an explanation of ⟨the location of⟩ the place where the box was deposited would be required in order that the history be satisfactory. J.M." On the reverse side of the note, also in Mulholland's hand: "Convenient to the ~~little~~ village of Manchester, Ontario County, New York, stands a hill of considerable size, and the most elevated of any in the neighborhood. On the west side of this hill not far from the top"

he told me that I should come to that place precisely in one year from that time, and that he would there meet with me, and that I should continue to do so untill the time should come for obtaining the plates. Accordingly as I had been commanded I went at the end of each year, and at each time I found the same messenger there and received instruction and intelligence from him at each of our interviews respecting what the Lord was going to do, and how and in what manner his kingdom was to be conducted in the last days. As my father's worldly circumstances were very, ⟨limited⟩ we were under the necessity of laboring with our hands, hiring by days works and otherwise as we could get opportunity, sometimes we were at home and some times abroad and by continued labor were enabled to get a comfortable maintenance.

In the year Eighteen hundred and twenty four my fathers family met with a great affliction by the death of my eldest brother Alvin.[1] In the month of October Eighteen hundred and twenty five I hired with an old Gentleman, by name of Josiah Stoal [Stowell] [p. 7] who lived in Chenango County, State of New York. He had heard something of a silver mine having been opened by the Spaniards in Harmony, Susquahana County, State of Pensylvania, and had previous to my hiring with him been digging in order if possible to discover the mine. After I went to live with ⟨him⟩ he took me among the rest of his hands to dig for the silver mine, at which I continued to work for nearly a month without success in our undertaking, and finally I prevailed with the old gentleman to cease digging after it. Hence arose the very prevalent story of my having been a money digger.

During the time that I was thus employed I was put to board with a Mr Isaac Hale of that place, Twas there that I first saw my wife, (his daughter) Emma Hale. On the eighteenth of January Eighteen hundred and twenty seven we were

1. Alvin's death occurred 19 November 1823.

married while yet I was employed in the service of Mr Stoal. Owing to my still continuing to assert that I had seen a vision, persecution still followed me, ⟨and my wife's father's family was very much⟩ ~~and so much was my wife's father excited, that he was greatly~~ opposed to our being married, ~~in so much that he would not suffer us to be married at his house~~, I was therefore under the necessity of taking her elsewhere, so we went and were married at ~~Mr St~~ the house of ~~Mr Stoal.~~ ⟨Squire Tarbill.[1] in South Bainbridge. Chenango County, New York.⟩ Immediately after my marriage I left Mr Stoals, and went to my father's and farmed with him that season.

At length the time arrived for obtaining the plates, the Urim and Thummin and the breastplate. On the twenty second day of September, One thousand Eight hundred and twenty seven, having went as usual at the end of another year to the place where they were deposited, the same heavenly messenger delivered them up to me with this charge that I should be responsible for them. That if I should let them go carelessly or ⟨through⟩ any neglect of mine I should be cut off, but that if I would use all my endeavours to preserve them untill ⟨he⟩ (the messenger) ~~called~~ should call for them, they should be protected.

I soon found out the reason why I had received such strict charges to keep them safe and why it was that the messenger had said that when I had done what was required at my hand, he would call for them, for no sooner was it known that I had them than the most strenious exertions were used to get them from me. Every stratagem that could be ~~resorted~~ invented was resorted to for that purpose. The persecution became more bitter and severe than before, and multitudes were on the alert continualy to get them from me if possible but by the wisdom

1. The identity of the justice of the peace who married Joseph Smith and Emma Hale is not certain. It was probably either Thomas or Zachariah Tarbell. (Porter, "A Study of the Origins of the Church," 188-90.)

of God they remained safe in my hands untill I had accomplished by them what was required at my hand, when according to arrangement the messenger called for them, I delivered them up to him and he has them in his charge untill this day, being the Second day of May, One thousand Eight hundred and thirty eight.[1]

The excitement however still continued, and rumour with her thousand tongues was all the time employed in circulating tales about my father's family and about myself. If I were to relate a thousan⟨d⟩th part of them it would fill up volumes. The persecution however became so intolerable that I was under the necessity of leaving Manchester and going with my wife ⟨to⟩ Susquahanah County in the State of Pensyllvania. While preparing to start (being very poor and the persecution so heavy upon us that there was no probability that we would ever be otherwise) in the midst of our afflictions we found a friend in a Gentleman by ⟨the⟩ name of Martin Harris, who came to us and gave me fifty dollars [p. 8] to assist us in our affliction, Mr Harris was a resident of Palmyra township Wayne County in the State of New York and a farmer of respectability. By this timely aid was I enabled to reach the place of my destination in Pensylvania,[2] and immediately after my arrival there I commenced copying the characters of ~~all~~ the plates. I copyed a considerable number of them and by means of the Urim and Thummin I translated some of them which I did between the time I arrived at the house of my wife's father in the month of December, and the February following. Sometime in this month of February the aforementioned Mr Martin Harris came to our place, got the characters which I had drawn off ~~of~~ the plates and started with them to the City of New York. For

1. See Diary of Joseph Smith, 30 April–4 May 1838 for references to the original writing of the text of this part of the manuscript. The introductory editorial note, pp. 230-231, explains why I have dated this manuscript 1839 despite references to 1838 in the writing of its beginning pages.

2. Joseph Smith moved to Harmony, Pennsylvania, in December 1827.

what took place relative to him and the characters I refer to his own account of the circumstances as he related them to me after his return which was as follows. "I went to the City of New York and presented the Characters which had been translated, with the translation thereof, to Professor ⟨Charles⟩ Anthon~~y~~[1] a gentleman celebrated for his literary attainments. Professor Anthon~~y~~ stated that the translation was correct, more so than any he had before seen translated from the Egyptian.

I then shewed him those which were not yet translated, and he said that they were Egyptian, Chaldeak, Assyriac, and Arabac, and he said that they were true characters. He gave me a certificate certifying to the people of Palmyra that they were true characters and that the translation of such of them as had been translated was also correct. I took the Certificate and put it into my pocket, and was just leaving the house, when Mr Anthon~~y~~ called me back and asked me how the young man found out that there were gold plates in the place where he found them. I answered that an Angel of God had revealed it unto him. He then said to me, let me see that certificate, I accordingly took it out of my pocket and gave it [to] him when he took it and tore it to pieces, saying that there was no such thing now as ministring of angels, and that if I would bring the plates to him, he would translate them.* ⟨I informed him that part of the plates were sealed, and that I was forbidden to bring them. he replied "I cannot read a sealed book".⟩[2] I left him and went to Dr Mitchel [Samuel L. Mitchill] who sanc-

---

1. The insertion is penciled in another hand.

2. Martin Harris's visits to Charles Anthon, and the later notoriety attached to him in connection with Mormonism, brought reaction from the Professor on two known occasions: the first, a letter dated 17 February 1834 to E.D. Howe, published in Howe's *Mormonism Unvailed*, 270-72; and the second, a letter dated 3 April 1841 to Rev. Dr. Coit, New Rochelle, New York, published in John A. Clark, *Gleanings by the Way* (Philadelphia: W.J. and J.K. Simon, 1842), 233-38. (See also, Kimball, "The Anthon Transcript.")

tioned what Professor ~~Anthony~~ had said respecting both the Characters and the translation."

Mr Harris having returned from this tour he left me and went home to Palmyra, arranged his affairs, and returned again to my house about the twelfth of April, Eighteen hundred and twenty eight, and commenced writing for me while I translated from the plates, which we continued untill the fourteenth of June following, by which time he had written one hundred and sixteen ⟨pages⟩ of manuscript on foolscap paper. Some time after Mr Harris had began to write for me, he began to tease me to give him liberty to carry the writings home and shew them, and desired of me that I would enquire of the Lord through the Urim and Thummin if he might not do so. I did enquire, and the answer was that he must not. However he was not satisfied with this answer, and desired that I should enquire again. I did so, and the answer was as before. Still he could not be contented but insisted that I should enquire once more⟨.⟩ ~~after~~ After much solicitation I again enquired of the Lord, and permission was granted him to have the writings on certain conditions, which were, that he shew them only to his brother. Preserved Harris, his own wife [Lucy Harris], his father [Nathan], and his mother [Rhoda L. Harris], and a Mrs [Polly Harris] Cobb a sister to his wife. In accordance with this last answer I required of him that he should bind himself in a covenant to me [p. 9] in the most solemn manner that he would not do otherwise than had been directed. He did so. He bound himself as I required of him, took the writings and went his way.

Notwithstanding however the great restrictions which he had been laid under, and the solemnity of the covenant which he had made with me, he did shew them to others and by stratagem they got them away from him, and they never have been recovered nor obtained back again untill this day.[1] In the

1. May 1838. (See Diary of Joseph Smith, 30 April–4 May 1838.)

mean time while Martin Harris was gone with the writings, I went to visit my father's family at Manchester. I continued there for a short season and then returned to my place in Pensylvania. Immediately after my return home I was walking out a little distance, when Behold the former heavenly messenger appeared and handed to me the Urim and Thummin again (for it had been taken from me in consequence of my having wearied the Lord in asking for the privilege of letting Martin Harris take the writings which he lost by transgression) and I enquired of the Lord through them and obtained the folowing revelation.

Revelation to Joseph Smith jr, given July 1828 concerning certain manuscripts on the first part of the book of Mormon which had been taken from the possession of Martin Harris.

[D&C 3]

After I had obtained the above revelation, both the plates, and the Urim and Thummin were taken from me again, but in a few days they were returned to me.[1] ⟨*when I enquired of the Lord, and the Lord said thus unto me*

N.B. This Revelation will read, after the interlined words in page 11 & line 17th

*Revelation given to Joseph Smith Jr. May 1829 informing

In his Preface to the 1830 edition of the Book of Mormon Joseph Smith wrote: "I would inform you that I translated, by the gift and power of God, and caused to be written, one hundred and sixteen pages, the which I took from the Book of Lehi, which was an account abridged from the plates of Lehi, by the hand of Mormon; which said account, some person or persons have stolen and kept from me, notwithstanding my utmost exertions to recover it again."

Joseph Smith's mother gives additional detail on the loss of the manuscript, Lucy Smith, *Biographical Sketches*, 117-27.

1. A revelation (D&C 10) has been inserted at this point in the manuscript. It appears that the document may have been overlooked, or that Mulholland failed to copy it at the proper place in the text. Hence, it was copied on a separate piece of folded paper, marked by asterisks for insertion here, and attached at the top of page 11 of the manuscript with sealing wax.

him of the alteration of the manuscript of the fore part of the Book of Mormon.⟩

⟨[D&C 10]⟩

I did not however go immediately to translating, but went to laboring with my hands upon a small farm which I had purchased of my wife's father, in order to provide for my family.[1] In the month of February, Eighteen hundred and twenty nine my father came to visit us at which time I received the following revelation for him.

Revelation to Joseph Smith Senr. given February 1829.

[D&C 4]

The following I applied for at the request of the aforementioned Martin Harris and obtained.

Revelation given March, 1829.

[D&C 5]

On the fifth day of Aprile Eighteen hundred and twenty nine Oliver Cowdery came to my house, untill when I had never seen him. He stated to me that having been teaching school in the neighborhood where my father resided, and my father being one of those who sent to the school, he had went to board for a season at my father's house, and while there the family related to him the circumstance of my having received the plates, and accordingly he had came to make enquiries of me.[2]

Two days after the arrival of Mr Cowdery (being the seventh of April) I commenced to translate the book of Mormon and he commenced to write for me, which having continued for

1. On the property and home acquired by Joseph Smith from the Hales in Harmony, Pennsylvania, see Porter, "A Study of the Origins of the Church," 132-38.

2. Further detail on the circumstances of Oliver Cowdery's meeting the Smith family is in Lucy Smith, *Biographical Sketches*, 128-31.

some time I enquired of the Lord through the Urim and Thummin and obtained the following revelation.

Revelation given April 1829, to Oliver Cowdery and Joseph Smith Jr.

[D&C 6]

After we had received this revelation he (Oliver Cowdery) stated to me that after he had gone to my father's to board, and after the family communicated to him concerning my having got the plates, that one night after he had retired to bed, he called upon the Lord to know if these things were so, and that the Lord had manifested to him that they were true, but that he had kept the circumstance entirely secret, and had mentioned it to no being, so that after this revelation having been given, he knew that the work was true, because that no ~~mortal~~ being living knew of the thing alluded ⟨to⟩ in the revelation but God and himself. During the month of April I continued to translate, and he to write with little cessation, during which time we received several revelations. A difference of opinion arising between us about the account of John the Apostle, mentioned in the new testament, John, twenty first chapter and twenty second verse, whether he died, or whether he continued; ~~We~~ We mutually agreed to settle ⟨it⟩ by the Urim and Thummin, and the following is the word which we received.

A Revelation given to Joseph Smith jr, and Oliver Cowdery in Harmony Pensylvania April 1829. when they desired to know whether John, the beloved disciple, tarried on earth.– Translated from parchment, written and hid up by himself.

[D&C 7]

Whilst continuing the work of translation during this month of April; Oliver Cowdery became exceedingly anxious to have the power to translate bestowed upon him and in relation to this desire the folowing revelations were obtained.

Revelation given April 1829.

[D&C 8]

Revelation given to Oliver Cowdery, April 1829.

[D&C 9]

We still continued the ⟨work of⟩ translation, when in the ensuing month (May, Eighteen hundred and twenty nine) we on a certain day went into the woods to pray and inquire of the Lord respecting baptism for the remission of sins as we found mentioned in the translation of the plates. While we were thus employed praying and calling upon the Lord, a Messenger from heaven, descended in a cloud of light, and having laid his hands upon us, he ordained us, saying unto us; "Upon you my fellow servants in the name of Messiah I confer the priesthood of Aaron, which holds the keys of the ministring of angels and of the gospel of repentance, and of baptism by immersion for the remission of sins, and this shall never be taken again from the earth, untill the sons of Levi do offer again an offering unto the Lord in righteousness." He said this Aaronic priesthood had not [p. 17] the power of laying on of hands, for the gift of the Holy Ghost, but that this should be conferred on ⟨us⟩ hereafter and he commanded us to go and be baptized, and gave us directions that I should baptize Oliver Cowdery, and afterward that he should baptize me. ~~and that I should be called the first elder of the the Church and he the second.~~

Accordingly we went and were baptized, I baptized him first, and afterwards he baptized me, after which I laid my hands upon his head and ordained him to the Aaronick priesthood, and afterward he laid his hands on me and ordained me to the same priesthood, for so we were commanded.

The messenger who visited us on this occasion and conferred this priesthood upon us said that his name was John, the same that is called John the Baptist in the new Testament, and that he acted under the direction ⟨of⟩ Peter, James, and John, who held the keys of the priesthood of Melchisedeck, whi[c]h priesthood he said should in due time be conferred on us. And that I should be called the first Elder of the Church and he the second. It was on the fifteenth day of May, Eighteen hundred and twentynine that we were baptized; ~~under~~ and ordained under the hand of the Messenger.[1]

Immediately upon our coming up out of the water after we had been baptized we experienced great and glorious blessings from our Heavenly Father.

No sooner had I baptized Oliver Cowdery than the Holy Ghost fell upon him and he stood up and prophecied many things which should shortly come to pass: And again so soon as I had been baptized by him, I also had the Spirit of Prophecy, when standing up I prophecied concerning the rise of this Church, and many other things connected with the Church and this generation of the children of men. We were filled with the Holy Ghost, and rejoiced in the God of our Salvation.

Our minds being now enlightened, we began to have the Scriptures laid open to our understandings, and the true meaning and intention of their more mysterious passages revealed unto us, in a manner which we never could attain to previously, nor ever before ⟨had⟩ thought of. In the meantime we were forced to keep secret the circumstances of our having been baptized, and having received this priesthood; owing to a spirit of persecution which had already manifested itself in the neighborhood. We had been threatened with being mobbed, from time to time, and this too by professors of religion, and their intentions of mobbing us, were only counteracted by the influence of my wife's father's family (under Divine Providence) who had became very friendly to me and were opposed to mobs; and were willing that I should be allowed to continue the work of translation without interruption: And therefore offered and

1. Oliver Cowdery's report of this experience is on pp. 30-32.

promised us protection from all unlawful proceedings as far as in them lay.

After a few days however, feeling it to be our duty, we commenced to reason out of the scriptures, with our acquaintances and friends, as we happened to meet with them. About this time my brother, Samuel, H. Smith ~~came~~ came [p. 18] to visit us. We informed him of what the Lord was about to do for the children of men; and to reason with him out of the Bible: we also showed him that part of the work which we had translated, and labored to persuade him concerning the Gospel of Jesus Christ which was now about to be revealed in it's fulness. He was not however very easily persuaded of these things, but after much enquiry and explanation, he retired to the woods, in order that by secret and fervent prayer he might obtain of a merciful God, wisdom to enable him to judge for himself: The result was that he obtained revelation for himself sufficient to convince him of the truth of our assertions to him and on the twenty fifth day of that same month in which we had been baptized and ordained; Oliver Cowdery baptized him, And he returned to his father's house greatly glorifying and praising God, being filled with the Holy Spirit. Not many days afterwards, my brother Hyrum Smith came to us to enquire concerning these things, when at his earnest request, I enquired of the Lord through the Urim and Thummin, and received for him the following

Revelation given to Hyrum Smith, at Harmony, Susquehanah County, Pensys~~sy~~lvania. May 1829.

[D&C 11]

About the same time came an old Gentleman to visit us, of whose name I wish to make honorable mention; Mr Joseph Knight Senr. of Colesville, Broom County, New York;[1] who having heard of the manner in which we were occupying our

1. MS. reads "Penn."

time, very kindly and considerately brought us, a quantity of provisions, in order that we might not be interrupted in the work of translation, by the want of such necessaries of life: and I would just [p. 20] mention here (as in duty bound) that he several times brought us supplies (a distance of at least thirty miles) which enabled us to continue the work when otherwise we must have relinquished it for a season.

Being very anxious to know his duty as to this work, I enquired of the Lord for him, and obtained as follows.

Revelation given to Joseph Knight Senr. at Harmony Susquehanah County, Pennsylvania. May 1829.

[D&C 12]

Shortly after commencing to translate, I became acquainted with Mr Peter Whitmer of Fayette, Seneca County New York, and also with some of his family. In the beginning of the month of June, his son, David Whitmer came to the place where we were residing, and brought with him a two horse waggon, for the purpose of having us accompany him to his father's place and there remain untill we should finish the work. He proposed that we should have our board free of charge, and the assistance of one of his brothers to write for me, as also his own assistance when convenient.

Having much need of such timely aid in an undertaking so arduous, and being informed that the people of the neighborhood were anxiously ~~the~~ awaiting the opportunity to enquire into these things; we accepted the invitation and accompanied Mr Whitmer to his father's house, and there resided [p. 21] untill the translation was finished, and the copyright secured. Upon our arrival, we found Mr Whitmer's family very anxious concerning the work, and very friendly towards ourselves. They continued so, boarded and lodged us according to proposal, and John Whitmer, in particular, assisted us very much in writing during the remainder of the work.

In the meantime, David, John, and Peter Whitmer Jr became our zealous friends and assistants in the work; and being anxious to know their respective duties, and having desired with much earnestness that I should enquire of the Lord concerning them, I did so, through the means of the Urim and Thummin and obtained for them in succession the folowing Revelations.

Revelation given to David Whitmer, at Fayette, Seneca County New York. June 1829.

[D&C 14]

Revelation given to John Whitmer, at Fayette, Seneca County, New York, June 1829.

[D&C 15]

Revelation given to Peter Whitmer Jr at Fayette, Seneca County, New York. June 1829.

[D&C 16]

We found the people of Seneca County in general friendly and disposed to enquire into the truth of these strange matters which now began to be noised abroad: many opened their houses to us in order that we might have an opportunity of meeting with our friends for the purposes of instruction and explanation. We met with many from time to time, who were willing to hear us, and wishful to find out the truth as it is in Christ Jesus, and apparently willing to obey the Gospel when once fairly convinced and satisfied in their own minds; and in this same month of June, my brother Hyrum Smith, David Whitmer, and Peter Whitmer Jr were baptized, ⟨in Seneca lake⟩ the two former by myself; the latter by Oliver Cowdery –

From this time forth many became believers, and were baptized, whilst we continued to instruct and persuade as many as ⟨applied.⟩ for information.

In the course of the work of translation, we ascertained that three special witnesses were to be provided by the Lord, to whom he would grant, that they should see the plates from which this work (the Book of Mormon) should be translated, and that these witnesses should bear record of the same; as will be found recorded, Book of Mormon First edition ⟨second book of Nephi, chap. 11.⟩[1] Page ⟨110⟩ and ⟨third european edition section 17, page 102.⟩[2] ~~second edition Page~~ .

Almost immediately after we had made this discovery; it occurred to Oliver Cowdery, David Whitmer, and the aforementioned Martin Harris (who had came to enquire after our progress in the work) that they would have me enquire of the Lord, to know if they might not obtain of him to be these three special witnesses; and finally they became so very solicitious, and teazed me so much, that at length ⟨I⟩ complied, and through the Urim and Thummin, I obtained of the Lord for them the folowing Revelation. [p. 23]

Revelation to Oliver Cowdery, David Whitmer, and Martin Harris, at Fayette, Seneca County, New York, June 1829. Given previous to their viewing the plates containing the Book of Mormon.

[D&C 17]

Not many days after the above commandment was given, we four, viz Martin Harris, David Whitmer, Oliver Cowdery and myself, agreed to retire into the woods, and try to obtain by fervent and humble prayer, the fulfilment of the promises given in this revelation; that they should have a view of the plates. we accordingly made choice of a piece of woods convenient to Mr Whitmer's house, to which we retired, and having knelt down, we began to pray in much faith, to Almighty God to bestow upon us a realization of those promises. Ac-

1. 2 Nephi 25 in the current edition. The insertion is penciled in another hand.

2. This and the previous insertion are written in ink in another hand, possibly that of Robert Campbell.

cording to previous arrangement, I commenced by vocal prayer to our Heavenly Father and was folowed by each of the rest in succession; we did not yet however obtain any answer or manifestation of the divine favour in our behalf. We again observed the same order of prayer each calling on and praying fervently to God in rotation; but with the same result as before. Upon this our second failure, Martin Harris proposed that he would withdraw himself from us, believing as he expressed himself that his presence was the cause of our not obtaining what we wished for: He accordingly withdrew from us, and we knelt down again, and had not been [p. 24] many minutes engaged in prayer when presently we beheld a light above us in the air of exceeding brightness, and behold, an angel stood before us; in his hands he held the plates which we had been praying for these to have a view of: he turned over the leaves one by one, so that we could see them, and discern the engravings thereon distinctly: He addressed himself to David Whitmer, and said, "David, blessed is the Lord, and he that keeps ~~all~~ his commandments:" when immediately afterwards we heard a voice from out of the bright light above us, saying "These plates have been revealed by the power of God, and they have been translated by the power of God; the translation of them which you have seen is correct, and I command you to bear record of what you now see and hear".—I now left David and Oliver, and went in pursuit of Martin Harris, who I found at a Considerable distance fervently engaged in prayer; he soon told me however that he had not yet prevailed with the Lord, And earnestly requested me, to join him in prayer, that he also might realize the same blessings which we had just recieved: we accordingly joined in prayer, and ultimately obtained our desires, for before we had yet finished, the same vision was opened to our view; at least it was again to me, and I once more beheld, and seen, and heard the same things; whilst at the same moment, Martin Harris cried out, apparently in an ecstasy of Joy " 'Tis enough, 'tis enough; mine eyes have beheld, mine eyes have beheld", And jumping up he shouted, Hosanna, blessing God; and otherwise rejoiced exceedingly. Having thus through the mercy of God, obtained these glorious manifestations, it now remained for these three individuals to fulfil the commandment which they had received, viz: to bear record of these things; in order to accomplish which, they drew up and subscribed the following document.

The Testimony of Three Witnesses.

Be it known unto all nations, kindreds, tongues, and people, unto whom this work shall come, that we through the grace of God the Father, and our lord, Jesus Christ, have seen the plates which contain this record, which is a record of the people of Nephi, and also of the Lamanites, their brethren, and also of the people of Jared, who came from the tower of which hath been spoken; and we also know that they have been translated by the gift and power of God, for his voice hath declared it unto us; wherefore we know of a surety, that the work is true. And we also testify that we have seen the engravings which are upon the plates; and they have been shewn unto us by the power of God and not of man. And we declare with words of soberness, that an angel of God came down from Heaven, and he brought and laid before our eyes, that we beheld and saw the plates, and the engravings ther⟨e⟩on; and we know that it is by the grace of God the Father, and our Lord Jesus Christ, that we beheld and b⟨e⟩ar record that these things are true; and it is marvelous in our eyes, nevertheless, the voice [p. 25] of the Lord commanded us, that we should bear record of it; wherefore, to be obedient unto the commandments of God, we bear testimony of these things. And we know that if we are faithful in Christ, we shall rid our garments of the blood of all men, and be found spotless before the judgement seat of Christ, and shall dwell with him eternally in the heavens. And the honor be to the Father, and to the Son, and to the Holy Ghost, which is one God. Amen.

OLIVER COWDERY
DAVID WHITMER
MARTIN HARRIS.

Soon after these things had transpired the following additional tes[t]imony was obtained.

And also the Testimony of Eight Witnesses.

Be it known unto all nations, kindreds, tongues, and people, unto whom this work shall come, that Joseph Smith Jr, the translator of this work has shewn unto us, the plates of which hath been spoken, which have the appearance of gold; and as many of the leaves as the said Smith has translated, we did handle with our hands: and we also saw the engravings thereon, all of which has the appearance of ancient work, and of curious workmanship. And this we bear record with words of soberness, that the said Smith has shewn unto us, for we have seen and hefted, and know of a surety, that the said Smith has got the plates of which we have spoken. And we give our names unto the world, to witness unto the world, that which we have seen; and we lie not, God bearing witness of it.

CHRISTIAN WHITMER
JACOB WHITMER
PETER WHITMER JR
JOHN WHITMER
HIRAM PAGE
JOSEPH SMITH SEN
HYRUM SMITH
SAMUEL H. SMITH.

Mean time we continued to translate, at intervals, when not necessitated to attend to the numerous enquirers, that now began to visit us; some for the sake of finding the truth, others for the purpose of putting hard questions, and trying to confound us, Among the latter class, were several learned Priests ⟨who⟩ generally came for the purpose of disputation: However the Lord continued to pour out upon us his Holy Spirit, and as often as we had need, he gave us in that moment what so say; so that although unlearned, and inexperienced in religious Controversies, yet were we able to confound those learned Rabbi's of the day, whilst at the same time, we were enabled to convince the honest in heart, that we had obtained (through the mercy of God) to the true and everlasting gospel of Jesus Christ, So that almost daily we administered the ordinance of Baptism for the remission of sins, to[1] such as believed. We now became anxious to have that promise realized to us, which the Angel that conferred upon us the Aaronick Priesthood [p. 26] had given us, viz: that provided we continued faithful; we should also have the Melchesidec Priesthood, which holds the authority of the laying on of hands for the gift of the Holy Ghost. We had for some time made this matter a subject of humble prayer, and at length we got together in the Chamber of Mr Whitmer's house in order more particularly to seek of the Lord what we now so earnestly desired: and here to our unspeakable satisfaction did we realize the truth of the Saviour's promise; "Ask, and you shall recieve, seek, and you shall find, knock and it shall be opened unto you;" for we had not long been engaged in solemn and fervent prayer, when the word of the Lord, came unto us in the Chamber, commanding us; that I should ordain Oliver Cowdery to be an Elder in the Church of Jesus Christ, And that he also should ordain me to the same office, ~~accordin~~ and then ⟨to⟩ ordain others as it should be made known unto us, from time to time: we were however commanded to defer this our ordination untill, such times, as it should be practicable to have our brethren, who had been and who should be baptized, assembled together, when we must have their sanction to our thus proceeding to ordain each other, and have them decide by vote whether they were willing to accept us as spiritual teachers, or not, when also we were commanded to bless bread and break it with them, and to take wine, bless it, and drink it with them, afterward proceed to ordain each other according to commandment, then call out such men as the Spirit should dictate, and ordain them, and

1. MS. reads "so."

then attend to the laying on of hands for the gift of the Holy Ghost, upon all those whom we had previously baptized; doing all things in the name of the Lord.

The following commandment will further illustrate the nature of our calling to this Priesthood as well as that of others who were yet to be sought after.

Revelation to Joseph Smith Jr, Oliver Cowdery, and David Whitmer, making known the calling of twelve apostles in these last days, and also instructions relative to building up the Church of Christ, according to the fulness of the gospel: Given in Fayette, Seneca County New York, June 1829.

[D&C 18]

In this manner did the Lord continue to give us instructions from time to time, concerning ~~our~~ ⟨the⟩ duties which now devolved upon us, and among many other things of the kind, we obtained of him the folowing, by the Spirit of Prophecy and revelation; which not only gave us much information, but also pointed out to us the precise day upon which, according to his will and commandment, we should proceed ~~to organize~~ to organize his Church once again, here upon the earth. [p. 29]

[D&C 20]

Mean time our translation drawing to a close, we went to Palmyra, Wayne County, N.Y: Secured the Copyright; and agreed with Mr Egbert Grandon to print five thousand Copies, for the sum of three thousand dollars.

I wish also to mention here, that the Title Page of the Book of Mormon is a literal translation, taken from the very last leaf, on the left hand side of the collection or book of plates, which contained the record which has been translated; ~~and not by any means~~ the language of the whole running same as all Hebrew writing in general; and that, said Title Page is not by any means a modern composition either of mine or of any other man's who has lived or does live in this generation.

Therefore, in order to correct an error which generally exists concerning it, I give below that part of the Title Page of the English Version of the Book of Mormon, which is a genuine and literal translation of the Title Page of the Original Book of Mormon, as recorded on the plates.

The
BOOK OF MORMON

An account written by the hand of Mormon, upon plates, Taken from the plates of Nephi.[1]

Wherefore it is an abridgement of the record of the people of Nephi, and also of the Lamanites; written to the Lamanites, who are a remnant of the house of Israel; and also to Jew and Gentile: written by way of commandment, and also by the spirit of prophecy and of revelation.

Written, and sealed up, and hid up unto the Lord, that they might not be destroyed; to come forth by the gift and power of God unto the interpretation thereof: sealed by the hand of Moroni, and hid up unto the Lord, to come forth in due time by the way of [the] Gentile; the interpretation thereof by the gift of God.

An abridgement taken from the book of Ether, also; which is a record of the people of Jared; who were scattered at the time the Lord confounded the language of the people when they [p. 34] were building a tower to get to Heaven: which is to shew unto the remnant of the house of Israel what great things the Lord hath done for their fathers; and that they may know the Covenants of the Lord, that they are not cast off forever; and also to the convincing of ⟨the⟩ Jew and Gentile that Jesus is the Christ, the Eternal God, manifesting himself unto all nations. And now if there are faults, they are the mistakes of men; wherefore condemn not the things of God, that ye may be found spotless at the judgement seat of Christ.

---

1. This heading is written in large script in MS.

(The remainder ⟨of the Title Page⟩ is of course, modern)

A commandment of God and not of man to Martin Harris, given (Manchester New York, March, 1830) by him who is eternal.

[D&C 19]

Whilst the Book of Mormon was in the hands of the printer, we still continued to bear testimony, and give information, as far as we had opportunity; and also made known to our brethren, that we had received commandment to organize the Church And accordingly we met together for that purpose, at the house of the above mentioned Mr Whitmer (being six in number)[1] on Tuesday the sixth day of April, AD One thousand, eight hundred and thirty.

Having opened the meeting by solemn prayer to our Heavenly Father we proceeded, (according to previous commandment) to call on our brethren to know whether they accepted

---

1. The following note, in the hand of John V. Long, has been pasted on this page of the MS.:

"Names of the six members of the Church as they were organized Apr. 6, 1830

Oliver Cowdery
Joseph Smith
Hyrum Smith
Peter Whitmer Jun.
Samuel H. Smith
David Whitmer

"Some of these had been baptized previously; but were all baptized on the day of organization.

"These names were given to Joseph Knight by Oliver Cowdery.

(Signed) Joseph Knight

"G.S.L. City
"Aug. 11th 1862

(Copy) (Witnesses) G.A. Smith
Robt. L. Campbell
Thos. Bullock
John V. Long"

On references to the six who were present when the Church was organized, see note 5 on p. 241.

us as their teachers in the things of the Kingdom of God, and whether they were satisfied that we should proceed and be organized as a Church according to said commandment which we had received. To these they consented by an unanimous vote. I then laid my hands upon Oliver Cowdery and ordained him an Elder of the "Church of Jesus Christ of Latter Day Saints." after which he ordained me also to the office of an Elder of said Church. We then took bread, blessed it, and brake it with them, also wine, blessed it, and drank it with them. We then laid our hands on each individual member of the Church present that they might receive the gift of the Holy Ghost, and be confirmed members of the Church of Christ. The Holy Ghost was poured out upon us to a very great degree. Some prop⟨h⟩esied, whilst we all praised the Lord and rejoiced exceedingly. Whilst yet together I received the following commandment.

Revelation to Joseph Smith Jr, Given at Fayette, Seneca Co N Y. April 6th 1830.

[D&C 21]

We now proceeded to call out and ordain some others of the brethren to different offices of the Priesthood, according as the Spirit manifested unto us; and after a happy time spent in witnessing and feeling for ourselves the ~~proces~~ ⟨powers &⟩ the blessings of the Holy Ghost, through the grace of God bestowed upon us, we dismissed with the pleasing knowledge that we were now individually, members of, and acknowledged of God, "The Church of Jesus Christ," organized in accordance with commandments and revelations, given by him to ourselves, in these last days, as well as according to the order of the Church as recorded in the New Testament.

Several persons who had attended the above meeting, and got convinced of the truth, came forward shortly after, and were received into the Church, among the rest My own Father and Mother were baptized to my great joy and consolation, and about the same time, Martin Harris and a Orrin Porter[1] Rockwell.

Revelation to the Church of Christ, which was established in these last days, in the year of our Lord One thousand eight hundred and thirty: Given ⟨at⟩ Manchester New York, April 1830, in consequence of some desiring to unite with the Church without re-baptism, who had previously been baptized.

[D&C 22]

The following persons being anxious to know of the Lord what might be their respective duties, in relation to this work, I enquired of the Lord and received for them the following—

Revelation to Oliver Cowdery, Hyrum Smith, Samuel H. Smith, Joseph [p. 38] Smith Sen, and Joseph Knight Senr, given at Manchester, New York, April 1830.

[D&C 23]

On Sunday April 11th 1830, Oliver Cowdery preached the first public discourse, that was delivered by any ⟨of⟩ our number. Our meeting was held by previous appointment at the house of Mr Whitmer, Fayette, large numbers of people attended, and the same day the following were baptized; viz: Hyrum Page, Kathrine Page, Christian Whitmer, Anne Whitmer Jacob Whitmer, Elizabeth Whitmer, and on the 18th Do [ditto] Peter Whitmer, Snr. Mary Whitmer, William Jolly, Elizabeth Jolly, Vincent Jolly, Richard B. Peterson and Elizabeth Anne Whitmer, all by Oliver Cowdery in Seneca Lake.

During this month of April I went on a visit to the residence of Mr Joseph Knight, of Colesville, Broom Co N.Y. with whom and his family I had been previously acquainted, and of whose name I have above mentioned, as having been so kind and thoughtful towards us, while translating the book of Mormon. Mr Knights and his family were Universalists, but were willing

1. "Orrin Porter" written later in a different hand.

to reason with me upon ⟨my⟩ religious views, and were as usual friendly and hospitable. We held several meetings in the neighbourhood, we had many friends, and some enemies. Our meetings were well attended, and many began to pray fervently [p. 39] to Almighty God, that He would give them wisdom to understand the truth.

Amongst those who attended our meetings regularly, was Newel Knight son to Joseph Knight. He and I had ~~now~~ many and serious conversations on the important subject of man's eternal salvation: we had got into the habit of praying much at our meetings and Newel had said that he would try and take up his cross, and pray vocally during meeting; but when we again met together, he rather excused himself; I tryed to prevail upon him, making use of the figure, supposing that he should get into a mudhole would he not try and help himself out, and that we were willing now to help him out of the mudhole, he replied that provided he had got into a mudhole through carelessness, he would rather wait and get out himself, than have others to help him, and so he would wait untill he should get into the woods by himself, And there he would pray. Accordingly he deferred praying untill next morning, when he retired into the woods, where (according to his own account afterwards) he made several attempts to pray, but could scarcely do so, feeling that he had not done his duty, but that he should have prayed in the presence of others. He began to feel uneasy, and continued to feel worse both in mind and body, untill, upon reaching his own house, his appearance was such as to alarm his wife very much. He requested her to go and bring me to him. I went and found him suffering very much in his mind, and his body acted upon in a very strange manner. His visage and limbs distorted and twisted in every shape and appearance possible to imagine; and finally he was caught up off the floor of the apartment and tossed about most fearfully. His situation was soon made known to his neighbours and relatives, and in a short time as many as eight or nine grown persons had got together to witness the scene. After he had thus suffered for a time, I succeeded in getting hold ⟨of⟩ him by the hand, when almost immediately he spoke to me, and with great earnestness requested of me, that I should cast the Devil out of him, saying that he knew he was in him, and that he also knew that I could cast him out. I replied "If you know that I can, it shall be done" And then almost unconsciously I rebuked the devil, and commanded him in the name of Jesus Christ to depart from him; when immediately Newel spoke out and said that he saw the devil leave him and vanish from his sight. This was the first miracle which was done in this Church, ~~and it~~ or by any member of it, and it was done, not by man nor by the power of man, but it was done by God, and by the power of Godliness: Therefore let the honour and the praise, the dominion and the glory be ascribed to the Father, Son, and Holy Spirit for ever and ever Amen.

The scene was now entirely changed for as soon as the devil had departed from our friend, his countenance became natural, his distortions of body ceased, and almost immediately the Spirit of the Lord descended upon him, and the visions of eternity were opened to his view. He afterwards related his experience as follows. "I now began to feel a most pleasing sensation resting upon me, and [p. 40] immediately the visions of heaven were opened to my view. I felt myself attracted upward and remained for some time enwrapt in contemplation in so much that I knew not what was going on in the room. By and by I felt some weight pressing upon my shoulder and the side of my head; which served to recall me to a sense of my situation, and I found that the Spirit of the Lord had actually caught me up off the floor, and that my shoulder and head were pressing against the beams."

All this was witnessed by many, to their great astonishment and satisfaction when they saw the devil thus cast out; and the power of God and his holy spirit thus made manifest. So soon as consciousness returned, his bodily weakness was such that we were obliged to lay him upon his bed, and wait upon him for some time. As may be expected, such a scene as this contributed much to make believers of those who witnessed it, and finally, the greater part of them became members of the Church.

Soon after this occurrence I returned to Fayette, Seneca County. The Book of Mormon ("The Stick of Joseph in the hands of Ephraim") had now been published for some time, and as the ancient Prophet had predicted of it; "It was accounted as a strange thing." No small stir was created by its appearance; great opposition, ⟨and⟩ much persecution followed the believers of its authenticity; but it had now come to pass that, Truth had sprung out of the earth; and Righteousness had looked down from Heaven, so we feared not our opponents, knowing that we had both Truth and righteousness on our side; that we had both the Father and the Son, because we had the doctrines of Christ and abided in them; and therefore ⟨we⟩ continued to preach and to give information to all who were willing to hear.

During the last week in May the above mentioned Newel Knight came to visit us, at Fayette and was baptized by David Whitmer.

On the first day of June 1830,[1] we held our first conference as an organized Church. Our numbers were about thirty, besides whom, many assembled with us, who were either believers or anxious to learn.

Having opened by singing and prayer, we partook together of the emblems of the body and blood of our Lord Jesus Christ, we then ~~called~~ proceeded to confirm several who had lately been baptized; after which we called out and ordained severals to the various offices of the Priesthood. Much exhortation and instruction was given; and the Holy Ghost was poured out

1. "Conference as an" has been written and partially erased at the beginning of this line.

upon us in a miraculous manner many of our number prophecied, whilst others had the Heavens opened to their view, and were so over come that we had to lay them on beds, or other convenient places: Among the rest was Brother Newel Knights who had to be placed on a bed, being unable to help himself. By his own account of the transaction, He could not understand why we should lay him on the bed, ⟨as⟩ he felt no sensibility of weakness. He felt his heart filled with love, with glory and pleasure [p. 41][1] unspeakable, and could discern all that was going on in the room, when all of a sudden a vision of futurity burst upon him. He saw there represented, the great work which through my instrumentality was yet to be accomplished. He saw Heaven opened and beheld the Lord Jesus Christ, seated at the right hand of the Majesty on high, and had it made plain to his understanding that the time would come whe[n] he would be admitted into his presence to enjoy his society for ever and ever. When their bodily strength was restored to these brethren, they shouted "hosannas to God and the lamb" and rehearsed the glorious things which they had seen and felt, whilst they were yet in the Spirit.

Such scenes as these were calculated to inspire our hearts with joy unspeakable, and fill us with awe and reverence for that Almighty Being, by whose grace we had been called to be instrumental in bringing about for the children of men, the enjoyment of such glorious blessings as were now at this time poured out upon us. To find ourselves engaged in the very same order of things, as observed by the holy Apostles of old; To realize the importance and solemnity of such proceedings, and to witness and feel with our own natural senses, the like glorious manifestations of the powers of the Priesthood; the gifts and blessings of the Holy Ghost; and the goodness and condescension of a merciful God, unto such as obey the ever-

1. At the top of page 42 "1841 April 1—commenced reading" is written in pencil.

lasting gospel of our Lord Jesus Christ, combined to create within us, sensations of rapturous gratitude, and inspire ⟨us⟩ with fresh zeal and energy, in the cause of truth.

Shortly after this conference David Whitmer baptized the following persons in Seneca lake. viz: John Poorman, John Jolly, Julia Anne Jolly—and Harriett Jolly, Jerushee Smith, Kathrine Smith, William Smith, Don C Smith—Peter [Porter] Rockwell—Caroline Rockwell and Electa Rockwell.

Immediately after conference, I returned to my own house, and from thence (accompanied by my wife, Oliver Cowdery, John Whitmer and David Whitmer) journeyed again on a visit to Mr Knight's of Colesville, Broom Co. We found a number in the neighborhood still believing and now anxious to be baptized.

We appointed a meeting for the Sabbath, and on the afternoon of Saturday we erected a dam across a stream of water which was convenient, for the purpose of there attending to the ordinance, but during the night a mob collected, and tore down our dam which hindered us of attending to the baptism on the sabbath.

We afterward found out that this mob had been instigated to this act of molestation, by certain Sectarian Priests of the neighborhood, who began to consider their craft in danger, and took this plan to stop the progress of the truth, and the sequel will show how determinedly they prosecuted their opposition, as well as to how little purpose in the end.

The Sabbath arrived and we held our meeting, Oliver Cowdery preached, and others of us bore testimony to the truth of the Book of Mormon, the doctrine of [p. 42] repentance, baptism for the remission of sins, and laying on of hands for the gift of the Holy Ghost &c &c, Amongst our Audience were those who had torn down our dam and who seemed wishful to give us trouble, but did not untill after the meeting was dismissed, when they immediately commenced talking to those whom they considered our friends, to try to turn them against us and our doctrines.

Amongst the many present at this meeting was one Emily Coburn [Colburn] sister to the wife of Newel Knight. The Revd. Mr Shearer, a ~~divine~~⟨Priest⟩[1] of the presbyterian faith, who had considered himself her pastor,[2] came to understand that she was likely to believe our doctrine, and had a short ⟨time⟩ previous to this, ~~our~~ meeting, came to labor with her, but having spent some time with her without being able to persuade her against us, he endeavored to have her leave her sisters house, and go with him to her father's, who lived at a distance ~~of at least some miles off~~: For this purpose he had recourse to stratagem, he told her that one of her brothers was waiting at a certain place, wishful to have her go home with him. He succeeded thus to get her a little distance from the house when, seeing that her brother was not in waiting for her, She refused to go any further with him; upon which he got hold of her by the arm to force her along; but her sister, was soon with them; ~~and~~ the two women were too many for him and he was forced to sneak off without his ⟨Prey⟩[3] ~~errand~~, after all his labor and

1. Insertion in another hand.

2. An extant letter written by John Sherer to Absalom Peters, Corresponding Secretary of the American Home Missionary Society in New York, confirms this story in the history and reveals Sherer's motivation: "I will relate a circumstance that has given me pain. A member of the church in Sandford a young female, has renounced her connexion with the church, and joined another in Colesville founded by Joseph Smith. this man has been known, in these parts, for some time, as a kind of juggler, who has pretended, through a glass, to see money under ground &c &c. The book, on which he founds his new religion, is called the "Book of Mormon." It contains not much, and is rather calculated to suit the marvelous, and unthinking. No man in his right mind can think the Book or the doctrines it contains, worthy of the least notice; yet there are a number who profess to believe in it. Since the church was formed, which was some time in July, about twenty have gathered around their standard, and have subscribed themselves to be the followers [of] Christ; for they call themselves a church of Christ, and the only church of Christ." (John Sherer to Absalom Peters, 18 November 1830, MS., The Amistad Research Center, Dillard University, New Orleans, Louisiana.)

3. Insertion in another hand.

ingenuity. Nothing daunted however he went to her Father,[1] represented to him something or other, which induced the Old Gentleman to give him a power of Attorney, which, as soon as our meeting was over, on the above named sunday evening, he immediately served upon her and carried her off to her father's residence, by open violence, against her will. All his labor was in vain however, for the said Emily Coburn, in a short time afterwards, was baptized and confirmed, a member of "the Church of Jesus Christ of Latter Day Saints."

However, early on Monday morning we were on the alert, and before our enemies were aware we had repaired the dam, and proceeded to baptize, when the following thirteen persons were baptized under the hands of Oliver Cowdery viz: Emma Smith, Hezekiah Peck and wife [Martha], Joseph Knight and wife [Polly]—William Stringham and wife [Esther]—Joseph Knight Jr Aa~~r~~ron Culver and wife [Esther]—Levi Hall—Polly Knight and Julia Stringham. –Before the baptism was entirely finished, the mob began again to collect, and shortly after we had retired, they amounted to about fifty men. They surrounded the house of Mr Knight (whither[2] we had retired ~~to~~) raging with anger and apparently wishful to commit violence upon us. Some asked us questions, others threatened us, so that we thought it wisdom to leave and go to the house of Newel Knight.

There also they followed us, and it was only by the exercise of great prudence on our part, and reliance on our heavenly Father that they were kept [p. 43] from laying violent hands upon us, and so long as they chose to stay, we were obliged to answer them various unprofitable questions, and bear with insults and threatenings without number.

---

1. Amasa Colburn. Emily's account of the incident is in Emily M. Austin, *Mormonism; or Life Among the Mormons* (Madison, Wisconsin: M.J. Cantwell, 1882), 30-48; see also, Porter, "A Study of the Origins of the Church," 199-201.
2. "whither" written over "where"

We had appointed a meeting for this evening, for the purpose of attending to the confirmation of those who had been the same morning baptized; the time appointed had arrived, and our friends had nearly all collected together, when to my surprise, I was visited by a constable, and arrested by him on a warrant, on charge of being a disorderly person; of setting the country in an uproar by preaching the Book of Mormon, &c &c. The Constable informed me (soon after I had been arrested) that the plan of those who had got out the warrant, was to get me into the hands of the mob, who were now lying in ambush for me; but that he was determined to save me from them, as he had found me to be a different sort of person from what I had been represented to him. I soon found that he had told me the truth in this matter, for not far from Mr Knight's house, the waggon in which we had set out; was surrounded by the mob, who seemed only to await some signal from the Constable; but to their great disappointment—he gave the horse the whip and drove me out of their reach. Whilst driving ~~along pretty quickly~~, ⟨in great haste⟩ one of the waggon wheels came off, which left us, once more, very nearly surrounded by them, as they had came on, in close pursuit; however we ~~now~~ managed to ~~get~~ ⟨replace⟩ the wheel ~~on again~~ and, again left them behind us. He drove on to the Town of South Bainbridge, Chenango County, where he lodged me for the time being, in an upper room of a Tavern, and in order that all might be right with himself and with me also, he slept during the night with his feet against the door, and a loaded musket by his side, whilst I occupied a bed which was in the room, he having declared that if we were interrupted unlawfully, that he would fight for me, and defend me as far as in his power.

On the day following a court was convened for the purpose of investigating those charges which had been preferred against me, A great excitement prevailed on account of the scandalous falsehoods which had been circulated, the nature of which will ~~come out~~ ⟨appear⟩[1] in the sequel.

In the mean time, my friend, Joseph Knight, had repaired to two of his neighbours viz: James Davidson and John Reid Esqrs, (respectable farmers; men renowned for their integrity, and well versed in the laws of their country,) and retained them on my behalf during my trial. At ⟨length⟩ the trial commenced amidst a multitude of spectators who in general evinced a belief that I was guilty of all that had been reported concerning me, and of course were very zealous, that I should be punished according to my crimes. Among many witnesses called up against me, was Mr Josiah Sto~~al~~⟨wel⟩ (of whom I have made mention, as having worked for him some time) and examined to the following effect. Q—Did not the prisoner Joseph Smith have a horse of you? Ansr. Yes. Q. Did not he go to you and tell you, that an angel had appeared unto him, and authorised him to get [p. 44] the horse from you? Ansr. No, he told me no such story. Q—Well; How ~~did~~ had he the horse of you? Ansr. He bought him of me, as an~~yther~~⟨other⟩[2] man would ~~do~~. Q—Have you had your pay? Ansr. That is not your business. The question being again put, the witness replied, "I hold his note for the price of the horse, which I consider as good as the pay—for I am well acquainted with Joseph Smith Jr, and know him to be an honest man; and if he wishes I am ready to let him have another horse on the same terms".

Mr. Jonathan Thompson was next called up, and examined—Q—Has not the prisoner, Joseph Smith Jr had a yoke of oxen of you? Ansr. Yes. Q—Did he not obtain them of you by telling you that he had a revelation to the effect that he was to have them? Ansr. No. He did not mention a word of

---

1. Alterations in this and previous paragraph in another hand, possibly that of Willard Richards.

2. Here, and in the next paragraph, "y" has been written over "o" to make "any." These alterations are in a different hand, possibly that of Willard Richards.

the kind concerning the oxen; he purchased them, same as any~~ther~~ ⟨other⟩ man would.

After a few more such attempts, the court was detained for a time, in order that two young women (daughters of Mr Sto~~al~~⟨wel⟩ with whom I had at times kept Company; might be sent for, in order, if possible to elicit something from them which might be made a pretext against me. The young Ladies arrived and were severally examined, touching my character, and conduct in general but particularly as to my behaviour towards them both in publick and private, when they both bore such testimony in my favor, as left my enemies without a pretext on their account.– Several attempts were now made to prove something against me, and even circumstances which were alleged to have taken place in Broom County were brought forward; but these, my lawyers would not ~~here~~ admit of ⟨as testimony⟩ against me, ⟨~~in this~~⟩ in consequence of which, my persecutors managed to detain the court, untill they had succeeded in obtaining a warrant from Broom Co, and which warrant they served upon me, at the very moment ~~in which I had been~~ ⟨that I was⟩ acquitted by this court.[1]

The constable who served this second warrant upon me, had no sooner arrested me, than he began to abuse and insult me, and so unfeeling was he with me, that although I had been kept all the day in court, without any thing to eat since ~~the~~ morning, yet he hurried me off to Broom Co, a distance of about fifteen miles before he allowed me any kind of food whatever.

He took me to a tavern, and gathered in a number of men, who used every means to abuse, ridicule, and insult me. They spit upon me, pointed their fingers at me, saying prophesy, prophesy, and thus did they imitate those who crucified the Saviour of mankind, not knowing what they did. We were at this time not far distant from my own house. I wished to be

1. Alterations in this paragraph are probably by Willard Richards.

allowed the privilege of spending the night with my wife at home, offering any wished for security, for my appearance, but this was denied me. I applied for something to eat. ~~the~~ The Constable ordered me some crusts of bread, and water, which was the only ~~fare~~ ⟨~~Pr~~ food⟩ I ~~that night~~ received ⟨that night⟩. At length we retired to bed; the constable [p. 45] made me lie next the wall; He then laid himself down by me, and put his arm around me; and upon my moving in the least, would clench me fast, fearing that I intended to escape from him: And in this ~~{not~~ very ⟨dis⟩agreeable} manner did we pass the night.– ⟨The⟩ next[1] day I was brought before the Magistrate's Court of Colesville, Broom Co, and put upon my trial. My former faithful friends and lawyers were again at my side, my former persecutors were arrayed against me. Many witnesses were again called forward and examined; some of whom swore to the most palpable falsehoods, and like to the false witnesses which had appeared against me the day previous; they contradicted themselves so plainly, that the Court would not admit their testimony. Others were called who shewed by their zeal, that they were willing enough to prove something against me; but all they could do, was to tell somethings which some body else had told them. In this frivolous and vexatious[2] manner did they proceed for a considerable time, when ~~finally~~ Newel Knight was called up, and examined by Lawyer Seymour, who had been especially sent for on this occasion. One Lawyer Burch, also was on the side of the prosecution; but Mr Seymour seemed to ⟨be⟩[3] a more zealous Presbyterian, and appeared very anxious and determined that the people should not be deluded by any one professing the power of Godliness; and not "denying the power thereof."

1. "n" written over "N."

2. Quotations around "frivolous and vexatious" have been crossed out in MS.

3. With this exception, alterations in this paragraph are apparently by Willard Richards.

~~So soon as~~ Mr Knight ~~had been~~ ⟨was⟩ sworn, ⟨&⟩ Mr Seymour ~~proceeded to~~ interrogate⟨d⟩ him as follows.[1] Q– Did the prisoner, Joseph Smith, Jr cast the devil out of you? Ansr. No sir. Q– Why, have not you had the devil cast out of you? Ansr. Yes Sir. ~~Q. And did he not cast~~ Q– And had not Joe Smith some hand in its being done? Ansr. Yes Sir. Q And did not he cast him out of you? Ansr. No Sir it was done by the power of God, and Joseph Smith was the instrument in the hands of God on the occasion; He commanded him ⟨to come⟩ out of me in the name of Jesus Christ. Q, And are you sure that it was the devil? Ansr. Yes Sir. Q Did you see him, after he was cast out of you? Ansr. Yes Sir I saw him. Q Pray, what did he look like?– (Here one of my lawyers, informed the witness that he need not answer the question,) The witness replied, I believe I need not answer your last question, but I will do it, provided I be allowed to ask you one question first, and you answer me. viz: Do you, Mr. Seymour, understand the things of the Spirit? No (answered Mr Seymour) I do not pretend to such big things. Well then (replied Knight,) it would be of no use to tell you what the devil looked like, for it was a[2] spiritual sight, and spiritually discerned; and of course you would not understand it, were I to tell you of it. The Lawyer dropped his head, whilst the loud laugh of the audience proclaimed his discomfiture. Mr Seymour now addressed the court, and in a long and violent harangue endeavored to blacken my character and bring me in guilty of the charges which had been brought against me; among other things, he brought up the story of my having been a money digger, and in this manner proceeded, in hopes to influence the Court and the people against me. Mr Davidson [p. 46] and Mr Reid followed on my behalf. They held forth in true colours, the nature of the prosecution; the malignancy of intention, and the apparent disposition to persecute their

1. Alterations in this sentence appear to be by Willard Richards.
2. "a" repeated in MS.

client, rather than to afford him justice. They took up the different arguments which had been brought by the lawyers for the prosecution and having shewed their utter futility and misapplication; then proceeded to scrutinise the evidence which had been adduced, and each in his turn, thanked God that He had been engaged in so good a cause, as that of defending a man whose character stood so well the test of such a strict investigation. In fact, these men, (although not regular lawyers) were upon this occasion able to put to silence their opponents, and convince the court that I was innocent.

They spoke like men inspired of God, whilst those who were arrayed against me, trembled under the sound of their voices, and quailed before them like criminals before a bar of justice.

The majority of the assembled multitude had now began to find that nothing could be sustained against me: even the Constable who arrested ⟨me,⟩ and treated me so badly—now came and apologized to me, and asked my forgiveness ~~of~~ ⟨for⟩[1] his behaviour towards me; and so far was he changed that he informed me that the mob were determined, that if the Court acquitted me; that they would have me, and rail ride me, and tar and feather me; and further, that he was willing to favour me, and lead me out in safety by ~~another~~ ⟨a private⟩ way.

The Court finding the charges against me, not sustained, I was accordingly acquitted, to the great satisfaction of my friends, and vexation of my enemies, who were still determined upon molesting me, but through the instrumentality of my new friend, the Constable; I was enabled to escape them, and make my way in safety to my wifes sister's house, where I found my wife awaiting with much anxiety the issue of those ungodly proceedings: And with her in company next day arrived in safety at my own house.

After a few days however, I again returned to Colesville,

1. Insertion in another hand in blue ink.

in company with Oliver Cowdery, for the purpose of confirming those whom we had thus been forced to ~~abandon~~ ⟨leave⟩[1] for a time. We had scarcely arrived at Mr. Knight's when the mob was seen collecting together to oppose us, and we considered it wisdom to leave for home, which we did, without even waiting for any refreshment. Our enemies pursued us, and it was oftentimes as much as we could do to elude them; however we managed to get home, after having travelled all night, except a short time, during which we were forced to rest ourselve[s] under a large tree by the way side, sleeping and watching alternately. And thus were we persecuted on account of our religious faith—in a country, the constitution of which, guarantees to every man the indefeasible right, to worship God according to the dictates of his own conscience; and by men too, who were professors [p. 47] of religion, and who were not backward to maintain this privilege for themselves; though they thus wantonly could deny it to us. For instance Cyrus McMaster a Presbyterian of high standing in his church was one of the chief instigators of these persecutions, and he at one time told me personally, that he considered me guilty without judge or jury. The celebrated Doctr Boyington [Nathan Boynton], also a presbyterian, was another instigator to those deeds of outrage: Whilst a young man named [Abram W.] Benton, of the same religious faith swore out the first warrant against me. I could mention many others also, but for brevity's sake, will make these suffice for the present. [there insert the sheet marked A.1.][2]

Mean time, notwithstanding all the rage of our enemies, still we had much consolation, and many things occurred to strengthen our faith, and cheer our hearts. After our return ~~from Colesville~~, the Church ~~there, were,~~ ⟨at Colesville⟩ as might

1. Insertion in another hand.

2. Notation, including brackets, in the hand of William W. Phelps, but there is no sheet marked "A.1."

be expected, ⟨were⟩ very anxious concerning our again visiting them, during which time, Sister [Sally] Knight, (wife to Newel Knight) had a dream, which enabled her to say that we would visit them that day, which really came to pass, for a few hours afterwards we arrived, and thus was ~~our~~ ⟨the⟩ faith ~~much~~ ⟨of the Saints⟩[1] strengthened, concerning dreams and visions in the last days, foretold by the ancient Prophet Joel: And although we, this time, were forced to seek safety from our enemies by flight, yet did we feel confidence that eventualy we should come off victorious, if we only continued faithful to Him who had called us forth from darkness, into the marvellous light of the Everlasting Gospel of our Lord Jesus Christ.

Shortly after our return home, we received the following commandments.

Revelation given to Joseph Smith Jr, and Oliver Cowderry, Given at Harmony, Pennsylvania, July, 1830.

[D&C 24]

Revelation given at Harmony, Penn. July 1830.

[D&C 25]

Revelation to Joseph Smith Jr. Oliver Cowdery and John Whitmer, given at Harmony, Penn, July 1830.

[D&C 26]

Shortly after we had received the above revelations, Oliver Cowdery returned to Mr Whitmers, and I began to arrange and copy the revelations which we had received from time to time; in which I was assisted by John Whitmer, who now resided with me. Whilst thus (~~and otherwise at intervals~~) employed in the work appointed me, by my Heavenly Father; I received a letter from Oliver Cowdery—the contents of which, gave me

1. First two alterations in this paragraph appear to be by Thomas Bullock; the last two by Willard Richards.

both sorrow and uneasiness. Not having that letter ⟨now⟩ in my possession, I cannot, of course give it here in full, but merely an extract of the most prominent parts, which I can yet, and expect long to remember. He wrote to inform me, that he had discovered an error in one of the commandments, Book [p. 50] of "Doctrine and Covenants" Sect. 2nd Par. 7th "and truly manifest by their works that they have received of the Spirit of Christ unto the remission of their sins"[1]

The above quotation he said was erroneous, and added; "I command you in the name of God to erase those words, that no priestcraft be amongst us."

I immediately wrote to him in reply, in which I asked him, by what authority he took upon him to command me to alter, or erase, to add or diminish to or from a revelation or commandment from Almighty God. In a few days afterwards I visited him and Mr Whitmer's family, when I found the family in general of his opinion concerning the words above quoted; and it was not without both labor and perseverance that I could prevail with any of them to reason calmly on the subject; however Christian Whitmer, at length got convinced that it was reasonable and according to scripture, and finally, with his assistance I succeeded in bringing not only the Whitmer family, but also Oliver Cowdery ~~also~~ to acknowledge that they had been in error, and that the sentence in dispute was in accordance ⟨with⟩ ~~of~~ the rest of the commandment. And thus was this error rooted out, which having its rise in presumption and rash judgement, was the more particularly calculated (when once fairly understood) to teach each and all of ~~the~~ us the necessity of humility, and meekness before the Lord, that he might teach us of his ways; that we might walk in his paths, and live by every word which proceedeth forth from his mouth.

Early in the month of August, Newel Knight and his wife paid us a visit, at my place at Harmony, Penn; and as neither

1. See D&C 20:37.

his wife nor mine had been as yet confirmed, ~~and~~ it was proposed that we should confirm them, and partake together of the sacrament, before he and his wife should leave us.– In order to prepare for this; I set out to go to procure some wine for the occasion, but had gone ~~but~~ ⟨only⟩ a short distance when I was met by a heavenly messenger, and received the following revelation; the first paragraph of which was written at this time, and the remainder in the September following.

Revelation given at Harmony Penn, August 1830.

[D&C 27]

In obedience to the above commandment we prepared some wine of our own make, and held out meeting, consisting only of five viz: Newel Knight and wife, myself and my wife, and John Whitmer. We partook together of the sacrament, after which we confirmed these two sisters into the Church, and spent the evening in a glorious manner. The Spirit of the Lord was poured out [p. 52] upon us, we praised the Lord God, and rejoiced exceedingly.

About this time a spirit of persecution began ⟨again⟩ to manifest itself against us in the neighborhood where I now resided, which was commenced by a man of the methodist persuasion, who professed to be a minister of God [Nathaniel C. Lewis], ~~and whose name was~~ [*blank*]. This man ~~came to~~ understood,[1] that my father in law and his family had promised us protection, and were friendly; and enquiring into the work, and knowing that if he could get him turned against me, my friends in that place would be but few, he accordingly went to visit my father in law, and told him falsehoods concerning me, of the most shameful nature, which turned the Old gentleman and his family so much against us, that they would no longer promise us protection, nor believe our doctrines.

Towards the latter end of August I (in company with John

1. "Understood" written over "understand."

and David Whitmer, and my brother Hyrum Smith) visited the church at Colesville, N.Y. Well knowing the determined hostility of our enemies in that quarter, and also knowing that it was our duty to visit the church, we had called upon our Heavenly Father in mighty prayer, that he would grant us an opportunity of meeting with them; that he would blind the eyes of our enemies, so that they would not know us, and that we might on this occasion return unmolested.– Our prayers were not in vain, for, when within a little distance of Mr Knights place, we encountered a large company at work upon the public road, among ⟨whom⟩ were several of our most bitter enemies. They looked earnestly at us, but not knowing us. we passed on with out interruption. We that evening assembled the church, and confirmed them, partook of the sacrament, and held a happy meeting, having much reason to rejoice in the God of our salvation, and sing Hosannas to his holy name.

Next morning we set out on our return home, and although our enemies had offered a reward of five dollars, to any one who would give them information of our arrival, yet did we get clear ~~out~~ of the neighborhood, without the least annoyance, and arrived at home in safety.– Some few days afterwards however, Newel Knight came to my place, and from him we learnt that very shortly after our departure the mob ~~had~~ came to know of our having been there, when they immediately collected together, and ~~had~~ threatened the brethren and very much annoyed them during all that day.

Mean time Brother Knight had came, with his waggon, prepared to move my family, &c, &c, to Fayette, N Y. Mr Whitmer having heard of the persecutions which had been got up against us at Harmony, Penn, had invited ⟨us⟩ to go and live with him; and during the last week of August we arrived at Fayette, amidst the congratulations of our brethren and friends.

To our great grief however, we soon found that Satan had been lying in wait to deceive, and seeking whom he might devour. Brother Hyrum [p. 53] Page had got in his possession, a certain stone, by which he had obtained ~~to certain~~ ⟨two⟩ revelations, concerning the upbuilding of Zion, the order of the Church &c &c, all of which were entirely at variance with the order of Gods house, as laid down in the new Testament, as well as in our late revelations.

As a conference meeting had been appointed for the first day of September, I thought it wisdom not to do much more than to converse with the brethren on the subject, untill the conference should meet. Finding however that many (especially the Whitmer family and Oliver Cowdery) were believing much in the things set forth by this stone, we thought best to enquire of the Lord concerning so important a matter, and before conference convened, we received the following,

Revelation to Oliver Cowdery, Given at Fayette, N,Y. September 1830.

[D&C 28]

Revelation given in the presence of six elders, in Fayette, N,Y. September 1830.

[D&C 29]

At length, our conference assembled; the subject of the stone above mentioned, was discussed, and after considerable investigation, Brother Page, as well as the whole church who were present, renounced the said stone, and all things connected therewith, much to our mutual satisfaction and happiness. We now partook of the sacrament, confirmed, and ordained many, and attended to a great variety of Church business on that and the following day; during which time we had much of the power of God manifested amongst us; the Holy Ghost came upon us, and filled us with joy unspeakable; and peace, and faith, and hope, and charity abounded in our midst. Before we separated we obtained the following,

Revelation to David Whitmer, Peter Whitmer Jr. and John Whitmer given at Fayette, New York, September, 1830.

[D&C 30]

Revelation to Thomas B. Marsh, given at Fayette, September 1830.

[D&C 31]

[p. 59] /[1]During this Conference which continued three days the utmost harmony prevailed and all things were settled satisfactory to all present, and a desire was manifest by all the saints to go forward and labor with all their power to spread the great and glorious principles of truth which had been revealed by our heavenly father. A number were baptized during the conference and the work of the Lord spread and prevailed.

At this time a great desire was manifest by several of the Elders respecting the remnants of the house of Joseph—the Lamanites residing in the west, knowing that the purposes of God were great to that people and hoping that the time had come when the promises of the Almighty in regard to that people were about to be accomplished, and that they would receive the gospel and enjoy its blessings. The desire being so great that it was agreed upon we should enquire of the Lord respecting the propriety of sending some of the Elders among them, which we accordingly did and received the following revelation

Revelation to Parley P. Pratt and Ziba Peterson given Octr. 1830

[D&C 32]

Immediately on ~~the receipt~~ receiving[2] this revelation preparations were made for the journey of the brethren therein

1. James Mulholland's handwriting ends, and Robert B. Thompson's begins.
2. "Receiving" written over "of."

designated to the boarders of the Lamanites[1] and a copy of the revelation was given them: [p. 60]

~~Having got ready for their journey~~ They[2] bade adieu to their Brethren and friends and commenced their journey, preaching by the way and leaving a sealing testimony behind them lifting up their voice[s] like a trump in the different villages through which they passed. They continued their journey until they came to ~~Kirtland~~ ⟨Mentor⟩ Ohio,[3] where they tarried some time there being quite a number in that place ⟨& vicinity⟩ who believed their testimony and came forward and obeyed the gospel among the number was ~~Elder~~ Sidney S. Rigdon and a large portion of the Church over which he presided.[4]

---

1. Known as the Lamanite Mission, Oliver Cowdery, Peter Whitmer, Jr., Parley Pratt, and Ziba Peterson traveled to Missouri in the fall and winter of 1830-31, where they sought to deliver the message of the Book of Mormon to the Indians on the American frontier. Although the sojourn among the Indians produced limited results, the mission foreshadowed the establishment of dual Mormon gathering places in Ohio and Missouri in 1831. While passing through Ohio, the missionaries converted Parley Pratt's minister friend, Sidney Rigdon, at Mentor, and a large number of his congregation. These converts formed the nucleus of the Kirtland congregation. (Parley P. Pratt, Jr., ed., *Autobiography of Parley Parker Pratt* [Salt Lake City: Deseret Book Company, 1961], 47-58. See also, Warren A. Jennings, "The First Mormon Mission to the Indians," *Kansas Historical Quarterly* 38 [Autumn 1971]: 288-99; and Richard L. Anderson, "The Impact of the First Preaching in Ohio," *BYU Studies* 11 [Summer 1971]: 474-96.)

2. This and the following cancellation are in pencil. "T" is written over the "t" in "they."

3. The extensive autobiographical data on Sidney Rigdon that follows indicates his probable involvement in the History when it was first written (see Diary of Joseph Smith, 30 April–2 May 1838), his prominence in the Church at the time, and the need to respond to charges that he had played a role in the writing of the Book of Mormon. Later, however, at the beginning of the twentieth century, when the History was edited for publication in its present form, Rigdon's prominence had diminished. Theories connecting Rigdon to the Book of Mormon's origin had lost their credibility, the lengthy data on Rigdon was evidently felt to be too extensive to be a featured part of the text; hence it was drastically condensed.

At this point in the MS., a penciled insertion (* to page 72) directs the reader forward to page 72, and a penciled line cancels the intervening twelve pages of text, thus designating the Rigdon material that was deleted from the text of the published History. (See Smith, *History of the Church*, 1:120-21.)

4. The alterations, including insertions, in this paragraph are apparently by Willard Richards.

Sidney Rigdon. Engraving. Charles W. Carter Collection. LDS Church Archives.

As there has been a great rumor and many false statements have been given to the world respecting Elder Rigdons' connexion with the church of Jesus Christ,[1] it is necessary that a correct account of the same be given so, that the public mind may be disabused on the subject. I shall therefore proceed to give a brief history of his life drawn from Authentic sources, as also an account of his connexion with the Church of Christ.

Sidney S Rigdon was born in Saint Clair Township Allegany County state of Pensylvania on the 19th Feby A.D. 1793, and was the youngest son of William and Nancy Rigdon. William Rigdon his father was a native of Hartford County, State of Maryland, was born A.D. 1749 and died May 26th A.D. 1810, in the 62nd year of his age. William Rigdon was the son of Thomas Baker and Ann Lacy Rigdon. Thomas Baker Rigdon was a native of the State of Maryland and was the son of Thomas Baker Rigdon who came from Great Britain.

Ann Lacy Rigdon, Grandmother of Sidney ~~S~~ Rigdon was a native of Ireland and emigrated to the City of Boston Mass and was there married to Thomas Baker Rigdon.

Nancy Rigdon his mother was a native of Freehold Monmouth County, New Jersey was born March 16, 1759 and died Octr. 3rd 1839 and was the eldest daughter of Bryant Gallaher who was a native of Ireland. Elisabeth Gallaher

1. A popular theme among early writers who could not accept Joseph Smith's explanation for the origin of the Book of Mormon was that Sidney Rigdon, a man of considerable literary ability residing in Pennsylvania, had contact with Joseph Smith before Mormon missionaries converted Rigdon at Mentor, Ohio, in 1830, and that he played a key role in writing the Book of Mormon. Efforts to connect Rigdon with the Book of Mormon stem from the Spalding theory, first published in E.D. Howe's *Mormonism Unvailed* in 1834. Although Rigdon denied the Book of Mormon connection attributed to him, the theory persisted into the twentieth century.

A review of early criticism of the Book of Mormon is in Hugh Nibley, "Mixed Voices: A Study in Book of Mormon Criticism," *Improvement Era* 62 (March-August, October, November, 1959); Bushman, *Joseph Smith and the Beginnings of Mormonism*, 119-28. On the Spalding theory see Bush, "The Spalding Theory Then and Now."

Mother to the said Nancy Rigdon was the second wife of the said Bryant Gallaher and whose maiden name was Reed and was a native of Monmouth County New Jersey. Her parents were natives of Scotland [p. 61]

In giving an account of his progenitors ~~Elder~~[1] Rigdon is of the opinion that he is of Norman Extraction, and thinks that the name of Rigdon was derived from the French word Rig-o-don which signifies a dance, which language was spoken by the Normans, and that his Ancestors came over to England with William the Conqueror.

His father William Rigdon was a farmer and he removed from the State of Maryland sometime prior to his marriage to the State of Pensylvania, and his Mother had removed some time prior to that from the State of New Jersey to the same state, where they were married and continued to follow agricultural pursuits. They had four children viz three sons and one Daughter. The eldest were sons called Carvel, Loami and Sidney S. the subject of this brief history. the fourth a Daughter named Lacy.

Nothing very remarkable took place in the youthful days of Elder Rigdon, suffice it to say that he continued at home with his parents following the occupation of a Farmer until he was seventeen years of age when his father died. After which event he continued on the same farm with his mother until he was 26 years of age.

In his 25th year he connected himself with a society which in that country[2] was called Regular Baptists. The church he united with was at that time under the charge of the Rev David Phillips a clergyman from Wales. The year following he left the farm and went to reside with the Rev Andrew Clark a Minister of the same order, during his continuance with him he received a licence to preach in that society and commenced

1. The cancellation here is in pencil.
2. "Country" written over "quarter."

from that time to preach and returned to farming occupations no more. this was in March A.D. 1819.

In the month of May of the same year, he left the State of Pensylvania and went to Trumball County State of Ohio, and took up his residence at the house of Adamson Bentley a preacher of the same faith, this [p. 62] was in July of the same year. While there he became acquainted with Phebe Brooks to whom he was married on the 12th of June A.D. 1820. She was a native of the State of New Jersey ⟨Bridge Town, Cumberland Co⟩ and had previously removed to Trumball Co Ohio After his marriage he continued to preach in that district of Country until Novr. 1821 when he was requested by the first Baptist Church of the City of Pitsburgh to take the pastoral charge of said Church, which invitation he accepted and in Feby A.D. 1822 he left Warren in Trumball Co and removed to that City and immediately entered upon his pastoral duties and continued to preach to that church with considerable success. At the time he commenced his labors in that church and for some time before, the Church was in a very low state and much confusion existed in consequence of the conduct of their former pastor. However, soon after Mr.[1] Rigdon commenced his labours there was soon a ple[a]sing change effected, for by his incessant labors and his peculiar style of preaching the church was crowded with anxious listners. the number of members rapidly encreased and it soon became one of the most respectable churches in that City. He was now a popular minister and was much respected in that City and all classes and persuasions sought his society.

After he had been in that City some time his mind was troubled and much perplexed with the idea that the doctrines maintained by that Society were not altogether in accordance with the scriptures, this thing continued to agitate his mind more and more and his reflections on these occasions were

1. "Mr." written over "Elder."

peculiarly trying. For according to his views of the word of God, no other Church that he was aquainted with was right or with whom he could associate. Consequently if he was to disavow the doctrine of the Church with whom he was then associated, he knew of no other way of[1] obtaining a liv[e]lihood except by manual labor, and at that time had a wife and three children to support.

On the one hand was wealth, popularity & honor, on the other ⟨appeared⟩ nothing but poverty and hard labour—[p. 63] But notwithstanding his great ministerial success and the prospect of ease and affluence, (which frequently swerve the mind and have an undue influence on too many who wear the sacred garb of religion, who for the sake of popularity and of wealth can calm and lull to rest their conscientuous scruples and succomb to the popular faith,) yet his mind~~s~~ rose superior to all these considerations, Truth was his pursuit and for truth he was prepared to make every sacrifice in his power. After mature deliberation, deep reflection & solemn prayer to his heavenly father, the resolve was made and the important step was taken and in the month of August A.D. 1824 after laboring among that people Two years and six months he made know[n] his determination to withdraw from that Church as he could no longer uphold the doctrines taught and maintained by it, this announcement was like a clap of thunder Amazement seized the congregation which was then collected which at last gave way for a flood of tears It would be in vain to attempt to describe the feelings of the Church on that occasion who were zealously attached to their beloved pastor, or the feelings of their minister on his part it was indeed a struggle of principle over affection and kindness.

There was at the time of his seperation from that Church a gentleman of the name of Alexander Camp[b]ell who was formerly from Ireland and who has since obtained considerable

1. "of" written over "to."

notriety in the religious world, who was then a member of the same association and who afterwards separated from it. There was also another gentleman of the name of Walter Scott a Scotchman by birth who was ~~at that time~~ a member of the Sandamenian church[1] in that City and who seperated from the same about that time.

Prior to these seperations, Mr Camp[b]ell resided in Bethany Brook County Virginia where he published a mont[h]ly periodical called the Christian Baptist. After they had seperated from the different Churches these gentlemen were on terms of the greatest friendship and frequently met together to discus the subject of religion being yet undetermined respecting [p. 64] the principles of the doctrine of Christ or what course to pursue. However from this connexion sprang up a new sect in the world known by the name of Camp[b]ellites, they call themselves "desciples." the reason why they were called Camp[b]ellites was in consequence of Mr. Camp[b]ell's publishing the periodical above mentioned and it being the means through which they communicated their sentiments to the world, other than this Mr Camp[b]ell was no more the originater of that sect than ~~Elder~~ ⟨Mr⟩ Rigdon[2]

Having now retired from the ministry, and having no way by which to sustain his family besides his own industry, he was necessi[t]ated to find other imployment in order to provide

---

1. "Sandamenian" written over "Scandinavian" in MS.

The Sandemanians, originally Glasites, were a Christian sect founded about 1730 in Scotland by John Glas, a Presbyterian minister in the Church of Scotland. Deposed for believing that the Christian Church could not be upheld by political or secular influence, and that the kingdom of Christ is essentially spiritual, Glas founded his own church. Eventually, Robert Sandeman (1718-1771), Glas's son-in-law, became leader of the sect. Sandeman left England in 1764, established churches in New England, and settled in Danbury, Connecticut. Sandemanian churches attempted to conform to primitive Christianity as understood by them, which included lay priesthood, weekly observance of the Lord's Supper, washing of feet, and belief that accumulation of wealth was unscriptural. (*Encyclopedia Britannica Micropaedia*, 1979 ed., s.v. "Sandemanians.")

2. Alteration in MS. apparently by Willard Richards.

for their maintainance; and for this purpose he engaged in the humble capacity of a Journeyman Tanner in that City, and followed his new employment ⟨without⟩ murmering for two years. ⟨1826 Aug⟩[1] During which ⟨time⟩ he both saw and experienced, that by resigning his pastoral vocation in that city and engaging in the humble occupation of a tanner he had lost many who once professed the greatest friendship, and who manifested the greatest love for his society—that when he was seen by them in the garb suited to the employment of a tanner there was no longer that freedom, courtesy, and friendship manifested ⟨& that⟩;– many of his friends became estranged, and looked upon him ⟨with⟩ coolness and indiferance; too obvious to admit of deception. To a well regulated and enlightened mind, to one, who soars above the arbitrary and vain lines of distinction which pride or envy may have drawn, such conduct appears ridiculous; while at the same time it cannot but cause feelings of a peculiar nature in those who, for their honesty and integrity of heart have brought themselves into situations to be made the subjects of it.

These things, however ⟨did not⟩ affect his mind, so as to change his purpose. He had counted the cost before his separation and had made his mind known to his wife who cheefully shared his sorrow and humiliation; believing that all things would work together for their good, being conscious that what they had ⟨done,⟩ was for conscience sake, and in the fear of the Lord.

After laboring for two years [p. 65] as a Tanner, he removed to Bainbridge, G[e]auga County, Ohio, where it was known that he had been a preacher and had gained considerable distinction as a public speaker, and the people soliciting ~~to~~ him[2] ~~him~~ to preach he complied with their requests. From this time forward he devoted himself to the work of the ministry, con-

1. This insertion is a penciled addition in another hand.
2. "him" written over "have."

fining himself to no creed but held up the Bible as the rule of faith, and advocated those Doctrines which had been the subject of his and Mr. Campbell's investigations, vis. Repentance and Baptism for the remission of sins.

He continued to labor in that vicinity one year[1] and, During the time, his former success attended his labors; large numbers invariably attended his meetings. While he labored in that neighborhood he was instrumental in building up a large and respectable church in the Town of Mantua Portage County, Ohio. The doctrines which he advanced being new public attention was awakened and great excitement prevailed throughout that whole section of country and frequently the ~~congregation~~ ⟨congregations⟩ which he addressed were so large that it was impossible to make himself audible to all. The subjects he proposed were presented, in such an impressive manner to the congregations that those who were unbiased by bigotry and prejudice had to exclaim "we never heard it in this manner before". There were however some that opposed the doctrines which he advanced but not with that ~~noble~~ oppos[i]tion which ⟨ever⟩ ought ⟨to⟩ characterize the nob[l]e and ingenuous, when they hold different views respecting religion. Those by whom he was c~~hiefly~~ opposed well knew that an honorable and public investigation would inevitably discover the weakness and falsity of their doctrines consequently they shuned it, but resorted to base slander and abuse and ⟨endeavored⟩ by ridiculing the doctrines which he promulgated, to suppress them. This, however, did not turn him from the path which he felt to be his[2] duty; for he continued to set forth the ⟨Mr Rigdon was teaching the⟩[3] doctrine of repentance & baptism for remission of [p.66] sins, and the gift of the Holy Ghost according to the teachings

1. "1827" penciled in the margin in a different hand.
2. "his" repeated in MS.
3. Insertion in a different hand and ink; probably Willard Richards; "the" written in pencil.

of *Peter,* on the day of Pentecost; exhorting his hearers, in the mean time, to throw away their creeds of faith, to take the Bible as their standard and search its sacred pages to learn to live by every word that proceedeth from the mouth of the Lord, and to rise above every sectarian sentiment and the tradition of the age, and explore the wide and glorious fields of truth which the scriptures holds out to view.

After labouring in that neighbourhood one year, he received a very pressing invitation to remove to the town of Mento[r] in the same county, ~~and~~ about thirty miles from Bainbridge and within a few miles from Lake Erie, which he sometime afterward complied with.

The persons by whom he was more particularly requested, to move to that place, were the remnants of a Baptist Church which was nearly broke up, the members of which had become attached to the doctrines promulgated by ~~Elder~~ ⟨Mr⟩ Rigdon.[1]

The Town of Mento[r] was settled by wealthy and enterprising individuals, who had by industry and good management made that township one of the most delightful in that county or probably in the Western Reserve. Its advantages for agricultural purposes could hardly be surpassed, while the splendid farms, fertile fields, and stately mansions make it particularly attractive to the eye of the traveller and gives evidence of enterprise and wealth.

In that beautiful location he took up his residence, and immediately commenced his labors, with that zeal and assiduity which had formerly characterized him. But being a stranger, and many reports being put in circulation, of a character calculated to lesson him in the estimation of the people and consequently destroy his influence. Some persons were even wicked enough to retail those slanderous reports which were promulgated, and endeavour to stir up persecution against him, consequently many of the citizens were jealous and did

1. Alteration apparently by Willard Richards.

not extend to him that confidence which he might otherwise be expected. [p. 67]

His path was not strewed with flowers, but the thorns of persecution beset him and he had to contend against much prejudice and opposition, whose swollen waves might have sunk one less courageous, resolute and determined; yet, notwithstanding these unfavorable circumstances he continued to meet the storm, to stem the torrent and bear up under the reproach for some time.

At length the storm subsided; for after laboring in that neighborhood about eight months,[1] he so won upon the feelings of the people by his consistant walk and conversation, his frankness and sociability, combined with his overwhelming eloquence, that a perfect calm succeeded, their evil apprehensions and surmizings were allayed, their predjudices gave way, and the man whom they had looked upon with jealousy, was now their theme of praise and their welcome guest: Those who had been most hostil[e] now became his warmest[2] admirers and most constant friends. The churches in which he preached which had heretofore been filled with anx[i]ous hearers, were now filled to overflowing: The poor flocked to the services and the rich throng'd the assemblies.

The doctrines he advanced were new, but at the same time were elucidated with such clearness, and enforced with an eloquence altogether superior to what they had been accustomed to before, that those, whose sectarian predjudices were not too deeply rooted, who listened to the deep and searching discourses, which he delivered from time to time, could not fail of being greatly affected, and convinced that the principles he advanced were true, and in accordance with the scriptures

Nor were his labors and success confined to that Township alone, but calls were made in every direction for him to preach,

1. "1828" penciled in margin in a different hand.
2. "Warmest" written over "Tha."

which he complied with as much as he possibly could, until his labors became very extensive and spread over a vast extent of country.

Wherever he went the same success attended his ministry, and he was every way received with kindness and welcomed by persons of all classes. Predjudice after prejudice gave way on every hand. Oppostion after opposition was broken down, and bigotry was [p. 68] routed from its strong holds: The truths he advanced were received with gladness, and the doctrines he taught had a glorious ascendancy, wherever he had the opportunity of promulgating them.

His fame as an orator, and deep reasoner in the scriptures continued to spread far and wide, and he soon gained a popularity, and an elevation, which has fallen to the lot of but few; consequently thousands flocked to hear his eloquent discourses.

When it was known where he was going to preach, there might be seen, long before the appointed time, persons of all classes, sects, and denominations flocking like doves to the windows, from a considerable distance—The humble pedestrian, and the rich in their splendid equipages might be seen crowding the roads.

The churches in the different places w[h]ere he preached, were now no longer large enough to contain the vast assemblies which congregated from time to time, so that he had to repair to the wide spread canopy of heaven, and in the woods, and in the groves he addressed the multitudes which flocked to hear him.

Nor was his preaching in vain. It was not empty sound that so closely engaged the attention of his audiences and with which they were so deeply interested, but it was the truths which were imparted, the intelligence which was conveyed, and the duties which were enforced.

Not only did the writings of the new testament occupy his attention, but occasionally those of the antient prophets; particularly their prophesies which had reference to the present, and to the future, were brought up to review, and treated in a manner entirely new and deeply interesting. No longer did he follow the old beaten tract which had been travelled for ages by the religious world; but he dared to enter upon new grounds, called in question the opinions of uninspired men, shewed the foolish ideas of many commentators on the sacred scriptures—exposed their [p. 69] their ignorance and contradictions—threw new light on the sacred volume, particularly those prophesies which so deeply interested this generation, and which had been entirely overlooked, or mystefied by the religious world—cleared up scriptures which had heretofore appeared inexplicable, and delighted his astonished audience with things "new and old"—proved to a demonstration the litteral fulfilment of prophesy, the gathering of Israel in the last days to their antient inheritances, with their ultimate splendour and glory.– The situation of the world at the coming of the son of man.– The Judgments which Almighty God would pour out upon the ungodly prior to that event, and the reign of Christ with his saints on the earth in the mellenium.

These important subjects could not fail to have their weight on the minds of his hearers, who clearly discerned the situation in which they were placed, by the sound and logical arguments which he adduced, and soon, numbers felt the importance of obeying, that form of doctrine, which had been delivered them, so that they might be accounted worthy to escape those things which were coming on the earth and many came forward desiring to be baptized for the remission of sins. He accordingly commenced to baptize, and like John of old, there flocked to him people from all the region round about,– persons of all ranks and standings in society,– the rich the poor, the noble and the brave, flocked to be baptized of him.

Nor was this desire confined to individuals or families, but whole societies, threw away their creeds an[d] articles of faith, and became obedient to the faith he promulgated; and he soon had large and florishing societies throughout that whole region of country.

He now was a welcome visitor wherever he travelled, ~~and~~ his society was courted by the learned and intelligent, and the highest encomiums were bestowed upon him, for his biblical lore and his eloquence.

The work of the ministry engaged all his time and attention; he felt deeply for the salvation of his fellow man and for the attainment of which, he labored [p. 70] with unceasing diligence.

During this state of unexampled success, the prospect of wealth and afluence was fairly open before him, but he looked upon it with indifference and made every thing subserviant to the promotion of correct principles; and having food and raiment he learnt therewith to be content. As a proof of this his family were in no better circumstances, made no greater appearance in the world, than whe[n] he labored at the occupation of tanning. His family consisted of his wife and six children, and lived in a very small unfinished frame house, hardly capable of making a family comfortable, which affords an evident proof that his affections were not set upon things of a worldly nature, or secular agrandizement.

After he had labored in that vicinity some time and having received but little pecuniary aid; the members of the churches, which he had built up, held a meeting, to take into consideration his circumstances, and provide for his wants and place him in a situation suitable to the high and important office which he sustained in the church. They resolved upon erecting him a sui[t]able residence, where he could make his family comfortable and accomodate his numerous friends who visited him. A committe[e] was appointed to make a purchase of land and to erect such buildings as were necessary.

The committee soon made a purchase of a farm in a beautiful situation in that township and made contracts for erecting a sui[t]able dwelling house, stable, barn &c &c. and soon made a commencement on the house and had a quantity of the building materials on the spot. He being held in the highest respect by that people, they entered into the work with pleasure, and seemed to vie with each other in their labor of love, believing it a duty to make their beloved pastor and his family comfortablc.

His prospects with regard to temporal things, were now brighter than ever they had been [p. 71] before, and he felt happy in the midst of a people who had every disposition to promote his welfare.

Under these pleasing circumstances and enjoying this full tide of prosperity, he hardly thought, that for his attachment to truth, he would soon see the prospect blasted, and himself and family reduced to a more humble situation than before.

At this time, it being in the fall of A.D. 1830, Elders Parley P. Pratt, Ziba Peterson, Oliver Cowdery and Peter Whitmer, called at that town, on their way to the western boundaries of the State of Missouri, testifying to the truth of the "Book of Mormon," and that the Lord had raised up a prophet, and restored the Priesthood.

Previous to this Mr[1] ⟨Elder Parley P.⟩ Pratt had been a preacher in the same church with ~~Elder~~ ⟨Mr⟩ Rigdon and resided in the town of Amherst, Lorain Co. in that State, and had been sent into the State of New York on a mission, where he became aquainted with the circumstances of the coming forth of the book of Mormon, and was introduced to Joseph Smith Junr. and others of the Church of Latter Day Saints. After listening to the testimony of the witnesses, and reading the "Book" he became convinced that it was of God, and that the principles

1. "Mr" written over "Elder" here and in the next line are in ink in another hand. The following insertion ("Elder Parley P.") appears to be in the hand of Thomas Bullock.

A penciled cross in the MS. at the beginning of this paragraph marks the end of the Sidney Rigdon material designated for omission in the published history. (See Smith, *History of the Church*, 1:120-21.)

which they taught were the principles of truth, he was then baptized and shortly after was ordained an Elder and began to preach, and from that time became a streneous advocate of the truth.

Believing there were many in the church with whom he had formerly been united who were honest seekers after truth, induced him while on his journey to the west, to call upon his friends and make known the great things which the Lord had brought to pass[1]

*[2]The first house at which they called, was ~~Elder~~ ⟨Mr⟩ Rigdons, and after the usual salutations presented him with the Book of Mormon, stating that it was a revelation from God. [3]This being the first time ~~he~~ ⟨Mr Rigdon⟩[4] had ever heard of or seen the Book of Mormon, he felt very much surprised at the assertion, and replied that he had the Bible which he believed was a revelation from [p. 72] God, and which he pretended to have some aquaintance, but with respect to the book they had presented him, he must say that he had considerable doubts. Upon which they expressed a desire to investigate the subject, and argue the matter, but he replied; No! Young gentlemen, "you must not argue with me on the subject, but I will read your book and see what claims it has upon my faith, and will endeavour to ascertain, whether it be a revelation from God or not.

After some further conversation ~~on the subject~~ they expressed a desire to lay the subject before the people, and requested the privilege of preaching in ~~Elder~~ ⟨Mr⟩[5] Rigdon's chapel to which he readily consented. The appointment was accord-

1. "see four lines below—This being" is penciled sideways in the margin here, in another hand.

2. The asterisk is in pencil. The following insertion is in ink in another hand.

3. A penciled cross here and the words "see 2 paragraphs above–" refers to the cross preceding the paragraph that begins with "Previous."

4. This alteration is in pencil in another hand.

5. This cancellation and insertion are in ink in another hand; the following ones in this paragraph are in pencil.

ingly published and a large and respectable congregation assembled. Oliver Cowdery and Parley P. Pratt severally addressed the meeting. At the conclusion ~~Elder~~ ⟨Mr⟩ Rigdon arose and stated to the congregation, that the information they had that evening received was of an extraordinary character, and certainly demanded their most serious consideration, and as the Apostle advised his brethren "to prove all things and hold fast that which was good,"[1] so he would exhort his brethren to do likewise and give the matter a careful investigation, and not turn against without being fully convinced of its being an imposition, lest they should possibly resist the truth.

[2]This was indeed generous on the part of Elder Rigdon and gave evidence, of his entire freedom from any sectarian bias; but allowing his mind full scope to range untramelled through the scriptures, embracing every principle of truth and rejecting error under whatever guise it should appear, he was perfectly willing to allow his members the same privilege. Having received great light on the scriptures he felt desireous to receive more from whatever quarter it should come from. This was ⟨his prevailing⟩ characteristic, and if any sentiment was advanced by any one, that was new or tended to throw light on the scriptures or the dealings of God with the children of men, it was allways treasured up in his mind, and gladly received it. [p. 73]

After the meeting broke up, the brethren returned home with Mr.[3] Rigdon, and conversed upon the important things which they had proclaimed. He informed them that he should read the Book of Mormon, give it a full investigation, and then would frankly tell them his mind and belief on the subject,–

1. See 1 Thessalonians 5:21.

2. "See p. 74—" is penciled here in another hand, and a line is drawn through this and the next paragraph.

3. "Mr." written over "Elder" in another hand in this and the two following paragraphs.

Told them they were welcome to abide at his house until he had oppertunity of reading it.

~~About two~~ ⟨A few⟩[1] miles from Mr. Rigdons, at the town of Kirtland were a number of the members of his Church, who lived together and had all things common from which circumstance has arisen the idea that this was the case with the Church of Jesus Christ; to which place they immediately repaired and proclaimed the gospel unto them with considerable success for their testimony was received by many of the people and seventeen came forward in obedience to the gospel.

While thus engaged they visited Mr. Rigdon occassionally, and found him very earnestly engaged in reading the "Book of Mormon", praying to the Lord for direction, and meditating on the things he heard and read; and after a fortnight from the time the Book was put into his hands, he was fully convinced of the truth of the work, by a revelation from Jesus Christ which was made known to him in a remarkable manner, so that he could exclaim, "flesh and blood hath not revealed it unto me but my father which is in heaven."[2]

Being now fully satisfied in his own mind of the truth of the work and the necessity of obedience thereto he informed his wife of the same, and was happy to find that she was not only diligently investigating the subject but was believing with all her heart, and was desireous of obeying the truth, which, undoubtedly was a great satisfaction to his mind.[3]

The consequence ⟨of⟩ obeying the truth, and embracing a system of religion so unpopular as that of the church of Jesus Christ at that time was, presented itself in the strongest possible light. At present the honors and [p. 74] applause of the world, were showered down upon him, his wants were abun-

1. Insertion in pencil in another hand.
2. Matthew 16:17.
3. A pencil line is drawn through the text from the beginning of this paragraph to the point on page 75 where W. W. Phelps's handwriting begins.

dantly supplied, and even anticipated. He was respected by the entire community, and his name was a tower[1] of strength; His council was sought for, respected and esteemed. But if he should unite with the Church of Christ, his prospect of wealth and affluence would vanish, his family dependant upon him for support must necessarily share his humiliation and poverty. He was aware that his character and his reputation must suffer in the estimation of the community.

Aware of all these things, there must have been feelings of no ordinary kind, agitating[2] his bosom at that particular crisis, but yet they did not deter him from the path of duty. He had formerly made a sarifice for truth and conscience sake and had been sustained, consequently he felt great confidence in the Lord, believing that if he pursued the path of duty, no good thing would be withheld from him.

Although he felt great confidence in the Lord yet he felt it a trial of some magnitude when he avowed his determination to his beloved companion, who had before shared in his poverty and who had cheerfully struggled through it without murmuring or repining. He informed her what the consequences would undoubtedly be respecting their worldly circumstances if they obeyed the gospel and then said "My Dear you have once followed me into poverty, are you again willing to do the same" she answered I have weighed the matter, I have contemplated ⟨on⟩ the circumstances in which we may be placed, I have counted the cost, and I am perfectly satisfied to follow you. yea, it is my desire to do the will of God, come life or come death.[3] Accordingly they ⟨Mr Rigdon & wife⟩[4] were both baptized into the church of Jesus Christ;[5] and, together with

1. MS. reads "tour."
2. "Agitating" written over "agitate."
3. Handwriting of Robert B. Thompson ends and that of William W. Phelps begins.
4. Penciled insertion in another hand.
5. Sidney Rigdon was baptized 14 November 1830.

those who had been previously admitted to baptism, made a little branch in this section of Ohio, of about twenty members; whom the brethren, bound for the borders of the Lamanites, after adding to their [p. 75] number, one of their converts, Dr Frederic G. Williams, bid an affectionate farewell, and went on their way rejoicing.

The Lord, who is ever ready to instruct such as diligently seek in faith, gave the following revelation at Fayette New York.

A revelation to Ezra Thayre and Northrop Sweet given October, 1830.

[D&C 33]

In the forepart of November, Orson Pratt, a young man, of 19 years, who had been baptised at the first preaching of his brother, Parley P. Pratt, September 19 (his birth day) about six weeks previous, in Canaan N.Y., came to inquire of the Lord what his duty was, and received the following answer:

A revelation to Orson Pratt given November 1830.

[D&C 34]

~~It was~~[1] in December. ~~that~~ Elder Sidney Rigdon, ~~a sketch of whose history I have before mentioned,~~ came to inquire of the Lord, and with ⟨him⟩ came ~~that man, (of whom I will hereafter speak more fully,) named~~ Edward Partridge; he was a pattern of piety, and one of ⟨the⟩ Lord's great men, ~~known by his steadfastness and patient endurance to the end.~~ Shortly after the arrival of these two brethren, thus spake the Lord:–

A revelation to Joseph Smith Junr. and Sidney Rigdon given at Fayette, N.Y. December 1830.

[D&C 35]

And the voice of the Lord to Edward Partridge was,

1. Except for this first one, the cancellations in this paragraph are in pencil.

A Revelation to Edward Partridge given December 1830.

[D&C 36]

It may be well to observe here, that the Lord greatly encouraged, and strengthened the faith of his little flock which had embraced the fulness of the everlasting gospel, as revealed to them in the book of Mormon, by giving some more extended information upon the Scriptures; a translation of which had already commenced.[1] Much conjecture and conversation frequently occurred among the Saints, concerning the books mentioned and referred to, in various ⟨places⟩ in the old and new testaments, which were now no where to be found.[2] [p. 80] The common remark was, they are "lost books"; but it seems the apostolic churches had some of these writings, as Jude mentions or quotes the prophecy of Enoch the seventh from Adam.[3] To the joy of the little flock, which in all, from Colesville to Canandaigua, numbered about seventy members, did the Lord reveal the following doings of olden time from the prophecy of Enoch:

Extract from the prophesy of Enoch. ⟨Given by Revelation to Joseph Smith Jr.⟩[4]

[Moses 7]

Soon after the words of Enoch were given, the Lord gave the following commandment:

---

1. As early as 1830 Joseph Smith began a textual revision of the Old and New Testaments, a work that continued for more than two years. (See Robert J. Matthews, *A Plainer Translation: Joseph Smith's Translation of the Bible: A History and Commentary* [Provo, Utah: Brigham Young University Press, 1975], chapter 2.)

2. See, for example, Numbers 21:14; Joshua 10:13; 1 Kings 11:41; 1 Chronicles 29:29; 2 Chronicles 9:29; 2 Chronicles 20:34; 1 Corinthians 5:9; Colossians 4:16.

3. Jude 1:14-15.

4. Insertion in a different hand from surrounding text.

A Revelation to Joseph Smith and Sidney Rigdon, given December, 1830.

[D&C 37]

The year opened with a prospect, great and glorious, for the welfare of the Kingdom; for, on the 2d of January, 1831, a conference was held in the town of Fayette, N.Y., at which was received, besides the ordinary business transacted for the church, the following revelation:

[D&C 38]
[p. 90]

Not long after the conference closed, there was a man came to me, by the name of James Covill, who had been a baptist minister for about forty years, and covena[n]ted with the Lord that he would obey any command that the Lord would give through me as his servant, and I received the following Revelation, ⟨to James Covill⟩[1] given at Fayette N.Y. January 5, 1831.

[D&C 39]

As James Covill rejected the word of the Lord, and returned to his former principles and people, the Lord gave unto me and Sidney Rigdon the following revelation, explaining why he obeyed not the word: given at Fayette N.Y. January, ⟨6,⟩ 1831.

[D&C 40]

The latter part of January, in company ⟨with⟩ Brother Sidney Rigdon and Edward Partridge, I started with my wife for Kirtland, Ohio, where we arrived about the first of February, and were kindly received [p. 92] and welcomed into the house of

1. Penciled insertion in another hand.

brother N.K. Whitney.[1] I and my wife lived in the family of Brother Whitney several weeks, and received every kindness and attention, which could be expected, and especially from Sister [Elizabeth Ann] Whitney. The branch of the church ~~of church,~~ in this part of the Lord's vineyard, which had increased to nearly one hundred members, were striving to do the will of God, so far as they knew it; though some strange notions and false spirits had crept in among them. With a little caution, and some wisdom, I soon assisted the brethren and sisters to overcome them. The plan of "common stock", which had existed in what was called "the family," whose members generally had ~~embraced~~ embraced the ever-lasting gospel, was readily abandoned for the more perfect law of the Lord: and the false spirits were easily discerned and rejected by the light of revelation.[2]

The Lord gave unto the church the following revelation at Kirtland, Ohio, February 4, 1831.

[D&C 41]

1. The arrival of Joseph Smith in Kirtland, Ohio, marks the shift of Church headquarters from New York to Ohio. On the Mormon experience in Ohio see Backman, *The Heavens Resound*; James B. Allen and Glen M. Leonard, *The Story of the Latter-day Saints* (Salt Lake City: Deseret Book Company, 1976), chapters 3, 4; and Parkin, "Conflict at Kirtland."

2. Nearly all of those converted to Mormonism in Ohio by the Lamanite missionaries in the fall of 1830 had been disciples of Sidney Rigdon. Some of these converts were practicing a communal order called "the family," wherein they pooled their property in an attempt to follow the New Testament example of Acts 4:32. Upon learning of the success of the missionaries as they had passed through Ohio, Joseph Smith sent John Whitmer there to oversee the Ohio converts until the Prophet could go there himself. When Whitmer arrived, he observed that the "family" were "going to destruction very fast" because of the excesses of their communal living. "They considered from reading the scripture that what belonged to one brother, belonged to any of the brethren, therefore they would take each other's clothes and other property and use it without leave, which brought confusion and disappointments." The situation was corrected when Joseph Smith arrived in Ohio in February 1831. (Whitmer, "The Book of John Whitmer," chapter 2; Cook, *Joseph Smith and the Law of Consecration*, 6-7; Backman, *The Heavens Resound*, 15, 64.)

As Edward Partridge now appears by revelation as one of the heads of the church,[1] I will give a sketch of his history. He was born in Pittsfield, Berkshire county, Massachusetts, on the 27th of August, 1793, of William and Jemima Partridge. His fathers ancesters emigrated from Berwick, in Scotland during the seventeenth century, and settled at Hadley Mass., on Connecticut river. Nothing worthy of note transpired in his youth, with this exception,[2] that he remembers (though the precise time he cannot recollect.) that the spirit of the Lord strove with him a number of times, insomuch that his heart was made tender, and he went and wept: and that sometimes he went silently and poured the effusions of his soul to God, in prayer.

At the age of sixteen he went to learn the hatting trade, and continued as an apprentice for about four years. At the age of twenty he had become disgusted with the religious world. He saw no beauty, comeliness, or loveliness in the character of the god that was preached up by the sects. He, however, heard a universal Restorationer preach upon the love of God: this sermon gave him exalted opinions of God, and he concluded, that Universal Restoration was right according to the bible. He continued in this belief till 1828, when he and his wife were baptised into the Campbellite church by ~~elder~~ Sidney Rigdon, in Mentor, though they resided in Painesvill[e], (Ohio). He continued a member of this church, though doubting at times its being the ⟨true⟩ one, till ⟨Elders⟩ P.P. Pratt, O. Cowdery, P. Whitmer and Z Peterson came along with the book of Mormon, when he began to investigate the subject of religion anew; went with Sidney Rigdon to Fayette, N.Y. where on the 11th of December I baptised him in the Seneca river.[3] Other incidents of his life will be noticed in their time and place. [p. 94]

---

1. In a revelation dated 4 February 1831, Partridge had been called as bishop of the Church. (D&C 41:9.)

2. "Excepting" changed to "exception."

3. Lucy Smith wrote that Partridge and Rigdon arrived at the Smith home

On the 9th of February, 1831, at Kirtland, in the presence of twelve elders, and according to the promise heretofore made the Lord gave the following revelation, embracing the law of the church.

[D&C 42]

Soon after the foregoing revelation was received, a woman came with great pretensions to revealing commandments, laws, and other curious matters;[1] and, as every person (almost) has advocates for both theory and practice, in the various notions and projects of the age, it became necessary to inquire of the Lord, when I received the following. Revelation, given at Kirtland, February, 1831.[2] to Joseph Smith Jr.

[D&C 43]

The latter part of February I received the following revelation which caused the church to appoint a conference to be

---

during a preaching service, and that upon finishing his discourse Joseph Smith gave all who had anything to say an opportunity to speak. Then Edward Partridge arose, Lucy noted, "and stated that he had been to Manchester, with the view of obtaining further information respecting the doctrine which we preached; but, not finding us, he had made some inquiry of our neighbours concerning our characters, which they stated had been unimpeachable, until Joseph deceived us relative to the Book of Mormon. He also said, that he had walked over our farm, and observed the good order and industry which it exhibited; and, having seen what we had sacrificed for the sake of our faith, and having heard that our veracity was not questioned upon any other point than that of our religion, he believed our testimony, and was ready to be baptized." (*Biographical Sketches*, 170.)

1. According to John Whitmer, the woman's name was Hubble, a "prophetess," who "professed to have many revelations and knew that the Book of Mormon was true; and that she should become a teacher in the Church of Christ. She appeared very sanctimonious and deceived some, who were not able to detect her in her hypocrisy." (Whitmer, "The Book of John Whitmer," chapter 3.)

Ezra Booth wrote that Hubble "so ingratiated herself" into the favor of some of the elders "that they received her as a person commissioned to act a conspicuous part in Mormonizing the world." Even Sidney Rigdon "gave her the right hand of fellowship, and literally saluted her with what they called the 'kiss' of charity." But Joseph Smith put the matter in order. (See Cook, *Revelations*, 61-62.)

2. The following four words were added by Willard Richards.

held on the 6th of June ensuing. It was given at Kirtland February, 1831, to ~~me~~ ⟨Joseph Smith Jr.⟩[1] and Sidney Rigdon.

[D&C 44]

At this age of the church many false reports, lies, and fo[o]lish stories were published in the newspapers, and circulated in every direction, to prevent people from investigating the work, or embracing the faith. A great earthquake in China, which destroyed from one to two hundred thousand inhabitants, was burlesqued in some papers, as "Mormonism in China."[2] But to the joy of the saints who had to struggle against every thing that prejudice and wickedness could invent, I received the following. Revelation at Kirtland. March 7. 1831. Given to Joseph Smith, Jr—[3]

[D&C 45]

The next day after the above was received, I also received the following revelation relative to the gifts of the Holy Ghost. Given at Kirtland, March 8, 1831. To Joseph Smith Jr.

---

1. Alteration to the text appears to have been by Willard Richards.

2. In March and April 1831, American newspapers reported news from a collection of papers from Calcutta, India, and Canton and Peking, China. Reports included one from the Peking *Gazette* referring to an earthquake presumed to have occurred in China claiming the lives of 500,000 to 1,000,000 people in the provinces of "Peohe-li and Ho-nan." Another report dated 17 July from Canton stated that a "sort of revelation from the gods" was being disseminated, declaring that "in the 8th, 9th & 10th months, a great pestilence will prevail, and cause the death of persons innumerable. . . . The virtuous shall be spared, but the wicked will find it impossible to escape." On 5 April 1831 the Painesville *Telegraph*, under the heading "Mormonism in China," extracted from the New York *Journal of Commerce* the July 17 report from Canton dealing with the revelation. (See "From Canton," *Western Star* [Lebanon, Ohio], 9 April 1831, reporting an item from the New York *Journal of Commerce*, 23 March 1831; "Great Earthquakes," *Ohio State Journal* [Columbus, Ohio], 7 April 1831.)

In reality nineteenth-century China had no earthquakes of the magnitude reported. (See *Encyclopedia Britannica*, 1979 ed., s.v. "Earthquake.")

3. The last five words in this paragraph, and the last four in the next, were added by Willard Richards.

[D&C 46]

The same day that I received the foregoing revelation I also received the following, setting apart John Whitmer as a historian inasmuch as he was faithful.

Given at Kirtland, March 8, 1831, to ~~me~~(Joseph Smith Jr.)[1] and John Whitmer.

[D&C 47]

Upon inquiry how the brethren should act in regard to purchasing lands to settle upon; and where they should finally make a permanent location, I received the following. Revelation.

Given at Kirtland March, 1831. to Joseph Smith Jr.[2]

[D&C 48]

About this time came Leman Copley, one of the sect called shaking Quakers,[3] and embraced the fulness of the everlasting gospel, apparently honest hearted, but still retained ideas that the Shakers were right in some particulars of their faith; and, in order to have more perfect understanding on the subject, I inquired of the Lord and received the following revelation:

Given to Sidney Rigdon, Parley P. Pratt and Leman Copley at Kirtland, March, 1831.

---

1. Alteration by Willard Richards.
2. Last four words added by Willard Richards.
3. The United Society of Believers in Christ's Second Appearing (Shakers) were a celibate millenarian sect that had its origins among radical English Quakers, with ritual practices of shaking, shouting, dancing, whirling, and singing in tongues. Shaker doctrine was canonized from older traditions by Ann Lee, a Manchester textile worker, converted in 1758. In 1774 Lee established the Shaker movement in America. Upon her death in 1784, Joseph Meacham and Lucy Wright perfected the Shaker communal social organization, and by 1826 there were eighteen Shaker villages, including the one near Cleveland, Ohio. Shakers were noted for their model farms and orderly communities. Their industry produced numerous inventions, including the circular saw, a threshing machine, and the common clothespin. (*Encyclopedia Britannica Micropaedia*, 1979 edition, s.v. "Shakers.")

[D&C 49]

During the month of April I continued to translate the scriptures as time would allow; in May, a number of elders being present, and not understanding the different spirits abroad in the earth,[1] I inquired and received from the Lord the following

Revelation, given May 1831. [2]To Joseph Smith Jr.

[D&C 50]

Not long after the foregoing was received: and the saints from the state of New York began to come on,[3] and it seemed necessary to settle them, at the solicitation of Bishop Partridge, I inquired and received the following

Revelation, given May, 1831.[4] To Joseph Smith Jr.

[D&C 51]

On the 6th of June, the elders from the various parts of the country where they were laboring, came in and the conference before appointed, convened in Kirtland,[5] and the Lord

---

1. John Whitmer described a spirit of "error and enthusiasm" under which some of the early converts had fallen. "Some had visions and could not tell what they saw. Some would fancy to themselves that they had the sword of Laban, and would wield it as expert as a light dragoon; some would act like an Indian in the act of scalping; some would slide or scoot on the floor with the rapidity of a serpent, which they termed sailing in the boat to the Lamanites, preaching the gospel. And many other vain and foolish maneuvers that are unseeming and unprofitable to mention. Thus the Devil blinded the eyes of some good and honest disciples." (Whitmer, "The Book of John Whitmer," chapter 6; see also, Parkin, "Conflict at Kirtland," 66-76.)

2. The following four words added by Willard Richards.

3. Although Joseph Smith and a few others from New York had arrived in Kirtland, Ohio, in February 1831, the bulk of the New York Saints did not arrive there until May. (See Porter, "Origins of the Church," 296-322; Backman, *The Heaven's Resound*, 42-51; William G. Hartley, *They Are My Friends: A History of the Joseph Knight Family, 1825-1850* [Provo, Utah: Grandin Book Company, 1986], chapter 9.)

4. Remainder of line added by Willard Richards.

5. The official minutes date this conference 3 June 1831. (Cannon and Cook, *Far West Record*, 6-7.) John Whitmer also designates 3 June and indicates the conference may have lasted more than one day. (Whitmer, "Book of John Whitmer," chapter 7.)

displayed his power ⟨to the most perfect satisfaction, of the saints⟩[1] ~~in a manner that could not be mistaken. The man of sin was revealed, and the authority of the Melchisedec ⟨priesthood⟩ was manifested and~~ ⟨I⟩ conferred, ⟨the high priesthood⟩ for the first time, upon several of the elders.[2] It was clearly evident that the Lord gave us power in proportion to the work to be done and strength according to the race set before us; and grace and help as our needs required. Great harmony prevailed. Several were ordained; Faith was strengthened: and humility, so necessary for the blessing of God to follow prayer, characterized the saints. The next day as a kind continuation of this great work of the last days, I received the following: Revelation, given June 1831. ⟨To Joseph Smith Jr.⟩

[D&C 52]

Shortly after the above was received, at his request I ⟨Joseph Smith Jr⟩ inquired ⟨of the Lord⟩[3] and received the following

Revelation to Sidney Gilbert, given June, 1831.

[D&C 53]

The branch of the church in Thompson on account of breaking the covenant, and not knowing what to do, sent in

1. The alterations in this paragraph are by Willard Richards.

John Whitmer clarifies this reference, noting that the day previous, Joseph Smith had prophesied that the "man of sin" would be revealed. Then, during the conference, "while the Lord poured out His Spirit upon His servants, the devil took a notion to make known his power. He bound Harvey Whitlock and John Murdock so that they could not speak, and others were affected but the Lord showed to Joseph, the seer, the design of the thing; he commanded the devil in the name of Christ, and he departed, to our joy and comfort." (Whitmer, "Book of John Whitmer," chapter 7.)

2. The minutes of the conference list the twenty-three who were the first to be ordained high priests in the Church. (Cannon and Cook, *Far West Record*, 6-8.)

3. Insertions by Willard Richards.

their elders for me to inquire of the Lord for them which [p. 121] I did and received the following[1]

Revelation to Newel Knight, given June, 1831.

[D&C 54]

The elders now began to go to the western country, two and two, according to the ~~previous~~ word of the Lord ⟨about this time⟩ ~~From~~P.P. Pratt, ~~who had~~ returned from ~~t~~his ~~expedition~~ ⟨mission⟩ of last fall.[2] ~~during the spring, we had verbal information; and from letters from the still remaining elders we had written intelligence; and as this was the most important subject which then engrossed the attention of the saints, I will here insert the copy of a letter received~~ about this ~~from that Section,~~ ⟨time we received the following letter⟩ dated at Kaw township (Mo.) May 7, 1831.[3]

Kaw township (Mo.) May 7. 1831.

Our dearly beloved Brethren, I have nothing particular to write as concerning the Lamanites; and because of a short Journey which I have Just returned from; in consequence of which I have not written to you, since the 16th of last [p. 122] month. I ⟨myself⟩ and br. Ziba ⟨Petersen⟩ went into the county east, which is Fayette and is about 40 miles; and in the name of Jesus we called on the people to repent, many of whom are, I believe, earnestly searching for truth, and if sincerely, I pray they may find that precious treasure;– for it seems to be wholly fallen in the streets ⟨so⟩ that equity. ⟨cannot enter.⟩

The Letter we received from you informed us that the opposition was great against you; now our beloved brethren

---

1. The branch of the Church at Thompson comprising the Saints gathered there from Colesville, New York, had settled upon and begun improving land promised to the Church by Leman Copley. After Copley backed out of his agreement, the Thompson Saints sent a delegation led by Branch President Newel Knight to lay the matter before Joseph Smith. (Hartley, *They Are My Friends*, chapter 8.)

2. Parley Pratt returned to Kirtland from Missouri in March 1831.

3. Alterations in this and the next paragraph by Willard Richards.

we verily believe that we also can rejoice that we are counted worthy to suffer shame for his name, for almost the whole country, which consists of universalists, Atheists, Deists, Presbyterians, Methodists, Baptists, and professed Christian priests, and people, with all the devils from the infernal pit, are united, and foaming out their own shame; God forbid that I should bring a railing accusation against them, for vengeance belongeth to him who is able to repay: and herein, brethren, we confide.

I am informed of an other tribe of Lamanites, lately, who have abundance of flocks of the best kind of sheep and cattle, and they manufacture blankets of a superior quality. The tribe is very numerous; they live three hundred miles west of Santa Fe, and are called Navashoes. Why I mention this tribe is, because I feel under obligations to communicate to my brethren every information concerning the Lamanites, that I meet with in ⟨my⟩ labors and travels, believing as I do that much is expected from me, in the cause of our Lord; and doubting not but I am daily remembered before the throne of the most High, by all of my brethren, as well those who have not seen my face in the flesh, as those who have.

We begin to expect our brother Pratt soon; we have heard from him only when he was at St. Louis. We are all well, (bless the Lord!) and preach the gospel we will, if earth and hell oppose our way, and we dwell in the midst of scorpions: for in Jesus we trust: grace be with you all. Amen.

P.S. I beseech br. Whitney to remember and write, and direct to me, Independence, Jackson Co. Missouri

OLIVER COWDERY [P. 123]

While we were preparing for our Journey to Missouri, about the middle of June, W.W. Phelps and his family arrived among us, and, ⟨as⟩ he said, "to do the will of ⟨the⟩ Lord." I inquired and received the following

Revelation to W.W. Phelps, given June, 1831

[D&C 55]

Soon after I received the foregoing, Elder T.B. Marsh came, to inquire what he should do, as elder Ezra Thayre his yoke-fellow in the ministry, could not get ready for his mission to start as soon as he (Marsh) would;[1] and I enquired of the Lord and received the following.

Revelation, given June 1831.[2] To Joseph Smith Jr.

[D&C 56]

On the 19th of June, in company with Sidney Rigdon, Martin Harris, Edward Partridge, W.W. Phelps Joseph Coe, A.S. Gilbert and his wife,[3] I started from Kirtland, Ohio, for the land of Missouri, agreeable to the commandment before received, wherein it was promised, that if we were faithful the land of our inheritance, even the place for the city of the New Jerusalem, should be revealed.[4] We went by wagon, canal boats and stages to Cincinnati, where I had an interview with the Rev. Walter Scott, one of the fathers of the Campbellite, or Newlite church. Before the close of our interview, he manifested one of the bitterest spirits against the doctrine of the New Testament, ("that these signs shall follow them that believe," as recorded in the 16th chapter of the gospel according to St. Mark,) that I ever witnessed among men.

We left Cincinnati in a steamer and landed at Louisville, Ky. where we were detained three days in waiting for a steamer to convey us to St. Louis. At St. Louis, myself, Br. Harris, Phelp[s], Partridge, and Coe, went on foot by land to Inde-

1. At the June 1831 Kirtland conference, Marsh and Thayer had been paired as missionaries to travel to Missouri proselyting on their way. An uncanonized revelation given for Joseph Smith, Sr., and Ezra Thayer focuses upon the situation that prevented Thayer's mission with Marsh. (See Kirtland Revelation Book, 91-92, MS. LDS Church Archives; published in Cook, *Revelations*, 88-91.)

2. Remainder of line added by Willard Richards.

3. Elizabeth Van Benthusen Gilbert (1800-1891).

4. D&C 28:9.

pendence Jackson county, Missouri, where we arrived about the middle of July; and the residue of the company came by water a few days after. Notwithstanding the corruptions and abominations of the times, and the evil spirits manifested towards us on [p. 126] account of our belief in the Book of Mormon, at many places, and among various persons, yet the Lord continued his watchful care and loving kindness to us day by day: and we made it a rule, wherever there was an opportunity, to read a chapter in the bible, and pray, and these seasons of worship gave us great consolation.

The meeting of our brethren, who had long waited our arrival, was a glorious ⟨one⟩ and moistened with many tears. It seemed good and pleasant for brethren to meet to gether in unity. But our reflections were great: coming as we had from a highly cultivated state of society in the east, and sta⟨n⟩ding now upon the confines or western limits of the United States, and looking into the vast wilderness of those that sat in darkness, how natural it was to observe the degradation, leanness of intellect, ferocity and jealousy of a people that were nearly a century behind the times; and to feel for those who roamed about with out the benefit of civilization, refinement or religion!—yea, and exclaim in the language of the prophets:—when will the wilderness blossom as the rose; when will Zion be built up in her glory, and where will thy Temple stand unto which all nations shall come in the last days? Our anxiety was soon relieved by receiving the following

Revelation given in Zion, July 1831.

[D&C 57]
[p. 128]

The first Sabbath after our arrival in Jackson county, brother W W Phelps preached to a western audience, over the boundary of the United States, wherein were present specimens of "all the families of the earth:" ~~Shem, Ham, and Japheth:~~ for there were several of the ~~Lamanites as descendants~~

~~of Shem,~~ ⟨Indians⟩ quite a respectable number of Negros ~~as descendants of Ham,~~ and the balance was made up of citizens of the surrounding country, and fully represented them[1] ~~great progenitor, Japheth.~~ ⟨selves as pioneers of the west.⟩ At this meeting two were baptised, who had previously believed in the fulness of the gospel. During this week the Colesville branch referred to in the latter part of the last revelation,[2] and Sidney Rigdon, Sidney Gilbert and wife, and elders Morley and Booth arrived, and I also received the the following

Revelation, given Zion, August, 1831.

[D&C 58]

On the 2d day of August, I assisted the Colesville branch of the church[3] to lay the first log for a house as a foundation of Zion, in Kaw township, twelve miles west of Independence. The log was carried and placed by twelve men in honor of the twelve tribes of Israel.[4] At the same time, through prayer, the land of Zion was consecrated and dedicated for the gathering of the Saints by Elder Rigdon; and it was a season of joy to those present, and afforded a glimpse of the future, which time will yet unfold to the satisfaction of the faithful.

As we had received a commandment for elder Rigdon to

---

1. "them" written over "their"

2. Insertion, "see note to be inserted," penciled in another hand.

3. According to Oliver Cowdery, the Colesville Branch consisted of "about sixty souls." (Whitmer, "The Book of John Whitmer," chapter 9.)

4. John Whitmer reported Oliver Cowdery's description of this event: "On the second day of August, 1831, Brother Sidney Rigdon stood up and asked, saying, Do you receive this land for the land of your inheritance with thankful hearts from the Lord? Answer from all, We do. Do you pledge yourselves to keep the laws of God on this land which you have never kept in your own land? We do. Do you pledge yourselves to see that others of your brethren who shall come hither do keep the laws of God? We do. After prayer he arose and said, I now pronounce this land consecrated and dedicated to the Lord for a possession and inheritance for the Saints, (in the name of Jesus Christ, having authority from him.) And for all the fiathful servants of the Lord to the remotest ages of time. Amen." (Whitmer, "The Book of John Whitmer," chapter 9.)

write a description of the land of Zion,[1] we sought for all the information necessary to accomplish so desirable an object. Unlike the timbered states in the east, except upon the rivers and water courses, which were verdantly dotted with trees from one to three miles wide, – as far as [p. 137] the eye can glance the beautiful rolling prairies lay spread around like a sea of meadows. The timber is a mixture of oak, hickory, black walnut, elm, ash, cherry, honey locust, mulberry, coffee-bean, hackberry, box elder, and basswood, together with the addition of Cotton wood, butter wood, pecan soft and hard maple upon the bottoms. The shrubbery was beautiful, and consisted in part of plumbs, grapes, crab apples and persimmons. The prairies were decorated with a growth of flowers that seemed as georgeous grand as the brilliance of stars in the heavens, and exceed description. The soil is rich and fertile, from three to ten feet deep, and generally composed of a rich black mould, intermingled with clay and sand. It produces in abundance, wheat, corn, and many other common agricultural commodities, together with sweet potatoes and cotton. Horses, cattle and hogs, though of an inferior breed, are tolerable plenty and seem nearly to raise themselves by grazing in the vast prairie range in summer, and feeding upon the bottoms in winter. The wild game is less plenty where man has commenced the cultivation of the soil, than it is a little distance furthe[r] in the wild prairies. Buffaloe, elk, deer, bear, wolves, beaver, and many lesser animals, roam at pleasure. Turkies, geese, swans, ducks; yea a variety of the feathered race, are among the rich abundance that graces the delightful regions of this goodly land of the heritage of the children of God. Nothing is more fruitful or a richer stock holder in the blooming prairies, than the honey bee. Honey is but about twenty-five cents a gallon.

The season is mild and delightful nearly three quarters of the year, and as the land of Zion situated at about ⟨equal⟩ dis-

1. D&C (1835 edition) 18:11; (current edition) 58:50.

tances from the Atlantic and Pacific oceans, as well as from the Allegany and Rocky mountains, in the 39th degree of north latitude, and between the 16th and 17th degrees of[1] west longitude, it bids fair to become one of the most blessed places on the globe, when the curse is taken from the land, if not before. The winters are milder than in the Atlantic States of the same parallel of latitude; and the weather is more agreeable, so that were the virtues of the inhabitants only equal to the blessings of the Lord which he permits to [p. 138] crown the industry and efforts of those inhabitants, there would be a measure of the good things of life, for the benefit of the saints, full, press[ed] down and running over, even an hundred fold.

The disadvantages here, like all new countries, are self evident: lack of mills and schools, together with the natural privations and inconveniences, which the hand of industry, and the refinement of society with the polish of science, overcome. But all these impediments, vanish when it is recollected what the prophets have said concerning Zion in the last days: how the glory of Lebanon is to come upon her, the fir tree, the pine tree, and the box together, to beautify the place of his sanctuary, that he may make the place of his feet glorious: where, for brass he will bring gold, and for iron he will bring silver, and for wood brass, and for stones iron:– and where the feast of fat things will be given to the just: yea when the splendor of the Lord, is brought to our consideration for the good of his people, the calculations of men and the vain glory of the world vanishes, and we exclaim: God will shine the perfection of beauty out of Zion.

On the third day of August, ⟨I proceeded to dedicate⟩ the spot[2] for the Temple, a little west of Independence, ~~was dedicated in~~ ⟨and there were⟩ presen~~ce~~⟨t⟩ ~~of eight men, among whom were myself,~~ Sidney Rigdon, Edward Partridge, W.W. Phelps,

1. "of" repeated in MS.
2. "spot" written over "ground."

Oliver Cowdery, Martin Harris and Joseph Coe.[1] The 87,th Psalm was read, and the scene was solemn and impresive. On the 4th I attended the first conference in the land of Zion.[2] It was held at the house of brother Joshua Lewis in Kaw Township, in presence of the Colesville branch of the church. The spirit of the Lord was there. On the 7th I attended the funeral of sister Polly Knight, the wife of Joseph Knight Sen.[3] This was the first death in the church in this land. And I can say a worthy member sleeps in Jesus till the resurrection. I also received the following

Revelation given in Zion, August 1831.

[D&C 59]

On the 8th, as ⟨there⟩[4] had been some inquiry among the elders, what they were to do, I received the following

Revelation given August 1831.

[D&C 60]

On the 9th, in company with ten elders,[5] I left Independence Landing for Kirtland. We started down the river in canoes, and went the first day as far as Fort Osage where we had an excellent wild turkey for supper. Nothing very important occurred till the third day, when many of the dangers, so common upon the western waters, manifested themselves; and after we

---

1. Alterations in this sentence by Willard Richards.

2. The minutes of the conference list fourteen elders present. (See Cannon and Cook, *Far West Record*, 9-10.)

3. Although terminally ill when she left Kirtland, Polly Knight desired to see the land of Zion and be buried there. Her condition was such during the trip to Missouri that her son stopped and bought lumber for a coffin. She arrived in Jackson County two weeks before her death. (Hartley, *The Joseph Knight Family*, 80-81.)

4. Insertion in another hand.

5. Those accompanying Joseph Smith to Kirtland were Samuel H. Smith, Oliver Cowdery, Sidney Rigdon, William W. Phelps, Frederick G. Williams, Reynolds Cahoon, Sidney Gilbert, Joseph Coe, Ezra Booth, and Peter Whitmer, Jr.

had encamped upon the bank of the river, at McIlwaine's bend, brother Phelps, in an open vision, by daylight, saw the Destroyer, in his most horrible power, ride upon the face of the waters. Others heard the noise, but saw not the vision. The next morning, after prayer, I received the following [p. 142]

Revelation given August 1831.

[D&C 61]

On the 13th I met several of the Elders on their way to the land of Zion,[1] and after the joyful salutation ⟨with⟩ which brethren meet each other ~~with,~~ who are actually "contending for the faith once delivered to the saints," I received the following

Revelation given August, 1831.

[D&C 62]

After this little meeting of the elders, myself and Sidney Rigdon, and Oliver Cowdery continued our journey by land to Saint Louis, where we overtook Brothers Phelps and Gilbert. From this place we took stage, and they went by water, to Kirtland, where we arrived safe and well on the 27th. Many things transpired upon this journey to strengthen our faith, and ⟨which⟩[2] displayed the goodness of God in such a marvellous manner, that we could not help beholding the exertions of Satan to blind the eyes of the people so as to hide the true light that lights every man that comes unto the world. In these infant days of the church, there was a great anxiety to obtain the word of the Lord upon every subject that in any way concerned our salvation; and as "the land of Zion" was now the most important temporal object in view, I inquired of the Lord

1. After the revelation instructing them to leave the river, Joseph Smith and his associates crossed the Missouri River at Chariton, Saline County, where they met Hyrum Smith, John Murdock, David Whitmer, and Harvey Whitlock, who were en route to Jackson County. (Cook, *Revelations*, 97-98.)

2. "which" inserted in pencil in another hand.

for further information upon the gathering of the Saints and the purchase of the land and other matters, and received the following

Revelation given in Kirtland, August, 1831.

[D&C 63]

The forepart of September was spent in making preparations to remove to the town of Hiram and commence the translation of [the] bible. The brethren who were commanded to go up to Zion were earnestly engaged in getting ready to start in the coming October. On the 11th of September I received the following

Revelation given in Kirtland, September 1831.

D&C 64]

On the 12th of September I removed with my family to the township of Hiram, and commenced living with John Johnson. Hiram was in Portage county and about thirty miles southeasterly from Kirtland. From this time until the fore part of October I did little more than to prepare to recom⟨m⟩ence the translation of the bible. About this time, Ezra Booth came out as an apostate. He came into the church upon seeing a person healed of an infirmaty of many years standing.[1] He had been a methodist priest for some ⟨time⟩ previous to his embracing the fulness of the gospel, as developed in the book of Mormon, and upon his admission into the church [p. 153] he was ordained an elder. As will be seen by the foregoing revelations, he went up to Missouri as a companion of Elder Morley; but when he actually learned that faith, humility, patience and tribulation, were before blessing; and that God brought

1. Earlier in 1831, Booth had witnessed the healing by Joseph Smith of Elsa Johnson, John Johnson's wife. She had suffered from an attack of chronic rheumatism in her shoulder that for two years had prevented the raising of her hand to her head. (Smith, *History of the Church*, 1:215-16; "History of Luke Johnson," *Deseret News*, 19 May 1858.)

low before ⟨he⟩ exalted; that instead of "the Savior's granting him power to smite men and make them believe", (as he said he wanted God to do him,) he found he must become all things to all men, that he might peradventure save some, and that too, by all diligence, by perils by sea and land. As was the case in the days of Jesus, which appears in the 6th chapter of St. John's gospel, he said, verily, verily I say unto you, ye seek me, not because ye saw the miracles, but because ye did eat of the loaves, and were filled:[1] so was it ⟨with⟩ Booth, and when he was disappointed by his own evil heart, he turned away. And as said before became an apostate, and wrote a series of Letters[2] which by their coloring, falsity, and vain calculations to overthrow the work of the Lord, exposed his weakness, wickedness and folly and left him a monument of his own shame for the world to wonder at.

A conference was held in which brother W.W Phelps was instructed to stop at Cincinnati, on his way to Missouri, and purchase a press and types, for the purpose of establishing and publishing a monthly paper at Independence, Jackson county, Missouri, to be called "The Evening and Morning Star." The first Sunday in October Orson Hyde, a clerk in Brothers Sidney Gilbert and Newel K. Whitney's store ⟨in Kirtland⟩, was baptised, and became a member of the church. As he was soon after designated as one of the chosen men of the Lord to bear his word to the nations, I feel a desire to notice him as he was and as he is. He was ⟨in his own words⟩ left in his infancy an orphan, with none to look upon him with a father's eye, and feel for him with a mother's heart. The hand that wiped his

1. John 6:26.

2. Nine Booth letters were published between 13 October and 8 December 1831. (Ezra Booth, Nelson, Portage County, Ohio, to Reverend Ira Eddy, 12 September; 2, 24, 31 October; 7, 14, 21, 29 November; 6 December, 1831, as published under the title, "Mormonism," in the *Ohio Star* (Ravenna, Portage County, Ohio), 13, 20, 27 October; 3, 10, 17, 24, November; 8 December, 1831. The letters also appeared in other newspapers, and in E.D. Howe, *Mormonism Unvailed*, 175-221.)

infant tears was still; the breasts that gave him suck, was cold, and slumbered in the arms of death. He was thrust abroad upon the cold and friendless bosom of an unfeeling world, so that for twenty long years, he saw no one in whose veins flowed a drop of kindred blood, and consequently grew up as a wild and uncultivated plant of nature, and now had come unto the new and everlasting covenant to be renewed and receive grace for grace, [p. 154] and put himself under the fatherly care of him whose yoke is easy and whose burden is light, and who rewardeth his sons and daughters, who serve him faithfully to the end, with eternal life.–

To continue, in his own figure, he now stood before the world to feed the fowls of the Lord, in the same manner that he had done in early life, to feed the poultry of the gentleman with whom he resided. for says he, "when I poured the corn upon the ground, the fowls all came together en masse, but after the corn was exhausted, and the stream stayed, the fowls all turned away, going in different directions each one singing his own song: so with religion, while God poured out the stream of revelation upon the ancient church, they were all united and ate the living bread; but when he withheld revelations, in latter times, because of unbelief of man, they turned and went their own course, and sung their own song; some a methodist song; some a baptist song; some a presbyterian song, &c, but if they had had revelation they would have sung one of the songs of Zion."– ~~His further history will come in, in place, hereafter.~~

In the forepart of October I received the following Revelation on prayer, given October 1831.

[D&C 65]

Soon after the above revelation was received, I recommenced the translation of the scriptures, in company with Elder Rigdon, who had removed to Hiram, to act in his office of scribe to me. On the 11th of October a conference was held at brother Johnson's[1] where I was living, at which the elders were instructed into the ancient ⟨manner⟩ of conducting meetings, of which knowledge the most of them were ignorant: a committee of six were appointed to instruct the several branches of the church. Elders David Whitmer and Reynolds Cahoon were appointed as two of the said Committee with the fu[r]ther duty, on their mission, of setting forth the condition of brs. Joseph Smith Jr. and Sidney Rigdon, that they might obtain means to continue the translation. this Conference was adjourned till the 25th October, to meet at the house of Serenus Burnett, in Orange, Cuyahoga county. On the 21st first I attended a special conference to settle a difficulty which had occurred in Kirtland on account that William Cahoon and Peter Devolue had abused one of Br Whitneys children.[2] Myself and Elder Rigdon were appointed to go to Kirtland and settle the difficulty, which we did.

At the conference on the 25, at Orange, 12 high-priests, 17 elders, 4 priests, 3 teachers, and 4 deacons, together with a large congregation attended.[3] Much business was done, and the four remaining committee, authorised by the conference at Hiram on the 11th, were appointed and consisted of Simeon Carter, Orson Hyde, Hyrum Smith and Emer Harris. At the request of Wm. E. McLellin I inquired of the Lord and received the following

Revelation given October, 1831,

[D&C 66]

I returned from the conference at Orange to Hiram, and as Oliver Cowdery and John Whitmer were to start for Inde-

---

1. Minutes of the 11 October conference are in Cannon and Cook, *Far West Record*, 16-17.

2. Minutes of the 21 October conference are in Cannon and Cook, *Far West Record*, 18.

3. Three conference meetings were held on 25 and 26 October. (See minutes in Cannon and Cook, *Far West Record*, 19-26.)

pendence, Missouri, a Special Conference was appointed for the first of November,[1] at which I received the following. [2]Revelation [p. 157]

[D&C 1]

After this revelation was received some conversation was had concerning Revelations and language, and I received the following,

Revelation given November, 1831.

[D&C 67]

After the above was received Wm. E. McLellin, as the wisest man in his own estimation, having more learning than sense, endeavored to write a commandment like unto one of the least of the Lord's, but failed; it was an awful responsibility to write in the name of the Lord. The elders, and all present, that witnessed this vain attempt of a man to imitate the language of Jesus Christ, renewed their faith in the fulness of the gospel and in the truth of the commandments and revelations which the Lord had given to the Church through my instrumentality; and the elders signified a willingness to bear testimony of their truth to all the world. Accordingly I received the following.

"The testimony of the witnesses to the book of the Lord's commandments, which he gave to his church through Joseph Smith, Jr. who was appointed by the voice of the church for this purpose: we therefore feel willing to bear testimony to all the world of mankind, to every creature upon the face of ⟨all⟩

1. Oliver Cowdery and John Whitmer were appointed in November 1831 to take Church revelations to Missouri for publication. Six conference meetings were held at Hiram, Ohio, between 1 and 13 November to make arrangements for their mission. During the conference, a preface and appendix for the Book of Commandments was received by revelation, and the number of volumes to be printed was designated at 10,000. (D&C 68:32; 69:1; 70:1; Minutes of the November conferences are in Cannon and Cook, *Far West Record*, 26-33.)

2. At this point in the MS., the handwriting of William W. Phelps ends and Willard Richards begins.

the earth, and upon the islands of the sea, that the Lord has borne record to our souls, through the Holy Ghost shed forth upon us, that these commandments [p. 162] were given by inspiration of God, and are profitable for all men, and are verily true. We give this testimony unto the world, the Lord being our helper: and it is through the grace of God, the Father, and his Son Jesus Christ, that we are permitted to have this privilege of bearing this testimony unto the world, that the children of men may be profited thereby."

As the following Elders were desirous to know the mind of the Lord concerning themselves, I enquired and received:–

A Revelation, given November, 1831, To Orson Hyde, Luke Johnson, Lyman Johnson, and William E. McLellin. The mind and will of the Lord, as made known by the voice of the Spirit to a conference concerning certain Elders; and also certain items, as made known, in addition to the Covenants and Commandments.

[D&C 68]

It had been decided by the conference that Elder Oliver Cowdery should carry the commandments and revelations to Independence, Missouri, for printing, and that I should arrange and get them in readiness by the time that he left, which was to be by the 15th of the month and possibly before, At this time there were many things which the elders desired to know relative to preaching the gospel to the inhabitants of the earth, and concerning the gathering: and, in order to walk by the true light, and be instructed from on high, on the 3d of November 1831. I enquired of the Lord and received the following *Revelation*, which ~~by way of~~ ⟨from its⟩ importance, and ⟨for⟩ distinction has since been ~~called the Appendix, and~~ added to the Book of Doctrine and Covenants, and called the Appendix

[D&C 133]

The Book of Commandments and Revelations was to be

dedicated, by prayer, to the service of Almighty God, by me; and after I had done this, I enquired of the Lord concerning these things, and received the following

Revelation, given November, 1831.

[D&C 69]

My time was occupied closely in reviewing the commandments and sitting in conference for nearly two weeks; for we held from the first [p. 172] to the twelfth of November, four special conferences. In the last,[1] which was held at Brother Johnson's in Hiram, after deliberate consideration, in consequence of the book of Revelations, now to be printed, being the foundation of the church in these last days; and a benefit to the world, showing that the keys of the mysteries of the Kingdom of our Savior, are again entrusted to man, and the riches of eternity within the compass of those who are willing to live by every word that proceedeth out of the mouth of God: ~~therefore~~ the conference priced the Revelations to be worth to the church, the riches of the whole earth, speaking temporally. The great benefits to the world, which result from the Book of Mormon and the Revelations, which the Lord has seen fit, in his infinite wisdom, to grant unto us for our salvation, and for the salvation of all that will believe, were duly appreciated: and in answer to an enquiry, I received the following.

Revelation, Given November, 1831.

[D&C 70]
[p. 174]

After Oliver Cowdery and John Whitmer had departed for Jackson County, Missouri,[2] I resumed the translation of the Scriptures and continued to labor in this branch of my, ⟨calling⟩

1. The minutes for the conference of 12-13 November are in Cannon and Cook, *Far West Record*, 31-32.

2. Cowdery and Whitmer started for Missouri on 20 November 1831 and arrived at Independence on 5 January 1832.

with elder Sidney Rigdon as my scribe untill ~~the first day of December when~~ I received the following

Revelation, given December 1, 1831.

D&C 71]

[p. 175]

Knowing now the mind of the Lord, that the time had come that the gospel should be proclaimed in power and demonstration to the world, from the scriptures, reasoning with men as in days of old, I took a journey to Kirtland, in company with Elder Sidney Rigdon, on the 3d day of December to fulfil the above Revelation.[1] On the 4th several of the Elders and ~~brethren~~ members assembled together to learn their duty and for edification, and, after some time had been spent in conversing about our temporal and Spiritual welfare, I received the following

Revelation, given December 4th 1831.

[D&C 72]

From this time until the 8th or 10th of January 1832 myself and Elder Rigdon continued to preach in Shalersville, Ravenna, and other places, setting forth the truth; vindicating the cause of our Redeemer: shewing that the day of vengeance was coming upon this generation like a thief in the night: that prejudice, blindness, and darkness, filled the minds of many, and caused them to persecute the true church, and reject the true light: by which means we did much towards allaying the excited feelings which were growing out of the scandalous letters then being published in the "Ohio Star," at Ravenna, by the before mentioned Apostate Ezra Booth. On the 10th of January, ~~1832~~ I received the following

---

1. The revelation, dated December 1831, directed Joseph Smith and Sidney Rigdon to discontinue the revision of the Bible "for a season" and travel through the area preaching in an effort to counteract the influence of Ezra Booth, whose anti-Mormon letters had commenced publication in the *Ohio Star* on 13 October.

Revelation to Joseph Smith, Jr. and Sidney Rigdon, January, 1832. The word of the Lord unto them concerning the church of the Living God, established in the last days, making known the will of the Lord [p. 179] unto the elders, what they shall do until conference.

[D&C 73]

[1]Upon the reception of the foregoing word of the Lord, I re-commenced the translation of the scriptures, and labored diligently till ~~just (about the first) before the Conference which was to commence on the 25th of~~ January. During this period I also received the following as

An Explanation of the epistle to the first Corinthians, 7th Chapter, 14th verse.

[D&C 74]

A few day[s] before the conference was to commence in Amherst Lorain County, I started in company with the elders that lived in my own vicinity, and arrived in due time. At this conference much harmony prevailed, and considerable business was done to advance the kingdom, and promulgate the gospel to the inhabitants of the surrounding country. The Elders seemed anxious for me to enquire of the Lord, that they might know his will, or learn what would be most pleasing to him, for them to do, in order to bring men to a sense of their condition: for, as it was written, all men had gone out of the way, so that none doth good; no, not one.[2] I enquired and received the following

Revelation, given January, 1832.

[D&C 75]

---

1. In the MS., the following lines introducing section 74 follow section 72 with a note indicating they should be inserted here.
2. Romans 3:12.

Upon my return from Amherst Conference, I resumed the translation of the scriptures. From sundry revelations which had been received, it was apparent that many important points, touching the salvation of man, had been taken from the Bible, or lost before it was compiled. It appeared self evident from what truths were left, that if God rewarded every one according to the deeds done in the body, the term "heaven," as intended for the Saints eternal home, must include more kingdoms than one. Accordingly on the 16th of February, 1832, while translating St John's Gospel, myself and Elder Rigdon saw the following *VISION*

[D&C 76]

Nothing could be more pleasing to the Saint, upon the order of the kingdom of the Lord, than the light which burst upon the world, through the foregoing vision. Every law, every commandment, every promise, every truth, and every point, touching the destiny of man, from Genesis to Revelation, where the purity of either remains unsullied from the wisdom of men, goes to shew the perfection of the theory, and witnesses the fact that that document is a transcript from the Records of the eternal world. The sublimity of the ideas; the purity of the language; the scope for action; the continued duration for completion, in order that the heirs of salvation, may confess the Lord and bow the knee; The rewards for faithfulness. & the punishments for sins, are so much beyond the narrow mindedness of men, that, every honest man is constrained to exclaim; *It came from God*.

About the first of march, in connection with the translation of the scriptures, I received the following explanation of the Revelations of Saint John.

[D&C 77]

Previous to the 20th of March I received the four following Revelations, besides the work of translating.

Revelation, given, March, 1832. The order ⟨given⟩ of the Lord to Enoch, for the purpose of establishing the poor.

[D&C 78]
[p. 197]

Revelation, Given March, 1832.

[D&C 79.]

Revelation Given, March, 1832.

[D&C 80.]

Revelation Given March, 1832.

[D&C 81]

I received a letter from the brethren who went up to the Land of Zion, stating that they had arrived at Independence, Missouri, in good health and spirits, with a printing press, and a store of goods. They also sent me the prospectus for the monthly paper agreeably to the instructions of the fall conference; it read as follows:

[Prospectus for *The Evening and the Morning Star*]

According to previous calculation we now began to make preparations to visit the brethren who had removed to the land of Missouri. Before going to Hiram, to live with Father Johnson, my wife had taken two children (twins) of John Murdock, to bring up. She received them ⟨when⟩ only nine days old; they were now nearly eleven months. I would remark that nothing important had occurred since I came to reside in Father Johnson's house in Hiram; I had held meetings on the sabbaths and evenings. and baptized a number. Father Johnsons son, Olmsted Johnson, came home on a visit, during which I told him if he did not obey the gospel, [p. 204] the spirit he was of would lead him to destruction, and when he went away, he would never return or see his father again. He went to the southern states and Mexico, and on his return, took sick, and di⟨e⟩d in Virginia. In addition to the apostate Booth, Simonds Rider [Ryder], Eli Johnson, Edward Johnson[1] and John Johnson Jr. had apostatized.

On the 25th of March; the twins before mentioned, which had been sick of the meazles for some time, causing us to be broke of our rest in taking care of them, especially my wife, in the evening I told her she had better retire to rest with one of the children and I would watch with the sickest child. In the night she told me I had better lie down on the trundle bed, and I did so, and was soon after awoke by her screaming *Murder!* when I found myself going out of the door, in the hands of about a dozen men; some of whose hands were in my hair, and some hold of my shirt, drawers and limbs, The foot of the trundle bed was towards the door, leaving only room enough for the door to swing. My wife heard a gentle tapping on the window which she then took no particular notice of, (but which was unquestionably design'd for ascertaining whether we were all asleep,) and soon after the mob burst open the door and surrounded the bed in an instant, and, as I said, the first I knew I was going out of the door in the hands of an infuriated mob. I made a desperate struggle, as I was forced out, to extricate myself, but only cleared one leg, with which I made a pass at one man and he fell on the door steps. I was immediately confined again; and they swore, by God, they would kill me if I did not be still, which quieted me. As they passed around the house with me, the fellow that I kicked came to me, and thrust his hand into my face, all covered with blood, (for I hit him on the nose,) and with an exulting horse laugh, muttered,—"Ge . . . Gee . . . *God dam ye; I'll fix ye.*"

They then seized me by the throat, and held on till [p. 205]

1. Eli and Edward Johnson may have been relatives but were not children of John Johnson, Sr.

I lost my breath. After I came to, as they passed along with me, about thirty rods from the house, I saw Elder Rigdon stretched out on the ground, whither they had dragged him by his heels. I supposed he was dead.

I began to plead with them, saying, you will have mercy and spare my life, I hope:– To which they replied, *"God dam ye;* call on yer *God* for help, *we'll* show ye no mercy:"– and the people began to shew themselves in every direction: one coming from the orchard had a plank, and I expected they would kill me, and carry me off on the plank.

They then turned to the right and went on about thirty rods further;– about sixty rods from the house, and thirty from whence I saw Elder Rigdon;– into the meadow, where they stopped, and one said, "Simonds, Simonds" (meaning I supposed Simonds Rider,) "pull up his drawers, pull up his drawers, he will take cold." Another replied *"A'nt ye goin to kill 'im,"*? *"a'nt ye goin to kill 'im"*? when a group of mobbers collected a little way off and said, "Simonds, Simonds come here;" and Simonds charged those who had hold of me to keep me from touching the ground, (as they had done all the time) lest I should get a spring upon them. They went and held a council, and as I could occasionally over-hear a word, I suppose it was to know. whether it was best to kill me.

They returned after a while when I learned that they had concluded not to kill me, but pound and scratch me well, tear of[f] my shirt and drawers and leave me naked. One cried *"Simonds, Simonds where's the tar bucket"*? *"I don't know"* answered one, *"where 'tis, Eli's left it."* They ran back and fetched the bucket of tar, when one exclaimed *"God dam it,– let us tar up his mouth;"* and they tried to force the tar paddle into my mouth; I twisted my head around so that they could not; and they cried out *"God dam ye, hold up yer head, and let us give* [p. 206] *ye some tar."* They then tried to force a phial into my mouth, and broke it in my teeth. All my clothes were torn off me except my shirt collar; and one man fell on me and scratched my body with his nails like a mad cat, and then muttered out, *"God dam ye, that's the way the Holy Ghost falls on folks."*

They then left me, and I attempted to rise, but fell again. I pulled the tar away from my lips &c, so that I ⟨could⟩ breathe more freely, and after a while I began to recover, and raised myself up, when I saw two lights: I made my way towards one of them, and found it was father Johnson's. When I came to the door, I was naked, and the tar made me look as though I had been covered with blood, and when my wife saw me she thought I was all mashed to pieces, and fainted. during the affray abroad, the sisters of the neighborhood had collected at my room. I called for a blanket, they threw me one, and shut the door; I wrapped it around me, and went in.

In the mean time, Brother John Poorman heard an outcry across the cornfield and running that way met father Johnson, who had been fastened in his house at the commencement of the assault, by having his door barred by the mob, but on calling to his wife to bring his gun, saying, he would blow a hole through the door, the mob fled, and father ⟨Johnson⟩ seizing a club, ran after the party that had Elder Rigdon, and knocked down one man, and raised his club to level another, exclaiming *"What are you doing here"*? when they left Elder Rigdon and turned upon father Johnson, who, turning to run towards his own house, met Brother Poorman coming out of the cornfield; each supposing the other to be a mobber, an encounter ensued, and Poorman gave Johnson a severe blow on the left shoulder with a stick or stone which brought him to the ground. Poorman ran immediately towards father Johnsons, and arriving while I was waiting for the blanket, exclaimed. "I'm [p. 207] afraid I've killed him."—Killed who? asked some one; when Poorman hastily related the circumstance of the encounter near the cornfield, and went into the shed and hid himself. Father Johnson soon recovered so as to come to the house, when the whole my[s]tery was quickly solved concerning the difficulty between him and Poorman, who, on learning, the facts, joyfully came from his hiding place[1]

My friends spent the night in scraping and removing the tar, and washing and cleansing my body, so that by morning I was ready to be clothed again. This being sabbath morning, the people assembled for meeting at the usual hour of worship, and among them came also the mobbers; viz, Simonds Rider, a campbellite Preacher, and leader of the mob; one McClintic,[2]

1. Luke Johnson, son of John Johnson, also described the Hiram mobbing: " . . . while Joseph was yet at my father's, a mob of forty or fifty came to his house, a few entered his room in the middle of the night, and Carnot Mason dragged Joseph out of bed by the hair of his head; he was then seized by as many as could get hold of him, and taken about forty rods from the house, stretched on a board, and tantalized in the most insulting and brutal manner; they tore off the few night clothes that he had on, for the purpose of emasculating him, and had Dr. Dennison there to perform the operation; but when the Dr. saw the Prophet stripped and stretched on the plank, his heart failed him, and he refused to operate; the mob then scratched his body all over, saying, 'Damn you, this is the way the Holy Ghost falls upon you.' And in attempting to force open his jaws, they broke one of his front teeth, to pour a vial of some obnoxious drug into his mouth.

"The mob became divided, and did not succeed; but poured tar over him and then stuck feathers in it and left him, and went to an old brick yard to wash themselves and bury their filthy clothes. At this place a vial was dropped, the contents of which ran out and killed the grass. About the same time, part of the mob went to the house Sidney Rigdon occupied, and dragged him out, and besmeared him with tar and feathers. My father, hearing the outcry of the family, went to the door, but finding it held by some one on the outside, he called for his gun, when those who held the door left; he pursued, and was knocked down; his collar bone was broken; he was taken back to the house, and hands laid upon him by David Whitmer, and immediately healed. A few minutes after this accident, we heard the voice of Joseph calling for a blanket; some person handed him one, and he came in, the tar trickling down his face; his wife was very much alarmed, supposing it to be blood, until he came near enough to see that it was tar. My mother got some lard, and rubbed it upon him to get the tar off, which they succeeded in removing.

"Waste, who was the strongest man on the Western Reserve, had boasted that he could take Joseph out alone; at the time they were taking him out of the house, Waste had hold of one foot, Joseph drew up his leg and gave him a kick, which sent him sprawling in the street. He afterwards said that the Prophet was the most powerful man he ever had hold of in his life." ("History of Luke Johnson.")

2. Possibly William McClintock at Freedom, Portage County. No McClintocks are listed in the 1831, 1835, or 1839 census of Hiram Township.

who had his hands in my hair; one Streeter, son of a Campbellite Minister; and Felatiah Allen, Esquire,[1] who gave the mob a barrel of whiskey to raise their spirits; and many others;

With my flesh all scarfied and defaced, I preached to the congregation as usual, and on the afternoon of the same day baptized three individuals.

The next morning I went to see Elder Rigdon, and found him crazy, and his head highly inflamed, for they had dragged him by his heels, and those, too, so high from the earth he could not raise his head from the rough frozen surface, which lacerated it exceedingly; and when he saw me he called to his wife, to bring him his razor. She asked him what he wanted of it? and he replied, to kill *me*. Sister Rigdon left the room and he asked *me* to bring his razor. I asked him what he wanted of it, and he replied he wanted to kill his wife, and he continued delirious some days. The feathers which were used with the tar on this occasion, the mob took out of Elder Rigdons house. After they had seized him, and dragged him out. one of the banditti returned to get some pillows, when the women shut him in and kept him some time. [p. 208]

During the mob[bing] one of the twins received a severe cold, and continued to grow worse till friday, and died[2] The Mobbers were composed of various religious parties but mostly Campbellites, Methodists and Baptists, who continued to molest and menace father Johnson's house for a long time. Elder Rigdon removed to Kirtland with his family, then sick with the meazles, the following wednesday; and, on account of the mob he went to Chardon, Saturday April first. Sunday, April second, I started for Missouri in company with Newel K. Whitney Peter Whitmer, and Jesse Gause; To fulfill the revelation. Not wishing to go by Kirtland, as another mob existed in that

1. Possibly Peletiah Allyn/Allen (1785-1856).

2. Joseph Murdock Smith died 29 March 1832. (Smith, *History of the Church*, 1:265.)

neighborhood. (and indeed the spirit of mobocracy was very prevalent through that region of country at that time) Brother George Pitkin took us in his waggon, by the most expeditious route to Warren, where we arrived the same day, and were there joined by Elder Rigdon, who left Chardon in the morning; and proceeding onward we arrived at Wellsville. the next day, and the day following at Stubenville where we left the waggon; and on wednesday the fifth of April we took passage on board a steam packet for Wheeling, Virginia; where we purchased a lot of Paper for the Press in Zion, then in care of W.W. Phelps.

After we left Hiram, fearing for the safety of my family, on account of the mob, I wrote to my wife, in connection with Bishop Whitney, to have her go to Kirtland and tarry with his family till our return. She went to Kirtland to Bro Whitney's, and Sister Whitney's Aunt, Sarah Smith, (who was then living with her,) enquired of her Neice if my wife was going to stay there; and, on being answered in the affirmative, said she should go away, for there was not room enough for both of them: accordingly Sister Whitney invited my wife to leave, which she did immediately, having enjoyed about two hours visit.[1] She then went to Brother Reynolds Cahoon's—and fa-

---

1. When Sarah Smith's niece, Elizabeth Ann Whitney, with whom she had traveled to Kirtland, Ohio, in 1818, joined the Latter-day Saints, Sarah remained aloof. The two women were the closest of friends, as indicated by Elizabeth's willingness to leave her own family and settle in a new land with her aunt. Elizabeth noted that Sarah was "true and affectionate . . . and had great influence over me in molding my character and developing my strongest attributes." Sarah regarded all religion as priestcraft, and when Joseph Smith sent his family to live with the Whitneys during his absence, Sarah considered it an unacceptable intrusion and sent Emma Smith away. Describing the incident, Elizabeth Ann Whitney explained that Sarah "had a good motive in it, and really thought she was consulting the best interests of those who were far dearer to her than her own life; her devotion and her power of self-sacrifice towards us individually were unlimited, but her efforts, like those of many other sincere and ardent friends, were misdirected." Sarah died at Kirtland, Ohio. ("A Leaf from an Autobiography," *Woman's Exponent* 7 [15 August, 1 September, 1 November 1878]: 41, 51, 83.)

ther Smiths and Doctor Williams, where I found her, very disconsolate, on my return. [p. 209]

From Wheeling we took passage on board the steamer Trenton. While at the Dock, during the night, the boat was twice on fire, burning the whole width of the boat through into the cabin, but with so little damage the boat went on in the morning; and when we arrived at Cincinati, some of the mob, which had followed us all the way round, left us, and we arrived at Louisville the same night. Captain Brittle offered us protection, on board of his boat, & gave us supper and breakfast, gratuitously. At Louisville we were joined by Elder Titus Billings, who was journeying with a company of Saints from Kirtland, to Zion, and we took passage on the Steamer Charleston for St Louis, where we parted with Brother Billings and company, and by stage, arrived at Indepen[d]ence, Missouri, on the Twenty fourth of April, a distance of about 300 miles from St Louis. We found the brethren generally enjoying health and faith, and extremely glad to welcome us among them.

On the 26th ⟨of April⟩[1] I called a general council of the church,[2] and was acknowledged as the President of the High priesthood, according to a previous ordination at a Conference of High-priests, elders, and members, held at Amherst, Ohio, on the 25th of January 1832. The right hand of fellowship was given to me by the Bishop. Edward Partridge, in behalf of the Church. The scene was solemn, impressive, and delightful. During the intermission, a difficulty or hardness which had existed between Bishop Partridge and Elder Rigdon was amicably settled,[3] and when we came together in the afternoon all hearts seemed to rejoice, and I received the following

---

1. Insertion in another hand, probably that of Thomas Bullock.

2. Minutes of this 26 April 1832 meeting are published in Cannon and Cook, *Far West Record*, 43-45.

3. An eight-month disagreement between Sidney Rigdon and Edward Partridge evidently grew out of inconveniences suffered during Rigdon's trip to Missouri the previous year. (See Cook, *Revelations*, 172-75.)

Revelation given April, 1832, shewing the order given to Enoch and the church in his day.

[D&C 82]

On the 27th we transacted considerable [p. 212] business for the salvation of the saints who were settling among a ferocious set of mobbers, like lambs among wolves. It was my endeavor to so organize the church, that the brethren might eventually be independent of every incumbrance beneath the celestial Kingdom, by bonds and covenants of mutual friendship, and mutual love.

On the 28th and 29th I visited the brethren above Big Blue river, in Kaw Township, Twelve miles west of Independence, and received a welcome only ~~known~~ known by brethren and sisters united as one in the same faith, and by the same baptism and supported by the same Lord. The Colesville Branch, in particular, rejoiced as the Ancient Saints did with Paul. It is good to rejoice with the people of God. On the 30th I returned to independence, and again sat in council with the brethren and received the following

Revelation given April, 1832.

[D&C 83]
[p. 213]

Our council was continued on the 1st of May when it was ordered that three thousand copies of the Book of Commandments be printed the first Edition;[1] that William W. Phelps, Oliver Cowdery, and John Whitmer be appointed to review and prepare such revelations as shall be deemed proper for publication, for the press, and print them as soon as possible at Independence, Mo.– "Published by W.W. Phelps & Co." It

1. This action altered the decision of the conference at Hiram, Ohio, on 1 November 1831 that had designated a first edition of ten thousand copies of the Book of Commandments. See p. 367.

was also ordered that W.W. Phelps correct and print the Hymns which had been selected by Emma Smith, in fulfillment of the revelation.[1]

Arrangements were also made for supplying the saints with stores in Missouri and Ohio, which, with a few exceptions, was hailed with joy by the brethren.[2] Before we left Independence, Elder Rigdon preached two ~~most powerful~~[3] discourses, which, so far as outward appearance is concerned, gave great satisfaction to the people.

On the 6th of May I gave the parting hand to the brethren in Independence, and in company with Brothers Rigdon and Whitney, commenced a return to Kirtland, by stage, to St. Louis; from thence to Vincennes, Indiana; and from thence to New Albany, near the falls of Ohio River.

Before we arrived at the latter place the horses became frightened, and while going at full speed, Bishop Whitney attempted to Jump out of the coach, but having his coat fast, caught his foot in the wheel and had his leg & foot broken in several places;[4] ⟨at the same time I Jumped out unhurt⟩ and we put up at Mr Porter's public house,[5] in Greenville, ~~for~~ for four

---

1. See D&C 25.

2. One of the purposes of the April 1832 trip to Missouri by Joseph Smith, Sidney Rigdon, Jesse Gause, and Newel K. Whitney was to incorporate the mercantile pursuits in Kirtland and Independence into branches of a single firm, the Ohio branch under the name "Newel K. Whitney and Company," and the Missouri branch, "Gilbert, Whitney and Company." (See Cook, *Revelations*, 167-68.)

3. The cancellation here is in pencil.

4. Whitney wrote that the breaking of his leg came in consequence of "the upsetting of the stage." (Newel K. Whitney, statement dictated to Willard Richards, n.d., MS. LDS Church Archives.)

5. Daniel P. Porter, (1794-1866), merchant, tavernkeeper, postmaster, was born at Rutland, Rutland County, Vermont. One of the early settlers of Greenville, he came to Indiana from New England sometime before 1826. He was followed in a few years by his brothers, James W., a physician, b. 1796 at Rutland, Vermont; and Julius R., tavernkeeper, b. 1799, also at Rutland. James, the doctor, was evidently the one who attended to Whitney. Julius R. took his brother Daniel's place in the tavern business and also suceeded him as postmaster. (Albert Alonzo Pomeroy, *History and Genealogy of the Pomeroy Family* (Toledo,

weeks, while Elder Rigdon went directly forward to Kirtland. During all this time, Bro Whitney lost not a meal of victuals or a night's sleep; and Dr Porter, (our landlord's brother,) who attended him, said it was "a [p. 214] dam'd pity we had not got some Mormon there, they can set broken bones, or do any thing else."–[1]

I tarried with brother Whitney, and administered to him till he was able to be moved. While at this place I frequently walked out in the woods, where I saw several fresh graves; and one day when I arose from the dinner-table. I walked directly to the door and commenced vomiting most profusely. I raised large quantities of blood and poisonous matter, and so great were the muscular contorsions of my system that my jaw was dislocated in a few moments; this I succeeded in replacing with my own hands, and made my way to Brother Whitney, (who was on the bed,) as speedily as possible, he laid his hands on me and administered in the name of the Lord, and I was healed in an instant, although the effect of the poison had been so powerful, as to cause much of the[2] hair to become loosened from my head. Thanks be to my heavenly father for his interference in my behalf at this critical moment, in the name of Jesus Christ; Amen.

Brother Whitney had not had his foot moved from the bed for near four weeks. when I went into his room after a walk in the grove, and told him if *he would agree* to start for home in the morning, we would take a waggon to the river about four miles, and there would be a ferry boat in waiting which would take us quickly across, where we would find a hack which would take us directly to the landing, where we should

---

Ohio: Franklin Printing and Engraving Company, 1912), 406-7; *History of the Ohio Falls Cities and Their Counties* (Cleveland: L.A. Williams and Company, 1882), 2:282, 295, 296; US Federal Census, Floyd County, Indiana, 1830, 1840, 1850.)

1. Cancellation in this paragraph is in pencil.
2. "the" written over "my"

find a boat in waiting, and we will be going up the River before 10 o'clock and have a prosperous journey home. He took courage and told me he would go. We started the next morning and found every thing as I had told him, for we were passing rapidly up the river before 10 oclock, and landing at Wellsville, took stage coach to Chardon, from thence in a waggon to Kirtland where ⟨~~where~~ we arrived some time in June &⟩ I found [p. 215] my wife as before mentioned

As soon as I could arrange my affairs I ⟨re⟩commenced the translation of the scriptures, and thus I spent most of the summer. In July we rece⟨i⟩ved the first number of "The Evening and Morning Star"; which was a joyous treat to the Saints. Delightful indeed, was it, to contemplate, that the little band of brethren had become so large, and grown so strong, in so short a space as to be able to issue a paper of their own, which contained not only some of the revelations, but other information, also, which would gratify, and enlighten the humble enquirer after truth. So embittered was the public mind against the truth, that the press universally had been arrayed against us; and although many News-papers published the prospectus of our new paper, yet it appeared to have been done more to calumniate the Editor, than give ~~give~~ publicity to the sheet,[1]

---

1. The *Painesville Telegraph*, quoting the New York *Whig*, reported: "The Mormonites have found a resting place in Independence, Jackson County, Missouri, whence we have received the prospectus of a newspaper from W.W. Phelps, formerly of the Ontario Phenix. We make a few extracts for the singularity of the thing." [Then follow extracts from the prospectus of *The Evening and the Morning Star*.] The paper continues: "It is painful to see intelligent men carried away with strange conceits. The belief of the book of Mormon is *one* of the strangest superstitions of the present day. Greater have been, and perhaps now are. The folly of *Freemasonry divine*, surpasses it in the egregiousness of the imposition practised by or upon the most intelligent and well informed minds. The delusion of the false prophet, and the gift of *unknown* tongues, and of the St. Simonites in France, seem to be all of the same character with this, now taking up its abode in Jackson County, Missouri." (*Painesville Telegraph* [Ohio], 17 April 1832.)

Editors thought to do us harm, while the saints rejoiced that they could do nothing against the truth but for it.

The following are extracts from "the Evening and Morning Star; Independence, Mo. June 1832. 1st No.

[The extracts are titled: "To Man"; "To the Church of Christ Abroad in the Earth"; "Common Schools" [p. 221]]

In August we were again delighted to receive the Star. The following is extracted from the second number.

["The Elders in the Land of Zion to the Church of Christ Scattered Abroad"; "To the Elders who Preach Good Tidings to the World"; "Foreign News" [p. 226]]

The August number of the "Star" contained the following

["The Cholera"; "To the Honorable Men of the World"]

⟨Sep. 10 George A. Smith baptized by Joseph H. Wakefield a Potsdam, St. Lawrence Co New York. confirmed by Elder Solomon Humphrey⟩[1]

The elders began to return from their missions to the eastern states, and present the histories of their several stewar[d]ships in the Lord's vineyard; and while together in these seasons of Joy, I enquired of the Lord and received the following;

Revelation, given the 22d and 23d of September 1832, On Priesthood.

[D&C 84]

The following is extracted from the "Evening and Morning Star," of September 1832. (No—4.)

["Writing Letters"]

I continued the translations, and ministering to the church,

1. Insertion in the handwriting of Thomas Bullock.

through the fall, excepting a rapid journey to Albany, New York, and Boston, in company with bishop whitney,[1] from which I returned on the sixth of November, immediately after the birth of my son, Joseph Smith, 3d ⟨Note A addenda page 2⟩.[2] In answer to Letters received from the brethren in Missouri I wrote as follows;

[Joseph Smith to W.W. Phelps, November 27, 1832.]

1. In the fall of 1832, Newel K. Whitney and Joseph Smith traveled to New York and Massachusetts on business connected with the mercantile firm and to fulfill the revelation directing the bishop to warn eastern cities of desolation that would follow the rejection of the gospel. Whitney recalled, "My leg was not perfectly well, but I proceeded with Joseph . . . to New York, Providence and Boston, and through New England. We visited Bishop [Benjamin T.] Onderdonk of the Episcopal Church of the United States while at N. York, and returned back to Kirtland. This journey was taken to fulfill the revelation." (D&C 84:114; Joseph to Emma Smith, 13 October 1832; N.K. Whitney, undated manuscript dictated to Willard Richards, MS., LDS Church Archives.)

2. Note A is in the handwriting of Thomas Bullock in volume A-1 of the MS.: "About the 8th of November I received a visit from Elders Joseph Young, Brigham Young, and Heber C. Kimball from Mendon, Munroe County, New York. They spent four or five days at Kirtland, during which we had many interesting moments. At one of our interviews, Brother Brigham Young, and John P. Greene spoke in Tongues, which was the first time I had heard this gift among the brethren, and others also spoke, and I received the gift myself. Brother Joseph Young is a great man, but Brigham is a greater, and the time will come when he will preside over the whole Church. (see page 240)"

ORSON PRATT, *A INTERESTING ACCOUNT*, 1840

Orson Pratt. A Interesting Account of Several Remarkable Visions, and of The Late Discovery of Ancient American Records. *(Edinburgh, 1840.) The same edition appears with and without the "A" in the title.*

Editorial Note

Among the members of the Quorum of Twelve who helped introduce Mormonism in the British Isles in 1840-41 was Apostle Orson Pratt. After arriving in Edinburgh, Scotland, in May 1840, Elder Pratt ascended a hill above the city, dedicated the country for the message of the restored gospel, and implored the powers of heaven to reward his work. His hard labor during the next nine months resulted in more than 200 converts.

To arouse interest in his message in this northern city of learning and art, Pratt published in September 1840 a thirty-one-page pamphlet titled *A Interesting Account of Several Remarkable Visions, and of the Late Discovery of Ancient American Records Giving an Account of the Commencement of the Work of the Lord in this Generation*. (Breck England, *The Life and Thought of Orson Pratt* [Salt Lake City: University of Utah Press, 1985], 66-71; Peter Crawley and David J. Whittaker, *Mormon Imprints in Great Britain and the Empire 1836-1857* [Provo, Utah: Friends of the Brigham Young University Library, 1987], 19-21.)

The significance of the Orson Pratt pamphlet is that it contained the first publication of Joseph Smith's 1820 Vision. Pratt drew from his personal acquaintance and the Prophet's early writings for the material recounting Joseph's experience, and his narrative is sufficiently different to warrant inclusion here.

Orson Pratt, c.1865. Photograph by G. Wunsch, Austria. LDS Church Archives.

Mr. Joseph Smith, jun., who made the following important discovery, was born in the town of Sharon, Windsor county, Vermont, on the 23d of December, A.D. 1805. When ten years old, his parents, with their family, moved to Palmyra, New York; in the vicinity of which he resided for about eleven years, the latter part in the town of Manchester. Cultivating the earth for a livelihood was his occupation, in which he employed the most of his time. His advantages, for acquiring literary knowledge, were exceedingly small; hence, his education was limited to a slight acquaintance with two or three of the common branches of learning. He could read without much difficulty, and write a very imperfect hand; and had a very limited understanding of the ground rules of arithmetic.[1] These were his highest and only attainments; while the rest of those branches, so universally taught in the common schools throughout the United States, were entirely unknown to him. When somewhere about fourteen or fifteen years old, he began seriously to reflect upon the necessity of being prepared for a future state of existence: but how, or in what way, to prepare himself, was a question, as yet, undetermined in his own mind: he perceived that it was a question of infinite importance, and that the salvation of his soul depended upon a correct understanding of the same. He saw, that if he understood not the [p. 3] way, it would be impossible to walk in it, except by chance; and the thought of resting his hopes of eternal life upon chance, or uncertainties, was more than he could endure. If he went to the religious denominations to seek information, each one pointed to its particular tenets, saying—"This is the way, walk ye in it;" while, at the same time, the doctrines of each were, in many respects, in direct opposition to one another. It, also, occurred to his mind, that God was not the author of but one doctrine, and therefore could not acknowledge but one de-

1. Wording here suggests that Pratt may have had access to the Joseph Smith 1832 History when he produced this work. See p. 5.

nomination as his church; and that such denomination must be a people, who believe, and teach, that one doctrine, (whatever it may be,) and build upon the same. He then reflected upon the immense number of doctrines, now, in the world, which had given rise to many hundreds of different denominations. The great question to be decided in his mind, was— if any one of these denominations be the Church of Christ, which one is it? Until he could become satisfied, in relation to this question, he could not rest contented. To trust to the decisions of fallible man, and build his hopes upon the same, without any certainty, and knowledge, of his own, would not satisfy the anxious desires that pervaded his breast. To decide, without any positive and definite evidence, on which he could rely, upon a subject involving the future welfare of his soul, was revolting to his feelings. The only alternative, that seemed to be left him, was to read the Scriptures, and endeavor to follow their directions. He, accordingly, commenced perusing the sacred pages of the Bible, with sincerity, believing the things that he read. His mind soon caught hold of the following passage:— "If any of you lack wisdom, let him ask of God, that giveth to all *men* liberally, and upbraideth not; and it shall be given him." —James i.5. From this promise he learned, that it was the privilege of all men to ask God for wisdom, with the sure and certain expectation of receiving, liberally; without being upbraided for so doing. This was cheering information to him: tidings that gave him great joy. It was like a light shining forth in a dark place, to guide him to the path in which he should walk. He, now, saw that if he inquired of God, there was, not only, a possibility, but a probability; yea, more, a certainty, that he should [p. 4] obtain a knowledge, which, of all the doctrines, was the doctrine of Christ; and, which, of all the churches, was the church of Christ. He, therefore, retired to a secret place, in a grove, but a short distance from his father's house, and knelt down, and began to call upon the Lord. At first, he was severely tempted by the powers of darkness, which endeavored to overcome him; but he continued to seek for deliverance, until darkness gave way from his mind; and he was enabled to pray, in fervency of the spirit, and in faith. And, while thus pouring out his soul, anxiously desiring an answer from God, he, at length, saw a very bright and glorious light in the heavens above; which, at first, seemed to be at a considerable distance. He continued praying, while the light appeared to be gradually descending towards him; and, as it drew nearer, it increased in brightness, and magnitude, so that, by the time that it reached the tops of the trees, the whole wilderness, for some distance around, was illuminated in a most glorious and brilliant manner. He expected to have seen the leaves and boughs of the trees consumed, as soon as the light came in contact with them; but, perceiving that it did not produce that effect, he was encouraged with the hopes of being able to endure its presence. It continued descending, slowly, until it rested upon the earth, and he was enveloped in the midst of it. When it first came upon him, it produced a peculiar sensation throughout his whole system; and, immediately, his mind was caught away, from the natural objects with which he was surrounded; and he was enwrapped in a heavenly vision, and saw two glorious personages, who exactly resembled each other in their features or likeness. He was informed, that his sins were forgiven. He was also informed upon the subjects, which had for some time previously agitated his mind, viz.—that all the religious denominations were believing in incorrect doctrines; and, consequently, that none of them was acknowledged of God, as his church and kingdom. And he was expressly commanded, to go not after them; and he received a promise that the true doctrine—the fullness of the gospel, should, at some future time, be made known to him; after which the vision withdrew, leaving his mind in a state of calmness and peace, indescribable. Some time after having received this glorious [p. 5] manifestation, being young, he was again entangled in the vanities of the world, of which he afterwards sincerely and truly repented.

And it pleased God, on the evening of the 21st of September, A.D. 1823, to again hear his prayers. For he had retired to rest, as usual, only that his mind was drawn out, in fervent prayer, and his soul was filled with the most earnest desire,[1] "to commune with some kind messenger, who could communicate to him the desired information of his acceptance with God," and also unfold the principles of the doctrine of Christ, according to the promise which he had received in the former vision. While he thus continued to pour out his desires before the Father of all good; endeavoring to exercise faith in his precious promises; "on a sudden, a light like that of day, only of a purer and far more glorious appearance and brightness, burst into the room. Indeed, the first sight was as though the house was filled with consuming fire. This sudden appearance of a light so bright, as must naturally be expected, occasioned a shock or sensation visible to the extremities of the body. It was, however, followed with a calmness and serenity of mind, and an overwhelming rapture of joy, that surpassed understanding, and, in a moment, a personage stood before him."

Notwithstanding the brightness of the light which previously illuminated the room, "yet there seemed to be an additional glory surrounding or accompanying this personage, which shone with an increased degree of brilliancy, of which he was in the midst; and though his countenance was as lightning, yet, it was of a pleasing, innocent, and glorious appearance; so much so, that every fear was banished from the heart, and nothing but calmness pervaded the soul."

"The stature of this personage was a little above the common size of men in this age; his garment was perfectly white, and had the appearance of being without seam."

1. The quotations that follow are from the 1834-36 History.

This glorious being declared himself to be an Angel of God, sent forth, by commandment, to communicate to him that his sins were forgiven, and that his prayers were heard; and also, to bring the joyful tidings, that the covenant which God made with ancient Israel, concerning their [p. 6] posterity, was at hand to be fulfilled; that the great preparatory work for the second coming of the Messiah, was speedily to commence; that the time was at hand for the gospel, in its fullness, to be preached in power unto all nations; that a people might be prepared with faith and righteousness, for the Millennial reign of universal peace and joy.

He was informed, that he was called and chosen to be an instrument in the hands of God, to bring about some of his marvelous purposes in this glorious dispensation. It was also made manifest to him, that the "American Indians" were a remnant of Israel; that when they first emigrated to America, they were an enlightened people, possessing a knowledge of the true God, enjoying his favor, and peculiar blessings from his hand; that the prophets, and inspired writers among them, were required to keep a sacred history of the most important events transpiring among them: which history was handed down for many generations, till at length they fell into great wickedness: the most part of them were destroyed, and the records, (by commandment of God, to one of the last prophets among them,) were safely deposited, to preserve them from the hands of the wicked, who sought to destroy them. He was informed, that these records contained many sacred revelations pertaining to the gospel of the kingdom, as well as prophecies relating to the great events of the last days; and that to fulfil his promises to the ancients, who wrote the records, and to accomplish his purposes, in the restitution of their children, &c., they were to come forth to the knowledge of the people. If faithful, he was to be the instrument, who should be thus highly favored in bringing these sacred things to light: at the same time, being expressly informed, that it must be done with an eye single to the glory of God, that no one could be entrusted with those sacred writings, who should endeavor to aggrandize himself, by converting sacred things to unrighteous and speculative purposes. After giving him many instructions concerning things past and to come, which would be foreign to our purpose to mention here, he disappeared, and the light and glory of God withdrew, leaving his mind in perfect peace, while a calmness and serenity indescribable pervaded the soul. But, before morning, the vision was [p. 7] twice renewed, instructing him further, and still further, concerning the great work of God, about to be performed on the earth. In the morning, he went out to his labor as usual; but soon the vision was renewed—the Angel again appeared; and having been informed by the previous visions of the night, concerning the place where those records were deposited, he was instructed to go immediately and view them.

Accordingly, he repaired to the place, a brief description of which shall be given, in the words of a gentleman, by the name of Oliver Cowdery, who has visited the spot.

"As you pass on the mail-road, from Palmyra, Wayne county, to Canandaigua, Ontario county, New York, before arriving at the little village of Manchester, say from three to four, or about four miles from Palmyra, you pass a large hill on the east side of the road. Why I say large, is because it is as large, perhaps, as any in that country.

"The north end rises quite suddenly until it assumes a level with the more southerly extremity; and I think, I may say, an elevation higher than at the south, a short distance, say half or three-fourths of a mile. As you pass towards Canandaigua, it lessens gradually, until the surface assumes its common level, or is broken by other smaller hills or ridges, water-courses and ravines. I think I am justified in saying, that this is the highest hill for some distance round, and I am certain, that its appearance, as it rises so suddenly from a plain on the north, must attract the notice of the traveller as he passes by."—"The north end," which has been described as rising suddenly from the plain, forms " a promontory without timber, but covered with grass. As you pass to the south, you soon come to scattering timber, the surface having been cleared by art or wind; and a short distance further left, you are surrounded with the common forest of the country. It is necessary to observe, that even the part cleared, was only occupied for pasturage; its steep ascent, and narrow summit not admitting the plough of the husbandman, with any degree of ease or profit. It was at the second mentioned place, where the record was found to be deposited, on the west side of the hill, not far from the top down its side; and when myself visited the place in the year 1830, there were several trees standing—enough to cause a shade in [p. 8] summer, but not so much as to prevent the surface being covered with grass—which was also the case when the record was first found.

"How far below the surface these records were" anciently "placed, I am unable to say; but from the fact, that they had been some fourteen hundred years buried, and that, too, on the side of a hill so steep, one is ready to conclude, that they were some feet below, as the earth would naturally wear, more or less, in that length of time. But they, being placed toward the top of the hill, the ground would not remove as much as at two-thirds, perhaps. Another circumstance would prevent a wearing of the earth: in all probability, as soon as timber had time to grow, the hill was covered," "and the roots of the same would hold the surface. However, on this point, I shall leave every man to draw his own conclusion, and form his own speculation." But, suffice to say, "a hole of sufficient depth was dug. At the bottom of this was laid a stone of suitable size, the upper surface being smooth. At each edge, was placed a large quantity of cement, and into this cement, at the four edges of this stone, were placed erect four others; *their* bottom edges resting *in* the cement, at the outer edges of the first stone. The four last named, when placed erect, formed a box:

the corners, or where the edges of the four came in contact, were also cemented so firmly, that the moisture from without was prevented from entering. It is to be observed, also, that the inner surfaces of the four erect or side stones, were smooth. This box was sufficiently large to admit a breastplate, such as was used by the ancients, to defend the chest, &c., from the arrows and weapons of their enemy. From the bottom of the box, or from the breastplate, arose three small pillars, composed of the same description of cement used on the edges; and upon these three pillars were placed the records." —"This box, containing the records, was covered with another stone, the bottom surface being flat, and the upper crowning." When it was first visited by Mr Smith, on the morning of the 22d of September 1823, "a part of the crowning stone was visible above the surface, while the edges were concealed by the soil and grass." From which circumstance, it may be seen, "that however deep this box might have been placed at first, the time had been [p. 9] sufficient to wear the earth, so that it was easily discovered, when once directed, and yet, not enough to make a perceivable difference to the passer-by."—"After arriving at the repository, a little exertion in removing the soil from the edges of the top of the box, and a light pry, brought to his natural vision its contents." While viewing and contemplating this sacred treasure with wonder and astonishment, behold! the Angel of the Lord, who had previously visited him, again stood in his presence, and his soul was again enlightened as it was the evening before, and he was filled with the Holy Spirit, and the heavens were opened, and the glory of the Lord shone round about and rested upon him. While he thus stood gazing and admiring, the Angel said, "Look!" And as he thus spake, he beheld the Prince of Darkness, surrounded by his innumerable train of associates. All this passed before him, and the heavenly messenger said, "All this is shown, the good and the evil, the holy and impure, the glory of God, and the power of darkness, that you may know hereafter the two pow-

ers, and never be influenced or overcome by that wicked one. Behold, whatsoever enticeth and leadeth to good and to do good, is of God, and whatsoever doth not, is of that wicked one. It is he that filleth the hearts of men with evil, to walk in darkness and blaspheme God; and you may learn from henceforth, that his ways are to destruction, but the way of holiness is peace and rest. You cannot at this time obtain this record, for the commandment of God is strict, and if ever these sacred things are obtained, they must be by prayer and faithfulness in obeying the Lord. They are not deposited here for the sake of accumulating gain and wealth for the glory of this world; they were sealed by the prayer of faith, and because of the knowledge which they contain, they are of no worth among the children of men, only for their knowledge. On them is contained the fulness of the gospel of Jesus Christ, as it was given to his people on this land; and when it shall be brought forth by the power of God, it shall be carried to the Gentiles, of whom many will receive it, and after will the seed of Israel be brought into the fold of their Redeemer by obeying it also. Those who kept the commandments of the Lord on this land, desired this at his hand, and through the prayer of faith obtained the promise, that [p. 10] if their descendants should transgress and fall away, that a record should be kept, and in the last days come to their children. These things are sacred, and must be kept so, for the promise of the Lord concerning them must be fulfilled. No man can obtain them if his heart is impure, because they contain that which is sacred." ***
"By them will the Lord work a great and marvelous work; the wisdom of the wise shall become as naught, and the understanding of the prudent shall be hid, and because the power of God shall be displayed, those who profess to know the truth, but walk in deceit, shall tremble with anger; but with signs and with wonders, with gifts and with healings, with the manifestations of the power of God, and with the Holy Ghost, shall the hearts of the faithful be comforted. You have now beheld

the power of God manifested, and the power of Satan; you see that there is nothing desirable in the works of darkness; that they cannot bring happiness; that those who are overcome therewith are miserable; while, on the other hand, the righteous are blessed with a place in the kingdom of God, where joy unspeakable surrounds them. There they rest beyond the power of the enemy of truth, where no evil can disturb them. The glory of God crowns them, and they continually feast upon his goodness, and enjoy his smiles. Behold, notwithstanding you have seen this great display of power, by which you may ever be able to detect the evil one, yet I give unto you another sign, and when it comes to pass then know that the Lord is God, and that he will fulfil his purposes, and that the knowledge which this record contains will go to every nation, and kindred, and tongue, and people under the whole heaven. This is the sign: when these things begin to be known, that is, when it is known that the lord has shown you these things, the workers of iniquity will seek your overthrow. They will circulate falsehoods to destroy your reputation; and also will seek to take your life; but remember this, if you are faithful, and shall hereafter continue to keep the commandments of the Lord, you shall be preserved to bring these things forth; for in due time he will give you a commandment to come and take them. When they are interpreted, the Lord will give the holy priesthood to some, and they shall begin to proclaim this gospel and baptize by water, and after that, they shall have power to give the Holy Ghost by the laying on of their [p. 11] hands. Then will persecution rage more and more; for the iniquities of men shall be revealed, and those who are not built upon the Rock will seek to overthrow the church; but it will increase the more opposed, and spread farther and farther, increasing in knowledge till they shall be sanctified, and receive an inheritance where the glory of God will rest upon them; and when this takes place, and all things are prepared, the ten tribes of Israel will be revealed in the north country, whither they have been for a long season; and when this is fulfilled will be brought to pass that saying of the prophet,—'And the Redeemer shall come to Zion, and unto them that turn from transgression in Jacob, saith the Lord.' But, notwithstanding the workers of iniquity shall seek your destruction, the arm of the Lord will be extended, and you will be borne off conqueror if you keep all his commandments. Your name shall be known among the nations, for the work which the Lord will perform by your hands shall cause the righteous to rejoice and the wicked to rage; with the one it shall be had in honor, and with the other in reproach; yet, with these it shall be a terror, because of the great and marvelous work which shall follow the coming forth of this fullness of the gospel. Now, go thy way, remembering what the Lord has done for thee, and be diligent in keeping his commandments, and he will deliver thee from temptations and all the arts and devices of the wicked one. Forget not to pray, that thy mind may become strong that when he shall manifest unto thee, thou mayest have power to escape the evil, and obtain these precious things."

We here remark, that the above quotation is an extract from a letter written by Elder Oliver Cowdery, which was published in one of the numbers of the "Latter Day Saints' Messenger and Advocate."

Although many more instructions were given by the mouth of the angel to Mr Smith, which we do not write in this book, yet the most important items are contained in the foregoing relation. During the period of the four following years, he frequently received instruction from the mouth of the heavenly messenger. And on the morning of the 22d of September, A.D. 1827, the angel of the Lord delivered the records into his hands.

These records were engraven on plates, which had the [p. 12] appearance of gold. Each plate was not far from seven by eight inches in width and length, being not quite as thick as common tin. They were filled on both sides with engravings, in Egyptian characters, and bound together in a volume, as the leaves of a book, and fastened at one edge with three rings running through the whole. This volume was something near six inches in thickness, a part of which was sealed. The characters or letters upon the unsealed part were small, and beautifully engraved. The whole book exhibited many marks of antiquity in its construction, as well as much skill in the art of engraving. With the records was found "a curious instrument, called by the ancients the Urim and Thummim, which consisted of two transparent stones, clear as crystal, set in the two rims of a bow. This was in use, in ancient times, by persons called seers. It was an instrument, by the use of which, they received revelation of things distant, or of things past or future."

In the meantime, the inhabitants of that vicinity, having been informed that Mr Smith had seen heavenly visions, and that he had discovered sacred records, began to ridicule and mock at those things. And after having obtained those sacred things, while proceeding home through the wilderness and fields, he was waylaid by two ruffians, who had secreted themselves for the purpose of robbing him of the records. One of them struck him with a club before he perceived them; but being a strong man, and large in stature, with great exertion he cleared himself from them, and ran towards home, being closely pursued until he came near his father's house, when his pursuers, for fear of being detected, turned and fled the other way.

Soon the news of his discoveries spread abroad throughout all those parts. False reports, misrepresentations, and base slanders, flew as if upon the wings of the wind in every direction. The house was frequently beset by mobs and evil designing persons. Several times he was shot at, and very narrowly escaped. Every device was used to get the plates away from him. And being continually in danger of his life, from a gang of abandoned wretches, he at length concluded to leave the place, and go to Pennsylvania; and accordingly, packed up his goods, putting the plates into a barrel of beans, and proceeded upon his journey. [p. 13] He had not gone far, before he was overtaken by an officer with a search-warrant, who flattered himself with the idea, that he should surely obtain the plates; after searching very diligently, he was sadly disappointed at not finding them. Mr Smith then drove on; but before he got to his journey's end, he was again overtaken by an officer on the same business, and after ransacking the wagon very carefully, he went his way, as much chagrined as the first, at not being able to discover the object of his research. Without any further molestation, he pursued his journey until he came into the northern part of Pennsylvania, near the Susquehanna river, in which part his father-in-law resided.

Having provided himself with a home, he commenced translating the record, by the gift and power of God, through the means of the Urim and Thummim; and being a poor writer, he was under the necessity of employing a scribe, to write the translation as it came from his mouth.

In the meantime, a few of the original characters were accurately transcribed and translated by Mr Smith, which, with the translation, were taken by a gentleman by the name of Martin Harris, to the city of New York, where they were presented to a learned gentleman by the name of Anthon, who professed to be extensively acquainted with many languages, both ancient and modern. He examined them; but was unable to decipher them correctly; but he presumed, that if the original records could be brought, he could assist in translating them.

But to return. Mr Smith continued the work of translation, as his pecuniary circumstances would permit, until he finished the unsealed part of the records. The part translated is entitled the "Book of Mormon," which contains nearly as much reading as the Old Testament.

ORSON HYDE, *EIN RUF AUS DER WÜSTE*, 1842

Orson Hyde, Ein Ruf aus der Wüste, eine Stimme aus dem Schoose der Erde [A Cry from the Wilderness, a Voice from the Dust of the Earth] *(Frankfurt, 1842).*

Editorial Note

Speaking at the 6 April 1840 conference of the Church held at Nauvoo, Illinois, Orson Hyde referred to a prophecy "some years ago" indicating that he had "a great work to perform among the Jews," a work that would "prepare the way, and greatly facilitate the gathering together of that people." He said he felt the time had now come to visit the Jews in New York, London, Amsterdam, Constantinople, and the Holy Land and report to the Church information about their "movements, expectations, &c." It was then resolved by the conference that Elder Hyde should proceed on his mission with letters of recommendation by the President and Clerk of the conference. (Joseph Smith Letter book 2, 197-206; also in Smith, *History of the Church*, 4:105-6.)

From Columbus, Ohio, on 1 May 1840, two weeks after starting with John E. Page on his mission, Hyde sought the sanction of the Church presidency for a plan "manifested to us by the Spirit" that would add another dimension to his mission to Europe: "As there is a great work to be done in Germany, . . . the following plan has been suggested to us; viz., to write a set of lectures upon the faith and doctrine of our Church, giving a brief history of the coming forth of the Book of Mormon, and an account of its contents . . . together with the outlines and organization and government of the Church . . . and get the same translated into German, and publish it when we arrive in Germany, and scatter it through the German empire." Two weeks later, Joseph Smith responded to the inquiry, "I entirely approve of the same, and give my consent." (Orson Hyde and John E. Page to Joseph Smith, 1 May 1840,

Joseph Smith Letterbook 2:144-45; Joseph Smith to Orson Hyde and John E. Page, 14 May 1840, Joseph Smith Letterbook 2:146-47; published in Smith, *History of the Church*, 4:123-124, 129.)

Having proceeded to Europe without John Page, Hyde wrote to Joseph Smith from London a year later, informing him, "I have written a book to publish in the German language, setting forth our doctrine and principles in as clear and concise a manner as I possibly could. After giving a history of the rise of the Church in something the manner that Brother Orson Pratt did, I have written a snug little article on every point of doctrine believed by the Saints." (Orson Hyde to Joseph Smith, 15 June 1841; published in *Times and Seasons* 2 [1 October 1841]: 551-55; and Smith, *History of the Church*, 4:373-74.) En route to Constantinople a short time later, Elder Hyde stopped at Regensburg, Germany, while awaiting a visa to enter the Austrian Empire. During his stay he exchanged instruction in English for lessons in the German language. Then, continuing his mission, he journeyed to Turkey, Syria, Palestine, and Egypt; and on 24 October 1841, standing on the Mount of Olives, he dedicated the land of Palestine for the return of the Jews. Upon completing his purpose in the Holy Land, Hyde returned to Regensburg in February 1842 by way of Egypt and Italy. He wrote that having wandered "through the thorns and thistles of an uncivilized world," he found it desirable to stay in Regensburg "for a season or two in order to partake of the flowers of German literature." To use his "idle hours" profitably, he resumed giving English lessons. With the help of one of his students, he translated the work he had written in England the previous year into German. When authorities at Regensburg denied the Mormon elder permission to publish and distribute his work in that city because its principles "were so different from those of the predominant religion of this country," and for fear "it would only cause excitement and unrest among the people," Hyde published his book in August that year at Frankfurt. (Smith, *History of the Church*, 4:386; Hyde, *Ein Ruf*, 107-8; 113-14; Marvin S. Hill, "An Historical Study of the Life of Orson Hyde, Early Mormon Missionary and Apostle from 1805-1852" [Master's thesis, Brigham Young University, 1955]; "Items of News," *The Latter-day Saints' Millennial Star* 3 [September 1842]: 96.)

Orson Hyde's publication was the first foreign-language printing of Joseph Smith's 1820 vision and his experience in producing the Book of Mormon. And although Hyde used Orson Pratt's 1840 Edinburgh publication as a model, his work is sufficiently different to warrant inclusion here. The German text contains misspellings, inconsistencies, grammatical errors, occasional phrases and word choices patterned after English usage, and evidence of the use of the King James Bible as a source text, all of which substantiate Hyde's statement, "I do not claim that this work is perfect in its mechanism; I do not understand the

German language perfectly, however, the principles which are emphasized in it are true and good." (Hyde, *Ein Ruf*, 224. For a detailed analysis of the Orson Hyde work see Marvin H. Folsom, "The Language of Orson Hyde's *Ein Ruf aus der Wüste*," in *Proceedings of the Deseret Language and Linguistic Society*, Fifteenth Annual Symposium, 13 March 1989, Provo, Utah.) The English translation below is by Marvin H. Folsom, professor of German, Brigham Young University.

Joseph Smith jun., die Person, zu welcher der Engel des Herrn zuerst gesandt ward, wurde geboren den 23. Dezember A.D. 1805 in der Stadt Sharon, Grafschaft Windsor Vermont. Als er zehn Jahre alt war, zogen seine Eltern nach Palmyra in den Staat New-York. In dieser und in der nahe gelegenen Stadt Manchester verlebte er beinahe eilf Jahre. Seine einzige Beschäftigung war, den Boden zu pflügen und ihn zu bebauen. Da seine Eltern arm waren, und eine zahlreiche Familie zu ernähren hatten, so war seine Erziehung sehr mangelhaft. Er konnte ziemlich gut lesen, dafür schrieb er aber höchst nothdürftig, und hatte nur geringe Kenntnisse von Redebildern. Höher reichte sein literarisches Wissen nicht. Die meisten der Gegenstände, welche so allgemein in den vereinigten Staaten Amerika's gelehrt werden, waren ihm in jener Zeit gänzlich unbekannt, wo er mit einer Himmels-Botschaft begünstigt wurde. [p. 13]

Als er sein fünfzehntes Jahr er reicht hatte, fing er ernsten Sinnes über das Wichtige einer Vorbereitung für die Zukunft nachzudenken an; doch schwer ward es ihm zu entscheiden, wie er sich an ein so bedeutungsvolles Werk zu setzen hätte. Er sah klar ein, daß es ihm unmöglich sein würde, auf dem rechten Wege zu wandeln, ohne ihn zuvor zu kennen; und seine Hofnungen des ewigen Lebens auf einen Zufall oder eine blinde Ungewißheit zu stützen, das wäre mehr gewesen, als er je zu thun gesinnt war.

Er entdeckte die religiöse Welt arbeitend unter dem Andrange von Irrthümern, die durch ihre widersprechenden Mei-

ORSON HYDE, *A CRY FROM THE WILDERNESS*, 1842

Joseph Smith jun[ior], the person to whom the angel of the Lord was first sent, was born on December 23 in the year of our Lord 1805 in the town of Sharon, Windsor County, Vermont. When he was ten years old, his parents moved to Palmyra in the state of New York. For almost eleven years he lived here [in Palmyra] and in the neighboring town of Manchester. His only occupation was to plow and cultivate the soil. Because his parents were poor and had to feed a large family, his education was meager. He was able to read fairly well, but his ability to write was very limited and had only little literary knowledge. His knowledge of letters did not go any further. Most of the subjects which were generally taught in the United States of America were completely unknown to him at the time he was favored with a heavenly message. [p. 13]

When he had reached his fifteenth year, he began to think seriously about the importance of preparing for a future [existence]; but it was very difficult for him to decide how he should go about such an important undertaking. He recognized clearly that it would be impossible for him to walk the proper path without being acquainted with it beforehand; and to base his hopes for eternal life on chance or blind uncertainty would have been more than he had ever been inclined to do.

He discovered the world of religion working under a flood of errors which by virtue of their contradictory opinions and

nungen und Grundsätze den Grund zur Entstehung so verschiedener Sekten und Parteien legten, und deren Gefühle gegen einander nur zu oft durch Haß, Streit, Groll und Muth vergiftet waren. Er fühlte daß es nur eine Wahrheit gäbe, und daß diejenigen, welche sie recht verständen, sie auch gleichmäßig verständen. Die Natur hatte ihn mit einem starken, beurtheilenden Verstande begabt, und so sah er denn durch das Glas der Vernunft und des guten Sinnes mit Mitleid und Verachtung auf jene Religionssysteme hin, welche einander so entgegen gesetzt, und dennoch alle offenbar aus den Schriften der Wahrheit gezogen sind. [p. 14]

Nachdem er sich zu seiner eigenen Genugthuung hinlänglich überzeugt hatte, daß Finsterniß die Erde bedeckte, und grosse Dunkelheit die Völker, da verließ ihn die hoffnung, je eine Sekte oder Partei zu finden, die im Besitze der reinen Wahrheit wäre.

In Folge dessen machte er sich denn selber glaubensvoll an die Untersuchung des Wortes Gottes, als die beste Art und Weise zur Erkenntniß der Wahrheit zu gelangen. In dieser lobenswürdigen Beschäftigung hatte er noch night lange fortgefahren, also seine Augen auf folgende Stelle des heiligen Jakobus fielen: "Wenn Jemand von euch der Weisheit bedarf, so laßt sie ihn von Gott begehren, der da allen Menschen freigebig gibt und nichts vorwirft, und es soll ihm gegeben werden."—Diese Stelle betrachtete er als eine Vollmacht zu einem feierlichen Aufrufe an seinen Erschaffer, um vor Ihm seine Bedürfnisse ausbreiten zu dürfen, mit sicherer Hoffnung zum gewissen Erfolge. Und so fing er denn an, die heißen Wünsche seiner Seele mit glaubensvoller Entschlossenheit zum Herrn hinauf zu senden. Bei einer gewissen Gelegenheit begab er sich in ein kleines Wäldchen nahe an seines Vaters Wohnung, und knieete nieder zum feierlichen Gebete vor Gott. Da machte der Widersacher verschiedene mächtige Versuche, den Eifer seines Gemüthes zu erkalten. Er umnachtete seinen Verstand mit Zweifeln, [p. 15] und führte seiner Seele allerlei

principles laid the foundation for the rise of such different sects and denominations whose feelings toward each other all too often were poisoned by hate, contention, resentment and anger. He felt that there was only one truth and that those who understood it correctly, all understood it in the same way. Nature had endowed him with a keen critical intellect and so he looked through the lens of reason and common sense and with pity and contempt upon those systems of religion, which were so opposed to each other and yet were all obviously based on the scriptures. [p. 14]

After he had sufficiently convinced himself to his own satisfaction that darkness covered the earth and gross darkness [covered] the nations, the hope of ever finding a sect or denomination that was in possession of unadulterated truth left him.

Consequently he began in an attitude of faith his own investigation of the word of God [feeling that it was] the best way to arrive at a knowledge of the truth. He had not proceeded very far in this laudable endeavor when his eyes fell upon the following verse of St. James [1:5]: "If any of you lack wisdom, let him ask of God, that giveth to all men liberally, and upbraideth not; and it shall be given him." He considered this scripture an authorization for him to solemnly call upon his creator to present his needs before him with the certain expectation of some success. And so he began to pour out to the Lord with fervent determination the earnest desires of his soul. On one occasion, he went to a small grove of trees near his father's home and knelt down before God in solemn prayer. The adversary then made several strenuous efforts to cool his ardent soul. He filled his mind with doubts [p. 15] and brought

unpassende Bilder vor, um ihn an der Erreichung des Gegenstandes seiner Bestrebungen zu hindern; allein die überfließende Gnade unseres Gottes kam ihn aufzurichten, und verschaffte neue Triebe seinen schwindenden Kräften. Bald theilte sich jedoch die trübe Wolke, und Licht und Friede füllte sein geängstigtes Herz. Und von Neuem rief er wieder mit Glauben und Kraft des Geistes zum Herrn.

In diesem heiligen Momente schloß sich die, ihn umgebende Natur vor seinen Blicken, um der Darstellung himmlischer und geistiger Dinge freien Raum zu geben. Zwei glorreiche, himmlische Personen stunden vor ihm, die sich in Gesicht und Gestalt ganz einander glichen. Diese unterrichteten ihn, daß seine Gebete erhört seien, und daß der Herr beschloßen habe, ihn mit besonderer Gunst ze beglücken. Es wurde ihm auch gesagt, daß er keiner Religions-Secte oder Parthei anhängen solle, da alle derselben in ihrer Lehre irrten, und keine von Gott also Seine Kirche und Sein Reich angesehen wäre. Ferner ward ihm noch befohlen, in Geduld zu harren bis zu einer künftigen Zeit, wo die wahre Lehre Christi und die ganze Vollheit des Evangeliums ihm soll geoffenbaret werden. Das Gesicht schloß sich, und Friede und Ruhe stiegen in sein Gemüth. [p. 16]

Einige Zeit nachher als ihm diese himmlische Offenbarungen geworden sind (in seinen früheren Jahren), verfiel er in die Fehler und Eitelkeiten der Welt, welche er später jedoch aufrichtig bereute.

Am abende des 21. Septembers A.D. 1823 gefiel es dem Herrn sein Flehen wieder zu erhören, und den Bitten seines Herzens zu antworten. Er begab sich wie gewöhnlich, in dieser merkwürdigen Nacht zur Ruhe mit dem betenden Wunsche, daß ihm wieder eine Unterredung mit irgend einem himmlischen Boten gewährt werden möchte, der ihm die gewünschte Unterweisung über seine Unnahme vor Gott, so wie auch über die zu enthüllenden Grundsätze der Lehre Christi geben würde, der Verheißung gemäß, die ihm in dem früheren

to mind all manner of inappropriate images to prevent him from obtaining the object of his endeavors; but the overflowing mercy of God came to buoy him up and gave new impetus to his failing strength. However, the dark cloud soon parted and light and peace filled his frightened heart. Once again he called upon the Lord with faith and fervency of spirit.

At this sacred moment, the natural world around him was excluded from his view, so that he would be open to the presentation of heavenly and spiritual things. Two glorious heavenly personages stood before him, resembling each other exactly in features and stature. They told him that his prayers had been answered and that the Lord had decided to grant him a special blessing. He was also told that he should not join any of the religious sects or denominations, because all of them erred in doctrine and none was recognized by God as his church and kingdom. He was further commanded, to wait patiently until some future time, when the true doctrine of Christ and the complete truth of the gospel would be revealed to him. The vision closed and peace and calm filled his mind. [p. 16]

Some time after he had been given these heavenly revelations (in his earlier years), he lapsed into the errors and vanities of the world, which he later was genuinely sorry for.

On the evening of September 21 in the year of our Lord 1823, it pleased the Lord to hear his pleading once again and to answer the desires of his heart. On this noteworthy night, he retired to bed with the prayerful desire of being granted communion with some kind of heavenly messenger, who might give him the desired instruction concerning his acceptance before God as well as the revealed principles of the doctrine of Christ according to the promise which had been given to him in the early vision. As he continued to offer up his

Gesichte ward. Als er so fortfuhr sein Gebet dem himmlischen Vater zuzusenden, da füllte plötzliches Licht, gleich dem des Tages, nur noch reiner und verklärter, das Zimmer. Der erste Anblick war in Wahrheit, als ob das Haus in verzehrendem Feuer stünde. Das plötzliche Erscheinen dieses Lichtes, hatte eine Wirkung, gleich der eines heftigen Stoßes, auf seinen Körper, die bis an dessen Extremitäten fühlbar war.

Sein Gemüth jedoch fühlte sich sogleich mit Ruhe und Heiterkeit übergoßen, und sein Zustand erhob sich zu einem Entzücken der Freude das jede Beschreibung [p. 17] übersteigt. In derselben Minute stand eine Person vor ihm, deren Gestalt, ohngeachtet des Lichtes, welches das Zimmer erhellte, von noch strahlenderem Glanze umfloßen war. Ihr Gesicht, obgleich dem Blitze änlich, war lieblichen, unschuldigen und gewinnenden Anblickes, so daß jede Furcht aus seinem Herzen verbannt war.

Die Figur dieser Person war etwas über die gewöhnliche Höhe der Männer im jugendlichen Alter; ihre Kleidung war vollkommen weiß, und schien ohne Nacht zu sein.

Dieses glorreiche Wesen gab sich selber als einen Engel Gottes kund, gesandt auf Befehl des Herrn, ihm zu verkünden, daß sein Gebet nun wirklich erhöret sei, und daß er ihm die frohe Botschaft bringe, daß der Bund, welchen Gott mit den Alten in Israel in Betreff ihrer Nachkommenschaft gemacht hatte, nun der Zeit seiner Erfüllung nahe sei; daß das grosse Vorbereitungs-Werk zur zweiten Ankunft des Messias, seinnen Anfang nehmen werde, daß die Vollheit des Evangeliums mit Macht unter allen Nationen gepredigt werden werde, um ein Volk zu bilden mit Glauben und Gerechtigkeit für das tausendjährige Reich allgemeinen Friedens und ungestörter Freude.

Diese Belehrungen wurden ihm hier gegeben, das mit er als ein von Gott Berufener und Auserwählter [p. 18] die wunderbaren Absichten erkenne, die Gott durch ihn bewirken wolle. Es ward ihm auch gesagt, daß die "Amerikanischen

prayer to Heavenly Father, sudden[ly] light, like that of day, only purer and more radiant, filled the room. In truth, it appeared at first as though the house were engulfed in a consuming fire. The sudden appearance of this light had an effect like that of a violent force on his body which was felt even in his extremities.

However, his mind was immediately flooded with calmness and serenity and his state of mind was elevated to an ecstacy of joy that surpasses all description. [p. 17] At that instant a personage stood before him whose person, notwithstanding the light that filled the room, was encompassed about with even more brilliant light. His countenance though like lightning was of a pleasant, innocent and engaging aspect so that all fear was banished from his heart.

The stature of this person was somewhat taller than that of men in their youth; his clothes were perfectly white and appeared to have no seams.

This glorious being declared himself to be an angel of God, sent at the command of the Lord to tell him that his prayer had now really been answered and that he was bringing him [Joseph Smith] the glad tiding that the covenant which God had made with the ancient ones in Israel concerning their posterity was now about to be fulfilled; that the great work of preparation for the second coming of the Messiah was about to begin, that the fullness of the gospel would be preached with power among all nations to prepare a people of faith and righteousness for the millennial reign of universal peace and uninterrupted joy.

These doctrines were given to him now so that he as one called and chosen of God might recognize [p. 18] the wonderful purposes that God wanted to bring about through him. He was also told that the "American Indians" were remnants of

Indier", Trümmer des Hauses Israel wären, und daß selbe, als sie Jerusalem verließen, um nach Amerika auszewandern, ein erleuchtetes Volk waren, im Besitze der Kenntniß des wahren Gottes, seines Segens und seiner besondern Gunst genießend. Die Propheten und begeisterten Schriftsteller unter ihnen waren beauftragt, eine Geschichte über die unter ihnen statt findenden wichtigen Ereigniße zu führen, und sie so von Generation zu Generation zu überliefern.

In Länge der Zeit verfiel dieses Volk in große Gottlosigkeit, und der größere Theil desselben ward vertilgt: aber ihre Urkunden wurden auf Befehl des Herrn durch einen ihrer letzten Propheten schützend in den Schoos der Erde niedergelegt, um sie vor den Händen der Gottlosen zu bewahren, die sie zu zerstören suchten. Es ward ihm gesagt, daß diese Urkunden viele heil. Offenbarungen enthielten, die zur Ergänzung des Evangeliums gehörten, und die als Prophezeihungen im großen Bezuge auf die Ereigniße der letzten Tage stünden, und dass sie ferner um der, den Alten gegebenen Verheißung willen, die diese Urkunden niedergeschrieben haben, zur Kenntniß der Wölker gelangen müßen, um so den Absichten Gottes zur Wiedereinsetzung ihrer Kinder den Weg zu bahnen. [p. 19]

Auch ward ihm versprochen, daß wenn er gläubig befunden würde, er das doch begünstigte Werkzeug sein sollte, diese heiligen Dinge ans Licht zu bringen. Er ward noch besonders aufmerksam gemacht, daß dies Werk im enzigen Hinblicke auf Gott gethan werden müße, und daß da keiner mit diesen heil. Schriften vertraut gemacht werden könnte, der sich bemühen würde, sich selbst zu erheben, bei Verwendung dieser heiligen Dinge zu ungerechten und speculativen Zwecken.

Nachdem der Engel dem Joseph Smith noch viele andere Verlehrungen, gegenwärtige und künftige Dinge betreffend gegeben hatte, die aber in diesem Werke nicht alle aufgezeichnet werden, verschwand er, und die Glorie des Herrn mit ihm, jedoch sein Gemüth blieb beseligt mit himmlischen Frieden.

Bis zum anbrechenden Morgen ward dies Gesicht noch

the House of Israel and that they were an enlightened people when they left Jerusalem to emigrate to America, possessing a knowledge of the true God and enjoying his blessing and special favor. The prophets and inspired writers among them were commissioned to write a history of the important events among them and to hand it down from generation to generation.

In the course of time, this people fell into great wickedness and the greater portion of them was destroyed; but at the Lord's direction their records were deposited for protection into the bosom of the earth by one of their last prophets, to preserve them from the hands of the wicked who sought to destroy them. He was told that these records contained many sacred revelations pertaining to the fullness of the gospel and which stood as prophecies on a grand scale concerning the events of the last days and that they furthermore must be made known unto the nations for the sake of the promise given to the ancients in order to fulfill the purposes of God in restoring his children. [p. 19]

He was also promised that if he were faithful, he would be the favored instrument to bring these sacred things to light. It was especially pointed out to him that this work must be done with an eye single to God and that no one could be entrusted with these sacred scriptures who would try to aggrandize himself by using these sacred things for unrighteous or speculative purposes.

After the angel had given Joseph Smith many other instructions concerning present and future things which are not all recorded in this work, he disappeared and the glory of the Lord with him; however his mind remained filled with heavenly peace.

Before dawn this vision was repeated twice, each time with

zweimal wiederholt, und immer mit neuen Belehrungen, das Vollbringen des grossen Werkes Gottes auf Erden betreffend.

Am nächsten Morgen ging Joseph Smith hinaus ins Freie an seine Arbeit wie gewöhnlich; und hier erneuerte sich das Gesicht zum wiederholten Male. Der Gesandte des Herrn erschien ihm auf dem Felde und zeigte ihm den Fleck, wo die heil. Urkunden, von deren [p. 20] Wichtigkeit er Nachts vorher schon unterrichtet worden war, niedergelegt wurden, und er befahl ihm, sogleich zu gehen und nach denselben zu sehen. Dem zufolge begab er sich an den bezeichneten Platz, welcher nicht weit von seines Vaters Wohnung entfernt war. Es war am 22. Sept. A.D. 1823, wo er nach einer kleinen Anstrengung beim Aufgraben der Erde und Hinwegräumung mehrerer über einander gelegter Steine, die mit Maurerkitt verbunden waren, endlich die heiligen Urkanden seinen natürlichen Augen dargegeben sah. Während er staunend und bewundernd diese geheiligten Schätze betrachtete, sieh! da stand der Engel des Herrn, der ihn vorhin schon besucht hatte, wieder an seiner Seite. Und seine Seele ward wieder erleuchtet wie Abends vorher, er ward erfüllet mit dem heiligen Geiste, der Himmel öffnete sich und die Glorie des Herrn erschien um ihn.

Und als er so dastand in Entzücken versunken in Gegenwart des Boten himmlischer Glückseligkeit, da sprach der Engel zu ihm: "Sieh!"– Und als er dieß desagt hatte, sah Joseph Smith den Fürsten der Finsterniß vorbeiziehen mit einem zahllosen Heere seiner Verbündeten; und der Himmelsbote sagte abermals zu ihm: "Dir ist nun gezeiget worden das Gute und das Böse, das Heilige and Unreine, die Glorie Gottes und die Macht der Finsterniß, damit du hernach [p. 21] erkennen möchtest, die beiden Gewalten, um nicht von dem Bösen bethört zu werden. Sieh, was da immer dich zum Guten ausmuntert, das kommt von Gott, was es aber nicht thut, das ist vom Bösen. Er ist es, der der Menschen Herz mit übel füllt, damit sie wandeln in Finsterniß und Lästerung des Herrn; du aber wirst von nun an erkennen, daß seine Wege zum Ver-

new instructions concerning the bringing about of the great work of God on earth.

The next morning, Joseph Smith went out into the field to work as usual; here the vision was renewed once again. The messenger of the Lord appeared to him in the field and showed him the place where the sacred records were deposited, [p. 20] about whose importance he had been instructed the night before and he commanded him to go immediately to look for them. Accordingly he went to the designated spot which was not far from his father's home. It was on the 22nd of September in the year of our Lord 1823, when after some effort digging away the earth and removing several stones stacked on each other and held together by mortar, he finally beheld the sacred records with his natural eyes. As he looked upon these sacred treasures in amazement and awe, behold, the angel of the Lord who had already visited him previously, again stood at his side. And his soul was again enlightened as on the previous evening, he was filled with the Holy Ghost, the heavens were opened and the glory of the Lord shone around him.

And as he stood there engrossed in ecstasy in the presence of the messenger of heavenly bliss, the angel spoke to him: "Behold," and when he had said this, Joseph Smith saw the prince of darkness pass by with a numberless host of his associates; and the heavenly messenger once again said unto him: "You have now been shown the good and the evil, the holy and the unclean, the glory of God and the power of darkness, so that you may hereafter [p. 21] recognize the two powers and not be deceived by the evil one. Behold, whatever entices you to do good comes of God, but what does not is of the evil one. He is the one who fills the hearts of men with evil, so that they walk in darkness and blaspheme the Lord; from now on you shall know that his ways lead to destruction, but that

derben führen, jener aber der Heiligkeit zu Friede und Ruhe. Jetzt ist es dir noch nicht erlaubt, diese Urkunden in Empfang zu nehmen, denn es ist der Befehl des Herrn, daß, wenn diese heiligen Dinge erlangt werden wollen, es durch Gebet, Glauben und Gehorsam gegen den Herrn geschehen müße. Sie wurden [nicht] hier niedergelegt als Mittel zur Anhäufung irdischen Gewinnes, oder zur Verherrlichung dieser Welt. Sie wurden versiegelt und eingegraben unter Gebeten des Glaubens, und haben für die Menschenkinder keinen andern Werth als den ihres Inhaltes. Auf ihnen ist niedergeschrieben die Vollheit des Evangeliums Jesus Christi so wie es gegeben ward seinem Volke in diesem Lande (Amerika.) Und wenn es verbreitet werden soll durch die Macht Gottes, so wird es hingebracht werden zu den Völkern, die nicht aus dem Hause Israel sind. Viele derselben werden es annehmen, und nachher wird der Samen Israels gebracht werden in die Hürde ihres Erlösers, wenn sie diese geoffenbarten Dinge befolgen. Jene Vorfahren, welche die Gebote des Herrn in diesem [p. 22] Lande (Amerika) beobachteten, erlangten von seiner Gnade, durch glaubensvolle Gebete die Verheißung: daß, wenn ihre Abkömmlinge in Irrthümer und Abfall geriethen, sie die heiligen Urkunden nicht erhalten möchten, sondern daß selbe aufbewahret würden bis zu den letzten Tagen ihrer Kinder. Diese Dinge sind geheiliget, und müssen so gehalten werden, denn die Verheißung des Herrn in Betreff derselben wird erfüllet werden. Doch Niemand wird sie erlangen, dessen Herz unrein ist; denn ihr Inhalt ist heilig, durch sie will der Herr ein großes und wunderbares Werk vollbringen: Die Weisheit des Weisen soll zu nichte werden, und der Verstand des Klugen mit Dunkelheit umhüllet sein. Und wenn die Macht Gottes sich offenbaret, so werden jene, die da in Wahrheit zu wandeln glauben, mit Täuschung ringen und im Aerger zittern. Die Herzen der Gläubigen aber werden mit Zeichen und Wunder, mit Geschenken und Heilungen, mit Kundmachung der Macht Gottes und mit dem heiligen Geiste getröstet werden. Dir ist nun gezeiget

the way of holiness leads to peace and rest. You are not permitted at this time to receive these records, for it is the command of the Lord, that when these sacred things shall be received, it shall be through prayer, faith and obedience to the Lord. They were [not] placed here as a means of accumulating worldly gain or for the glorification of this world. They were sealed and buried amid the prayers of faith and are of no value unto the children of men except for what they contain. The fullness of the gospel of Jesus Christ is written upon them as it was given to the people in this land (America). And when it shall go forth by the power of God, it shall be carried to the nations which are not of the House of Israel. Many of them will accept it and afterward the seed of Israel shall be brought into the fold of their redeemer, if they follow these revelations. Those ancestors who kept the commandments of the Lord in this [p. 22] land (America), received through his mercy and through faithful prayers the promise that when their descendants should fall into error and apostasy, they would not receive the sacred records but that they would be preserved unto the last days of their children. These things are sacred and must be kept that way, for the promise of the Lord concerning them shall be fulfilled. For no one will receive them whose heart is unclean, for their content is sacred, through them the Lord wants to bring about a great and marvelous work. The wisdom of the wise shall come to naught and the understanding of the prudent shall be clothed in darkness. And when the power of God is revealed, then those who think they are walking in truth will struggle against deception and tremble with anger. But the hearts of the faithful will be comforted with signs and wonders, with gifts and healings, with the revelation of the power of God and with the Holy Ghost. You have been

worden, die Macht des Herrn und die des Satans. Du siehst, daß nichts wünschenwerthes in den Werken der Finsterniß ist, daß sie keine Glückseligkeit gewähren können, und daß jene, welche in selbe verfallen, nur elend und unglücklich sind, — während auf der andern Seite die Gerechten beglückt werden mit einem Platze in dem Reiche Gottes, wo unausprechliche Freude sie [p. 23] umgibt. Dort sind sie erhaben über die Macht des Feindes der Wahrheit, und kein Uebel kann sie mehr stören. Die Glorie Gottes krönet sie, sie feiern ein ewiges Fest seiner Güte und sonnen sich in dem Lächeln seines Angesichtes. Obgleich dir geoffenbaret worden ist, auf welche Art du immer fähig sein wirst, das Böse zu entdecken, so will ich dir dennoch ein Zeichen geben. Und wenn es geschehen soll, dann wisse, daß der Herr Gott ist, daß Er Seine Absichten vollziehen will, und daß der Inhalt dieser Urkunden zu allen Nationen, Zungen, Stämmen und Völkern unter den weiten Himmel gehen soll. Dieß ist das Zeichen: Wenn diese Dinge anfangen bekannt zu werden, das heißt, wenn es bekannt wird, daß der Herr dir diese Dinge gezeigt hat, dann werden die Vollbringer der Ungerechtigkeit deinen Untergang suchen. Sie werden Falschheiten in Umlauf bringen, um deinen Ruf zu zerstören, auch werden sie nach deinem Leben streben. Doch merke, daß, wenn du glaubensvoll bist, und die Befehle des Herrn vollziehest, du bewahrt werden wirst, um diese Dinge zur Kenntniß zu bringen, denn in gemessener Zeit wird dir Befehl gegeben werden, zu kommen und sie zu holen. Wenn sie ausgelegt sind, so will der Herr einigen die Priesterwürde verleihen, und diese werden anfangen das Evangelium zu erklären und mit Wasser zu taufen, auch werden sie Gewalt haben den heiligen Geist zu geben, durch Auflegung [p. 24] ihrer Hände. Dann wird die Verfolgung immer mehr und mehr wüthen, denn die Bosheiten der Menschen werden offenbar werden, und jene, welche nicht auf den Felsen gebaut sind, werden die Kirche Christi zu überwältigen suchen. Aber je mehr Hinderniße, desto mehr wird sie anwachsen, und sich

shown the power of God and the power of Satan. You see that there is nothing desirable in the works of darkness, that they cannot bring happiness and that those who succumb to them are only miserable and unhappy, whereas on the other hand the righteous are given a place in the kingdom of God where they are filled with unspeakable joy. [p. 23] There they are beyond the power of the enemy of truth and no evil can harm them. They are crowned with the glory of God, they celebrate an eternal feast of his goodness and bask in the smile of his countenance. Even though the manner by which you can discover wickedness has been revealed to you, nevertheless I will give you a sign. And when it shall come to pass, then know that the Lord is God, that he will fulfill his purposes and that the content of these records shall go to every nation, tongue, kindred and people under all of heaven. This is the sign: When these things begin to be known, that is, when it becomes known that the Lord has shown these things unto you, then the workers of iniquity shall seek your overthrow. They will spread falsehoods to destroy your reputation, and they will also seek to take your life. But remember that if you are faithful and keep the commandments of the Lord, you shall be preserved in order to bring these things to light, for in due time you shall be commanded to come and get them. When they are interpreted, the Lord will grant the priesthood unto some and these will begin to preach the gospel and to baptize with water, and they will have the power to bestow the Holy Ghost by the laying on of their [p. 24] hands. Then persecution will rage more and more, for the iniquities of men will become manifest and those who are not founded upon the rock, will seek to overthrow the Church of Christ. But the more obstacles there are, the more it will grow and come to the knowledge of

ausbreiten zur Kenntniß der Menschen, bis sie werden geheiliget sein, und eine Erbschaft besitzen, wo der Ruhm des Herrn über ihnen verweilen wird. Und wenn dies Statt finden wird, und alle Dinge verbereitet sind, dann sollen die zehn Stämme Israels wieder entdeckt werden in den nördlichen Gegenden, wo sie verweilt hatten, für so lange Zeit. Dann wird erfüllet werden, was der Prophet sagte: 'Und der Erlöser wird zu Sion kommen und zu denen, welche aus Jakob von der Ungerechtigkeit wieder zurückkehren.'— Und obgleich die Vollbringer der Ungerechtigkeiten deine Zerstörung suchen werden, so wird doch der schützende Arm des Herrn über dich ausgestreckt sein, und du sollst als Sieger hervor gehen aus dem Kampfe, wenn du alle Seine Gebote hältst. Dein name soll gekannt sein, unter den Nationen, denn das Werk, welches der Herr durch deine Hände vollbringen will, wird den Gerechten zur Freude, den Bösen aber zur Wuth gereichen. Bei den Ersteren wird dein Name in Ehren stehen, den Letztern aber zum Vorwurf sein. Ja für diese soll er ein Schrecken sein, um des großen und wundervollen Werkes [p. 25] wegen, das vorausgehen soll zur Vollfüllung des Evangeliums. Gehe nun deinen Weg, und erinnere dich, was der Herr für dich gethan hat. Sei eifrig in Befolgung seiner Gebote und Er wird dich befreien von den Versuchungen, Nachstellungen und Fallstricken des Bösen. Vergiß nicht zu beten, damit dein Gemüth stark werde, auf daß du Macht habest dem Bösen zu entkommen, wenn sich der Herr dir offenbaren will zur Erlangung dieser köstlichen Dinge."—

Während der Zeitdauer der vier folgenden Jahre empfing Joseph Smith noch manche Belehrung aus dem Munde des himmlischen Boten. Und am Morgen des 22. Septembers A.D. 1827 erlaubte ihm der Engel des Herrn, diese Urkunden in Empfang zu nehmen. Diese waren auf gleichförmige Platten eingegraben, welche wie Gold erschienen. Jede Platte war beinahe 7 Zoll breit, und beinahe 8 Zoll lang, und an Dicke etwas geringer als gewöhnliches Blech. Diese waren eingegraben mit

men, until they shall be sanctified and receive an inheritance where the glory of the Lord shall rest upon them. And when this shall come to pass and all things are prepared, then shall the ten tribes of Israel again be revealed in the northern regions where they had remained for so long. Then the saying of the prophet shall be fulfilled: 'And the Redeemer shall come to Zion and unto them in Jacob who shall turn from their unrighteousness.' [Isa. 59:20] And even though the workers of iniquity shall seek your destruction, the protecting arm of the Lord shall be over you and you shall be borne off victorious, if you keep all his commandments. Your name shall be known among the nations, for the work which the Lord shall perform by your hands shall prove to be a joy unto the righteous, but rage unto the wicked. Among the former, your name shall be honored, but among the latter it shall be a reproach. Yea, for them it shall be terrible, because of the great and marvelous work [p. 25] which shall go forth unto the fulfilling of the gospel. Now go your way and remember what the Lord has done for you. Be diligent in keeping his commandments and he will deliver you from the temptations, persecutions and snares of the evil one. Don't forget to pray that your mind may become strong, that you may have power to escape the evil when the Lord shall reveal himself unto you, so that you may receive these precious things."

During the course of the following four years Joseph Smith received many instructions from the mouth of the heavenly messenger. And on the morning of the 22nd of September in the year of our Lord 1827 the angel of the Lord permitted him to take possession of these records. These were engraved on uniform plates which had the appearance of gold. Each plate was almost 7 inches wide and almost 8 inches long and in thickness somewhat less than common tin. They were en-

sauberer Schrift ähnlich den ägyptischen Hieroglyphen und in Form eines Bandes dreimal mit Draht zusammen geheftet, der mittelst kleiner Löcher an den Enden durch das Ganze gezogen war. Das ganze Buch war beiläufig 8 Zoll dick und ein Theil desselben war versiegelt. Die Charaktere oder Buchstaben des unversiegelten Theiles waren (nach den Worten Mr. Pratt, aus dessen Schriften ich vorhergehende [p. 26] Erzählung entnommen) klein und künstlich schön eingegraben. Der ganze Band trug viele Anzeichen des Alterthums so wie der Geschicklichkeit im Graviren. Mit den Urkunden wurden zwei durchsichtige Steine gefunden, klar wie Krystall, die von den Männern der Vorzeit 'Seher' genannt, gebraucht wurden. Die Art, auf welche sie selbe benützten, war folgende: Diese zwei Steine, genannt Urim und Thummim, im Durchmesser einer englischen Krone (Münze) nur etwas dicker, wurden dahin gelegt, wo alles Licht ausgeschlossen war. Die handelnden Personen opferten alsdann ihre Gebete dem Herrn und die Antwort erschien, geschrieben mit Buchstaben des Lichts auf den Urim und Thummim, verschwand aber sehr bald wieder. So: "Kam Licht in Finsterniß, allein die Finsternisse begriffen es nicht." — Auf diese Art wurden diese geheiligten Urkunden in's Englische übersetzt. [p. 27]

Nachdem es bekannt geworden war, daß Joseph Smith himmlische Erscheinungen gehabt hatte, und daß ihm die Kenntniß der heiligen Urkunden gewährt worden war, fingen viele an, darüber zu spotten, und diese Idee lächerlich zu machen. Andere waren geschäftig, niedrige Verläumdungen und Falschheiten gegen ihn in Umlauf zu bringen; manche waren geneigt ihn mit Gewalt zu behandeln, und wieder andere glaubten und waren verlangend, mehr zu sehen und zu hören. In der That, es brachte eine solche Aufregung in dem Volke hervor, gleich jener in Jerusalem, als Christus geboren ward, wovon gesagt worden: "Herodes erschrack und ganze Jerusalem mit ihm." —

In Folge dieser grossen Aufregung denn fand Joseph Smith

graven with a fine script similar to Egyptian hieroglyphs and fastened together in the form of a book by three rings, which were drawn through the whole by means of small holes on the ends. The entire book was approximately 8 inches thick and one part of it was sealed. The characters or letters of the unsealed part were small and artistically beautifully engraved (according to the words of Mr. Pratt, from whose writings [p. 26] I have taken the foregoing account). The whole book exhibited many signs of antiquity such as the skill of engraving. Two transparent stones, clear as crystal, were found with the records. They were called "seers" and were used by the ancients. The manner in which they were used is as follows: These two stones, called Urim and Thummim, in diameter the size of an English crown (coin) but a little thicker, were placed where there was no light. Those using them then offered prayers unto the Lord and the answer appeared written with letters of light on the Urim and Thummim, but disappeared again soon after. Thus: "The light shineth in darkness, and the darkness comprehended it not" [John 1:5] – In this manner these records were translated into English. [p. 27]

After it had become known that Joseph Smith had received heavenly manifestations and that he had been granted the knowledge of the sacred records, many began to mock and to ridicule this idea. Others were busy spreading slanderous rumors and misrepresentations about him; many were inclined to treat him with violence and others were believing and desirous of seeing and hearing more. Indeed, it brought forth such an excitement among the people like unto that in Jerusalem when Christ was born, of which has been said: "Herod was afraid and all Jerusalem with him." [Matt. 2:3]

In consequence of this great excitement, Joseph Smith

es geeigneter, mit seinem Weibe, das [p. 28] er kurz vorher geheirathet hatte, in die Nähe seines Schwiegervaters hinzuziehen in den Staat Pennsylvania an die Ufer des herrlichen Jusquehannah-Flusses. Ehe er Palmyra verließ, ward zu verschiedenen Malen nach ihm geschossen, er entkam aber immer unbeschädigt durch göttliche Fügung. Jedoch einmal ward er von zwei Männern so heftig mit Knütteln geschlagen, daß er noch bis zu diesem Tage die Spuren davon an seinem Körper trägt. Die öffentlichen Blätter fingen an zu grübeln, zu vermuthen und zu fragen, was wohl der Endschluß des Ganzen werden soll.

Nachdem er sich also eine Heimath in diesem Theile des Landes verschafft hatte, fing er an, die Urkunden unter der Leitung Gottes und mit Hilfe des "Urim's und Thummim's," die schon früher beschrieben wurden, aus der "reformirten egyptischen" Sprache zu übersetzen. Da er in der Kunst des Schreibens sehr mangelhaft gebildet war, so war er genöthigt, einen Schreiber zu verwenden, der es niederschrieb, so wie es aus seinem Munde kam.

In der Zwischenzeit jedoch kopirte Joseph Smith mehrere Charaktere von dem Originale und übersetzte sie, welche beide, die Kopie und die Uebersetzung, in die Stadt New-York gebracht wurden, um dort einem Manne vorgelegt zu werden, der unter dem Titel eines [p. 29] Autors als ein, in allen alten und neuen Sprachen viel erfahrener Mann bekannt war. Er untersuchte sie beide, und es ward ihm unmöglich sie zu entziffern; jedoch meinte er, daß, wenn die Original-Urkunde gebracht würde, er bei deren Uebersetzung behülflich sein könnte.

Doch um wieder umzukehren; Joseph Smith fuhr in seinem übersetzungs-Werke so fort, also es ihm seine pekuniären Verhältnisse erlaubten, bis daß er den unversiegelten Theil der Urkunden fertig hatte. Dieser übersetzte Theil ist betitelt: "Das Buch Mormon", dessen Inhalt etwas mehr als das neue Testament umfaßt. . . .

found it more expedient to move with his wife, [p. 28] whom he had married shortly before, to the vicinity of his father-in-law in the state of Pennsylvania on the shores of the magnificent Susquehannah River. Before he left Palmyra, he was shot at several times, but each time divine providence helped him to escape unharmed. However, on one occasion he was beaten by two men with clubs so violently, that he still bears the scars on his body to this day. The newspapers began to ponder, speculate and to wonder what the outcome of the whole affair might be.

After he had made a home for himself in this part of the country, he began to translate the records from the "reformed Egyptian" under the direction of God and with the help of the Urim and Thummim which were described earlier. Since he hadn't learned to write well, he was required to use a scribe who wrote it down as it came from his mouth.

In the meantime, however, Joseph Smith copied several characters from the original and translated them; both the copy and the translation were taken to the city of New York to be presented to a man who [p. 29] was known as one who was well versed in all ancient and modern languages. He examined them both, but it was impossible for him to decipher them; however he felt that if the original were brought to him, he could help with the translation.

But to return [to the story]; Joseph Smith continued with the work of translation as his pecuniary circumstances allowed, until he had completed the unsealed portion of the records. This translated portion is entitled: "The Book of Mormon," which contains somewhat more than the New Testament.

Orson Hyde, c.1853. Daguerreotype Collection. LDS Church Archives.

"CHURCH HISTORY," 1842

Joseph Smith, "Church History," Times and Seasons *3 (March 1, 1842): 706-10.*

Editorial Note

John Wentworth, born at Sandwich, Carroll County, New Hampshire, in 1815, graduated from Dartmouth College in 1836 and then went to Michigan to find a job teaching school. Disappointed in his prospects, he traveled later that year to Chicago, Illinois, a village of twenty-five hundred, in search of other employment. Within a month, he became editor and, within three years, owner of the weekly *Chicago Democrat*, the town's first newspaper. Wentworth eventually became one of Illinois' foremost citizens, both in accomplishment and stature. At six foot six and three hundred pounds, "Long John" Wentworth was elected to the United States House of Representatives in 1843, and at twenty-eight years of age he was the youngest member of that body. He later served five more terms in the Congress and was elected mayor of Chicago in 1857. Prior to his death in 1888, he was appointed to the Illinois state board of education. He was also appointed police commissioner, and at one time he held title to more Cook County real estate than anyone else in Chicago. Wentworth was a strong supporter of history as a patron of the Chicago Historical Society and a lecturer on the early days of Chicago. He wrote a three-volume *Wentworth Genealogy*. He took pride in the collection of his papers, including a diary "somewhat in the style of John Quincy Adams," and he lamented their loss in the Chicago fire of 1871. In 1844 he married Roxanna Marie Loomis, who died in 1870. Of their five children, only one grew to maturity. (A.T. Andreas, *History of Chicago* [Chicago: A.T. Andreas, Publisher, 1884], 622-28; Arba Nelson Waterman, *Historical Review of Chicago and Cook County* [Chicago and New York: The Lewis Publishing Company, 1908], 99-103; Dumas

John Wentworth, 1847. Chicago Historical Society.

Malone, *Dictionary of American Biography* [New York, Charles Scribner's Sons, 1936], 19:657-59; Don E. Fehrenbacher, *Chicago Giant: A Biography of "Long John" Wentworth* [Madison, Wisconsin: American History Research Center, 1957].)

In 1842, Wentworth, then the twenty-six-year-old Chicago editor, wrote to Joseph Smith, requesting a "sketch of the rise, progress, persecution and faith of the Latter-day Saints" for a New Hampshire friend of his, George Barstow, who was writing a history of New Hampshire.

Barstow, born in 1812 at Haverhill, Grafton County, New Hampshire, was educated at Dartmouth College and practiced law in Massachusetts and New Hampshire. In 1842 he published a history of New Hampshire that reached a second edition in 1851. About 1850 he moved to San Francisco, California, where he practiced law and was professor of medical jurisprudence at the University of the Pacific; he served in the California House of Representatives and was president of the Young Men's Christian Association. He died in San Francisco in 1883, leaving a wife but no children. (Charles H. Bell, *Bench and Bar of New Hampshire* [New York, 1894], 171.)

Joseph Smith's answer to Wentworth was apparently not used by Barstow but was published in the 1 March 1842 issue of the Nauvoo, Illinois, paper, *Times and Seasons*.

I was born in the town of Sharon Windsor co., Vermont, on the 23d of December, A.D. 1805. When ten years old my parents removed to Palmyra New York, where we resided about four years, and from thence we removed to the town of Manhester.

My father was a farmer and taught me the art of husbandry. When about fourteen years of age I began to reflect upon the importance of being prepared for a future state, and upon enquiring the plan of salvation I found that there was a great clash in religious sentiment; if I went to one society they referred me to one plan, and another to another; each one pointing to his own particular creed as the summum bonum of perfection: considering that all could not be right, and that God could not be the author of so much confusion I determined to investigate the subject more fully, believing that if God had a church it would not be split up into factions, and that if he taught one society to worship one way, and administer in one set of ordinances, he would not teach another principles which were diametrically opposed. Believing the word of God I had confidence in the declaration of James; "If any man lack wisdom let him ask of God who giveth to all men liberally and upbraideth not and it shall be given him," I retired to a secret place in a grove and began to call upon the Lord, while fervently engaged in supplication my mind was taken away from the objects with which I was surrounded, and I was enwrapped in a [p. 706] heavenly vision and saw two glorious personages who exactly resembled each other in features, and likeness, surrounded with a brilliant light which eclipsed the sun at noon-day. They told me that all religious denominations were believing in incorrect doctrines, and that none of them was acknowledged of God as his church and kingdom. And I was expressly commanded to "go not after them," at the same time receiving a promise that the fulness of the gospel should at some future time be made known unto me.

On the evening of the 21st of September, A.D. 1823, while I was praying unto God, and endeavoring to exercise faith in the precious promises of scripture on a sudden a light like that of day, only of a far purer and more glorious appearance, and brightness burst into the room, indeed the first sight was as though the house was filled with consuming fire; the appearance produced a shock that affected the whole body; in a moment a personage stood before me surrounded with a glory yet greater than that with which I was already surrounded. This messenger proclaimed himself to be an angel of God sent to bring the joyful tidings, that the covenant which God made with ancient Israel was at hand to be fulfilled, that the preparatory work for the second coming of the Messiah was speedily to commence; that the time was at hand for the gospel, in all its fulness to be preached in power, unto all nations that a people might be prepared for the millennial reign.

I was informed that I was chosen to be an instrument in

the hands of God to bring about some of his purposes in this glorious dispensation.

I was also informed concerning the aboriginal inhabitants of this country, and shown who they were, and from whence they came; a brief sketch of their origin, progress, civilization, laws, governments, of their righteousness and iniquity, and the blessings of God being finally withdrawn from them as a people was made known unto me: I was also told where there was deposited some plates on which were engraven an abridgement of the records of the ancient prophets that had existed on this continent. The angel appeared to me three times the same night and unfolded the same things. After having received many visits from the angels of God unfolding the majesty, and glory of the events that should transpire in the last days, on the morning of the 22d of September A.D. 1827, the angel of the Lord delivered the records into my hands.

These records were engraven on plates which had the appearance of gold, each plate was six inches wide and eight inches long and not quite so thick as common tin. They were filled with engravings, in Egyptian characters and bound together in a volume, as the leaves of a book with three rings running through the whole. The volume was something near six inches in thickness, a part of which was sealed. The characters on the unsealed part were small, and beautifully engraved. The whole book exhibited many marks of antiquity in its construction and much skill in the art of engraving. With the records was found a curious instrument which the ancients called "Urim and Thummim," which consisted of two transparent stones set in the rim of a bow fastened to a breastplate.

Through the medium of the Urim and Thummim I translated the record by the gift, and power of God.

In this important and interesting book the history of ancient America is unfolded, from its first settlement by a colony that came from the tower of Babel, at the confusion of languages to the beginning of the fifth century of the Christian era. We are informed by these records that America in ancient times has been inhabited by two distinct races of people. The first were called Jaredites and came directly from the tower of Babel. The second race came directly from the city of Jerusalem, about six hundred years before Christ. They were principally Israelites, of the descendants of Joseph. The Jaredites were destroyed about the time that the Israelites came from Jerusalem, who succeeded them in the inheritance of the country. The principal nation of the second race fell in battle towards the close of the fourth century. The remnant are the Indians that now inhabit this country. This book also tells us that our Saviour made his appearance upon this continent after his resurrection, that he planted the gospel here in all its fulness, and richness, and power, and blessing; that they had apostles, prophets, pastors, teachers and evangelists; the same order, the same priesthood, the [p. 707] same ordinances, gifts, powers, and blessing, as was enjoyed on the eastern continent, that the people were cut off in consequence of their transgressions, that the last of their prophets who existed among them was commanded to write an abridgement of their prophesies, history &c., and to hide it up in the earth, and that it should come forth and be united with the bible for the accomplishment of the purposes of God in the last days. For a more particular account I would refer to the Book of Mormon, which can be purchased at Nauvoo, or from any of our traveling elders.

As soon as the news of this discovery was made known, false reports, misrepresentation and slander flew as on the wings of the wind in every direction, the house was frequently beset by mobs, and evil designing persons, several times I was shot at, and very narrowly escaped, and every device was made use of to get the plates away from me, but the power and blessing of God attended me, and several began to believe my testimony.

On the 6th of April, 1830, the "Church of Jesus Christ of Latter-Day Saints," was first organized in the town of Manchester, Ontario co., state of New York.[1] Some few were called and ordained by the spirit of revelation, and prophesy, and began to preach as the spirit gave them utterance, and though weak, yet were they strengthened by the power of God, and many were brought to repentance, were immersed in the water, and were filled with the Holy Ghost by the laying on of hands. They saw visions and prophesied, devils were cast out and the sick healed by the laying on of hands. From that time the work rolled forth with astonishing rapidity, and churches were soon formed in the states of New York, Pennsylvania, Ohio, Indiana, Illinois and Missouri; in the last named state a considerable settlement was formed in Jackson co.; numbers joined the church and we were increasing rapidly; we made large purchases of land, our farms teemed with plenty, and peace and happiness was enjoyed in our domestic circle and throughout our neighborhood; but as we could not associate with our neighbors who were many of them of the basest of men and had fled from the face of civilized society, to the frontier country to escape the hand of justice, in their midnight revels, their sabbath breaking, horseracing, and gambling, they commenced at first to ridicule, then to persecute, and finally an organized mob assembled and burned our houses, tarred, and feathered, and whipped many of our brethren and finally drove them from their habitations; who houseless, and homeless, contrary to law, justice and humanity, had to wander on the bleak prairies till the children left the tracks of their blood on the prairie, this took place in the month of November, and they had no other covering but the canopy of heaven, in this inclement season of the year; this proceeding was winked at by the government and although we had warrantee deeds for our land, and had violated no law we could obtain no redress.

There were many sick, who were thus inhumanly driven

1. The church was organized at Fayette, Seneca County, New York at the home of Peter Whitmer, Sr. See p. 242, note 2.

from their houses, and had to endure all this abuse and to seek homes where they could be found. The result was, that a great many of them being deprived of the comforts of life, and the necessary attendances, died; many children were left orphans; wives, widows; and husbands widowers. – Our farms were taken possession of by the mob, many thousands of cattle, sheep, horses, and hogs, were taken and our household goods, store goods, and printing press, and type were broken, taken, or otherwise destroyed.

Many of our brethren removed to Clay where they continued until 1836, three years; there was no violence offered but there were threatnings of violence. But in the summer of 1836, these threatnings began to assume a more serious form; from threats, public meetings were called, resolutions were passed, vengeance and destruction were threatened, and affairs again assumed a fearful attitude, Jackson county was a sufficient precedent, and as the authorities in that county did not interfere, they boasted that they would not in this, which on application to the authorities we found to be too true, and after much violence, privation and loss of property we were again driven from our homes.

We next settled in Caldwell, and Davies counties, where we made large and extensive settlements, thinking to free ourselves from the power of oppression, by settling in new counties, with very few inhabitants in them; but here we were not allowed to live in peace, but in 1838 we were again attacked by mobs [p. 708] an exterminating order was issued by Gov. Boggs, and under the sanction of law an organized banditti ranged through the country, robbed us of our cattle, sheep, horses, hogs &c., many of our people were murdered in cold blood, the chastity of our women was violated, and we were forced to sign away our property at the point of the sword, and after enduring every indignity that could be heaped upon us by an inhuman, ungodly band of maurauders, from twelve to fifteen thousand souls men, women, and children were driven from their own fire sides, and from lands that they had warrantee deeds of, houseless, friendless, and homeless (in the depth of winter,) to wander as exiles on the earth or to seek an asylum in a more genial clime, and among a less barbarous people.

Many sickened and died, in consequence of the cold, and hardships they had to endure; many wives were left widows, and children orphans, and destitute. It would take more time than is allotted me here to describe the injustice, the wrongs, the murders, the bloodshed, the theft, misery and woe that has been caused by the barbarous, inhuman, and lawless, proceedings of the state of Missouri.

In the situation before alluded to we arrived in the state of Illinois in 1839, where we found a hospitable people and a friendly home; a people who were willing to be governed by the principles of law and humanity. We have commenced to build a city called "Nauvoo" in Hancock co., we number from six to eight thousand here besides vast numbers in the county around and in almost every county of the state. We have a city charter granted us and a charter for a legion the troops of which now number 1500. We have also a charter for a university, for an agricultural and manufacturing society, have our own laws and administrators, and possess all the privileges that other free and enlightened citizens enjoy.[1]

Persecution has not stopped the progress of truth, but has only added fuel to the flame, it has spread with increasing rapidity, proud of the cause which they have espoused and conscious of their innocence and of the truth of their system amidst calumny and reproach have the elders of this church

1. On the Mormon sojourn in Illinois see Leonard J. Arrington and Davis Bitton, *The Mormon Experience: A History of the Latter-day Saints* (New York, 1979), chapter 4; Robert Bruce Flanders, *Nauvoo: Kingdom on the Mississippi* (Urbana, Illinois, 1965); David E. Miller and Della S. Miller, *Nauvoo: The City of Joseph* (Salt Lake City, 1974); Roberts, *Comprehensive History*, volume 2; Allen and Leonard, *Story of the Latter-day Saints*, chapters 5, 6.

gone forth, and planted the gospel in almost every state in the Union; it has penetrated our cities, it has spread over our villages, and has caused thousands of our intelligent, noble, and patriotic citizens to obey its divine mandates, and be governed by its sacred truths. It has also spread into England, Ireland, Scotland and Wales: in the year of 1839 where a few of our missionaries were sent over five thousand joined the standard of truth, there are numbers now joining in every land.

Our missionaries are going forth to different nations, and in Germany, Palestine, New Holland, the East Indies, and other places, the standard of truth has been erected: no unhallowed hand can stop the work from progressing, persecutions may rage, mobs may combine, armies may assemble, calumny may defame, but the truth of God will go forth boldly, nobly, and independent till it has penetrated every continent, visited every clime, swept every country, and sounded in every ear, till the purposes of God shall be accomplished and the great Jehovah shall say the work is done.

We believe in God the Eternal Father, and in his son Jesus Christ, and in the Holy Ghost.[1]

We believe that men will be punished for their own sins and not for Adam's transgression.

We believe that through the atonement of Christ all mankind may be saved by obedience to the laws and ordinances of the Gospel.

We believe that these ordinances are 1st, Faith in the Lord Jesus Christ; 2d, Repentance; 3d, Baptism by immersion for the remission of sins; 4th, Laying on of hands for the gift of the Holy Ghost.

We believe that a man must be called of God by "prophesy,

---

1. The thirteen statements of belief given here are textually close to those in Orson Pratt's tract and were added to the canon of Mormon scripture in 1880. See Whittaker, "The 'Articles of Faith' in Early Mormon Literature and Thought."

and by laying on of hands" by those who are in authority to preach the gospel and administer in the ordinances thereof.

We believe in the same organization that existed in the primitive church, viz: apostles, prophets, pastors, teachers, evangelists &c.

We believe in the gift of tongues, prophesy, revelation, visions, healing, interpretation of tongues &c.

We believe the bible to be the word of God as far as it is translated correctly; we also believe the Book of Mormon to be the word of God.

We believe all that God has revealed, all that he does now reveal, and we believe [p. 709] that he will yet reveal many great and important things pertaining to the kingdom of God.

We believe in the literal gathering of Israel and in the restoration of the Ten Tribes. That Zion will be built upon this continent. That Christ will reign personally upon the earth, and that the earth will be renewed and receive its paradasaic glory.

We claim the privilege of worshipping Almighty God according to the dictates of our conscience, and allow all men the same privilege let them worship how, where, or what they may.

We believe in being subject to kings, presidents, rulers, and magistrates, in obeying, honoring and sustaining the law.

We believe in being honest, true, chaste, benevolent, virtuous, and in doing good to *all men*; indeed we may say that we follow the admonition of Paul "we believe all things we hope all things," we have endured many things and hope to be able to endure all things. If there is any thing virtuous, lovely, or of good report or praise worthy we seek after these things. Respectfully &c.,

JOSEPH SMITH

PITTSBURGH GAZETTE INTERVIEW, 1843

"The Prairies, Nauvoo, Joe Smith, the Temple, the Mormons, &c.," The Pittsburgh Weekly Gazette *58 (September 15, 1843): 3.*

Editorial Note

In August 1843 David Nye White, senior editor of the *Pittsburgh Weekly Gazette*, Pittsburgh, Pennsylvania, visited Joseph Smith at his home in Nauvoo, Illinois. His report of that visit contains one of the distinctive accounts of the Prophet's 1820 vision published during his lifetime.

David White was born at Wareham, Plymouth County, Massachusetts, in 1803. He was engaged in the book and job printing business at Pittsburgh several years before he purchased the *Gazette* in 1841. After fifteen years of involvement with the newspaper, he retired, but he continued to fill positions of public trust in Allegheny County. Besides serving as school director, town councilman, and burgess of Sewickley, White was also appointed collector of internal revenue of the Pennsylvania twenty-third district, and as a member of the Pennsylvania House of Representatives from Allegheny County.

White took an active part and exercised a potent influence in the formation of the Republican Party. After the repeal of the Missouri Compromise in 1854, anti-slavery advocates felt that the only way to prevent the spread of slavery was to form a national organization. When Salmon P. Chase, U.S. senator from Ohio, visited Pittsburgh in 1855, he consulted David N. White, then editor of the *Gazette*, and they decided to call a national convention to form a party opposing the extension of slavery. White corresponded with anti-slavery leaders throughout the country, which resulted in the convening of a national convention at Pittsburgh in February 1856 to unite groups opposed to slavery. This gathering was followed by a national nominating convention in Philadelphia in June at which the Republican Party was formed, candidates

David Nye White. Carnegie Library, Pittsburgh, Pennsylvania.

nominated, and resolutions passed against the further spread of slavery. Although White sold the *Gazette* in 1856 before the triumph of the party—the election of Abraham Lincoln—he was an active supporter of its principles. David N. White died at Sewickley, Allegheny County, Pennsylvania, 1 April 1888. ("Death of Hon. D.N. White," *Pittsburgh Commercial Gazette*, 2 April 1888, p. 2; *History of Allegheny County, Pennsylvania* [Chicago: A. Warner and Company, Publishers, 1889], 1:240, 657.)

On 28 August 1843, while traveling through the western frontier, White stopped at Nauvoo, Illinois, and visited the Mormon prophet. Two days later at Warsaw, Illinois, the editor wrote his perceptions of the "far-famed kingdom of the 'Latter-day Saints,'" which were published in the 15 September issue of the *Gazette*. His account contains a graphic contemporary description of the community and its people: "We travelled over vast prairies, extending in every direction as far as the eye could reach, except on our right, where lay the bluff which intervened between us and the river. . . . As we approached the 'kingdom,' as Nauvoo is denominated here, the country again began to be settled, while the luxuriant herbage of the prairie was cropped quite short by the herds of cattle belonging to the Mormons. Most of the prairie, near Nauvoo, is fenced with turf. A ditch some two feet deep is dug on each side of the fence, and the turf piled up between, making a very good and durable fence. These fences are broad enough on the top for a foot path. Quite a number of the houses or huts in which the inhabitants on the prairies live, are also made of turf, and covered with clapboards. As this turf is black, as is all the soil on the prairies, these huts present a very sombre appearance, and as there is not a tree, and scarcely a hillock to ward off the scorching sun of summer, or the cold blast of winter, they present a very bleak and desolate appearance."

White and his party spent nearly two days viewing Nauvoo and talking to its people. He estimated the city was "about four miles long, up and down the river, and three miles broad. The part near the prairie, about a mile and a half from the river, is quite broken up with ravines; nevertheless it is all laid out in acre lots, and more or less settled. . . . The site of Nauvoo is one of the most beautiful on the Mississippi river. The river at this place makes a large bend, forming a semi-circle, within which lies the lower part of the city, running back to the bluff. This semi-circular piece of ground is perfectly level, and lies above high water mark, extending at the widest place about three-fourths of a mile back from the river, and is about a mile and a half in length along the bluff. The bluff rises gradually, and is not very high, and presents most beautiful building sites. On the bluff immediately opposite the centre of the semi-circle, and about a mile from the river, stands the temple. The site is beautifully chosen, as it is in a central and elevated position, and can

Nauvoo Temple. Photograph of model at original temple site,
Nauvoo, Hancock County, Illinois.

be seen from the river, all around the bend, and from every part of the town. All over the bluff and bottom, are buildings, either erected, or in progress of erection, but no part of the town is compactly built. The whole space is a conglomeration of houses, fences, gardens, corn fields, stables, huts, &c. One looks in vain for any thing like a compactly built street. The object seems to have been to scatter as widely as at all convenient, and to cover as much ground as possible. The ground is sold out in acre lots, and every man builds his house, or shantee, or hut, as the case may be, and plants his ground in corn and vegetables for the support of his family. The houses are of all sorts, shapes and sizes. Some, very many, are fine brick dwellings. Others are quite respectable looking frames. Others, again, are mere shantees, some log, some turf, and some mere sheds of boards. There are very few stores, mechanic shops, or business houses, and no trade going on. There is nothing to export, and no ability to import. Every body seems engaged in putting up houses, taking care of gardens, and getting in hay from the prairies. As crowds of emigrants are flocking in daily, the whole community is employed in providing shelter, and in procuring the barest necessaries for existence. It is hard to estimate the number of the population, it is scattered over so large a space, and several families are frequently crowded into one house. The prophet stated to me, that he estimated their number at 12,000. . . .

"There must be a great deal of suffering in the winter season, from cold and hunger; and there is considerable sickness in the community at this time. One sees many pale faces about the streets. . . ."

Of particular interest to the visitors was the temple: "This modern structure, which is to revive the departed glories of the temple of Jerusalem, and which is as apparently dear to every Mormon heart, as was that famous and venerated house to the devout Jew, is building, as we stated before, on the bluff, and is indeed 'beautiful for situation.' It is about 120 feet long by 90 broad. When finished it is to consist of a basement, and two twenty-five feet stories. The basement and one twenty-five feet story is up, and the remainder in process of completion. The basement story is about 12 feet in the clear, the half of which is under ground. It is divided off into various sized rooms running along each side, with a large hall or room in the centre. In this large room, stands the consecrated laver, supported by twelve oxen, carved with great fidelity to the living original. Four of the oxen face the north, four the south, and two each, east and west. They, as well as the laver, are composed of wood, and are to be overlaid with gold.

"The laver is of oblong shape, some four or five feet deep, and large enough for two priests to officiate at the rite of baptism, for which it is intended, at once. A pump stands by it to supply it with water. Stairs approach it from either side. I walked up and looked in. It contained nothing but a few inches of water. The laver, oxen, &c., are at present protected from the weather by a temporary roof. What the numerous rooms in this basement are intended for I did not learn. The walls are all exceedingly strong and massy, even the partition walls, generally from two to three feet thick. The basement is lighted by numerous windows, about five feet high, and as many wide, arched over the top. Between these windows are very heavy pilasters, on the top of which rest the basement stones of the less heavy pilasters between the windows of the upper stories. On each of these basement stones is carved a crescent or figure of the new moon, with the profile of a man's face, as seen in old Almanacs. The windows of the upper stories are some fifteen or eighteen feet high, arched over the top in a perfect semicircle.—The first story above the basement is divided into two apartments, called the outer and inner courts. The walls between these courts are three feet thick, of solid mason work, with two immense doors for passage between them.— The outer court is some twenty-five feet wide by ninety feet long—the inner court is about ninety feet square. These facts about the dimensions of the building I obtained from Joe himself. All the work is of good cut stone, almost white, and it will present a fine appearance when finished. How the second 25 feet story is to be finished I did not learn." (On the Nauvoo Temple see Don F. Colvin, "A Historical Study of the Mormon Temple at Nauvoo, Illinois" [Master's thesis, Brigham Young University, 1962].)

Upon visiting Joseph Smith on Aug. 29th, White noted that "the house of the prophet . . . has a very good garden containing about an acre, with a very fine fence around it, painted white, as is also the house, a moderate sized, and humble looking frame dwelling." During the conversation that ensued, the Prophet related the circumstances of his 1820 vision. (I am indebted to Noel R. Barton for locating a copy of the original Pittsburgh Gazette *interview.)*

Speaking of revelations, he stated that when he was in a "quandary," he asked the Lord for a revelation, and when he could not get it, he "followed the dictates of his own judgment, which were as good as a revelation to him; but he never gave anything to his people as revelation, unless it was a revelation, and the Lord did reveal himself to him." Running on in his voluble style, he said: "The world persecutes me, it has always persecuted me. The people at Carthage, in a public meeting lately, said, 'as for Joe, he's a fool, but he's got some smart men about him.'[1] I'm glad they give me so much credit. It is not every fool that has sense enough to get smart men about him. The Lord does reveal himself to me. I know it. He revealed himself first to me when I was about fourteen years old, a mere boy. I will tell you about it. There was a reformation among the different religious denominations in the neighborhood where I lived, and I became serious, and was desirous to know what Church to join. While thinking of this matter, I opened the Testament promiscuously on these words, in James, 'Ask of the Lord who giveth to all men liberally and upbraideth not.' I just determined I'd ask him. I immediately went out into the woods where my father had a clearing, and went to the stump where I had stuck my axe when I had quit work, and I kneeled down, and prayed, saying, 'O Lord, what Church shall I join?' Directly I saw a light, and then a glorious personage in the light, and then another personage, and the first personage said to the second, "Behold my beloved Son, hear him." I then, addressed this second person, saying, "O Lord, what Church shall I join." He replied, "don't join any of them, they are all corrupt." The vision then vanished, and when I came to myself, I was sprawling on my back; and it was some time before my strength returned. When I went home and told the people that I had a revelation, and that all the churches were corrupt, they persecuted me, and they have persecuted me ever since. They thought to put me down, but they hav'nt succeeded, and they can't do it. . . .

---

1. An anti-Mormon meeting was held at Carthage, Illinois, on 19 August 1843. See Smith, *History of the Church*, 5:537-38.

I. DANIEL RUPP, *AN ORIGINAL HISTORY*, 1844

Joseph Smith, "Latter Day Saints," in I. Daniel Rupp, An Original History of the Religious Denominations at Present Existing in the United States *(Philadelphia, 1844), 404-10.*

Editorial Note

Israel Daniel Rupp, historian and translator, was born 10 July 1803 at East Pennsboro (now Hampden), Cumberland County, Pennsylvania. Rupp was the fourth of fourteen children born to a German farmer, whose parents had immigrated from Germany in 1751. A voracious reader and student of the past, Rupp mastered several languages, and he became interested in history after reading a biography of Benjamin Franklin in German. He married Caroline Aristide in 1827, and they became parents of eight children. That same year he originated a plan for a history of the Germans of Pennsylvania. Since there were no local county histories, and the voluminous archival material of the state had not been published, he moved to Harrisburg and opened a private school in order to have better access to the historical sources. In 1829 he translated Foxe's *Book of Martyrs* into German, the first of eleven works he translated from English to German or from German to English. He also began to travel extensively through the German counties of Pennsylvania collecting material for his proposed history. His genial personality, coupled with his flair for research and meeting people, contributed to his success in gathering source material. While residing in Lancaster, Pennsylvania, in 1842, he published a *History of Lancaster County*, which was the first of six works devoted to twenty-three Pennsylvania counties. The volume was well received and brought a clamor from other counties for similar treatment. Although he produced some twenty-five volumes during his lifetime, his *History of the Germans of Pennsylvania*, which was to be the crowning contribution of his life, was never

Israel Daniel Rupp. The Historical Society of Pennsylvania.

completed. His published works included an *Early History of Western Pennsylvania* (1846); *A Collection of Thirty Thousand Names of German . . . Immigrants in Pennsylvania . . . 1727 to 1778* (1856); *The Geographical Catechism of Pennsylvania and the Western States* (1836); and *He Pasa Ekklesia: An Original History of the Religious Denominations at Present Existing in the United States* (1844). In addition to his publications, Rupp organized libraries, debating societies, and county lyceums; lectured on temperance; addressed teachers' institutes; and acted as a delegate to political conventions. But his main contribution lies in the foundation he laid for the study of local history. Stricken with paralysis, he died at Philadelphia on 31 May 1878. (Oswald Seidensticker, "Memoir of Israel Daniel Rupp, The Historian," *The Pennsylvania Magazine of History and Biography* 14 [1890]: 403-13; "Israel Daniel Rupp," *New England Historical and Genealogical Register* 33 [January 1879]: 116-17; William H. Egle, "I. Daniel Rupp," *Historical Magazine* 9 [February 1871]: 111-15; Malone, *Dictionary of American Biography*, 16:225-26.)

While residing in Lancaster, Pennsylvania, in 1843, Rupp had conceived a work containing history and doctrines of religious denominations in the United States written by representatives of each organization for the purpose of giving each "an opportunity of telling its own story . . . in its own way." In July he wrote Joseph Smith requesting a chapter about the Mormons. The Prophet responded by sending a statement derived partly from the material sent to John Wentworth the previous year but containing additional information about himself and Nauvoo. On 5 June 1844, three weeks before he was killed, the Prophet acknowledged having received a copy of Rupp's *An Original History of the Religious Denominations at Present Existing in the United States*: "I feel very thankful for so valuable a treasure. The design, the propriety, the wisdom of letting every sect tell its own story, and the elegant manner in which the work appears, have filled my breast with encomiums upon it, wishing you God speed. Although all is not gold that shines, any more than every religious creed is sanctioned with the so eternally sure word of prophecy, satisfying all doubt with 'Thus saith the Lord;' yet, 'by proving contraries,' truth is made manifest, and a wise man can search out 'old paths,' wherein righteous men held communion with Jehovah, and were exalted through obedience. I shall be pleased to furnish further information at a proper time, and render you such further service as the work and vast extension of our Church may demand for the benefit of truth, virtue and holiness." (Joseph Smith to I. Daniel Rupp, 5 June 1844, published in Smith, *History of the Church*, 6:428.)

The Church of Jesus Christ of Latter Day Saints, was founded upon direct revelation, as the true church of God has ever been, according to the scriptures (Amos, iii. 7, and Acts i.2.) And through the will and blessings of God, I have been an instrument in his hands, thus far, to move forward the cause of Zion. Therefore, in order to fulfil the solicitation of your letter of July last, I shall commence with my life.

I was born in the town of Sharon, Windsor county, Vermont, on the 23d of December, A.D. 1805. When ten years old, my parents removed to Palmyra, New York, where we resided about four years, and from thence we removed to the town of Manchester, a distance of six miles.

My father was a farmer, and taught me the art of husbandry. When about fourteen years of age, I began to reflect upon the importance of being prepared for a future state; and upon inquiring the place of salvation, I found that there was a great clash in religious sentiment; if I went to one society they referred me to one place, and another to another; each one pointing to his own particular creed as the "summum bonum" of perfection. Considering that all could not be right, and that God could not be the author of so much confusion, I determined to investigate the subject more fully, believing that if God had a church, it would not be split up into factions, and that if he taught one society to worship one way, and administer in one set of ordinances, he would not teach another principles which were diametrically opposed. Believing the word of God, I had confidence in the declaration of James, "If any man lack wisdom let him ask of God, who giveth to all men liberally and upbraideth not, and it shall be given him."

I retired to a secret place in a grove, and began to call upon the [p. 404] Lord. While fervently engaged in supplication, my mind was taken away from the objects with which I was surrounded, and I was enrapt in a heavenly vision, and saw two glorious personages, who exactly resembled each other in features and likeness, surrounded with a brilliant light, which eclipsed the sun at noonday. They told me that all the religious denominations were believing in incorrect doctrines, and that none of them was acknowledged of God as his church and kingdom. And I was expressly commanded to "go not after them," at the same time receiving a promise that the fulness of the gospel should at some future time be made known unto me.

On the evening of the 21st September, A.D. 1823, while I was praying unto God and endeavoring to exercise faith in the precious promises of scripture, on a sudden a light like that of day, only of a far purer and more glorious appearance and brightness, burst into the room; indeed the first sight was as though the house was filled with consuming fire. The appearance produced a shock that affected the whole body. In a moment a personage stood before me surrounded with a glory yet greater than that with which I was already surrounded. This messenger proclaimed himself to be an angel of God, sent to bring the joyful tidings, that the covenant which God made with ancient Israel was at hand to be fulfilled; that the preparatory work for the second coming of the Messiah was speedily to commence; that the time was at hand for the gospel in all its fulness to be preached in power, unto all nations, that a people might be prepared for the millennial reign.

I was informed that I was chosen to be an instrument in the hands of God to bring about some of his purposes in this glorious dispensation.

I was informed also concerning the aboriginal inhabitants of this country, and shown who they were, and from whence they came;—a brief sketch of their origin, progress, civilization, laws, governments, of their righteousness and iniquity, and the blessings of God being finally withdrawn from them as a people, was made known unto me. I was also told where there was deposited some plates, on which was engraven an abridgment of the records of the ancient prophets that had existed on this continent. The angel appeared to me three times the same night and unfolded the same things. After having received many visits from the angels of God, unfolding the majesty and glory of the events that should transpire in the last days, on the morning of the 22d of September, A.D. 1827, the angel of the Lord delivered the records into my hands.

These records were engraven on plates which had the appearance of gold; each plate was six inches wide and eight inches long, and [p. 405] not quite so thick as common tin. They were filled with engravings in Egyptian characters, and bound together in a volume, as the leaves of a book, with three rings running through the whole. The volume was something near six inches in thickness, a part of which was sealed. The characters on the unsealed part were small and beautifully engraved. The whole book exhibited many marks of antiquity in its construction, and much skill in the art of engraving. With the records was found a curious instrument which the ancients called "Urim and Thummim," which consisted of two transparent stones set in the rim on a bow fastened to a breastplate.

Through the medium of the Urim and Thummim I translated the record, by the gift and power of God.

In this important and interesting book the history of ancient America is unfolded, from its first settlement by a colony that came from the tower of Babel, at the confusion of languages, to the beginning of the fifth century of the Christian era.

We are informed by these records, that America, in ancient times, has been inhabited by two distinct races of people. The first were called Jaredites, and came directly from the tower of Babel. The second race came directly from the city of Jerusalem, about six hundred years before Christ. They were principally Israelites, of the descendants of Joseph. The Jaredites were destroyed, about the time that the Israelites came from Jerusalem, who succeeded them in the inheritance of the country. The principal nation of the second race fell in battle towards the close of the fourth century. The remnant are the Indians who now inhabit this country. This book also tells us that our Saviour made his appearance upon this continent after his resurrection; that he planted the gospel here in all its fulness, and richness, and power, and blessing; that they had apostles, prophets, pastors, teachers, and evangelists; the same order, the same priesthood, the same ordinances, gifts, powers, and blessing, as was enjoyed on the eastern continent; that the people were cut off in consequence of their transgressions; that the last of their prophets who existed among them was commanded to write an abridgment of their prophecies, history, &c., and to hide it up in the earth, and that it should come forth and be united with the Bible, for the accomplishment of the purposes of God, in the last days. For a more particular account, I would refer to the Book of Mormon, which can be purchased at Nauvoo, or from any of our travelling elders.

As soon as the news of this discovery was made known, false reports, misrepresentation and slander flew, as on the wings of the wind, in every direction; my house was frequently beset by mobs, [p. 406] and evil designing persons; several times I was shot at, and very narrowly escaped, and every device was made use of to get the plates away from me; but the power and blessing of God attended me, and several began to believe my testimony.

On the 6th April, 1830, the "Church of Jesus Christ of Latter Day Saints," was first organized, in the town of Manchester, Ontario Co., State of New York.[1] Some few were called and ordained by the Spirit of revelation and prophecy, and began to preach as the Spirit gave them utterance, and though weak, yet were they strengthened by the power of God; and many were brought to repentance, were immersed in the water,

1. See note 2 on p. 242.

and were filled with the Holy Ghost by the laying on of hands. They saw visions and prophesied, devils were cast out, and the sick healed by the laying on of hands. From that time the work rolled forth with astonishing rapidity, and churches were soon formed in the States of New York, Pennsylvania, Ohio, Indiana, Illinois, and Missouri; in the last named state a considerable settlement was formed in Jackson county; numbers joined the church and we were increasing rapidly; we made large purchases of land, our farms teemed with plenty, and peace and happiness were enjoyed in our domestic circle and throughout our neighborhood; but as we could not associate with our neighbours, – who were, many of them, of the basest or men, and had fled from the face of civilized society to the frontier country, to escape the hand of justice – in their midnight revels, their sabbath-breaking, horse-racing, and gambling, they commenced at first to ridicule, then to persecute, and finally an organized mob assembled and burned our houses, tarred and feathered and whipped many of our brethren, and finally drove them from their habitations; these, houseless and homeless, contrary to law, justice, and humanity, had to wander on the bleak prairies till the children left the tracks of their blood on the prairie. This took place in the month of November, and they had no other covering but the canopy of heaven, in that inclement season of the year. This proceeding was winked at by the government; and although we had warrantee deeds for our land, and had violated no law, we could obtain no redress. There were many sick who were thus inhumanly driven from their houses, and had to endure all this abuse, and to seek homes where they could be found. The result was, that a great many of them being deprived of the comforts of life, and the necessary attendance, died; many children were left orphans; wives, widows; and husbands, widowers. Our farms were taken possession of by the mob, many thousands of cattle, sheep, horses, and hogs were taken, and our household goods, store goods, and printing press and types were broken, taken, or otherwise destroyed. [p. 407]

Many of our brethren removed to Clay county, where they continued until 1836 (three years); there was no violence offered, but there were threatenings of violence. But in the summer of 1836 these threatenings began to assume a more serious aspect; from threats, public meetings were called, resolutions were passed, vengeance and destruction were threatened, and affairs again assumed a fearful attitude; Jackson county was a sufficient precedent, and as the authorities in that county did not interfere, they boasted that they would not in this; which on application to the authorities we found to be too true; and, after much violence, privation, and loss of property, we were again driven from our homes.

We next settled in Caldwell and Davies counties, where we made large and extensive settlements thinking to free ourselves from the power of oppression by settling in new counties, with a very few inhabitants in them; but here we were not allowed to live in peace; and in 1838 were again attacked by mobs; an exterminating order was issued by Governor Boggs, and under the sanction of law, an organized banditti ravaged the country, robbing us of our cattle, sheep, horses, hogs, &c.; many of our people were murdered in cold blood, the chastity of our women was violated, and we were forced to sign away our property at the point of the sword; and after enduring every indignity that could be heaped upon us by an inhuman, ungodly band of marauders,—from twelve to fifteen thousand souls, men, women, and children, were driven from their own firesides, and from lands for which they had warrantee deeds, to wander houseless, friendless, and homeless, (in the depth of winter,) as exiles on the earth, or to seek an asylum in a more genial clime, and among a less barbarous people.

Many sickened and died in consequence of the cold and hardships they had to endure, many wives were left widows, and children orphans and destitute.

It would take more time than I am able to devote to your service, at present, to describe the injustice, the wrongs, the murders, the bloodshed, thefts, misery and wo that have been committed upon our people by the barbarous, inhuman, and lawless proceedings of the State of Missouri. And I would refer you, and the readers of your history who may be desirous of further information on this topic, to the evidence taken on my recent trial before the Municipal Court of Nauvoo, on Saturday, July 1st, 1843, on a writ of habeas corpus, which is published in pamphlet form by Messrs. Taylor & Woodruff, of this city.

After being thus inhumanly expelled by the government and people from Missouri, we found an asylum and friends in the State of [p. 408] Illinois. Here, in the fall of 1839, we commenced a city called Nauvoo, in Hancock county, which, in December, 1840, received an act of incorporation from the Legislature of Illinois, and is endowed with as liberal powers as any city in the United States. Nauvoo, in every respect, connected with increase and prosperity, has exceeded the most sanguine expectations of thousands. It now contains near 1500 houses, and more than 15,000 inhabitants. The charter contains, amongst its important powers, privileges, or immunities, a grant for the "University of Nauvoo," with the same liberal powers of the city, where all the arts and sciences will grow with the growth, and strengthen the strength of this beloved city of the "saints of the last days." Another very commendatory provision of the charter is, that that portion of the citizens subject to military duty are organized into a body of independent military men, styled the "Nauvoo Legion," whose highest officer holds the rank, and is commissioned lieutenant-general. This legion, like other independent bodies of troops in this republican government, is at the disposal of the Governor of this State, and President of the United States. There is also an act of incorporation for an agricultural and manufacturing association, as well as the Nauvoo House Association.

Nauvoo, Hancock County, Illinois, c.1846. Daguerreotype.
Charles W. Carter Collection. LDS Church Archives.

The temple of God, now in the course of erection, being already raised one story, and which is 120 feet by 80 feet, of stone, with polished pilasters, of an entire new order of architecture, will be a splendid house for the worship of God, as well as an unique wonder for the world, it being built by the direct revelation of Jesus Christ for the salvation of the living and the dead.[1]

Since the organization of this church its progress has been rapid, and its gain in numbers regular. Besides these United States, where nearly every place of notoriety has heard the glad tidings of the gospel of the Son of God, England, Ireland, and Scotland, have shared largely in the fulness of the everlasting gospel, and thousands have already gathered with their kindred saints, to this the cornerstone of Zion. Missionaries of this church have gone to the East Indies, to Australia, Germany, Constantinople, Egypt, Palestine, the Islands of the Pacific, and are now preparing to open the door in the extensive dominions of Russia.

There are no correct data by which the exact number of members composing this now extensive, and still extending, Church of Jesus Christ of Latter Day Saints can be known. Should it be supposed at 150,000, it might still be short of the truth.

Believing the Bible to say what it means and mean what it says; and guided by revelation according to the ancient order of the fathers [p. 409] to whom came what little light we enjoy; and circumscribed only by the eternal limits of truth: this church must continue the even tenor of her way, and "spread undivided, and operate unspent."

We believe in God the Eternal Father, and in his son Jesus Christ, and in the Holy Ghost.

We believe that men will be punished for their own sins and not for Adam's transgression.

1. See D&C 124:26-28.

We believe that through the atonement of Christ all men may be saved by obedience to the laws and ordinances of the gospel.

We believe that these ordinances are: 1st, Faith in the Lord Jesus Christ; 2d, Repentance; 3d, Baptism by immersion for the remission of sins; 4th, Laying on of hands for the gift of the Holy Ghost.

We believe that a man must be called of God by "prophecy, and by laying on of hands," by those who are in authority to preach the gospel and administer in the ordinances thereof.

We believe in the same organization that existed in the primitive church, viz. apostles, prophets, pastors, teachers, evangelists, &c.

We believe in the gift of tongues, prophecy, revelation, visions, healing, interpretation of tongues, &c.

We believe the Bible to be the word of God as far as it is translated correctly; we also believe the Book of Mormon to be the word of God.

We believe all that God has revealed, all that he does now reveal, and we believe that he will yet reveal many great and important things pertaining to the kingdom of God.

We believe in the literal gathering of Israel, and in the restoration of the Ten Tribes. That Zion will be built upon this continent. That Christ will reign personally upon the earth, and that the earth will be renewed and receive its paradisal glory.

We claim the privilege of worshipping Almighty God according to the dictates of our conscience, and allow all men the same privilege, let them worship how, where, or what they may.

We believe in being subject to kings, presidents, rulers, and magistrates; in obeying, honouring, and sustaining the law.

We believe in being honest, true, chaste, benevolent, virtuous, and in doing good to all men; indeed we may say that we follow the admonition of Paul; "we believe all things: we hope all things:" we have endured many things, and hope to be able to endure all things. If there is any thing virtuous, lovely, or of good report, or praiseworthy, we seek thereafter.

ALEXANDER NEIBAUR REPORT, 1844

Alexander Neibaur Journal, 24 May 1844. MS. LDS Church Archives, Salt Lake City, Utah.

Editorial Note

Alexander Neibaur was born in Ehrenbreitstein, Germany, on 8 January 1808. He studied dentistry at the University of Berlin, after which he set up his practice in Preston, England. In 1834, he met and married Ellen Breakel. When the first Mormon missionaries, Heber C. Kimball, Willard Richards, Orson Hyde, and others arrived in England in 1837, the young dentist was among the first converts. Four years later, Neibaur and his family emigrated to Nauvoo, Illinois, where he pursued his profession as a dentist and also made matches. The Neibaurs crossed the plains to Winter Quarters in 1847 and arrived in the Great Basin with the Brigham Young company of 1848. He settled in the Salt Lake City 4th Ward, where he raised a large family of fourteen children and was the first dentist and match manufacturer in the Salt Lake Valley. He died in Salt Lake City on 15 December 1883. ("Alexander Neibaur," *The Utah Genealogical Magazine and Historical Magazine* 5 [April 1914]: 53-63; Preston Nibley, *Stalwarts of Mormonism* [Salt Lake City: Deseret Book Company, 1954], 111-12.)

As a linguist, Alexander Neibaur taught German and Hebrew to Joseph Smith while in Nauvoo. On 24 May 1844, Neibaur visited Joseph at his home, where he met Edward Bonney and the two men heard the Prophet relate the experience of his First Vision.

May 24 called at J: Smith 10 oc'lk foren[oon] took Dinner ⟨read German⟩ after Dinner met the Sax & fox Indians Dancet

Alexander Neibaur.

heir Waar Danc[1] = 24 called at Br J.S met Mr Bonnie = Br Joseph tolt us the first call he had a Revival meeting his mother & Br & Sist got Religion, he wanted to get Religion too wanted to feel & ~~sho~~ shout like the Rest but could feel nothing, opened his Bible ~~f~~ the first Passage that struck him was if any man lack wisdom let him ask of God who giveth to all men liberallity & upbraidat not went into the Wood to pray kneelt himself down his tongue was closet cleavet to his roof—could utter not a word, felt easier after a while = saw a fire towards heaven came near & nearer saw a personage in the fire light complexion blue eyes a piece of white cloth drawn over his shoulders his right arm bear after a wile a other person came to the side of the first Mr Smith then asked must I join the Methodist Church = No = they are not my People, ~~sl~~ have gone astray there is none that doeth good no not one, but this is my Beloved son harken ye him, the fire drew nigher Rested upon the tree enveloped him [*page torn*] comforted Indeavoured to arise but felt uncomen feeble = got into the house told the Methodist priest, said this was not a age for God to Reveal himself in Vision Revelation has ceased with the New Testament

---

1. MS. reads "dany."

Sac (Sauk) and Fox Indians were of Algonquian linguistic stock. By 1844, they had united and were living in Iowa. Earlier, minor Sauk chiefs had ceded tribal lands east of the Mississippi to the United States. In 1832, this led to the Black Hawk War, after which the Indians moved to Iowa. These Indians at one time had inhabited the land upon which Nauvoo was settled. The Diary of Joseph Smith, 23 May 1844, gives an account of the council between the Prophet and the Indians held at the Prophet's home in Nauvoo on that day.

May 24 called at J: Smith 10 silk [illegible]
took Dinner read German after Dinner met the Sax & fox Indian
Dancet their Waar Danz = 24 called at Br J..
met Mr Bonnie = Br Joseph tolt us the first call
he had a Revival Meeting his Mother & Br & Sist
got Religion, he wanted to get Religion too
wanted to feel & sho shout like the Rest but
could feel nothing, opened his Bible of the first
Passage that struck him was if any man
lack Wisdom let him ask of God who giveth
to all Men liberallity & upbraidat not
went into the Wood to pray kneelt himself down
his tongue was closet cleavet to his roof—could
utter not a word, felt easier after a while = saw
a fire towards heaven came near & nearer
saw a personage in the fire light complexion
blue eyes a piece of white cloth drawn over
his shoulders his right arm bear after a while
a other person came to the side of the first
Mr Smith then asked must I join the Methodist
Church = No = they are not my People, th
have gone astray there is none that doeth
good no not one, but this is my Beloved
son harken ye him, the fire drew nigher
Rested upon the tree enveloped him

Alexander Neibaur Diary, 24 May 1844. LDS Church Archives.

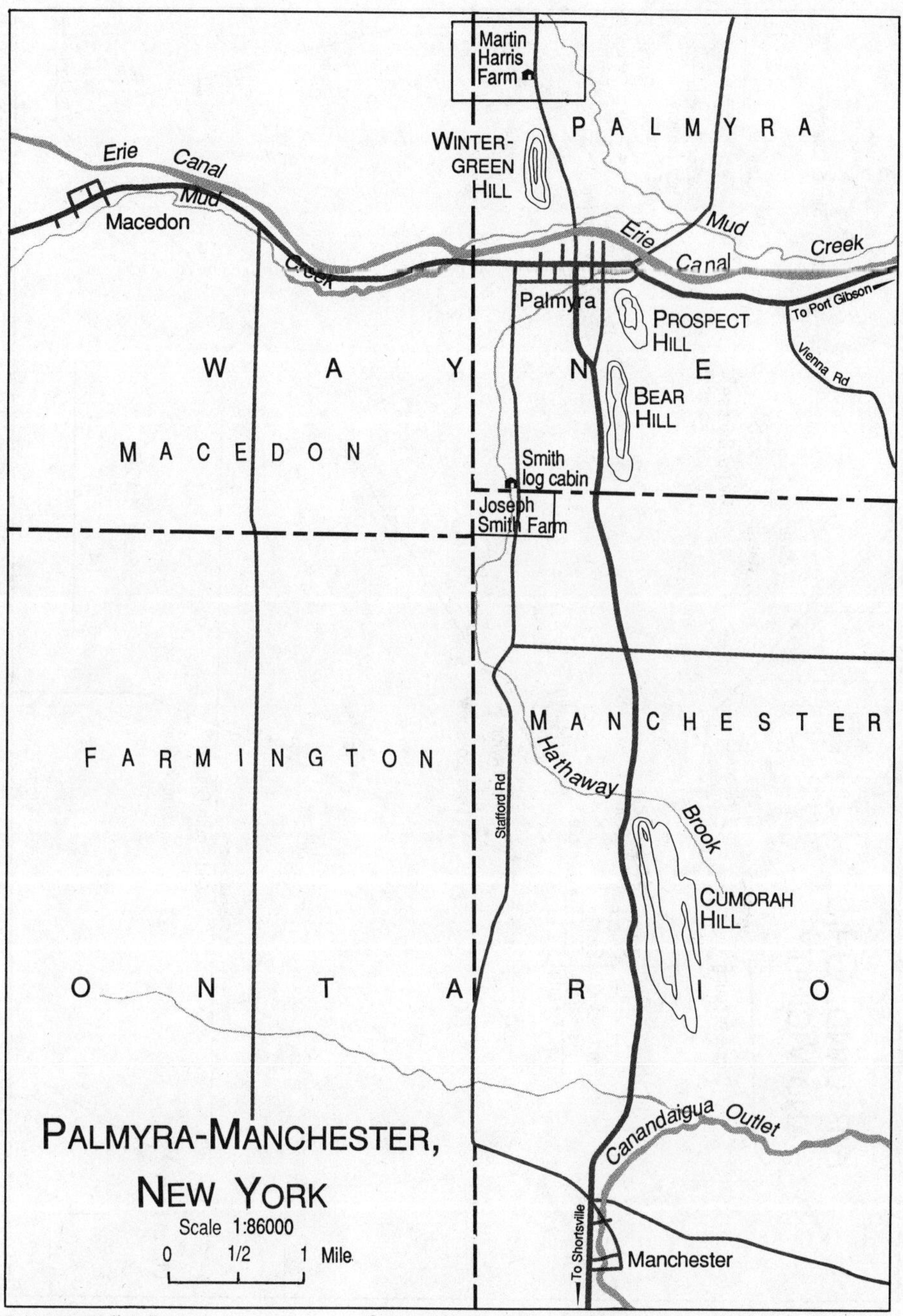

Research by Don Enders

Cartography by Steven R. Thomas, University of Utah, DIGIT Lab

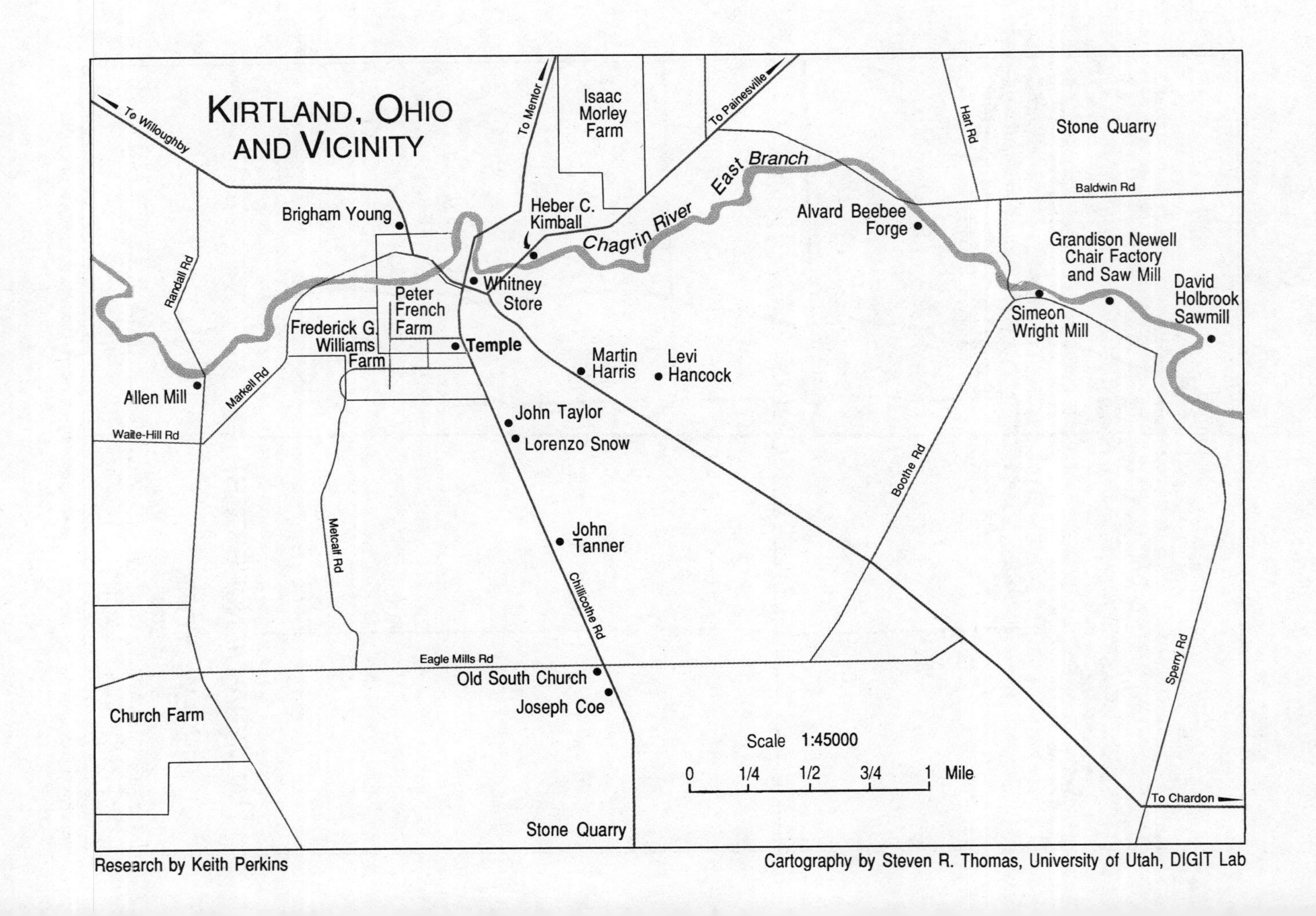

Research by Keith Perkins

Cartography by Steven R. Thomas, University of Utah, DIGIT Lab

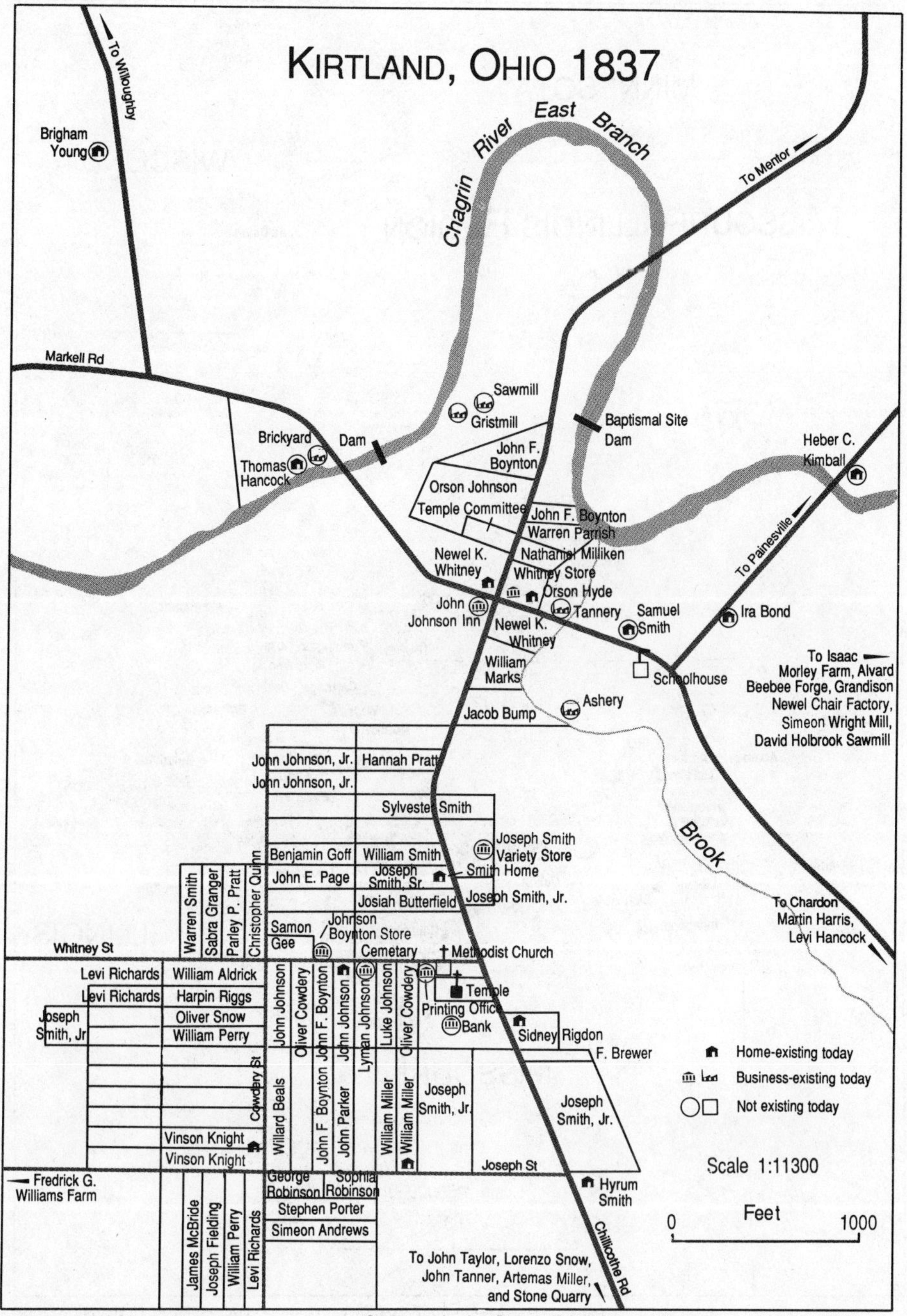

Research by Keith Perkins

Cartography by Steven R. Thomas, University of Utah, DIGIT Lab

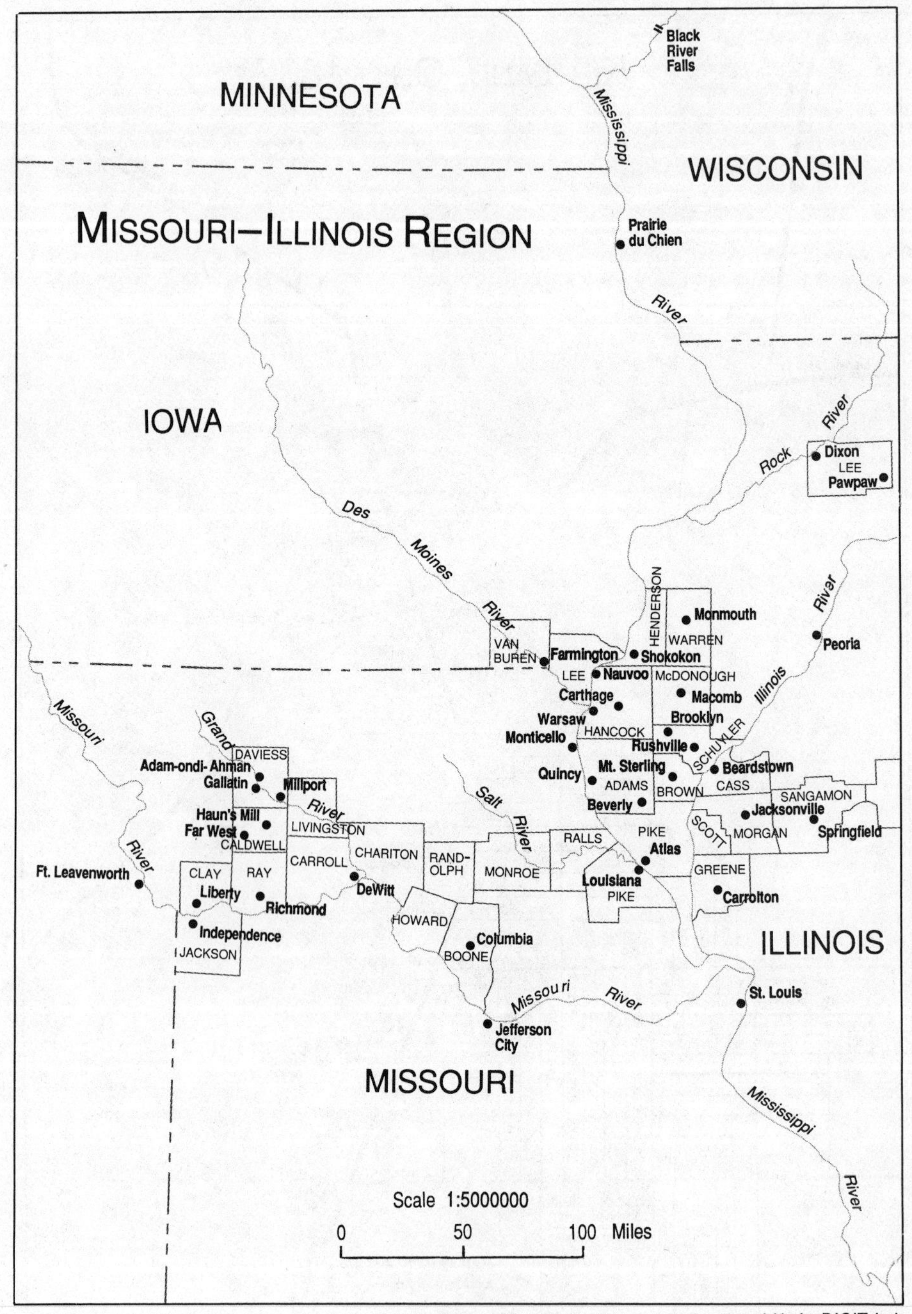

Cartography by Steven R. Thomas, University of Utah, DIGIT Lab

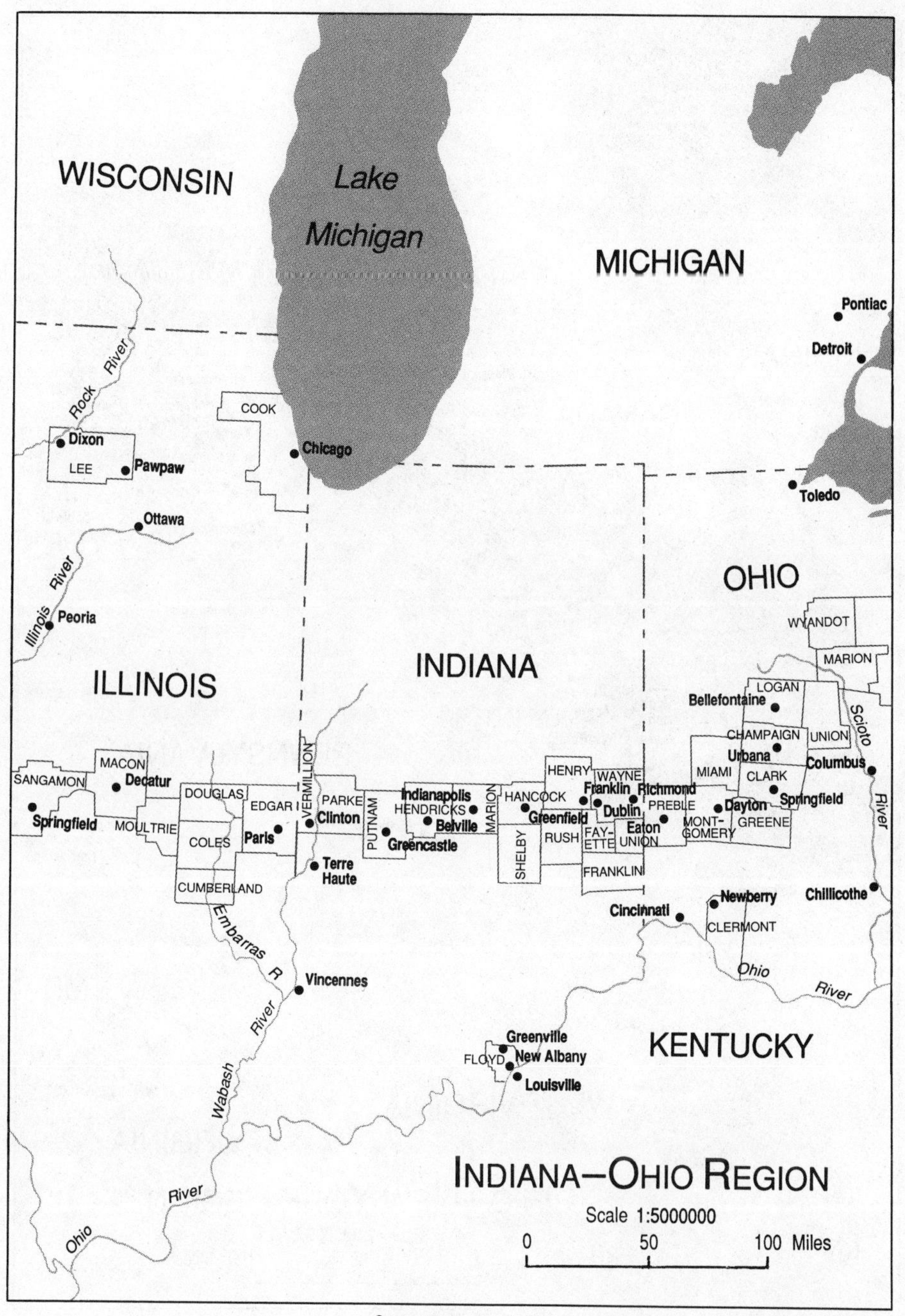

Cartography by Steven R. Thomas, University of Utah, DIGIT Lab

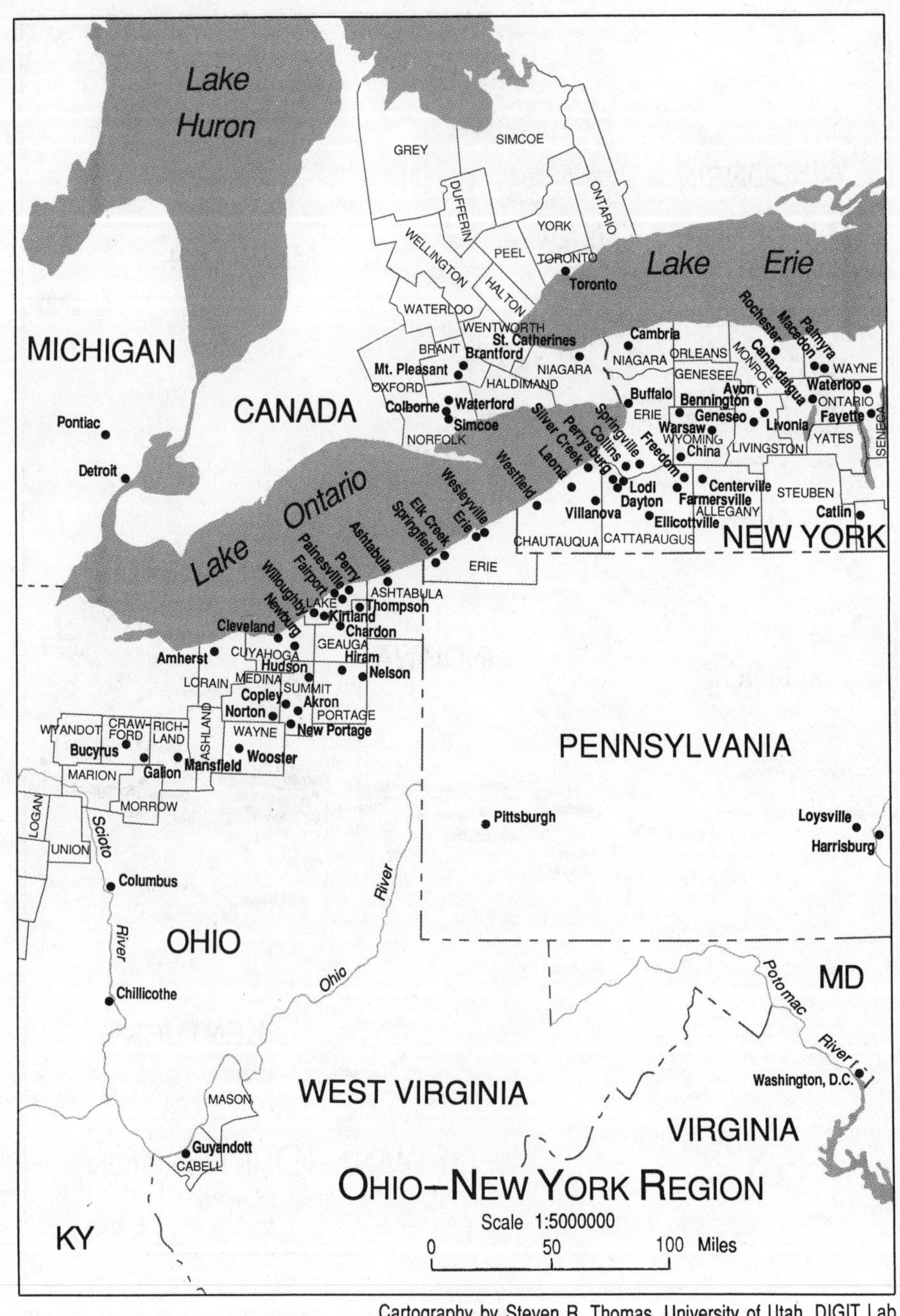

Cartography by Steven R. Thomas, University of Utah, DIGIT Lab

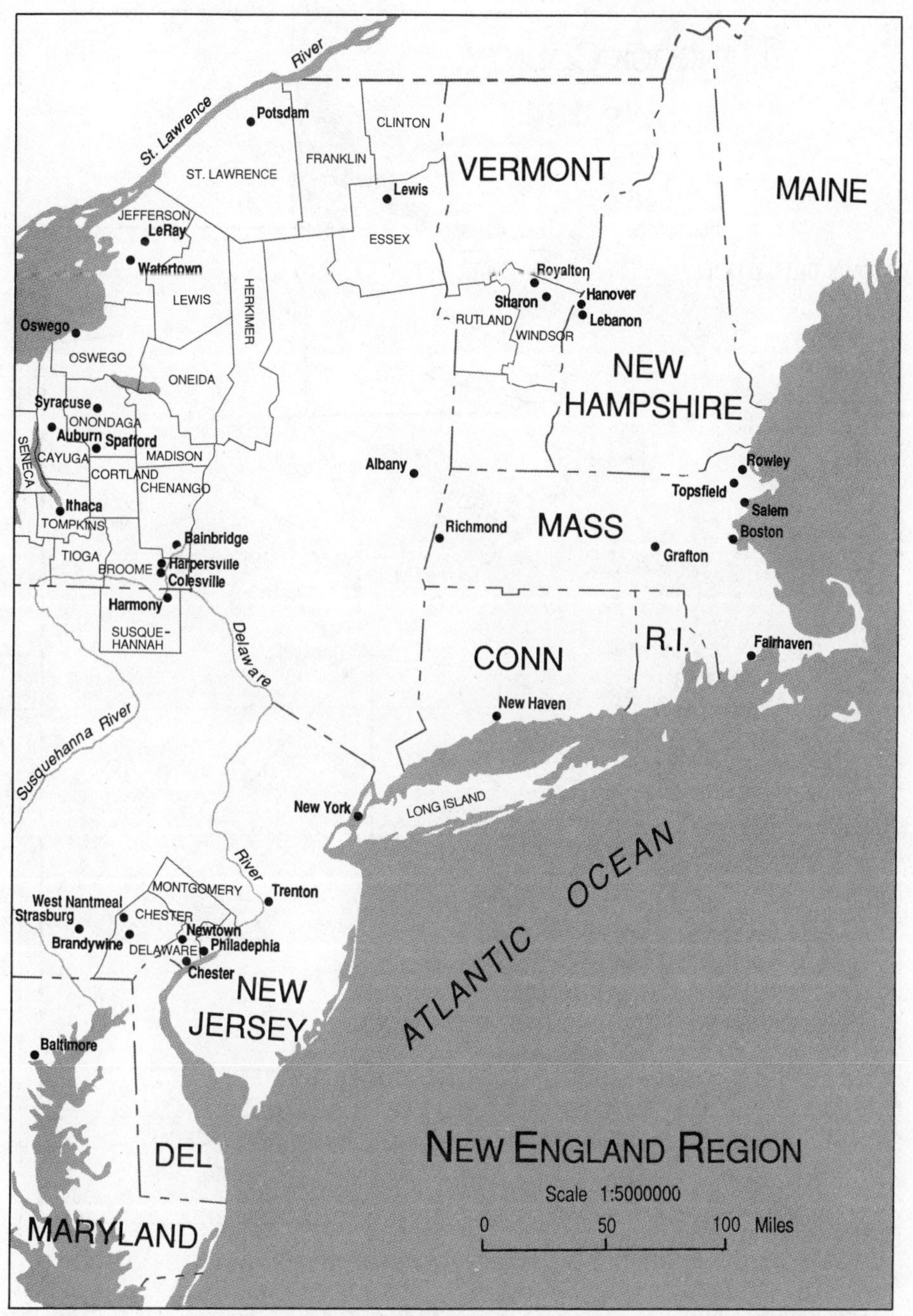

Cartography by Steven R. Thomas, University of Utah, DIGIT Lab

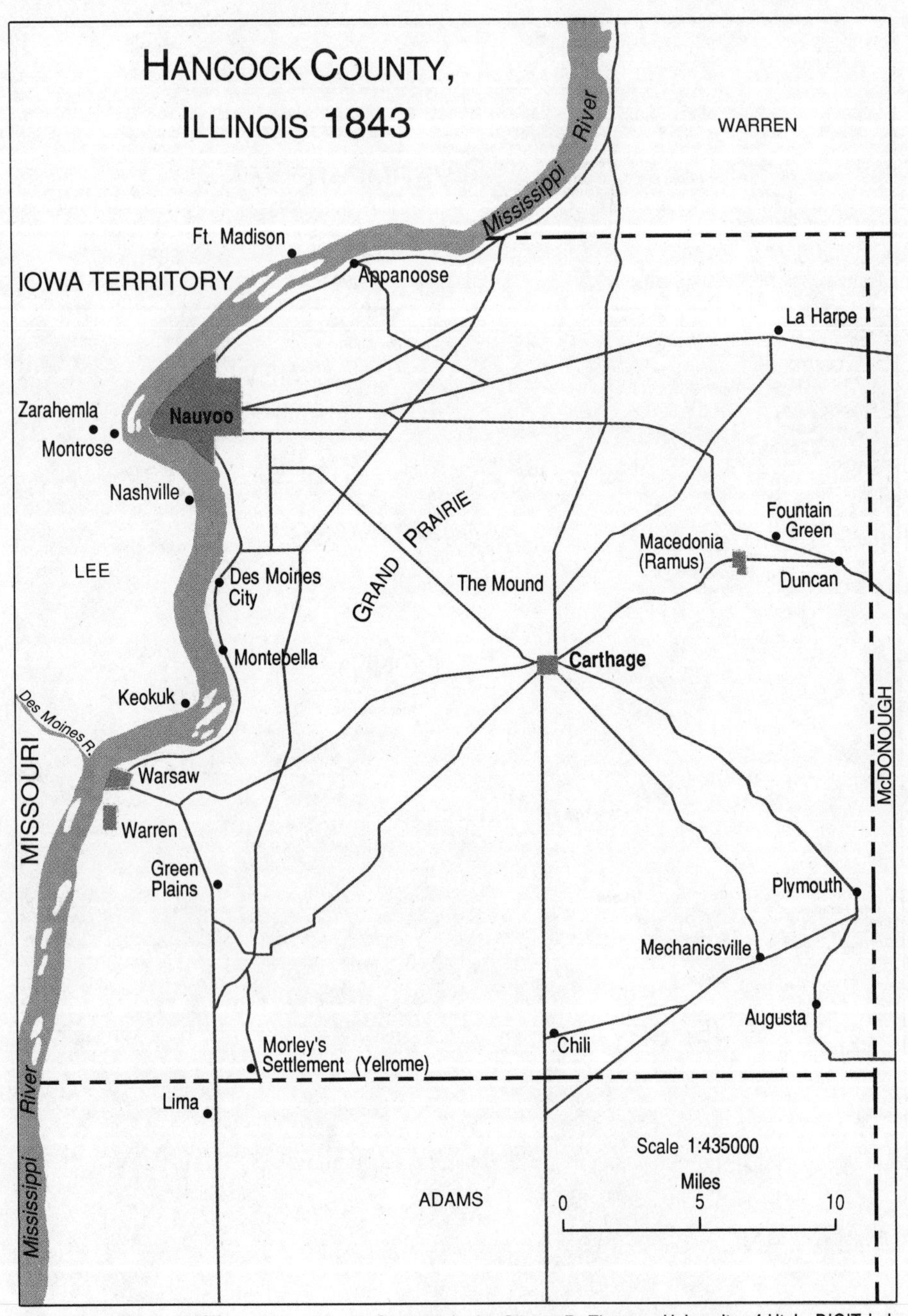

Research by Rowena Miller

Cartography by Steven R. Thomas, University of Utah, DIGIT Lab

BIOGRAPHICAL REGISTER

Aldrich, James H., taken prisoner by a mob during difficulties in Jackson County, Missouri, in 1833; living in Kirtland, Ohio, in 1835; and Nauvoo 3rd Ward, 1846. (Black, "Membership," 1:445-46.)

Allen/Allyn, Peletiah (1785-1856), born at Barkhamsted, Litchfield County, Connecticut. Married Amelia Joslin in Trumbull County, Ohio, 1835. Died at Hiram, Portage County, Ohio. (Michael Clegg, *Portage County, Ohio Newspaper Obituary Abstracts 1825-1870* [Fort Wayne, Indiana: Published by author, 1982], 31, 59; International Genealogical Index.)

Angell, Truman O. (1810-1887), carpenter, joiner, architect. Brother-in-law to Brigham Young. Born at Providence, Rhode Island. Married Polly Johnson, 1832. Living in China, New York, when converted to Mormonism, 1833. Moved to Kirtland, Ohio in 1835 and worked on the temple. Member of the second quorum of seventy. Moved to Missouri, 1837; and Illinois, 1839. Supervised joiner work on Nauvoo Temple. Arrived in Salt Lake Valley with pioneers of 1847. Appointed Church architect; supervised construction of many buildings, including Salt Lake Temple. ("Truman O. Angell – Master Builder," *Our Pioneer Heritage* 10:194-204; Orson F. Whitney, *History of Utah* [Salt Lake City: George Q. Cannon and Sons, 1892-1904], 4:60-61; Paul L. Anderson, "Truman O. Angell: Architect and Saint," in *Supporting Saints: Life Stories of Nineteenth-Century Mormons*, edited by Donald Q. Cannon and David J. Whittaker [Religious Studies Center: Brigham Young University, 1985].)

Anthon, Charles (1797-1867), educator, classical scholar, born in New York City. Entered Columbia College at age fourteen; he so far excelled above his classmates that he was excluded from further competition and graduated in 1815. Studied law; admitted to the New York bar, 1819. A master of Greek and Latin, he was professor of classical studies and literature at Columbia College from 1820 until his death. Widely acclaimed for his scholarship, for thirty years he published at least one volume annually. Died in New York City. (Kimball, "The Anthon Transcript," *BYU Studies*, 10:325-52; Malone, *Dictionary of American Biography*, 1:313-14; Henry Drisler, *A Commemorative Dis-*

course [New York: D. Van Nostrand, 1868]; "The Late Doctor Anthon," *Harper's Weekly*, 17 August 1867, 525-26.)

Avery, Arvin Allen (1812-1877) was born at Spafford, Onondaga County, New York. He married Francis Maria Babbitt 25 September 1835. He was living in Nauvoo, Illinois, in 1846. Evidently did not go west with the Latter-day Saints. (Elroy M. Avery and Catharine H. Avery, *The Groton Avery Clan* [Cleveland, 1912], 1:565; "Nauvoo Temple Endowment Register," 1845-1846, 219, Typescript, LDS Church Family History Library.)

Babbitt, Almon W. (1813-1856), attorney. Born at Cheshire, Berkshire County, Massachusetts. Converted to Mormonism, 1833. Married Julia Ann Johnson, 1834. Participant in the march of Zion's Camp to Missouri later that same year. Proselyting mission to Upper Canada, 1837-1838. Appointed president of Kirtland Stake, 1841. Presiding elder at Ramus, Hancock County, Illinois, 1843. Elected to Illinois state legislature from Hancock County, 1844. Appointed to the committee to sell the property of Latter-day Saints departing from Nauvoo, 1845; and postmaster of Nauvoo, 1846. Crossed the plains to Utah in 1848. Disfellowshipped, 1851. Appointed secretary of Utah Territory, 1852. Killed by Cheyenne Indians in Nebraska. (Lyndon W. Cook, *The Revelations of the Prophet Joseph Smith: A Historical and Biographical Commentary of the Doctrine and Covenants* [Provo, Utah: Seventies Mission Bookstore, 1981], 251-52; Kate B. Carter, ed., "Almon Whiting Babbitt," *Our Pioneer Heritage*, 11:513-72; Jay Donald Ridd, "Almon W. Babbitt, Mormon Emissary" [M.A. thesis, University of Utah, 1953].)

Badlam, Alexander (1808-1894), coachmaker. Born at Norfolk, Norfolk County, Massachusetts. Married Mary Ann Brannan, sister of Samuel Brannan. Participant in Zion's Camp, 1834. Appointed to the First Quorum of seventy, 1835. Presided over Boston branch of the Church, 1846-1848. Migrated to Utah, 1850. Mission to California, 1852; studying Chinese in Sacramento, 1853-1855. President of Sixth Quorum of Seventy. By 1872 he had left the Church. (Smith, *History of the Church*, 2:183, 204; Susan Easton Black, "Membership of the Church of Jesus Christ of Latter-day Saints, 1830-1848" [Provo, Utah: Religious Studies Center, Brigham Young University, 1984], 3:146-47; "Journal History of the Church of Jesus Christ of Latter-day Saints," 9 February 1853; 12 January, 4 April 1855; 16 September 1872.)

Bailey, Joshua (1772?–1849), born at Andover, Essex County, Massachusetts. Married Hannah Boutwell. Died at Dracut, Middlesex County, Massachusetts. (Family Group Records Collection, LDS Church Genealogical Department.)

Bailey, Mary (1808-1841), born at Bedford, Hillsborough County, New Hampshire. Converted to Mormonism in Boston by Orson Hyde and Samuel Harrison Smith, 1832. Married Samuel H. Smith on 13 August 1834. Mother of four children. Died at Nauvoo, Illinois. (Family Group Records Collection; *Utah Genealogical and Historical Magazine*, 28:103.)

Beman, Alvah (1775-1837) was born at New Marlboro, Berkshire County, Massachusetts. Married Sally Burtts in 1796. Moved from Massachusetts to Livonia, Livingston County, New York, 1799. Had a large farm, sheep, cattle; made cloth. Later the family moved to Avon, Livingston County, New York. He was among the first to be acquainted with Joseph Smith and his work in Palmyra, New York. Assisted Joseph in concealing Book of Mormon plates from a Palmyra mob. In 1830 he and his family of six, including four daughters, resided at Livonia, New York. Appointed to preside over elders of the Church at Kirtland, 1836. Died at Kirtland, Ohio. (Milton V. Backman, Jr., *A Profile of Latter-day Saints of Kirtland, Ohio, and Members of Zion's Camp* [Provo, Utah: Brigham Young University, 1982], 6; Smith, *History of the Church*, 2:370; Mary B. Noble, Autobiography, Ms. LDS Church Archives.)

Benton, Abram Willard (1805-1867), physician, studied medicine with Dr. Nathan Boynton at Bettsburgh and settled in Afton, Chenango County, New York, where he practised several years. In 1830 he was a member of the Chenango County Medical Society. Seven years later he sold out and moved to Illinois. Became a director of the Mississippi and Rock River Junction Railroad, 1852. Died at Fulton, Whiteside County, Illinois. While in New York he wrote his perceptions of Joseph Smith, including a summary of the 1830 Bainbridge trial, in a letter to the editors of the *Evangelical Magazine and Gospel Advocate* in Utica, New York. His piece appeared under the title "Mormonites" in the issue of 9 April 1831. (James M. Smith, *History of Chenango and Madison Counties, New York* [Syracuse, 1880], 100, 144; Charles Bent, ed., *History of Whiteside County, Illinois* [Morrison, Illinois, 1887], 166; Whiteside County, Illinois, Cemetery Records, Typescript, 44, LDS Church Family History Library.)

Billings, Titus (1793-1866), born at Greenfield, Franklin County, Massachusetts. Married Diantha Morley in 1817. One of the first converts to Mormonism in Kirtland, Ohio, 1830. Moved to Jackson County, Missouri, 1832; remained in Missouri until 1838. Participant in the Battle of Crooked River in October 1838. Member of the Nauvoo Legion in Illinois. Crossed the plains to Salt Lake City in 1848. Pioneer settler of Manti, Utah. About 1863 moved to Provo, Utah, where he died. (Cook, *Revelations*, 102.)

Bishop, Francis Gladden (1809-1878), watch repairer, born at Greece, Monroe County, New York. After joining the Latter-day Saints in July 1832, he was engaged in extensive missionary work from North Carolina to Canada, 1833-1840, and was president of the branch at

Westfield, New York. Heretical tendencies and subsequent repentance resulted in excommunication and readmittance to the Church on three occasions. On 28 September 1835 he was charged with "advancing heretical doctrines . . . derogatory to the character of the Church." He was excommunicated in 1842 for purveying his own revelations as doctrine. Later formed a church of his own, which existed in Iowa until about 1860. (Kirtland Council Minutes, 28 September 1835; Smith, *History of the Church*, 2:284-85; Kate B. Carter, *Our Pioneer Heritage* [Salt Lake City: Utah Printing Company, 1958-1977], 5:335-36; *Messenger and Advocate*, 1:63-64, 167, 186; 2:335; 3:476, 519; *Times and Seasons*, 1:77-78.)

Bogart, Samuel (1797-1861), farmer, was born in Carter County, Tennessee. He fought in the Battle of New Orleans in 1815 and the Black Hawk War in 1832. Moved to Missouri, 1833; and Washington County, Texas, 1839. Commanded a company of Rangers in the Mier Expedition into Old Mexico in 1842-1843. Settled in Collin County, Texas, 1845; represented the county in the state legislature, 1847, 1849, 1851, 1859. Died at Woodlawn, Collin County.

Bogart was Captain of Ray County, Missouri volunteers ("minute men") under Hiram G. Parks's command during the conflict with the Mormons in 1838. He led the force that engaged David Patten's men at Crooked River on 25 October 1838, which resulted in Patten's death. (*Document Containing the Correspondence, Orders, &c. in Relation to the Disturbances with the Mormons; and the Evidence Given before the Hon. Austin A. King* [Fayette, Missouri: Boones Lick Democrat, 1841], 42, 108; Smith, *History of the Church*, 3:170-71; Roy F. Hall and Helen G. Hall, *Collin County: Pioneering in North Texas* [Quanah, Texas: Nortex Press, 1975], 153; Louis J. Wortham, *A History of Texas: From Wilderness to Commonwealth* [Fort Worth: Wortham-Molyneaux Company, Texas, 1924], 4:92-101.)

Boggs, Lilburn W. (1798-1861) was the fifth governor of Missouri, 1837-1841. He was born in Kentucky; moved to Missouri, where he engaged in business. Missouri state senator, 1826-32, elected lieutenant-governor in 1832 and became governor upon the resignation of his predecessor, Daniel Dunklin. He played a prominent roll in the expulsion of the Mormons from the state in 1838. He was severely wounded by an assassin in 1842 and accused Joseph Smith of complicity in the crime. In 1846 moved to California, where he became alcalde of the Sonoma district, 1847-1849. He died at Sacramento. (*The National Cyclopedia of American Biography* [New York: James Whites and Company, 1904], 12:303; William M. Boggs, "A Short Biographical Sketch of Lilburn W. Boggs, by his Son," *Missouri Historical Review* 4 [January 1910]: 106-10; Joseph F. Gordon, "The Life of Governor Lilburn W. Boggs" [Ph.D. diss., University of Missouri, 1956]; L. Dean Marriott,

"Lilburn W. Boggs: Interaction with Mormons Following Their Expulsion from Missouri" [Ph.D. diss., Brigham Young University, 1979].)

Bond, Ira (1798-1887), farmer, born at Caldwell, Essex County, New Jersey. Married Charlotte Wilcox. After moving to Mendon, New York, he was among the first Mormon converts there in 1832. Called to preside over the deacons in Kirtland, 1836. Owned 178 acres and a dwelling house valued at $465 at Kirtland in 1836. Remained in Kirtland after Mormons left, and died there. ("Journal History," 14 April 1832; Smith, *History of the Church*, 2:371; Geauga County, Ohio, Tax Records; A. E. Sherman, comp., Cemetery Inscriptions, Lake County, Ohio, 22, Typescript, LDS Church Family History Library.)

Bonney, Edward (1807-1864), lawyer, adventurer, farmer, born in Essex County, New York. Married Maria L. Van Frank in Homer, New York, 1832. Settled at Montrose, Iowa, about 1834. Counsel for the prosecution when the Nauvoo *Expositor* case came before Daniel H. Wells, 17 June 1844. Appointed aide-de-camp to Joseph Smith in the Nauvoo Legion, 18 June 1844. Listed as a witness by Joseph for his prospective trial in the *Expositor* case, 26 June 1844. Apparently affiliated with Mormonism for a while but did not remain. After the death of the Prophet, he became a self-appointed agent of justice, or bounty-hunter. Instrumental in the arrest and conviction of the Hodge brothers of Nauvoo for the killing of John Miller and Henry Leicy in Lee County, Iowa, in 1845. After the murder of George Davenport at Rock Island, Illinois, in 1845, he volunteered to bring to justice a gang of murderers and thieves operating in the Mississippi Valley. Lived at Rock Island, Prospect Park, York, and Aurora, Illinois. Restaurant keeper at Hannibal, Missouri, in 1860. Joined the Union army during the Civil War and was assigned to the secret service. Died at Chicago, Illinois. Published an account of his adventures under the title *The Banditti of the Prairies* in the late 1840s. (Smith, *History of the Church*, 6:488-91, 500, 576; Philip D. Jordan's Introduction in Edward Bonney, *The Banditti of the Prairies* [Norman, Oklahoma: University of Oklahoma Press, 1963]; Russel B. Nye, *A Baker's Dozen: Thirteen Unusual Americans* [East Lansing: Michigan State University Press, 1956], 73-94; James G. Wilson and John Fiske, *Appletons' Cyclopaedia of American Biography* [New York, 1888], 1:29; Doris M. Reed, "Edward Bonney, Detective," *The Indiana University Bookman* [November 1957]: 5-17; U.S. Census: York, DuPage County, Illinois, 1850; Hannibal, Marion County, Missouri, 1860.)

Booth, Ezra (1792- ?), born in Connecticut. Married Dorcas Taylor, 1819. A Methodist minister when converted to Mormonism in 1831. He accompanied Isaac Morley to Missouri and attended the August 1831 conference in Jackson County. After returning to Ohio in September, he was called on another mission to Missouri, where he became disaffected and left the Church. Published a series of nine anti-Mormon letters in the *Ohio Star* in 1831. Residing on a farm in Mantua, Portage County, Ohio in 1860. (Cook, *Revelations*, 72-73.)

Boutwell, Hannah (1773-1835), born at Wilmington, Middlesex County, Massachusetts. Married Joshua Bailey. Died at Dracut, Middlesex County, Massachusetts. (Family Group Records Collection.)

Boynton, John Farnham (1811-1890), merchant, lecturer, scientist, inventor. Born at Bradford (now Groveland) Essex County, Massachusetts. Converted to Mormonism in 1832. Member of the Council of Twelve, 1835-1837. Married Susan Lowell, 1836. Established a mercantile business in Kirtland, Ohio with Lyman Johnson. Left the Church in 1837. Settled in Syracuse, New York. Lecturer on natural history, geology, and science. Delivered more than 4,000 lectures. Sent by U.S. government to California in 1849. Assisted in running boundary line between United States and Mexico. Developed the torpedo that destroyed the Confederate ram Albemarle during U.S. Civil War. Author of 36 patents. Avid collector of Boynton genealogy. Died at Syracuse, New York. (Andrew Jenson, *Biographical Encyclopedia*, 1:91; *National Cyclopedia of American Biography*, 4:91-92; John F. Boynton and Caroline H. Boynton, *The Boynton Family* [n.p.: Caroline H. Boynton, 1897], xix-xxxv.)

Boynton, Nathan (1788-1860), born in Hampshire County, Massachusetts. Married Lepha Stowell of Bainbridge, Chenango County, New York about 1818. Boynton lived for many years in Chenango County, where he was a prominent physician and lumber dealer. About 1833 he moved to Elmira, Chemung County, New York, where he died. (John Boynton and Caroline Boynton, *The Boynton Family*, 29.)

Brown, Albert (1807-1902), carpenter. Born at Windsor, Hartford County, Connecticut. Living in Hoosick, Rensselaer County, New York, in 1830. Converted to Mormonism, 1832. Participant in march of Zion's Camp, 1834. Married Sarah Campbell, 1839. Member of the Nauvoo Legion. Migrated to Utah in 1863. He was a patriarch at time of his death in East Mill Creek, Utah. (Family Group Records Collection; U.S. Census: Rensselaer County, New York, 1830; *Deseret Evening News*, 29 January 1902; Frank E. Esshom, *Pioneers and Prominent Men of Utah* [Salt Lake City: Pioneers Book Publishing Company, 1913], 772.)

Brown, Eliza (1808- ?), was born in Chenango County, New York. She married William C. Perry, 1835. (Patriarchal Blessing Index, LDS Church Archives; "Nauvoo Temple Endowment Register.")

Brunson, Seymour (1798-1840), born at Plattsburgh, Clinton County, New York. Veteran of War of 1812. Married Harriet Gould, 1820. Joined Latter-day Saints in Ohio in 1831. He was a temporary member of the high council at Far West, Missouri, in 1838 and was appointed to the Nauvoo, Illinois, high council the following year. He was a captain in the 53rd regiment of Missouri militia and lieutenant colonel in the Hancock County, Illinois, militia. Died at Nauvoo. (Cook, *Revelations*, 153; Family Group Records Collection.)

Bump, Jacob (1791- ?), born at Butternuts, Otsego County, New York, where he lived until 1824. Participant in Zion's Camp, 1834. Married Abigail Pettingill. Contracted to do the plastering on the temple at Kirtland, Ohio. Joined dissenters in Kirtland to depose Joseph Smith in 1837. Used his influence with Kirtland dissenters to prevent mob violence against Mormons leaving Kirtland in 1838. He was associated with William E. McLellin and the Church of Christ in Kirtland in 1847 and was still living at Kirtland in 1860. (*Deseret Weekly* (Salt Lake City), 10 February 1858; Black, "Membership," 7:534-36; "Journal History," 6 July 1838.)

Burdick, Thomas (1795-1877), farmer, born at Canajoharie, Montgomery County, New York. Married Anna Higley, 1828. Appointed Church clerk to record membership licenses, February 1836. Kirtland schoolteacher, justice of the peace, and member of the Kirtland high council, 1837. Teaching school at Burlington, Iowa, 1845. In 1846 moved to Council Bluffs, where he was clerk and the first judge of Pottawattamie County; also postmaster at Kanesville. Crossed the plains in 1853 to San Bernardino. Moved to San Gabriel. Member of the board of supervisors of Los Angeles County. Died in Los Angeles. His son, Cyrus, was a cofounder of the city of Pomona. (*An Illustrated History of Los Angeles County California* [Chicago: The Lewis Publishing Company, 1889], 402; J. M. Guinn, *Historical and Biographical Record of Los Angeles and Vicinity* [Chicago: Chapman Publishing Company, 1901], 370; Nellie Johnson, *The Descendants of Robert Burdick* [Syracuse, New York: Syracuse Typesetting Company, 1937], 132-34, 328-30; Smith, *History of the Church*, 2:400, 522; Black, "Membership," 5:650-51; U.S. Census: Pottowattamie County, Iowa, 1850.)

Burnet, Serenus (1787/8-1858), farmer, born in New Jersey. One of the first settlers at Orange, Cayahoga County, Ohio, in 1815. He remained there until his death. Between 1820 and 1854 he was repeatedly elected to offices of trust, including trustee, treasurer, and clerk of the town. (Crisfield Johnson, *History of Cuyahoga County, Ohio* [Cleveland: D. W. Ensign and Co., 1879], 491-95; U.S. Census: Cuyahoga County, Ohio, 1820-1850; Cuyahoga County, Ohio, Probate Record of Wills, Vol. A, 391-93.)

Cahoon, Mary (1810- ?), daughter of William Cahoon, born at Albany, Albany County, New York. Married David Elliot, 1831. (Black, "Membership," 8:248-49; Family Group Records Collection.)

Cahoon, Reynolds (1790-1862), farmer, tanner, builder, was born at Cambridge, Washington County, New York. Participant in the War of 1812. Married Thirza Stiles, 1810. Among the first converts to Mormonism in Ohio in 1830. Appointed counselor to Bishop Newel K. Whitney at Kirtland, Ohio, 10 February 1832. Member of the committee to oversee building of the Kirtland Temple, and manager of the Kirtland store through which business connected with temple construction was transacted. Moved to Iowa after the 1838 expulsion of Mormons from Missouri. Crossed the plains to Utah in 1848. Died in South Cottonwood Ward, Salt Lake County. (Cook, *Revelations*, 73; Stella C. Shurtleff and Brent F. Cahoon, *Reynolds Cahoon and his Stalwart Sons* [Salt Lake City: Paragon Press, 1960]; U.S. Census: Salt Lake County, Utah, 1850, 1860; Family Group Records Collection.)

Cahoon, William F. (1813-1893), shoemaker, carpenter, joiner, eldest son of Reynolds Cahoon. Born at Harpersfield, Ashtabula County, Ohio. Baptized at Kirtland, Ohio, in 1830. Proselyting in Ohio, Pennsylvania, and New York, 1833. Participant in Zion's Camp march, 1834. Member of first quorum of seventy, 1835. Married Nancy Miranda Gibbs, 1836. Carpenter on Nauvoo temple, 1844. Migrated to Utah, 1849. President of second quorum of seventy. Died in Salt Lake City. (Jenson, *Biographical Encyclopedia*, 4:687-88; Shurtleff and Cahoon, *Reynolds Cahoon*, 79ff; *Deseret Evening News*, 7 April 1893.)

Campbell, Alexander (1788-1866), clergyman, writer, born at Shaw's Castle, County Antrim, Ireland. Trained for the ministry by his father, a Presbyterian minister, and further educated at Glasgow University. Joined his father in America and settled in western Pennsylvania, 1809. In 1810 the Campbells formed an independent society based on Baptist views and usages. But they believed baptism was necessary for the remission of sins. They repudiated human creeds and proposed to unite all believers in one church, with the Bible as their standard. In 1832 his followers joined Kentucky "Christians" to form the Disciples of Christ. Founded Bethany College, 1840. For forty years, 1823-1863, edited a religious magazine, first named *The Christian Baptist*, then, in 1830, *The Millennial Harbinger*. Preached extensively in the United States and Britain. Died at Bethany, Brooke County, West Virginia.

Followers of Campbell under the leadership of Sidney Rigdon were the first converts to Mormonism in Ohio in 1831. (Amos S. Hayden, *Early History of the Disciples in the Western Reserve* [Cincinnati: Chase and Hall, 1876], 45-53; Malone, *Dictionary of American Biography*, 3:446-48; *Encyclopedia Brittanica Micropaedia*, 15th ed., s.v. "Alexander Campbell"; Louis Cochran, *Alexander Campbell: The Man and His Mission* [Dallas, Texas: Wilkinson Publishing Co., 1965].)

Capron, Henry (1798-1875), farmer, born in New York. Spent most of his life at Ava, Oneida County, New York. Married Betsey Kent. Veteran of the War of 1812. He was supervisor and justice of the town for many years. (Daniel E. Wager, ed., *Our County and Its People: A Descriptive Work on Oneida County, New York* [Boston: The Boston

History Co., Publishers, 1896], 109, 394; U.S. Census: Oneida County, New York, 1830-1850.)

Carrico, Thomas (1802-?), born at Beverly, Essex County, Massachusetts. Baptized in 1834 by John F. Boynton. Settled at Kirtland, Ohio, 1835. Married Betsey Baker, 1836. Appointed doorkeeper of the Kirtland Temple. Traveled to Missouri with the Kirtland Camp, 1838. Settled at Nauvoo, Illinois, in 1842. Appointed counselor to Bishop Jonathan H. Hale, 1842. No known record of him after the Latter-day Saints left Nauvoo. (Nauvoo Ninth Ward High Priests Record, Ms., 12.)

Carter, Gideon (1798-1838), born at Killingworth, Middlesex County, Connecticut. Married Hilda Burwell. Baptized by Joseph Smith in 1831. Proselyting mission with Sylvester Smith in eastern states and New England, 1832. Member of Kirtland Safety Society and Kirtland high council, 1837. Moved to Far West, Missouri, 1838. Killed in battle at Crooked River, Ray County, Missouri. (Jenson, *Biographical Encyclopedia*, 3:615-16; Cook, *Revelations*, 154.)

Carter, Jared (1801-1849), shoemaker, cordwainer, born at Benson, Rutland County, Vermont. Married Lydia Ames, 1825. Joined the Church and was ordained an elder, 1831. Proselyting in eastern states, New York, and Michigan, 1831-33. Appointed to the Kirtland high council, 1837; and Far West, Missouri, high council, 1838. Member of the committee to oversee construction of the Kirtland Temple. Became disaffected and was disfellowshipped at Nauvoo but promised to return. Died in DeKalb County, Illinois. (Cook, *Revelations*, 73-74; Smith, *History of the Church*, 2:277-80, 333; Kirtland, Ohio, High Council Minutes, 19 September 1835; Illinois Mortality Schedule, 1850, Typescript, LDS Church Family History Library.)

Carter, Simeon (1794-1869), farmer, born at Killingworth, Middlesex County, Connecticut. Married Lydia Kenyon, 1818. Converted to Mormonism in Ohio in 1831. Member of the Clay County, Missouri, high council, 1834, and Far West, Missouri, high council, 1836. Missionary to England, 1846-49. Arrived in Salt Lake Valley, 1850. Settled at Brigham City, Box Elder County, Utah, where he died. (Cook, *Revelations*, 74-75; U.S. Census: Box Elder County, Utah, 1860; Esshom *Pioneers and Prominent Men*, 796-97.)

Clark, John B. (1802-1885), lawyer, born in Madison County, Kentucky. Moved to Howard County, Missouri, in 1818. Appointed clerk of the county court in 1823, colonel of militia in 1825, and major-general in 1836. He fought in the Black Hawk War. In 1849 Clark was elected to the state legislature and, beginning in 1854, served three terms in the U.S. Congress. He was a Confederate brigadier-general during the Civil War. Practiced law until his death at Fayette, Missouri.

Clark was given supreme command of the militia forces operating against the Mormons in Missouri in the summer of 1838, and he was the recipient on 27 October of Governor Boggs's extermination order. Although Clark did not arrive at Far West, Caldwell County, until after the Mormon defenders had surrendered to General Lucas, he presided over the dismantling of the community. (*History of Howard and Chariton Counties, Missouri* [St. Louis: National Historical Company, 1883], 252-53; Floyd Shoemaker, *Missouri and Missourians* [Chicago: The Lewis Publishing Co., 1943], 1:413, 641, 647-48, 824-25, 830, 917; *The Bench and Bar of St. Louis, Kansas City, Jefferson City, and Other Missouri Cities* [St. Louis: American Biographical Publishing Co., 1884], 310-11.)

Cobb, Polly Harris (1794- ?), was the youngest of ten children born to Rufus and Lucy Harris. Her sister Lucy, two years older, married Martin Harris. Polly married Freeman Cobb in 1812 at Palmyra, New York. (Family Group Records Collection.)

Coe, Joseph (1774-1854), was born at Genoa, Cayuga County, New York. Living in Essex County, New Jersey in 1830. Proselyting in New York, 1831. Appointed agent to purchase Church property, 1833. Member of the Kirtland high council, 1834-1837. Assisted in purchase of Egyptian mummies for the Church in 1835. Left the Church in 1838. Remained in Kirtland, Ohio, where he died. (Cook, *Revelations*, 86-87; Kirtland, Ohio Cemetery Records, 26, microfilm of typescript, LDS Church Family History Library.)

Colburn, Emily (1813- ?), born apparently in Pennsylvania. Sister of Newel Knight's wife, Sally Colburn. Joined the Latter-day Saints at Colesville, New York, after a local Presbyterian priest, John Sherer, tried to forcibly restrain her from doing so. Married Clark Slade, 1833. Experienced the difficulties of the Church in Missouri before moving to Illinois. Became disillusioned and left the Church. Later lived in Ohio, Wisconsin, and Iowa. Authored autobiographical sketch of her Mormon experience in 1882. (Emily M. Austin, *Mormonism; or, Life Among the Mormons*.)

Copley, Leman (1781-1862), born in Connecticut. Joined the Latter-day Saints in 1831. Owned 759 acres of land at Thompson, Ohio. When the New York Mormons moved to Ohio in 1831, he allowed them to settle on his land but afterward rescinded his agreement. He testified against Joseph Smith at the 1834 Philastus Hurlbut trial and was later disfellowshipped. Reinstated in 1836 but remained in Ohio. Died at Thompson, Ohio. (Geauga County, Ohio, tax lists; Cook, *Revelations*, 67; Violet Warren and Jeannette Grosvenor, "Inscriptions and Interments in Geauga County, Ohio, through 1983," 591, Typescript.)

Corrill, John (1794-1843), carriage builder, was born at Barre, Worcester County, Massachusetts. Living in Harpersville, Ashtabula County, Ohio, when converted to Mormonism in 1830. Moved to Jackson County, Missouri, 1831. Second counselor to Bishop Edward Partridge; presided over a branch of the Church at Independence. A Kirtland, Ohio, blessing stated that none "surpass him in understanding pertaining to architecture," and that he would "build the house of the Lord in Zion." Directed later stages of construction of the Kirtland Temple. Elected state representative from Caldwell County, Missouri, 1838. Appointed Church historian in 1838 but soon afterward left the Church. Published *A Brief History of the Church of Christ*, 1839. Died at Quincy, Adams County, Illinois. (Cook, *Revelations*, 68-69; Joseph Smith, Sr., Patriarchal Blessing Book, Vol. 1, Ms. LDS Church Archives; Adams County, Illinois, Probate Records.)

Covell, James (1756-1844), was born at Dover, New York. Married Lydia Black. Living in Chautauqua County, New York in 1830. Died at Mayville, Chautauqua County, New York. (Cook, *Revelations*, 57.)

Cowdery, Maria Louise (1835-1892), born at Kirtland, Geauga County, Ohio. The only child of Oliver Cowdery and Elizabeth Whitmer who grew to maturity. Married Charles Johnson, a medical doctor, in Richmond, Missouri, 1856; no children. Lived successively in Colorado, Kansas, and Missouri. She died at Southwest City, Missouri. (*Utah Genealogical Magazine*, 26:106, 141; *History of Ray County, Missouri* [St. Louis: Missouri Historical Co., 1881], 566; *Journal of History* [Lamoni, Iowa], 13:19.)

Cowdery, Oliver (1806-1850), teacher, lawyer, newspaper editor, was born at Wells, Rutland County, Vermont. He assisted Joseph Smith as a scribe during translation of the Book of Mormon and with other church writings. Witness to early events connected with the foundation of Mormonism. One of the Three Witnesses to the Book of Mormon, and a participant in the priesthood restoration. Married Elizabeth Ann Whitmer, 1832. Member of the Kirtland high council. Appointed assistant president of the Church in 1834. He left the Church in 1838 but returned ten years later. Practiced law in Ohio and Wisconsin. Died at Richmond, Ray County, Missouri. (Cook, *Revelations*, 14; Jenson, *Biographical Encyclopedia*, 1:246-51; R. L. Anderson, *Investigating the Book of Mormon Witnesses*, 37-65; Stanley P. Gunn, *Oliver Cowdery, Second Elder and Scribe* [Salt Lake City: Bookcraft, Inc., 1962].)

Cowdery, Warren A. (1788-1851), physician, druggist, farmer. Older brother of Oliver Cowdery, born at Poultney, Rutland County, Vermont. Married Patience Simonds, 1814. Practiced medicine in Vermont and Freedom, New York. Moved to Freedom in 1815; became postmaster, 1824. Converted to Mormonism, 1831. Appointed president of the Church at Freedom, 1834. Moved to Kirtland, Ohio, in 1836 and was involved in managing the book bindery and printing office. Also editor of the *Messenger and Advocate* and clerk to Joseph Smith. Became disaffected and left the Church in 1838. In 1850 farmed at Kirtland, where he died. (Carl C. Curtis, Cowdery Genealogical Material, Typescript, LDS Church Family History Library; Cook, *Revelations*, 214-15.)

Cowdery, William (1765-1847), father of Oliver Cowdery. Born at East Haddam, Middlesex County, Connecticut. Married Rebecca Fuller about 1787. Parents of eight children. Resided at Wells, Vermont, prior to joining Latter-day Saints and moving to Kirtland, Ohio. He died at Kirtland, Ohio. (Family Group Records Collection; Curtis, Cowdery Genealogy.)

Crosier, Harlow (1812- ?), farmer, carpenter. Born in Berkshire County, Massachusetts. Cousin of Almon W. Babbitt. Moved to Mentor, Ohio, 1837. Married Mary S. Fowler in 1839 in Lake County, Ohio. Soon after marriage, moved to Naperville, DuPage County, Illinois, where he was living in 1882. (Lake County, Ohio, Marriage Record, 59, microfilm of typescript, LDS Church Family History Library; Rufus Blanchard, *History of DuPage County, Illinois* [Chicago: O. L. Baskin & Co., 1882]: 7; U.S. Census: DuPage County, Illinois, 1850, 1860.)

Culver, Aaron (c.1766-1831), residing at Colesville, New York, in 1830. Married Esther Peck. Sold a hundred-acre farm and traveled to Jackson County, Missouri, with the Colesville Mormons in 1831. He was one of twelve men to lay "the first log as a foundation for Zion" at the 2 August dedication of that land. He died shortly thereafter. (*Utah Genealogical Magazine*, 27:77; Hartley, *They Are My Friends*.)

Culver, Esther Peck (1766-1836), born at Attleborough, Bristol County, Massachusetts. After her baptism, moved with her husband, Aaron Culver, to Jackson County, Missouri, with the Colesville Saints in 1831. She was widowed when her husband died in 1831. Died at Gallatin, Daviess County, Missouri. (*Utah Genealogical Magazine*, 27:77; Hartley, *They Are My Friends*.)

Daley, Moses (1794-1865), born at Wallkill, Ulster County, New York. Married Almira Barber, 1819. Missionary in Michigan, 1832. Settled at Adam-ondi-Ahman, Caldwell County, Missouri. Participant in the Gallatin election fight in Caldwell County, Missouri, 1838. Crossed plains, 1848. Settled at San Bernardino, California. Died at Riverside, California. (Carter, *Our Pioneer Heritage* 4:433; Black, "Membership," 13:79-82; Journal History, 4 June, 6 August 1838.)

Davidson, James (1779-1847), one of the "Vermont Sufferers" who settled on 500 acres of land near Bainbridge, Chenango County, New York, about 1797. Living in proximity of Josiah Stowell in Bainbridge in 1830. Died at Afton, Chenango County, New York. (U.S. Census: Chenango County, New York, 1820-1840; James H. Smith, *History of Chenango and Madison Counties, New York*, 149, 156-57, 164; Cemetery, Church, and Town records of Chenango County, New York, in Mrs. Frank H. Parcells, "Unpublished Cemetery, Church and Town Records . . . of the National Society Daughters of the American Revolution, 1930-31," 4, Microfilm of typescript, LDS Church Family History Library.)

Davis, Marvel Chapin (1801-1877), physician, born at Wardsboro, Windham County, Vermont. Married Rebecca Jane Sloan, 1823. Died at Seville, Medina County, Ohio. (Family Group Records Collection; U.S. Census: Medina County, Ohio, 1850.)

Dayton, Hiram (1798-1881), farmer, born at Herkimer, Herkimer County, New York. Married Permelia Bundy, 1820. Living in Parkman, Geauga County, Ohio in 1830. Joined Latter-day Saints in 1832. Moved to Kirtland, Ohio in 1834; Far West, Missouri, in 1838; Nauvoo, Illinois, in 1839. President of twelfth quorum of elders at Nauvoo. Crossed plains to Salt Lake Valley, 1849. Settled at Cedar Fort. Died at American Fork, Utah. (Family Group Records Collection; Black, "Membership," 13:642-48; Leland M. Dayton and Alta A. Dayton, "Record of the Posterity of Hiram Dayton and Permelia Bundy Dayton," September 1961, 9-17, Typescript, LDS Church Family History Library.)

Denton, Solomon Wilbur (1816-1864), born at Fitchville, Huron County, Ohio. Participated in the march of Zion's Camp, 1834. Married Fanny M. Stanley in 1835. Proselyting with Don Carlos Smith in New York, 1836. He was employed in the Kirtland printing office until he left the Church in 1837. Co-editor of the Pontiac (Michigan) *Jacksonian*, 1838-1844. Postmaster at Pontiac, 1844-1848, 1853-1860. Discharged from Civil War service, 1862. Died at Pontiac, Oakland County, Michigan. (International Genealogical Index; Robinson, "Items of Personal History," 1 [August 1889]; Backman, *Profiles*, 21; *History of Oakland County, Michigan* [Philadelphia: L. H. Everts & Co., 1877]: xvii, 86, 702.)

Doniphan, Alexander William (1808-1887), born in Mason County, Kentucky. Graduate of Augusta College. Opened a law office in Lexington, Missouri, 1830. In 1833 moved to Liberty, Clay County, Missouri, where he became a prominent lawyer. Elected to the state legislature in 1836, 1840, 1854. Employed as legal counsel by the Mormons in Missouri beginning in 1833. During the Mormon difficulties of 1838, he commanded the first brigade of David Atchison's third division of Missouri militia. Later that year he refused to carry out an execution order against Mormon leaders. He fought in the Mexican War and later refused a general's commission in both the Union and Confederate armies during the Civil War. He died at Richmond, Missouri. (David C. Roller and Robert W. Twyman, eds., *The Encyclopedia of Southern History* [Baton Rouge: Louisana State University, 1979], 367; Smith, *History of the Church*, 1:425; 3:190-91; Gregory Maynard, "Alexander Doniphan: Man of Justice," *BYU Studies* 13 (Summer 1973): 462-72; also Maynard, "Alexander William Doniphan, the Forgotten Man from Missouri" M.A. thesis, Brigham Young University, 1973;

André Paul DuChateau, "Missouri Colossus, Alexander William Doniphan, 1808-1887" (Ph.D. diss., Oklahoma State University, 1973.)

Dort, David (1793-1841), miller, was born at Surry, Cheshire County, New Hampshire. Moved to Michigan about 1822. Married Joseph Smith's cousin, Mary, and later her sister Fanny, daughters of Joseph's maternal uncle and aunt Stephen and Temperance Mack. Converted to Mormonism by Lucy Mack Smith, 1831. Participant in march of Zion's Camp from Michigan, 1834. Member of Kirtland high council, 1837; Far West high council, 1838; and Nauvoo high council, 1839. Left Church and joined Methodists. Died in Nauvoo, Illinois. (Cook, *Revelations*, 256; John and Audrey Cumming, *The Pilgrimage of Temperance Mack* [Mount Pleasant, Michigan: Published by authors, 1967], 5,7,48-49.)

Draper, Zemira (1812-1876), farmer, miller, born at Crambe, Northumberland County, Ontario, Canada. Baptized in 1834. Moved to Kirtland, Ohio, 1835. Married Ellen Bradshaw, 1838. With the Church in Ohio, Missouri, Illinois. Migrated to Utah in 1848; settled in the tenth ward. Moved to Willow Creek, later renamed Draper, Utah, in 1850. Appointed first counselor in bishopric. In 1862 sent to colonize Rockville, Washington County, Utah, where he died after serving as bishop's counselor and justice of the peace. (Family Group Records Collection; Delbert M. Draper, *The Mormon Drapers* [Salt Lake City: Published by author, 1958], 295-305; Esshom, *Pioneers and Prominent Men*, 848.)

Eaton, Frazier (1780- ?), sexton, born in New Hampshire. Living in Alleghany County, New York, both before and after his association with the Latter-day Saints. He evidently lived for a time in Kirtland, Ohio, in the 1830s, and in Hancock County, Illinois, in 1840, but by 1850 he was back in Rushford. According to George A. Smith, Eaton had donated $700 for the building of the Kirtland Temple, but when he was unable to attend the dedication, after arriving late, he left the Church. (U.S. Census: Alleghany County, New York, 1820-1850; New York State Census: Alleghany County, 1855; George A. Smith Discourse, 15 November 1864, in *Journal of Discourses*, 11:9.)

Elliott, David (1799-1855), blacksmith, born at Charleston, Montgomery County, New York; moved to Ithaca, New York. Joined the Latter-day Saints in 1831. Married Mary Cahoon, 1831. Participated in march of Zion's Camp, 1834. Member of the first quorum of seventy. Moved to Missouri with the Kirtland Camp, 1838. Settled at Springfield, Illinois after departure from Missouri. He died at Salt Lake City. (Backman, *Profiles*, 23, 93, 117, 121; Smith, *History of the Church*, 2:203; Family Group Record Collection.)

Emmett, James (1803-1852/3), born in Boone County, Kentucky. Joined the Church in Illinois in 1832. Moved to Clay County, Missouri,

1836. Proselyting in states between Ohio and Missouri, 1835-1837. Disfellowshipped and reinstated, 1837. Appointed to Iowa high council, 1841. Policeman at Nauvoo, 1843. Named to western exploring expedition by Joseph Smith in February 1844. After the death of the Prophet, Emmett led a company west that eventually stopped in what became South Dakota. Most of the company later reunited with the Church. In 1849 Emmett went to California, where he died. (Family Group Record Collection; Smith, *History of the Church*, 4:352; 6:149; 7:135; Dale Morgan, "Reminiscences of James Holt: A Narrative of the Emmett Company," *Utah Historical Quarterly* 23 [January, April 1955]: 1-33, 151-79; Gerald E. Jones, "An Early Mormon Settlement in South Dakota," *South Dakota History* 1 [Spring 1971]: 119-31.)

Felshaw, William (1800-1867), contractor and builder. Born at Granville, Washington County, New York. Married Mary Gilbert, 1826. Converted to Mormonism in Boston by Orson Hyde and Samuel H. Smith in 1832. Lived at Hoosick, Rensselaer County, New York, before moving to Kirtland, Ohio, about 1833. Carpenter on Kirtland, Nauvoo, and Salt Lake temples. Migrated to Utah in 1851. Member of Utah territorial legislature, 1854. Traveled to Wyoming to help relieve stranded handcart companies in 1856. Died at Fillmore, Utah. (Family Group Records Collection; Smith, *History of the Church*, 7:326; Esshom, *Pioneers and Prominent Men*, 868.)

Follett, King (1788-1844), born at Winchester, Cheshire County, New Hampshire. Married Louisa Tanner prior to 1816. Living in Cayahoga County, Ohio, when he joined the Latter-day Saints in 1831. Member of second quorum of seventy. During the difficulties in Missouri in 1838, Follett was imprisoned in Richmond and Columbia. He was a Hancock County, Illinois, constable. Killed digging a well at Nauvoo. His funeral sermon became the occasion for the Joseph Smith "King Follett discourse." (Family Group Records Collection; Smith, *History of the Church*, 3:335, 401-2; 6:248-49; Andrew Jenson, *The Historical Record* [Salt Lake City, 1882-1890], 5:31; Donald Q. Cannon, "The King Follett Discourse: Joseph Smith's Greatest Sermon in Historical Perspective," *BYU Studies* 18 [Winter 1978]: 179-225.)

Fordham, Elijah (1798-1879), lumber dealer, carpenter. Born in New York City. Married Jane Ann Fisher, 1822. Living in Pontiac, Michigan, 1831-33. Participant in march of Zion's Camp in 1834. As the only Church member in New York City in 1837, he assisted the missionaries en route to Great Britain. Miraculously healed by Joseph Smith, 1839. Appointed to Iowa high council, 1839. Migrated to Utah in 1850. Died at Wellsville, Cache County, Utah. (Family Group Records Collection; Smith, *History of the Church*, 2:183, 494; 4:14; Black, "Membership," 10:736-42.)

Foster, Solon (1811-1896), farmer, born at Danby, Tompkins

County, New York. Joined the Latter-day Saints, 1833. Went to Missouri with Zion's Camp, 1834. Called to first quorum of seventy, 1837. Married Sarah Downing in Nauvoo, 1841. Arrived in Salt Lake Valley, 1850. Called to help colonize St. George, Utah, 1861. Died at Salt Lake City, Utah. (Black, "Membership," 10:917-18.)

Gause, Jesse, born Jesse Goss (1784?–1836?), served as a counselor with Sidney Rigdon to Joseph Smith in the Church presidency from 8 March 1832 until his disaffection later the same year. Born at East Marlborough, Chester County, Pennsylvania, Gause had been a member of the Society of Friends before joining the Latter-day Saints. He accompanied Joseph Smith to Missouri in 1832 and, upon his return to Kirtland, Ohio, joined Zebedee Coltrin on a proselyting mission to the eastern states in August. At this point Gause fades from the annals of Mormon history. (D. Michael Quinn, "Jesse Gause: Joseph Smith's Little-known Counselor," *BYU Studies* 23 [Fall 1983]: 487-93.)

Gee, Salmon (1792-1845), born at Lyme, New London County, Connecticut. Married Sarah Watson Crane, 1814. Living in Geauga County, Ohio, when converted to Mormonism in 1832. One of the presidents of the seventy, 1837-38. Member of the Kirtland high council, 1841-44. Died at Ambrosia, Lee County, Iowa. (Family Group Records Collection; Jenson, *Biographical Encyclopedia*, 1:192-93.)

Gilbert, Algernon Sidney (1789-1834), born at New Haven, Connecticut. Married Elizabeth Van Benthusen, 1823. Merchant at Painesville, Ohio, and subsequently a partner with Newel K. Whitney in the firm Gilbert & Whitney at Kirtland, Ohio. Joined the Latter-day Saints in 1830. Operated a branch of the Gilbert-Whitney store in Independence, Missouri, 1831-33. Among the Saints driven from Jackson County, Missouri, 1833. Authored correspondence between Church leaders and Missouri Governor Dunklin during this crisis. Died of cholera during the march of Zion's Camp in 1834. (Cook, *Revelations*, 84; Smith, *History of the Church*, 2:118-19.)

Gilbert, Elizabeth Van Benthusen (1800-1891), born at Albany, Albany County, New York. Her sister, Keziah, was the mother of Mary Elizabeth Rollins Lightner. Married Algernon S. Gilbert, 1823. Baptized at Kirtland, Ohio, by Oliver Cowdery, 1830. She was the first Mormon woman to enter Jackson County, Missouri, traveling there with her husband and Joseph Smith in 1831. Lived with the Lightners after the death of her husband. Migrated to Utah in 1863. "Ordained" a midwife at Minersville, Utah, 1870. Died at Minersville. (*Deseret Evening News*, 26 June 1891; "Mary Elizabeth Rollins Lightner," *Utah Genealogical Magazine*, 26:250-53; "Organization of the Ward Relief Societies: Beaver County," *Our Pioneer Heritage*, 14:102; Black, "Membership," 44:195-96.)

Gilliam, Cornelius (1798-1848), born at Mt. Pisgah, Florida. Attracted by the frontier and fond of hunting, he settled consecutively in five western Missouri counties. Married Mary Crawford, 1820. He became a part-time Baptist minister in Clinton County and was sheriff of Clay County, 1830-34. Member of the committee that helped locate the Latter-day Saints in Clay County in 1833. Represented Platte County in the Missouri state senate, 1838-1842. Fought in the Black Hawk and Seminole Indian wars, 1832, 1835, and came to regard the natives as a nuisance and a threat. Led a wagon train to Oregon in 1844, where he became prominent in local government. While leading a strike against Cayuse Indians who had killed Marcus Whitman, Gilliam was killed at Wells Springs near the Umatilla River when a loaded rifle accidentally discharged. Gilliam County, Oregon, was named in his honor.

During the 1838 Mormon conflict in Missouri, Gilliam commanded men from the Platte purchase who were painted, feathered, and dressed like Indians. "Gilliam himself wore a full Indian costume, had his war paint on, and called himself 'the Delaware Chief,' and his men 'the Delaware amarujans.' They would whoop and yell, and otherwise comport themselves as savages.' " (*History of Caldwell and Livingston Counties, Missouri* [St. Louis: National Historical Company, 1886], 134; LeSueur, *The 1838 Mormon War*, 22-23, 25, 92, 128-29, 258; Fred Lockley, "Reminiscences of Mrs. Frank Collins Nee Martha Elizabeth Gilliam," *Oregon Historical Quarterly* 17 [December 1916]: 358-72.)

Goldthwaite, Lydia (1812-1884), was born at Sutton, Worcester County, Massachusetts. Married Calvin Bailey in 1828 but was deserted by her husband three years later. While visiting friends in Mt. Pleasant, Ontario, Canada, in 1833, she was converted by Joseph Smith. After returning to her parents in New York in 1834 and being derided for her religion, she gathered with the Saints at Kirtland in 1835. While working for Hyrum Smith, she met and married Newel Knight, who was boarding at Hyrum's home. Followed the Church through Missouri and Illinois. After the death of her husband in 1847 during the Mormon exodus, Lydia and seven children arrived in Utah in 1850. Died at St. George, Utah. (Jenson, *Biographical Encyclopedia*, 2:775-76; Hartley, *They Are My Friends*; "Homespun" [Susa Young Gates], *Lydia Knight's History*, Noble Women's Lives Series [Salt Lake City, Juvenile Instructor Office, 1883].)

Gould, Dean, son of John Gould, was a non-Mormon member of Zion's Camp in 1834. He was baptized upon his arrival in Missouri. (Smith, *History of the Church*, 2:72, 95.)

Gould, John (1808-1851), was born in Ontario, Canada. Baptized in June 1833. Proselyting in New York, 1834-35. Appointed a president in the first council of seventy, 1837. Married Abigail Harrington. Died at Cooley's Mill, Pottawatamie County, Iowa. (Cook, *Revelations*, 204; Jenson, *Biographical Encyclopedia*, 1:191.)

Grandin, Egbert B. (1806-1845), printer, publisher. Youngest of ten children. Grew up on a farm twelve miles north of Palmyra, New York. At age eighteen he began learning the printing trade at the weekly Palmyra newspaper, the *Wayne Sentinel*. Purchased the *Sentinel* and a bookstore in 1827. Married Harriet Rogers in 1828. In August 1829 Grandin contracted to print the Book of Mormon. The book came off the press the following March. Died at Palmyra. ("Historic Discoveries at the Grandin Building," *Ensign* 10 [July 1980]: 48-50; Golden A. Buchmiller, "Grandin Building Opens to Visitors in Palmyra," *Church News*, 30 October 1982; John H. Gilbert, "Memorandum," 8 September 1892, Typescript, King's Daughter's Free Library, Inc., Palmyra, New York.)

Greene, John P. (1793-1844), shoemaker. Born in Herkimer County, New York. Married Brigham Young's sister, Rhoda. Living in Mendon, New York, when he joined the Church. Appointed to the Kirtland, Ohio high council, 1836. Published *Facts Relative to the Expulsion of the Mormons . . . from Missouri,* 1839. Presided over the branch of the Church at New York City, 1839. Elected to the Nauvoo, Illinois, city council, 1841, and became city marshal, 1843. Under his direction as marshal, the Nauvoo *Expositor* was destroyed in June 1844. He was among those arrested in the *Expositor* case. Died a short time later at Nauvoo. (Jenson, *Biographical Encyclopedia*, 2:633-36; Smith, *History of the Church*, 3:347; 6:124; 6:124; 7:63, 487ff.)

Grover, Thomas (1807-1886), riverboat captain. Born at Whitehall, Washington County, New York. Married Caroline Whiting, 1828. Converted to Mormonism in 1834. Appointed to Kirtland, Ohio, high council, 1836; Far West, Missouri, high council, 1837; and Nauvoo, Illinois, high council, 1839. Arrived in Salt Lake Valley, 1847; settled at Farmington, Utah. Member of Utah legislature and probate judge of Davis County. Died at Farmington, Davis County, Utah. (Cook, *Revelations*, 259; Jenson, *Biographical Encyclopedia*, 4:137-40.)

Hale, Emma (1804-1879), born at Harmony, Susquehanna County, Pennsylvania. Married Joseph Smith, 1827. Assisted her husband as scribe during early translation work on the Book of Mormon. An 1830 revelation directed her to select hymns for a Church hymn book. Followed her husband during the movement of the Church from New York to Illinois. Appointed president of the Female Relief Society at Nauvoo, Illinois, in 1842. Remained in Illinois after the death of her husband in 1844. In 1847 she married Lewis Bidamon. Died at Nauvoo, Illinois. (Cook, *Revelations*, 37; Linda K. Newell and Valeen T. Avery, *Mormon Enigma: Emma Hale Smith* [Garden City, New York: Doubleday and Company, 1984].)

Hale, Isaac (1763-1839), hunter, farmer. Born at Waterbury, Connecticut, and raised in Wells, Vermont. He served in the Revolutionary

War. Married Elizabeth Lewis, 1789, and they became parents of nine children. Moved to Harmony, Pennsylvania, in 1791. In 1828 when persecution hampered work on the Book of Mormon in Manchester, New York, Joseph Smith continued the work under the protection of his father-in-law, Isaac Hale, in Harmony, Pennsylvania. But the following year Hale became embittered against Joseph and his work, forcing Joseph to move to Fayette, New York. Died in Pennsylvania. (Newell and Avery, *Mormon Enigma*, 1-8, 102; Porter, "A Study of the Origins of the Church," 114-18.)

Hall, Levi (1801-1867), farmer, born in Canada. Wife's name, Ruth. Converted to Mormonism and baptized in Broome County, New York, 1830. He apparently did not go to Ohio with the Colesville, New York, Saints in 1831. In 1850 farmed at Windsor, Broome County, New York, where he died. (U.S. Census: Broome County, New York, 1830, 1850; New York State Census: Broome County, 1835; Broome County, New York, Probate Records.)

Hancock, Solomon (1793-1847), born at Springfield, Hampden County, Massachusetts. Married Alta Adams, 1815. Converted to Mormonism in Ohio in 1830. Moved to Jackson County, Missouri, 1832. Appointed to Missouri high council, 1834. Presided over Yelrome branch in Hancock County, Illinois, 1844. Died in Iowa during Mormon exodus from Nauvoo. (Cook, *Revelations*, 77-78.)

Harris, Emer (1781-1869), farmer, carpenter. Born at Cambridge, Washington County, New York. Elder brother of Martin Harris. Married Roxana Peas, 1802. Joined the Latter-day Saints and moved to Kirtland, Ohio, 1831. Proselyting in Susquehanna County, Pennsylvania, with Martin Harris, 1832. Worked on Kirtland and Nauvoo temples. Member of Nauvoo Legion. Migrated to Utah, 1852. Appointed patriarch, 1853. Presided over high priests at Provo, Utah, 1855. Died at Logan, Cache County, Utah. (Family Group Records Collection; Emer Harris Biographical Sketch, Typescript, BYU Library; Cook, *Revelations*, 154-55; *Deseret Evening News*, 8 December 1869.)

Harris, Martin (1783-1875), farmer. Born at Easttown, Saratoga County, New York. In 1792 moved to Palmyra, New York, where he became a respected landowner. Assisted Joseph Smith as a scribe during translation of the Book of Mormon; paid printing costs for publication of the book. One of the Three Witnesses to the Book of Mormon. Participant in the march of Zion's Camp to Missouri, 1834. Member of the Kirtland high council. Left the Church in 1837; remained in the East until 1870, when he came to Salt Lake City and was rebaptized. Died at Clarkston, Cache County, Utah. (Cook, *Revelations*, 9; Jenson, *Biographical Encyclopedia*, 1:271-76; Wayne C. Gunnell, "Martin Harris—Witness and Benefactor to the Book of Mormon" [Master's thesis, Brigham Young University, 1955]; Anderson, *Investigating the Book of*

Mormon Witnesses, chapters 7, 8; Ronald W. Walker, "Martin Harris: Mormonism's Early Convert," *Dialogue* 19 [Winter 1986]: 29-43.)

Harris, Lucy (1792-1837), the ninth of ten children born to Rufus and Lucy Harris, brother of Nathan Harris; hence a cousin of her husband, Martin Harris. Probably born in Palmyra, New York. Married Martin Harris, 1808. Died at Palmyra, New York. (Family Group Records Collection.)

Harris, Nathan (1758-1835), farmer, hunter, fisherman; father of Martin Harris. Born at Smithfield, Providence County, Rhode Island. Married Rhoda Lapham prior to 1781. Among the first settlers at Palmyra, New York, where he moved from Rhode Island in 1893 and bought 600 acres. Died at Mentor, Lake County, Ohio. (Family Group Records Collection; "Old Newspapers – No. 23," *Palmyra Courier* [New York], 3, 10 May 1872.)

Harris, Preserved (1785-1867), a younger brother of Martin Harris, was born at Palmyra, Wayne County, New York. Married Nancy Warren prior to 1811. Died at Mentor, Lake County, Ohio. (Family Group Records Collection.)

Harris, Rhoda Lapham (1759-1849), wife of Nathan Harris. Born in Providence, Rhode Island. Moved with her husband to Palmyra, New York, 1793. Died at Mentor, Lake County, Ohio. (Family Group Records Collection; Thomas L. Cook, *Palmyra and Vicinity* [Palmyra, New York: Palmyra Courier-Journal, 1930], 202.)

Herritt, John (? -1840), member of the second quorum of seventies in Kirtland. Died while on a proselyting mission to the Fox Islands in Maine. (Black, "Membership," 22:452.)

Higbee, Elias (1795-1843), born at Galloway, Gloucester County, New Jersey. Married Elizabeth Ward, 1818. Baptized, 1832. Among the Saints driven from Jackson County, Missouri, 1833. Worked on Kirtland Temple, 1835. Member of Clay County, Missouri, high council, 1836; Far West, Missouri, high council, 1837. Church Recorder, 1838-1843. Traveled to Washington, D.C., with Joseph Smith in 1839 to seek redress for Missouri grievances. Died of cholera in Hancock County, Illinois. (Cook, *Revelations*, 225; Jenson, *Biographical Encyclopedia*, 1:253.)

Hill, Isaac (1806-1879), blacksmith, brickmaker. Born near Brighton, Beaver County, Pennsylvania. Married Mary Bell, 1827. Converted to Mormonism, 1833. Participated in march of Zion's Camp to Missouri, 1834. With Latter-day Saints in Missouri and Illinois. Migrated to Utah, 1850. Bishop of Salt Lake City 2nd Ward, 1854-1864. Missionary to Canada, 1857-1858. Moved to Bear Lake, 1864. Died at Fish Haven, Bear Lake County, Idaho. (Family Group Records Collection; Smith, *History of the Church*, 2:149; Jenson, *Biographical Encyclopedia*, 4:509; Journal of Isaac Hill, MS., LDS Church Archives.)

Hinkle, George M. (1802-1861), merchant, born in Kentucky. Appointed to the Missouri high council in January 1836 to replace Orson Pratt. During the Missouri conflict in 1838, he commanded the Mormon militia defending Far West, Caldwell County. Under the guise of a truce, he surrendered Church leaders to opposing forces, which resulted in the imprisonment of Joseph Smith and others. Hinkle testified for the state against his former associates at the November 1838 hearing in Richmond, Ray County. He was excommunicated in 1839. In later years he practiced medicine, kept a drugstore, and farmed. He died in Iowa. (Smith, *History of the Church*, 2:357; 3:188-89, 196-98, 210, 284; Pratt, *Autobiography*, 186; S.J. Hinkle, "A Biographical Sketch of G.M. Hinkle"; *Document Containing the Correspondence*, 125-29.)

Hitchcock, Jesse (1801-c.1846), born in Ash County, North Carolina. Member of the Missouri high council, 1836-37. Appointed acting scribe for Joseph Smith during illness of Warren Parrish in 1836. Called on mission in Illinois to disabuse public mind over arrest of the Prophet in 1843. Died at Mt. Pisgah, Iowa, while crossing the plains between 1846-1848. (Smith, *History of the Church*, 2:482; 5:485; Black, "Membership," 23:236; Susan W. Easton, "Inscriptions Found on Tombstones and Monuments in Early Latter-day Saint Burial Grounds," 11, Typescript, BYU Library.)

Hollister, John (1792-1839), born at Marbletown, Kingston County, New York. Married Lavina Clearwater, 1817. Living in Caroline, Tompkins County, New York, 1818-1835. Evidently moved to Portage County, Ohio, investigated Mormonism, joined the Church, then moved to Illinois, where he died before the 1840 census. A daughter, Sarah Ann, is listed in the Nauvoo temple records in 1846. (Family Group Records Collection; U.S. Census: Tompkins County, New York, 1830.)

Holmes, Erastus (1801-1863), was born in Pennsylvania. He settled at Newberry (later Mulberry), Clermont County, Ohio. Holmes apparently did not join the Latter-day Saints. He was postmaster of Mulberry, 1839-1847, and also a merchant in the town. In 1850 he was living in Cincinatti. He died at Milford, Clermont County. (U.S. Census: Clermont County, Ohio, 1830, 1840; Hamilton County, 1850; *History of Clermont County, Ohio* [Philadelphia: Lewis H. Everts, 1880], 465, 469; Whitt, *Clermont County, Ohio, Wills, Estates, and Guardianships, 1800-1851* [New Richmond, Ohio: A. M. Whitt, 1986], 3:144; Daughters of the American Revolution, "Monument Inscriptions Prior to 1900 from Cemeteries in Clermont County, Ohio," Milford I.O.O.F. Cemetery.)

Holmes, Milton (1811-1863), shoemaker. Born at Rowley, Essex County, Massachusetts. Married Aphia Woodman. He was living at Napoli, Cattaraugus County, New York, in 1830. Proselyting mission to Canada with Lyman Johnson in February 1834. Participated in the march of Zion's Camp to Missouri, 1834. Member of the second quorum of seventy. Missionary in England, 1840-41, 1844-45. Lived remainder of his life in Franklin County, Maine. (Smith, *History of the Church*, 2:35; Black, "Membership," 23:673-74; U.S. Census: Franklin County, Maine, 1850.)

Howe, Harriet, a Church member in Painesville, Ohio. Sister of Eber D. Howe, publisher of the Painesville *Telegraph*. Harriet helped make clothing for workmen and the veil for the Kirtland Temple. ("Journal History," 22 October 1867; Diary of Joseph Smith, 30 April 1834.)

Humphrey, Solomon (1775-1834), born at Canton, Hartford County, Connecticut. Married Ursula Andrews. Converted to Mormonism, 1831. Proselyting in eastern states, 1831-1832. Participated in march of Zion's Camp to Missouri, 1834. Died in Clay County, Missouri. (Jenson, *Biographical Encyclopedia*, 4:689-90; Cook, *Revelations*, 78.)

Hyde, Orson (1805-1878), clerk, schoolteacher, businessman, lawyer. Born at Oxford, New Haven County, Connecticut. Converted by Sidney Rigdon, 1831. Baptized sixty during proselyting mission with Samuel Smith in eastern states, 1832. Appointed clerk to First Presidency, 1833. Participant in Zion's Camp, 1834. Married Marinda Nancy Johnson, 1834. Member of the Council of Twelve, 1835-1878. Mission to England, 1837-1838, 1846-1847; Palestine, 1841-1842. Member of the Nauvoo city council, 1841. Presided over Mormons at Winter Quarters, Nebraska, 1847-50. Published *Frontier Guardian*. Moved to Utah in 1852. Appointed associate judge of the supreme court for Utah; member of territorial legislature; president of the senate. He died at Spring City, Sanpete County, Utah. (Cook, *Revelations*, 109-10; Jenson, *Biographical Encyclopedia*, 1:80-82; Hill, "Historical Study of the Life of Orson Hyde.")

Jackman, Levi (1797-1876), carpenter. Born at Vershire, Orange County, Vermont. Married Angeline Myers Brady. Living in Portage County, Ohio, when he joined the Church in 1831. Settled in Jackson County, Missouri, 1832. Appointed to Missouri high council, 1834; Far West high council, 1837; Salt Lake City high council, 1848. Returned to Kirtland from Missouri in July 1835 and worked on the temple. Arrived in Salt Lake Valley with Mormon pioneers, 1847. Counselor in Salt Lake City 16th Ward bishopric. Died at Salem, Utah County, Utah. (Jenson, *Biographical Encyclopedia*, 2:769-70; Smith, *History of the Church*, 2:124, 524; 7:629; *Deseret Evening News*, 26 July 1876.)

Jackson, Truman (1802- ?), farmer. Born in Vermont. Evidently joined the Latter-day Saints in Ohio but did not follow the Church west. Member of elders quorum in Kirtland, 1836; and seventies quorum, 1837. Married Ann Brown, 1837; living at Gold, Bureau County, Illinois, 1860. (U.S. Census: Bureau County, Illinois, 1860; Smith, *History*, 2:400; *Messenger and Advocate* 3:676.)

James, Samuel (1814-1876), born in Pennsylvania. Appointed to the Kirtland, Ohio high council, 1836. Married Marian Evans, 1841. Extensive proselyting in eastern states, 1835-1844. He followed Sidney Rigdon after death of Joseph Smith. At a conference in Pittsburgh, Pennsylvania, in April 1845, Rigdon appointed James one of his counselors. Listed as Bible agent in 1860, 1870 census. Died at Steubenville, Jefferson County, Ohio. (Smith, *History of the Church*, 2:366; 5:386; *The History of the Reorganized Church of Jesus Christ of Latter Day Saints* [Independence, Missouri: Herald House, 1967], 3:8.)

Johnson, Edward (1809-1890), born at Morristown, Morris County, New Jersey. Married Matilda Archer, 1833. (Black, "Membership," 25:519.)

Johnson, John (1779-1843), farmer. Born at Chesterfield, Cheshire County, New Hampshire. Married Mary Elsa Jacobs, 1800. Settled at Hiram, Ohio, in 1818 and joined the Latter-day Saints in 1831. Joseph Smith resided at the Johnson home in Hiram during work on Bible revision. Johnson moved to Kirtland, Ohio, in 1832. Member of the Kirtland high council, 1834-37. Became disaffected and withdrew from the Church, 1838. Died at Kirtland, Ohio. (Cook, *Revelations*, 199; *Deseret Weekly*, 26 May 1858; Keith Perkins, "A House Divided: The John Johnson Family," *Ensign* 9 [1979]: 54-59.

Johnson, John, Jr. (1805-1887), farmer, born at Pomfret, Windsor County, Vermont. Living at Hiram, Portage County, Ohio, 1850. In 1855 moved to vicinity of Council Bluffs, Pottawattamie County, Iowa, where he died. (Family Group Records Collection; U.S. Census: Portage County, Ohio, 1850; Pottawattamie Co., Iowa, Probate Index.)

Johnson, Luke (1807-1861), farmer, teacher, doctor; son of John Johnson. Born at Pomfret, Windsor County, Vermont. Living in Hiram, Ohio, when converted in 1831. Proselyting in Pennsylvania, Virginia, and Kentucky, 1831-1833. Married Susan Poteet, 1833. Accompanied Zion's Camp to Missouri, 1834. Member of Quorum of Twelve, 1835-1837. Left the Church in 1838. Rebaptized in 1846. Arrived in Salt Lake Valley with Mormon pioneers, 1847. Became bishop in St. John, Tooele County, Utah. Died at Salt Lake City. (Cook, *Revelations*, 110-11; Jenson, *Biographical Encyclopedia*, 1:85-86.)

Johnson, Lyman Eugene (1811-1856), merchant, lawyer; son of John Johnson. Born at Pomfret, Windsor County, Vermont. Baptized in 1831. Missionary with Orson Pratt to the eastern states, New England, and Canada, 1832-1833. Married Sarah Lang. One of eight men named in an 1834 revelation to solicit funds and volunteers to assist the Saints driven from Jackson County. Member of Zion's Camp, 1834. Member of the Council of Twelve, 1835-1838. Left the Church, 1838. Living in Iowa, 1842. Died by drowning at Prairie du Chien, Wisconsin. (Cook, *Revelations*, 111; Jenson, *Biographical Encyclopedia*, 1:91-92.)

Johnson, Olmstead (1809-1834), son of John Johnson, Sr., was born at Pomfret, Windsor County, Vermont. (Family Group Records Collection.)

Johnson, Orson (1803/4-1883), innkeeper, farmer. Born at Bath, Grafton County, New Hampshire, where he was living in 1830. Converted to Mormonism in 1832. Participated in the march of Zion's Camp in 1834. Member of the Kirtland high council in 1834. Left the Church in 1837. Living at Peoria, Illinois, 1840, 1850; and, in 1880, at Altona, Knox County, Illinois, where he died. (Smith, *History of the Church*, 2:151; U.S. Census: Peoria County, Illinois, 1840, 1850; Knox County, 1880; "Journal History," 3 February 1832.)

Jolly, Elizabeth (1788-1843), wife of William Jolly. Died at Parkman, Geauga County, Ohio. (Warren and Grosvenor, "A Monumental Work," 482.)

Jolly, Harriet (1816-1865), born in New York, a daughter of William and Elizabeth Jolly. Married Arza Bisbee in Geauga County, Ohio, 1833. Moved to Missouri about 1837. Living in Richmond, Ray County, 1840-1850, and probably died there. (Geauga County, Ohio, Marriage Records, 132; U.S. Census: Ray County, Missouri, 1840, 1850; *History of Ray County, Missouri*, 695.)

Jolly, John (1812-1885), farmer; born in New York. Son of William and Elizabeth Jolly. Married Hamuthiel Rowler in Trumbull County, Ohio, 1849. Settled in Parkman, Geauga County, Ohio, where he died. After moving to Ohio he apparently left the LDS Church. (Warren and Grosvenor, "A Monumental Work," 512; U.S. Census: Geauga County, Ohio, 1850, 1860; International Genealogical Index.)

Jolly, Julia Ann (1815-1889), daughter of William and Elizabeth Jolly, born in New York. Married David Whitmer, 1831. Died at Richmond, Ray County, Missouri. (Mary C. Dear, *Two Hundred Thirty-Eight Years of the Whitmer Family: 1737-1976* [Richmond, Missouri: Beck Printing Co., 1976], 41; U.S. Census: Ray County, Missouri, 1850.)

Jolly, Vincent (1809-1866), farmer; born in New York. Son of William and Elizabeth Jolly. Apparantly left the church after settling in Geauga County, Ohio. Married Betsy Curtis, 1834. Died at Parkman, Geauga County, Ohio. (Warren and Grosvenor, "A Monumental Work," 489; "Geauga County Marriage Records, 132;" U.S. Census: Geauga County, Ohio, 1830, 1850.)

Jolly, William (1777-1863), farmer; father-in-law of David Whitmer. Born in Massachusetts. Daughter, Julia Ann, married David, 1831. Living in Parkman, Geauga, County, Ohio, when he joined the Latter-day Saints. He apparently did not remain with the Church. Died at Parkman, Ohio. (Warren and Grosvenor, "A Monumental Work," 482; U.S. Census: Geauga County, Ohio, 1830, 1850.)

Kimball, Heber C. (1801-1868), blacksmith, potter. Born at Sheldon, Franklin County, Vermont. Married Vilate Murray, 1822. Converted to Mormonism, 1832 at Mendon, New York. Participant in march of Zion's Camp, 1834. Member of the Council of the Twelve, 1835-47. Missionary to England, 1837-38, 1839-41. Elected to Nauvoo city council, 1841. Arrived in Salt Lake Valley with Mormon pioneers, 1847. Counselor to Brigham Young in the First Presidency, 1847-68. Died at Salt Lake City. (Cook, *Revelations*, 263-64; Jenson, *Biographical Encyclopedia*, 1:34-37. Stanley B. Kimball, *Heber C. Kimball: Mormon Patriarch and Pioneer* [Urbana, Illinois: University of Illinois Press, 1981].)

Kimball, Susanna (1767-1859), mother of Newel K. Whitney, was born at Mendon, Worcester County, Massachusetts. Married Samuel Whitney, 1792. Joined the Latter-day Saints, 1835. Died at Kirtland, Ohio. (Larry N. Poulsen, "The Life and Contributions of Newel K. Whitney" [Master's thesis, Brigham Young University, 1966], 66.)

King, Austin A. (1802-1870), governor of Missouri, 1848-1852. Born in Sullivan County, Tennessee. In 1830 he moved to Missouri, where he practiced law at Columbia. In 1837, upon his appointment to a circuit judgeship by Governor Lilburn Boggs, he moved to Richmond, Ray County. Between 1837 and 1848 he served as judge of Missouri's fifth judicial circuit, consisting of the counties of Clinton, Ray, Caldwell, Clay, Platte, and Buchanan. In November 1838 he presided at the preliminary hearing of Joseph Smith and other Mormon leaders at Richmond. Represented Missouri as a Union Democrat in the U.S. Congress, 1862-64. Had a successful law practice in St. Louis prior to his death. (*History of Ray County, Missouri*, 259-61; Howard Conard, *Encyclopedia of the History of Missouri* [St. Louis: The Southern History Company, 1901], 3:537; Dumas Malone, *Dictionary of American Biography*, 10:382.)

Kingsbury, Horace (1798-1853), jeweler, silversmith; born in New Hampshire. Married Diantha Stiles, 1826. In 1827 he moved to Painesville, Ohio, where he died. Mayor of Painesville, 1848. (U.S. Census: Lake County, Ohio, 1850; Joseph A. Kingsbury, *A Pendulous Edition of Kingsbury Genealogy* [Pittsburgh: Murdoch-Kerr Press, 1901], 230; Benjamin W. Dwight, *History of the Descendants of Elder John Strong* [Albany: Joel Munsell, 1871], 1039; *History of Geauga and Lake Counties, Ohio* [Philadelphia: Williams Brothers, 1878], 214.)

Kingsbury, Joseph (1812-1898), born at Enfield, Hartford County, Connecticut. Converted to Mormonism in Kirtland, Ohio, 1832. Married Caroline Whitney, daughter of Newel K. Whitney, 1836. Clerk in Newel K. Whitney store at Kirtland. Appointed to the Kirtland high council, 1835, and Iowa high council, 1841. Among Saints expelled from Missouri, 1838. Clerk in Joseph Smith's Nauvoo store. Arrived in Salt Lake Valley, 1847. Bishop of Salt Lake City 2nd Ward, 1851-1852. Appointed superintendent of the Church Tithing Office, 1867. Ordained a patriarch,

1883. Died at Salt Lake City. (Edward Tullidge, *History of Salt Lake City* [Salt Lake City: Star Printing Co., 1886], 121-23; Whitney, *History of Utah*, 4:114-15; Lyndon W. Cook, *Joseph C. Kingsbury: A Biography* [Provo, Utah: Grandin Book Co., 1985].)

Knight, Joseph, Sr. (1772-1847), born at Oakham, Worcester County, Massachusetts. Married Polly Peck about 1795. Moved to Bainbridge, Chenango County, New York, in 1808 and two years later, to Colesville, Broome County, New York, where he remained nineteen years. Owned a farm, gristmill, and carding machines, and, according to his son, "was not rich, yet possessed enough of this world's goods to secure himself and family the necessities and comforts of life." When Joseph Smith obtained the Book of Mormon plates in 1827, Knight was visiting the Smith home in Manchester, New York, and Joseph used Knight's horse and buggy as a means of conveyance on that occasion. Among the first converts to Mormonism, his family formed the nucleus of a small branch of the Church at Colesville. Helped pioneer the Mormon settlement at Independence, Missouri, in 1831. Died at Mt. Pisgah, Iowa, during the Mormon exodus from Illinois. (Journal of Newel Knight, 1, MS., LDS Church Archives; Smith, *History of the Church*, 1:47; Cook, *Revelations*, 20-22; Hartley, *They Are My Friends*; Jessee, "Joseph Knight's Recollection.")

Knight, Joseph, Jr. (1808-1866), miller, farmer, wheelwright; youngest son of Joseph Knight, Sr. Born at Halifax, Windham County, Vermont. Family moved to Chenango County, New York, the year he was born. Worked with Joseph Smith on his father's farm in Broome County, New York. Transported Joseph and Oliver Cowdery from Harmony, Pennsylvania to Fayette, New York, in 1829, where work on the Book of Mormon was completed. Moved to Ohio and on to Missouri in 1831. Married Betsy Covert, 1832. Built the first mill used by the Church in Jackson County, Missouri; also the printing office. Among those driven from Jackson County, 1833. Later lived at Lima, Nauvoo, and Laharpe, Illinois. Bishop at Winter Quarters during Mormon exodus west. Arrived in Utah, 1851. Missionary to Moqui Indians, 1862. Died in Salt Lake City. (Joseph Knight autobiographical sketch, MS. LDS Church Archives; Hartley, *They Are My Friends*; "Journal History," 26 Oct., 16 Nov. 1862; Black, "Membership," 26:4-8.)

Knight, Newel (1800-1847), miller. Born at Marlborough, Windham County, Vermont. Living at Colesville, New York, when converted by Joseph Smith. Moved to Ohio, then Missouri, in 1831. Among those expelled from Jackson County, Missouri, 1833. Member of Clay County high council, 1834; Far West high council, 1836; and Nauvoo high council, 1839-1845. His first wife, Sally Coburn, died in Missouri in September 1834. Returning to Ohio, he worked on the Kirtland Temple and boarded at the Hyrum Smith home, where he met Lydia Bailey.

Died during the Mormon exodus from Nauvoo to Salt Lake Valley. (Journal of Newel Knight, MS.; Jenson, *Biographical Encyclopedia*, 2:773-75; Cook, *Revelations*, 78-79; Hartley, *They Are My Friends*; "Newel Knight's Journal," *Scraps of Biography*, Tenth Book of the Faith-Promoting Series [Salt Lake City: Juvenile Instructor Office, 1883], 47-104.)

Knight, Polly (1811-1844), born at Bainbridge, Chenango County, New York. Traveled with her family and other Colesville Saints to Jackson County, Missouri, 1831. Married William Stringham after the death of his first wife, her sister, Esther. Died at Nauvoo, Hancock County, Illinois. (*Utah Genealogical and Historical Magazine*, 26:148; Hartley, *They Are My Friends*.)

Knight, Polly Peck (1774-1831), sister of Hezekiah Peck. Born at Guilford, Windham County, Vermont. Married Joseph Knight, Sr., about 1795. Died in Jackson County, Missouri. (*Utah Genealogical and Historical Magazine*, 27:77-78; Hartley, *They Are My Friends*.)

Knight, Sally Colburn (1804-1834), born at Guilford, Chenango County, New York. Married Newel Knight, 1825. Died at Turnham's Landing, Clay County, Missouri. (Family Group Records Collection; *Messenger and Advocate*, 1:12; Hartley, *They Are My Friends*, 12, 102.)

Knight, Vinson (1804-1842) born at Chester, Washington County, New York. Married Martha McBride, 1826. Owned a farm at Perrysburg, New York, when converted in 1834. Appointed counselor to Bishop Newel K. Whitney in Kirtland, 1836. Church land agent, 1839. Appointed bishop of Nauvoo Lower Ward, 1839, and presiding bishop of the Church, 1841. Elected to Nauvoo city council, 1841. Died at Nauvoo. (Cook, *Revelations*, 265.)

Lane, George (1784-1859), Methodist minister; born near Kingston, Ulster County, New York. In the summer of 1819 Lane attended the Genesee Conference at Vienna (later Phelps), Ontario County, New York, a convocation of more than a hundred ministers representing New York, Pennsylvania, and the Upper and Lower Canada District. At this conference Lane was appointed presiding elder of the Susquehanna District, where he served until July 1824, when he was appointed to preside over the Ontario District. This included the circuits of Lyons, Ontario, Seneca, and Canandaigua, the area of Smith family residence. (Porter, "Reverend George Lane.")

Lewis, Job, in his fifties, owned a tavern in Westfield, Chautauqua County, New York, in 1833. Wife's name was Margaret. He apparently joined the Church in the early 1830s. Excommunicated for treating the Church with contempt in 1836. (U.S. Census: Chautauqua County, New York, 1830; "Journal History," 23 May 1836.)

Lewis, Joshua (1795-1835), among the early settlers of Jackson County, Missouri. He was converted to Mormonism by the Lamanite missionaries who came there in the fall of 1830. Died in Clay County, Missouri. ("Journal History," 3 February 1931; Cannon and Cook, *Far West Record*, 274.)

Lucas, Samuel D. (1799-1868), born in Washington County, Kentucky. One of the early settlers of Independence, Missouri, where he owned a store. Judge of Jackson County court, 1831. Major-general of the fourth division of Missouri militia. One of the organizers of the Independence masonic lodge, 1847. Married Myra Symington in 1850 after the death of his first wife. Served as Jackson County clerk, 1842-1848. Held office continuously until 1865.

Lucas and David R. Atchison were commanding third- and fourth-division militia units during the Mormon conflict in Caldwell County, Missouri, in October 1838, when Atchison was dismissed from his post. This left Lucas as the senior officer. Apparently unaware that Major-general John B. Clark (at the time proceeding toward the scene of action from Howard County with militia of his first division) had been named supreme commander of the forces operating against the Saints, Lucas presided at the Mormon surrender at Far West. (*History of Caldwell and Livingston Counties, Missouri*, 132-33; *Document Containing the Correspondence*, 70-72; Elizabeth P. Ellsberry, "Marriage Records of Jackson Co., Missouri" [Chillicothe, Missouri: n.d.], 51; *History of Jackson County*, [Kansas City: Union Historical Company, 1881], 105, 170, 179, 643, 806-7; Pearl Wilcox, *Jackson County Pioneers* [Independence: Published by author, 1975], 204-5.)

Lyman, Amasa M. (1813-1877), farmer; born at Lyman, Grafton County, New Hampshire. Joined Latter-day Saints and moved to Kirtland, Ohio, 1832. Participant in march of Zion's Camp, 1834. Married Maria Tanner, 1835. Although arrested with Joseph Smith at Far West, Missouri, in 1838, he was not charged at the Richmond hearing. Appointed an apostle in 1842, a member of the First Presidency the following year, and the Council of Twelve, 1844. Arrived with pioneer company in Salt Lake Valley in 1847. Assisted in colonization of, and presided over settlement at San Bernardino, California, 1851-1857. President of European mission, 1860-1862. Colonized Fillmore, Utah, 1863. Excommunicated in 1870 for teaching false doctrine. Died at Fillmore, Utah. (Cook, *Revelations*, 266-67; *Deseret Weekly* 8 (1858): 117-18, 121-22.)

Mack, Almira (1805-1886), youngest daughter of Joseph Smith's maternal uncle Steven Mack and his wife Temperance Bond. Born at Tunbridge, Orange County, Vermont. Baptized by David Whitmer, 1830. Married William Scobey, who died in 1832 a year after their marriage. Married Benjamin Covey, 1836. Involved with Latter-day Saints in Ohio, Missouri, Illinois. Crossed the plains to Utah, 1848. Settled in the Salt Lake City 12th Ward, where her husband presided as bishop. Accompanied her husband on colonizing mission to Carson Valley, 1856-1857. Died at Salt Lake City. (Locke A. Sprague, "The Progenitors and Descendants of Col. Steven Mack and Temperance Bond Mack," MS. LDS Family History Library; *Deseret Evening News*, 11 March 1886; *An Enduring Legacy* [Salt Lake City, 1980], 3:123-24; John and Audrey Cumming, *The Pilgrimage of Temperance Mack*.)

Mack, Lucy (1775-1856), daughter of Solomon Mack and Lydia Gates. Married Joseph Smith, Sr., 1796. Mother of eight sons and three daughters. Seven of her sons preceded her in death. Her *Biographical Sketches of Joseph Smith*, written in 1845, is an important source for family and church history. After the violent death of her sons Joseph and Hyrum and the departure of the Saints to the West, she remained in Illinois with her family until her death. (Jenson, *Biographical Encyclopedia*, 1:690-92.)

Mack, Solomon (1732-1820), farmer, merchant, shipmaster, mill operator. Born at Lyme, New London County, Connecticut. When financial tragedy disorganized his father's family, Solomon was given out as a child to a neighborhood farmer, where he learned hard work but little else. Enlisted in the French and Indian War, 1755. Married Lydia Gates, 1759. He farmed successively at northern New York; Lyme, Connecticut; Marlow and Gilsum, New Hampshire. Served in the Revolutionary War. Crippled by a falling tree, he continued an active life, spending four years at sea, then farming, dam building, milling. Deprived of religion in his youth, he had a remarkable conversion experience at age eighty. Died at Gilsum, New Hampshire. (Solomon Mack, *A Naraitve [sic] of the Life of Solomon Mack* [Windsor, Vermont: Printed at the expence of the author, (1811?)]; Anderson, *Joseph Smith's New England Heritage*, chapter 2.)

Marsh, Thomas B. (1799-1866), born at Acton, Middlesex County, Massachusetts. Married Elizabeth Godkin, 1820. Converted to Mormonism in 1830. Moved to Kirtland, Ohio, in 1831, and Jackson County, Missouri, 1832. Among those expelled from Jackson County in 1833. Member of the Clay County, Missouri, high council, 1834. Named president of the Quorum of Twelve at its inception in 1835. Marsh left the Church in 1838 and remained in Missouri but returned to the Church in Utah in 1857. Settled at Spanish Fork, where he taught school. Died at Ogden, Utah. (Jenson, *Biographical Encyclopedia*, 1:74-76; Cook, *Revelations*, 42-43; *Deseret Weekly* 8 [1858]: 18; Lyndon W. Cook, " 'I Have Sinned Against Heaven . . . .': Thomas B. Marsh Returns to the Church," *BYU Studies*, 20 [Summer 1980]: 389-400.)

Matthews, Robert (1788-1841), alias Robert Matthias, alias Joshua the Jewish minister. Joiner and merchant; born at Cambridge, Washington County, New York. Resided at Albany in 1830 with his wife and family of five. He was a religious eccentric who claimed to be God the

Father reincarnated in the body of Matthias the ancient apostle. In 1830 he prophesied the destruction of Albany. Taught that no man who shaved could be a true Christian. Left Albany and his family to embark on a grand apostolic preaching tour through the East and South. Upon his return to New York, he joined with kindred spirits—Elijah Pierson and Benjamin T. Folger. He was described as "one of the most striking figures in the New York of the early Thirties." Committed to the hospital for the insane at Bellevue for a time. Brought to trial in April 1835 at White Plains, New York, on murder charges following the death, in August 1834, of Mr. Pierson after he ate blackberries prepared by Matthias. Matthias was acquitted of the murder charge but was confined in jail three months for brutality on a charge of beating his daughter with a whip. Little is known of Matthias after his visit with Joseph Smith at Kirtland, Ohio, in 1835. An 1839 newspaper reported that the people of Little Rock, Arkansas, had seized him, shaved his beard, and threatened him with a closer shave by "Dr. Lynch" if he did not leave town. (Gilbert Seldes, *The Stammering Century* [New York, 1928], 118-31; *Alton Commercial Gazette*, 19 February 1839; Parkin, "Conflict at Kirtland," 244-47; William L. Stone, *Matthias and his Impostures* [New York: Harper & Brothers, 1835]; Scott H. Faulring, "Prophet Meets Prophet: Robert Matthias Visits Joseph Smith," Typescript, Brigham Young University. The trial is reported in the "Trial of Matthias," New York *Evening Post*, 17, 18, 20 April 1835.)

McBride, Reuben (1803-1891) was born at Chester, Washington County, New York. Married Mary Ann Anderson, 1833. Baptized in 1834 and participated later that year in the march of Zion's Camp. Resided at Kirtland, Ohio, 1836-1848, to oversee Church interests there after the departure of the main body of the Saints in 1838. Migrated to Utah, 1850. Returned to Kirtland in 1851 and led a remnant of Church members to Utah the next year. Settled at Fillmore, Millard County, Utah, 1852. Member of Millard Stake high council. Missionary in England, 1867. Died at Fillmore. (Jenson, *Biographical Encyclopedia*, 4:690; *Deseret Evening News*, 9 March 1891.)

McLellin, William E. (1806-1883), schoolteacher, born in Smith County, Tennessee. Joined the Church in Missouri, 1831. Married Emeline Miller, 1832. Member of the Council of Twelve, 1835-1838. Left the Church in Missouri. Attempted to organize a new church in Kirtland, Ohio, 1847. Published *Ensign of Liberty* at Kirtland, Ohio, 1847-1849. Joined Hedrickites, 1869. Died at Independence, Missouri. (Jenson, *Biographical Encyclopedia*, 1:82-83; Cook, *Revelations*, 106-7.)

McLellin spelled his name four different ways during his lifetime.

McMaster, Cyrus (1801-1879), farmer, born at Sidney, Delaware County, New York. Wife's name: Electa. Living at Bainbridge, Chenango County, 1850. Died at Afton, Chenango County. (Smith, *History of*

Chenango and Madison Counties, 163; U.S. Census: Chenango County, New York, 1850.)

McWithey, Eliza Ann (1817- ?), daughter of Isaac McWithey; born in New York. Married Edwin D. Webb, 1835, in Kirtland, Ohio. Living in the Nauvoo 1st Ward, 1842, and in Marquette County, Wisconsin, 1850. Arrived in Utah, 1853. Probably died prior to 1860 when her husband was living alone at Fillmore, Millard County. (Family Group Records Collection; U.S. Census: Marquette County, Wisconsin, 1850; Millard County, Utah, 1860.)

McWithey, Isaac (c.1786-1851) and family of four were living in Bennington, Genessee County, New York, in 1830, and in Kirtland, Ohio, in 1835. Appointed to Missouri high council, 1836. Back in Kirtland by 1840. (Smith *History of the Church*, 2:367; U.S. Census: Genessee County, New York, 1830; Sherman, Lake County, Ohio, Cemetery Inspriptions, 29.)

Millet, Artemus (1790-1874), builder, farmer, stonemason. Born at Westmoreland, Cheshire County, New Hampshire. Married Ruth Granis, 1815. Converted to Mormonism by Brigham Young, 1833. Resident of Kirtland, Ohio, 1834-1838. Worked on Kirtland and Nauvoo temples. Crossed plains to Utah, 1850. Resided at Manti; president of high council. Died at Scipio, Utah. (Family Group Records Collection; Artemus Millet, Autobiography, MS. LDS Church Archives.)

Milliken, Nathaniel (1793-1874), farmer; born at Buxton, York County, Maine. A cousin of Arthur Milliken, who married Lucy Smith, Joseph Smith's youngest sister. Married Mary F. Hayes, 1819. Died at Kirtland, Ohio. (Family Group Records Collection; U.S. Census: Lake County, Ohio, 1850, 1870; Black, "Membership," 31:135-36.)

Mitchill, Samuel Latham (1764-1831), physician, U.S. senator and representative. Born at North Hempstead, Long Island. Educated in the classics; studied medicine, law, chemistry. Graduated from the University of Edinburgh, 1786. Professor of natural history, chemistry, and agriculture at Columbia College, 1793-1795. Married Catherine Akerly, 1799. Elected to the U.S. Congress in 1801; served in the House: 1801-1804, 1810-1813; and Senate, 1804-1809. Helped found the New York Literary and Philosophical Society, 1814; Lyceum of Natural History, 1817; and Rutgers Medical College, 1826. Characterized as a "living encyclopedia," he was a prolific writer in the field of science and medicine. Advocated the name "Fredonia" for the United States. Died at New York City. (Kimball, "The Anthon Transcript"; Malone, *Dictionary of American Biography*, 13:69-71.)

Morey, George (1803-1875), born at Pittsford, Monroe County, New York. Living in Vermillion County, Indiana, in 1830. Married Sylvia Butterfield. Member of the Missouri high council, 1837-1838. Constable at Nauvoo, Illinois, 1841. Left the Church in 1844 and moved to Brown

County, Illinois. Settled at Hamilton, Decatur County, Iowa in 1852; presided over the Reorganized LDS Church there. Died at Hamilton. (Smith, *History of the Church*, 2:504; *Biographical and Historical Record of Ringgold and Decatur Counties, Iowa* [Chicago: The Lewis Publishing Co., 1887], 682; *History of the Reorganized Church*, 3:238, 252, 276, 339; 4:129.)

Morley, Isaac (1786-1865), farmer, cooper. Born at Montague, Hampshire County, Massachusetts. Married Lucy Gunn, 1812. Settled at Kirtland, Ohio, 1812. Veteran of the War of 1812. One of first converts to Mormonism in Kirtland. Migrating Saints settled on his farm. Appointed counselor to Bishop Edward Partridge in Missouri, 1831. Among those driven from Jackson County, Missouri, 1833. President of the LDS community at Lima, Hancock County, Illinois, 1840. Crossed the plains to Utah, 1848. Member of Salt Lake high council, 1849; and Utah Territorial Legislature, 1851-1855. Settled in Fairview, Sanpete County, Utah. (Jenson, *Biographical Encyclopedia*, 1:235-36; Cook, *Revelations*, 79-80; Backman, *Heavens Resound*, 35-36, 70; Richard H. Morley, "The Life and Contributions of Isaac Morley" [M.A. thesis, Brigham Young University, 1965].)

Murdock, John (1792-1871), farmer; born at Kortright, Delaware County, New York. Married Julia Clapp, 1823. A Campbellite in Ohio when converted to Mormonism in 1830. Wife died following the birth of twins on 30 April 1831. The twins, Joseph and Julia, were adopted by Joseph and Emma Smith. Participant in Zion's Camp, 1834. Appointed to Clay County, Missouri, high council, 1834. Bishop of Nauvoo Ward, 1842-1844. Arrived with Mormon pioneers in Salt Lake Valley, 1847. Appointed bishop of Salt Lake City 14th Ward, 1849. Missionary to Australia, 1851-1853. Settled at Lehi, Utah, 1854-1867. Died at Beaver, Beaver County, Utah. (Cook, *Revelations*, 80; Jenson, *Biographical Encyclopedia*, 2:362-64; Black, "Membership," 32:20.)

Murdock, Julia (1831-1880), one of twins born to John Murdock and Julia Clapp Murdock at Warrensville, Cuyahoga County, Ohio. After their mother died in childbirth, these twins, born the same day as those of Joseph and Emma Smith's, were adopted into the Smith family. Joseph Murdock Smith, Julia's twin brother, died a year later as a result of exposure during the mobbing of the Prophet at Hiram, Ohio. Julia's first husband, Elisha Dixon, was killed in a steamboat explosion in Texas. In 1858 she married John J. Middleton, a lawyer and Catholic, and joined his church. She had no children. Died of cancer at Nauvoo, Illinois. (*Utah Genealogical and Historical Magazine*, 38:61, 63.)

Olney, Oliver (1796-c.1843), born at Eastford, Windham County, Connecticut; residing at Shalersville, Portage County, Ohio, in 1830. Married Else Johnson, 1820. President of the teachers quorum in Kirtland, 1836-1838. Excommunicated at Nauvoo for claiming to be a prophet, 1842. Published an expose on polygamy in St. Louis, 1845. By 1850 Olney children were living with their maternal grandfather, John Johnson, in Hiram, Portage County, Ohio, indicating Olney's possible death prior to that time. (Family Group Records Collection; Olney, *Genealogy of the Descendants of Thomas Olney*, 40; Smith, *History of the Church*, 2:371; 4:552.)

Orton, Amos R. (1792-1847), born at Tyringham, Berkshire County, Massachusetts. Living in Olean, Cattaraugus County, New York, in 1830. He was a member of the seventies quorum at Kirtland, Ohio, and worked on the temple. His wife, Elizabeth, died in 1837. Excommunicated from the Church in 1838. (Edward Orton, *An Account of the Descendants of Thomas Orton* [Columbus, Ohio: Nitschke Brothers Press, 1896], 48-50, 58, 61, 74; U.S. Census: Cattaraugus County, Ohio, 1830; Smith, *History*, 2:206; "Journal History," 7 January 1838; *Messenger and Advocate*, 3:544.)

Packard, Noah (1796-1860), farmer, miner; born at Plainfield, Hampshire County, Massachusetts. Married Sophia Bundy, 1820. Living in Parkman, Geauga County, Ohio, when converted to Mormonism, 1832. Proselyting in the eastern states , 1833. Appointed president of Parkman Branch, 1833. Member of the Kirtland high council, 1836-1838. Counselor in the high priest's quorum at Nauvoo, Illinois, 1841-1846. Worked in Wisconsin lead mines, 1846-1850. Crossed plains to Utah in 1850. Settled at Springville, Utah, 1851. (Jenson, *Biographical Encyclopedia*, 2:684; Cook, *Revelations*, 269-70.)

Page, Catherine Whitmer (1807- ?), daughter of Peter Whitmer, Sr., and wife of Hiram Page. Born in Pennsylvania. Living in Richmond, Ray County, Missouri, 1880. (U.S. Census: Ray County, Missouri, 1880; Family Group Records Collection.)

Page, Hiram (1800-1852), physician, farmer; native of Vermont. Married Catherine Whitmer, 1825. Parents of nine children. One of the Eight Witnesses to the Book of Mormon. Among the first members of the Church. In the fall of 1830 he deceived several associates with false revelations received through a seerstone. Suffered mob violence during the trials of the Saints in Missouri. Left the Church in 1838. Died at Excelsior Springs, Ray County, Missouri. (Jenson, *Biographical Encyclopedia*, 1:277-78; Anderson, *Investigating the Book of Mormon Witnesses*, chapter 9.)

Page, Mary, identification not known. Possibly related to Hiram Page, who married Catherine Whitmer.

Parks, Hiram G. (180?- ?). Married Nancy McGhee, 1828. Ray County, Missouri, treasurer in 1835 and one of the original trustees when the town was incorporated that same year. In 1838 he was commander of the second brigade of David Atchison's third division of Missouri militia. (*History of Ray County*, 256; 384; *Document Con-*

taining the Correspondence, Orders, &c., 32; U.S. Census: Ray County, Missouri, 1840; International Genealogical Index.)

Parrish, Warren (1803-1887), brother-in-law of David Patten; born in New York. Residing at Alexandria, Jefferson County, New York, in 1830. Baptized by Brigham Young, May 1833. Participant in march of Zion's Camp to Missouri, 1834. Married Martha H. Raymond, 1835. Proselyting in Kentucky and Tennessee with Wilford Woodruff, 1835-1836. Member of the first quorum of seventy. Engaged in clerical work for Joseph Smith, 1835-1836. Treasurer of Kirtland Safety Society, 1836. In 1837 he renounced his Church membership and led dissenters against Joseph Smith. Clergyman living at Mendon, Monroe County, New York, in 1850. In 1870 he was insane, residing at Emporia, Lyon County, Kansas, where he died. (Smith, *History of the Church*, 2:184, 203, 293, 484-86, 528; Carter, *Our Pioneer Heritage*, 5:333-34; U.S. Census: Jefferson County, New York, 1830; Geauga County, Ohio, 1840; Lyon County, Kansas, 1870; Lyon County, Kansas, Cemetery Records, Typescript, 104, LDS Family History Library.)

Partridge, Edward (1793-1840), hatter. Born at Pittsfield, Berkshire County, Massachusetts. Married Lydia Clisbee, 1819. Living in Painesville, Ohio, when converted by Mormon missionaries in 1830. Named first bishop in the Church, 1831. Called to oversee settlement of the Saints in Zion (Jackson County, Missouri), 1831. Victim of mob violence in Jackson County, 1833. Proselyting in the eastern states and New England, 1835. Witnessed the expulsion of the Saints from Missouri in 1838 and was himself jailed. Appointed bishop of the Nauvoo Upper Ward, 1839. Died at Nauvoo. (Jenson, *Biographical Encyclopedia*, 1:218-22; Cook, *Revelations*, 53-54.)

Patten, David (1799-1838), farmer. Born in Vermont. Living in Monroe County, Michigan when he married Phoebe Ann Babcock, 1828. Converted to Mormonism, 1832. Proselyting in eastern states, 1832-1833, and in Tennessee with Warren Parrish, 1834. Member of the Council of Twelve, 1835-1838. Shot at Crooked River, Ray County, during the Missouri difficulties in October 1838. Died shortly thereafter near Far West, Missouri. (Cook, *Revelations*, 226; Jenson, *Biographical Encyclopedia*, 1:76-80; "History of David Patten," *Deseret Weekly* 8 (1858): 18-19.)

Peck, Hezekiah (1782-1850), millwright; brother of Polly Peck, who married Joseph Knight, Sr. Born at Guilford, Windham County, Vermont. Married Martha Long. Living at Bainbridge, Chenango County, New York, in 1830 when converted to Mormonism. Moved to Jackson County, Missouri, 1831. Named counselor to Bishop John Corrill in Missouri, 1833. Counselor in the priests quorum at Nauvoo, 1841. Bishop of Nauvoo 10th Ward, 1844. Died at Jackson, Andrew County, Missouri. (*Utah Genealogical and Historical Magazine*, 27:78; Smith,

History of the Church, 1:88, 363; 4:312; 7:298; U.S. Census: Chenango County, New York, 1830; Porter, "Origins of the Church," 212; Hartley, *They Are My Friends*.)

Peck, Martha Long (1789- ?), sister-in-law of Joseph Knight, Sr. Born at Wilmington, Windham County, Vermont. Married Hezekiah Peck at Bainbridge, Chenango County, New York. Moved with the Church through Ohio and Missouri and was living in Nauvoo, Illinois, by 1846. Not listed with her family at Jackson, Andrew County, Missouri, in 1850 census. (*Utah Genealogical and Historical Magazine*, 27:78-79; U.S. Census: Andrew County, Missouri, 1850; Hartley, *They Are My Friends*.)

Perry, William Chadwick (1812-1893), farmer, carpenter, born at Madison, Madison County, New York. Father's family moved to Middlebury, Genesee County, 1815. Converted to Mormonism, 1832. Married Eliza Brown, 1835. Worked on the temple at Kirtland, Ohio. Perry and family of four were among those who migrated to Missouri with the Kirtland Camp in 1838. Member of second quorum of seventy. Alternate high councilman in Nauvoo. Living in Nodaway County, Missouri, 1850-1860. (Ivan Perry, *Perry Family History* [Provo, Utah: J. Grant Stevenson, 1966], 1:14-19; Smith, *History of the Church*, 3:92.)

Peterson, Richard Ziba (? -1849), numbered among the first members of the Church. Accompanied Oliver Cowdery, David Whitmer, and Parley Pratt on the Lamanite Mission to Missouri in October 1830. Married Rebecca Hooper, 1831. Eight known children. Left the Church in 1833. Migrated to California, 1848. Sheriff of Placerville, Eldorado County, 1848-49. There, he died. (Cook, *Revelations*, 45.)

Phelps, William W. (1792-1872), newspaper editor. Born at Hanover, Morris County, New Jersey. Married Sally Waterman, 1815. Converted to Mormonism in New York, 1831. After arriving in Kirtland, Ohio, in 1831, he was appointed to assist in the Church printing office. Editor of *The Evening and the Morning Star* at Independence, Missouri; published the Book of Commandments; helped compile the 1835 Doctrine and Covenants and the first Mormon hymn book. Counselor to David Whitmer in the Missouri Church presidency, 1834. Assisted Joseph Smith as a clerk and ghostwriter. Left the Church in 1838 but returned in 1840. Came to Utah in 1849. Elected to the territorial legislative assembly, 1851. Died in Salt Lake City. (Jenson, *Biographical Encyclopedia*, 3:692-97; Cook, *Revelations*, 87-88; Walter D. Bowen, "The Versatile W. W. Phelps—Mormon Writer, Educator, and Pioneer" [M.A. thesis, Brigham Young University, 1958].)

Piexotto, Daniel Levy Maduro (1800-1843), physician, author, linguist. Born at Amsterdam, Holland. Came to New York City in 1807. When Gershom Seixas, father of Joshua Seixas, died while serving as rabbi of the Congregation Shearith Israel, Daniel's father, Moses, succeeded him. Married Rachel M. Seixas, cousin of Joshua Seixas, 1823. Received his M.D. and M.A. degrees from Columbia College, 1819 and 1825. Pioneer in the field of preventive medicine. Physician at the New York City Dispensary; lectured on abdominal diseases and complaints of females. President of the New York County Medical Society, 1830-32. Advocate of reform of faulty medical practices. Helped in founding of Academy of Medicine. Member of Washington masonic lodge. Editor of *The New York Medical and Physical Journal*, first quarterly medical journal printed in English language. In 1836 he was called to the presidency of the Willoughby Medical College and moved to Cleveland, Ohio. Later returned to New York, where he died. (Solomon R. Kagan, *Jewish Contributions to Medicine in America* [Boston: Boston Medical Publishing Co., 1889], 10-12; Daniel P. Hays, "Daniel L.M. Peixotto, M.D.," *Publications of the American Jewish Historical Society* 26 [1918]: 219-30.)

When Joseph Smith met him, Peixotto was Professor of Theory and Practice of Physics and Obstetrics at Willoughby Medical College. (Louis C. Zucker, "Joseph Smith as a Student of Hebrew," *Dialogue* 2 [Summer 1968], 44; *History of Geauga and Lake Counties, Ohio*, 40.)

Pitkin, George W. (1801-1873), born at Hartford, Windsor County, Vermont. Married Amanda Eglestone in 1829. Converted to Mormonism, 1831. Living at Hiram, Ohio while serving as sheriff of Portage County. Later, sheriff of Caldwell County, Missouri. Settled at Nauvoo, Illinois, 1839. Crossed the plains to Utah, 1848. Moved to Ogden, Utah in 1850, and to Cache Valley in 1859. One of the pioneer settlers of Millville where he lived until his death. (Family Group Records Collection; George O. Pitkin, Biographical Sketch, Typescript, LDS Church Family History Library.)

Poorman, John (c.1784- ?), neighbor to Peter Whitmer and William Jolly at Fayette, Seneca County, New York, in 1810, 1820 census records. After his baptism, he moved to Ohio in 1832, and Missouri, in 1833. He was involved in the confrontation with a mob that tarred and feathered Joseph Smith at Hiram, Ohio on 25 March 1832. Married Nancy Bancroft in Clay County, Missouri, 1836; probably a second marriage. The birth of a child in Clay County, 1840 is the last known reference to him. (Nanon L. Carr, "Marriage Records of Clay County, Missouri, 1822-1852," Kansas City, Mo.: by author, 1957], 44; Smith, *History of the Church*, 1:263.)

Porter, Francis (1787/8-1866), farmer; born in New Hampshire. He had assisted in organizing and was a trustee of the second society of the Methodist Episcopal Church at LeRay, Jefferson County, New York in 1824. Died in Jefferson County. (U.S. Census: Jefferson County, New York, 1850; Franklin B. Hough, *A History of Jefferson County* [Watertown, New York: Sterling and Riddell, 1854], 194.)

Pratt, Orson (1811-1881), writer, teacher, surveyor, historian. Born at Hartford, Washington County, New York. Younger brother of Parley Pratt. After joining the Church, he left Kirtland, Ohio with Lyman Johnson in February 1832 on missionary assignment in the East; returned in February 1833 after traveling four thousand miles, baptizing 104 people, and organizing several branches of the Church. Participant in Zion's Camp, 1834. Member of the Council of Twelve, 1835- 1881. Married Sarah Marinda Bates, 1836. Elected to Nauvoo, Illinois city council, 1843. Entered Salt Lake Valley with Mormon pioneers, 1847. Presided over Church in Great Britain, 1848. Member of Utah Territorial legislature. Appointed Church historian, 1874. Died at Salt Lake City. (*The Deseret Weekly*, 9 June 1858; Cook, *Revelations*, 49-51; England, *The Life and Thought of Orson Pratt*; David J. Whittaker, "Orson Pratt: Prolific Pamphleteer," *Dialogue* 15 [Autumn 1982]: 27-41.)

Pratt, Parley Parker (1807-1857), farmer, editor, legislator; elder brother of Orson Pratt. Born at Burlington, Otsego County, New York. Married Thankful Halsey, 1827. Participant in Lamanite mission to Missouri, 1830. Traveled to Missouri with Zion's Camp, 1834. Member of the Quroum of Twelve, 1835-57. Jailed at Richmond and Columbia, Missouri during difficulties of 1838-39. Proselyting in England, 1839, 1847. A prolific writer; edited *The Latter-day Saints' Millennial Star*, 1840. Directed affairs of the Church in New York City, 1844-45. Returned to Utah, 1847. Led exploration party into southern Utah, 1850. Mission to South America, 1851-52. Murdered at Van Buren, Crawford County, Arkansas. (Cook, *Revelations*, 46-47; Jenson, *Biographical Encyclopedia*, 1:83-85; Parley P. Pratt, ed., *Autobiography of Parley P. Pratt* [New York: Russell Brothers, 1874; 3rd edl, 1938; reprinted, Salt Lake City: Deseret Book Co., 1961].)

Price, Sterling (1809-1867), born in Prince Edward County, Virginia. Moved to Chariton County, Missouri in 1831 and engaged in merchandising and farming. Elected to the state legislature and chosen Speaker of the House, 1840. Elected to the U.S. Congress in 1844 but resigned his seat in 1846 to participate in the Mexican War. His service brought him a commission of brigadier general. Beginning in 1852 he served a term as governor of Missouri. His influence placed Missouri on the side of the South in the Civil War. Commanded Confederate forces in a series of defeats. Died at St. Louis. (Conard, *Encyclopedia of the History of Missouri*, 5:229-31.)

In the conflict with the Mormons in Missouri in 1838, a contingent of Missouri militia under Price guarded Mormon prisoners, including Joseph Smith, from Independence, Jackson County to Richmond, Ray County, and was involved in guard duty at the Richmond court of inquiry in November.

Redfield, David Harvey (1807-1879), farmer, merchant. Born at

Herkimer, Herkimer County, New York. Joined the Latter-day Saints by 1831. Married Fanny McAtherton, 1837. Traveled from Ohio to Missouri with the Kirtland Camp in 1838. Petitioned Missouri authorities, including Governor Boggs, in behalf of the Mormon people during the difficulties of 1838. One of those charged with riot in the destruction of the Nauvoo *Expositor* in 1844. Crossed the plains to Salt Lake Valley, 1848. By 1854 he was living in Nicolaus, Sutter County, California where he was Sutter County Coroner, and where he evidently died. (Family Group Records Collection; Smith, *History of the Church*, 3:234-35; 6:487ff; Black, "Membership," 36:235-37; John H. Redfield, *Genealogical History of the Redfield Family* [Albany, New York: Munsell and Rowland, 1860], 144, 242; *History of Sutter County, California* [Oakland, California, 1879], 77; U.S. Census: Sutter County, California, 1860, 1870.)

Reed, John S. (c.1785- ?), farmer; born in Massachusetts. Visited Nauvoo, Illinois in 1844 and related his experience in defending Joseph Smith in 1830. Reed stated that he met the Prophet about 1823 when the young man first came to Bainbridge, Chenango County, New York at about the age of 18; that he "moved in the first circles of the community" until after he related his experience with the gold plates, and formed a church in the locality; whereupon, a bigoted element of the community united against him; made a false accusation and arraigned Joseph Smith before Justice of the Peace, Joseph Chamberlain. Reed was called to defend the prisoner, and the prosecution "ransacked the . . . county of Chenango for witnesses that would swear hard" to convict him, but nothing was found against his character. Immediately after he was discharged by the court, Joseph was served with another writ and tried at Colesville with the same result. Residing at Mexico, Oswego County, New York, in 1860. (U.S. Census: Oswego County, New York, 1860; "Some of the Remarks of John S. Reed, Esq., as Delivered before the State Convention," *Times and Seasons* 5 [1 June 1844]: 549-51.)

In 1861, Amos Reed, son of John S., accompanied James D. Doty, President Lincoln's appointee as superintendent of Indian affairs for Utah Territory, to serve as his clerk. This occasioned a letter from 77-year-old John S. Reed, living at Mexico, Oswego County, New York, to Brigham Young introducing his son, and again rehearsing his early legal defense of Joseph Smith at South Bainbridge, and Colesville, New York. (John S. Reed to Brigham Young, 6 December 1861, Ms., Brigham Young Papers, LDS Church Archives.)

Rich, Leonard (1800-1856), farmer; born in New York. Residing at Warsaw, Genesee County, New York, in 1830. One of the presidents of the seventies, 1835-37. Participant in the march of Zion's Camp to Missouri, 1834. Left the Church and was living in Kirtland, Ohio after

1845. Wife's name, Keziah. Died at Kirtland. (Family Group Records Collection; Smith, *History of the Church*, 2:184, 203; Jenson, *Biographical Encyclopedia*, 1:189-190; Black, "Membership," 36:582-83; U.S. Census: Genesee County, New York, 1830; Lake County, Ohio, 1850; Kirtland, Ohio cemetery record, Typescript, 18, LDS Church Family History Library.)

Rigdon, Sidney (1793-1876), tanner; Campbellite minister. Born at St. Clair, Alleghany County, Pennsylvania. Married Phoebe Brook, 1820. Converted by Mormon missionaries at Mentor, Ohio in November 1830. Scribe for Joseph Smith. Accompanied the Prophet to Upper Canada on proselyting mission and helped keep his diary during the trip, 1833. Counselor in Church presidency, 1833-44. With Joseph in jail at Liberty, Clay County, Missouri, 1838-39. Among those who went to Washington, D.C., to seek redress of Missouri grievances, 1839. Member of Nauvoo city council; postmaster of Nauvoo. Claimed right to lead the Church after death of the Prophet; excommunicated, 1844. Died at Friendship, New York. (Cook, *Revelations*, 52-53; Jenson, *Biographical Encyclopedia*, 1:31-34; F. Mark McKiernan, *A Voice of One Crying in the Wilderness: Sidney Rigdon, Religious Reformer, 1793-1876* [Lawrence, Kansas: Coronado Press, 1971].)

Robinson, Ebenezer (1816-1891), printer. Born at Floyd, Oneida County, New York. Learned printing trade in Utica, New York, and Ravenna, Ohio. Came to Kirtland, Ohio in May 1835 and began work in the printing office. Church clerk and recorder, and clerk of the Missouri high council, 1838. Publisher and co-editor of the *Times and Seasons*, 1839-40. Left Nauvoo and affiliated with Sidney Rigdon in the east for a time after the death of Joseph Smith. Moved to Iowa and joined the Reorganized Church, 1863. Became a follower of David Whitmer in 1888. Published *The Return*, a publication of Whitmer's Church of Christ, 1889-1891. (Robinson, "Items of Personal History;" Pearl Wilcox, *The Latter Day Saints on the Missouri Frontier* [Independence, Mo.: by author, 1972], 279-280.)

Robinson, George W. (1814-1878), merchant, miller, banker. Born at Pawlet, Rutland County, Vermont. Married Athalia Rigdon, oldest daughter of Sidney Rigdon, 1837. In September 1837 elected general Church recorder to replace Oliver Cowdery. Sustained as general Church recorder and clerk to the First Presidency at Far West, Missouri in April 1838. Imprisoned with Joseph Smith and other Church leaders at Richmond, Missouri, 1838. First postmaster at Commerce, later Nauvoo, Illinois, 1839. Helped establish the Nauvoo Agricultural and Manufacturing Association, 1841. Left the Church, 1842. Moved to Friendship, Allegany County, New York, 1847. Founded First National Bank there, 1864. Died at Friendship. (Jenson, *Biographical Encyclopedia*, 1:252-53; Smith, *History of the Church*, 6:464; Arlene Hess, "Collected Materials Relative to Sidney Rigdon and his Descendants, and other Subjects used in Preparation for the History of Friendship, New York," Typescript, Brigham Young University.)

Rockwell, Caroline (1812-1887), sister of Orrin P. Rockwell; born at Belchertown, Hampshire County, Massachusetts. Married Horton Smith, a farmer living in Hambden, Geauga County, Ohio, 1834. Died at Hambden. (U.S. Census: Geauga County, Ohio, 1850, 1860; Warren and Grosvenor, "A Monumental Work," 285; Family Group Records Collection.)

Rockwell, Electa (1814-1900), sister of Orrin P. Rockwell; born at Belchertown, Hampshire County, Massachusetts. Married Samuel M. Ousley, a native of Kentucky, farming in Clay County, Missouri, 1837. Resided in Andrew County, Missouri, 1839-1852. Crossed plains to California in 1852; settled the following year at Gilroy, Santa Clara County. When her husband was killed in 1855, Electa continued to improve the 630 acre farm and raise her nine children until death. (Family Group Records Collection; Eugene T. Sawyer, *History of Santa Clara County, California* [Los Angeles: Historic Record Company, 1922], 407.)

Rockwell, Orrin Porter (1813-1878), scout, pioneer, frontiersman, lawman, rancher. Born at Belchertown, Hampshire County, Massachusetts. Porter was four years old when the family moved to Manchester, New York, where he befriended Joseph Smith. Among the first converts to Mormonism. Went to Missouri in 1831 and experienced the difficulties there. Married Luana Beebe, 1832. Assisted in Mormon exodus from Missouri, 1839. Member of the Mormon party who went to Washington, D.C., to seek redress for Missouri wrongs, 1839-40. Accused, imprisoned, and later acquitted in the 1842 assassination attempt of former Missouri Governor, Lilburn Boggs. Scout and hunter for the Mormon pioneers crossing the plains, 1846-47. Deputy marshal in Utah, 1849-78. Died at Salt Lake City. (Harold Schindler, *Orrin Porter Rockwell* [Salt Lake City: University of Utah Press, 1966]; Richard L. Dewey, *Porter Rockwell: A Biography* [New York: Paramount Books, 1986]; Nicholas Van Alfen, "The Trusted Messenger," *Our Pioneer Heritage*, 15:375-89; *Utah Genealogical and Historical Magazine*, 26:154-56.)

Rolfe, Samuel Jones (1794-1867), joiner, carpenter. Born at Concord, Merrimack County, New Hampshire. Married Elizabeth Hathaway, 1818. Residing in Rumford, Oxford County, Maine when converted. Moved to Kirtland, Ohio, 1835. Worked on Kirtland and Nauvoo temples. Appointed president of priests quorum in Nauvoo, 1841. Bishop at Winter Quarters, Nebraska, 1846-47. Arrived in Salt Lake Valley, 1847. Settled in San Bernardino, California, 1851; county treasurer, counselor in stake presidency. (Family Group Records Collection; Cook, *Revelations*, 272-273.)

Rose, Joseph (1792- ?), born in Orange County, New York. Member of the 2nd quorum of seventy at Kirtland, Ohio. Proselyting in Missouri, Indiana, and Illinois, 1836-37; and Ohio, 1844. No evidence that he followed the Church after Nauvoo. A Joseph Rose living at Union, Fulton County, Illinois in 1850 could be this man. (U.S. Federal Census; *Messenger and Advocate*, 3 [June, July 1837]; 519, 535; Smith, *History of the Church*, 3:253; 6:339.)

Roundy, Shadrach (1788-1872), was born at Rockingham, Windham County, Vermont. Married Betsy Quimby, 1814. Family records show him in Spafford, Onondaga County, New York, between 1815 and 1831, and in Willoughby, Ohio, between 1834 and 1838. Converted to Mormonism, 1831. Member of Nauvoo, Illinois, bishopric, and Legion, 1841; policeman, 1843. Bodyguard to Joseph Smith. Arrived in Salt Lake Valley, 1847. Member of Salt Lake high council, 1847-48. Bishop of the Salt Lake City 16th Ward, 1849-56. Died at Salt Lake City. (Cook, *Revelations*, 273; Smith, *History of the Church*, 2:298.)

Rudd, John (1779- ?), was born in Bennington, Vermont. Family members were among the pioneer settlers of Springfield, Erie County, Pennsylvania. John Rudd, Sr. (1748-1830) came to Springfield in 1805 from Otsego County, New York and settled on 350 acres of lake front land. John Jr. had preceded his father and others of the family to Springfield in 1802 and established a distillery. After John Sr.'s death, some of the family joined the Latter-day Saints. Joseph Smith stayed at the Rudd home traveling to and from the East in 1833. In 1836 the mother, Chloe Hill Rudd, died at Independence, Cuyahoga County, Ohio. At a conference held in Kirtland, Ohio in August 1834 to investigate charges of misconduct against Joseph Smith during the march of Zion's Camp, John, Jr. signed his name exonerating the Prophet's actions. Beyond this, there appears to be no further reference to him in Church annals. (Benjamin Whitman, *History of Erie County, Pennsylvania* [Chicago: Warner, Beers & Co., 1884], 160-161; 751; *Messenger and Advocate*, 2:382; *Evening and Morning Star*, 2:182.)

Ryder, Symonds (1792-1870), farmer; born at Hartford, Windsor County, Vermont. Moved to Hiram, Portage County, Ohio in 1814. Married Mehetable Loomis, 1818. Ryder joined the Campbellites in 1828, and for thirty years was overseer of that church in Hiram except for the short time he was affiliated with the Latter-day Saints in 1831. His association with Mormonism followed the miraculous healing of John Johnson's wife by Joseph Smith; but after a letter calling him to preach misspelled his name he left the Church. He died at Hiram, Ohio. (Hayden, *Early History of the Disciples*, 245-256; Cook, *Revelations*, 81.)

Salisbury, Wilkins Jenkins (1809-1856), blacksmith. Born at Lebanon, Madison County, New York. Member of the first quorum of the seventy. He married Joseph Smith's sister, Katherine, at Kirtland, Ohio, 1831. Parents of eight children. Participated in the march of Zion's Camp to Missouri, 1834. Expelled from the Church for un-Christian conduct in 1836. Moved with the Church to Missouri and Illinois. Remained at Plymouth, Hancock County, Illinois where he died. (Mary A. Anderson, *Ancestry and Posterity of Joseph Smith* [Independence: Herald Printing House, 1929], 75; E. Cecil McGavin, *The Family of Joseph Smith* [Salt Lake City: Bookcraft, 1963], 95-108; Richard L. Anderson, "What Were Joseph Smith's Sisters Like?" *The Ensign* 9 [March 1979]: 42-44.)

Scott, Walter (1796-1861), preacher and religious reformer, was born at Moffat, Dumfriesshire, Scotland. Educated at Edinburgh University. Scott emigrated to America in 1818, and taught school in New York. Three years later in Pittsburgh he met Alexander Campbell, a Baptist minister. Together they studied the scriptures and determined that Christendom had departed from New Testament purity. As independent preachers they labored to correct the evils they saw. Largely due to Scott's influence the "Reformers" ceased to regard themselves Baptists. As a partner of Campbell's, Scott wrote extensively for the *Christian Baptist*, and *Millennial Harbinger*. Scott established the evangelistic pattern and method of propaganda that characterized the Disciples.

While in Pittsburgh, Scott met Sidney Rigdon, then pastor of a small Baptist church in the city, and the congregations of the two men were united into one body. Scott died at Mayslick, Mason County, Kentucky. (Hayden, *Early History of the Disciples*, 61-65; Malone, *Dictionary of American Biography*, 502-503.)

Seixas, Joshua (1802-187?), Hebraist, textbook writer. Lived in New York City. Attracted attention by promising a reading knowledge of Hebrew in six weeks, classes meeting one hour a day. Taught Hebrew in New York, Philadelphia, Washington, at Princeton Theological Seminary, the Seminary at Brunswick, New Jersey, and Andover Theological Seminary. His *A Manual Hebrew Grammar for the Use of Beginners* was published in 1833. In 1835 he taught at Oberlin College, Ohio. After completing the course at Oberlin, Seixas was hired for a six-week term of instruction at the Western Reserve College in Hudson, beginning in December and ending 23 January 1836. Three days later he arrived at Kirtland where he taught Hebrew from 26 January—29 March 1836. (LeRoi C. Snow, "Who Was Professor Joshua Seixas?" *Improvement Era* 39 (February 1936): 67-71; Zucker, "Joseph Smith as a Student of Hebrew;" Malcolm H. Stern, *First American Jewish Families* [Cincinnati: American Jewish Archives, 1978], 264; James H. Fairchild, *Oberlin: The Colony and the College, 1833-1883* [Oberlin, Ohio: E.J. Goodrich, 1883], 368-70.)

Seymour, William (1780-1848), congressman, jurist; born in Norwalk, Fairfield County, Connecticut. Moved to Windsor, Broome County, New York, 1793 and Binghamton, 1802, where he studied law. Returned to Windsor, 1807. Prosecution lawyer in the 1830 Joseph Smith trial in Chenango County. Justice of the Peace, 1812-1828; appointed first judge of the court of common pleas of Broome County, 1833-35, 1837-47. Elected as a Democrat to the U.S. House of Representatives, 1835-37. Practiced law at Binghamton until his death there. (*Biographical Directory of the American Congress* [Washington, D.C.: U.S. Government Printing Office, 1971], 1680; William S. Lawyer, *Binghamton* [Binghamton, New York, 1900], 325-26.)

Sherman, Lyman R. (1804-1839), born at Monkton, Addison County, Vermont. Married Delcena Didamia Johnson, 1829. Converted to Mormonism, 1832. Participant in Zion's Camp, 1834. One of the presidents of the seventy, 1835-37. Appointed to Kirtland high council, 1837. Moved to Far West, Missouri, 1838. Called to apostleship in 1839 but died before he could be notified and ordained. (Cook, *Revelations*, 217; Jenson, *Biographical Encyclopedia*, 1:190.)

Smith, Alvin (1798-1823), farmer; brother of Joseph Smith. Born at Tunbridge, Orange County, Vermont. After his parents moved to Palmyra, New York from Vermont, Alvin played a prominent role in the family economy, working hard to pay for and clear land, and build a home. Joseph referred to him as "the noblest of my father's family." According to his mother, Alvin died of an overdose of calomel administered by a local physician for a stomach ailment, possibly appendicitis. His death date is 19 November 1823 in his twenty-fifth year. (Lucy Smith, *Biographical Sketches*, 87ff; Richard L. Anderson, "The Alvin Smith Story," *The Ensign* 17 [August 1987]: 67-69.)

Smith, Don Carlos (1816-1841), farmer, printer; born at Norwich, Windsor County, Vermont. Married Agnes M. Coolbrith, 1835. President of the high priests quorum in Kirtland, Ohio, 1836, and in Nauvoo, Illinois, 1841. Editor of the *Times and Seasons* in Nauvoo, 1839-41. Member of the Nauvoo city council, 1841. A major in the Hancock County militia, and brigadier general in Nauvoo Legion, 1841. He died at Nauvoo. (Cook, *Revelations*, 274-75; Smith, *History of the Church*, 4:393-94; 398-99; Anderson, "Joseph Smith's Brothers, *The Ensign* 9 [September 1979]: 30.)

Smith, George A. (1817-1875), farmer; cousin of Joseph Smith. Born at Potsdam, St. Lawrence County, New York. Baptized, 1832; moved to Kirtland, Ohio, 1833. Participant in march of Zion's Camp, 1834. Appointed to first quorum of seventy, 1835. Member of Council of Twelve, 1839-75. Mission to England, 1839-41. Married Bathsheba Bigler, 1841. Member of Nauvoo Legion. Arrived in Salt Lake Valley with Mormon pioneers, 1847. Directed southern Utah settlement. Appointed Church Historian, 1854. Member of Utah Territorial Supreme

Court, 1855. Counselor to Brigham Young, 1868. (*The Deseret Weekly*, 18 August 1858; Cook, *Revelations*, 275-76; Jenson, *Biographical Encyclopedia*, 37-42; C. Kent Dunford, "The Contributions of George A. Smith to the Establishment of the Mormon Society in the Territory of Utah" [Ph.D. diss., Brigham Young University, 1970].)

Smith, Hyrum (1800-1844), farmer; born at Tunbridge, Orange County, Vermont. Married Jerusha Barden, 1826. One of the Eight Witnesses to the Book of Mormon. Member of the committee to supervise construction of the temple at Kirtland, Ohio. Participant in the march of Zion's Camp, 1834. Appointed second counselor in First Presidency, 1837. Imprisoned at Liberty, Missouri with his brother Joseph, 1838-39. Appointed patriarch and assistant Church president, 1841. Member of Nauvoo city council. Among those charged in the destruction of the Nauvoo *Expositor*, 1844. Killed in the attack upon the jail that took his brother Joseph's life at Carthage, Illinois. (Cook, *Revelations*, 19-20; Jenson, *Biographical Encyclopedia*, 1:52; Pearson H. Corbett, *Hyrum Smith Patriarch* [Salt Lake City: Deseret Book Co., 1963].)

Smith, Jerusha Barden (1805-1837), born at Norfolk, Litchfield County, Connecticut. Married Hyrum Smith at Manchester, New York, 1826. Mother of six children. Died 13 October 1837 at Kirtland, Ohio. (Smith, *History of the Church*, 2:519; *Utah Genealogical and Historical Magazine*, 26:102-103.)

Smith, John (1781-1854), farmer; born at Derryfield, Rockingham County, New Hampshire. Uncle of Joseph Smith. Baptized, 1832. Member of the Kirtland high council, 1834. Presided over Church communities in Lee County, Iowa, 1839; Ramus, Hancock County, Illinois, 1843; Nauvoo, Illinois, 1844; Salt Lake City, 1847-48. Accompanied the first Mormon pioneer company to Utah, 1847. Church patriarch, 1849-54. Died at Salt Lake City. (Jenson, *Biographical Encyclopedia*, 1:182-83; Cook, *Revelations*, 208; Irene M. Bates, "Uncle John Smith, 1781- 1854: Patriarchal Bridge," *Dialogue: A Journal of Mormon Thought* 20 [Fall 1987]: 79-89.)

Smith, Joseph (1771-1840), cooper; born at Topsfield, Essex County, Massachusetts. Married Lucy Mack, 1796, in Tunbridge, Vermont. After three crop failures, he moved his family to Palmyra, New York in 1816. One of the Eight Witnesses to the Book of Mormon. Moved to Kirtland, Ohio, 1831. Appointed Church patriarch, 1833. Member of the Kirtland high council. Appointed assistant counselor to the First Presidency, 1837. Died at Nauvoo, Illinois. (Cook, *Revelations*, 11; Earnest M. Skinner, "Joseph Smith, Sr., the First Patriarch to the Church" [M.A. thesis, Brigham Young University, 1958].)

Smith, Joseph (1832-1914), farmer; President of the Reorganized Church, 1860-1914. He remained with his mother in Nauvoo, Illinois after his father was killed in 1844, and most of the saints migrated west with Brigham Young. Married Emmeline Griswold, 1856. Accepted call as president of the Reorganized Church of Jesus Christ of Latter Day Saints in 1860. Moved to Plano, Illinois in 1865 and began editing the *Saints' Herald*. Moved to Lamoni, Iowa in 1881 and helped found Graceland College. Outspoken critic of the practice of plural marriage. Traveled to Utah in 1879 where he challenged LDS teachings about his father's involement in polygamy. Died at Independence, Missouri. Facial neuralgia resulted in blindness during the last four years of his life. (Malone, *Dictionary of American Biography*, 17: 312-13; Anderson, *Ancestry and Posterity of Joseph Smith*, 567-78; Richard P. Howard, *The Memoirs of President Joseph Smith III (1832-1914)* [Independence, Missouri, 1979; Robert D. Hutchins, "Joseph Smith III: Moderate Mormon" [M.A. thesis, Brigham Young University, 1977]; Roger D. Launius, "And There Came Prophets in the Land Again: The Life of Joseph Smith III, 1832-1914, Mormon Reformer" [Ph.D. diss., Louisiana State U., 1982].)

Smith, Katherine (1813-1900), born at Lebanon, Grafton County, New Hampshire. Married Wilkins Jenkins Salisbury, 1831. Parents of eight children. The family moved to Missouri in 1838, then to Illinois. After the death of her husband in 1856, she remained at Plymouth, Hancock County, Illinois. Although affiliated with the Reorganized Church, she maintained contact with relatives and friends in Utah until her death. (*Utah Genealogical and Historical Magazine*, 26:102, 151-52; Anderson, "What were Joseph Smith's Sister's Like?" 42-44.)

Smith, Lucy (1821-1882), youngest sister of Joseph Smith; born at Palmyra, Ontario County, New York. Living with her parents during the migration of the Church from New York to Illinois. Married Arthur Millikin in 1840; parents of nine children. After her father's death, she and her husband cared for her mother seven years. Joined the Reorganized Church in 1873. Died in Illinois. (Anderson, "What were Joseph Smith's Sisters Like?" 42-44.)

Smith, Lyman (1817-1837), born at Potsdam, St. Lawrence County, New York. Member of Zion's Camp, 1834. Married Clarissa Lyman, 1834. Proselyting in Ohio and New York with his second cousin, George A. Smith, 1835. Appointed to first quorum of seventy, 1835. Died in Illinois. (Family Group Records Collection; Journal of George A. Smith, 1817-1874, Ms., LDS Church Archives; "Journal History," 14, 28 February 1835.)

Smith, Sarah (1767-1850), was born in Connecticut. Died at Kirtland, Ohio. (Sherman, Lake County, Ohio Cemetery Inscriptions, 21.)

Smith, Samuel Harrison (1808-1844), farmer; younger brother of Joseph Smith. Born at Tunbridge, Orange County, Vermont. One of the Eight Witnesses to the Book of Mormon. Proselyting with Orson Hyde in the eastern states, 1832. Hyde said of him, he was "a man slow of speech and unlearned, yet a man of good faith and extreme integrity."

Member of the Kirtland high council, 1834-38. Married Mary Bailey, 1834. Appointed a bishop at Nauvoo in 1841. Nauvoo city alderman, and member of Nauvoo Legion, 1841. Married Levira Clark, 1841. Moved to Plymouth, Illinois, 1842. Died at Nauvoo, Illinois. (Cook, *Revelations*, 34; Jenson, *Biographical Encyclopedia*, 1:278-82. See also, Anderson, *Investigating the Book of Mormon Witnesses*, 140-141; and Anderson, "Joseph Smith's Brothers," 30-33; Dean Jarman, "The Life and Contributions of Samuel Harrison Smith" [M.A. thesis, Brigham Young University, 1961].)

Smith, Sophronia (1803-1876), born at Tunbridge, Orange County, Vermont. Married Calvin W. Stoddard at Palmyra, New York, 1828. Mother of two known daughters. After Calvin's death in 1836, Sophronia married William McCleary in 1838. She was numbered with the saints in Ohio, Missouri, and Illinois, but did not follow Brigham Young west. Died in Illinois. (*Utah Genealogical and Historical Magazine*, 26:102, 151; Stoddard Family Bible, in possession of Buddy Youngreen; Richard L. Anderson, "What were Joseph Smith's Sisters Like . . . ?" 42- 44.)

Smith, Sylvester (c.1805- ?), born in Connecticut. Converted to Mormonism, 1831. One of the presidents of seventy, 1835-37. Missionary to New England with Jared Carter in 1832. Quarrelsome participant in Zion's Camp, 1834. Temporary scribe to Joseph Smith in 1836 during illness of Warren Parrish. Member of the Kirtland high council, 1835-36. Left the Church in 1837. Living in Kirtland, Ohio, 1840, and Willoughby, 1850. (Jenson, *Biographical Encyclopedia*, 1:191; Cook, *Revelations*, 156; U.S. Census: Lake County, Ohio, 1840, 1950.)

Smith, William (1811-1893), farmer, newspaper editor. Married Caroline Amanda Grant in 1833. Participant in march of Zion's Camp, 1834. Member of the Quorum of Twelve, 1835-45. Settled at Plymouth, Illinois, 1839. Represented Hancock County in the Illinois State House of Representatives, 1842. Editor of Nauvoo newspaper, *The Wasp*, 1842. Appointed presiding patriarch, 1845. Rebellious and headstrong, he was excommunicated in 1845. Associated with James J. Strang, 1846-47; joined Reorganized LDS Church, 1878. Died at Osterdock, Clay County, Iowa. (Cook, *Revelations*, 276-77; Jenson, *Biographical Encyclopedia*, 1:86- 87; Anderson, "Joseph Smith's Brothers," 32-33; Calvin P. Rudd, "William Smith: Brother of the Prophet Joseph Smith" [M.A. thesis, Brigham Young University, 1973].)

Snow, Zerubbabel (1809-1888), school teacher, merchant, lawyer; elder brother of Erastus Snow. Born at St. Johnsbury, Caledonia County, Vermont. Converted to Mormonism and moved to Ohio, 1832. Commissary of Zion's Camp, 1834. Practiced law in Ohio, 1839-50. Associate Justice of Utah Territory, 1851-54. Missionary to Australia, 1856-58. Probate judge of Cedar County, Utah, 1859-61; and Utah County, 1862-64. Salt Lake County prosecuting attorney, 1865-84. (Jenson, *Biographical Encyclopedia*, 4:691; Tullidge, *History of Salt Lake City*, 160-166.)

Squires, Andrew Jackson (1815- ?), physician; born at Aurora, Portage County, Ohio. Studied medicine at the Medical University at Willoughby, Ohio, 1840-41. Married Martha Wilmot, 1850. Began practice of medicine at Mantua in 1864; still practicing in Hiram, Ohio, 1885. Served in Ohio state legislature, 1859-61. (*History of Portage County, Ohio* [Chicago: Warncr, Bccrs and Co., 1885], 750.)

Stanley, Harvey (1811-1862), stone cutter, dairyman; born in New York. Member of the first quorum of seventy. Participant in march of Zion's Camp to Missouri, 1834. Married Lerona Eliza Cahoon, daughter of Reynolds Cahoon, in Kirtland, Ohio, 1836. Lerona died, 1840. Worked on Nauvoo Temple. Living at Keokuk, Lee County, Iowa, 1850. Migrated in the 1850s to Petaluma, Marin County, California where he died. (U.S. Census: Lee County, Iowa, 1850; Marin County, California, 1860; Marin County, California, Probate Register, Vol. B, 29; Shurtleff and Cahoon, *Reynolds Cahoon and his Stalwart Sons*, 93-94.)

Stoddard, Calvin (1801-1836), married Joseph Smith's sister Sophronia in Palmyra, New York, 1828. Parents of two daughters. Assisted in building the Kirtland Temple. Died at Palmyra, New York. (*Utah Genealogical and Historical Magazine*, 26:102, 151; Stoddard family bible; Smith, *History of the Church*, 2:206; Anderson, "What were Joseph Smith's Sisters Like?")

Stowell, Josiah (1770-184?), farmer, miller; born at Winchester, Cheshire County, New Hampshire. Married Miriam Bridgeman. Parents of eight children. Stowell owned a farm and saw mill two miles south of Bainbridge, New York. Employed Joseph Smith on his farm, and in search for lost Spanish treasure in northern Pennsylvania in 1820s. Stowell did not follow the Latter-day Saints west from New York, although he remained friendly toward them. He died at Smithboro, Tioga County, New York. (William H.H. Stowell, *Stowell Genealogy* [Rutland, Vermont, 1922], 229-30; Porter, "Origins of the Church," 121-23; 177-78, 207-210.)

Stowell, Miriam (1807-1878), daughter of Josiah Stowell; married Benjamin Richards in 1837. Died in Tioga County, New York. (Stowell, *Stowell Genealogy*, 229-30.)

Stowell, Rhoda (1805-1844), daughter of Josiah Stowell; married Ward Bovier in 1835. Died at Elmira, Chemung County, New York. (Stowell, *Stowell Genealogy*, 229-30.)

Stringham, Esther Knight (1798-1831), daughter of Joseph Knight, Sr., was born at Marlborough, Windham County, Vermont. Married William Stringham. Parents of four children. She died in Jackson County, Missouri. (*Utah Genealogical and Historical Magazine*, 26:148-149; Hartley, *They Are My Friends*.)

Stringham, Julia Ann (1817-1886), granddaughter of Joseph Knight, Sr. Born in Broome County, New York. One of four children of William Stringham and Esther Knight. (*Utah Genealogical and Historical Magazine*, 26:147-149.)

Stringham, William (1788-1868), tailor; born at North Hempstead, Queens County, Long Island, New York. Married Esther Knight, daughter of Joseph Knight, Sr. After her death in 1833, he married Esther's sister, Polly. Polly's death in 1844 was followed by a third marriage to Eliza Lake in Nauvoo, Illinois. Moved with the Latter-day Saints to Garden Grove, Iowa for a time, but returned to Illinois where he worked as a tailor. Contacted by Mormon missionaries in 1855 and rebaptized, the Stringhams crossed the plains to Utah in 1856. William died at Manti, Sanpete County, Utah. (Family Group Records Collection; *Utah Genealogical and Historical Magazine*, 26:146-149; Hartley, *They Are My Friends*, 187-189.)

Strong, Elial (c.1810-1834), born at Sullivan, Tioga County, Pennsylvania. One of the first Mormon converts from Tioga County, 1831. One of the missionaries who converted Heber C. Kimball, Brigham Young, and others at Mendon, New York, 1832. He died in Missouri. ("Journal History," 31 December 1831; 15 April 1832; Backman, *Profile*, 69.)

Sweet, Northrop (1802-1881), was born in New York. Married Elathan Harris, daughter of Emer Harris. Living in Palmyra, New York, 1830. Baptized by Parley Pratt in October 1830. Shortly after moving to Ohio in 1831, he left the Church, and with Wycom Clark and others organized a church, "The Pure Church of Christ," which did not exist long. Moved to Branch County, Michigan about 1845. He died at Batavia, Branch County. (Cook, *Revelations*, 48.)

Tanner, John (1778-1850), farmer; born at Hopkinton, Washington County, Rhode Island. Living in Bolton, Warren County, New York when converted through the miraculous healing of his leg by Mormon missionaries in 1832. Contributed substantial of his wealth for the benefit of the Church. Moved to Kirtland, Ohio, 1835, and Missouri, 1838, where he suffered mob violence. Settled at Montrose, Iowa, 1840-46. Crossed the plains to Utah in 1848 and settled at South Cottonwood, where he died. (Jenson, *Biographical Encyclopedia*, 2:799-802; Maurice Tanner, *Descendants of John Tanner* [n.p.: The Tanner Family Association, 1942], 14-23.)

Thayre, Ezra (1791- ?), born at Randolph, Windsor County, Vermont. Builder of bridges, dams, mills in area of Palmyra, New York. Married Polly Wales, 1810. Baptized by Parley Pratt, 1830. Member of the committee to purchase land for Mormon settlement at Kirtland, Ohio, 1833. Participant in march of Zion's Camp, 1834. Did not support leadership of the Quorum of Twelve after the death of Joseph Smith.

Moved to Michigan, 1849; residing in Ottawa County, 1860. Joined the RLDS Church. (Cook, *Revelations*, 47-48; Smith, *History of the Church*, 1:335; 2:185.)

Thompson, Jonathan (1787- ?), shoemaker, born in Massachusetts. Had been a town supervisor at Norwich, Chenango County, New York, 1821-22. Living at Plymouth, Chenango County, New York in 1830. (U.S. Census: Chenango County, New York, 1830; Smith, *History of Chenango and Madison Counties, New York*, 322.)

Tippets, John Harvey (1810-1890), farmer; born in Rockingham County, New Hampshire. Converted to Mormonism, 1832. Married Abby Jane Smith, 1834. Involved with the Church in Missouri and Illinois. Member of Mormon Battalion, 1846. Accompanied sick detachment to Pueblo, Colorado, then joined the saints at Winter Quarters. Left pioneer company at Fort Laramie to lead Battalion members and Mississippi saints to Salt Lake Valley in 1847. Moved to Farmington, Davis County, Utah, 1864. Ordained patriarch, 1878. Died at Farmington. (Family Group Records Collection; Carter, *Our Pioneer Heritage*, 2:606-607.)

Tippets, Joseph H. (1814-1868), farmer; a cousin of John H. and William Tippets. Born at Lewis, Essex County, New York. Participated in construction of the temple at Kirtland, Ohio. Married Rosella Elvira Perry, 1837. At Quincy, Illinois in 1840. Crossed plains to Utah, 1848. Resided at Kaysville, Farmington, and Brigham City, where he died. (Family Group Records Collection; Backman, *Profile*, 72, 99; U.S. Census: Adams County, Illinois, 1840.)

Tippets, William (1812-1877), farmer; born at Groton, Hillsboro County, New Hampshire. Married Sophia Mead, 1842. Residing in Liberty, Clay County, Missouri, 1844-50; Salt Lake City, Utah, 1850-60. Died at Perry, Box Elder County, Utah. (Family Group Records Collection; Lydia Walker Forsgren, *History of Box Elder County* [Box Elder County Daughters of the Utah Pioneers, 1937], 14.)

Turnham, Joel (1784-1862), farmer; born in Virginia. Moved to Clay County, Missouri by 1820. Built a tobacco warehouse at Liberty Landing, 1830. County commissioner in 1829. Served as judge of the Clay County court 1827-30; 1838-44; and 1854-56. Living at Fishing River, Clay County, 1850. Appointed to a committee to warn abolitionists from Clay County, 1855. Died at Cameron, Milam County, Texas. (Woodson, *History of Clay County*, 331-32; *History of Clay and Platte Counties, Missouri* [St. Louis: National Historical Company, 1885], 118, 123, 170-173; John T. Martin and Louis C. Hill, "Milam County, Texas Records," Typescript [Waco, Texas, 1968], 2:149; U.S. Census: Clay County, Missouri, 1850; Milam County Texas, 1860.)

Wakefield, Joseph H. (1792-1835), born at Dublin, Cheshire County, New Hampshire. Married Eunice Sawyer, 1812. Resided in

Watertown, Jefferson County, New York prior to joining the Latter-day Saints in 1831. Proselyting in St. Lawrence County, New York in 1832 where he baptized George A. Smith. Moved to Kirtland, Ohio in 1833 and a short time later left the church. In January 1834 he associated with a Kirtland anti-Mormon committee dedicated to the defamation of Joseph Smith's character, and advocated the Spalding theory of Book of Mormon origins. Died at Willoughby, Ohio. (Homer Wakefield, *Wakefield Memorial Comprising an Historical, Genealogical and Biographical Register of the Name and Family of Wakefield* [Bloomington, Illinois: privately printed, 1897], 57; Cook, *Revelations*, 69; *Painesville Telegraph* 5 (31 January 1834): 3.)

Weaver, Russell (1789-1865), farmer, settled in Cambria, Niagara County, New York, by 1810; lived there all his life. (William Pool, *Landmarks of Niagara County, New York* [Syracuse: D. Mason, 1897]: 245; U.S. Census: Niagara County, New York, 1850, 1860.)

Webb, Edwin Densmore (1813-?), carpenter; born at Hanover, Chautauqua County, New York. One of the seventies in Kirtland, Ohio, 1836. Living in the Nauvoo, Illinois 1st Ward, 1842, and in Racine, Wisconsin, 1842-50. Crossed plains to Utah, 1853. Living at Fillmore, Millard County, Utah, 1860 where he probably died. (Family Group Records Collection; Backman, *Profile*, 74; U.S. Census: Marquette County, Wisconsin, 1850; Millard County, Utah, 1860.)

Webb, John (1808-1894), wagon maker, farmer; born at Manham, Herkimer County, New York. Married Catharine Wilcox, 1836. Baptized in 1839. Living in Adams County, Illinois in early 1840s. The federal census lists him in Salt Lake Valley, 1850; Fillmore, Millard County, Utah, 1860; and Petersburgh, Millard County in 1870. In 1855 he was one of the pioneer settlers of Holden, Millard County. He died at Coyote, Garfield County, Utah. (Family Group Records Collection; *Deseret Evening News*, 12 June 1894; Daughters of the Utah Pioneers, *An Enduring Legacy* [Salt Lake City: Utah Printing Company, 1982], 5:333.)

Whitlock, Harvey (1809- ?), born in Massachusetts. Joined the Church and moved to Jackson County, Missouri, 1831. Victim of the expulsion from Jackson County, 1833. Excommunicated, 1835; rebaptized, 1836. Withdrew from Church, 1838. Living in Cedar County, Iowa in 1840. Medical doctor in Salt Lake City, 1850. Moved to California in 1864; joined the Reorganized Church. (Cook, *Revelations*, 81.)

Whitmer, Christian (1798-1835), shoemaker. Born in Pennsylvania, the oldest son of Peter Whitmer. Married Anne Schott in 1825. Officer in the New York militia, 1825. One of the Eight Witnesses to the Book of Mormon. Moved to Ohio and Missouri, and was among those driven from Jackson County in 1833. Appointed to the Missouri high council, 1834. Died in Clay County, Missouri. (Jenson, *Biograph-*

ical Encyclopedia, 1:276; Smith, *History of the Church*, 2:357; Anderson, *Investigating the Book of Mormon Witnesses*, chapter 9.)

Whitmer, David (1805-1888), born near Harrisburg, Dauphin County, Pennsylvania. One of the Three Witnesses to the Book of Mormon. First met Joseph Smith during a business trip to Palmyra, New York in 1828. Baptized in June 1829. Married Julia Ann Jolly, 1831. Appointed president of the Church in Missouri, 1834. Left the Church in Missouri in 1838 and spent the remainder of his life there. Operated a livery stable at Richmond, Ray County. Elected mayor of Richmond, 1867-68. (Cook, *Revelations*, 24-25; Jenson, *Biographical Encyclopedia*, 1:263-71; Anderson, *Investigating the Book of Mormon Witnesses*, 67-92.)

Whitmer, Anne Schott (1801-1866), wife of Christian Whitmer. After the death of her husband in 1835 she married Francis Hulett. Following a divorce she returned to Fayette, Seneca County, where she died. (*Utah Genealogical and Historical Magazine*, 26:107; Jenson, *Historical Record*, 7:610.)

Whitmer, Elizabeth Ann Schott (1803- ?), was born in Pennsylvania. Married Jacob Whitmer, 1825. Living with her family in Richmond, Ray County Missouri in 1850. Following the death of her husband in 1856, she was living with her daughter's family (J.P. Bisbee) in Ray County in 1860. (U.S. Census: Ray County, Missouri, 1850, 1860; Porter, "Origins of the Church," 225-26.)

Whitmer, Elizabeth Ann (1815-1892), daughter of Peter Whitmer, Sr. and Mary Musselman. Born at Fayette, Seneca County, New York. Baptized by Oliver Cowdery, 1830. Married Oliver Cowdery, 1832; parents of six children, only one of whom grew to maturity. Living in Southwest City, Missouri in 1887. (*Utah Genealogical and Historical Magazine*, 26:106.)

Whitmer, Jacob (1800-1856), shoemaker, farmer. Born in Pennsylvania. Married Elizabeth Ann Schott, 1825. One of the Eight Witnesses to the Book of Mormon. Engaged with the Latter-day Saints in Ohio and Missouri. Among those driven from Jackson County, 1833. Left the Church in 1838 and settled near Richmond, Ray County, Missouri, where he remained until his death. (Jenson, *Biographical Encyclopedia*, 1:276-77; Anderson, *Investigating the Book of Mormon Witnesses*, Chapter 9.)

Whitmer, John (1802-1878), farmer, stock raiser. Born in Pennsylvania. Among the first converts to Mormonism. One of the Eight Witnesses to the Book of Mormon. Scribe to Joseph Smith. Appointed Church historian, 1831. Wrote a history titled, "The Book of John Whitmer," covering the years 1831-38. Married Sarah Jackson, 1833. Appointed counselor to his brother, David, in the Missouri Church presidency, 1834. Editor of the *Messenger and Advocate*, 1835-36. Left the church in 1838; remained at Far West, Caldwell County, Missouri, where he died. (Cook, *Revelations*, 25-26; Jenson, *Biographical Encyclopedia*, 1:251-52.)

Whitmer, Mary Musselman (1778-1856), a native of Germany, wife of Peter Whitmer, Sr. Five of her eight children were witnesses to the Book of Mormon. In addition to her own large family, she had the added charge of Joseph Smith, his wife, and Oliver Cowdery during translation work on the Book of Mormon at her Fayette, New York home. She claimed to have been shown the Book of Mormon plates by a divine messenger during this time. She died at Richmond, Ray County, Missouri. (Jenson, *Biographical Encyclopedia*, 1:283; Anderson, *Investigating the Book of Mormon Witnesses*, 30-32; *Utah Genealogical and Historical Magazine*, 26:107.)

Whitmer, Peter, Jr. (1809-1836), tailor. Born at Fayette, Seneca County, New York. One of the Eight Witnesses to the Book of Mormon. Baptized in June 1830. Participant in the Lamanite mission to Ohio and Missouri, 1830-31. Married Vashti Higley, 1832. Appointed to the Missouri high council, 1836. Died in Clay County, Missouri. (Cook, *Revelations*, 26-27; Jenson, *Biographical Encyclopedia*, 1:277.)

Whitmer, Peter, Sr. (1773-1854), farmer; born in Pennsylvania. Moved to Fayette, Seneca County, New York about 1809. Overseer of highways, 1826-27. He was among the first converts to Mormonism in 1830. The Church was organized in his log house at Fayette on 6 April 1830. Followed the Church into Ohio and Missouri, but fell away in 1838. Died at Richmond, Ray County, Missouri. (Jenson, *Biographical Encyclopedia*, 1:282-83; Anderson, "The Whitmers," *The Ensign* 9 (August 1979): 35-40; and *Investigating the Book of Mormon Witnesses*, 125; Porter, "Origins of the Church," 224-234.)

Whitney, Elizabeth Ann Smith (1800-1882), born at Derby, New Haven County, Connecticut. When her Aunt Sarah Smith left Connecticut in 1818 to make her home in Ohio, Sarah persuaded her brother Gibson to allow her neice, Elizabeth Ann, to go with her. The two women settled in Kirtland, Ohio where Elizabeth married Newel K. Whitney in 1822. She and her husband were converted by Mormon missionaries in November 1830. Appointed first counselor to Emma Smith at the organization of the Relief Society in Nauvoo, 1842. Her husband's death in 1850 left her with a family of eleven. (*Utah Genealogical and Historical Magazine*, 28:66; Whitney, "A Leaf From an Autobiography," 41.)

Whitney, Newel K. (1795-1850), merchant. Born at Marlborough, Windham County, Vermont. Partner with Sidney Gilbert in a mercantile firm at Painesville and later, Kirtland, Ohio. Married Elizabeth Ann Smith, 1822. Appointed bishop at Kirtland, 1831; Nauvoo Middle Ward, 1839; Salt Lake City 18th Ward, 1849. Traveled with Joseph Smith to

Missouri and New York, 1832. Elected alderman at Nauvoo, 1841. Crossed the plains to Utah, in 1848. Died at Salt Lake City. (Cook, *Revelations*, 102-103; Jenson, *Biographical Encyclopedia*, 1:222-27; Larry N. Poulsen, "The Life and Contributions of Newel K. Whitney" [M.A. thesis, Brigham Young University, 1966].)

Whitney, Samuel (1772-1846), father of Newel K. Whitney, was born at Marlborough, Windham County, Vermont. Married Susanna Kimball, 1792. Joined the Latter-day Saints, November 1835. Died at Kirtland, Ohio. (Poulsen, "The Life and Contributions of Newel K. Whitney," 66; *Progressive Men of Bingham, Fremont and Oneida Counties, Idaho* [Chicago, 1904], 467.)

Wight, Lyman (1796-1858), farmer; born at Fairfield, Herkimer County, New York. Married Harriet Benton, 1823. Affiliated with the Campbellites in Kirtland, Ohio when converted to Mormonism in 1830. Among the Latter-day Saints driven from Jackson County, Missouri, 1833. The revelation that called missionaries to solicit volunteers for Zion's camp listed Wight and Sidney Rigdon as companions. Member of the Clay County, Missouri high council, 1834. Imprisoned with Joseph Smith at Liberty, Missouri, 1838-39. Member of Council of Twelve, 1841-48. Moved to Texas, 1845. Excommunicated, 1848. Chief Justice of Gillespie County, Texas, 1850. Died at Dexter, Medina County, Texas. (Cook, *Revelations*, 82-83; *Doctrine and Covenants* 103:38; Jenson, *Biographical Encyclopedia*, 1:93; U.S. Census: Gillespie County, Texas, 1850.)

Wilcox, Catherine Noramore (1809-1884), was born at Kremina, New York. Married Eber Wilcox in 1826, who died of cholera in Clay County, Missouri in 1834. Married John Webb, 1836. Lived in Illinois and Missouri. Crossed plains to Utah in 1848. By the 1860 census, Catherine had apparently separated from John Webb. (Family Group Records Collection; U.S. Census: Salt Lake County, 1850; Millard County, 1860.)

Williams, Frederick Granger (1787-1842), physician. Born at Suffield, Hartford County, Connecticut. Married Rebecca Swain, 1815. Converted by Mormon missionaries who came through Kirtland, Ohio, in November 1830. Appointed clerk to Joseph Smith in July 1832. Counselor in the First Presidency, 1833-37. Participated in march of Zion's Camp, 1834. Disaffected from the Church and later restored to fellowship, 1837- 39. Died at Quincy, Illinois. (Jenson, *Biographical Encyclopedia*, 1:51-52; Cook, *Revelations*, 104-5; Frederick G. Williams III, "Frederick Granger Williams of the First Presidency of the Church," *BYU Studies* 12 [September 1972]: 243-61].)

Wilson, Robert (1800-1870), born near Staunton, Augusta County, Virginia. Moved to Franklin, Howard County, Missouri in 1820. Probate judge of Howard County, 1824-27. Married Peggy Snoddy, 1825. Clerk of the Randolph circuit and county courts, 1828-1840. Wilson was a brigadier general in the 2nd brigade of John B. Clark's 1st Division of Missouri militia during the Mormon conflict of 1838. Prominent lawyer of central and western Missouri. Represented Randolph County in the Missouri legislature, 1844-45, and later served two sessions in the state senate representing the district containing Andrew, Holt, and Atchison Counties. Appointed U.S. senator in 1862. Died at Marshall, Missouri. (William Bay, *Reminiscences of the Bench and Bar of Missouri* [St. Louis: F.H. Thomas and Co., 1878], 561-63.)

Works, Angeline Eliza (1814-1880), born at Aurelius, Cayuga County, New York. A sister to Brigham Young's wife, Miriam. Married Ebenezer Robinson in Kirtland, Ohio, 1835. Died at Hamilton, Decatur County, Iowa. (Family Group Records Collection; *Biographical and Historical Record of Ringgold and Decatur Counties, Iowa*, 651-52.)

Young, Brigham (1801-1877), carpenter, painter, glazier. Born at Whitingham, Windham County, Vermont. Married Miriam Works, 1824. Living in Mendon, New York when he joined the Latter-day Saints in 1832. Moved to Kirtland, Ohio, 1832. With Zion's Camp, 1834. His Kirtland years were divided between missionary work and labor on the temple. He succeeded Thomas Marsh as president of the Quorum of Twelve. Member of the Quorum of Twelve, 1835-1847; Church President, 1848-1877. Directed Mormon evacuation from Missouri, 1838-39. Mission to England, 1839-41. Elected to Nauvoo city council, 1841. Directed Mormon migration from Nauvoo to Utah, 1846-48. Governor of Utah Territory, 1850; Superintendent of Indian Affairs, 1851-57. Directed colonization of hundreds of communities in western U.S.. Died in Salt Lake City. (Jenson, *Biographical Encyclopedia*, 1:8-14; Cook, *Revelations*, 279-81. Leonard J. Arrington, *Brigham Young: American Moses* [New York, 1985].)

Young, Joseph (1797-1881), painter, glazier; brother of Brigham Young. Born at Hopkinton, Middlesex County, Massachusetts. Converted to Mormonism in 1832. Married Jane A. Bicknell, 1834. A president of the First Quorum of Seventy, 1835-1881. Participant in Zion's Camp march to Missouri, 1834; and Kirtland Camp, 1838. Witnessed the Haun's Mill Massacre, in Caldwell County, Missouri, 1838. Moved to Nauvoo, Illinois, 1840. Crossed the plains to Utah in 1850. Missionary in England, 1870. Died at Salt Lake City, Utah. (Jenson, *Biographical Encyclopedia*, 1:187-88; Cook, *Revelations*, 281.)

Young, Lorenzo Dow (1807-1895), farmer, nurseryman. Brother of Brigham Young. Born at Smyrna, Chenango County, New York. Married Persis Goodall, 1826. Converted to Mormonism, 1832. During his Ohio years he was a member of Zion's Camp and supervised plastering of the temple at Kirtland, Ohio. Arrived in Utah with Mormon pioneers of 1847. Bishop of Salt Lake City 18th Ward, 1851-78. Ordained patriarch, 1877. Died at Salt Lake City. (Family Group Records Collection; Jenson, *Biographical Encyclopedia*, 4:724-25; Whitney, *History of Utah*, 4:53-55.)

Young, Phineas (1799-1879), printer, lawyer, saddler; born at Hopkinton, Middlesex County, Massachusetts. Brother of Brigham Young. Married Clarissa Hamilton, 1818; and later, Lucy Cowdery. Joined the Church in April 1832 and was en route to Jackson County, Missouri, in 1833 when he received news of the driving of the Saints from that place. Returned to Kirtland, Ohio, and worked in the printing office. Arrived in Utah with the Mormon pioneer company of 1847. Instrumental in the return of Oliver Cowdery to the Church, 1848. Missionary in Canada and England. Bishop of Salt Lake City 2nd Ward, 1864-71. He died at Salt Lake City. (*Deseret Weekly*, 3 February 1858; Jenson, *Biographical Encyclopedia*, 4:511; Carter, *Our Pioneer Heritage*, 2:509.)

WORKS CITED

Published Works

Ahlstrom, Sidney E. *A Religious History of the American People*. New Haven and London: Yale University Press, 1972.

"Alexander Neibaur." *Utah Genealogical Magazine and Historical Magazine* 5 (April 1914): 53-63.

Alexander, Thomas G. *Mormonism in Transition: A History of the Latter-day Saints, 1890-1930*. Urbana and Chicago: University of Illinois Press, 1986.

Allen, James B., and Glen M Leonard. *The Story of the Latter-day Saints*. Salt Lake City: Deseret Book Company, 1976.

Alton Commercial Gazette (Alton, Illinois), 19 February 1839.

Anderson, Mary A. *Ancestry and Posterity of Joseph Smith*. Independence: Herald Printing House, 1929.

Anderson, Paul L. "Truman O. Angell: Architect and Saint," in *Supporting Saints: Life Stories of Nineteenth-Century Mormons*, edited by Donald Q. Cannon and David J. Whittaker. Religious Studies Center: Brigham Young University, 1985.

Anderson, Richard L. "The Alvin Smith Story." *Ensign* 17 (August 1987): 58-72.

————. "Atchison's Letters and the Causes of Mormon Expulsion from Missouri." *BYU Studies* 26 (Summer 1986): 3-47.

————. "Confirming Records of Moroni's Coming." *Improvement Era* 73 (September 1970): 4-9.

————. "The House Where the Church was Organized." *Improvement Era* 73 (April 1970): 16-25.

————. "The Impact of the First Preaching in Ohio." *BYU Studies* 11 (Summer 1971): 474-96.

————. *Investigating the Book of Mormon Witnesses*. Salt Lake City: Deseret Book Company, 1981.

————. "Joseph Smith's Brothers. *Ensign* 9 (September 1979): 30-33.

————. *Joseph Smith's New England Heritage*. Salt Lake City: Deseret Book Company, 1971.

————. "Joseph Smith's New York Reputation Reappraised." *BYU Studies* 10 (Spring 1970): 283-314.

————. "The Mature Joseph Smith and Treasure Searching." *BYU Studies* 24 (Fall 1984): 489-560.

————. "The Reliability of the Early History of Lucy and Joseph Smith."

Dialogue 4 (Summer 1969): 13-28.
———. "The Second Witness of Priesthood Restoration." *Improvement Era* 71 (September 1968): 15-24.
———. "What Were Joseph Smith's Sisters Like?" *Ensign* 9 (March 1979): 42-44.
———. "The Whitmers." *Ensign* 9 (August 1979): 35-40.
———. "Who Were the Six who Organized the Church on 6 April 1830?" *Ensign* 10 (June 1980): 44-45.
Andreas, A.T. *History of Chicago*. Chicago: A.T. Andreas, Publisher, 1884.
Arrington, Leonard J. "Oliver Cowdery's Kirtland, Ohio, 'Sketch Book.' " *BYU Studies* 12 (Summer 1972): 410-26.
———. *Brigham Young: American Moses*. New York: Alfred A. Knopf, 1985.
Arrington, Leonard J. and Davis Bitton. *The Mormon Experience: A History of the Latter-day Saints*. New York: Alfred A. Knopf, 1979.
Ashment, Edward H. "The Facsimiles of the Book of Abraham: A Reappraisal." *Sunstone* 4 (December 1979): 33-48.
Austin, Emily M. *Mormonism; or Life Among the Mormons*. Madison, Wisconsin: M.J. Cantwell, 1882.
Avery, Elroy M. and Catharine H. Avery. *The Groton Avery Clan*. Cleveland, 1912.
Backman, Milton V., Jr. *American Religions and the Rise of Mormonism*. Salt Lake City: Deseret Book Company, 1965.
———. *The Heavens Resound: A History of the Latter-day Saints in Ohio 1830-1838*. Salt Lake City: Deseret Book Company, 1983.
———. *Joseph Smith's First Vision: The First Vision in its Historical Context*. Salt Lake City: Bookcraft, 1971.
———. *A Profile of Latter-day Saints of Kirtland, Ohio and Members of Zion's Camp*. Provo, Utah: Brigham Young University, 1982.
Barnes, Joseph W. "Obediah Dogberry: Rochester Freethinker." *Rochester History* 36 (July 1974): 1-24.
Bates, Irene M. "Uncle John Smith, 1781-1854: Patriarchal Bridge." *Dialogue: A Journal of Mormon Thought* 20 (Fall 1987): 79-89.
Bay, William. *Reminiscences of the Bench and Bar of Missouri*. St. Louis: F.H. Thomas and Company, 1878.
Bell, Charles H. *Bench and Bar of New Hampshire*. New York, 1894.
The Bench and Bar of St. Louis, Kansas City, Jefferson City, and Other Missouri Cities. St. Louis: American Biographical Publishing Company, 1884.
Bennett, James G. "The Mormons—A Leaf From Joe Smith." *New York Herald*, 3 April 1842.
Bent, Charles, ed. *History of Whiteside County, Illinois*. Morrison, Illinois: L.P. Allen, 1887.
Biographical Directory of the American Congress. Washington, D.C.: U.S. Government Printing Office, 1971.
Biographical and Historical Record of Ringgold and Decatur Counties, Iowa Chicago: The Lewis Publishing Company, 1887.
Blair, Alma R. "The Haun's Mill Massacre." *BYU Studies* 13 (Autumn 1972): 62-67.
Blanchard, Rufus. *History of DuPage County, Illinois.* Chicago: O.L. Baskin & Co., 1882

WORKS CITED

Bode, Carl. *The American Lyceum: Town Meeting of the Mind*. New York: Oxford University Press, 1956.

Boggs, William M. "A Short Biographical Sketch of Lilburn W. Boggs, by his Son." *Missouri Historical Review* 4 (January 1910): 106-10.

Bonney, Edward. *The Banditti of the Prairies*. Norman, Oklahoma: University of Oklahoma Press, 1963.

"The Book of Mormon." *Wayne County Sentinel* (Palmyra, New York), 26 March 1830.

The Book of Mormon: Another Testament of Jesus Christ. Translated by Joseph Smith, Jr., rev. ed. Salt Lake City: The Church of Jesus Christ of Latter-day Saints, 1986.

"The Book of Pukei." *Reflector* (Palmyra, New York), 12 June; 7 July 1830.

Booth, Ezra. Letters dated Nelson, Portage County, Ohio, to Reverend Ira Eddy, 12 September; 2, 24, 31 October; 7, 14, 21, 29 November; 6 December, 1831. Published in "Mormonism." *Ohio Star* (Ravenna, Portage County, Ohio), 13, 20, 27 October; 3, 10, 17, 24, November; 8 December, 1831.

Boynton, John F. and Caroline H. Boynton. *The Boynton Family*. Caroline H. Boynton, Publisher, 1897.

Buchmiller, Golden A. "Grandin Building Opens to Visitors in Palmyra." *Church News*, 30 October 1982.

Bush, Lester. "The Spalding Theory Then and Now." *Dialogue: A Journal of Mormon Thought* 10 (Autumn 1977): 40-69.

Bushman, Richard L. "The Book of Mormon in Early Mormon History." In *New Views of Mormon History: A Collection of Essays in Honor of Leonard J. Arrington*, edited by Davis Bitton and Maureen U. Beecher. Salt Lake City: University of Utah Press, 1987, 3-18.

———. *Joseph Smith and the Beginnings of Mormonism*. Urbana and Chicago: University of Illinois Press, 1984.

———. "Mormon Persecutions in Missouri, 1833." *BYU Studies* 3 (Autumn 1960): 11-20.

Butler, Jon. "Magic, Astrology and the Early American Religious Heritage, 1600-1760." *American Historical Review* 84 (April 1979): 317-46.

Butterfield, Lyman H. "The Adams Papers," in "Publishing the Papers of Great Men: A Session at the Sixty-Ninth Annual Meeting of the American Historical Association 30 December 1954." *Daedalus* 86 (May 1955): 64-65.

Cannon, Donald Q. "The King Follett Discourse: Joseph Smith's Greatest Sermon in Historical Perspective." *BYU Studies* 18 (Winter 1978): 179-225.

Cannon, Donald Q. and Lyndon W. Cook, eds. *Far West Record: Minutes of The Church of Jesus Christ of Latter-day Saints, 1830-1844*. Salt Lake City: Deseret Book Company, 1983.

Carmack, John K. "Fayette: The Place the Church was Organized." *Ensign* 19 (February 1989): 14-19.

Carter, Kate B., ed. *Our Pioneer Heritage*. 20 vols. Salt Lake City: Utah Printing Company, 1958-1977.

Clark, John A. *Gleanings by the Way*. Philadelphia: W.J. & J.K. Simon, 1842.

Clegg, Michael, *Portage County, Ohio Newspaper Obituary Abstracts*. Fort Wayne, Indiana: Published by author, 1982.

Cochran, Louis. *Alexander Campbell: The Man and His Mission*. Dallas, Texas: Wilkinson Publishing Company, 1965.

WORKS CITED

Conard, Howard. *Encyclopedia of the History of Missouri*. 6 vols. New York, Louisville, St. Louis: The Southern History Company, 1901.

Cook, Lyndon W. " 'I Have Sinned Against Heaven . . . .': Thomas B. Marsh Returns to the Church." *BYU Studies*, 20 (Summer 1980): 389-400.

———. *Joseph Smith and the Law of Consecration*. Provo, Utah: Grandin Book Company, 1985.

———. *Joseph C. Kingsbury: A Biography*. Provo, Utah: Grandin Book Company, 1985.

———. *The Revelations of the Prophet Joseph Smith: A Historical and Biographical Commentary of the Doctrine and Covenants*. Provo, Utah: Seventies Mission Bookstore, 1981.

Cook, Thomas L. *Palmyra and Vicinity*. Palmyra, New York: Palmyra Courier-Journal, 1930.

Corbett, Pearson H. *Hyrum Smith Patriarch*. Salt Lake City: Deseret Book Company, 1963

Crawley, Peter, and David J. Whittaker. *Mormon Imprints in Great Britain and the Empire 1836-1857*. Provo, Utah: Friends of the Brigham Young University Library, 1987.

Cross, Whitney R. *The Burned-over District: The Social and Intellectual History of Enthusiastic Religion in Western New York, 1800-1850*. New York: Cornell University Press, 1950.

Cumming, John and Audrey. *The Pilgrimage of Temperance Mack*. Mount Pleasant, Michigan: published by authors, 1967.

Daughters of the Utah Pioneers. *An Enduring Legacy*. 10 vols. Salt Lake City: Utah Printing Company, 1978-1987.

Dear, Mary C. *Two Hundred Thirty-Eight Years of the Whitmer Family: 1737-1976*. Richmond, Missouri: Beck Printing Company, 1976.

"Death of Hon. D.N. White." *Pittsburgh Commercial Gazette*, 2 April 1888.

Deseret Evening News. Salt Lake City, 1867-present.

Deseret Weekly. Salt Lake City: Deseret News Company, 1850-1898.

Dewey, Richard L. *Porter Rockwell: A Biography*. New York: Paramount Books, 1986.

The Doctrine and Covenants of the Church of Jesus Christ of Latter-day Saints. Rev. ed. Salt Lake City: The Church of Jesus Christ of Latter-day Saints, 1986.

Document Containing the Correspondence, Orders, &c. in Relation to the Disturbances with the Mormons; and the Evidence Given before the Hon. Austin A. King. Fayette, Missouri: Boon's Lick Democrat, 1841.

Draper, Delbert M. *The Mormon Drapers*. Salt Lake City: published by author, 1958.

Drisler, Henry. *A Commemorative Discourse, Prepared and Delivered at the Request of the Trustees and Alumni of the College*. Discourse in honor of Charles Anthon, Jay-Professor of the Greek Language and Literature at Columbia College. New York: D. Van Nostrand, 1868.

Dwight, Benjamin W. *History of the Descendants of Elder John Strong*. Albany: Joel Munsell, 1871.

Egle, William H. "I. Daniel Rupp." *Historical Magazine* 9 (February 1871): 111-15.

Ehat, Andrew F., and Lyndon W. Cook, eds. *The Words of Joseph Smith: The*

WORKS CITED

Contemporary Accounts of the Nauvoo Discourses of the Prophet Joseph. Provo, Utah: Religious Study Center, Brigham Young University, 1980.

Encyclopedia Britannica, 15th ed., s.v. "Earthquake."

Encyclopedia Britannica Micropaedia, 15th ed., s.v. "Sandemanians."

England, Breck. *The Life and Thought of Orson Pratt*. Salt Lake City: University of Utah Press, 1985.

The Ensign of Liberty of the Church of Christ. Kirtland, Ohio, March 1847–August 1849.

Esplin, Ronald K. "Joseph Smith's Mission and Timetable: 'God Will Protect Me until My Work Is Done.'" In *The Prophet Joseph: Essays on the Life and Mission of Joseph Smith*, edited by Larry C. Porter and Susan Easton Black. Salt Lake City: Deseret Book Company, 1988.

Esshom, Frank E. *Pioneers and Prominent Men of Utah*. Salt Lake City: Utah Pioneers Book Publishing Company, 1913.

Fairchild, James H. *Oberlin: The Colony and the College, 1833-1883*. Oberlin, Ohio: E.J. Goodrich, 1883.

Faulring, Scott H., ed. *An American Prophet's Record: The Diaries and Journals of Joseph Smith*. Salt Lake City: Signature Books, 1987.

Fehrenbacher, Don E. *Chicago Giant: A Biography of "Long John" Wentworth*. Wisconsin, 1957.

Flanders, Robert Bruce. *Nauvoo: Kingdom on the Mississippi*. Urbana, Illinois: University of Illinois Press, 1965.

Folsom, Marvin H. "The Language of Orson Hyde's *Ein Ruf aus der Wüste*." In *Proceedings of the Deseret Language and Linguistic Society*. Fifteenth Annual Symposium, 13 March 1989, Provo, Utah.

Ford, Thomas. *History of Illinois from Its Commencement as a State in 1818 to 1847*. Chicago: S.G. Griggs and Co., 1854.

Forsgren, Lydia Walker. *History of Box Elder County*. Box Elder County Daughters of the Utah Pioneers, 1937.

"From Canton." *Western Star* (Lebanon, Ohio), 9 April 1831.

The Gospel Reflector (Philadelphia) 1 (15 March 1841): 137-75.

"Great Earthquakes." *Ohio State Journal* (Columbus, Ohio), 7 April 1831.

Guinn, J.M. *Historical and Biographical Record of Los Angeles and Vicinity*. Chicago: Chapman Publishing Company, 1901.

Gunn, Stanley P. *Oliver Cowdery, Second Elder and Scribe*. Salt Lake City: Bookcraft, 1962.

Hall, Roy F. and Helen G. Hall. *Collin County: Pioneering in North Texas*. Quanah, Texas: Nortex Press, 1975.

Hartley, William G. *They Are My Friends: A History of the Joseph Knight Family, 1825-1850*. Provo, Utah: Grandin Book Company, 1986.

———. "Upon You My Fellow Servants." In *The Prophet Joseph: Essays on the Life and Mission of Joseph Smith*, edited by Larry C. Porter and Susan Easton Black. Salt Lake City: Deseret Book Company, 1988.

Hayden, Amos S. *Early History of the Disciples in the Western Reserve*. Cincinnati: Chase and Hall, 1876.

Hays, Daniel P. "Daniel L.M. Peixotto, M.D." *Publications of the American Jewish Historical Society* 26 (1918): 219-30.

Hill, Donna. *Joseph Smith: The First Mormon*. Garden City, New York: Doubleday & Company, 1977.

Hill, Marvin. "The First Vision Controversy: A Critique and Reconciliation." *Dialogue: A Journal of Mormon Thought* 15 (Summer 1982): 31-46.

———. "Joseph Smith and the 1826 Trial: New Evidence and New Difficulties." *BYU Studies* 12 (Winter 1972): 223-33.

———. "Joseph Smith the Man: Some Reflections on a Subject of Controversy." *BYU Studies* 21 (Spring 1981): 175-86.

Hinkle, S.J. "A Biographical Sketch of G.M. Hinkle." *Journal of History* 13 (October 1920): 448-53.

"Historic Discoveries at the Grandin Building." *Ensign* 10 (July 1980): 48-50.

History of Allegheny County, Pennsylvania. 2 vols. Chicago: A. Warner and Company, Publishers, 1889.

History of Caldwell and Livingston Counties, Missouri. St. Louis: National Historical Company, 1886.

History of Clay and Platte Counties, Missouri. St. Louis: National Historical Company, 1885.

History of Clermont County, Ohio. Philadelphia: Louis H. Everts, 1880.

"History of David Patten." *Deseret Weekly* 8 (1858): 18-19.

History of Geauga and Lake Counties, Ohio. Philadelphia: Williams Brothers, 1878.

History of Howard and Chariton Counties, Missouri. St. Louis: National Historical Company, 1883.

History of Jackson County, Missouri. Kansas City: Union Historical Company, 1881.

History of Oakland County, Michigan. Philadelphia: L. H. Everts & Co., 1877.

History of the Ohio Falls Cities and Their Counties. Cleveland: L.A. Williams & Company, 1882.

History of Portage County, Ohio. Chicago: Warner, Beers and Company, 1885.

History of Ray County, Missouri. St. Louis: Missouri Historical Company, 1881.

The History of the Reorganized Church of Jesus Christ of Latter Day Saints. 4 vols. Independence, Missouri: Herald House, 1967.

History of Sutter County, California. Oakland, California: Thompson and West, 1879.

"Homespun" [Susa Young Gates]. *Lydia Knight's History*. Noble Women's Lives Series. Salt Lake City, Juvenile Instructor Office, 1883.

Hough, Franklin B. *A History of Jefferson County in the State of New York*. Watertown, New York: Sterling and Riddell, 1854.

Howard, Richard P. *The Memoirs of President Joseph Smith III (1832- 1914)*. Independence, Missouri: Herald Publishing House, 1979.

———. *Restoration Scriptures: A Study of their Textual Development*. Independence: Herald Publishing House, 1969.

Howe, Eber D. *Mormonism Unvailed*. Painesville, Ohio: Printed and published by the author, 1834.

Hutchins, Robert D. "Joseph Smith III: Moderate Mormon." Master's thesis, Brigham Young University, 1977.

An Illustrated History of Los Angeles County California. Chicago: The Lewis Publishing Company, 1889.

International Genealogical Index. LDS Family History Library, Salt Lake City, Utah.

"Israel Daniel Rupp." *New England Historical and Genealogical Register* 33

(January 1879): 116-17.

Jennings, Warren A. "The Expulsion of the Mormons from Jackson County, Missouri." *Missouri Historical Review* 64 (October 1969): 41-63.

———. "The First Mormon Mission to the Indians." *Kansas Historical Quarterly* 38 (Autumn 1971): 288-99.

Jenson, Andrew. *Encyclopedic History of the Church of Jesus Christ of Latter-day Saints*. Salt Lake City: Deseret News, 1941.

———. *Latter-day Saint Biographical Encyclopedia*. 4 vols. Salt Lake City: Andrew Jenson History Company and Deseret News, 1901-1936.

———. *The Historical Record*. 9 vols. Salt Lake City, 1882-1890.

Jenson, Andrew, and Stevenson, Edward. *Infancy of the Church. An Elaborate and Detailed Description of Persons, Places and Incidents Connected with the Early Rise and Progress of the Church of Jesus Christ of Latter-day Saints. A Series of Letters written by Elders Andrew Jenson and Edward Stevenson*. Salt Lake City, 1889.

Jessee, Dean C. "Early Accounts of the First Vision." *BYU Studies* 9 (Spring 1969): 277-78.

———. "Joseph Knight's Recollection of Early Mormon History." *BYU Studies* 17 (Autumn, 1976): 29-39.

———. "The Original Book of Mormon Manuscript." *BYU Studies* 10 (Spring 1970): 259-78.

———, comp. and ed. *The Personal Writings of Joseph Smith*. Salt Lake City: Deseret Book Company, 1984.

———. "Joseph Smith and the Beginning of Mormon Record Keeping." In *The Prophet Joseph Smith: Essays on the Life and Mission of Joseph Smith*, edited by Larry C. Porter and Susan Easton Black. Salt Lake City: Deseret Book Company, 1988.

———. "'Walls, Grates, and Screeking Iron Doors': The Prison Experience of Mormon Leaders in Missouri, 1838-1839." In *New Views of Mormon History: A Collection of Essays in Honor of Leonard J. Arrington*, edited by Davis Bitton and Maureen Ursenbach Beecher. Salt Lake City: University of Utah Press, 1987.

———. "The Writing of Joseph Smith's History." *BYU Studies* 11 (Spring 1971): 439-73.

Jessee, Dean C. and David W. Whittaker. "The Last Months of Mormonism in Missouri: The Albert Perry Rockwood Journal." *BYU Studies* 28 (Winter 1988): 5-41.

Johnson, Crisfield. *History of Cuyahoga County, Ohio*. Cleveland: D.W. Ensign and Company, 1879.

Johnson, Nellie. *The Descendants of Robert Burdick of Rhode Island*. Syracuse, New York: Syracuse Typesetting Company, 1937.

Jones, Gerald E. "An Early Mormon Settlement in South Dakota." *South Dakota History* 1 (Spring 1971): 119-31.

Journal of Discourses. 26 vols. Liverpool, England: Printed and published by Albert Carrington [and others], 1853-1886.

Journal of History. 18 vols. Lamoni, Iowa: Board of Publication of the Reorganized Church of Jesus Christ of Latter Day Saints, 1908-1925.

Kagan, Solomon R. *Jewish Contributions to Medicine in America*. Boston: Boston Medical Publishing Company, 1889.

WORKS CITED

Kelly, Clyde. *United States Postal Policy*. New York and London: D. Appleton and Company, 1932.

Kimball, Stanley B. "The Anthon Transcript: People, Primary Sources and Problems." *BYU Studies* 10 (Spring 1970): 325-64.

———. *Heber C. Kimball: Mormon Patriarch and Pioneer*. Urbana, Illinois: University of Illinois Press, 1981.

Kingsbury, Joseph A. *A Pendulous Edition of Kingsbury Genealogy*. Pittsburgh: Murdoch-Kerr Press, 1901.

"The Late Doctor Anthon." *Harper's Weekly*, 17 August 1867, 525-26.

Latter Day Saints' Messenger and Advocate. 3 vols. Kirtland, Ohio. October 1834–September 1837.

The Latter-day Saints' Millennial Star. 132 vols. Manchester, Liverpool, London, England. 1840-1970.

Lawyer, William S. *Binghamton: Its Settlement, Growth and Development*. Binghamton, New York: Century Memorial Publishing Company, 1900.

"A Leaf from an Autobiography." *Woman's Exponent* 7 (15 August, 1 September, 1 November 1878).

Lemisch, Jesse. "The Papers of Great White Men." *Maryland Historian* 11 (Spring 1975): 44.

Letters by Oliver Cowdery to W.W. Phelps on the Origin of the Book of Mormon and the Rise of the Church of Jesus Christ of Latter-day Saints. Liverpool: Thomas Ward and John Cairns, 1844.

Lockley, Fred. "Reminiscences of Mrs. Frank Collins Nee Martha Elizabeth Gilliam." *Oregon Historical Quarterly* 17 (December 1916): 358-72.

London, Lena. "The Militia Fine, 1830-1860." *Military Affairs* 15 (1951): 133-44.

Mack, Solomon. *A Narraitve [sic] of the Life of Solomon Mack*. Windsor, Vermont: Printed at the expence of the author, [1811?]

Malone, Dumas. *Dictionary of American Biography*. 20 vols. New York: Charles Scribner's Sons, 1936.

———. "Tapping the Wisdom of the Founding Fathers." *New York Times Magazine*, 27 May 1954, 25-26.

Matthews, Robert J. *A Plainer Translation: Joseph Smith's Translation of the Bible: A History and Commentary*. Provo, Utah: Brigham Young University Press, 1975.

Maynard, Gregory Phillip. "Alexander Doniphan: Man of Justice." *BYU Studies* 13 (Summer 1973): 462-72.

McGavin, E. Cecil. *The Family of Joseph Smith*. Salt Lake City: Bookcraft, 1963.

McKiernan, F. Mark. *A Voice of One Crying in the Wilderness: Sidney Rigdon, Religious Reformer, 1793-1876*. Lawrence, Kansas: Coronado Press, 1971.

McKiernan, F. Mark, and Roger D.Launius, eds. *An Early Latter Day Saint History: The Book of John Whitmer*. Independence, Missouri: Herald House, 1980.

Miller, David E., and Della S. Miller. *Nauvoo: The City of Joseph*. Salt Lake City: Peregrine Smith, 1974.

Monroe, Haskell M. "Some Thoughts for an Aspiring Historical Editor." *American Archivist* 32 (April 1969): 147-59.

Morgan, Dale. "Reminiscences of James Holt: A Narrative of the Emmett Company." *Utah Historical Quarterly* 23 (January, April 1955): 1-33, 151-

79.

The National Cyclopedia of American Biography. 63 vols. New York: James Whites and Co., 1898-1984.

National Historical Publications and Records Commission. *Historical Documentary Editions*. Washington, D.C.: National Archives, 1986.

"Newel Knight's Journal." *Scraps of Biography*. Tenth Book of the Faith-Promoting Series, 47-104. Salt Lake City: Juvenile Instructor Office, 1883.

Newell, Linda K., and Valeen T. Avery. *Mormon Enigma: Emma Hale Smith*. Garden City, New York: Doubleday & Company, 1984.

Nibley, Hugh. "The Facsimiles of the Book of Abraham: A Response by H.W. Nibley to E.H. Ashment." *Sunstone* 4 (December 1979): 49-51.

———. "The Meaning of the Kirtland Egyptian Papers." *BYU Studies* 11 (Summer 1971): 350-99.

———. *The Message of the Joseph Smith Papyri: An Egyptian Endowment*. Salt Lake City: Deseret Book Company, 1975.

———. "Mixed Voices: A Study in Book of Mormon Criticism." *Improvement Era* 62 (March-August, October, November, 1959).

Nibley, Preston. *Stalwarts of Mormonism*. Salt Lake City: Deseret Book Company, 1954.

Nye, Russel B. *A Baker's Dozen: Thirteen Unusual Americans*. East Lansing, Michigan: Michigan State University Press, 1956.

"Old Newspapers—No. 23." *Palmyra Courier* (New York), 3, 10 May 1872.

Olney, James H. *Genealogy of the Descendants of Thomas Olney*. Providence, Rhode Island, 1889.

Orton, Edward. *An Account of the Descendants of Thomas Orton*. Columbus, Ohio: Nitschke Brothers Press, 1896.

Painesville Telegraph (Ohio).

Partridge, Elinore. "Nineteenth-century Spelling: The Rules and Writers." *Ensign* 5 (August 1975): 75-80.

Perkins, Keith. "A House Divided: The John Johnson Family," *Ensign* 9 (1979): 54-59.

Perrin, William H., ed. *History of Summit County, Ohio*. Chicago, 1881.

Perry, Ivan. *Perry Family History*. Provo, Utah: J. Grant Stevenson, 1966.

Pessen, Edward. *Jacksonian America: Society, Personality, and Politics*. rev. ed. Homewood, Illinois: The Dorsey Press, 1978.

Peterson, J.W. "William B. Smith's Last Statement." *Zion's Ensign* (Independence, Missouri), 1894.

Pomeroy, Albert Alonzo. *History and Genealogy of the Pomeroy Family*. Toledo, Ohio: Franklin Printing and Engraving Company, 1912.

Pool, William. *Landmarks of Niagara County, New York*. Syracuse: D. Mason, 1897

Porter, Larry C. "Dating the Melchizedek Priesthood." *Ensign* 9 (June 1979): 5-10.

———. "Reverend George Lane—Good 'Gifts,' much 'Grace,' and Marked 'Usefulness.' " *BYU Studies* 9 (Spring 1969): 321-40.

Pratt, Parley P., Jr., ed. *Autobiography of Parley Parker Pratt*. Salt Lake City: Deseret Book Company, 1961.

Progressive Men of Bingham, Fremont and Oneida Counties, Idaho. Chicago: A.W. Bowen, 1904.

WORKS CITED

Quincy, Josiah. *Figures of the Past From the Leaves of Old Journals*. Boston: Roberts Brothers, 1883.

Quinn, D. Michael. "Jesse Gause: Joseph Smith's Little-known Counselor." *BYU Studies* 23 (Fall 1983): 487-93.

Redfield, John H. *Genealogical History of the Redfield Family*. Albany, New York: Munsell and Rowland, 1860.

Reed, Doris M. "Edward Bonney, Detective." *The Indiana University Bookman* (November 1957): 5-17.

Reinders, Robert. "Militia and Public Order in Nineteenth Century America." *Journal of American Studies*. 11 (April 1977): 81-101.

Rich, Russell R. "The Dogberry Papers and the Book of Mormon." *BYU Studies* 10 (Spring 1970): 315-19.

Riker, William H. *Soldiers of the States: The Role of the National Guard in American Democracy*. Washington, D.C.: Public Affairs Press, 1957.

Roberts, Brigham H. *A Comprehensive History of the Church of Jesus Christ of Latter-day Saints*. 6 vols. Salt Lake City: The Church of Jesus Christ of Latter-day Saints, 1930.

Robinson, Ebenezer. "Items of Personal History of the Editor." *The Return* (Davis City, Iowa), 1889-1890.

Roller, David C., and Twyman, Robert W., eds., *The Encyclopedia of Southern History*. Baton Rouge: Louisiana State University, 1979.

Sawyer, Eugene T. *History of Santa Clara County, California*. Los Angeles: Historic Record Company, 1922.

Schindler, Harold. *Orrin Porter Rockwell: Man of God, Son of Thunder*. Salt Lake City: University of Utah Press, 1966.

Seidensticker, Oswald. "Memoir of Israel Daniel Rupp, The Historian." *Pennsylvania Magazine of History and Biography* 14 (1890): 403-13.

Seldes, Gilbert. *The Stammering Century*. New York: Peter Smith, 1928.

"Shakers." *Encyclopedia Britannica Micropaedia*, 15th ed.

Shipps, Jan. *Mormonism: The Story of a New Religious Tradition*. Urbana and Chicago: University of Illinois Press, 1985.

Shoemaker, Floyd. *Missouri and Missourians*. 5 vols. Chicago: The Lewis Publishing Company, 1943.

Shurtleff, Stella C., and Brent F. Cahoon. *Reynolds Cahoon and his Stalwart Sons*. Salt Lake City: Paragon Press, 1960.

"Sketch of the Autobiography of George Albert Smith." *Deseret Weekly* (Salt Lake City, Utah), 18 August 1858.

Smith, James H. *History of Chenango and Madison Counties, New York*. Syracuse: D. Mason and Co., 1880.

Smith, Joseph. *History of the Church of Jesus Christ of Latter-day Saints*. Edited by Brigham H. Roberts. 7 vols. Salt Lake City: Deseret Press, 1964.

Smith, Joseph, Sr. "To the Public." *Wayne Sentinel* (Palmyra, New York), 30 September; 6, 13, 20, 27 October; 3 November 1824.

Smith, Lucy. *Biographical Sketches of Joseph Smith the Prophet and his Progenitors for many Generations*. Liverpool: Published for Orson Pratt by S.W. Richards, 1853.

Snow, LeRoi C. "Who Was Professor Joshua Seixas?" *Improvement Era* 39 (February 1936): 67-71.

"Some of the Remarks of John S. Reed, Esq., as Delivered Before the State

Convention." *Times and Seasons* 5 (1 June 1844): 549-52.

Stern, Malcolm H. *First American Jewish Families*. Cincinnati: American Jewish Archives, 1978.

Stevens, Edward W., Jr. "Science, Culture, and Morality: Educating Adults in the Early Nineteenth Century." In *"Schools and The Means of Education Shall Forever Be Encouraged:" A History of Education in the Old Northwest, 1787-1880*, ed. Paul H. Mattingly and Edward W. Stevens, Jr., 69-83. Athens, Ohio: Ohio University Libraries, 1987.

Stone, William L. *Matthias and his Impostures*. New York: Harper & Brothers, 1835.

Stowell, William H.H. *Stowell Genealogy*. Rutland, Vermont: The Tuttle Company, 1922.

Summerfield, Arthur E. *U.S. Mail: The Story of the United States Postal Service*. New York: Holt, Rinehart and Winston, 1960.

Tanner, Maurice. *Descendants of John Tanner*. n.p.: The Tanner Family Association, 1942.

Thomas, Keith. *Religion and the Decline of Magic*. New York: Charles Scribner's Sons, 1971.

Times and Seasons (Nauvoo, Illinois). 6 vols., 1839-1846.

"Trial of Matthias." *Evening Post* (New York City), 17, 18, 20 April 1835.

"Truman O. Angell—Master Builder." *Our Pioneer Heritage* 10 (1967): 194-203.

Tullidge, Edward. *History of Salt Lake City*. Salt Lake City: Star Printing Company, 1886.

United States. 1792. *Statutes at Large*. Second Congress, session 1.

Utah Genealogical and Historical Magazine. 31 vols. Salt Lake City: Published by the Utah Genealogical and Historical Society, 1910-1940.

Van Tassel, David D. *Recording America's Past*. Chicago: The University of Chicago Press, 1960.

Van Wagoner, Richard, and Steven Walker. "Joseph Smith: 'The Gift of Seeing.' " *Dialogue* 15 (Summer 1982): 49-68.

Wager, Daniel E., ed. *Our County and its People: A Descriptive Work on Oneida County, New York*. Boston: The Boston History Company, Publishers, 1896.

Wakefield, Homer. *Wakefield Memorial Comprising an Historical, Genealogical and Biographical Register of the Name and Family of Wakefield*. Bloomington, Illinois: privately printed, 1897.

Walker, Ronald W. "Martin Harris: Mormonism's Early Convert." *Dialogue* 19 (Winter 1986): 29-43.

———. "The Persistent Idea of American Treasure Hunting." *BYU Studies* 24 (Fall 1984): 429-59.

Waterman, Arba Nelson. *Historical Review of Chicago and Cook County*. Chicago and New York: The Lewis Publishing Company, 1908.

Weigel, Gustave, S.J. *Churches in North America: An Introduction*. Baltimore: Helicon Press, 1961.

Whitman, Benjamin. *History of Erie County, Pennsylvania*. Chicago: Warner, Beers & Co., 1884.

Whitmer, David. *An Address to All Believers in Christ*. Richmond, Missouri, 1887.

Whitney, Elizabeth Ann. "A Leaf from an Autobiography." *Woman's Exponent*

7 (15 August 1878): 41.

Whitney, Orson F. *History of Utah*. 4 vols. Salt Lake City: George Q. Cannon and Sons, 1892-1904.

Whitt, Aileen M. *Clermont County, Ohio, Wills, Estates, and Guardianships, 1800-1851*. New Richmond, Ohio: A.M. Whitt, 1986.

Whittaker, David J. "The 'Articles of Faith' in Early Mormon Literature and Thought." In *New Views of Mormon History: A Collection of Essays in Honor of Leonard J. Arrington*, edited by Davis Bitton and Maureen U. Beecher. Salt Lake City: University of Utah Press, 1987.

———. "Orson Pratt: Prolific Pamphleteer." *Dialogue* 15 (Autumn 1982): 27-41.

Wilcox, Pearl. *Jackson County Pioneers*. Independence, Missouri: by author, 1975.

———. *The Latter Day Saints on the Missouri Frontier*. Independence, Missouri: by author, 1972.

Williams, Frederick G. III. "Frederick Granger Williams of the First Presidency of the Church." *BYU Studies* 12 (September 1972): 243-61.

Wilson, James G. and John Fiske. *Appletons' Cyclopaedia of American Biography*. 7 vols. New York, 1888.

Wirthlin, LeRoy S. "Joseph Smith's Boyhood Operation: An 1813 Surgical Success." *BYU Studies* 21 (Spring 1981): 131-54.

Woman's Exponent. 41 vols. Salt Lake City, 1872-1914.

Woodson, William H. *History of Clay County*. Topeka and Indianapolis: Historical Publishing Company, 1920.

Wortham, Louis J. *A History of Texas: From Wilderness to Commonwealth*. 5 vols. Fort Worth, Texas: Wortham-Molyneaux Company, 1924.

Wright, Esmond. "Making History." *The Listener* 63 (15 November 1962): 803.

Zion's Ensign (Independence, Missouri), 1891-1921.

Zucker, Louis C. "Joseph Smith as a Student of Hebrew." *Dialogue* 2 (Summer 1968): 41-55.

Unpublished Works

Black, Susan Easton. "Membership of the Church of Jesus Christ of Latter-day Saints, 1830-1848." 48 vols. Provo, Utah: Religious Studies Center, Brigham Young University, 1984.

Bowen, Walter D. "The Versatile W. W. Phelps – Mormon Writer, Educator, and Pioneer." Master's thesis, Brigham Young University, 1958.

California, Marin County, Probate Register. MS., LDS Church Family History Library.

Carr, Nanon L. "Marriage Records of Clay County, Missouri, 1822-1852." Typescript. Kansas City, Missouri: by author, 1957.

Colvin, Don F. "A Historical Study of the Mormon Temple at Nauvoo, Illinois." Master's thesis, Brigham Young University, 1962.

Cowdery, Oliver. Diary, 1 January – 27 March 1836. MS., Oliver Cowdery Papers, LDS Church Archives.

Crosby, Jonathan. "A Biographical Sketch of the Life of Jonathan Crosby written by himself." MS., Utah Historical Society.

WORKS CITED

Curtis, Carl C. Cowdery Genealogical Material. Typescript, LDS Church Family History Library.

Dayton, Leland M., and Alta A. Dayton. "Record of the Posterity of Hiram Dayton and Permelia Bundy Dayton." Typescript, September 1961. LDS Church Family History Library.

Daughters of the American Revolution. "Monument Inscriptions Prior to 1900 From Cemeteries in Clermont County, Ohio." Milford I.O.O.F. Cemetery. LDS Church Family History Library.

DuChateau, Andre Paul DuChateau. "Missouri Colossus, Alexander William Doniphan, 1808-1887." Ed.D. diss., Oklahoma State University, 1973.

Dunford, C. Kent. "The Contributions of George A. Smith to the Establishment of the Mormon Society in the Territory of Utah." Ph.D. diss., Brigham Young University, 1970.

Easton, Susan W. "Inscriptions Found on Tombstones and Monuments in Early Latter-day Saint Burial Grounds." Typescript, Brigham Young University Library.

Ellsberry, Elizabeth P. "Marriage Records of Jackson Co., Missouri." Chillicothe, Missouri: n.d.

Esplin, Ronald K. "The Emergence of Brigham Young and the Twelve to Mormon Leadership, 1830-1841." Ph.D. dissertation, Brigham Young University, 1981.

Faulring, Scott H. "Prophet Meets Prophet: Robert Matthias Visits Joseph Smith." Typescript, Brigham Young University.

Family Group Records Collection. LDS Church Family History Library, Salt Lake City, Utah.

Gentry, Leland H. "A History of the Latter-day Saints in Northern Missouri from 1836-39." Ph.D. dissertation, Brigham Young University, 1965.

Gilbert, John H. "Memorandum," 8 September 1892. Typescript, King's Daughter's Free Library, Palmyra, New York.

Gordon, Joseph F. "The Life of Governor Lilburn W. Boggs." Ph.D. diss., University of Missouri, 1956.

"Grammar and Alphabet of the Egyptian Language." 1 vol., MS., LDS Church Archives.

Gunnell, Wayne C. "Martin Harris—Witness and Benefactor to the Book of Mormon." Master's thesis, Brigham Young University, 1955.

Harris, Emer. Biographical Sketch. Typescript, BYU Library, Provo, Utah.

Hess, Arlene. "Collected Materials Relative to Sidney Rigdon and his Descendants, and other Subjects used in Preparation for the History of Friendship, New York." Typescript, Brigham Young University.

Hill, Isaac. Journal. MS., LDS Church Archives.

Hill, Marvin S. "An Historical Study of the Life of Orson Hyde, Early Mormon Missionary and Apostle from 1805-1852." Master's thesis, Brigham Young University, 1955.

Hodges, Nadine and Mrs. Howard W. Woodruff. "Genealogical Notes From the 'Liberty Tribune'." Typescript, LDS Church Family History Library.

Illinois Mortality Schedule, 1850. Typescript, LDS Church Family History Library.

Illinois. Whiteside County. Cemetery Records. Typescript, LDS Church Family History Library.

WORKS CITED

International Genealogical Index. LDS Church Family History Library.
Jarman, Dean. "The Life and Contributions of Samuel Harrison Smith." Master's thesis, Brigham Young University, 1961.
Jennings, Warren. "Zion is Fled: The Expulsion of the Mormons from Jackson County, Missouri." Ph.D. dissertation, University of Florida, 1962.
"Journal History of the Church of Jesus Christ of Latter-day Saints." 750+ vols. MS., LDS Church Archives, 1830-present.
Kansas, Lyon County. Cemetery Records. Typescript, LDS Church Family History Library.
Kimball, Heber C. "Journal and Record of Heber Chase Kimball an Apostle of Jesus Christ of Latter Day Saints." MS., Heber C. Kimball Papers, LDS Church Archives.
Kirtland, Ohio. High Council Minutes, December 1832–November 1837. MS., LDS Church Archives.
Kirtland Revelation Book, MS., LDS Church Archives.
Knecht, Charles. "Notes Written on 'Chamber's Life of Joseph Smith,' by William Smith." 1925, Typescript, LDS Church Archives.
Knight, Joseph. Autobiographical sketch. MS., LDS Church Archives.
Knight, Newel. Journal. MS., LDS Church Archives.
Launius, Roger D. "And There Came Prophets in the Land Again: The Life of Joseph Smith III, 1832-1914, Mormon Reformer." Ph.D. diss., Louisiana State University, 1982.
Madsen, Gordon. "Joseph Smith at Bainbridge: The Trial and the Law." Paper read at the 23rd Annual Conference of the Mormon History Association, 7 May 1988, at Logan, Utah.
Marriott, L. Dean. "Lilburn W. Boggs: Interaction with Mormons Following Their Expulsion from Missouri." Ph.D. diss., Brigham Young University, 1979.
Martin, John T., and Louis C. Hill. "Milam County, Texas Records." 2 vols. Typescript (Waco, Texas, 1968). LDS Church Family History Library.
Maynard, Gregory Phllip. "Alexander William Doniphan, The Forgotten Man from Missouri." Master's thesis, Brigham Young University, 1973.
Millet, Artemus. Autobiography. MS., LDS Church Archives.
Morley, Richard H. "The Life and Contributions of Isaac Morley." Master's thesis, Brigham Young University, 1965.
Mouritsen, Robert Glen. "The Office of Associate President of the Church of Jesus Christ of Latter-day Saints." Master's thesis, Brigham Young University, 1972.
Mulholland, James. Diary. MS., LDS Church Archives.
Nauvoo, Illinois. Ninth Ward High Priests Record. MS., LDS Church Archives.
"Nauvoo Temple Endowment Register," 1845-46. Typescript, LDS Church Family History Library.
Noble, Mary Beman. Autobiography. MS., LDS Church Archives.
New York, Broome County. Probate Records. Microfilm at LDS Church Family History Library.
Ohio. Cuyahoga County. Probate Record of Wills. Microfilm of MS., LDS Church Family History Library.
Ohio, Geauga County, Kirtland Cemetery Records. Typescript, LDS Church Family History Library.
Ohio, Geauga County. Court of Common Pleas, Final Record. Microfilm of MS.,

LDS Church Family History Library.
Ohio, Geauga County. Marriage Records. Microfilm, LDS Church Family History Library.
Ohio, Geauga County. Tax Records, 1830-1839. Microfilm, LDS Church Family History Library.
Ohio, Lake County. Marriage Record. Microfilm of typescript, LDS Church Family History Library.
Parcells, Mrs. Frank H. "Unpublished Cemetery, Church and Town Records Together with Genealogical Notes and Other Unpublished Data Compiled by (Mrs Henry) Alice Payne Garden, Chairman Genealogical Research Committee, New York State Conference of the National Society Daughters of the American Revolution." Brooklyn, New York. Microfilm of typescript, LDS Church Family History Library.
Parkin, Max H. "A History of the Latter-day Saints in Clay County, Missouri, from 1833 to 1837." Ph.D. dissertation, Brigham Young University, 1976.
———. "Conflict at Kirtland: A Study of the Nature and Causes of External and Internal Conflict of the Mormons in Ohio Between 1830 and 1838." Salt Lake City: Max H. Parkin, 1966.
Partridge, Elinore H. "Characteristics of Joseph Smith's Style." Task Papers in LDS History, No. 14, 1976. Typescript, LDS Church Archives.
Patriarchal Blessing Index. LDS Church Archives.
Peterson, Paul H. "An Historical Analysis of the Word of Wisdom." Master's thesis, Brigham Young University, 1972.
Phelps, William W. Diary. MS., W.W. Phelps Papers, LDS Church Archives.
Pitkin, George O. Biographical Sketch. Typescript, LDS Church Family History Library.
Poulsen, Larry N. "The Life and Contributions of Newel K. Whitney." Master's thesis, Brigham Young University, 1966.
Porter, Larry C. "A Study of the Origins of the Church of Jesus Christ of Latter-day Saints in the States of New York and Pennsylvania, 1816-1831." Ph.D. dissertation, Brigham Young University, 1971.
Pratt, Parley P. Letter to the Elders of the Church of Latter day Saints and Brethren in Canada, 27 November 1836. MS., Parley P. Pratt Papers, LDS Church Archives.
Pratt, Orson. Letter to John Christensen, 11 March 1876. MS., LDS Church Archives.
Pratt, Orson, and Joseph F. Smith. Letter to John Taylor, 18 December 1877. MS., LDS Church Archives.
Quinn, Dennis Michael. "Organizational Development and Social Origins of the Mormon Heirarchy, 1832-1932: A Prosopographical Study." Master's thesis, University of Utah, 1973.
"A Record of the Transactions of the Twelve Apostles of the Church of Christ of Latter day Saints from the Time of their Call to the Apostleship Which was on the 14th Day of February AD. 1835." 19pp. MS., LDS Church Archives.
Reed, John S. Letter to Brigham Young, 6 December 1861. MS., Brigham Young Papers, LDS Church Archives.
Richards, Willard. Diary, 1836-1852. MS., Willard Richards Papers, LDS Church Archives.

Ridd, Jay Donald. "Almon W. Babbitt, Mormon Emissary." Master's thesis, University of Utah, 1953.

Rudd, Calvin P. "William Smith: Brother of the Prophet Joseph Smith." Master's thesis, Brigham Young University, 1973.

Searle, Howard C. "Early Mormon Historiography: Writing the History of the Mormons 1830-1858." Ph.D. dissertation, UCLA, 1979.

Sherer, John. Letter to Absalom Peters, 18 November 1830, MS., The Amistad Research Center, Dillard University, New Orleans, Louisiana.

Sherman, A.F., comp. Lake County, Ohio, Cemetery Inscriptions. Typescript, LDS Family History Library.

Skinner, Earnest M. "Joseph Smith, Sr., the First Patriarch to the Church." Master's thesis, Brigham Young University, 1958.

Smith, George A. Journal, 1817-1874. MS., LDS Church Archives.

———. Letter to Wilford Woodruff, 21 April 1856. MS., Historian's Office Papers, LDS Church Archives.

Smith, Joseph. Diaries and Papers. LDS Church Archives, Salt Lake City, Utah.

Smith, Joseph, Sr., Patriarchal Blessing Book, vol. 1, MS., LDS Church Archives.

Sprague, Locke A. "The Progenitors and Descendants of Col. Steven Mack and Temperance Bond Mack as Related to the David Cooper and Rollin Sprague Families." MS., LDS Family History Library.

Stoddard Family Bible, in possession of Buddy Youngreen, Provo, Utah.

Warren, Violet, and Jeannette Grosvenor. "A Monumental Work: Inscriptions and Interments in Geauga County, Ohio Through 1983." Typescript, LDS Church Family History Library.

Whitmer, John. "The Book of John Whitmer: Kept by Commandment." MS., RLDS Church Archives, Independence, Missouri.

Whitney, Newel K. Statement dictated to Willard Richards, n.d., MS., LDS Church Archives.

Williams, Frederick G. Statement, n.d., MS., F.G. Williams Papers, LDS Church Archives.

Woodford, Robert J. "The Historical Development of the Doctrine and Covenants." Ph.D. dissertation, Brigham Young University, 1974.

Woodruff, Wilford. Diary. MS., Wilford Woodruff Papers, LDS Church Archives.

Young, Brigham. Letter to Brigham Young, Jr., 24 April 1866. Brigham Young Letterbook 8:327-330. MS., Brigham Young Papers, LDS Church Archives.

INDEX

Aaronic Priesthood, 21; restoration of, 31-32, 231 n. 1, 290-91
Abraham, 38
Agrippa, King, 274
Aldrich, James, 154
Allen, Felatiah, 378
Alphabet, Egyptian, 102, 143
Angell, Truman, 155
Angels: difficulty of describing, 55, 69; former mortals as, 56; ministrations of, among mortals, 56-57; role of, in plan of salvation, 57. *See also* Moroni
Anthon, Charles, characters taken to, 9, 285, 401
Anti-slavery advocates, 438, 440
Apostasy, general, from Christ's teachings, 5-6, 59
Apostles, ancient: professed belief in, 39; reviling of, by contemporaries, 43; eternal truths revealed to, 70
Arrests: of Church leaders at Far West, 218-19; of Joseph Smith, 252, 312
"Articles and Covenants" of the Church, 14, 260 n. 1
Articles of Faith, 436-47, 456-58
Assistant presidents of Church, 20 n. 1, 21, 24
Astronomy, 102, 163
Authority: lack of, to administer in ordinances, 30; restoration of, 31-32; Joseph Smith's search for, in religions, 47-48
Avery, Allen, 101
Babbitt, Almon, 179, 184
Badlam, Alexander, 155
Bailey, Joshua and Hannah Boutwell, 121 n. 3
Baker, Elizabeth, 197
Baptism: necessity for, shown in Book of Mormon, 30; of Ebenezer Robinson, 108-9 n. 1; of Joseph and Oliver, 231, 290-91; of many converts, 235, 238, 299; following Church organization meeting, 244, 303-4; mobs attempt to prevent, 250-51, 309-11; font for, in Nauvoo Temple, 442-43
Baptists, 270-71
Barstow, George, 429
Beaman, Alvah, 132, 138, 142, 188, 206; is appointed councilor pro tem, 190 n. 1, 192; is ordained elders quorum president, 200
Benton, Abram Willard, 259, 318
Bible: "any tune can be played upon," 71-72; corruption of, 72; Joseph Smith's revision of, 345, 363, 371; truths removed from, 372
Billings, Titus, 380
Bishop, F. G., 101
Bishop, Gladden, 202
Bissel, Benjamin, 111 n. 1
Blessings, priesthood: ordaining Oliver Cowdery as assistant president, 24; given to priesthood leaders, 25; given to Newel K. Whitney, 106-7; rebuking disease of Joseph Smith Sr., 107; given to

children by Joseph Smith, 109, 119; dictated for brethren, 109 n. 2; healing Thomas Burdick, 122; patriarchal, given by Joseph Smith Sr., 180; given to Sidney Rigdon, 193
Board-kiln, fires in, 157, 160
Bogart, Samuel, 215, 224
Boggs, Lilburn W., governor of Missouri, 212 n. 1, 214-15
Bond, Ira, 200
Bonney, Edward, 459
Book bindery, arrangements regarding, 120
Book of Commandments, 368, 381-82
Book of Mormon: plates of, 8-9; characters from, taken to New York, 9, 284-86, 401; manuscript loss of pages of, 9-10, 286-87; extracts from, pirated, 11-12; manuscript of, is chiefly in Oliver Cowdery's handwriting, 29 n. 2; Moroni tells Joseph Smith about, 53-54, 278, 393, 413; sacred knowledge contained in, 88, 397, 417; Three Witnesses of, 235-38, 294-98; Eight Witnesses of, 238, 298; printing of, 241, 248 n. 1, 300; title page of, 241, 300-302; controversy stirred by, 248, 307; Sidney Rigdon's supposed role in, 327 n. 1; translation of, 401, 425; brief summary of, 431-32, 450-51. *See also* Plates, gold
Booth, Ezra, 349 n. 1, 363-64, 370
Bosley, Edmund, 114 n. 4
Box, stone, containing gold plates, 83-84, 281, 395-96
Boynton, John F., 109, 114
Boynton, Nathan, 259, 318
Bradley, Mr., 108
Branum (Brannan?), Samuel, 161
Brittle, Captain, 380
Brother of Jared, 70
Brown, Albert, 155
Brown, Eliza, 110
Brunson, Seymour, 110
Bullock, Thomas, 302 n. 1, 386 n. 2
Bump, Jacob, 132
Burdick, Thomas, 122
Burnett, Serenus, 366

Cahoon, Reynolds, 25, 103 n. 1, 164,, 366; serves on temple construction committee, 105-6 n. 3; chastisement of, in revelation, 118-19, 207; Emma Smith stays with, 379
Cahoon, William F., 155, 366
Caldwell, A.C., 214 n. 2
Caldwell County, Missouri, 215-16
Calvinism, 180
Campbell, Alexander, 330-31
Campbell, Robert L., 302 n. 1
Canandaigua, Ontario County, New York, 77, 394
Capron, Henry, 149
Carpenter, Brother, 110
Carrico, Thomas, 150, to serve as doorkeeper, 190 n. 1, 192, 201; marriage of, 197
Carrill, John. *See* Corrill, John
Carter, Gideon, 153
Carter, Jared, 32, 145; serves on temple construction committee, 105-6 n. 3; as high councilor, 189 n. 1
Carter, Simeon, 145, 366
Chamberlain, Colonel, 180
Chamberlain, Joseph, Justice, 253 n. 1
Chandler, Michael, 102 n. 2
Charter members of Church, 241 n. 5, 302 n. 1
Chase, Salmon P., 438
China, earthquake in, 350
Church of Jesus Christ, uniformity of, in all ages, 35
Church of Jesus Christ of Latter-day Saints: slanders aimed at, 44-45, 350; conflicts within, 182; patience of members of, in persecutions, 225-27; organization of, 241-44, 302-3; charter members of, 241 n. 5, 302 n. 1; conferences of, 249-50, 307-8, 324, 352-53, 365-

66, 371, 380; rise of, described, 432-33, 435-36, 451-52, 456
City plan for Kirtland, 113 n. 3
Clark, John B., General, 221, 224
Clark, Josiah, 148
Cobb, Polly Harris, 286
Coe, Joseph, 189 n. 1, 356
Colburn, Amasa, 311 n. 1
Colburn, Emily, 251, 310-11
Cole, Abner, 11-12
Colesville, New York, 262, 317-18, 322; Saints from, arrive in Kirtland, 352; Saints from, arrive in Missouri, 358
Committee store, 105-6 n. 3, 113
Common stock, 116, 347
Constables: save Joseph Smith from mobs, 252-53, 258, 312, 317; insulting behavior of, 314-15
Copley, Leman, 351, 354 n. 1
Coriantumr, 79
Corrill, John, 103, 119, 155; chastisement of, 124; joins debate, 158-59; takes charge of house of Lord, 201
Court martial of Church leaders, 219
Covill, James, 346
Cowdery, Elizabeth Ann Whitmer, 19
Cowdery, Maria, 19
Cowdery, Oliver: earliest history attributed to, 1; Lord inspires, to write for Joseph, 10; edits Kirtland paper, 12; Joseph Smith's letter to, 13-14; 1834 history in hand of, 15; letters from, to W.W. Phelps, 15, 17, 26 n. 2, 113; genealogy of, 19; ordination of, as assistant president, 20, 24; attends conference, 27 n. 2, 28; meets and writes for Joseph Smith, 29, 288-89; as chief Book of Mormon scribe, 29-30; helps with Egyptian alphabet, 102; establishes printing office, 105 n. 2; blessing dictated for, 109 n. 2; attends Piexotto's lecture, 119; brings Hebrew books from New York, 144; unites with brethren in prayer, 147-48; studies Hebrew, 152; Joseph Smith visits relatives of, 177; preaches in meeting, 179; serves as convention delegate, 197 n. 1; summarizes leadership meeting, 199 n. 2; baptism of, 231, 290-91; becomes one of Three Witnesses, 235-38, 294-98; ordained as elder, 239, 242, 299, 303; preaches first official public sermon, 244, 304; eludes mob, 258, 318; commands Joseph to alter revelation, 260, 320; joins mission to Lamanites, 325 n. 1, 339; addresses Sidney Rigdon's congregation, 341; letter from, detailing Lamanite mission, 354-55; takes revelations for publication, 367 n. 1, 368, 381
Cowdery, Warren A., 97 n. 1, 101 n. 1, 202-3
Cowdery, William, 200
Critics of Joseph Smith, 11-12, 149-50, 258-59
Crozier, Harlow, 155
Culver, Aaron and Esther Peck, 251, 311
Cumorah, hill: physical description of, 77, 81-82; destruction of Jaredites and Nephites at, 78-81
Cushman, Mr., 119

Daley, Moses, 158
Daniel, vision of, 129
Davidson, James, 253, 257, 313, 316-17
Daviess County, Missouri, 216-17
Davis, Marvel C., 184
Dayton, Hyram, 186
Debates: on miracles, 143; advice regarding, 143-44; on revelation, 158-59, 163; decision to discontinue, 163-64, 171-72
Debts: Joseph Smith desires to repay, 98; prayer for deliverance from, 147; Joseph Smith pays, 151; recording of, 154 n. 1
Deer, brethren see, while traveling, 103

INDEX

Degrees of glory, vision of, 372
Dennison, Dr., 377
Denton, Solomon Wilber, 187
Devil cast out of Newel Knight, 247-48, 305-6
Devolue, Peter, 366
Dewitt, Carroll County, Missouri, 213-15
Diary of Joseph Smith: entries from, included in history, 17
Doctrine and Covenants, 368
Dog bite, man seeks healing of, 148
Doniphan, Alexander W., 216
Doorkeepers in house of Lord, 190 n. 1, 192, 201
Dort, David, 150
Draper, Brother, 153
Draper, Zemira, 155
Dreams contrasted with visions, 73-74
Dunklin, Daniel, governor of Missouri, 99

Earthquake in China, 350
Eaton, Frazier, 161
Education of Joseph Smith, 5, 389, 405
Egyptian alphabet, 102, 143
Egyptian papyri: acquisition of, 102 n. 2; exhibition of, 109-10, 142, 154, 158, 160, 188; translation of, 144, 145; Joseph Smith explains, to brethren, 163
Eight Witnesses of Book of Mormon, 238, 298
Elder's school. *See* School of the prophets
Elders: ordination of, 186, 239, 242, 299, 303; move into temple room, 207; seek to know will of Lord, 371
Elijah, 42, 123
Elliott, David, 113, 114 n. 4
Elliott, Mary Cahoon, 115
Emmett, James, 155
Endowment: preparing for, 133-34; blessings to follow, 135-36
Enoch, 35, 38, 58; prophecies of, restored, 345
Escape of Joseph Smith and fellow prisoners, 223-24
Evening and the Morning Star, The, 26 n. 2, 364, 373, 384-85
Extermination order, 218

F.G. Williams and Company, 26 n. 2, 105, 151
"Family, the," 347 n. 2
Far West, Caldwell County, Missouri, 210; Joseph Smith's hazardous journey to, 211-12; Saints flee to, 215-16; arrest of Church leaders at, 218-19; is plundered by mobs, 219
"Feasts" given by Newel K. Whitney, 186-87
Felshaw, William, 155
Fires: in board kiln, 157, 160; in shoemaker's shop, 157; mobs set, and blame Mormons, 217; on steamboat, 380
First Vision: Joseph Smith's 1832 account of, 6-7; Joseph describes, for Joshua, the Jewish Minister, 127; account of, in 1839 history, 272-73; impossibility of denying, 274-75; Orson Pratt's account of, 390-91; Orson Hyde's account of, 407-9; Joseph recounts, for John Wentworth, 429-30; Joseph recounts, for David White, 444; Joseph recounts, for I. Daniel Rupp, 448-49; Alexander Neibaur's report of, 461
Flag of truce, 218
Folsom, Marvin H., 404
Foolish, God chooses, to confound mighty, 52, 55, 95
Fordham, Elijah, 155, 186
Foster, Solon, 148

Gathering of Israel, 62-68, 399-400, 402
Gause, Jesse, 378, 382 n. 2
Gee, Salmon, 155
Gentiles: gospel taken to, 58-59; God's covenants with, 68

German, pamphlet published in, 402-25
Gilbert, Sidney, 353, 356
Glas, John, 331 n. 1
God: Joseph Smith's early testimony of, 6; works of, clarity and efficacy of, 33; regaining presence of, 72-73; eye single to glory of, 74-75
Gold, digging for, 93-94, 282. *See also* Plates, gold
Goldthwaite, Lydia, 145-46
Gospel: unchangeable nature of, 56-57; is taken to Gentiles, 58-59, 68; restoration of, 59; fulness of, contained in Book of Mormon, 88
Gould, John and Dean, 103
Governor, Saints petition, for aid, 214-15
Government, church, varying opinions regarding, 22-23
Grammar, Joseph Smith lectures on, 122, 132
Grandin, Egbert B., 241, 300
Greek, Joseph Smith studies, 177
Greene, John P., 189-90 n. 1, 191, 386 n. 2
Grover, Thomas, 186, 189-90 n. 1, 191
Gilliam, Cornelius, 224

Hale, Emma. *See* Smith, Emma Hale
Hale, Isaac, 9, 94, 282-83
Hall, Levi, 251, 311
Halsey, Thankful Cooper, 152 n. 1
Hancock, Solomon, 190 n. 1, 192
Harris, Emer, 155, 366
Harris, Lucy, 286
Harris, Martin, 160-61, 182; takes Book of Mormon characters to New York, 9, 284-86, 401; breaks covenant and loses manuscript, 9-10, 286-87; as high councilor, 189 n. 1; becomes one of Three Witnesses, 235-38, 294-98; baptism of, 244, 304; gives money to Joseph Smith, 284; revelation received for, 302; travels to Missouri, 356
Harris, Nathan, 143 n. 1, 286
Harris, Preserved, 143, 286
Harris, Rhoda L., 286
Hatch, Ebenezer, Constable, 252 n. 1
Haun's Mill massacre, 223 n. 1
Hawkes, Joseph B., 110 n. 2
Hayes, Ezra, 180 n. 1
Healing: of Joseph Smith Sr., 107; of Thomas Burdick, 122; power of, to follow endowment, 135; of Josiah Clark, 148; of Angeline Works, 157; of Elsa Johnson, 363 n. 1
Hebrew: studied in school of prophets, 104 n. 2; books in, 144-45; brethren study, 152, 178; teacher of, fails to show up, 185; school of, 186; new teacher of, is engaged, 186
Herritt, John, 186
Higbee, Elias, 155
High council. *See* Kirtland High Council
Hill, Isaac, 123-24, 137
Hinkle, George M., 216-18
Hiram, Ohio, 363
Histories of Church: earliest, by Oliver Cowdery, 1; in handwriting of Joseph Smith, 1-3; begun in 1834, 15, 17; serialized, to run in *Messenger and Advocate*, 26-27; begun in 1838, 230-31; of 1839, final draft of, 265, 267; brief, written for John Wentworth, 327-37; for I. Daniel Rupp, 445-58
Hitchcock, Jesse, 146, 155, 159
Hollister, John, 151-52, 153-54
Holmes, Erastus, 136-37, 142-43
Holmes, Milton, 153-54
Holy Ghost: role of, in understanding visions, 69-70; falls upon Joseph and Oliver following baptism, 231, 291; gift of , laying hands on for, 239, 242, 299; presence of, in Church organization meeting, 242-43, 302; Newel Knight feels, after devil is cast out, 248, 306; poured out in conference, 249-50, 307-8
Holy ground, 82

Horse: stolen from Joseph Smith, 224; bought from Josiah Stowell, 253-54, 313; runs away with coach, 382
House of the Lord. *See* Kirtland Temple
Howard, Caleb, 268-29 n. 1
Howe, Eber D., 11, 12
Howe, Harriet, 150, 161
Hubble, prophetess, 349 n. 1
Hudson Seminary, 185
Humility, 23; insufficient, of Twelve, 120-21
Humphrey, Solomon, 385
Hurlbut, Doctor Philastus, 11, 12
Hyde, Orson, 121, 122, 364-65, 366, 459; letter from, expressing dissatisfaction, 161, 164-67; reconciliation with, 167; hires new Hebrew teacher, 185; serves as clerk, 190 n. 1; pamphlet by, 402-25
Hymns, selection and printing of, 382

Imprisonment of Church leaders, 220-21
Independence, Missouri, 356-57
Indians, 79; Moroni describes forefathers of, 53, 393, 411-13, 431, 449; mission to, 324-25; war dance of, 459, 461
Inequality: Twelve chastised for, 121; complaints of, in Orson Hyde letter, 165-67
Isaiah: "sealed book" prophecy of, fulfilled, 9, 53-54, 285; gathering of Israel foreseen by, 64-65
Israel: perplexities of, 35; scattering of, 58, 63-64; rejection of Christ by, 58-59; God's promises to, 59-60; gathering of, 62-68, 399-400, 402; new covenant made with, 65-66

Jackman, Levi, 155
Jackson, Truman, 155
James, epistle of, 271
James, Samuel, 186, 189-90 n. 1, 192
Jared, brother of, 70
Jaredites, 79, 432
Jennings, Mr. (Ebenezer?), 159
Jesus Christ: contemporaries of, failed to recognize him, 38-39; excuses found for disbelieving, 40-41; perfection of, 43; rejection of, by Israel, 58-59; regaining presence of, 72-73; possibility of seeing, 135; Newel Knight sees vision of, 250, 308; ministry of, among Nephites, 432, 451
John the Baptist: priesthood restored by, 31-32, 231 n. 1, 290-91; disbelieving, excuses found for, 40, 41
John the Revelator, 289, 372
Johnson, Edward, 374
Johnson, Eli, 374
Johnson, Elsa, 363 n. 1
Johnson, John, Sr., 151, 189 n. 1; Joseph Smith lives with, 363, 373; confronts mob, 376; is mistaken for mobber, 376-77
Johnson, John, Jr., 374
Johnson, Luke, 189 n. 1, 191, 377 n. 1
Johnson, Lyman, 110
Johnson, Olmsted, 373-74
Johnson, Orson, 157, 183, 189 n. 1
Jolly, Elizabeth, 244, 304
Jolly, Harriet, 250, 309
Jolly, John, 250, 309
Jolly, Julia Anne, 250, 309
Jolly, Vincent, 244, 304
Jolly, William, 244, 304
Joseph, husband of Mary, 73
Joshua, 82
Joshua, the Jewish Minister, 125, 129-32

Kimball, Heber C., 101, 104 n. 2, 386 n. 2, 459
King, Austin A., Judge, 212
Kingsbury, Horace, 150
Kingsbury, Joseph, 189-90 n. 1, 192
Kirtland, Ohio: city plan for, 113 n.

3; presidency of Church in, 189 n. 1; Joseph Smith moves to, 346-47; New York Saints move to, 352; conference convened in, 352-53
Kirtland High Council, 25 n. 1; discusses redemption of Zion, 99-100; trials conducted by, 101-102, 103, 113-15; Joseph Smith's instructions to, 104; report of, on meeting to fill vacancies, 189-90 n. 1; new members of, ordained, 192
Kirtland Temple: donation for building, 99; workers on, compensation received by, 105-6 n. 3; finishing outside of, 132; committee overseeing construction of, 162 n. 1; instructions for finishing upper rooms of, 181; rules for regulation of, 190 n. 1, 192, 193, 196-97, 198-200; elders move into, 207

Knight, Joseph, Jr., 251, 311
Knight, Joseph, Sr., 233, 292-93; Joseph visits family of, 246, 304-5; baptism of, 251, 311; ; hires lawyers for Joseph, , 253, 313; lists charter members of Church, 302 n. 1
Knight, Newel, 145-46, 155; refuses to pray vocally, 246-47, 305; Joseph Smith casts devil out of, 247-48, 305-6; baptism of, 249, 307; sees vision at conference, 249-50, 308; testifies in trial, 256-57, 315-16; tells Joseph about mobs, 262, 322
Knight, Polly, 251, 311, 361
Knight, Sally Colburn, 259, 319
Knight, Vinson, 151, 186, 189 n. 1, 191

Lamanites, mission to, 324-25, 354-55
Lands, purchasing of, 115-16, 351, 363
Lane, George, 45-46
"Large journal" of Joseph Smith, 15, 17, 113
Last days, calamities of, 68-69
Latter Day Saints' Messenger and Advocate. See Messenger and Advocate
Lawyers: engaged for Joseph Smith, 253, 313; closing arguments of, 257, 316-17
Lee, Ann, 351 n. 3
Letters: from Joseph Smith to Oliver Cowdery, 13-14; from Oliver Cowdery to W.W. Phelps, 15, 17, 26 n. 2, 113; Joseph Smith writes, for publication, 102-3 n. 3, 137, 149; from Harvey Whitlock to Joseph Smith, 138-40; from Joseph Smith to Harvey Whitlock, 140-42; postage due on, 152-53; from Orson Hyde expressing dissatisfaction, 161, 164-67; from William Smith to Joseph, 168-70; from Joseph to William Smith, 170-75; from Dr. Piexotto to Warren Parrish, 207-8; from Warren Parrish to Dr. Piexotto, 208-9; from Oliver Cowdery demanding change in revelation, 260, 319-20; from John Sherer to Absalom Peters, 310 n. 2; from Oliver Cowdery detailing Lamanite mission, 354-55; to John Wentworth, 427-37; to I. Daniel Rupp, 447
Lewis, Job, 151
Lewis, Joshua, 361
Lewis, Lloyd, 144
Lewis, Lorenzo, 101, 144
Lewis, Nathaniel C., 261 n. 4, 321
Liberty jail, 221, 223
Long, John V., 302
Lucas, Samuel, 210, 220, 224
Lumber lost in kiln fire, 157
Lyceum movement, 159 n. 1
Lyman, Amasa, 220

Malachi, 278
Marriages, Joseph Smith performs, 145-46, 150-51, 159-60, 197, 207

Marsh, Thomas B., 101, 201-2, 206, 324, 356
Marvelous work and wonder, 52-53, 88
Mason, Carnot, 377 n. 1
Matthews, Robert, alias Robert Matthias, 125, 129-32
McBride, Reuben, 152
McClintock, William, 377 n. 2
McLellin, William E., 121, 122, 366; hires Hebrew teacher, 185, 186; attempts to imitate revelation, 367
McMaster, Cyrus, 258, 318
McWithy, Eliza A., 160
McWithy, Isaac, 160, 190 n. 1, 192
Melchizedek Priesthood: ordinations in, 238-39, 299
Messenger, Mr., 136
Messenger and Advocate, 12, 15; Oliver Cowdery's letters in, 15, 17, 26 n. 2, 113; commencing publication of, 26 n. 2; Joseph Smith writes letters for, 102-3 n. 3, 137, 149
Metcalf, George, 111 n. 1
Methodists, 46, 270-71
Michael, 56
Military duty, compulsory, 111 n. 1
Militia: are sent out to "protect" Mormons, 215; Far West besieged by, 218
Militia Act of 1792, 111 n. 1
Millet, Artemus, 132
Milliken, Nathaniel, 192, 201
Miracles, debate about, 143-44
Missionary work: among Lamanites, 324-25; of Joseph and Sidney, 370; among Jews, 402; in Germany, 402-3; in many nations, 436, 456
Mitchill, Samuel L., 285-86
Mobs: in Dewitt, Missouri, 213-15; Saints petition governor for help against, 214-15; Saints flee from, 215-16; in Daviess County, Missouri, 216-18; hellish cries of, upon capture of Church leaders, 218-19; Far West plundered by, 219; attempts of, to prevent baptism, 250-51, 309-11; constables save Joseph Smith from, 252-53, 258, 312, 317; Joseph and Oliver elude, 258, 318; brethren pass by, without detection, 262, 322; tar and feather Joseph and Sidney, 374-76, 377 n. 1. *See also* Persecutions
More sure word of prophecy, 72
Morey, George, 155, 180 n. 1
Morley, Isaac, 122, 148; revelation concerning, 123
Mormon: describes destruction of Nephites, 78-81
Mormonism Unvailed, 12
Moroni: appearances of, to Joseph Smith, 8, 51-54, 74, 127-28, 276-81, 392-94, 409-15, 430-31; visions seen by, 70; instructs Joseph concerning good vs. evil, 87-90, 396-99; confusion of, with Nephi, 277 n. 1
Moses, 37, 57; prophesies of Israel's afflictions, 59-60; visions of, 70; stood on holy ground, 82
Mulholland, James, 230-31, 265, 267; note from, attached to manuscript, 281 n. 1
Mummies, Egyptian, 102 n. 2, 110, 142
Murdock, Joseph, 18, 373, 378
Murdock, Julia, 18, 373
Murdock, John, 190 n. 1, 192, 353 n. 1

Nauvoo, Illinois, 435, 440, 442, 454
Nauvoo Temple, 442-43, 456
Nebuchadnezzar, 129
Neibaur, Alexander, 459-62
Nephi, 70, 277 n. 1
Nephites: twelve disciples among, 70; destruction of, at Cumorah, 78-81; Christ's ministry among, 432, 451
Newel K. Whitney and Company, 382 n. 2
Noah, 38

Olney, Oliver, 180, 200
Onderdonk, Benjamin T., 386 n. 1
Ordinances: washing of feet, 134
Ordinations: of Oliver Cowdery as assistant president, 24; authority for administering, 30-31; of elders, 186-87; first, of Melchizedek Priesthood, 238-39, 242, 299; in Kirtland, 353
Orton, Amos R., 201

Packard, Noah, 98, 154, 189-90 n. 1, 191
Page, Hiram, 244, 263, 298, 304, 322-23
Page, John E., 105 n. 1, 402-3
Page, Katharine, 244, 304
Page, Mary, 244
Painesville Telegraph, 384 n. 1
Parable of twelve sons, 121, 166
Parks, Hiram G., General, 215, 216-17
Parrish, Warren, 97 n. 1, 102 n. 2; acts as scribe, 17, 112-13; is asked to help settle dispute, 117; revelation concerning, 136-37; exchanges blessings with Joseph Smith, 147; marriage of, 150-51; gives money to Joseph Smith, 155; Joseph Smith prays for healing of, 177; studies Hebrew, 178; correspondence of, with Dr. Piexotto, 207-9
Partridge, Edward, 113, 114, 148; revelation concerning, 123, 344-45; preaches in meeting, 179; biographical sketch of, 348; travels to Missouri, 356; receives Joseph on behalf of Church in Zion, 380
Patriarchal blessings, 180
Patten, David W., 101, 121, 193, 217
Paul, 274
Peck, Martha Long, 251 n. 2, 311
Peck, Hezekiah, 136, 251, 311
Perry, William, 110
Persecutions: Oliver Cowdery on, 28; of Church, 44-45, 350; Moroni prophesies of, 89, 398, 419; Joseph Smith suffers, en route to Far West, 210-11; of Saints in Dewitt, 213-15; Joseph Smith discusses, 225-29, 432-35, 452-54; threats of, 232, 291; following announcement of First Vision, 274; during translation of Book of Mormon, 284. *See also* Mobs
Peters, Absalom, 310 n. 2
Peterson, Richard B. (Ziba), 244, 304, 324-25, 339
Phelps, William W., 114; Oliver Cowdery's letters to, 15, 17, 26 n. 2, 113; printing business of, 21, 26 n. 2, 364; brings charges against Lorenzo Young, 102 n. 1; helps with Egyptian grammar, 102 n. 2; blessing dictated for, 109 n. 2; addresses meeting, 119; condemnation of, 124; unites with brethren in prayer, 147-48; serves in Zion presidency, 189 n. 1; arrives in Kirtland, 355; travels to Missouri, 356; is to help review and publish materials, 381-82
Piexotto, Dr. Daniel, 119, 144-45, 185, 207-9
Pitkin, George, 379
Pittsburgh Weekly Gazette, 438-44
Plan of salvation: eternal nature of, 56-57
Plates, gold, of Book of Mormon: Joseph's failure to obtain, 8-9, 86-87, 281-82; Joseph obtains, 9, 283, 399; characters copied from, 9, 284-86, 401; are taken for a season, 9-10; obtaining, depended on eye single to God, 74-75, 88, 280; pecuniary desires regarding, 75-77, 85-86; description of location of, 77-78, 81-83, 281 n. 1, 394-95; stone box containing, 83-84, 281, 395-96; sacred contents of, 88, 397, 417; enemies attempt to steal, 283-84, 400-401, 432, 451; description of, 399-400, 421-23, 431, 450

Poison: elder preserved from effects of, 146; Joseph Smith vomits, 383
Poorman, John, 250, 309, 376-77
Porter, Daniel P., 382 n. 5
Porter, Francis, 115
Postage, Joseph Smith pays, on unwanted letters, 152-53
Pratt, Orson, 185-86, 277 n. 1, 344; pamphlet by, 387-401
Pratt, Parley P., 109, 218, 219 n. 1; imprisonment of, 220-21; is called to Lamanite mission, 324-25; visits Sidney Rigdon, 339-40; addresses Rigdon's congregation, 340-41
Presbyterians, 46, 270-71
Presidencies of Church in Kirtland and Zion, 189 n. 1
Price, Sterling, Colonel, 221, 224
Priesthood: presidency of, 21, 24; brethren ordained to offices in, 303, 307
Priests, sectarian, attempt to confound brethren, 238, 298
Printing office: of William W. Phelps, 21, 26 n. 2, 364; established at Kirtland, 26 n. 2, 105 n. 2; established in Missouri, 373
Prophets: ancient, are revered above living, 37-39, 41; excuses for refusal to believe, 39-41; are subject to human imperfections, 42, 94-95, 122-23

Quincy, Illinois: Joseph Smith escapes to, 224
Quorums: presidencies of, called and ordained, 200-201; relationships between, confusion regarding, 202 n. 2; take turns speaking, 207

Ramah, hill, 79
Raymond, Martha H., 150-51
Redfield, Harvey, 146
Reed, John, 253, 256 n. 1, 257, 313, 316-17
Reformation, religious, in Joseph Smith's youth, 46-47
Religion, pure: necessity of embracing, 36; unchangeable principles of, 36-37; Joseph Smith's search for, 46-48, 49, 125, 269-71, 389-90, 405-7
Religious excitement, 269-71
Repentance: First Presidency is called to, 22
Respect for priesthood offices, 23, 24-25
Rest of the Lord, 57-58
Revelation: necessity for, 71; debate concerning, 158-59, 163; Joseph describes seeking for, 443
Revelations: for Reynolds Cahoon, 118-19; for Twelve, 120-21; for Edward Partridge, 123, 344-45; for Warren Parrish, 136; for Harvey Whitlock, 140; for Lyman Sherman, 178; for Hyrum Smith, 233, 292; for Joseph Knight Sr., 233, 293; for David, John, and Peter Whitmer, 234-35, 294; for Oliver Cowdery, 236, 289-90; Oliver Cowdery demands change in, 260, 320; false, of Hiram Page, 263; on calling of Twelve, 300; for Martin Harris, 302, for Thomas B. Marsh, 324; concerning Lamanite mission, 324-25; for Orson Pratt, 344; false, of prophetess Hubble, 349 n. 1; impossibility of imitating, 367; publication of, 367 n. 1, 368-69, 381-82; testimony of, 367-68
Rich, Leonard, 154, 177
Richards, Willard, 268-69 n. 1, 273 n. 1, 459
Richmond, Missouri, imprisonment in, 221
Rigdon, Sidney: as counselor in First Presidency, 21, 189 n. 1; addresses conference, 32; is threatened and slandered, 103; blessing dictated for, 109 n. 2; preaches in meetings, 110, 137, 184; attends Piexotto's lecture, 119; speaks out in Isaac Hill case, 124; bears testimony to minister,

136; unites with brethren in prayer, 147-48; addresses leadership meeting, 190 n. 1, 193, 201; receives healing blessing, 193; asks forgiveness of Twelve, 205; arrested in Missouri, 218; imprisonment of, 220-21; missionaries visit, 325, 339; supposed role of, in writing Book of Mormon, 327 n. 1; biographical history of, 327-39; agrees to read Book of Mormon, 340, 341; conversion and baptism of, 342-44; dedicates land of Zion, 358 n. 4; missionary labors of, 370; sees vision of degrees of glory, 372; is tarred and feathered, 375; becomes delirious, 378
Road, Joseph Smith helps lay out, 177
Roberts, Brigham H., 20 n. 1, 265
Robinson, Ebenezer, 108-9 n. 1, 159
Robinson, George W., 218, 220, 230
Rockwell, Caroline, 250, 309
Rockwell, Electa, 250, 309
Rockwell, Orrin Porter, 250, 304, 309
Rolph, Samuel, 155, 201
Rose, Joseph, 189
Roundy, Shadrach, 118, 156
Rudd, John, 155
Rules and regulations governing House of the Lord, 193, 196-97, 198-200
Rupp, Israel Daniel, 445, 447
Ruth, covenant made by, 61-62
Ryder, Simonds, 374, 375

Sacrament: administered at Church organization meeting, 242, 299, 303; wine for, 261, 321
Salisbury, Wilkins J., 187
Salutations, respect lacking in, 23
Salvation. *See* Plan of salvation
Sandemanians, 331 n. 1
Satan: Joseph Smith sees hosts of, 87, 396, 415; recognizing devices of, 91, 397, 415-17; power of, over William Smith, 182; manifestations of, preceding First Vision, 272, 390-91, 407-9; Moroni warns Joseph Smith of, 280; binds two in conference, 353 n. 1; vision of, on waters, 361
Sauk Indians, 461
School of the prophets, 104, 119; dedication of, 121
Scientific revolution, skepticism engendered by, 11
Scoby, Almira Mack, 150
Scott, Walter, 356
Scriptures: Joseph Smith studies, as youth, 5-6; opened to understanding, 231, 291, 345; quoted by Moroni, 278-79
"Sealed book," 9, 53-54, 285
Seer stone of Hiram Page, 263, 322-23
Seixas, Joshua, 104 n. 2, 186, 193
Seventy, quorum of, 179
Seymour, William, 256-57, 315-16
Shakers, 351
Sherer, John, 310
Sherman, Lyman, 178
Shoal Creek, 223
Singing school, 186
Sins: Joseph Smith's concern over his, 7; youthful, of Joseph Smith, 13-14, 275-76, 409; Joseph prays for forgiveness of, 50-51, 127, 276, 392, 409; Harvey Whitlock confesses, in letter, 138-40; William Smith confesses, in letter, 169-70
Slander aimed at Joseph Smith, 91-92
Slavery, opponents of, 438, 440
Smith, Alvin, 7 n. 2, 19, 265; death of, 282
Smith, Don Carlos, 19, 25; accompanies brothers to court, 111; preaches in meeting, 188; is ordained president of high priests, 200; baptism of, 250, 309
Smith, Emma Hale: marriage of, to Joseph, 9, 18, 94, 282-83; acts as scribe, 10; character of, 94; is chastised for leaving meeting,

124; nurses man with swollen arm, 161; baptism of, 251, 311; nurses sick twins, 374; lodging of, in husband's absence, 379-80; hymns selected by, 382
Smith, Ephraim, 19
Smith, George A., 119, 302 n. 1, 385
Smith, Hyrum, 19, 182; as assistant president, 20 n. 1, 25, 189 n. 1; as high councilor, 25; travels to purchase store goods, 105; serves on temple construction committee, 105-6 n. 3; blessing dictated for, 109 n. 2; accompanies brothers to court, 111; tries to reconcile Joseph and William, 117; unites with brethren in prayer, 147-48; supports decision to discontinue debates, 163; Joseph's love for, 168; preaches in meeting, 179; blesses Sidney Rigdon, 193; imprisonment of, 220-21; revelation received for, 232-33, 292; baptism of, 235, 294; as one of Eight Witnesses, 298
Smith, Jerushee, 250, 309
Smith, John, 123-24, 182; as high councilor, 189 n. 1
Smith, Joseph, Jr.: birth and childhood of, 3, 5, 13, 268-69, 389, 405; limited education of, 5, 389, 405; marries Emma Hale, 9, 94, 282-83; genealogy of, 18-19; religious strivings of, as youth, 46-48, 49, 125, 270-72, 389-90, 405-7; prays for forgiveness of sins, 50-51, 392, 409; is instructed to view plates, 74, 394, 415; pecuniary desires of, regarding gold plates, 75-77, 85-86; fails to obtain plates, 86-87; evil men to seek overthrow of, 89, 398, 421; name of, to be known among nations, 90, 399, 421; character of, 91-92, 95; is employed to dig for gold, 93-94, 282; human failings of, 94-95; court trials of, 95, 221, 223, 253-57, 312-17; desires to repay debts, 98; meets with Twelve, 100-101, 133-36, 201-6; attends high council courts, 101-2, 103, 113-15; cares for sick father, 105, 107; conflicts of, with brother William, 115, 117-18, 163-64; attends school, 122, 132, 136, 187; relates history to Joshua, the Jewish Minister, 125, 126-28; performs marriages, 145-46, 150-51, 159-60, 197, 207; is insulted on journey, 149-50; studies Hebrew, 152, 178, 187; money and food given to, 154-56; expresses love for Hyrum, 168; New Year's thoughts of, 181-82; is reconciled with brother William, 182-83; arrest of, at Far West, 210; capture of, under flag of truce, 218; imprisonment of, 220-21; escapes to Illinois, 223-24; discusses persecution of Saints, 225-29; baptism of, 231, 290-91; ordained as elder, 239, 242, 299, 303; is mistreated by constable, 254-55, 314-15; contracts typhus, 268 n. 1; undergoes leg operation, 268 n. 1; missionary labors of, 370; is tarred and feathered, 374-76, 377 n. 1; vomits poison, 383; interview of, with David White, 443-44; interview of, with Alexander Neibaur, 461
—blessings given by: recording of, 98; to Newel K. Whitney, 106-7; rebuking father's disease, 107; to children, 109, 119; dictated for brethren, 109 n. 2; to newlywed couple, 110; to Warren Parrish, 147; casting devil out of Newel Knight, 247-48, 305-6
—preaching of: to high council, 104; in meetings of Saints, 110, 154, 159, 180; dedicating school of prophets, 121; on grammar, 122, 132; to Twelve, 133-36, 203-5; in funeral sermon, 143; in leadership

meeting, 191, 198-200; following mobbing, 378
—visions of: First Vision, 6-7, 127, 272-73, 390-91, 407-9, 430-31, 444, 448-49, 461; of Moroni, 8, 51-54, 74, 127-28, 276-81, 392-94, 409-15, 430-31, 449; of powers of darkness, 87, 396, 415; Moroni's instructions in, regarding good vs. evil, 87-90, 396-99, 415-21; of degrees of glory, 372
—writings of: of personal history, 1-3; of Egyptian alphabet, 102; for *Messenger and Advocate*, 102, 102-3 n. 3; letter to Harvey Whitlock, 140-42; letter to brother William, 170-75; detailing Missouri sufferings, 210, 211, 432-35, 452-54; letter to John Wentworth, 429-37; letter to I. Daniel Rupp, 447-58
Smith, Joseph, Sr.: family of, afflictions suffered by, 7; genealogy of, 18-19; as assistant president, 20 n. 1, 25, 189 n. 1; as high councilor, 25; falls ill, 105, 107; healing of, 107, 108; sorrow of, over William, 168; gives patriarchal blessings, 180; reconciles sons, 182-83; dedicates schoolroom, 185-86; baptism of, 244, 303; Joseph Jr. tells, of Moroni's visit, 281; as one of Eight Witnesses, 298
Smith, Joseph F., 277
Smith, Joseph III, 18, 386
Smith, Katharine, 19, 250, 309
Smith, Lucy, 19
Smith, Lucy Mack, 18, 115; baptism of, 244, 303; takes family to New York, 268-69 n. 1; tells of Edward Partridge, 348-49 n. 3
Smith, Lyman, 119
Smith, Mary Bailey, 112 n. 1
Smith, Samuel H., 19, 121; acts as scribe, 10; as high councilor, 25, 189 n. 1; appears before court, 111; wife of, delivers baby, 112; William Smith prejudices mind of, 118; prays with brethen, 147-48; preaches in meeting, 188; conversion and baptism of, 232, 292; as one of Eight Witnesses, 298
Smith, Sarah, 379
Smith, Sophronia, 19
Smith, Susanna Bailey, 112 n. 2, 121
Smith, Sylvester, 25 n. 1, 161, 185
Smith, William, 19, 25, 107; becomes enraged during high council court, 115; letter from, objecting to censuring, 116; rejects reconciliation attempts, 117-18; revelation prophesies return of, 120-21; attacks Joseph following debate, 163-64; Orson Hyde's complaint against, 165-66; family's feelings wounded by, 168; letter from, confessing sins, 168-70; letter to, from Joseph, 170-75; Satan's power over, 182; reconciliation of, with Joseph, 182-83; confesses sins to council, 183-84; baptism of, 250, 309
Snow, Zerubbabel, 123
Solemn assembly, 104, 135, 188
Spalding, Solomon, 12, 327 n. 1
Speaking, order in, 196, 199-200
Spirits, discerning of, 352
Squires, Andrew Jackson, 145
Stanley, Harvey, 155
Steamboat, fire on, 380
Stevens, Elder, 105
Stevens, Jonathan, Uzziel, and Lyman, 105 n. 1
Stoddard, Calvin, 182
Stone box containing gold plates, 83-84, 281, 395-96
Stowell, Josiah, 93, 253-54, 282, 313
Stores, brethren set up, 382
Stringham, Julia, 251, 311
Stringham, William and Esther Knight, 251, 311
Susquehanna County, Pennsylvania, 9

Tanner, John, 156

Tarring and feathering, 374-76, 377 n. 1
Temple. *See* Kirtland Temple; Nauvoo Temple
Tertullian, 36
Thayer, Ezra, 98, 356
Thompson, Jonathan, 254, 313-14
Three Witnesses of Book of Mormon, 235-38, 294-98
Time, passage of, 28
Tippets, William, John, and Joseph, 98-99
Title page of Book of Mormon, 241, 300-302
Tongues, gift of, 110, 386 n. 2
Translation of Book of Mormon, 233
Treasure seeking, 86, 93-94, 282
Trials, courtroom: of Joseph Smith, 95, 221, 223, 253-57, 312-17; of Samuel Smith, 111-12
Trials, high council, 101-2, 103, 113-15
Truce, flag of, 218
Truth: power of, 36; opposition to, 54-55; sprung out of earth, 307
Turnham, Joel, Judge, 221
Twelve apostles: return of, from East, 100; resolve differences with Sidney Rigdon, 101; revelation chastising, 120-21, 162; eastern mission of, 202 n. 1; objections of, to chastisement, 202-4; covenant with presidency, 206; revelation on calling of, 300

United Society of Believers in Christ's Second Appearing, 351 n. 3
Urim and Thummim, 233, 234, 278; brethren consult, about John the Beloved, 289; description of, 400, 423, 431, 450

Vacancies in Church leadership, meeting to fill, 189-93
Visions: Moroni appears in, 8, 51-54, 74, 127-28, 276-81, 392-94, 409-15, 430-31; difficulty of describing, 69-70; seen by ancient prophets, 70; promised to Saints, 70-71, 135; contrasted with dreams, 73-74; Daniel's, minister's explanation of, 129-30; seen by Newel Knight, 249-50, 308; discounted by minister, 273-74; false, 352 n. 1; of degrees of glory, 372. *See also* First Vision

Wakefield, Joseph H., 385
Wars, final, of Jaredites and Nephites, 78-81
Washing of feet, 104, 134
Waters, destroyer riding upon, 362
Wealth: desires for, in obtaining gold plates, 75-77, 85-86; equitable division of, 120
Weaver, Russell, 188
Webb, Edwin, 160
Webb, John, 197
Wentworth, John, 427, 429
Whispering in meetings, prohibition against, 192
Whitcher, Mary, 124-25
White, David Nye, 438-44
Whitlock, Harvey, 138-42, 353 n. 1
Whitmer, Anne, 244, 304
Whitmer, Christian, 244, 260, 298, 304, 320
Whitmer, David: assists in blessings, 107, 157; blessing dictated for, 109 n. 2; advises Alvah Beaman, 142; unites with brethren in prayer, 147-48; presides at sacrament meeting, 159; serves in Zion presidency, 189 n. 1; blesses Sidney Rigdon, 193; brings Joseph to father's home, 234, 293; revelation received for, 234-35, 294; becomes one of Three Witnesses, 235-38, 294-98; discusses organization of Church, 242 n. 2; baptism of, 294; mission of, 366
Whitmer, Elizabeth, 244, 304
Whitmer, Jacob, 244, 298, 304
Whitmer, John: as historian, 1, 351; edits *Messenger and Advocate*, 102 n. 3; on blessings dictated by

Joseph Smith, 109 n. 2; condemnation of, 124; unites with brethren in prayer, 147-48; serves in Zion presidency, 189 n. 1; assists in Book of Mormon production, 234; revelation received for, 234-35, 294; baptism of, 235; helps arrange and copy revelations, 259; as one of Eight Witnesses, 298; oversees converts in Ohio, 347 n. 2; describes false spirits, 352 n. 1; describes manifestations of Satan, 353 n. 1; describes dedication of Zion, 358 n. 4; helps review revelations for publication, 381

Whitmer, Mary, 244, 304

Whitmer, Peter, Jr., 159, revelation received for, 234-35, 294; baptism of, 235, 294; as one of Eight Witnesses, 298; joins mission to Lamanites, 325 n. 1, 339

Whitmer, Peter, Sr., 234, 244, 260, 293, 304

Whitney, Elizabeth Ann, 347, 379 n. 1

Whitney, Newel K., 151; travels to purchase store goods, 105; supervises temple committee storehouse, 105-6 n. 3; blessing given to, by Joseph Smith, 106-7; Joseph Smith teaches parents of, 114; shares hopes of Zion, 114-15; entertains Joseph Smith at "feasts," 186-87; ordains Vinson Knight, 189 n. 1, 191; Joseph and Emma live with, 347; is hurt in coach accident, 382-83; travels to New York, 386 n. 1

Whitney, Samuel and Susanna Kimball, 114 n. 2, 118

Wight, Lyman, 119, 180 n. 1, 216-17, 218; imprisonment of, 220-21

Wilcox, Catharine, 197

Williams, Frederick G.: manuscript in handwriting of, 15, 113 n. 1, 114; as counselor in First Presidency, 21; blessing dictated for, 109 n. 2; delivers baby of Samuel Smith's wife, 112; attends Piexotto's lecture, 119; is invited to warn relatives, 120; unites with brethren in prayer, 147-48; studies Hebrew, 152, 178; preaches in meeting, 159; addresses Twelve, 205

Wilson, Robert, General, 219, 220, 224

Wine: partaking of, at wedding, 197-98; procuring, for sacrament, 261, 321

Wise men, warning given to, in dream, 73

Witnesses: to Book of Mormon, 235-38, 294-98; in courtroom trials, 253-54, 256-57, 313-16; to revelations, 367-68

Wood, brethren gather, for Joseph Smith, 154, 156

Woodruff, Wilford, 113

Word of Wisdom, 198 n. 1

Works, Angeline, 157, 159

Writing, insufficiency of, to communicate visions, 70

Young, Brigham, 101, 122, 277 n. 1, 386 n. 2

Young, Joseph, 123, 386 n. 2

Young, Lorenzo, 101-2, 132

Young, Phineas, 101

Zion: Missouri designated as, 21, 99 n. 3, 210; plans for redemption of, 99-100; prayer for deliverance of, 147; presidency of Church in, 189; mass migration to, created conflicts, 210; dedication of, 358; description of land of, 359-60; conferences held in, 361, 380; temple in, spot dedicated for, 360

Zion's Camp, 100

THE PAPERS OF JOSEPH SMITH

Volume 1: Autobiographical and Historical Writings

Designed by Kent Ware

Maps by Steven R. Thomas,
University of Utah DIGIT Lab

Composed by Patricia J. Parkinson
on the Penta Publishing System
in Trump Mediaeval

Printed by Ringier America
on Miami Book, cream white text stock
(acid free)

Bound by Ringier America
in Roxite A Linen over Eska board
(acid free)
stamped with Kurz metallic
and pigment stamping foils
with
Rainbow Antique
endleaves